Using Paradox® 4
Special Edition

WALTER R. BRUCE III

with

Matthew Harris

Dana Greaves

Using Paradox 4, Special Edition

Copyright © 1992 by Que® Corporation.

All rights reserved. Printed in the United States of America. No part of this book may be used or reproduced in any form or by any means, or stored in a database or retrieval system, without prior written permission of the publisher except in the case of brief quotations embodied in critical articles and reviews. Making copies of any part of this book for any purpose other than your own personal use is a violation of United States copyright laws. For information, address Que Corporation, 11711 N. College Ave., Carmel, IN 46032.

Library of Congress Catalog No.: 91-68388

ISBN: 0-88022-822-9

92   5 4 3 2

Interpretation of the printing code: the rightmost double-digit number is the year of the book's printing; the rightmost single-digit number, the number of the book's printing. For example, a printing code of 92-1 shows that the first printing of the book occurred in 1992.

Screen reproductions in this book were created using Collage Plus from Inner Media, Inc., Hollis, NH.

Using Paradox 4, Special Edition, is based on Paradox through Version 4.0.

Publisher: Lloyd J. Short

Acquisitions Manager: Rick Ranucci

Product Development Manager: Thomas H. Bennett

Book Designer: Scott Cook

Production Team: Jeff Baker, Michelle Cleary, Christine Cook, Mark Enochs, Brook Farling, Kate Godfrey, Tim Groeling, Carla Hall-Batton, Phil Kitchel, Bob LaRoche, Joy Dean Lee, Laurie Lee, Jay Lesandrini, Juli Pavey, Cindy Phipps, Linda Quigley, Caroline Roop, Linda Seifert, Angie Trzepacz, Julie Walker, Allan Wimmer, Lisa Wilson, Phil Worthington

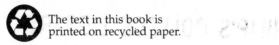

To Richey, Robby, Heather, and Heidi

CREDITS

Product Director
Walter R. Bruce III

Acquisitions Editor
Chris Katsaropoulos

Production Editor
Lori A. Lyons

Editors
Sara Allaei
Jo Anna Arnott
Diana R. Moore
Anne Owen
Colleen Totz

Technical Editor
Robert G. Stout

Composed in Cheltenham by Que Corporation.

Walter R. Bruce III is the author of *Using PC Tools 7.1*, *Que's Using Enable*, *Using Paradox 3*, *Using Paradox 3.5*, Special Edition, *Using DataEase*, *Using PROCOMM PLUS*, and *Using Carbon Copy PLUS*, and is coauthor of *Using MS-DOS 5*. He has written several instructional texts for use in intermediate and advanced workshops on using popular microcomputer software packages. He also has led workshops on the use of computer software for government and private-industry clients from coast to coast.

Mr. Bruce is a licensed attorney, who practiced for three years in North Carolina and for six years in the United States Air Force.

Matthew Harris is a consultant living in Oakland, California. He has been involved with the microcomputer industry since 1980, and began programming applications for IBM PCs and compatible computers in 1983. Mr. Harris has written commercially distributed applications as well as applications used in-house by several clients. He has provided consulting services to the 1990 International AIDS Conference, the University of California at San Francisco, and a variety of private companies. Mr. Harris has taught or assisted in teaching Pascal programming courses at the University of California Berkeley Extension Services. He has worked with the Paradox Application Language since Version 1.0 of Paradox. Mr. Harris also programs in Object-Oriented Pascal, dBASE, BASIC, and Assembler language.

Dana Greaves is a principal in Tsunami Systems, of San Jose, California, which provides database consulting and documentation services. He has engineered an extensive LAN-based manufacturing process control system using Paradox and the Paradox Engine. He has also worked as a consultant with Borland International to write and test programs for the Paradox 3.5 and Paradox 4.0 documentation. Before working with Paradox, Dana was a Process Engineer, designing test equipment and procedures for a major hard disk manufacturer.

TRADEMARK ACKNOWLEDGMENTS

ACKNOWLEDGMENTS

Thanks to the following individuals for their invaluable help in bringing this book together:

Lori Lyons for her outstanding work on this project.

Nan Borreson, Borland book department manager, for providing copies of Paradox and for all her timely assistance.

Robert Stout for providing timely technical advice.

The conventions used in this book have been established to help you learn to use Paradox quickly and easily.

Paradox highlights on-screen the first letter of each command. In this book, the first letter of each menu command is in boldface, as in **A**sk, to indicate that you can press A to select the command.

Many operations require a sequence of menu selections. This book lists the options you should select side by side, separated by commas, in the appropriate order. The following example means that you should select the **M**odify option and then the **R**estructure option:

Modify, **R**estructure

Every effort has been made to present menu options in this book exactly as they appear on-screen. To be consistent with Paradox menus, no spaces are shown between words of multiword commands if they appear with no spaces on-screen.

CONTENTS AT A GLANCE

TABLE OF CONTENTS

III Programming Paradox

Introduction

Welcome to *Using Paradox 4*, Special Edition. With this book as your guide, you are about to become a Paradox pro!

The program's authors christened their creation Paradox because they believed the program represents what others think to be a contradiction—a full-featured database program that is easy to learn and use. Although ease of use and ease of learning are relative to your previous experience, after you try Paradox, you will agree that the name fits the program's capabilities.

Traveling even a well-marked road for the first time is always easier if you follow someone who has been down that road before. As you journey through Paradox 4.0, this book points out the most direct route while showing you how to avoid hidden potholes and unnecessary tolls.

What Is Paradox 4.0?

Paradox 4.0 is the latest version of a relational database management system first released in 1985 by Ansa Software (since purchased by Borland International). This PC-based program enables you to collect, sort, and retrieve information on a computer and then generate reports that consolidate or summarize any or all of this information in nearly any order or format that you choose. You can even create representations of your numeric data by using color graphics.

The program is designed to enable you to work with your data in ways that seem natural and familiar and yet achieve quite sophisticated results. You probably know how to select choices from Paradox menus. The menus are similar in style to those found in Quattro Pro, a popular spreadsheet program by Borland. By reading these menus and using the on-line help documentation, you can learn how to use the basic features of Paradox without ever opening a book. But don't be content with just the basics. This book shows you how to use Paradox to converse with your data as if you were old friends, create reports from your data as if you were a seasoned mainframe programmer, and create graphic representations of your data that show relationships you didn't even realize existed.

Query By Example

Paradox 4.0 uses a method called Query By Example (QBE) to ask questions of your data. You first type into a table the information you want to save. Then you use QBE to get at your data when you need it. Query By Example doesn't require you to memorize any syntax and is so forgiving that you don't even have to know exactly how to spell the information you are trying to retrieve. QBE is the key to the simplicity and power of Paradox.

For example, you can use QBE to find the phone number of Joanne Smythe from a table of thousands of phone numbers, even if you think her name is Joan Smith.

Of course, Paradox has been designed to handle database problems much more complicated than retrieving a telephone number. Because of the program's *relational* design, you can work with more than one database table at a time just as easily as with one. By using the QBE methodology, you can create queries that generate answers from your data in seconds—answers that can take hours or even days to generate by hand. As easily as you can type a simple letter, you can design a custom report around your data that meets even the most demanding requirements of your chief executive officer.

Features for the Power User and Application Developer

For the power user or programmer, Paradox 4.0 also includes comprehensive form-design capabilities and a full procedural database application development environment called the *Paradox Application Language*, or *PAL*. A module called the *Application Workshop* enables even nonprogrammers to generate turnkey menu-driven systems customized to solve unique database management problems.

Borland International also sells Paradox SQL Link, a program that can be used with Paradox 4.0 to access data stored on Structured Query Language (SQL—pronounced *sequel*) database servers. Paradox SQL Link and Paradox 4.0 can act together as an SQL front end that enables use of Paradox queries against an SQL database server. PAL programs also can pass SQL queries directly to an SQL server. In addition, Borland has released Paradox Engine, a special version of Paradox intended for use by C, C++, or Pascal programmers.

What's New?

Since the program's introduction, Ansa-Borland has progressively enhanced Paradox while remaining true to the program's original design concepts. Paradox 4.0, released in 1992, includes a number of significant enhancements not found in earlier versions of the program. In fact, you would be hard pressed to find another PC-based relational database program with more impressive features. These features are summarized in table I.1.

Table I.1. New Features in Paradox 4.0	
Category	**Enhancement**
User Interface	Paradox objects presented in moveable, sizeable, stackable windows
	Pull-down menus
	Mouse support; scroll bars

continues

Table I.1. Continued

Category	Enhancement
	System menu always available to maximize, restore, size, move, and switch between windows; to control the appearance of the user interface; and to run the Text Editor, Personal Programmer, and Custom Configuration Program
New Field Types	Memo fields of unlimited length
	BLOB (Binary Large OBjects) fields
	Imported fields of unknown type
Network support	Coedit no longer generates a form lock or a link lock
	Option to create read-only directories on the network server
Presentation Enhancements	Enhanced report previewer
	Report reset and setup strings
	PostScript printer support
Text Editor	Available at all times
	Multiple editing windows
	Mouse support
	Cut-and-paste within and between editing windows
Video	New video modes including support for Super VGA video boards
Indexing	Secondary indexes
	Multifield
	Tables can be viewed in secondary index order

Category	Enhancement
Query/Report Restart	Option to have Paradox continue with a query or report even if source data changes
PAL/Script Enhancements	Event-driven programming: WAIT command can detect and trap for key presses, cursor movement, mouse movement, record posting, idle time, and message events
	Dialog box programming: ACCEPT can generate dialog boxes with push buttons, check boxes, radio buttons, sliders, file/table lists
	Unlimited dynamic arrays indexed by any data type
	System information available on demand
	Sizable, moveable, floating canvas windows
	LOCATE BESTMATCH in secondary index order
	Pop-up and pull-down menus
	WAIT WORKSPACE
	Paradox 3.5-compatible user interface toggle
	IFF(condition,true_exp,false_exp) in PAL, forms, and reports
	Capability to pass linear and dynamic arrays to procedures by reference
	Capability to program millisecond timing
	Capability to program sound
Miscellaneous Enhancements	Import and export Reflex 2 files

Paradox 4.0 recognizes several field types not recognized by earlier versions of the program; however, the program provides the option to create tables that are compatible with Paradox 3.5 and earlier. If you intend to use Paradox 4.0 database tables with an earlier version of Paradox, you must create or restructure the tables in this *compatible format.*

The standard user interface in Paradox 4.0 is significantly different than the interface found in Paradox 3.5 and previous versions. Consequently, many scripts written for use in Paradox 3.5 and earlier will not operate correctly in Paradox 4.0. You can use a menu option or a PAL command, however, to switch back to the Paradox 3.5 style user interface so that you can run existing scripts.

Paradox 4.0 runs only on IBM PC-compatible computers with one of the following CPUs: Intel 80286, 80386, 80386SX, 80486, or 80486SX. Paradox 4.0 runs in protected mode and uses all available extended memory, significantly enhancing performance during sorts, queries, scrolling, and PAL applications.

What Should Your System Have?

To run Paradox 4.0 as a single-user program, your system must have an 80286, 80386, 80386SX, 80486, or 80486SX CPU and at least 2M of RAM and DOS 3.0 or higher. The PC must have a hard disk and at least one floppy disk drive.

For network use, Paradox 4.0 requires an 80286, 80386, 80386SX, 80486, or 80486SX PC workstation with at least 2M RAM and DOS 3.1 or higher. The workstation must be connected to a network running one of the following network operating systems:

3Com 3+ network, Version 1.0 or higher

AT&T StarGROUP for DOS, Version 3.1 or higher

Banyan VINES, Version 2.0 or higher

DEC Pathworks, Version 1.0 or higher

IBM Token Ring or PC Network with IBM PC Local Area Network Program, Version 1.12 or higher

Microsoft LANMAN, Version 2.0 or higher

Novell Advanced NetWare, Version 2.0A or higher

Networks that are compatible with DOS 3.1 and with one of the networks listed in the preceding list

Performance and capacity are improved in standalone systems or network workstations if your system includes extended memory, expanded memory, or a math coprocessor.

New in Paradox 4.0 is the capability to make selections with a mouse. To use this capability, your PC must have a Microsoft mouse, Logitech mouse, PS/2 mouse, or a mouse that is 100 percent compatible with one of these brands of mice.

To take advantage of all the capabilities of Paradox, you also should have a graphics-capable monitor and graphics printer or plotter.

Who Should Read This Book?

Experienced users will find *Using Paradox 4,* Special Edition helpful in gaining a clear understanding of the Version 4.0 enhancements and may even learn a few tricks along the way.

The approach of this book mirrors that of the software. You don't have to be a programmer to learn and use Paradox. This book likewise makes no assumptions about your background or experience in using PCs or database management systems. If you are a new database user, start at the beginning of the book and move through it at a comfortable pace. More experienced users can skim Part I, "Paradox Fundamentals," and study the text more closely beginning in Part II, "Paradox Power Techniques." Power Paradox users may want to breeze through Parts I and II and concentrate on Part III, "Programming Paradox."

Because Paradox 4.0 is the most current version at the time of this writing, the book generally assumes that you are using this version. Discussions involving features new in Paradox 4.0 are marked with a Version 4 icon in the margin. If you have chosen not to upgrade, you should skip the sections that don't apply to your version of Paradox. Special considerations of interest to network users also are addressed where appopriate.

What Is Covered in This Book?

This book is divided into three major parts: Part I, "Paradox Fundamentals"; Part II, "Paradox Power Techniques"; and Part III, "Programming

Paradox." Parts I and II begin with quick start lessons that preview the topics to be discussed. Use the quick start lessons to get your feet wet and then examine the chapters that follow for detailed explanations.

Part I: Paradox Fundamentals

The first part of the book covers the most elementary aspects of creating a database with Paradox: entering data, editing data, asking questions of the data, and printing simple reports.

Quick Start 1, "Your First Paradox Session," tells you how to start Paradox and takes you through the creation of a simple database table. You then ask a few questions of the table and print two sorted lists derived from the table you create.

Chapter 1, "Navigating Paradox," explains how to use the keyboard, menus, screens, views, and prompts in Paradox.

Chapter 2, "Creating Database Tables," describes how to define and modify the structure of a Paradox database.

Chapter 3, "Entering, Editing, and Viewing Data," discusses the basics of entering new data into a database table and how to edit and sort the data.

Chapter 4, "Getting Started with Query By Example," takes a first look at the feature that makes Paradox powerful and easy to use: Query By Example (QBE).

Chapter 5, "Getting Started with Reports," covers how to create relatively simple tabular reports.

Chapter 6, "Getting Started with Scripts and Keyboard Macros," describes how you easily can automate frequently used Paradox operations by recording your keystrokes. This chapter describes how to record and play scripts and how to make changes by using the Script Editor.

Part II: Paradox Power Techniques

After you have an understanding of Paradox fundamentals, you are ready to tap the power of Paradox. The seven chapters in this part of the book discuss in detail all the capabilities of Paradox used interactively (without programming).

Quick Start 2, "Using Advanced Paradox Features," shows you how to perform multitable queries, design a data-entry form, add validity checking, design a custom report, and create a graph.

Chapter 7, "Using Advanced Query By Example and Multiple Tables," gets to the heart of Paradox. Although the basics of QBE are discussed in Chapter 4, this chapter explores queries that use multiple tables, group operations, set queries, and inclusive links. Master this chapter, and you are well on your way to mastering Paradox.

Chapter 8, "Using Advanced Form Techniques," explains how to create custom forms for entering, editing, and viewing Paradox data. In addition to discussing single-table forms with calculated numeric fields, word-wrap text fields, and multiple pages, this chapter describes how and why to create multitable and multirecord forms.

Chapter 9, "Using Power Entry and Editing Features," shows you how you can increase the ease and accuracy of your data entry by creating validation criteria. The chapter also discusses the nuances of editing data in multitable forms and on a network.

Chapter 10, "Using Tabular Reports," picks up where Chapter 5 leaves off. This chapter goes into detail about the use of the *table band* concept to customize tabular reports. The chapter covers summary fields, calculated fields, sorting, grouping, headings, report summaries, multifield columns, word wrap, and multitable reports.

Chapter 11, "Using Free-Form Reports," goes a step further and shows you how to design on-screen custom reports in which the fields can be placed anywhere on the form rather than in tabular fashion. Examples of this type of report are form letters, mailing labels, and invoices.

Chapter 12, "Using Paradox Graphics," discusses the business graphics module of Paradox 4.0. This chapter demonstrates how to create sophisticated graphs from your data with just a few keystrokes. The discussion includes the *crosstab* feature; graph types; graph elements; customizing color, grid, titles, labels, legends, fonts, and other graph settings; exploding pie slices; using scripts; and printing.

Chapter 13, "Using Paradox Tools," shows you how to rename Paradox tables; speed up queries; export data to formats compatible with other programs; import data from other program formats; copy tables, forms, reports, and scripts; delete tables, forms, reports, scripts, and graphs; choose image settings and use validity checks; display information about Paradox objects and network information; set and remove network locks and privileges; and set the autorefresh interval. A number of other Paradox tools also are discussed, such as password protection and temporary suspension of Paradox to go to DOS.

Part III: Programming Paradox

The final section of this book describes two of the most advanced and powerful parts of Paradox: the Application Workshop and the Paradox Application Language (PAL).

Chapter 14, "Using the Application Workshop," takes you through an Application Workshop session resulting in a complete menu-driven application. The chapter demonstrates menu building; selecting actions; specifying tables, records, fields, forms, and reports for use in the application; creating multitable views; the use of *tilde variables*; and running and modifying the completed application.

Chapter 15, "An Overview of the Paradox Application Language," discusses the fundamentals of PAL, the application development environment and programming language. This chapter also provides an overview of the programming capabilities of PAL.

Chapter 16, "Using the Paradox Application Language," delves into several of the most powerful and useful PAL programming techniques. Special attention is paid to capabilities that are new in Paradox 4.0, such as windows and event handling.

Chapter 17, "Using the Script Editor and PAL Debugger," explains how to use the special PAL Debugger programming tool to discover and fix errors in your PAL program.

Chapter 18, "Creating PAL Applications," takes you through the steps of building a sample application. This chapter covers in detail many of the most important programming techniques you need to know to create applications using PAL. This chapter focuses especially on the capabilities that are new in Version 4.0, including pull-down menus, dialog boxes, the new WAIT command, and event trapping.

Chapter 19, "PAL Command and Function Reference," indexes and briefly describes all the PAL commands and functions available in Paradox 4.0. This chapter provides a handy quick reference to assist PAL programmers in determining correct command and function syntax. In many cases, short examples are included.

Using the Appendixes and the Command Chart

Appendix A describes the steps necessary to install and start Paradox 4.0. Appendix B briefly discusses use of the Custom Configuration Program (CCP) to modify the video configuration, report settings, default working directory, international features, network features, and other settings. Appendix C presents a complete list of PAL keycodes and extended codes, which are used with several PAL commands. Appendix D lists the color attribute codes used with the PAL commands that can set or change colors or attributes of the screen.

Finally, at the back of the book, you can find a pull-out card showing a chart of the Paradox menu commands.

Now that you know what to expect, you are ready to get to the business at hand: learning Paradox. Get to know the program well, and Paradox will give you everything you could possibly want from a database management system.

PART

I

Paradox Fundamentals

Quick Start 1: Your First Paradox Session

This lesson is the first of two quick starts presented in this book. Each lesson is designed to help you get a running start with Paradox. Both quick starts take you step-by-step through simple examples of techniques and concepts discussed in the chapters that follow each quick start. This format gives you a preview of what is to come and enables you to begin using Paradox without much reading. The quick starts also may encourage you to experiment as you continue through the book.

Quick Start 1 walks you through Paradox start-up. You create a simple database table consisting of a list of company employees and enter several records. You then ask a few questions of the data. Finally, you print the list of employees, sorted first by employee number and then by name.

Before you can begin, you must install Paradox. Refer to Appendix A for information on how to ready the program for use on your system. Next, locate the appropriate keyboard template for your keyboard (enclosed in the box with the disks) and place the template on your keyboard. Finally, you are ready to begin the lesson.

Starting Paradox on a Hard Disk System

Paradox 4.0 is designed to work from a hard disk. To start Paradox from a hard disk, follow these steps:

1. Start your system and access the root directory on the hard disk that contains Paradox. From the DOS prompt (probably C> or C:\>), make a directory to hold your Paradox files. To create a directory with the name PDOXDATA, for example, type *md \pdoxdata* at the DOS prompt and press Enter. Change to the new directory by typing *cd \pdoxdata* and pressing Enter. Starting Paradox from this directory causes new database files to be stored in this location.

2. For DOS to find the Paradox program files, draw the system a "map" by defining the *path* to the Paradox directory with the DOS command PATH.

   Type *path c:\;c:\dos;c:\pdox40* and press Enter.

   This PATH statement assumes that your DOS files are in the directory C:\DOS. Insert the appropriate directory name into the PATH statement for your system.

3. To start Paradox 4.0, type *paradox* and press Enter.

As Paradox loads, you see a title screen similar to figure QS1.1 that shows the signature information you supplied during the installation process. As soon as you press a key, the first screen is followed by the screen in figure QS1.2, the menu bar.

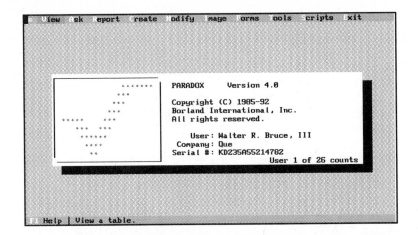

The Paradox 4.0
start-up screen.

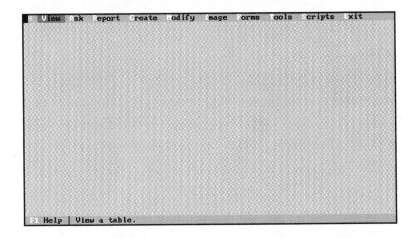

The Paradox
menu bar.

Creating the Employee Database

In some ways, entering information in a Paradox table is similar to typing the same data in columns using a typewriter, word processor, or spreadsheet. Unlike these methods, however, before you can begin entering information into a database table, you first must describe to Paradox the general nature of the data. You need to tell Paradox whether the data is alphanumeric (text), a memo (free-form text), numbers, currency, or dates; how long the longest name will be; how many characters are in the largest address, and so on. This description of the table is its *structure* or *definition*.

To define the Employee table, complete the following steps:

1. Select the **C**reate command from the menu bar. (Press C or click the **C**reate command in the menu bar with the mouse.) A small window opens on-screen with a blinking cursor to the right of the label `Table`. Type the table name, *Employee*, and press Enter. Paradox displays a table (a series of columns) entitled Struct (see fig. QS1.3). In this example, you define the structure of the Employee table.

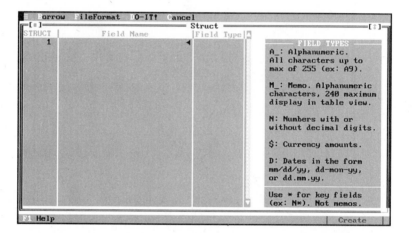

FIG. QS1.3

The Struct table.

2. The purpose of the Struct table is to define the columns in the table you are creating—the Employee table in this case. The entries you make in each row in Struct define a column, also called a *field*, that will appear in the Employee table. You must give each field a name. To name the first field in Employee, type *Emp ID #* beneath the Field Name heading and press Enter. The blinking cursor moves to the Field Type column.

3. The choices for field type are explained on the right side of your screen. To define the Emp ID # field as alphanumeric with a maximum length of 11, type *A11* and press Enter. Your screen then should look like figure QS1.4.

4. Following the same procedure, define the rest of the fields as indicated in figure QS1.5. To correct typing mistakes, erase the error with the Backspace key and retype the appropriate entry. You also can use the cursor-movement keys to move around the screen.

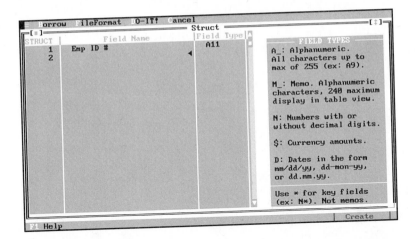

FIG. QS1.4

The Emp ID # field definition.

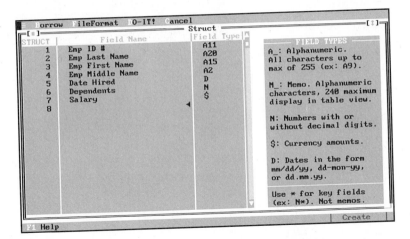

FIG. QS1.5

The completed Employee table.

5. After you have completed the definition, tell Paradox you are finished by pressing F2 (Do-It!) or by selecting **DO-IT!** from the menu bar. Paradox briefly displays a message that it is creating the Employee table and then returns to the menu bar. You are ready to begin entering data.

Entering Employee Data

Now that you have built a structure for your Employee table, you can enter data. If you have ever typed information in columns, you already know how to complete the next series of steps.

1. From the menu bar, select **M**odify, **D**ataEntry. (Press M and then D.) Type the name of your table, *Employee*, and press Enter. Paradox displays a window containing a table named Entry. This table contains an empty column for each field you defined for the Employee table (see fig. QS1.6).

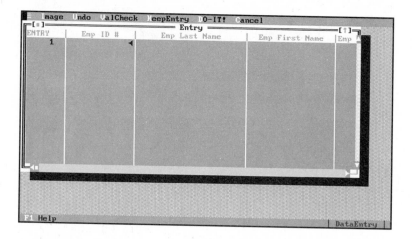

FIG. QS1.6

The DataEntry image.

2. Type the first employee ID number in the Emp ID # field:

   921-65-1234

   Press Enter. The cursor moves to the Emp Last Name field. Next, type the following data in the appropriate fields, pressing Enter at the end of each entry:

Emp Last Name	*English*
Emp First Name	*Gertrude*
Emp Middle Name	*M.*
Date Hired	*1/04/71*
Dependents	*2*
Salary	*36,750*

   As in the definition image, use the Backspace key to erase errors. After you press Enter at the Salary entry, Paradox starts a second row, and your screen should look like figure QS1.7.

3. Type the following data, using the same procedure:

Emp ID #	Emp Last Name	Emp First Name	Emp Middle Name	Date Hired	Depen-dents	Salary
541-67-5555	Kellogs	Emily	Q.	06/10/75	0	23,875.00
230-76-2376	Bronson	Tim	C.	11/23/69	3	41,400.00
111-33-8491	Jones	Harry	H.	06/07/78	2	32,250.00
329-76-2219	Albertson	Sharon	B.	03/04/81	1	21,870.00

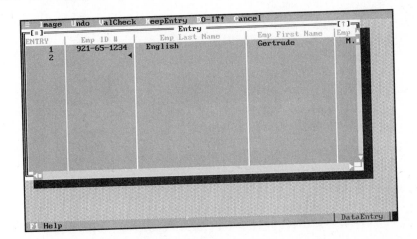

FIG. QS1.7

Beginning the second record.

4. Toggle on the built-in data-entry form (the Standard Form) by pressing F7. You now are looking at *Form view*, which shows you one record at a time. Use the form to enter the last three records, pressing Enter after every field. Pressing Enter at the last field on the form takes you to the next blank form. Use the PgUp and PgDn keys to move between forms if you need to make corrections.

Emp ID #	Emp Last Name	Emp First Name	Emp Middle Name	Date Hired	Depen-dents	Salary
448-09-6721	Green	George	H.	08/15/79	4	49,339.00
129-08-4562	Jones	Samantha	T.	10/02/65	1	75,900.00
987-31-9873	Quick	Joseph	L.	05/21/83	3	53,000.00

Press F7 again to return to the table view.

5. When finished, press F2 (Do-It!). Paradox saves the new data to disk, removes the Entry table from the screen and replaces it with the Employee table. Your screen should look similar to figure QS1.8. To clear the window from the screen, press F8 (Clear Image).

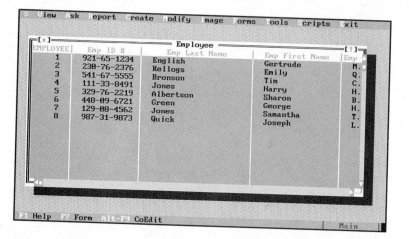

FIG. QS1.8

The Employee table.

Asking Questions of the Data

Imagine for a moment that you have entered data for 800 or even 8,000 employees, rather than only 8. With Paradox, you can easily search for one of those employees, regardless of how many you have, by using the Query By Example (QBE) method. The next several procedures in this lesson demonstrate a number of simple queries for your Employee table.

To find the name of the employee whose ID number is 111-33-8491, for example, do the following:

1. From the menu bar, select **Ask**.

2. Type the table name, *employee*, and press Enter. Paradox displays the Employee table again, but the table is empty. This window is a query form for the Employee table (see fig. QS1.9).

3. As indicated in the status bar at the bottom of the screen, you use the F6 key to check off the columns you want to see in the Answer table that results from your question. Use the mouse to click in the first row of the Emp ID # column, or use the right-arrow key to move the cursor to the Emp ID # column. Press the F6 key or use the mouse to click the F6 label in the status bar. Paradox places a

check mark (the ASCII square root symbol) in the column. Do the same thing in the first row of the Emp Last Name and Emp First Name columns.

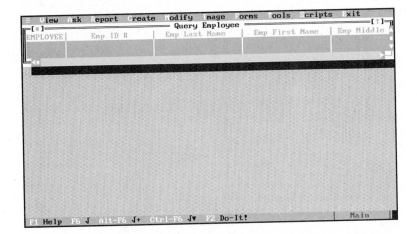

A query form for the Employee table.

4. Move the cursor back to the Emp ID # column and type the number that you want Paradox to match: *111-33-8491*. Press Enter and F2 (Do-It!). Paradox displays the Answer table in a window that overlaps the query form window, as shown in figure QS1.10. Harry Jones is your man. Press Alt-F8 (Clear) to clear the windows.

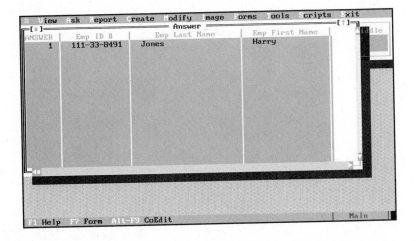

Finding an employee by searching for employee identification number.

Suppose that you need to find the salary for Tim Bronson, but you cannot remember whether the name is spelled Bronson or Brinson. Paradox enables you to look for text that is *like* the text you provide:

1. From the menu bar, select **Ask**, type *employee*, and press Enter. Use F6 to place check marks in the Emp Last Name, Emp First Name, and Salary columns.

2. Move the cursor to the Emp Last Name column, type *like Brinson*, and press F2 (Do-It!). Paradox displays the name and salary for Tim Bronson in the Answer table.

Suppose that you want to see the salary of Samantha Jones. Because more than one employee is named Jones, you must specify more than just the last name.

1. Press F8 (Clear Image) to clear the Answer table but not the query form.

2. Backspace over the entry in the Emp Last Name column and type *Jones*. Press Enter to move to the Emp First Name column and type *Samantha*. Press F2 (Do-It!). Paradox displays Ms. Jones's salary.

You also can use comparison operators in QBE. Assume that you want to see a list of all employees hired before January 1, 1980. You can do so by completing the following steps:

1. Clear all images with Alt-F8 and choose **Ask** from the menu bar. Type *employee* and then press Enter.

2. Use F6 to place a check mark in the Emp Last Name, Emp First Name, and Date Hired fields.

3. Type *<1/1/80* in the Date Hired field and press Enter. Then press F2 (Do-It!). The names and hire dates of the six employees hired before January 1, 1980 are displayed.

Sorting and Printing Your Data

Typically, you do not enter rows into a database table in any particular order. Paradox can retrieve any information from the table through the QBE process, regardless of the order of the rows in the table. When you display data on-screen or send data to the printer, however, you often want to see the information in order alphabetically, by date, by ID number, or in some other order. Follow these steps to sort the Employee table by ID number:

1. Start from a blank work area (press Alt-F8 to clear all images) and select **Modify**, **Sort**. Instead of typing *employee*, press Enter to see a list of available tables. Move the highlighted bar to Employee and press Enter.

2. To indicate that the results of the sort should replace the current contents of Employee, choose **S**ame from the menu that is attached to the bottom edge of the window. Paradox displays the form shown in figure QS1.11.

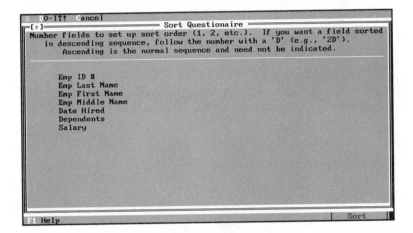

FIG. QS1.11

The sort form.

3. Paradox displays a cursor to the left of the Emp ID # field name. Type the number *1* to indicate that you want the table rows sorted by that field. Press F2 (Do-It!). Paradox sorts the data by ID number, as shown in figure QS1.12.

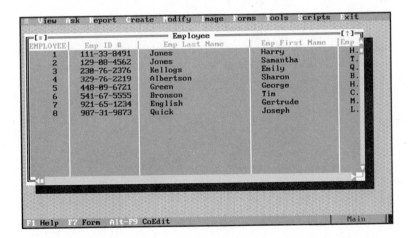

FIG. QS1.12

The Employee table viewed in order by Emp ID #.

Paradox has an *Instant Report* feature that immediately sends the currently viewed table to your printer. As your Employee table is currently displayed, however, it will not fit on normal 8 1/2-inch paper. You need to create an Answer table containing only each employee's ID number, name, and salary.

1. Clear the current image with F8 and then press F10 (Menu).

2. From the menu bar, select **Ask**. Type the table name *employee* (or press Enter and select the name).

3. Use F6 (Check Mark) to tell Paradox to display only the Emp ID #, Emp Last Name, Emp First Name, and Salary fields. Then press F2 (Do-It!). Paradox displays the Answer table.

4. Make sure that your printer is on and loaded with paper; then press Alt-F7 (Instant Report).

Suppose that you would rather see the list of employees in alphabetical order by name.

1. Display the menu by pressing F10 (Menu).

2. From the menu bar, select **Modify**, **Sort**. This time, indicate that you want to sort the Answer table (not Employee) by typing *answer* (or pressing Enter and selecting Answer from the list).

3. Select **Same**. Only the field names from the Answer table display.

4. Move the cursor to the Emp Last Name field and type the number *1*. Press Enter or the down-arrow key and type *2* next to Emp First Name. This setup causes the rows to be sorted in alphabetical order by last name and then by first name. ("Harry Jones" comes before "Samantha Jones," for example.)

5. Press F2 (Do-It!).

6. Finally, press Alt-F7 (Instant Print). Your report should look similar to figure QS1.13.

Quitting Paradox

You have almost completed your first Paradox session. Clear any remaining image on-screen by pressing Alt-F8 (Clear). To quit Paradox, select **Exit Yes**. Paradox displays the message Leaving Paradox in the bottom right corner of the screen, and returns you to DOS.

```
5/27/92              Standard Report           Page   1

 Emp ID #          Emp Last Name     Emp First Name      Salary
-----------        ----------------  ----------------   ----------
329-76-2219        Albertson         Sharon              21,870.00
230-76-2376        Bronson           Tim                 41,400.00
921-65-1234        English           Gertrude            36,750.00
448-09-6721        Green             George              49,339.00
111-33-8491        Jones             Harry               32,250.00
129-08-4562        Jones             Samantha            75,900.00
541-67-5555        Kellogs           Emily               23,875.00
987-31-9873        Quick             Joseph              53,000.00
```

FIG. QS1.13

The Employee table printed in alphabetical order by name.

Quick Start Summary

This first lesson gets you off to a flying start with Paradox. You practiced starting the program, creating a simple database table, querying, sorting the table, and quitting Paradox. Now you are ready to explore these topics in more detail. Chapter 1 begins the discussion by explaining how to find your way around Paradox.

Navigating Paradox

T his chapter helps you take an important first step in learning Paradox. You examine the program's *user interface*—how Paradox looks on-screen and how the program requests and responds to your actions. This chapter explains the Paradox screen, keyboard, menus, prompts, on-line help, and how you use these features to find your way around the program. Start with this chapter if you are new to Paradox, even if you are an experienced PC user.

If you have used other database programs, Paradox probably has a familiar feel to you. Paradox is unique in many ways, however. This chapter begins introducing you to the fundamental concepts of Paradox. You are ready to proceed with this chapter if you have started Paradox and displayed the Main menu on-screen. Refer to Appendix A if you need instructions for installing and running Paradox.

Familiarizing Yourself with the Paradox Screen

The first Paradox screen displayed is the Title screen. The Paradox logo and your signature information display as the program is loaded into the computer's memory. After the program is loaded, press any key, and Paradox removes the logo and signature information from the screen and displays a screen like the one shown in figure 1.1. The Main menu is the home base from which you begin many tasks in Paradox. The following paragraphs describe the various parts of the Paradox screen.

FIG. 1.1

The Paradox
Main menu.

The Menu Area

Reminder:
The line at the bottom of the screen displays a description of each menu option as it is highlighted.

Paradox makes heavy use of menus. The top line of the screen is the *menu bar*, which displays the Main menu options. The bottom line of the screen is the *status bar*, which displays a description of each menu option as it is highlighted. Note that in figure 1.1, the **View** option is highlighted, and the status line reads `View a table`. Refer to the section "Using Paradox Menus and Prompts" later in this chapter for a discussion of how best to select menu choices.

The Mode Indicator

The major Paradox functions are divided into 14 modes—the Main mode and 13 subordinate modes, including the following:

Report Design
Report Preview
Create
Sort
Edit
CoEdit

Editor
DataEntry
Restructure
Index
Form Design
Password
Graph Design

Paradox always displays the current mode in the bottom right corner of the screen. This message is the *mode indicator*. Figure 1.2, for example, shows that Paradox is in the Main mode. Paradox does not display a mode indicator at the Main menu (see fig. 1.1), but when the Main menu is displayed, the program is in Main mode.

Reminder:
Paradox displays the mode
in the bottom right corner.

```
  View  sk  eport  reate  odify  mage  orms  ools  cripts  xit
 [ ]                        Employee                        [↑]
EMPLOYEE    Emp  ID #         Emp Last Name        Emp First Name    Emp
      1   111-33-8491    Jones                Harry                  H.
      2   129-08-4562    Jones                Samantha               T.
      3   230-76-2376    Kellogs              Emily                  Q.
      4   329-76-2219    Albertson            Sharon                 B.
      5   448-09-6721    Green                George                 H.
      6   541-67-5555    Bronson              Tim                    C.
      7   921-65-1234    English              Gertrude               M.
      8   987-31-9873    Quick                Joseph                 L.




F1 Help   F7 Form  Alt-F9 CoEdit                           Main
```

FIG. 1.2

The mode
indicator.

Each Paradox mode has its own set of menus and prompts. (The pull-out menu map at the back of this book groups the menus according to mode.) For example, Paradox moves from Main mode to Sort mode when you decide to sort your data into an order different from the order in which the information was entered. To accomplish a sort, you select **M**odify, **S**ort from the Main menu (press M and then press S or use the mouse to click **M**odify and then **S**ort). Then enter the name of the table to be sorted and indicate whether the sorted data should be placed in the original table or in a new table. Paradox displays a screen like figure 1.3. Paradox is now in the Sort mode, as indicated by the word Sort in the mode indicator.

Reminder:
Each Paradox mode has its
own set of menus and
prompts.

Database terminology can be slightly confusing, and the purpose of these various modes may not at first be clear. One reason for the mode concept and the mode indicator, however, is to help prevent possible confusion without sacrificing a consistent user interface. Paradox is designed so that you can enter, view, and edit data from nearly identical screens but still tell one screen from another. Compare figures 1.4, 1.5, and 1.6. Moving between columns (fields) or rows (records) is the same in any of the three contexts, so you have less to learn. Keep in mind that these database management functions are distinct and should not be confused.

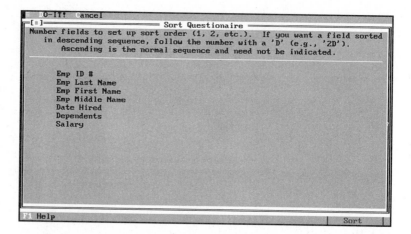

FIG. 1.3

The Sort mode.

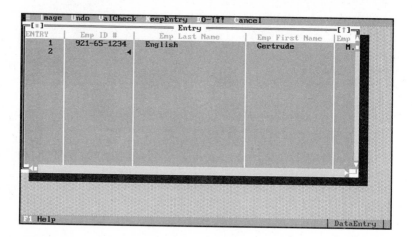

FIG. 1.4

The DataEntry mode.

The following rules apply to Paradox modes:

- ■ Paradox can be in only one mode at a time.

- ■ All modes are subordinate to the Main mode.

- ■ You can access subordinate modes only through the Main mode. You cannot, for example, go directly from the Edit mode to the Sort mode.

■ To leave a subordinate mode, you must execute the **Do-It!** command (F2) or select the Cancel option from the menu (*Note:* F2 (Do-It!) is the only way to exit CoEdit mode).

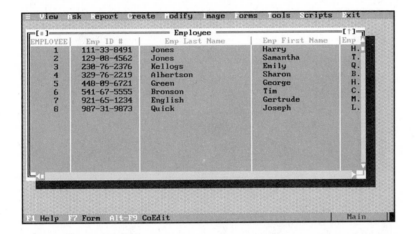

FIG. 1.5

The Main mode.

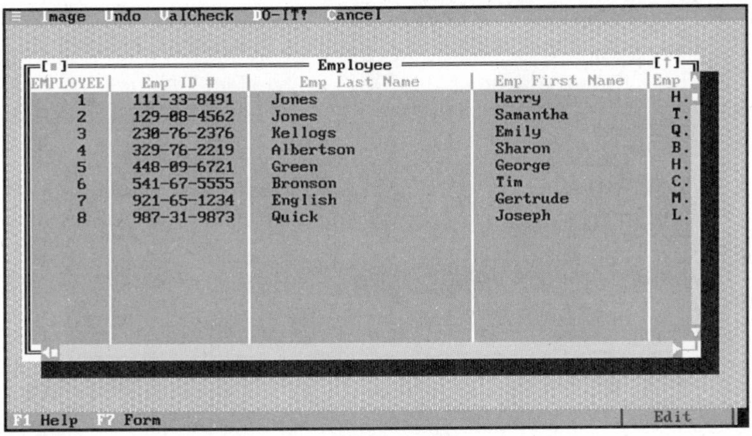

FIG. 1.6

The Edit mode.

The Message Area

At various times, Paradox displays messages on-screen. Information and error messages often appear just above the status bar, in the lower right corner of the screen, in inverse video (white letters on a red background, when viewed on a color monitor). Pressing F6 while at the Main menu, for example, results in the error message shown in figure 1.7. Keep an eye on this corner of the screen for messages from Paradox.

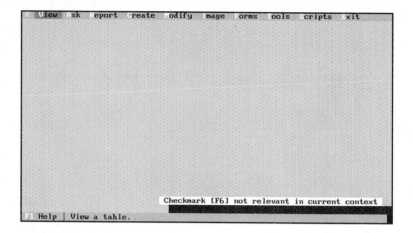

FIG. 1.7

An error message in the message area.

The Desktop

The largest portion of the initial Main menu screen, the *desktop*, is blank. This part of the screen is the area in which you enter, display, and edit your data. The Paradox desktop is similar in concept to the work area of a spreadsheet, and at times looks almost identical to a spreadsheet. Indeed, Paradox enables you to place *windows* on the desktop in a way that is similar in appearance and operation to the Borland spreadsheet program Quattro Pro.

Reminder:
Multiple windows can be on the desktop at the same time.

You can have multiple windows on the desktop at one time, and each on-screen window can display a different view of a particular table of data or a view of another table (see fig. 1.8). This capability is analogous to having more than one spreadsheet displayed on-screen at the same time.

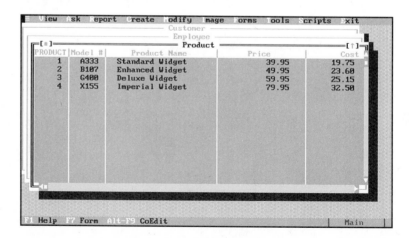

FIG. 1.8

The desktop with multiple windows.

The Paradox 4.0 window concept is discussed more fully in "Understanding Windows," later in this chapter. Think of each window on the desktop as a window into your data. Unless you have a very small amount of data in your table, you cannot display all the data on the desktop at the same time. At most, you can see one screen of information on the desktop at a time, but the actual data in your table is limited in size only by the capacity of your disk drive.

For Related Information:

▶▶ "Entering Data in DataEntry Mode," p. 99.

▶▶ "Entering and Editing Data in Edit Mode," p. 109.

▶▶ "Entering and Editing Data in CoEdit Mode," p. 119.

FROM HERE...

Using the Keyboard

Paradox works with any PC-, AT-, or PS/2-style keyboard or equivalent. The program uses practically every key on the keyboard in one way or another, so you need to be familiar with your keyboard (see fig. 1.9). This book uses the labels found on the IBM Enhanced Keyboard to describe the keys you should press.

Paradox Function-Key Commands

As with many other popular programs, Paradox makes heavy use of the function keys F1 through F10. A keyboard template for each of the two most popular function-key layouts (vertical and horizontal) is provided with the program. If you have not already done so, place the template on your keyboard and use it to help you learn Paradox. You soon will have the key commands committed to memory.

Eight of the ten function keys also are used with the Alt key, four with Ctrl, and two with Shift. In some cases, a function-key command has an equivalent menu command that you can execute through the Paradox menus. Using menus, however, always requires more keystrokes or mouse clicks, so you should use the function-key method whenever possible.

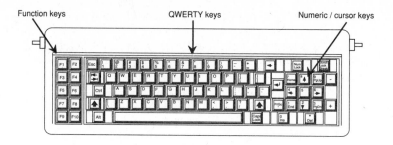

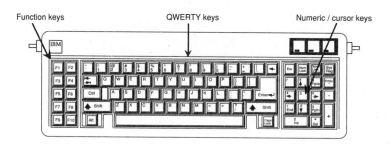

FIG. 1.9

The IBM PC
keyboard (top),
the IBM Personal
Computer AT
keyboard
(center), and the
IBM Enhanced
keyboard
(bottom).

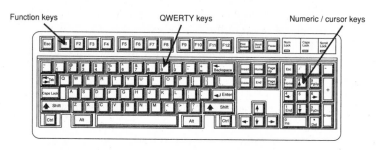

Table 1.1 includes a complete list of the function keys and function-key combinations along with the names assigned to them by Paradox. Several of these key combinations are used in Quick Start 1. The same list is provided for your convenience on the inside front cover of this book. Throughout the book, these keys are referenced by the labels you find on the keys, followed by the Paradox key name in parentheses, as in F2 (Do-It!) and Alt-F7 (Instant Report). (Note that Alt-F7 means that you should hold down the Alt key while you press the F7 key.)

Table 1.1. Paradox Function Key Names

Function key	Name
F1	Help
F2	DO-IT!
F3	Previous Image
Alt-F3	Instant Script Record
F4	Next Image
Alt-F4	Instant Script Play
Ctrl-F4	Next
F5	Example
Alt-F5	Field View
Ctrl-F5	Move/Size Active Window
Shift-F5	Maximize/Restore Active Window
F6	Check Mark
Alt-F6	Check Plus
Ctrl-F6	Check Descending
Shift-F6	Group By
F7	Form Toggle
Alt-F7	Instant Report
Ctrl-F7	View Graph
F8	Close Active Window
Alt-F8	Clear Desktop
Ctrl-F8	Close Active Window (or Canvas, if present)
F9	Edit
Alt-F9	CoEdit
F10	Menu Bar

The uses for these keys are explained in subsequent chapters.

Special Key Commands in Paradox

In addition to the function keys, Paradox uses several other keys in combination with the Ctrl or Alt key for special quick commands. Table 1.2 lists the key combinations and corresponding command names. (This table is also printed on the inside front cover.)

Table 1.2. Paradox Special Keys

Key	Name
Alt-C	Color Palette
Ctrl-D	Ditto
Alt-E	Editor
Ctrl-F	Field View (same as Alt-F5)
Alt-K	Key Viol
Alt-L	Lock Toggle
Ctrl-L	ReSync
Ctrl-O	DOS
Alt-O	DOS Big
Ctrl-R	Rotate
Alt-R	Refresh
Alt-S	Secondary Index
Ctrl-U	Undo
Ctrl-V	Vertical Ruler
Alt-X	Crosstab
Ctrl-Y	Delete Line
Ctrl-Z	Zoom
Alt-Z	Zoom Next

These special keystroke commands are explained fully and demonstrated in subsequent chapters. Like the function-key commands, they represent the quickest way to accomplish results. (Note that Ctrl-F, however, is equivalent to Alt-F5; both require the same number of keystrokes.)

For Related Information:

▶▶ "Entering and Editing Data in Edit Mode," p. 109.

▶▶ "Entering and Editing Data in CoEdit Mode," p. 119.

▶▶ "Selecting Fields in Query By Example," p. 160.

▶▶ "Using the Instant Report Feature," p. 187.

FROM HERE...

Using Paradox Menus and Prompts

Most PC-based programs are command-driven, menu-driven, or both. Paradox tends toward the menu-driven side, with the notable exception of the keyboard commands listed in tables 1.1 and 1.2.

Using the "Point-and-Shoot" Selection Method

Paradox menus are in the style of Borland's Quattro Pro. You can choose menu options by moving the inverse video bar (the highlight) to the appropriate choice and pressing Enter. This menu selection method is sometimes called the *point-and-shoot* method. While a choice is highlighted (and before you press Enter) Paradox displays a message in the status bar at the bottom of the screen that describes the effect of selecting the highlighted option. Moving the highlight to the **Ask** option on the Main menu, for example, displays the following message:

> Get a query form to ask questions about a table.

Often the effect of choosing a menu option is to display a pull-down submenu containing options that display still other submenus. Choosing **T**ools from the Main menu, for example, displays a submenu listing the following options:

> **R**ename
> **Q**uerySpeedup
> **E**xportImport
> **C**opy

Reminder:
You can choose menu options by moving the highlight and pressing Enter.

Delete
Info
Net
More

Selecting **M**ore from this submenu results in another pull-down submenu that includes the following options:

Add
MultiAdd
FormAdd
Subtract
Empty
Protect
Directory
ToDOS

You can think of the hierarchical structure of these menus as a tree, with each menu selection moving you out onto branches or sub-branches of the tree. (Refer to the pull-out menu map at the back of this book.)

You can easily tell which menu options have submenus. Each menu option that displays a triangular pointer (▶) to its right displays a submenu when you select that option.

If you get too far out on a limb, you can back out by pressing the Esc key. Pressing Esc uniformly reverses your steps, moving you back to your beginning point, one level at a time. To return to the first level, no matter how deep you are in the menu tree, press F10.

T I P   You can remove all submenus in one step by clicking an empty spot on the desktop.

 NOTE   Probably the most common mistake made by a new user of any software package is failing to read the prompts and messages provided on-screen. Get in the habit of reading thoroughly all screen messages, especially when you are working with a feature for the first time. This practice can prevent needless errors, and the screen prompts can help you learn Paradox faster and with less frustration.

Using the Mouse and First-Letter Selection Methods

When you are more familiar with the choices in the various Paradox menus, you can begin to use an alternative method of selecting menu options.

If you have attached a mouse pointing device to your computer, you can use your mouse to select a menu option. Move the mouse pointer to the menu option and click either mouse button.

With the appropriate menu displayed, another alternative to the point-and-shoot selection is to press the first letter of your choice regardless of the position of the highlight. If no highlight is displayed, you first must press F10 (Menu Bar) to activate the highlight in the menu bar. Then you can press the first letter of the menu choice.

The mouse and the first-letter methods are quicker and more accurate than the point-and-shoot method. Paradox highlights on-screen the first letter of each command. In this book, the first letter of each menu command is in boldface, as in **A**sk, to indicate that you can press A to select the command.

Cue:
Use the mouse or first-letter method for quick and accurate menu selection.

Many operations require a sequence of menu selections. This book lists the options you should select side by side, separated by commas, in the appropriate order. The following example means that you should select the **M**odify option and then the **R**estructure option:

Modify, **R**estructure

Every effort has been made to present menu options in this book exactly as they appear on-screen. To be consistent with Paradox menus, no spaces are shown between words of multiword commands if they appear with no spaces on-screen.

Using Paradox Screen Prompts

As you use Paradox, you often are presented with a prompt, rather than a menu or message, in a window. A *prompt* is different from a message in that a prompt requests your response, whereas a message is informative only.

Many times the prompt asks you to enter the name or number of a Paradox object (a table, form, report, and so on). To view the Employee table, for example, select **V**iew from the Main menu. Paradox displays the prompt Table followed by an empty *text box* (see fig. 1.10). A message in the status bar instructs you to enter the name of the table to

Cue:
Press Enter at a prompt to see a list of available tables.

view or to press Enter for a list. You can type the name, but, as the message suggests, you also can press Enter to see a list of available tables. Alternatively, you can use the mouse to click the OK command button. (A *command button* is a rectangular block on-screen that is labeled with a command—in this case, the word OK).

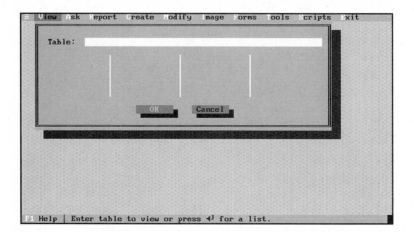

FIG. 1.10

A screen prompt asking for the table name.

When a list is displayed, such as the sample list of tables shown in figure 1.11, you can select from the list just as you select a menu option: click the name with the mouse, press the cursor-movement keys to move the highlight to the name of the item you want to view and then press Enter, or press the first letter of the item's name.

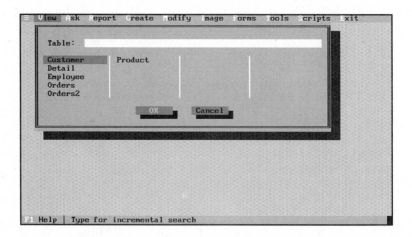

FIG. 1.11

A list of available tables.

Occasionally more than one item name begins with the same letter, as do the Orders and Orders2 tables in figure 1.11. Pressing the first letter causes Paradox to move the highlight to the first item that begins with that letter (see fig. 1.12). You then can use the point-and-shoot or mouse methods to complete the selection, or you can press the second letter in the item name to narrow the choices further, and so on.

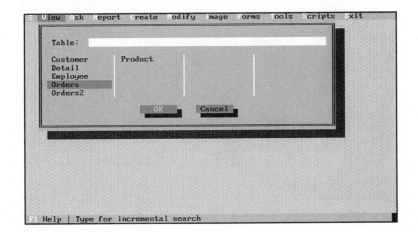

FIG. 1.12

Finding the first table name that begins with the letter O.

When Paradox asks for the name of an existing Paradox table or graph or for the number of a form or report, you can press Enter to display a list of available objects. Then use the first-letter, mouse, or point-and-shoot method to choose the object you want Paradox to use.

Understanding Paradox Views

One of the most important benefits of using a relational database is that you do not have to worry about how data is stored. You do, however, have to understand how to interpret what is displayed on-screen.

Working in Table View

Paradox normally displays data in the work area of the screen in a tabular fashion, called *table view* (see fig. 1.13). This view shows as many rows and columns as fit on-screen—up to 20 rows by 78 characters. Only one row or record is active at a time; this active record is indicated by the position of the blinking cursor. When the screen is not wide enough to display all field data, the last column is abbreviated.

Reminder:
Paradox normally displays data in table view.

If the content of the abbreviated field is numbers, the field appears filled with asterisks (see fig. 1.15, shown later in this chapter).

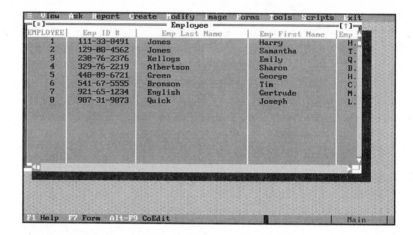

FIG. 1.13

An example of table view.

Moving the cursor in table view is easy. Use the cursor-movement keys to go from column to column and from row to row (see table 1.3).

Table 1.3. Using Cursor-Movement Keys in Table View

Key	Moves cursor
Home	To first record of table
Ctrl-Home	To first field of record
End	To last record of table
Ctrl-End	To last field of record
PgUp	Up one window screen
PgDn	Down one window screen
Left arrow	Left one field
Ctrl-left arrow	Left one screen
Right arrow	Right one field
Ctrl-right arrow	Right one screen
Up arrow	Up one record
Down arrow	Down one record
Enter	Right one field

Working in Form View

You may prefer to work with only one record on-screen at a time. With Paradox, this feat is as simple as pressing F7 (Form Toggle). Figure 1.14 shows the first record from the table in figure 1.13. The record now is displayed in *form view*—a window displays one record at a time from the selected table. In figure 1.14, the sample form view is displayed in a window on top of the window that contained the table view.

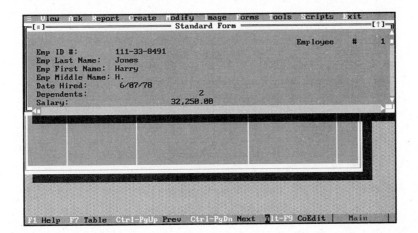

FIG. 1.14

A record displayed in form view.

Paradox automatically builds a form for use in form view. This *Standard Form* is *form F*. Paradox enables you to create up to 14 additional forms for use with each table. Chapter 8 covers in detail the many powerful form-design features available in Paradox. Paradox even can create forms for use with more than one table at a time.

Reminder:
You can create up to 15 forms per table.

As in table view, you can easily move around the screen by using the cursor-movement keys (see table 1.4).

Table 1.4. Using Cursor-Movement Keys in Form View

Key	Moves cursor
Home	To first record of table
Ctrl-Home	To first field of record
End	To last record of table
Ctrl-End	To last field of record
PgUp	To preceding page or record

continues

Table 1.4. Continued

Key	Moves cursor
Ctrl-PgUp	To same field of preceding record
PgDn	To next page or record
Ctrl-PgDn	To same field of next record
Left arrow	To preceding field
Right arrow	To next field
Up arrow	Up one field
Down arrow	Down one field
Enter	Next field

Working in Field View

Two basic tasks in database management are data entry and data editing. Chapter 3 explains the basics of both tasks. In either case, you always are entering or editing one field at a time. Paradox normally enables you to change an entry only from the end of the field. To correct a mistake, you back up to the point where the error was made, using the Backspace key, and type the correct data.

As an alternative to having to retype erroneous entries, Paradox provides *field view* for editing data. To activate this view, move the mouse pointer to the field and *double-click* either mouse button (press a button twice in quick succession). Alternatively, place the cursor in the field to be changed and press Alt-F5 (Field View) or Ctrl-F (Field View).

Cue:
To activate field view, press Alt-F5 (Field View). The cursor becomes an inverse video block.

In field view, the cursor becomes an inverse video block to remind you that you are using field view. Otherwise, the screen looks exactly as it did before you pressed Alt-F5 (Field View). You can use field view when entering and editing data within table view or form view. The cursor keys (listed in table 1.5) are available then for moving within the field without erasing the existing data. You also can use the Ins and Del keys to add or subtract characters or digits from the field.

Table 1.5. Using Cursor-Movement Keys in Field View

Key	Moves cursor
Home	To first character of field
End	To last character of field
Left arrow	One character left
Ctrl-left arrow	One word left
Right arrow	One character right
Ctrl-right arrow	One word right
Up arrow	Up one line (in wrapped fields)
Down arrow	Down one line (in wrapped fields)

When you finish correcting an entry, press Enter to return to the normal table or form view. You need to press Enter again to move to the next field (or next record, if you are editing the last field of a record). Refer to Chapter 3 for a more complete discussion of entering and editing data with Paradox.

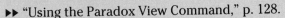

For Related Information:

▶▶ "Enjoying the View," p. 98.

▶▶ "Using the Paradox View Command," p. 128.

FROM HERE...

Understanding Windows

Understanding the window concept is fundamental to learning Paradox 4.0. A *window* is a rectangular area of the desktop containing data from one table. No windows appear on the opening Paradox desktop, but Paradox can display multiple windows on-screen (see fig. 1.15).

As you open multiple windows, Paradox creates a *stack* of overlapping windows on-screen. Windows that overlap are said to be *cascading*. Refer to "Creating Tiled and Cascading Windows" later in this chapter for a discussion of how to have windows appear side by side, rather than cascading.

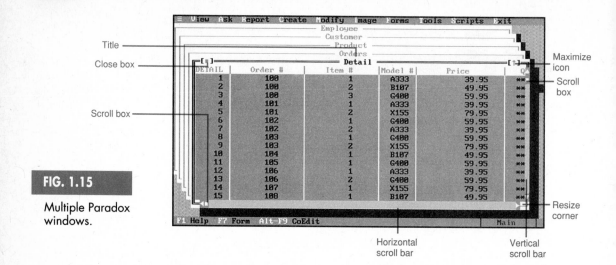

Title

Close box

Scroll box

Maximize icon

Scroll box

FIG. 1.15

Multiple Paradox windows.

Resize corner

Horizontal scroll bar

Vertical scroll bar

The border of every Paradox 4.0 window contains a title in the center of its top edge. When you are viewing a table in table view, Paradox displays the table name as the window title. In form view, however, Paradox uses the name of the form as the window title (refer back to fig. 1.14).

All windows on-screen are affected by the current mode. You cannot, for example, have one window in Main mode and another window in Edit mode on-screen at the same time.

Recognizing the Active Window

The *active window* is the topmost window—the one on top of the stack; it is surrounded by a double-line, highlighted border. You do all work in the active window, and you can edit data in the active window only.

Except in the case of a Report Preview window (discussed in Chapter 5, "Getting Started with Reports"), the active window contains a blinking cursor.

Closing a Window

The window border of the active window displays a *close box* near the upper left corner (see fig. 1.15). Click the close box with the mouse to close the active window. In some modes, such as Report mode, Paradox asks for confirmation before it closes the window. In other modes, such as Edit mode, you must choose DO-IT! or Cancel before you can close the window.

> **CAUTION:** You can use Ctrl-Break to close a window. You should use this keystroke with caution, however, because Paradox does not save any work that you have done and does not ask for confirmation before closing the window.

You also can close a window using the keyboard. The function key commands F8 and Ctrl-F8 (Close Active Window) close the active window. Alternatively, you can click the System menu button (in the upper-left corner of the screen) or press Alt-space bar to display the System menu, as shown in figure 1.16. Select the Close option to cause Paradox to close the active window.

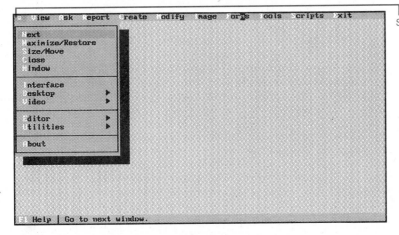

System menu button

FIG. 1.16

The System menu.

For Related Information:

▶▶ "Using the Image Options," p. 129.

▶▶ "Windows," p. 509.

▶▶ "Handling Windows," p. 577.

▶▶ "Using the Paradox Editor", p. 142.

Maximizing and Restoring a Window

When you first open a window, a *Maximize* icon—an upward-pointing arrow—appears near the upper right corner of the window border. If you click this icon, Paradox zooms the window to full-screen size (see fig 1.17). All other open windows are hidden from view.

Restore icon

DETAIL	Order #	Item #	Model #	Price	Quantity
1	100	1	A333	39.95	50
2	100	2	B107	49.95	25
3	100	3	G400	59.95	10
4	101	1	A333	39.95	15
5	101	2	X155	79.95	10
6	102	1	G400	59.95	35
7	102	2	A333	39.95	10
8	103	1	G400	59.95	22
9	103	2	X155	79.95	5
10	104	1	B107	49.95	45
11	105	1	G400	59.95	30
12	106	1	A333	39.95	15
13	106	2	G400	59.95	5
14	107	1	X155	79.95	10
15	108	1	B107	49.95	60
16	109	1	G400	59.95	25
17	109	2	B107	49.95	30
18	110	1	A333	39.95	5
19	110	2	B107	49.95	5
20	112	1	A333	39.95	29

F1 Help   F7 Form   Alt-F9 CoEdit   Main

FIG. 1.17

The Detail window after clicking the Maximize icon.

To maximize the active window using the keyboard, press Shift-F5 (Maximize/Restore Active Window). Alternatively, you can click the System menu button or press Ctrl-space bar to display the System menu and select **M**aximize/Restore.

After Paradox zooms a window to full-screen size, the Restore icon—a two-headed arrow—replaces the Maximize icon, as shown in figure 1.17. Use the mouse to click the Restore icon to shrink the active window to its original size (its size before you clicked the Maximize icon).

To restore the window using the keyboard, press Shift-F5 (Maximize/Restore), or display the System menu and choose **M**aximize/Restore.

Moving and Resizing a Window

When you have several windows open on the Paradox desktop, you may want to move one window to a different screen location in order to see data in another window. You also may want to shrink or expand the size of a window on the desktop. Paradox provides several methods for moving and sizing windows.

The easiest way to move a window is to use the mouse to *drag* the window to a new location. Move the mouse pointer to any point along the upper border of the active window. Click and hold down either mouse button. While holding the mouse button, move the mouse pointer to drag the window to its new location.

You also can resize the active window using the mouse. Paradox displays a *resize corner* at the lower right corner of each active window (refer to figs. 1.15 and 1.17). You can use this feature to change the dimensions of the active window on-screen.

Click the resize corner and hold the mouse button. Holding the button, move the mouse pointer to a different location on the desktop. As you move the pointer, Paradox resizes the window. To make the window smaller, move the mouse pointer up and/or to the left. To make the window larger, move the close corner down and/or to the right. Figure 1.18 shows the Employee table after resizing.

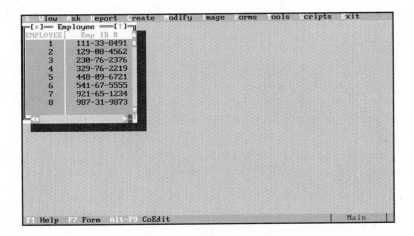

FIG. 1.18

The Employee table after resizing.

As an alternative to the mouse, you can use the keyboard to move or size the active window. Press Ctrl-F5 (Move/Size Active Window) or display the System menu and select **S**ize/Move. Paradox displays the following message in the Status bar:

← ↑ ↓ → move window, Shift-arrows resize it, then ↵

Use the arrow keys (←, ↑, ↓, and →) to move the window around the desktop. Hold Shift and use the arrow keys to expand or contract the size of the window.

Recognizing Inactive Windows

Inactive windows are surrounded by single-line borders that do not display a Close box, Maximize/Restore icon, or Resize corner. Inactive windows also do not display a blinking cursor.

When windows are overlapping, inactive windows appear to be beneath the active window.

Scrolling a Window

Because the desktop is larger than just one screen, sometimes a table (or more than one table) is on the desktop, but the table is not displayed fully on-screen. This situation is always the case when you are working in form view because form view displays only one record at a time.

You can use the cursor-movement keys listed in tables 1.3 and 1.4 to move around a table in table view or form view, respectively. While in table view, however, you also can use the mouse and the two *scroll bars* to move the cursor around the table—referred to as *scrolling* the table.

On the right side of the active window is the *vertical scroll bar* (refer to fig. 1.15). Use the mouse to click the down-scroll arrow to display records hidden below the bottom edge of the screen. Each time you click the arrow, Paradox scrolls one more record on-screen. Click the up-scroll arrow to display records hidden above the upper edge of the window.

Cue:
Drag the scroll box up or down in the scroll bar to move up or down quickly through the table.

To move up or down quickly through the table, you can *drag* the scroll box up or down in the scroll bar. Place the mouse pointer on the scroll box and press either mouse button. While holding the mouse button, move the mouse pointer up or down in the scroll bar, in the direction of the records you want Paradox to display. When the records of interest are visible, release the mouse button.

Moving between Windows

Cue:
To move between windows, click the mouse in any portion of the target.

To move between windows, click the mouse in any portion of what will become the new active window. To move from the Detail table displayed earlier in figure 1.15 to the Customer table, for example, you can click the window title `Customer`. Paradox brings the Customer window to the top of the stack, as shown in figure 1.19.

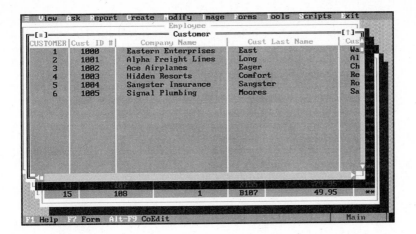

FIG. 1.19

Moving the
Customer table to
the top of the
stack.

If you want to use the keyboard to move between windows, you have
several alternatives:

- Press F3 (Previous Image) to move one window down in the
  stack—from Detail to Orders, for example, in the screen shown in
  figure 1.15.

- Press F4 (Next Image) to move to the next window up in the
  stack—from Orders to Detail, in the screen shown in figure 1.15.

- Press Ctrl-F4 (Next) to move the bottommost window in the stack
  to the top of the stack. Alternatively, select Next from the System
  menu.

For Related Information:

▶▶ "Using the Image Options," p. 129.

▶▶ "Windows," p. 509.

▶▶ "Handling Windows," p. 577.

FROM HERE...

Controlling the Desktop

As described in the preceding sections of this chapter, Paradox enables
you to control the size and position of each window on the desktop.

The program also provides several commands that enable you to control the position and size of all open windows in one step. The sections that follow describe these commands.

Redrawing the Screen

Cue:

From the Desktop menu, select **R**edraw to repaint the entire screen.

An interruption by a memory-resident program occasionally may cause your Paradox 4.0 screen to display bogus information—perhaps a message or data from the memory resident program. If you suspect that you have this problem, you can use the Redraw command to correct the display. Click the System menu icon or press Alt-space bar to display the System menu. Choose **D**esktop to display the Desktop menu (see fig. 1.20). Then select **R**edraw to cause Paradox 4.0 to repaint the entire screen.

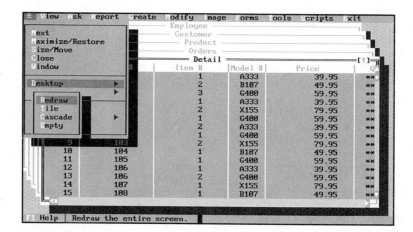

FIG. 1.20

The Desktop menu.

Creating Tiled and Cascading Windows

As you open multiple windows, Paradox creates a *stack* of overlapping windows on-screen. The contents of the topmost window are visible, but the other windows are obstructed by the active window. Windows that overlap in this fashion are said to be *cascading*. Sometimes you may want to see the contents of all open windows side by side. Windows displayed in a side-by-side format are said to be *tiled*.

To have Paradox display open windows in a tiled pattern, display the System menu and choose **D**esktop to display the Desktop menu. From the Desktop menu select **T**ile. Paradox moves and resizes all open windows into a side-by-side arrangement, as shown in figure 1.21.

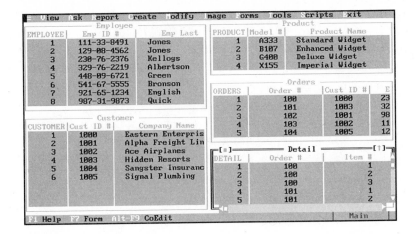

FIG. 1.21

Tiled windows.

 NOTE Even though you have selected Tile from the Desktop menu, any additional windows you open are displayed in the original cascading format.

To return the open windows to the cascading format, display the Desktop menu and choose Cascade.

Emptying (Clearing) the Desktop

As described earlier in this chapter, you can close each window, one at a time, by clicking the Close box, by pressing F8 (Close Active Window), or by choosing Close from the System menu. Paradox also enables you to close all open windows in one step, by *emptying* the desktop.

To close all open windows at once, press Alt-F8 (Clear Desktop) or select Empty from the Desktop menu.

 NOTE The Empty command on the Desktop menu abandons any unsaved changes that you may have made in the Edit or CoEdit modes. Alt-F8 (Clear Desktop) is not available in either mode.

Choosing an Enhanced Video Mode

By default, Paradox automatically detects the mode of the video adapter installed in your computer and displays on-screen the most appropriate number of rows and columns for that mode and adapter. In addition to this automatic setting, Paradox also offers several custom settings tailored for EGA and VGA adapters and for particular brands and models of video adapters with enhanced features, such as the capability to display 132 columns.

To activate one of the enhanced video modes, display the System menu and select **Video**. Choose from the following options:

- **A**: *Auto-detect*. The default option.

- **B**: *Monochrome*. Use with monochrome (single color) video adapters only.

- **C**: *EGA/VGA: 80 × 25*. Use with any EGA or VGA adapter. This option displays 80 characters by 25 lines.

- **D**: *EGA/VGA: 80 × 43/50*. Use with any EGA or VGA adapter. This option displays 80 characters by 43 lines on an EGA adapter and 80 characters by 50 lines on a VGA adapter.

- **E**: *Ahead Systems VGA Wizard*. Use only with an Ahead Systems VGA Wizard video adapter.

- **F**: *ATI VGA Wonder*. Use only with an ATI VGA Wonder adapter.

- **G**: *Compaq integrated (132 column) VGS*. Use only with a Compaq VGS adapter.

- **H**: *Everex Viewpoint VGA/EV-673 VGA*. Use only with an Everex Viewpoint VGA/EV-673 adapter.

- **I**: *Genoa Systems Super VGA*. Use only with the Genoa Systems Super VGA adapter.

- **J**: *Orchid ProDesigner VGA*. Use only with an Orchid ProDesigner VGA adapter.

- **K**: *Paradise EGA 480/VGA 1024*. Use only with a Paradise adapter.

- **L**: *Sigma VGA Legend/HP16*. Use only with a Sigma VGA Legend/HP16 adapter.

- **M**: *STB PowerGraph VGA*. Use only with an STB PowerGraph VGA adapter.

- **N**: *Video-7 VRAM VGA*. Use only with a Video-7 VRAM VGA adapter.

For Related Information:

▶▶ "Installing the Main Program," p. 988.

▶▶ "Setting Video Defaults," p. 997.

FROM HERE...

Switching to the 3.5 User Interface

Although the Paradox 4.0 user interface offers significant advantages over its predecessor, you may have already developed a PAL (Paradox Application Language) application that needs to be run in the Paradox 3.5 interface. To accommodate such a situation, Paradox 4.0 enables you to switch back to the Paradox 3.5 interface—referred to as *compatibility mode*.

To activate *compatibility mode*, display the System menu and select Interface. Paradox displays a pop-up menu in the center of the screen that asks Are you sure? Select **Yes**. Paradox switches to the Paradox 3.5-style user interface shown in figure 1.22.

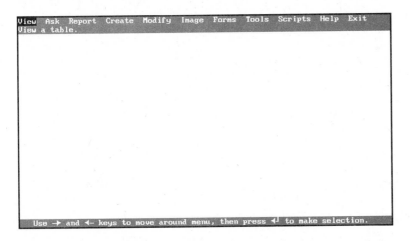

FIG. 1.22

The Paradox 3.5-style compatibility mode.

To return to the standard Paradox 4.0 user interface, press Alt-space bar to display the following short System menu:

```
Interface    About
```

Select Interface and then **Yes.** Paradox switches back to the Paradox 4.0 user interface.

NOTE When you switch between the standard Paradox 4.0 user interface and the compatibility mode, Paradox empties the desktop first. Be sure to save all changes before executing this operation.

FROM HERE...

For Related Information:

▶▶ "Installing the Main Program," p. 988.

▶▶ "Setting Video Defaults," p. 997.

Getting Help from Paradox

Cue:
Press F1 (Help) for on-line help.

Even though Paradox is an easy program to learn and use, you may not always be sure how to proceed. When you are looking for a brief explanation or a memory jogger, use the context-sensitive Paradox help system, which is available by pressing F1 (Help) at any screen. Paradox displays a screen of information specific to the task at hand.

Using the Help Screen

Reminder:
The Paradox help system is context-sensitive.

The Paradox help screen is divided into four areas: the menu area, the screen title, the message area, and the help information. The Help menu works in the same way as all other Paradox menus. Use the mouse, the point-and-shoot method, or the first-letter method to make your choices. The Esc key retraces your steps and takes you to the preceding help screen or the screen at which you started. Because the help system is context-sensitive, the choices on the menu depend on what you are doing when you ask for help. Press F1 (Help) at the Main menu to see the screen shown in figure 1.23.

When you select one of the options listed in the menu area, Paradox displays a help screen about the chosen topic, and another menu appears at the top of the screen, often presenting related topics of a more specific nature. Choosing **K**eys from the Help menu in figure 1.23, for example, displays the Paradox Keyboard screen shown in figure 1.24.

The information in this screen discusses how Paradox uses function keys, control keys, and arrow keys. For more detailed information about one of these groups of keys, select one of the options from the menu at the top of the screen. Selecting **P**aradox exits the help system.

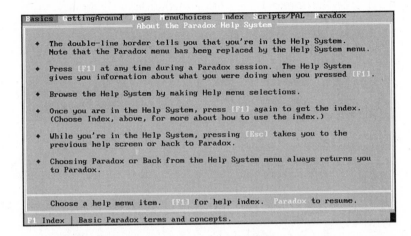

FIG. 1.23

Help screen describing the Paradox help system.

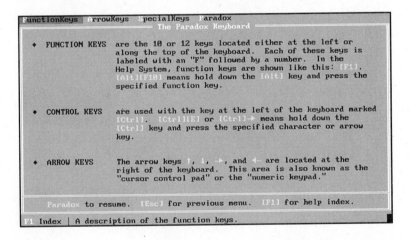

FIG. 1.24

Help screen describing the Paradox keyboard.

As you climb through this tree-like menu system, you often can find relevant information quickly. The information supplied by the help system is seldom as detailed, however, as that provided in the Paradox documentation or in this book.

Using the Help Index

The *help index* is an alternate way of finding a help screen about a specific topic. You first access the help system by pressing F1 (Help). A message at the bottom of the screen (the Status bar) instructs you to press F1 again for the help index. Do so, and Paradox displays an alphabetically arranged index of the help screens available in the help system.

Suppose that you are editing the Employee table and have forgotten how to use field view. First, from the Edit mode, press F1 (Help). Paradox displays the Editing a Table screen shown in figure 1.25. Press F1 again to access the help index (see fig. 1.26).

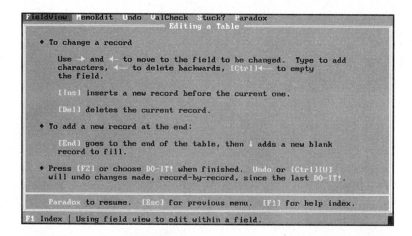

FIG. 1.25

Help screen describing how to edit a table.

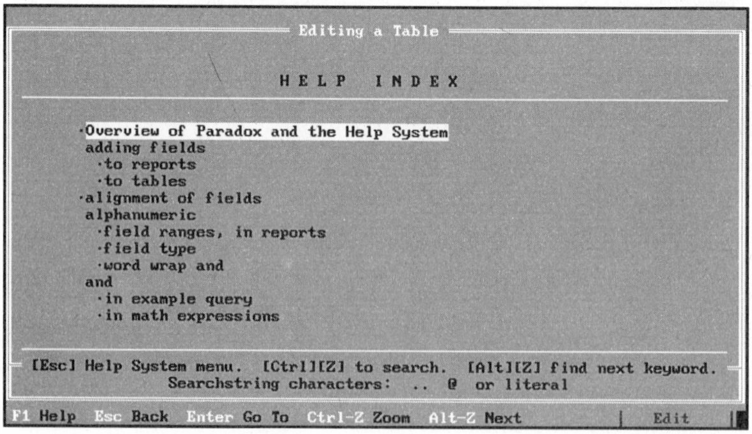

FIG. 1.26

The help index.

You now can use the *zoom search* feature to find any entries about field view. Press Ctrl-Z (Zoom), and Paradox displays a pop-up window containing a text box labeled Value. A message at the bottom of the screen reads Enter value or pattern to search for. Type *field view* and press Enter or click OK. Paradox searches the index and stops on the matching entry (see fig. 1.27).

Cue:
Press Ctrl-Z (Zoom) to use zoom search.

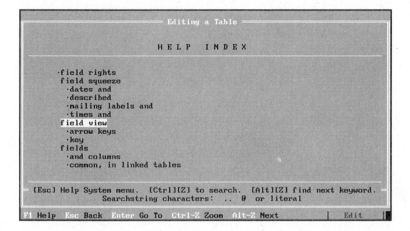

FIG. 1.27

Finding a field view entry.

This entry happens to be a *general topic*, not an *active entry*. General topics have no help screen and appear in the index to group the entries, whereas active entries are preceded by a dot and have a corresponding help screen. Move the highlight to the active entry and press Enter. Paradox displays the help screen shown in figure 1.28. Press F1 to return to the help index. To return to your work, press Esc or choose **P**aradox from the menu. Figure 1.29 shows the screen displayed when you select FieldView from the menu shown in Figure 1.25.

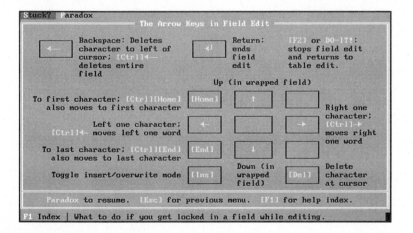

FIG. 1.28

Help screen describing how to use the arrow keys in field view.

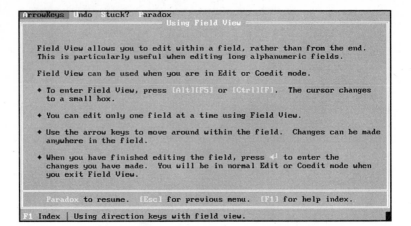

FIG. 1.29

Help screen
describing field
view.

NOTE   The two methods of locating help—by menu and by index—
are not exactly equivalent because only the menu method is
context sensitive. Using each method for the same topic
may even give you different screens. The screen in figure
1.25, for example, which you access by pressing F1 in Edit
mode, includes a menu choice called FieldView. Selecting
that option displays the screen shown in figure 1.29. This
screen is different from the one in figure 1.28, which you
access through the help index. Experiment with both Paradox help system methods to see which you prefer.

Chapter Summary

After completing this chapter, you probably have a better idea of how
Paradox presents itself and how you should respond. You are now familiar with the areas of the Paradox screen, you have a general understanding of how to begin tasks with Paradox using menu and keyboard
commands, you have been introduced to the fundamental concepts of
Paradox modes and windows, and you understand how to access the
Paradox help system. As you continue through this book, keep these
basic navigational aids in mind. The next chapter builds on this foundation and discusses the procedure for designing a new database with
Paradox.

Creating Database Tables

N ow that you are familiar with how to get around in Paradox, this chapter helps you develop a good theoretical and practical understanding of Paradox. If you are a new Paradox user, you should find this chapter especially helpful.

The first portion of this chapter briefly explains what is meant by the term *relational database*. The chapter then goes on to introduce several important Paradox concepts, such as table, object, family, structure, and network locking.

After this important, but mostly theoretical, discussion, the chapter turns to the more practical topic of how to create a Paradox database table. You learn how to define the structure of a Paradox table, define fields and keys, borrow structure from another table, modify the structure of an existing table, and change a table's name.

Understanding Database Terminology

Because of the great speed and storage capacity of computers, they always have been good candidates for storing large amounts of information. With microcomputer technology racing ahead at breakneck speed and the incredible popularity of PCs in business, the capability to store thousands of pages of information on your desktop has become the standard. The practical problem with storing that much information lies in developing a system to retrieve the data in some orderly fashion. Relational database programs are designed to solve this problem.

Although you may not be aware of the fact, you have built and used databases all your life. Whenever you collect information in some organized fashion so that you can access the data randomly, you are creating a database. Typical databases include the following:

> Telephone books
> Card catalogs
> Recipe cards
> Rolodex files
> Mailing lists

Computers enable you to store data electronically rather than on cards, in file cabinets, or in books. From this electronic storage, well-designed database programs can retrieve the data almost instantaneously.

Defining a Relational Database

Reminder:

Two tables are related when they have columns with the same names and field types.

A *relational database* consists of a collection of related tables made up of rows of data arranged in named columns. You can think of two tables as related when they have columns with the same names and field types. A relational database-management system, such as Paradox, enables you to use data from any number of related tables at the same time. This structure is a simplified distillation of the relational model, originally suggested in 1970 by Dr. Edgar F. Codd—then an IBM scientist, now the president of the Relational Institute and chief scientist of Codd and Date International. As PC implementations of the relational model go, Paradox is closer than most.

Paradox database terminology and the program's overall design are more faithful to the Codd relational model than such popular programs as dBASE III Plus and dBASE IV. Experienced dBASE users, therefore, may find some aspects of Paradox unfamiliar. Although understanding the relative merits of the various database models is not crucial, you do need to understand the terminology adopted by Paradox.

Understanding Paradox Objects

The term *object* in Paradox refers to any one of a number of database building blocks. The following are all Paradox objects:

The table *Employee*
The field *Emp ID #*
The form *F*
The report *R*
The script *Instant*

All data in Paradox is stored in *tables* made up of columns (*fields*) and rows (*records*), as shown in figure 2.1. A Paradox database consists of a collection of tables *related* or *linked* by common columns.

Reminder: Paradox stores data in tables.

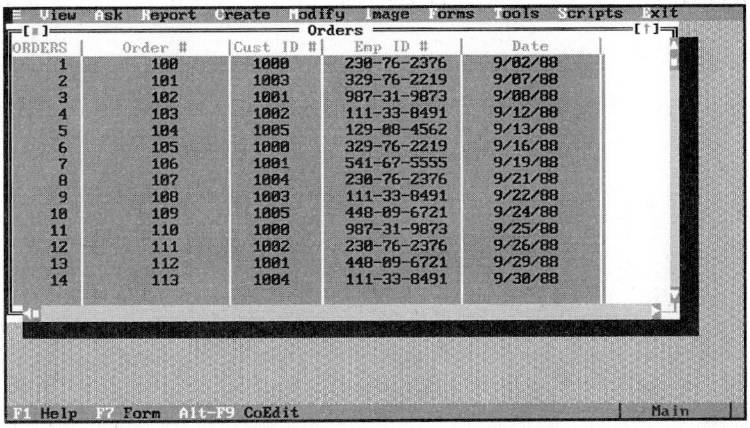

ORDERS	Order #	Cust ID #	Emp ID #	Date
1	100	1000	230-76-2376	9/02/88
2	101	1003	329-76-2219	9/07/88
3	102	1001	987-31-9873	9/08/88
4	103	1002	111-33-8491	9/12/88
5	104	1005	129-08-4562	9/13/88
6	105	1000	329-76-2219	9/16/88
7	106	1001	541-67-5555	9/19/88
8	107	1004	230-76-2376	9/21/88
9	108	1003	111-33-8491	9/22/88
10	109	1005	448-09-6721	9/24/88
11	110	1000	987-31-9873	9/25/88
12	111	1002	230-76-2376	9/26/88
13	112	1001	448-09-6721	9/29/88
14	113	1004	111-33-8491	9/30/88

FIG. 2.1

A Paradox table.

The table is to Paradox what the worksheet is to Lotus 1-2-3 or Quattro Pro. After you create a table, even the table definition is stored temporarily in a table (see fig. 2.2). Although you can enter and edit data in forms (*form view*), the majority of database tasks in Paradox are performed in a tabular format (*table view*). As in the Codd relational model, any query or other operation performed on a table returns an answer in the form of a table (see fig. 2.3), which in turn can be the object of further database operations.

Reminder: Any operation performed on a table returns a table.

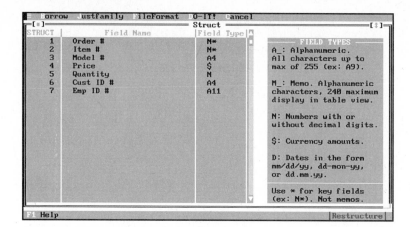

FIG. 2.2

The temporary
table.

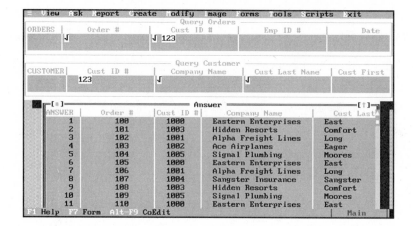

FIG. 2.3

The result of a
query of two
tables: the
temporary table
Answer.

A collection of tables make up a database, but Paradox does not provide an internal way to group tables. Instead, you should reserve a separate directory on your hard disk (or a separate floppy disk) for each database. Place tables from one, and only one, database in each directory. Otherwise, your working directory quickly becomes cluttered with unrelated tables, diluting the benefits of a relational database. Refer to Appendix A or Quick Start 1 for information on starting Paradox from the working directory. Refer also to the section, "Controlling the Interface Settings," in Appendix B for information on changing the default working directory.

Reminder:
All objects associated with a given table are a family of objects.

Most objects are associated with a particular table. You can, for example, design input forms and custom reports for each Paradox table. All the objects associated with a given table are a *family* of objects.

Objects, such as forms and reports, are stored as separate files on the disk. Paradox saves these files for you and uses the table name as the *base name* of these files, distinguishing among family members by using file name extensions. The exceptions to this rule are *scripts*, discussed in Chapter 6, and *graphs*, which are not part of a family of objects and do not necessarily have the same name as a table. The file name extensions assigned by Paradox are listed in table 2.1. This chapter discusses how to create a Paradox table. Creating and using these objects are discussed in later chapters of this book.

Table 2.1. Paradox Object File-Name Extensions

Object type	File-name extension
Table	DB
Memo file	MB
Form	F or Fn
Report	R or Rn
Graph	G
Image settings	SET
Validity checks	VAL
Primary index	PX
Query-speedup (secondary index)	Xm
Query-speedup (secondary index)	Ym
Script	SC

NOTE The letter n in the file-name extensions is replaced by an integer from 1 to 14 representing the name of the form or report. The letter m is replaced by two digits assigned by Paradox.

For Related Information:

▶▶ "Obtaining Information about Your Database," p. 426.

▶▶ "Getting Started," p. 990.

▶▶ "Controlling the Interface Settings," p. 1001.

FROM HERE...

Designing a Database

Cue:
Don't create a one-table database.

As you design your database, keep each table small, resisting the temptation to place everything but the kitchen sink into one giant table. The strength of relational database technology is that you can easily and simultaneously access data in multiple tables. You should almost never create a database consisting of only one Paradox table. Create multiple tables and use common columns to tie related information together.

Planning the Fields

Keep four goals in mind as you decide on the fields to include in each table:

- Collect all the information necessary for the reports that must be generated.

- Do not collect any information that will never be needed for a report.

- Divide the data into logical and manageable categories.

- Never enter the same information more than once.

You can meet the first two goals through thoughtful analysis of the real-life data you are collecting and the reports you currently generate or plan to generate. Careful attention to detail at this early stage of database design can save you countless hours of redesigning.

You can accomplish the last goal only if you do a good job with the third goal. In the example shown in figure 2.4, by comparing the Cust ID # columns in the two tables, you can see that customers often place more than one order. Recording Company Name, Cust Last Name, Cust Address, and so forth in the Orders table would require continual reentry of the same information. Dividing the data into two tables, Orders and Customer, enables you to enter the customer information one time only. Figure 2.3 shows an example of how Paradox can pull together the information for these two tables, using the Cust ID # column as a *link*.

Cue:
Normalize your tables.

This design process is sometimes called *normalization*. A *normalized* table is as small as possible, is easy to understand and change, contains no duplicate records, and contains little (if any) information already entered in another table.

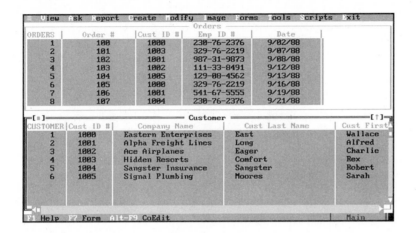

FIG. 2.4

The related
Orders and
Customer
tables.

Orders

Design your database on paper first. Write down the table names
and list the field names below them. This bird's-eye view of your
database is invaluable as you begin to define the structure of the
tables and to build forms and reports. Keep the layout next to your
keyboard as you work and file the paperwork away for later reference when you are finished. A worksheet for the two tables shown in
figure 2.4 would appear as follows:

T I P

Orders	Customer
Order #	Cust ID #
Cust ID #	Company Name
Emp ID #	Cust Address
Date	Cust City
	Cust State
	Cust ZIP
	Cust Phone

Understanding How Tables Are Related

An important step toward getting the most from any relational database management system like Paradox is to develop an understanding
of how the many tables in a database are related to each other.

Two tables are related if they have common field names and field types.
An example of related tables is shown in figure 2.4. The Orders and
Customer tables contain the field Cust ID #. This common field is the
link between the tables.

NOTE Fields used to link two tables do not actually have to have the same name, but the best practice is to give linking fields the same name. Paradox enables you to link tables with fields that have different names, provided that the fields have the same field type and size. Most database tables are intended, however, for use by people. To avoid confusing yourself or the people who will use the database you are designing, you should always give linking fields the same name because these fields will contain the same type of information. The Cust ID # field in Orders and the Cust ID # field in Customer both contain customer identification numbers. If you use different field names for these two fields, another user may assume that the fields contain different types of data.

The link between tables can be used to define more precisely the relationship between two tables. If the linking column contains unique data—as does the Cust ID # in the Customer table—the column is said to be on the *one-side* of the relationship. When the data in a linking column is not necessarily unique—as in the Cust ID # field in the Orders table—the column is on the *many-side* of the relationship. A *one-to-many* relationship, therefore, exists between Customer and Orders. You can enter data about a customer only once, and then use that same data many times when processing orders.

Typically, one table in a relationship is the *master* table. The other table is the *detail* table. Chapters 8 and 10, in the context of designing forms and reports, discuss how you decide which table is the master and which is the detail. In an order-placing system, such as the Customer/Orders example in figures 2.3 and 2.4, you can refer to Orders as the master table and Customer as the detail table. The relationship between two tables usually is expressed from the point of view of the master table, so the relationship between Orders and Customer is described as a *many-to-one* relationship. Four types of relationships are possible:

- *One-to-one.* A unique field in the master table is linked to a unique field in the detail table. One row in the master table corresponds to one (and only one) row in the detail table.

- *One-to-many.* A unique field in the master table is linked to a non-unique field in the detail table. One row in the master table links to a group of rows in the detail table.

- *Many-to-one.* A non-unique field in the master table is linked to a unique field in the detail table. A group of rows in the master table corresponds to only one row in the detail table.

■ *Many-to-many*. A non-unique field in the master table is linked to a non-unique field in the detail table. A group of rows in the master table corresponds to a group of rows in the detail table.

Relational database systems in general, and Paradox in particular, can be used most effectively if you avoid *many-to-many* relationships. Paradox can display data from both tables of one-to-one or one-to-many relationships on one screen, but the program cannot handle many-to-many relationships. Chapter 8 discusses what to do if you need to redesign a database to eliminate many-to-many relationships.

T I P

You can add links to your database worksheet (see the preceding tip on designing a database) by using lines and arrowheads. Draw lines on the worksheet between common field names. Place a single arrowhead on the *one-side* and a double arrowhead on the *many-side*. The worksheet for the Orders/Customer example, with lines and arrowheads, would appear as follows:

Orders	*Customer*
Order #	→Cust ID #
Cust ID #<←	Company Name
Emp ID #	Cust Address
Date	Cust City
	Cust State
	Cust ZIP
	Cust Phone

For Related Information:

▶▶ "Normalizing a Database," p. 262.

▶▶ "Creating a Multitable Form," p. 313.

▶▶ "Entering and Editing Data with Multitable Forms," p. 335.

FROM HERE...

Defining Table Structure

After you have designed your database, the next step is to create or define the *structure* of each table. Table definition is a task started from the Paradox Main menu. To begin defining a Paradox table, select Create from the Main menu. Paradox displays a dialog box containing a text box and two buttons. A prompt in the status line prompts you to Enter new table name. Type the table's name and press Enter or click the OK button. Use the following rules when naming the table:

- You can use up to eight characters (without file-name extensions).

- You can use letters, numbers, and the following special characters:

     $ # & @ ! % ( ) - _ { } ' ^

- You cannot include spaces.

- You cannot use duplicate names.

Paradox displays an image showing a temporary table named Struct (see fig. 2.5). Each row in this table represents the definition of a field in the table you are creating. The first column in Struct displays numbers assigned in the order that you define the fields. The second column holds the name of each field, and the third column contains field types. The next several sections discuss how to assign field names and field types.

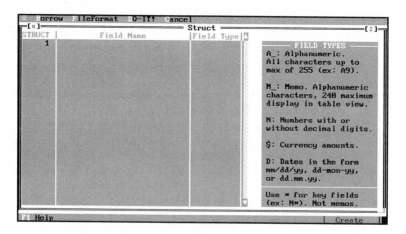

FIG. 2.5

The empty Struct table in Create mode.

Assigning Field Names

One of the more subtle aspects of database table definition is the assignment of field names. Planning is important in almost every step of database design, and the naming of fields is no exception. Use the following rules when you are deciding on field names:

■ You can use up to 25 characters.

■ You can use any printable character except the following:

[ ] ( )
the combination ->

■ You can include spaces, except as the first character.

■ You cannot use duplicate names in the same table.

Also consider the following guidelines when naming fields:

■ Field names should describe field contents.

■ Always use the same field name for fields used to link tables (see the note in the "Understanding How Tables Are Related" section earlier in this chapter).

■ If a field's contents will be looked up from another table, use the same field name as the field name in the other table. (Refer to the section "Borrowing Structure from Other Tables" later in this chapter for a naming shortcut for this type of field.)

■ Don't use a field name in more than one table of a database unless the field is intended to link tables or to be looked up from a linked table.

When you have decided on a field name, type the name in the Field Name column of the Struct table. You can correct mistakes by using the Backspace key to erase the incorrect entry and retyping it. You also can use the field view described in Chapter 1 (press Alt-F5 or Ctrl-F) to edit an errant field name.

Press Enter after the field name is as you want it. Paradox then moves the cursor to the column labeled Field Type (see fig. 2.6).

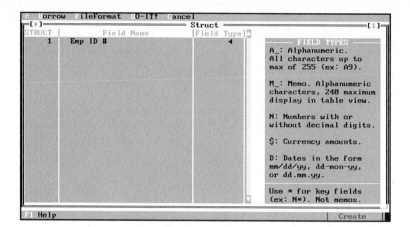

FIG. 2.6

Defining the field type.

Assigning Field Type

Much like a spreadsheet, Paradox can do calculations with number data. Unlike a spreadsheet, the program cannot determine on its own whether you intend data to be number or text. The purpose of the Field Type column in the Struct table is to inform Paradox whether the data to be entered will be text, number, currency, or dates. For text (*alphanumeric*) fields, you also must specify the maximum length of the data.

If you are familiar with spreadsheets or other database programs, you already may be wondering whether you can define field type even more specifically. You can cause numbers to display only as integers (with no decimal places), and you can force dates to print in a particular format, but not during the structure-definition process. Refer to Chapters 8, 10, and 11 for discussions of customizing the way data is displayed or printed.

Paradox Field Types

Paradox makes defining field types a simple task. The field type choices include the following:

> *Alphanumeric:* To define a field as alphanumeric, press A followed by the number of spaces (from 1 to 255) you want to reserve for the longest data entry. For example, *A20* indicates an alphanumeric field with a maximum length of 20. Any combination of characters, numbers, and spaces is a valid alphanumeric entry. The following entries are all valid in an alphanumeric field:

Every good boy
AB129878
#4&*00-123

Memo: Press M to indicate a memo field type. Like alphanumeric files, a memo field can contain any combination of characters, numbers, and spaces. Unlike alphanumeric fields, which are of fixed length from 1 to 255 characters, a memo field is of variable length and can be of practically unlimited length (64M). After you press M, type a number from 1 to 240 to indicate the number of characters you want Paradox to display in table view.

Number: Press N to define a field as number. Number data is any number with or without decimals. Paradox assigns the maximum length automatically. You can enter up to 15 significant digits (including decimal places). Numbers with more than 15 significant digits are rounded and stored in scientific notation. Numbers in number fields normally are displayed without commas and with only as many decimal places as are necessary to display the significant digits. Negative numbers are preceded by a minus sign. Refer to Chapters 3, 8, and 9 for information on changing the way numbers are displayed (formatted) on-screen in a table or form. The following are valid number entries:

12345
123.45
.12345
–12.345

Short number: Press S to specify the short number field type. This field type, used by advanced users and application developers who need to conserve disk storage, can contain only whole numbers (integers) in the range –32,767 to 32,767.

Binary: Press B to specify a binary field. Binary fields are of variable length and can hold *Binary Large OBjects (BLOBs)*. After you press B, type a number from 1 to 240 to indicate the number of characters you want Paradox to display in table view. You need to reserve only four spaces in table view, however. Whenever a field of the BLOB data type contains data, Paradox does not display the actual contents of the field. Rather, Paradox displays the word Blob in the field. Paradox 4.0 does not enable you to edit BLOB data directly, but you can use the Custom Configuration Program, discussed in Appendix B, to attach a BLOB editor to Paradox.

Currency: Press $ to indicate a currency field. Paradox treats currency fields the same as number fields, but displays currency data with commas and rounded to two decimal places. Negative numbers are displayed in parentheses. You do not type the dollar signs when entering currency data, but you can type the commas. All the following currency entries are valid:

12345
12,345
12,345.67
12345.678

Paradox displays the last currency entry rounded to 12,345.68, but stores and uses in internal calculations the number 12345.678.

Date: Press D to indicate a date field. Valid entries are any date from January 1, 100 to December 31, 9999, typed in the form mm/dd/yy, dd-mon-yy, or dd.mm.yy. If you enter dates that do not fall within the 20th Century, include the full year. The following are valid date entries, all for the same date:

3/09/78
9-Mar-78
9.03.78

Eight other date formats are available for use in reports. (See Chapters 10 and 11 for details on creating tabular and free-form reports).

When you press Enter after indicating field type, Paradox drops the cursor to the next row in the Struct table so that you can define another field. Paradox can handle up to a maximum of 255 fields per table.

Field Type Guidelines

Use the following guidelines to help you decide how to assign field types:

■ Use the *date* type when each entry in the field will be a date. For now, don't be concerned about how the date should be formatted for a report that you will need later. Paradox provides 11 different date formats at the reporting stage.

■ Use the *currency* field type when you want commas displayed within numbers.

■ Always use the *number* or *currency* field type when you may need to perform calculations with the data.

■ Assign the *alphanumeric* type for all fields that don't meet one of the preceding guidelines.

These guidelines seem obvious, but falling into a trap is easy if you are not careful. A five-digit ZIP code, for example, consists entirely of numbers, so you may be tempted to define a ZIP code field as number.

This definition presents a problem, however, for ZIP codes that begin with a 0, because Paradox drops any leading 0 in number data. You should define a ZIP code field as an alphanumeric field. This fact is more obvious with 9-digit ZIP codes because the hyphen, normally inserted between the fifth and sixth digits, cannot be entered in a number field.

Another trap laid at data-entry time is the reverse of the problem just described. Alphanumeric fields containing numbers—such as ZIP codes—present a special problem if you intend to sort the records in the table by that field. Alphanumeric columns are sorted from left to right within the field, even if the data happens to be numbers. Therefore, the number 123 entered into an alphanumeric field is sorted before the number 21. Avoid this problem by entering the same number of characters in this field in every record in the table. For example, you should enter *021* rather than *21*, because Paradox sorts 021 before 123.

Inserting and Deleting Fields

As you are building the table structure, you may decide that you don't like the order of the fields, or that you need to delete a field definition or insert a new field between existing definitions.

To delete a field from the structure, press the Del key. Inserting a blank row for a field is just as easy: you press the Ins key.

Cue:
Press Del to delete a field.

Paradox normally displays a table's data in the order, from left to right, that the fields are listed in the structure. For your convenience, define fields in the order you want them to appear on-screen. The only time field order matters to Paradox is when you are assigning key fields.

Assigning Key Fields

You may have noticed the last instruction on the Create mode screen shown in figures 2.5 and 2.6. That instruction states that you can use the asterisk (*) to indicate a *key field*.

Understanding Key Fields

Many database programs use the word *index* to describe the same concept that Paradox calls a *key*. An index for a database table is analogous to the index of a book. To look up discussions about Query By Example in this book, for example, you turn to the index and look up "Query By Example" alphabetically. The book index refers you to the appropriate pages. Much like a book's index, a Paradox table index keeps track of the data in the table, sorted in order alphabetically or numerically (according to field type). Just as a book index enables you to find information quickly on a particular subject, a database index speeds the computer's data search in a table.

Reminder:
A single key must be the first field in the structure.

Several aspects of Paradox key fields are unique. When you assign a single field as a key field, called a *single key*, it must be the first field in the definition (see fig. 2.7). In addition to creating an index on the values in the key field, Paradox does the following:

- Prevents duplicate values in the key field

- Keeps the table sorted according to the values in the field

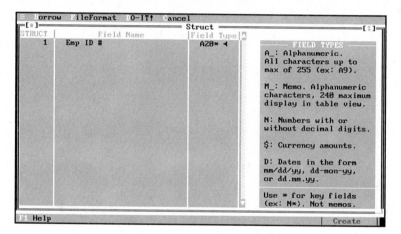

FIG. 2.7

Assigning a key field.

In the sample table whose structure is being created in figure 2.7, Paradox does not enable the Emp ID # field to have duplicate values when you enter data. Paradox also continually sorts the records so that they are stored in order by the ID number. Finally, the program creates an index on the Emp ID # field that speeds up queries of the table.

One disadvantage of keying a table is that the maximum potential size of each record is reduced from 4,000 bytes to 1,350 bytes. Another problem is that data entry can be slowed somewhat while Paradox sorts the table and updates the index.

Using Multifield Keys

In some situations, one field is not enough to prevent duplicate records. Figure 2.8 shows the Orders table and another table named

Detail. The Detail table includes the model numbers and quantity of merchandise making up each of the orders in the master table, Orders. Because more than one model can be ordered under the same order number, the Detail table potentially contains multiple records with the same Order # entry. This field cannot be used as a *single key*. By adding (or concatenating) the Item # field to the key, however, you can create unique key values. Although three records in Detail have order numbers equal to 100, for example, only one record has an order number of 100 *and* an item number of 1.

= View Ask Report Create Modify Image Forms Tools Scripts Exit

Orders				
ORDERS	Order #	Cust ID #	Emp ID #	Date
1	100	1000	230-76-2376	9/02/88
2	101	1003	329-76-2219	9/07/88
3	102	1001	987-31-9873	9/08/88
4	103	1002	111-33-8491	9/12/88
5	104	1005	129-08-4562	9/13/88
6	105	1000	329-76-2219	9/16/88
7	106	1001	541-67-5555	9/19/88
8	107	1004	230-76-2376	9/21/88

Detail				
DETAIL	Order #	Item #	Model #	Price	Quantity
1	100	1	A333	39.95	50
2	100	2	B107	49.95	25
3	100	3	G400	59.95	10
4	101	1	A333	39.95	15
5	101	2	X155	79.95	10
6	102	1	G400	59.95	35
7	102	2	A333	39.95	10
8	103	1	G400	59.95	22
9	103	2	X155	79.95	5

F1 Help F7 Form Alt-F9 CoEdit		Main

FIG. 2.8

The Detail table requires a multifield key.

To create a *multifield* or *concatenated* key, place the asterisk (*) after the field type of each key field. All key fields must come before any non-key field in the definition. The first key field is the *primary key*.

Cue:
To create a multifield key, place the * after each key field.

After you create a multifield key, Paradox does the following:

■ Prevents the entry of records that duplicate the exact entry in all key fields of an existing record

■ Keeps the table sorted first by the primary key field, then by the second key field in the definition, then by the third key field (if any), and so forth

■ Creates a primary index on the concatenation of the key fields

The definition of Detail is shown in figure 2.9. Notice that the Order # field and the Item # field are key fields and that they are the first two fields in the definition.

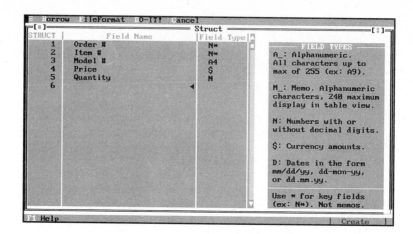

FIG. 2.9

The definition of the Detail table.

When Should You Assign a Key?

The following are two closely related reasons for keying a field or fields:

- To prevent duplicate records
- To allow a field or fields to be used as a link between tables on the one-side of a one-to-many or many-to-one relationship

Reminder:
Each record in every table should be unique.

A cardinal rule of relational databases is that each record in every table should be unique. When one field of a table is enough to determine the identity of a record, place that field first in the table definition and designate that field as the single key. As already discussed, some tables do not have a unique field. In those situations, you should use multifield keys to prevent duplicate records.

Cue:
Key the linking field in the one-side table.

The second reason for keying a field becomes important when you create multitable forms and reports. Because the one-side of a one-to-many or many-to-one relationship is, by definition, a table with unique records, you should key the linking field in the one-side table.

Every table should have at least one key field.

 NOTE   You cannot assign either a memo field or a binary field as a key field.

Borrowing Structure from Other Tables

This section describes how to borrow table structure (field definitions) from the definition of an existing table. The result is to give you fields in different tables with the same names and field types. Refer to the "Assigning Field Names" and "Assigning Field Type" sections earlier in this chapter to help you decide when you need to borrow table structure.

To borrow the table structure from another database, follow these steps:

1. Place the cursor in the Struct table at the position where the field definition(s) from the other table should start.

2. Use the mouse to click **B**orrow in the menu bar, or press F10 (Menu) to display the menu at the top of the screen and then select **B**orrow.

3. When Paradox displays a dialog box, press Enter or click OK to see a list of available tables.

4. Select the table from which you want to borrow. Paradox copies the field definitions from that table into Struct, beginning at the cursor position.

   Figure 2.10, for example, shows the result of using Borrow to copy the field definitions of the Orders table into the new structure of the Employee table.

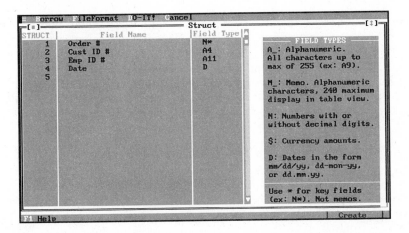

FIG. 2.10

Borrowing table structure.

Normally, you do not need all the borrowed field definitions. The Employee table shown in figure 2.10 is going to be linked to the Orders table through the Emp ID # field. The definition of Orders was borrowed to ensure that this linking field is defined exactly the same way in both tables. The other fields from Orders (Cust ID # and Date) are irrelevant to Employee. Delete those unwanted field definitions. Place the cursor in the row to be deleted and press the Del key. The field definition vanishes.

Selecting File Format

By default, when you create a new table in Paradox 4.0, the program saves the table in its native file format. This format is not compatible with previous versions of Paradox, however. If you intend to enable Paradox 3.5 users to access the table, you should cause Paradox to save the table structure in the so-called *compatible* file format.

Cue:
To use compatible table format, select **F**ileFormat, **C**ompatible.

To cause Paradox to use Paradox 3.5-compatible table format, select **F**ileFormat from the menu bar and choose **C**ompatible. If you later change your mind and decide that the table should be saved in standard Paradox 4.0 format, select **F**ileFormat from the menu bar and choose **S**tandard.

> **NOTE**   The FileFormat command sets table format, but does not save the table structure. Refer to the next section of this chapter for instructions on saving table structure.

Saving the Table Structure

As with most operations in Paradox, to complete the definition process and save the table structure, click **DO-IT!** in the menu bar, or press F2 (Do-It!). Paradox returns to Main mode. The field definitions that had been listed in the Struct table now are stored as the definition of the new table. At this point, you are ready to begin entering data into the table. When you define another table, Paradox clears the Struct table so that you can begin anew.

To abort the table-definition process without saving any of the table definition, select **C**ancel from the menu bar.

FROM HERE...

For Related Information:

▶▶ "Copying Paradox Objects," p. 430.

▶▶ "Developing Applications," p. 616.

Creating Tables on a Network

The major benefits of using Paradox on a network instead of most other PC-based database programs are summed up by two important properties: *data integrity* and *data consistency*.

Paradox prevents potentially damaging conflicts between two or more users attempting to access the same data in the same table at the same time. Paradox also dynamically ensures that all users of a particular table always are provided with the same correct version of the data, even if someone else is making changes to the table.

Reminder:
Paradox preserves data integrity and consistency.

The program accomplishes these feats primarily through a system of progressively more restrictive locks placed on shared Paradox objects. Following is a list of these locks, in order from most restrictive to least restrictive, and descriptions from the point of view of the user whose action caused the lock to be placed on a shared object:

Reminder:
Paradox automatically locks shared Paradox objects.

Lock	Description
Full lock	Totally prevents concurrent use by multiple users; the object can be used only by the current user.
Write lock	Other users have read-only access to the object; they can use the data but can neither change the data nor change the structure of the object.
Family lock	Same as write lock; the lock is placed on an entire Paradox database family when it is being copied through the Tools menu.
Group lock	A write lock placed on all detail records owned by a master record when you are coediting the primary key of the master record in a multi-table form.
Record lock	This write lock is placed on the individual record being edited in CoEdit mode.
Prevent write lock	Other users have complete access to the object but are prevented from placing a full lock or a write lock on the object.
Prevent full lock	Other users have complete access to an object but are prevented from placing a full lock on the object.

Paradox applies the lock or prevent lock that is least restrictive to concurrent use by multiple users and that is consistent with the operation you are performing.

As you create a Paradox table on a multiuser network, Paradox places a full lock (the most restrictive lock available) on the table being created. No other user can create or rename a table with the same name until you are finished creating the table structure and have returned to the Main mode.

Reminder:
Paradox places a full lock during table creation.

When you use the Borrow feature, however, Paradox places a prevent full lock on the table from which you are borrowing field definitions. This lock, the least restrictive type of lock or prevent lock, is effective only long enough to copy the definitions to the Struct table.

You also can cause Paradox to place a full lock on all tables in a particular DOS directory—referred to as a *dir lock*. A dir lock is not placed automatically by Paradox, but can be placed by a user with read/write/ access rights to the directory. While a dir lock is in place, Paradox potentially can run faster because the program does not have to continually update all files to disk. Use this lock with due consideration to other network users, however, because you are preventing all other users from making any changes to any table in the locked directory.

FROM HERE...

For Related Information:

▶▶ "Using CoEdit Mode on a Network," p. 125.

▶▶ "Using Reports on a Network," p. 217.

▶▶ "Using Scripts on a Network," p. 236.

Modifying Table Structure

You inevitably will need to make some adjustment to the structure of one or more tables in your database. Programmers always say that a program is never truly finished, and your database is never exactly as you want it. You can always think of improvements. This section of the chapter describes how to make changes to table structure by using the Restructure mode.

Enter the Restructure mode from the Main mode. From the Main menu, select **M**odify, **R**estructure and specify the name of the table whose structure needs to be changed. Paradox displays the existing definition with the word Restructure in the mode indicator (see fig. 2.11). The next several sections explain how to modify, insert, borrow, delete, and re-key field definitions and how to rearrange their order.

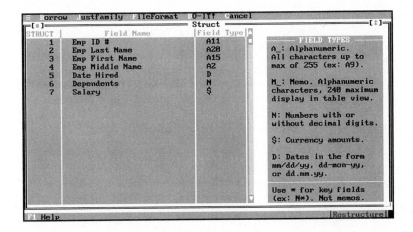

FIG. 2.11

The Restructure
mode.

> **CAUTION:** As with any database program, restructuring a table is a potentially disastrous undertaking that can result in a loss of data. Paradox, however, does a good job of warning you when the program is about to discard previously entered information, and to a certain extent, temporarily saves discarded information. Pay close attention to any messages displayed during the restructuring process.

You need to know that Paradox does not make a backup copy of your data before a restructure. You should back up the data yourself. If the power fails, your data may be corrupted. Use the Copy command, discussed in Chapter 13, to create this backup copy.

Renaming a Field

When the Struct table is displayed in the Restructure mode, the steps for modifying a field definition are the same as editing a definition during original creation. To change a field name, use the Backspace key to erase the current name and type the correction. You also can press Alt-F5 (Field View) and edit the name. Changing the name of a field has no effect on data already stored in the table.

Reassigning Field Type

Changing a field's type or length is just as easy as changing the field's name but can affect previously entered data. To change the field type,

Reminder:
Changing field type or
length can affect data.

use the Backspace key or the field view to edit the current entry in the Field Type column of the Struct table. Table 2.2 summarizes the effects of changes in the field type on existing data.

Reminder:
Paradox places inconsistent records in a Problems table.

When existing data is not consistent with the new definition, Paradox does not transfer the data to the newly defined table. Unlike many lesser database programs, however, Paradox does not altogether abandon the problem data (with one significant exception explained in the next section, "Changing Field Length"). Instead, the program places offending records in a temporary table called Problems. You later can edit and add the data back to the table or rename the Problems table so that it is saved permanently.

Table 2.2. The Effects of Reassigning Field Type

Old Field Type	New Field Type	Effect on existing data
Any type	A	None, if the new length is sufficient to handle existing data
Any type	M	None
N, $, or S	N, $, or S	None, unless an N field is converted to an S field and the data is not an integer or is outside the range $-32,767$ to $32,767$
A, M	N, $, or S	None for number entries; any entry containing non-number data or data with too many digits (more than 15 digits for a number or currency field, or more than 5 digits for a short number field) is placed in Problems table
D	N, $, or S	All records placed in Problems table
A, M	D	None for records containing a properly entered date value (mm/dd/yy, dd-mon-yy, or dd.mm.yy); records containing non-date values placed in Problems
N, $, or S	D	All records placed in Problems table

> **CAUTION:** All temporary tables in Paradox are just that—tempo-
> rary. For example, the Problems table created when you redefine
> the Employee table is replaced if problems arise later in redefining
> some other table in the database. If you are going to edit and use
> the discarded data or want to rename the table to save it, you
> must do so before Paradox replaces the temporary table. (See the
> section "Renaming Tables," later in this chapter.)

Changing Field Length

Only alphanumeric field definitions explicitly include field length. When
using the Restructure mode, you can increase the length of a field without being concerned about data loss. Shortening field length, however,
can be hazardous to your data.

Reminder:
Shortening field length can
cause loss of data.

Paradox warns you about possible data loss when you attempt to save
the new definition. When you press F2 (Do-It!), the program displays
the following message at the bottom of the screen:

```
Possible data loss for Xyz field
```

Xyz is the field name. In the center of the screen, Paradox also displays
the pop-up menu shown in figure 2.12.

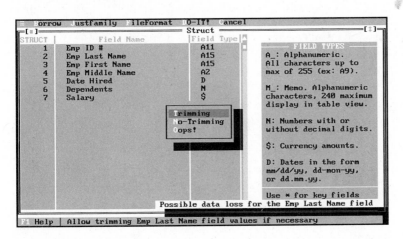

FIG. 2.12

Confirming
reduction of field
length.

To truncate all information beyond the new length, choose **Trimming**
from the pop-up menu.

> **CAUTION:** In this situation, offending data is not placed in the Problems table but is gone forever. Choose this option only when you are sure that the data is shorter than the new length or when you intend for the data to be erased.

If you are not sure whether the data in any record may be too long, or if you don't want any information trimmed away permanently, choose **No-Trimming**. Paradox places any offending records in Problems.

The last menu choice, **O**ops!, places you back in Restructure mode so that you can increase the length of the field again.

These same messages and choices are displayed when you convert a number field or currency field to a small number field.

Inserting and Borrowing Field Definitions

When you need to add another field to a table, position the cursor at the row in which you want to place the new field and press Ins. Paradox inserts a blank row in the Struct table, pushing the existing rows down one row. Suppose that you forgot to define a ZIP code field for the Customer table (which stores information about your customers). You want to insert that field just after the Cust State field, which is currently the fifth field in the structure. You first should position the cursor in row 6, because this spot is where you want the new field. Then press the Ins key. Paradox inserts a blank row 6 and pushes the existing sixth field, Cust Phone, down to row 7, as shown in figure 2.13.

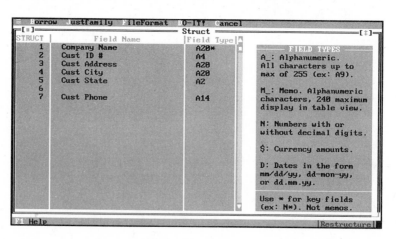

FIG. 2.13

Inserting a field.

Now you can define the field as usual (see fig. 2.14). The **B**orrow feature works in the same manner in the Restructure mode as it does in the Create mode.

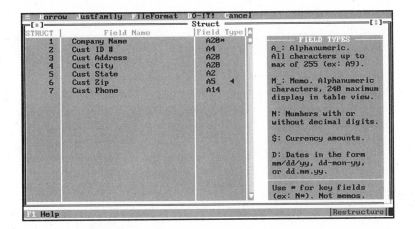

FIG. 2.14

The newly inserted field.

After you finish redefining the table, you can add data to the newly defined field(s) of existing records through the Edit mode. (For more information, refer to Chapter 3, "Entering, Editing, and Viewing Data.")

Deleting a Field

You may decide that you don't need to collect the data for a particular field or that you should have placed a certain field in another table. When you are in Restructure mode, place the cursor in the offending row and press Del. The row containing the field's definitions is deleted from Struct. When you finish redefining the table, Paradox warns you that data is about to be lost. For example, figure 2.15 shows the message and menu Paradox displays if you attempt to delete the Dependents field from the Employee table.

Cue:
In Restructure mode, press Del to delete a field.

To confirm deletion of the field, select **D**elete. If you don't want to delete the field, select **O**ops!, and (to undo the potential for data loss) reenter the definition of the deleted field or cancel Restructure by selecting **C**ancel from the menu bar.

CAUTION: Deleted data is *not* placed in a temporary table. When you confirm field deletion, you irrevocably abandon the data of the deleted field.

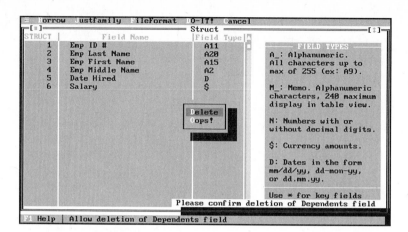

FIG. 2.15

Confirming
deletion of a
field.

Reassigning Keys

Cue:

Add an * to make a field
a key field.

To change a non-key field to a key field, add an asterisk (*) to the field
type. Conversely, removing the asterisk from the field type removes the
key. In either case, you may have to rearrange the rows in Struct somewhat to ensure that the primary key is first and that all subordinate
keys follow. Rearranging fields is discussed in the next section.

Changing keys also can create *key violations*, in which a record contains a value in the new key field that already occurs in the table—a
duplicate. Remember that key fields cannot contain duplicates. If this
problem occurs, Paradox places the violating records into a temporary
table called Keyviol. You then can edit the records to eliminate the
duplication, if appropriate, or rename Keyviol and save the offending
data as another table.

Rearranging Fields

The order of the fields in the table structure normally doesn't matter.
Because of the way you define key fields in Paradox, you probably will
have to rearrange field order when you change a table key. Paradox
handles this situation in a simple but elegant way.

Assume that you have defined the Customer table as shown in figure
2.16, with Company Name as the single key. Later, you decide that you
should have assigned Cust ID # as the key. To change a table key and
rearrange field order, follow these steps:

1. Remove the asterisk from the Field Type column of Company
   Name.

2. Rearrange the rows so that Cust ID # is first.
3. With the cursor in the first row, press Ins to insert a blank row 1.
4. Type *Cust ID #* in the Field Name column of that row and press Enter.

   Paradox recognizes that you already have a field by that name and moves the Cust ID # definition up to row 1 (see fig. 2.17).
5. Add the asterisk to the field type of Cust ID #, as the single key field.

Follow this procedure anytime you want to rearrange the order of the fields in a table structure.

Reminder:
The primary key field must be first in the structure.

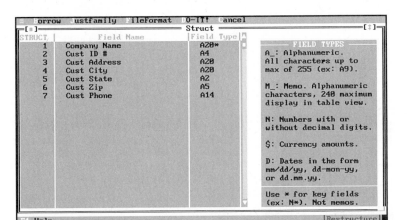

FIG. 2.16

The original order.

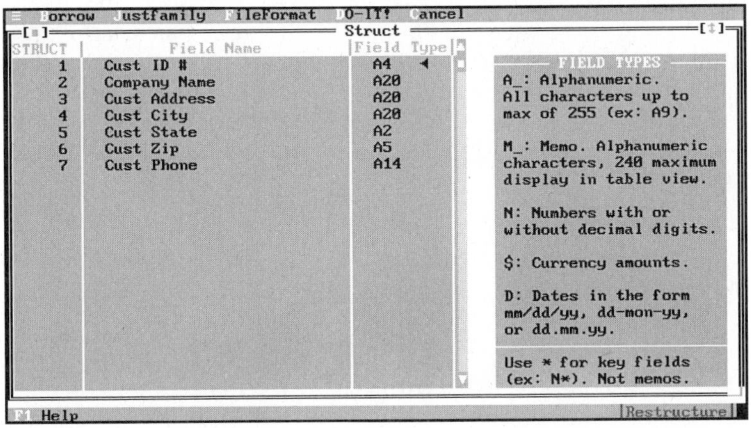

FIG. 2.17

The new order.

Modifying Table Structure on a Network

Reminder:
Paradox places a full lock on the table and its family during the restructuring of a shared table.

While you modify the structure of a shared table on a multiuser network, Paradox places a full lock on the table and all members of its family. Conversely, Paradox does not enable you to restructure a table while another network user is performing any operation with the shared table or any of its family members.

Saving Your Changes

Cue:
Press F2 (Do-It!) to save changes.

When you have made all the necessary changes, press F2 (Do-It!) to tell Paradox you are finished. Paradox then saves the new definition and rebuilds the table. When you alter a table's structure, Paradox makes corresponding adjustments to the entire family of objects associated with the table, including forms, reports, indexes, image settings, and validity check files.

FROM HERE...

For Related Information:

▶▶ "Copying Paradox Objects," p. 430.

Renaming Tables

You may want to change the name of a table. Because a table name cannot be used more than once in a DOS directory, for example, you may want to change a table name so that you can use the original name for another table. Perhaps the nature of the data has changed, and the current name doesn't reflect the contents of the table. Whatever the reason, you need a method of changing the table name, and Paradox provides one.

To change the name of a table, follow these steps:

1. Start at the Main menu and select **Tools**, **Rename**, **Table**.

2. Type the table name you want to change, or press Enter to see the list of tables, and then choose the appropriate table from the list.

   Remember that to choose from the list, you can click the table name, you can press the first letter of the table's name, or you can move the highlight to the table name and press Enter.

3. Paradox instructs you to enter a new name for the table. As usual, the table name must follow the rules listed in the section "Defining Table Structure."

4. When you have finished typing the name, press Enter. Paradox renames the table and the other family members.

For Related Information:

▶▶ "Renaming Paradox Objects," p. 428.

FROM HERE...

Understanding Temporary Tables

True to its relational origins, Paradox creates temporary tables in response to almost any situation. This chapter already has discussed the Struct table, the Problems table, and the Keyviol table, all of which are temporary. Paradox creates a total of 12 different temporary tables, as follows:

Answer
Changed
Crosstab
Deleted
Entry, Entry1, Entry2,...
Family
Inserted
Keyviol, Keyviol1, Keyviol2,...
List
Password
Problems
Struct

As implied by their collective name, temporary tables are short-lived. Three events can cause a temporary table to be wiped clean:

■ The table is overwritten by a newer temporary table of the same type.

■ You use the Tools menu to change the working directory.

■ You end the current Paradox session (by selecting **Exit**).

Cue:

Rename a temporary table to make it permanent.

Perhaps one of the most important uses for the renaming feature is to make one of these temporary tables permanent. To have Paradox permanently save the contents of a temporary table, just change its name to any valid table name (except one of the other 11 temporary table names, of course). For example, the Problems table may contain data discarded during table restructuring. To save the discarded data in Problems, you must give the table a new name before the program clears out the data. After you rename the table, Paradox treats the data in that table just as it does other nontemporary tables.

FROM HERE...

For Related Information:

▶▶ "Entering Data in DataEntry Mode", p. 99.

▶▶ "Displaying and Clearing the Answer Table," p. 159.

▶▶ "Using Crosstab," p. 408.

▶▶ "Renaming Paradox Objects," p. 428.

Adding Password Protection and Claiming Table Ownership on a Network

Reminder:

Password protection is important on a network.

Paradox includes an impressive password protection capability. When you create a table on a network, you protect your data against unauthorized access. The Paradox Protect option on the Tools/Move menu even enables you to permit some users full access to a table and to limit others to more restricted access. You may, for example, want to allow all employees to view the table that includes their personal and salary information but permit only the personnel department to make changes to the data. In a similar way, Paradox also enables you to control access to reports and forms.

Cue:

Assign a password to a shared table as soon as you create it.

To guarantee that you will have control over the granting of access to a table you have created, and to its family of objects, assign a password to a table when you create the table. Password protection is important when the table is in a shared directory accessible by other users on a network. The first network user to place a password on a table effectively becomes the table's owner and can lock all other users out, including you!

Refer to Chapter 13 for a complete description of how to use the Paradox protection features.

For Related Information:

▶▶ "Protecting Your Files," p. 443.

FROM HERE...

Chapter Summary

After completing this second chapter of the book, you are well on your way to becoming a Paradox pro, as promised. You now are armed with a fundamental understanding of database design and with detailed knowledge of Paradox table creation. You are ready to move on to Chapter 3 and to learn how to enter and edit Paradox data.

Entering, Editing, and Viewing Data

D ata entry and retrieval are the primary missions of any database management system. This chapter shows you several methods of entering, editing, and viewing data with Paradox tables, and Chapter 4 introduces you to the Query By Example (QBE) data-retrieval method. Both chapters build on the foundation of Chapters 1 and 2, so you should be familiar with basic Paradox terminology and know how to create a database of Paradox tables before you begin this chapter.

Paradox is considered a high-end database program, despite its ease of learning and use, because of the program's abundance of powerful features. This chapter does not introduce you to every data-entry and editing tool that Paradox has to offer but gives you the basic tools necessary to get up and running. The last portion of this chapter introduces the Paradox Editor, a full-screen text editor that is a new feature in Paradox 4.0. When you feel comfortable with the fundamentals presented in this chapter, turn to Chapter 8, "Using Advanced Form Techniques," and Chapter 9, "Using Power Entry and Editing Features," to discover the most potent entry and editing capabilities of Paradox.

Enjoying the View

Reminder:

Paradox presents data on-screen in table or form view.

As explained in the "Understanding Paradox Views" section of Chapter 1, Paradox presents data on-screen in one of two views. The *table view* is the familiar display of the data as a series of horizontal rows (see fig. 3.1). This view is the default view in which Paradox starts. You can switch to the *form view* by pressing F7 (Form Toggle). Paradox changes the screen to a vertical, single-record depiction of the same table.

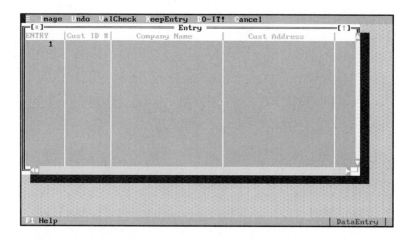

FIG. 3.1

The table view.

Reminder:

Paradox designs a standard form (form F) the first time you press F7 for a particular table.

Paradox designs a *standard form* (form F) the first time you press F7 for a particular table. Figure 3.2 shows the standard form for a table named Customer. You also can custom design as many as 14 additional forms per table. These custom forms are added to the table's family and are available for use any time you enter, edit, or view data from the table. Creating and using these custom forms is covered in detail in Chapter 8, "Using Advanced Form Techniques."

Whichever view you use, Paradox also provides a wide variety of features which can help you ensure that data is entered or edited correctly in table fields. Some features even enter data for you, as default data or data looked up from another table. These data entry and edit aids are *validity checks* and can be created for use in all the data-entry and editing modes. Refer to Chapter 9, "Using Power Entry and Editing Features," for a full discussion of these powerful features. Throughout this chapter, assume that you are using the standard table view or the standard form view with no validity checks, unless specifically stated otherwise.

Reminder:

You can enter data from three modes.

Paradox is an amazingly flexible database program. In addition to providing two views, Paradox enables you to enter data into database tables from three different modes—DataEntry, Edit, and CoEdit—and to edit data from the Edit and CoEdit modes. All these entry and edit options are introduced in this chapter.

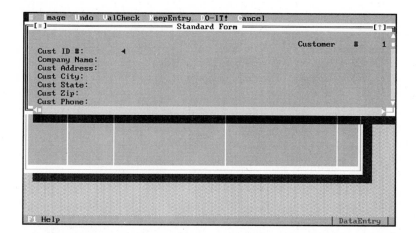

FIG. 3.2

The standard form view for the Customer table.

For Related Information:

▶▶ "An Overview of Form Design," p. 294.

FROM HERE...

Entering Data in DataEntry Mode

Of the three available modes for entering data, the DataEntry mode is the only one designed exclusively for that purpose. Paradox does not display existing records in DataEntry mode. The data already stored on disk, therefore, is protected from being changed accidentally.

To begin a DataEntry session, select **M**odify, **D**ataEntry from the Main menu. Specify the table to which the data should be added (the target table). Paradox displays an empty temporary table named Entry, which has the same structure as the target table (refer to fig. 3.1). A status message at the top of the screen states that you are working on Record 1 of 1. A pointer (a left-pointing triangle) indicates the current field into which you are about to enter data. (To switch to the form view, press F7.)

Reminder:

In DataEntry mode, you enter data in the temporary table named Entry.

Entering data in table or form view is as simple as typing your entry on-screen. Use the cursor-movement keys to move between fields and records. If you need to refresh your memory about how these keys operate in the table and form views, refer to tables 1.3 and 1.4 in Chapter 1.

Cue:
Press Alt-F5 or Ctrl-F to switch to field view.

You can use the Backspace key to erase your mistakes, one character at a time. The Ctrl-Backspace key combination deletes an entire field entry. You also can use the *field view* (by double-clicking the field or by pressing Alt-F5 or Ctrl-F) to edit entries while in DataEntry mode (see fig. 3.3).

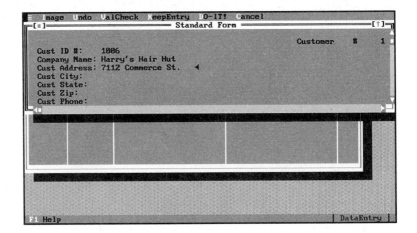

FIG. 3.3

Using the field view to edit entries.

To delete an entire record from the Entry table, place the cursor in the unwanted row and press the Del key.

T I P   As you enter data on-screen, Paradox holds the data in RAM (random-access memory), which is volatile—subject to loss if the power is interrupted before the data is saved to disk. By default, Paradox activates an autosave feature that periodically saves your data to disk as you work. You may notice your disk drive light momentarily coming on during your data-entry session. If you lose power during data entry, the Entry table in which you were working is safe in your working directory until you can restart your computer and return to Paradox. Be careful not to use the DataEntry mode again until you have copied the contents of Entry into the original target table. Use the **Add** command on the Tools/More menu.

Saving or Abandoning the Entered Data

As you enter data, the data does not go directly into the target table. The data is added to the Entry table. The records in figure 3.4, for example, are displayed in the Entry table and have not yet been added to Customer. When you are satisfied that the record or records are correct, press F2 (Do-It!). Paradox saves the data to disk, adding the records to the target table. The program displays the message Adding records from Entry to Customer... and returns you to Main mode with the Customer table as the active window, including new records.

Reminder:
Press F2 (Do-It!) to add the new records to the target table.

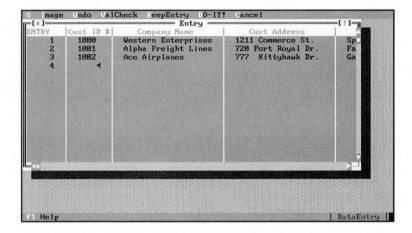

FIG. 3.4

Entering data in DataEntry mode.

You may decide that the data should not be added to the target table. In that case, select **C**ancel, **Y**es to cancel the data-entry session. Paradox abandons any information you entered into the Entry table and returns to the Main mode and the desktop, just as it was before you entered DataEntry mode.

Using Undo in DataEntry Mode

Paradox recognizes that nobody is perfect. The program has built in a life-saving *undo* feature. As you enter data, Paradox tracks your keystrokes in a *transaction log*. The Paradox undo feature enables you to undo one transaction at a time, starting with the most recent one, all the way back to the beginning of the current DataEntry session.

Reminder:
You can undo one transaction at a time.

A transaction is defined by its beginning and end points in time. The *transaction beginning point* is the moment you move the cursor into a new or existing field. The *transaction end point* is the moment you leave or delete the record. The transaction consists of any data entry or changes made to data in the Entry table that occurs between these two points in time.

Suppose that during data entry you realize that the first entry in the table shown in figure 3.4 is incorrect. The Company Name should be Eastern Enterprises rather than Western Enterprises. When attempting to edit the Company Name field, you mistakenly press the Del key before accessing field view, and you erase the entire record (see fig. 3.5).

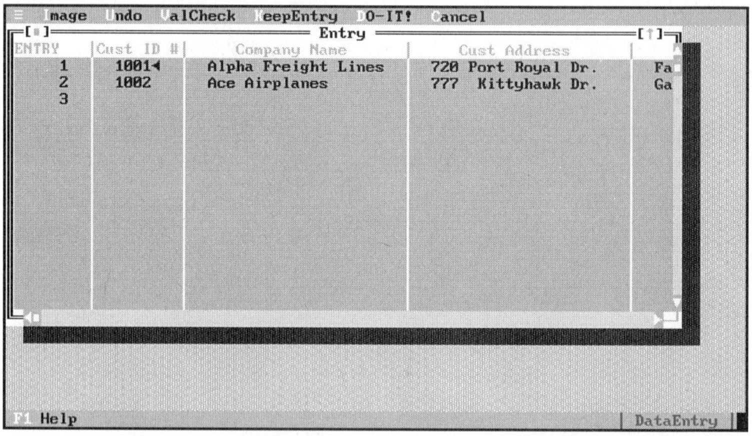

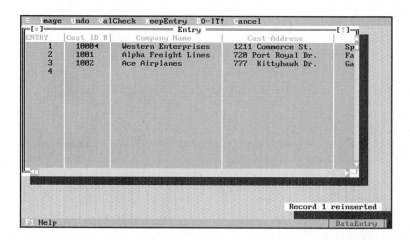

FIG. 3.5

Accidentally deleting a record.

Of course, you can retype the entire record. To conserve your energy, however, press the Undo keystroke command: Ctrl-U. Paradox quickly reinstates the missing record to the Entry table and displays a message telling you that the record was reinserted (see fig. 3.6).

FIG. 3.6

Using Undo to restore the deleted record.

Using Ditto in DataEntry Mode

Another labor-saving feature is Ctrl-D, the Ditto keystroke command. When you place the cursor in a blank field and press Ctrl-D, Paradox inserts into that field the entire contents of the same field from the preceding record. This feature works only for second and subsequent records in the Entry table.

Entering Data in a Memo Field

Paradox 4.0's memo field type enables you to add variable length text information to a table. The procedure for entering data in a memo field is distinctly different from the procedure for entering data in other field types.

Suppose that you restructure the Orders table and add a memo field named Notes. You want to provide your sales representatives the capability to enter, in the Orders table, free-form information about each order.

When you define the memo field (refer to Chapter 2 for more information on assigning field type), you specify a field length, just as you do with an alphanumeric field. But memo fields can have practically unlimited length (64M). The length specification you include in the memo field definition specifies the number of characters you want Paradox to display in table view. Regardless of the length you specify in the memo field's definition, and whether you are viewing the table in table view or form view, you enter data into a memo field using the Paradox Editor.

To enter data in a memo field, move the cursor to the field and double-click the field, or press Alt-F5 or Ctrl-F (Field View). Paradox opens an Editor window with the label Entry->Notes in the title bar. When you have finished entering data in the field, press F2 (Do-It!) to save your work and return to the original table.

Reminder:
Memo fields enable you to add variable length text information to a table.

Cue:
To enter data in a memo field, press Alt-F5 or Ctrl-F (Field View) to open an Editor window.

Refer to the "Using the Paradox Editor" section, later in this chapter, for more about using the Editor to enter or edit data.

Entering Data in a BLOB Field

The new BLOB (Binary Large OBject) field type enables you to add variable length files of nearly any format as field values. You can add graphic files (for example, TIFF, or PCX), spreadsheet files, word processing files, and so on. Suppose that you restructure the Employee table and add a BLOB field named Photo (refer to Chapter 2 for more information on assigning field type). You want to provide the capability to view a scanned image of each employee from within the Employee table.

Reminder:
BLOB fields enable you to add variable length files of any type to a table.

First, you must use the Custom Configuration Program to specify a Binary Large Object editor you want to use. (Refer to Appendix B for a complete discussion of how to specify a BLOB editor.) To view scanned photographs, for example, you should specify as the BLOB editor a program that is capable of viewing the graphics files created by your scanner.

Cue:
To enter data in a BLOB field, press Alt-F5 or Ctrl-F (Field View) to open a BLOB editor window.

The procedure for entering data in a BLOB field is similar to entering data in a memo field. To enter data in a BLOB field, move the cursor to the field and double-click on the field, or press Alt-F5 or Ctrl-F (Field View). Paradox suspends itself in the computer's memory and temporarily opens the BLOB editor and opens a new file with the file name $ZMEMZ$.ZZ. This is a temporary file that stores the file as you create it using the BLOB editor. If you want to import a pre-existing file—a scanned photograph of an employee, for example—make sure that you save the file with the name $ZMEMZ$.ZZ.

Reminder:
Save the BLOB file with the name $ZMEMZ$.ZZ.

When you have finished creating or importing the BLOB file, save the file (with the name $ZMEMZ$.ZZ) and exit from the BLOB editor. Paradox returns to the original table and inserts the word BLOB in the field to denote that the program has stored the new BLOB file in your database.

NOTE   The original file created by the BLOB editor is moved into the Paradox table. If you are working with graphics files that require substantial storage space, the Paradox table—EMPLOYEE in this example—can grow quite large.

Finding a Record with Zoom

When you are entering many records and want to take a look at a particular one in the Entry table, you can use the Zoom option to help you find the record. Refer to "Finding a Record with Zoom and Zoom Next," later in this chapter.

Working with the DataEntry Menu

Pressing F10 (Menu) in DataEntry mode activates the menu shown in figure 3.7.

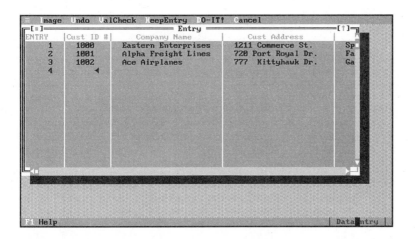

FIG. 3.7

The DataEntry menu.

The following are brief summaries of the options included on the DataEntry menu:

Option	Function
Image	This option provides access to Paradox window-customization features. These features work in the same manner in any mode, so refer to this chapter's section on "Using the Image Options."
Undo	This menu choice has the same effect as Ctrl-U (Undo).
ValCheck	Validity checks are one of the most useful features of Paradox, both in preventing entry of invalid data and in helping you enter data by providing default values and automatic lookup from other tables. This option is one of the power features covered in Chapter 9.

Option	Function
KeepEntry	This option temporarily saves the current Entry table to disk and ends the data-entry session. Refer to the section "Using DataEntry Mode on a Network" for more discussion of the **K**eepEntry option.
DO-IT!	This option is equivalent to the F2 (Do-It!) key.
Cancel	This option cancels data entry, discards all data entered during the session, and returns to the Main mode desktop, as you left it before starting data entry.

Handling Keys and Key Violations in DataEntry Mode

Reminder:
Paradox checks for key violations when you press F2 (Do-It!).

Chapter 2 introduces you to the concept of key fields. The two primary effects of a key field or fields are to keep the records in a particular order and to prevent duplicates, often called *key violations*. During DataEntry mode, Paradox does not continuously monitor the key field(s) for either purpose. Instead, the program waits until you press F2 (Do-It!), and then compares the new records with existing records.

Paradox stores the new records in their proper key order and looks for duplicates in the key field(s). Any duplicate records—records with a match in all key fields—are not added to the target table but are placed in the temporary table named Keyviol. Paradox displays the target table as a window in the Main mode desktop and displays Keyviol, if duplicates were found, just below the target table. In the example shown in figure 3.8, the number *1000* inadvertently was reused in Cust ID #, a single key field. Paradox prevents this record from being added to Customer, placing the problem entry in the Keyviol table.

To add records from Keyviol to the target table, first edit the offending entry, and then add the corrected record to the target table. For example, to edit the violating record shown in figure 3.8, press F9 (Edit), change the Cust ID # to *1005*, and press F2 (Do-It!). To add the record to the Customer table, press F10 (Menu) and select **T**ools, **M**ore, **A**dd. Specify that Keyviol is the source table and that Customer is the target table. (The **A**dd command is discussed fully in Chapter 13, "Using Paradox Tools.") For keyed target tables (target tables with one or more key fields), Paradox displays a pop-up menu with the choices **N**ewEntries and **U**pdate. Select **N**ewEntries to instruct Paradox to insert the record into Customer. Paradox displays the message Adding records from Keyviol to Customer, and then displays the screen shown in figure 3.9.

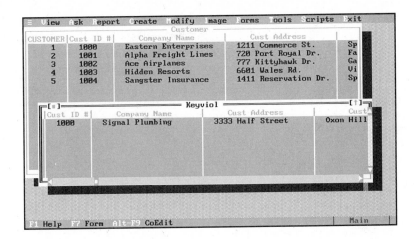

FIG. 3.8

Handling key violations in DataEntry mode.

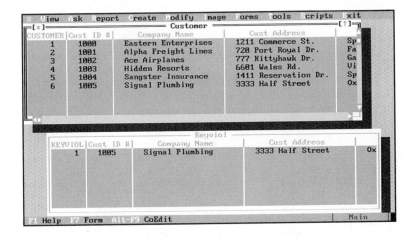

FIG. 3.9

Adding the corrected entry to Customer.

The method Paradox uses to prevent key violations differs drastically among modes. Understanding the methods used in each of the three modes is essential.

T I P

Using DataEntry Mode on a Network

When you select the **D**ataEntry option on a network, Paradox places a *prevent full lock* on the table. No other network user can set a lock that requires exclusive use of the database. All other users have full access

Reminder:
In DataEntry mode on a network, Paradox places a prevent full lock on the table.

to the table. If a full lock is already in place on the shared table, Paradox does not enable you to begin a DataEntry session until the other user finishes the operation that required a full lock.

Reminder:

KeepEntry temporarily saves the current Entry table to disk and ends the data-entry session.

When you attempt to complete your data-entry session by pressing F2 (Do-It!), Paradox places a *prevent write lock* on the target table. No other user can write to the table until your Entry table records have been added. You may get a message, however, that the file is locked. This message indicates that another user is performing some operation with the shared table that placed a write lock on the file. You have to wait until the other user is finished or use the **KeepEntry** option on the DataEntry menu. KeepEntry temporarily saves the current Entry table to disk and ends the data-entry session, returning you to the Main mode desktop. No changes are made to the target table. You later can use the **Add** option to add the records from Entry to the shared target file.

To terminate a data-entry session with **KeepEntry**, select **KeepEntry** from the menu bar. Paradox informs you that it is Saving Entry table.... The Entry table remains as the active window but in Main mode rather than DataEntry mode. After the other user has unlocked the target table, you can add the records from Entry. To do so, select **Tools, More, Add** from the Main menu. Specify *Entry* as the source table and the shared table as the target. Paradox displays a message telling you that the program is adding records from Entry to the target table and then displays the target table with new records added. If the target table is a keyed table, Paradox displays a submenu with the choices **NewEntries** and **Update**. Select **NewEntries**.

> **CAUTION:** Make a practice of immediately renaming the Entry table when you use the **KeepEntry** command. The Entry table is one of several temporary tables created by Paradox, so this table is never a secure home for your data. A subsequent DataEntry session or the Paradox Exit command wipes the Entry table clean. All data saved by **KeepEntry** then is gone. Changing the name of the table, however, completely protects the data from these disasters.

To rename the Entry table, start from the Main menu and select **Tools, Rename, Table**. Specify *Entry* as the current name of the table, type a new table name, and press Enter. When you later use the **Add** command to place the data in the target table on the network, remember to use the new name as the source file.

For Related Information:

▶▶ "Using DataEntry Mode with Multitable Forms," p. 335.

▶▶ "Customizing PAL Settings," p. 1004.

FROM HERE...

Entering and Editing Data in Edit Mode

In Edit mode, Paradox displays and enables you to change existing data. Making changes to your data is the primary purpose for the mode, but you also can use Edit mode to enter new data.

You have two ways to begin Edit mode: through the Main menu or with the F9 (Edit) key. The method you use depends on whether the table you want to edit is already on the desktop. If the subject table is not currently displayed in a table on the desktop, you must use the menu method. From the Paradox Main menu, select **M**odify, **E**dit and indicate the table to be edited. Often, however, the table you want to edit is already a window in the Main mode desktop. You can use the Modify menu to start Edit mode, but a much easier way is to press F9 (Edit). Paradox almost imperceptibly changes the mode from Main to Edit, and you are ready to make alterations or additions.

Cue:
Press F9 (Edit) to switch to Edit mode.

All tables on the desktop are placed into Edit mode together, but you can make changes only to the current table. (Query forms, discussed in Chapter 4, "Getting Started with Query By Example," cannot be edited during Edit mode.) You can press F3 (Previous Image) or F4 (Next Image) before or after entering Edit mode until the table you want to edit is active, and then you can make changes (see figs. 3.10 and 3.11).

Reminder:
All tables on the desktop are placed into Edit mode together.

Paradox displays the existing records of the table in the active window in Edit mode, starting with record number 1. If the table is keyed, the records are in order by the key field(s). Paradox removes multiple copies of any table from the screen to prevent inconsistent versions of the same table.

> **CAUTION:** The table you edit in Edit mode is not the temporary Entry table used by DataEntry mode. Additions and changes are made directly to the permanent table. Paradox does, however, maintain a transaction log during Edit mode so that the undo feature can return you to the original version of your table if you make a drastic mistake.

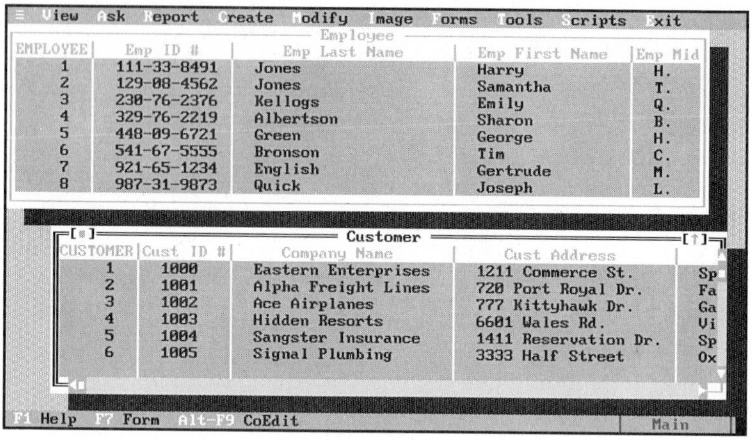

FIG. 3.10

Making the
Employee table
current in Main
mode.

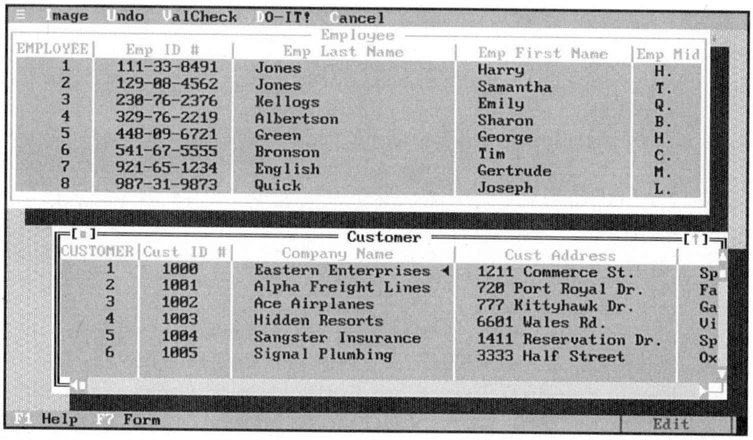

```
≡  View  Ask  Report  Create  Modify  Image  Forms  Tools  Scripts  Exit
┌EMPLOYEE┬──────────────────── Employee ─────────────────────────────────┐
│        │   Emp ID #        Emp Last Name      Emp First Name  │Emp Mid│
│    1   │ 111-33-8491    Jones              Harry              H.     │
│    2   │ 129-08-4562    Jones              Samantha           T.     │
│    3   │ 230-76-2376    Kellogs            Emily              Q.     │
│    4   │ 329-76-2219    Albertson          Sharon             B.     │
│    5   │ 448-09-6721    Green              George             H.     │
│    6   │ 541-67-5555    Bronson            Tim                C.     │
│    7   │ 921-65-1234    English            Gertrude           M.     │
│    8   │ 987-31-9873    Quick              Joseph             L.     │
└────────┴──────────────────────────────────────────────────────────────┘
   ┌[■]─────────────────── Customer ──────────────────────────[↑]┐
   │CUSTOMER│Cust ID #│    Company Name        │   Cust Address      │
   │    1   │ 1000    Eastern Enterprises    1211 Commerce St.    Sp │
   │    2   │ 1001    Alpha Freight Lines    720 Port Royal Dr.   Fa │
   │    3   │ 1002    Ace Airplanes          777 Kittyhawk Dr.    Ga │
   │    4   │ 1003    Hidden Resorts         6601 Wales Rd.       Vi │
   │    5   │ 1004    Sangster Insurance     1411 Reservation Dr. Sp │
   │    6   │ 1005    Signal Plumbing        3333 Half Street     Ox │
   └──────────────────────────────────────────────────────────────┘
 F1 Help   F7 Form   Alt-F9 CoEdit                         │ Main │
```

FIG. 3.11

Editing the
Employee table
with multiple
windows on the
desktop.

```
≡  Image  Undo  ValCheck  DO-IT!  Cancel
┌EMPLOYEE┬──────────────────── Employee ─────────────────────────────────┐
│        │   Emp ID #        Emp Last Name      Emp First Name  │Emp Mid│
│    1   │ 111-33-8491    Jones              Harry              H.     │
│    2   │ 129-08-4562    Jones              Samantha           T.     │
│    3   │ 230-76-2376    Kellogs            Emily              Q.     │
│    4   │ 329-76-2219    Albertson          Sharon             B.     │
│    5   │ 448-09-6721    Green              George             H.     │
│    6   │ 541-67-5555    Bronson            Tim                C.     │
│    7   │ 921-65-1234    English            Gertrude           M.     │
│    8   │ 987-31-9873    Quick              Joseph             L.     │
└────────┴──────────────────────────────────────────────────────────────┘
   ┌[■]─────────────────── Customer ──────────────────────────[↑]┐
   │CUSTOMER│Cust ID #│    Company Name        │   Cust Address      │
   │    1   │ 1000    Eastern Enterprises ◄  1211 Commerce St.    Sp │
   │    2   │ 1001    Alpha Freight Lines    720 Port Royal Dr.   Fa │
   │    3   │ 1002    Ace Airplanes          777 Kittyhawk Dr.    Ga │
   │    4   │ 1003    Hidden Resorts         6601 Wales Rd.       Vi │
   │    5   │ 1004    Sangster Insurance     1411 Reservation Dr. Sp │
   │    6   │ 1005    Signal Plumbing        3333 Half Street     Ox │
   └──────────────────────────────────────────────────────────────┘
 F1 Help   F7 Form                                        │ Edit │
```

T I P   When entering data from Edit mode, you may accidentally modify
existing records. A good way to reduce the risk is to always switch to
form view (by pressing F7) if you are going to enter new records.
While in table view, an errant keystroke may place you in the wrong
record. With multiple records on-screen, you may not immediately
notice that you are in the wrong row. In form view, you would be
more apt to notice an accidental PgUp or PgDn because the entire
screen would change, and the record number is conspicuous in the
upper right corner of the form.

If your table is keyed, however, you have a compelling reason *not* to
use Edit mode to enter new data. For more information, refer to the
"Handling Keys and Key Violations in Edit Mode" section later in this
chapter.

Finding a Record with Zoom and Zoom Next

You may want to edit one particular record out of hundreds, or even thousands, in your database table. Paradox provides a number of ways to help you find the record quickly, but the easiest way is to use the zoom feature. Zoom works best if the table contains a single key field.

Suppose that you know the value of one of the fields in the record you want to edit. Place the cursor in that field in any record and press Ctrl-Z (Zoom). Paradox displays a small dialog box containing a text box labeled `Value:` and two command buttons—OK and Cancel. A message in the status line reads `Enter value (exact match or pattern) to search for`. Type the value for the field and press Enter or select the OK button. Paradox scans the field from the top of the table to the bottom. When the program finds a match, it moves the cursor to that record so that you can edit the record. If Paradox doesn't find a match, you see the message `Match not found` in the bottom right corner of the screen, and Paradox does not move the cursor.

Cue:
Press Ctrl-Z to activate the Zoom feature.

Sometimes the value in the field you are searching is not unique, and Paradox may not find the correct record on the first try. In that case, press Alt-Z (Zoom Next). Paradox continues scanning the field throughout the table until the program finds a match or reaches the end of the table.

Cue:
Press Alt-Z for the Zoom Next feature.

The zoom feature works well in tandem with a single key. The value in a single key field is, by definition, unique, so you always find the record you want on the first try. Refer to the "Reordering the Table with OrderTable" section, later in this chapter, for information on how to create a secondary index that speeds up the zoom feature when you are searching fields other than the key field.

You also can access the zoom feature through Paradox's menu. Refer to the "Using the Image Options" section later in this chapter for a complete discussion of the Zoom menu options and for a discussion of using wild cards to find particular items.

Ctrl-Z (Zoom) and Alt-Z (Zoom Next) also work in DataEntry and CoEdit modes.

Editing Fields

Cursor-movement and editing keys work the same way in Edit mode as in DataEntry mode. Review tables 1.3 and 1.4 in Chapter 1 for descriptions of how the cursor-movement keys operate in the table and form views. Recall that some of these keys have different effects in the two views. The PgUp key, for example, moves you to the preceding screen of records in table view but moves up no more than one record in form view.

Use the Backspace key to erase your mistakes one character at a time, and use the Ctrl-Backspace keystroke combination to delete an entire field entry. You also can use the field view (double-click the field, or press Alt-F5 or Ctrl-F) to edit errant entries while in Edit mode. Accessing and using the field view is described in Chapter 1.

You must use field view to edit a memo field or a BLOB field. If you attempt to edit either type of field in form view or table view, Paradox reminds you to press Alt-F5 or Ctrl-F (you also can double-click the field to switch to field view).

When you invoke field view in a memo field, Paradox displays the memo data in a Paradox Editor window. Refer to the "Using the Paradox Editor" section, later in this chapter, for more about editing data using the Editor. Press F2 (Do-It!) to save your changes and return to the original table.

If you toggle field view in a BLOB field, Paradox loads the stored BLOB file into the BLOB editor you identified in the Custom Configuration Program. After you make any desired changes to the file, be sure to save the modified file as $ZMEMZ$.ZZ, and then exit the BLOB editor. Paradox returns to the original table and stores the modified BLOB file in this Paradox table.

Deleting a Record

Cue:
Press Del to delete a record.

Almost any data in a Paradox table eventually can become obsolete. When you no longer have any reason to keep certain data in your database, delete that data. Deleting data is extremely easy to do. Fortunately, the undo feature is as simple.

Cue:
Press Ctrl-U to Undo a deletion.

To delete a record, place the cursor in the target record (in table or form view) and press the Del key. If you didn't mean to delete the record, use Ctrl-U (Undo) to recover the lost record.

Deleting records in Paradox discards the data but does not recover the disk space used by the data. This feature may not seem to be a significant problem for small tables. The lack of a space recovery feature can be a real and serious problem if your Paradox table is large, and you regularly delete many records. Ultimately, you may run out of disk space.

T I P

The easiest way to recover the lost space is to restructure the table, without changing the table definition. To be on the safe side, make a copy of the table, using the Copy option on the Tools menu, and then follow the procedure outlined in Chapter 2 for restructuring a table. Be careful not to change the definition of any field. Access the Restructure mode and press F2 (Do-It!). Paradox makes a new copy of the table that takes up less room on the disk. Check the table when Paradox is done. Do not get rid of the backup copy you made until you are sure that the new table is OK.

Saving and Canceling Changes

As with DataEntry mode, in Edit mode, you can accept or discard changes made during an edit session. To save the changes and return to Main mode, press F2 (Do-It!). To throw away the edits, select Cancel, Yes from the menu.

Cue:
Press F2 (Do-It!) to save changes in Edit mode.

Either approach returns you to the Main mode. The table you were editing is in the active window.

The autosave feature mentioned in one of the preceding tips also operates during the Edit mode. Even though changes made during the edit session are not saved to disk until you press F2 (Do-It!), the autosave feature still protects you from an unexpected power outage. You lose, at most, a few keystrokes if the power is interrupted while you are entering or editing data in the Edit mode. Because changes are being saved directly to the target table, you do not have to go through a copy procedure after a power loss.

T I P

Using Undo in Edit Mode

The undo feature in Edit mode is identical to the undo feature in DataEntry mode. Keep in mind that the transaction log is cleared when you press F2 (Do-It!). You have the opportunity to undo one transaction at a time, starting from the most recent transaction to the time you entered Edit mode. After you confirm the changes by pressing F2, however, the edits are permanent and can be undone only through a subsequent editing session.

Using Ditto in Edit Mode

The Ditto command works practically the same way in Edit mode as it does in DataEntry mode. You first must clear any existing data from the field (with Ctrl-Backspace), and then press Ctrl-D (Ditto). Paradox reproduces the contents of the same field from the immediately preceding record.

Entering New Records

The Paradox Edit mode, although designed for making alterations to existing records, also can be used to enter new data. You can insert records within the table or add the records to the end of the table. For keyed fields, the location of the records doesn't matter because Paradox inserts them in the proper order when you press F2 (Do-It!).

Inserting Records within the Table

Cue:
Press Ins to insert
a new record.

To insert a blank row in the table, position the cursor (in table or form view) anywhere in the record that should follow your new record, and then press the Ins key. Starting at the cursor, Paradox moves all rows down one row, incrementing the record numbers accordingly (see figs. 3.12 and 3.13). Use the blank row to enter a new record, as shown in figure 3.14.

Adding Records to the End of the Table

You probably will add records routinely to the end of the table rather than continually inserting them within the table. To add a blank row at the end of the table during Edit mode, press the End key to move the cursor to the last record and then press the down-arrow key. Paradox adds a new blank row, giving that row the next record number in sequence (see fig. 3.15). You now are free to enter another record.

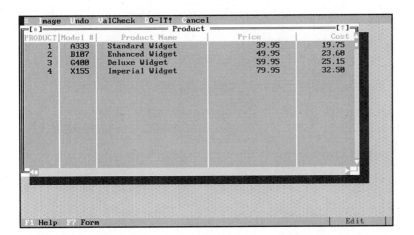

FIG. 3.12

Before inserting a blank row during Edit mode.

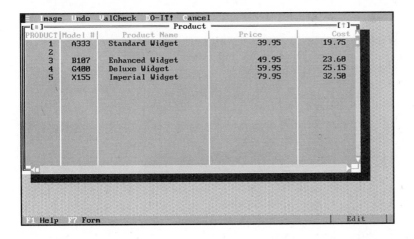

FIG. 3.13

After inserting a blank row during Edit mode.

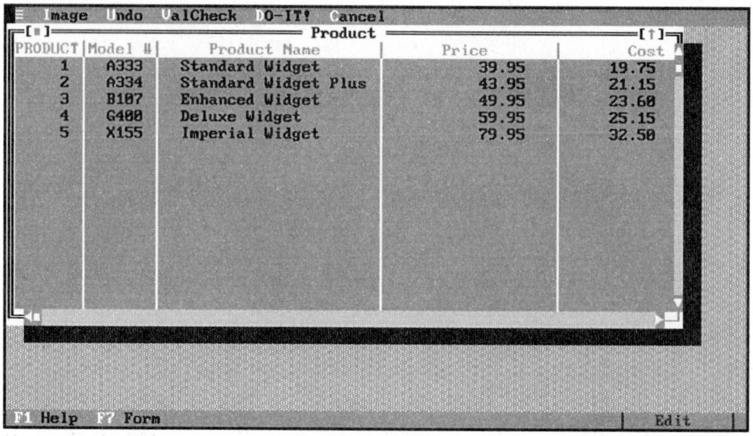

FIG. 3.14

The newly entered record.

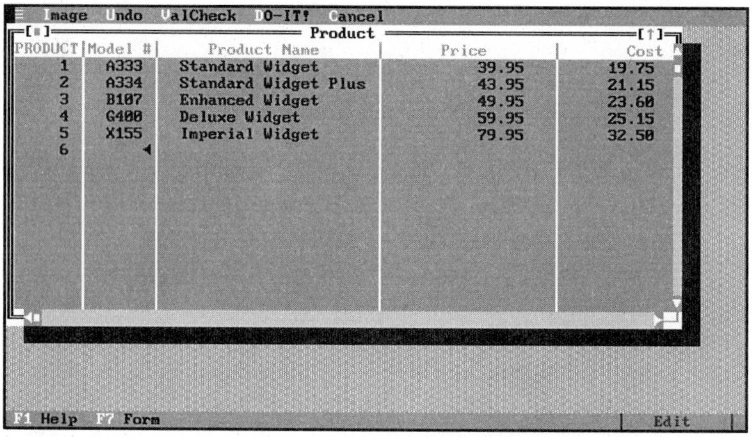

FIG. 3.15

Adding a new row to the end of the table during Edit mode.

Handling Keys and Key Violations in Edit Mode

Reminder:
DataEntry mode checks key violations when you press F2.

As in DataEntry mode, Paradox does not reorder the table or check for key violations in Edit mode until you press F2 (Do-It!). You may be surprised, however, by the way Paradox handles key violations. The following example demonstrates the problem.

The Product table shown in figure 3.16 is keyed on the Model # field. Suppose that during the current editing session you add records 6 and 7. Notice that Paradox has neither placed them in order by the key field nor prevented entry of a record with the same model number as an existing record. You don't have a problem at this point because you haven't accepted the changes.

Figure 3.17 shows the same table after you press F2. Two things have happened. First, Paradox moved Model # C777 to the fourth position, before G400 and after B107, which is what you would expect to happen. Second, the last entry shown in figure 3.16 has replaced the record that had the same model number—*without giving you any warning!*

> **CAUTION:** Beware of key fields when using Edit mode. Better yet, read the discussion of the CoEdit mode—you may decide to use that mode instead.

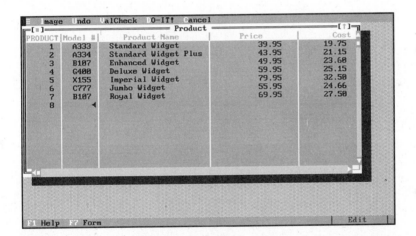

FIG. 3.16

Entering a key violation in Edit mode.

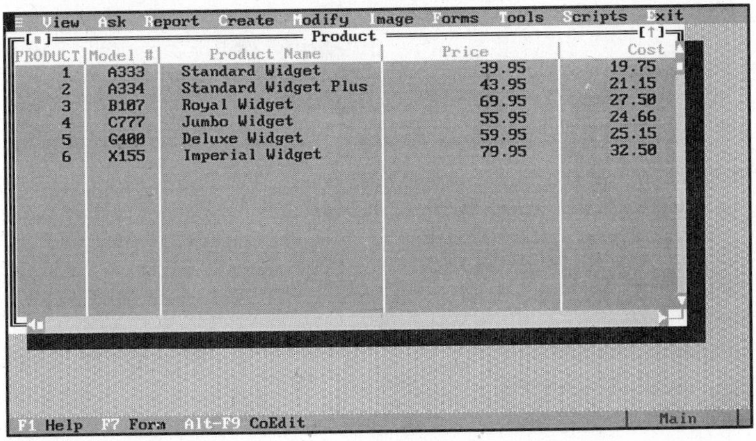

FIG. 3.17

How Paradox handles a key violation in Edit mode.

Using the Edit Menu

While in Edit mode, press F10 (Menu) to access the Edit menu, which includes the following options:

Option	Function
Image	This option provides access to Paradox window-customization features. These features work in the same manner in any mode, so refer to the "Using the Image Options" section later in this chapter.
Undo	This menu choice has the same effect as Ctrl-U (Undo).
ValCheck	Validity checks are one of the most useful features of Paradox, both in preventing entry of invalid data and in assisting you in data entry. They can provide default values and automatic lookup from other tables. Validity checks are covered in detail in Chapter 9, "Using Power Entry and Editing Features."
DO-IT!	This option is equivalent to F2 (Do-It!).
Cancel	Choosing this option cancels Edit mode, discards all changes made or data entered during the session, and returns to Main mode. The last table that you were editing remains the active window.

Using Edit Mode on a Network

Reminder:
Paradox places a full lock on a shared table in Edit mode.

Paradox places a full lock on a shared table when you access the table in Edit mode. No one else can use the table until you finish your edit session. Conversely, Paradox does not enable you to use Edit mode on a table already in use by any other individual on the network. For both of these reasons, you should use the CoEdit mode rather than Edit mode when editing shared network tables.

FROM HERE...

For Related Information:

▶▶ "Using Edit Mode with Multitable Forms," p. 335.

Entering and Editing Data in CoEdit Mode

This option's name derives from the fact that you can edit a shared table on a multiuser network at the same time that another network user is using the same table. The CoEdit mode is one of the jewels of the Paradox program. Not only can multiple users edit the same table at the same time, but everyone's screen is regularly updated to reflect changes made by other users.

You do not have to access a network, however, to make good use of this feature. On the contrary, CoEdit may be the best overall mode for entering and editing data with Paradox. As you can see from figure 3.18, CoEdit mode works in the actual target table, just as Edit does, rather than in an Entry table. The CoEdit mode is nearly identical in appearance to Edit mode.

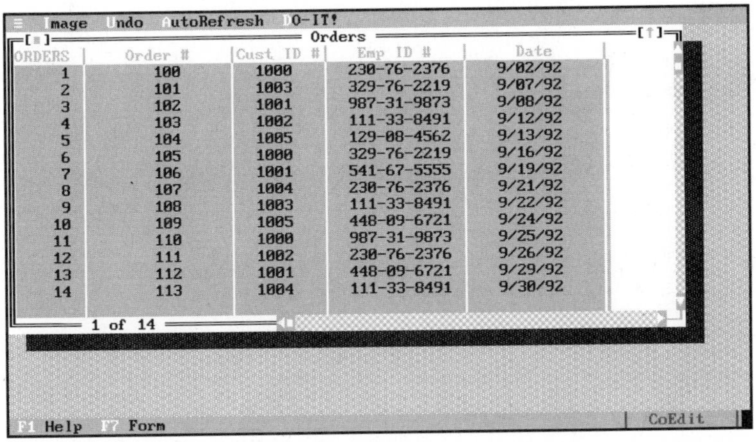

ORDERS	Order #	Cust ID #	Emp ID #	Date
1	100	1000	230-76-2376	9/02/92
2	101	1003	329-76-2219	9/07/92
3	102	1001	987-31-9873	9/08/92
4	103	1002	111-33-8491	9/12/92
5	104	1005	129-08-4562	9/13/92
6	105	1000	329-76-2219	9/16/92
7	106	1001	541-67-5555	9/19/92
8	107	1004	230-76-2376	9/21/92
9	108	1003	111-33-8491	9/22/92
10	109	1005	448-09-6721	9/24/92
11	110	1000	987-31-9873	9/25/92
12	111	1002	230-76-2376	9/26/92
13	112	1001	448-09-6721	9/29/92
14	113	1004	111-33-8491	9/30/92

FIG. 3.18

Coediting the Orders table.

As with Edit mode, you can start CoEdit mode from the Main menu or through a function-key command. To start CoEdit mode from the Main menu, select **M**odify, **C**oEdit and specify the table to be edited. If the chosen table is already on the desktop, Paradox enters CoEdit mode and makes the table's window active. Otherwise, the program adds the table to the desktop as the active window (see fig. 3.19).

When the table to be edited is already on the desktop, you can press Alt-F9 (CoEdit) to begin CoEdit mode. Like Edit mode, all tables on the desktop are in CoEdit mode at the same time. You can use the mouse or the function key commands F3 (Previous Image) and F4 (Next Image) before and after you enter CoEdit mode to move between windows.

Cue:
Press Alt-F9 to begin CoEdit mode.

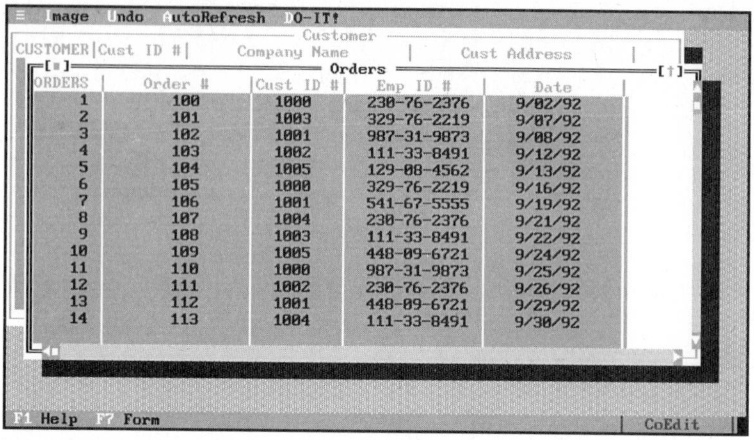

FIG. 3.19

Coediting with multiple tables on the desktop.

If you are using Paradox as a stand-alone system or using a nonshared database (directory) on a network, Paradox removes multiple windows of any table from the desktop when you begin CoEdit mode. The program, however, does not remove multiple windows of shared network tables. Refer to the section "Using CoEdit Mode on a Network" later in this chapter for an explanation of this apparent inconsistency.

All the fundamental operations for entering and editing data in Edit mode are done the same way in CoEdit mode: finding records to edit with Ctrl-Z (Zoom), moving around fields and records with the cursor keys, entering and editing data in a field, using field view, inserting new records, deleting records, and using Ctrl-D (Ditto). A few operations, however, are a bit different in CoEdit mode.

Saving and Canceling Changes

Reminder:

F2 (Do-It!) is the only way to terminate a CoEdit session. CoEdit offers no Cancel option.

You use F2 (Do-It!) to complete CoEdit mode, just as you do in Edit mode. Unlike in Edit, using F2 is the *only* way to terminate a CoEdit session.

In CoEdit mode, Paradox posts data to disk after every record rather than at the end of the session. This difference is related directly to the goal of maximum concurrency for network users—enabling multiple users on a network to safely edit a shared table at the same time. Even for nonnetwork users, this frequency of posting to disk directly limits the number of transactions that can be undone. In CoEdit mode, changes are posted to disk after every record, so the CoEdit menu contains no Cancel option. In addition, the CoEdit mode's Undo command (Ctrl-U) backs out of one and only one transaction—the most recent one.

You also can use Ctrl-Break to cancel CoEdit, but Paradox does not save unposted changes to the current record. The best practice, therefore, is to use F2 (Do-It!) instead of Ctrl-Break to complete a CoEdit session. Pressing Ctrl-Break while in Co-Edit mode has the same effect as pressing Ctrl-U (UnDo) and then pressing F2 (Do-It!).

Using the CoEdit Menu

While in CoEdit mode, press F10 (Menu) to access the CoEdit menu, which contains the following options:

Option	Function
Image	The first menu option provides access to Paradox window-customization features. These features work in the same manner in any mode, so refer to "Using the Image Options" later in this chapter.
Undo	This menu choice has the same effect as Ctrl-U (Undo). In CoEdit mode, this feature cancels the most recent transaction only. Undo cannot go back more than one transaction.
AutoRefresh	By default, Paradox refreshes your screen every three seconds with the most current content of the tables on the desktop. Through this menu option, you can vary the autorefresh interval to as little as one second or as long as one hour.
DO-IT!	Choosing this option is equivalent to pressing F2 (Do-It!).

Adding New Records to Keyed and Nonkeyed Tables

For nonkeyed tables, adding a record during CoEdit mode is the same as the equivalent procedure in Edit mode. You move to the last record, press the down-arrow key, and enter the new record. In CoEdit mode, Paradox monitors keys and key violations record-by-record rather than waiting for you to press F2 (Do-It!).

Reminder:
CoEdit monitors keys and key violations record by record.

When you enter a new record into a keyed table during CoEdit mode and move to the next record, Paradox checks for key violations. If none are found, the new record is inserted in proper sorted order in the table. Figure 3.20, for example, shows a new record being entered in the Product table from CoEdit mode. After the record is entered and you move to the next record, Paradox posts the entry in the correct sorted order—in this case by the Model # field (see fig. 3.21).

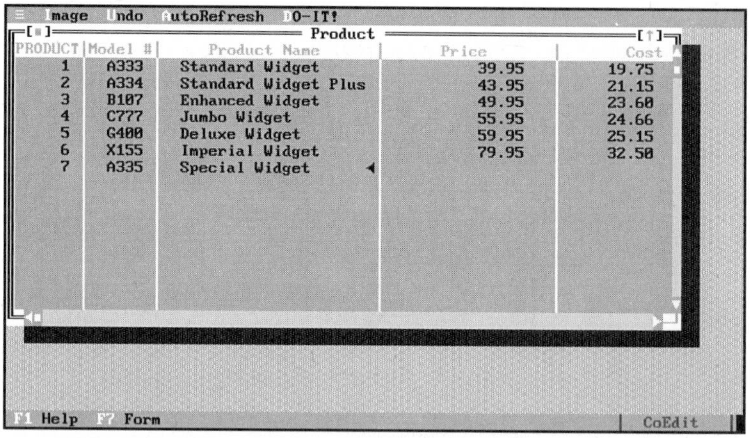

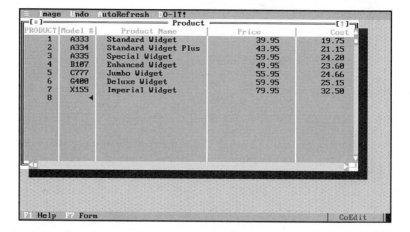

FIG. 3.20

Entering a new record with CoEdit mode.

FIG. 3.21

The new record posted in order by model number.

For large keyed tables, the immediate posting that occurs in CoEdit mode can make new records seem to disappear when you press Enter. Don't be concerned. The records aren't gone; they have been placed in the appropriate sorted order, which happens to be off the screen.

T I P

Handling Key Violations in CoEdit Mode

Figure 3.22 shows another record being entered in the same table, but this time a key violation has occurred. In sharp contrast to the way Paradox handles a key violation in Edit mode, in CoEdit mode, the program gives you ample warning. Paradox also provides several alternatives to help you resolve the conflict:

Reminder:
CoEdit warns you of a key violation.

■ The keystroke combination Alt-L (Lock Toggle) has the effect in CoEdit mode of placing and removing a lock on an individual record. When you are making changes to a record, the record is already locked, so pressing Alt-L removes the lock and causes the new record to be posted. At this point, the new record replaces the one that has the same key value (Model # B107). This result is the normal effect of a key violation in the Edit mode. (*Note:* You can use Ctrl-U (Undo) to reverse the effect of Alt-L, replacing the new record with the old version.)

Cue:
Press Alt-L to post the new record.

■ The keystroke combination Alt-K (Key Viol) is a toggle that alternately displays the new entry and the old entry so that you can decide which is correct. Press Alt-K once to see figure 3.23, showing the existing values in the last row of the table. Pressing Alt-K again switches back to the new value that is causing the conflict (see fig. 3.24).

Cue:
Press Alt-K to toggle between new and old entries.

Suppose that you made a mistake in the Model # field. The number should be V107 rather than B107. The Model # field in the new record needs to be corrected. After you fix the error, press Alt-L (Lock Toggle) to post the corrected record (see fig. 3.25).

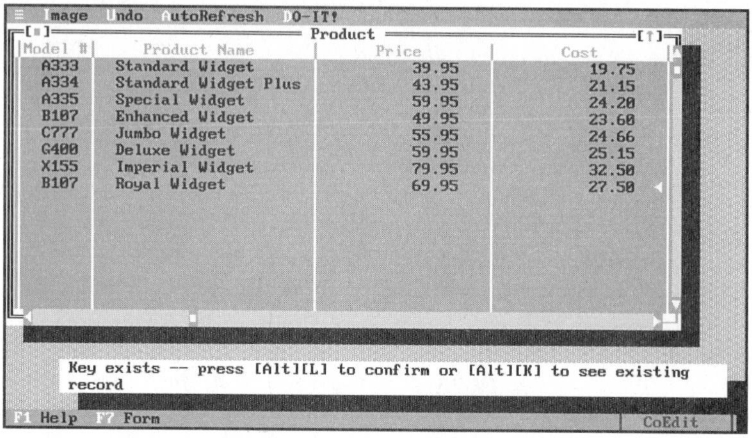

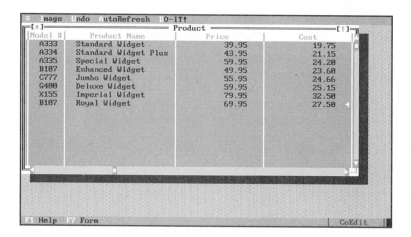

FIG. 3.22

Handling a key violation in CoEdit mode.

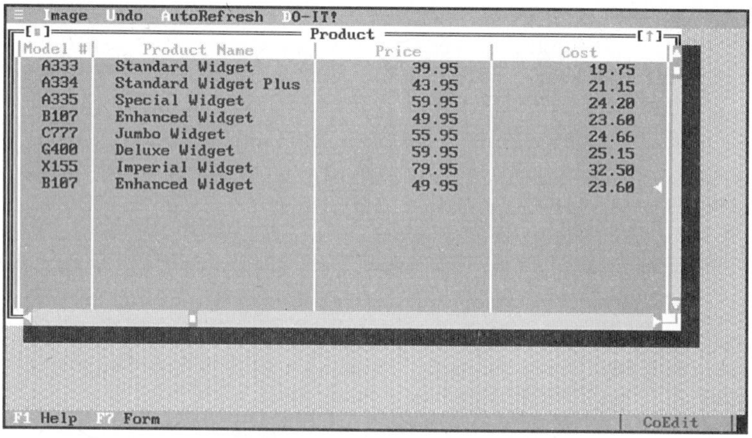

FIG. 3.23

Viewing the existing record with the conflicting key.

FIG. 3.24

Viewing the new record with the conflicting key.

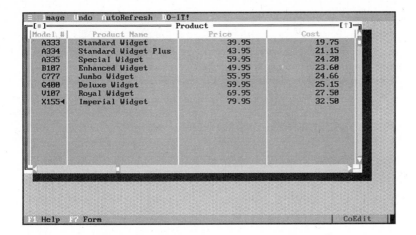

FIG. 3.25

After the key
violation has
been reconciled.

Using CoEdit Mode on a Network

CoEdit is specifically designed for editing shared tables on a network. Although this mode is the preferred method for editing keyed tables on a stand-alone system, CoEdit shines in a network environment. Before further study of the specifics of using CoEdit mode, however, you need to be familiar with the concept of network privileges.

Understanding Network Privileges

The owner of a shared table on a network, usually the person who created the table, can place certain restrictions on the use of the table by other network users. The **P**rotect option on the Tools menu and the separate Protection Generator program provide several sophisticated tools for this purpose.

Reminder:
The owner of a shared table can restrict usage of the table.

When you are the owner of a table, you should have no problem accessing the table in the CoEdit mode. You may run into certain restrictions, however, when you attempt to edit tables created by other network users. The owner of a Paradox table can grant or deny the following rights to the table (table rights):

■ *ReadOnly.* The right to view but not edit a table.

■ *Update.* The right to change only nonkey fields in existing records.

■ *Entry.* The right to enter new records and alter key fields using DataEntry mode or the **A**dd command; does not include the right to delete records.

- *InsDel.* The right to change and delete existing records and to add new records.

- *All.* Complete access to the table.

The table owner also can assign the following levels of *field rights*:

- *ReadOnly.* The right to view the field values but to make no changes.

- *All.* The right to view and change values in the field.

If the table owner has placed any restrictions on the table or fields, you may be asked for a password before you are granted access.

Refer to Chapter 2 and the discussion of the Protect option on the Tools/More menu for details on how to assign table and field rights.

Understanding the Locking System

Reminder:
On a network, CoEdit uses record-level locking, and Edit locks the entire table.

The essential difference between using CoEdit mode and using Edit mode on a network is that CoEdit uses record-level locking, and Edit locks the entire table. Paradox places a *prevent full lock* on the table you are editing in CoEdit mode. All other network users with appropriate table and field rights can have full access to the table but cannot place a full lock on the table. Until you begin to make a change to an existing record or begin to add a new record, no further lock is placed.

When you begin to edit or change a record, Paradox places a record-level lock that prevents any other user from having access to the record until you are finished. The record is unlocked when you press F2 (Do-It!) to leave CoEdit mode or when you move the cursor to another record.

When an individual record is locked, other users have complete access to all the other records in the table. Contrast this flexibility with how network access is handled by the Edit command. With Edit mode, the entire table is locked (with a full lock) for the entire time you are using the table.

Using Explicit Record Locking

Cue:
Use Alt-L (Lock Toggle) to lock a record explicitly.

If you want to preempt another user from changing a record and if you aren't ready to change the table yourself, you can use Alt-L (Lock Toggle) to lock a record explicitly. Move the cursor to the record that you want locked against any changes and press Alt-L. Paradox displays in inverse video the current-field pointer, the triangular pointer that appears at the right end of the current field.

When you finally make your changes or are ready to unlock the record, you can remove the lock by doing one of the following:

■ Press F2 (Do-It!), indicating that you are finished with CoEdit mode. Paradox displays the message Ending CoEdit.

■ Press Alt-L to toggle the lock. Paradox displays the current-field pointer in normal video.

■ Move the cursor to a different record.

Paradox posts the changes to the table and frees the record for access by other users.

T I P

If you want to lock more than one record in a particular table, open multiple windows containing the table. You can then lock a different record in each window.

Refreshing the Screen

Paradox was the first PC-based database program to provide real-time screen refresh for all users on a network. Other programs provide concurrent access to database tables, but a change made by one user is not written immediately to the screen of other users who are displaying the same record. dBASE IV has added this capability, but Paradox has included the capability since the program's inception.

Reminder:
Paradox provides real-time screen refresh for networked users.

For practical reasons, Paradox refreshes your screen at set intervals unless some other event causes the windows on your Paradox desktop to be brought up-to-date. You should be aware of the following events:

■ Paradox refreshes your screen every three seconds unless you change this interval through the **A**utorefresh choice on the CoEdit menu. You can adjust the refresh interval to as little as one second or to as long as one hour.

■ Between automatic screen refreshes, you can press Alt-R (Refresh) to see all changes that have been made by other users to the tables visible on-screen.

■ Each time you explicitly lock a record by pressing Alt-L (Lock Toggle), Paradox updates your screen. Because this procedure locks out other users, another user cannot change the data in the record while you are working with the record.

■ When you begin to change a record in a shared table, Paradox refreshes your screen so that you are sure to be working with the most current version of the record. The program also locks out other users until you are finished making your changes.

T I P   When you are using a shared keyed table in CoEdit mode, the record number is not a reliable identifier for particular records. Each time you (or any other users) enter a record, delete a record, or change a key value, many record numbers also may be altered. As Paradox refreshes your screen, don't be surprised to see record numbers continually changing as records are added to or deleted from the table.

FROM HERE...

For Related Information:

▶▶ "Using CoEdit Mode with Multitable Forms," p. 340.

Using the Paradox View Command

After you have entered data into a Paradox table, you may want to view the table's contents on the desktop. Chapter 4 discusses how to use Query By Example (QBE) to ask for specific records and fields to be displayed. This section describes how to view an entire table.

Viewing a Paradox Table

Reminder:
Table view is the default view.

To view a table, select **View** from the Main menu and specify the table you want to see. Paradox adds the table to the desktop as the active window. The desktop remains in Main mode. The default view is table view, but after a table is on the desktop, you can switch to the default form view by pressing F7 (Form Toggle). Each time you view another table, Paradox switches back to table view.

You can think of this look at your table as *home base*. Most other commands eventually return you here. When you are finished viewing the table, clear the screen by pressing either F8 (Close Active Window) or Alt-F8 (Close All Windows). (Alt-F8 clears the entire screen.)

Viewing Multiple Tables

With Paradox, you can have any number of tables on the desktop, each as a separate window. Each time you use View, Paradox adds another window to the screen (unless you press F8 or Alt-F8 to clear the screen). If you are viewing a table in form view and add another table to the desktop, Paradox switches back to table view when the program displays the new window.

Move between windows by using F3 (Previous Image) and F4 (Next Image). You can use the cursor keys to move around in the table in table or form view.

Reminder:
You can view any number of Paradox tables on the desktop.

Using the Image Options

The menu for each of the modes discussed in this chapter includes the option Image. This option is used to give you some control over just how each window looks on the desktop. The discussion here is applicable to the DataEntry, Edit, CoEdit, and Main modes, with a few variations.

To access the Image menu from any of these modes, select Image from the Main menu. Paradox displays the following menu options, or a subset of these options, depending on the program's current mode and view:

TableSize
ColumnSize
Format
Zoom
Move
PickForm
KeepSet
OrderTable
Graph

In form view and Edit mode, for example, Paradox displays the following options on the Image menu:

Format
Zoom
PickForm
KeepSet

The **KeepSet**, **OrderTable**, and **G**raph options are not available in either view from DataEntry mode.

Modifying Table Size

Paradox includes enough rows in the active window to display all the records of the current table, up to a maximum of 22 rows. Recall from the "Moving and Resizing a Window" section in Chapter 1, you can use either the mouse or the System menu to size a window. You also can use the **T**ableSize option on the Image menu to change window size.

To change the number of records displayed in the active window using the Image menu, access the table view Image menu and select **T**ableSize. Paradox displays a screen similar to figure 3.26. Use the keys listed in table 3.1 to size the table.

Table 3.1. Paradox TableSize Keys	
Key	**Effect**
Up arrow	Decrease the number of rows displayed (min. 2)
Down arrow	Increase the number of rows displayed (max. 22)
Home	Move to minimum number of rows (2)
End	Move to maximum number of rows (20)
Enter	Accept the new table size
Esc	Abort and return to preceding table size

For example, the window of the Detail table shown in figure 3.26 completely fills the screen. Suppose that you also want to see a couple of other related tables—Product and Orders—on the same screen. Using the mouse and Resize corner or the **T**ableSize option on the Image menu, you can reduce the size of each table until you can see portions of all three tables at the same time (see fig. 3.27). Paradox, however, uses the default length when displaying the table again.

Changing Column Size

Column widths in the table view are set according to the field definitions. The **C**olumnSize option on the table view Image menu gives you the ability to increase or decrease this width. Paradox 4.0 also enables you to use the mouse to change column width. Several factors, however, limit how wide or narrow you can make a column.

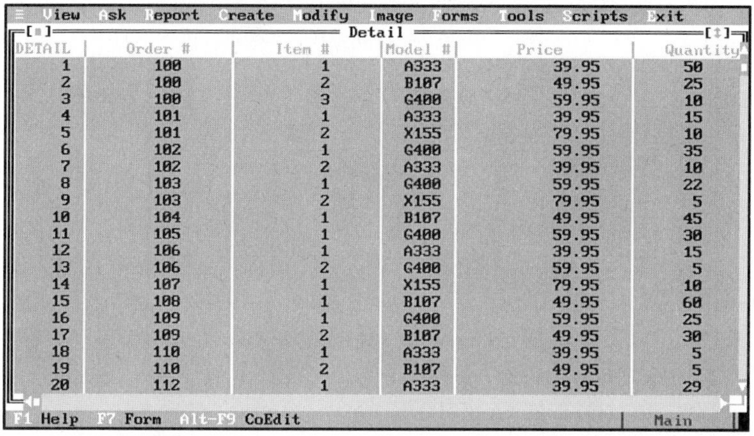

FIG. 3.26

The Detail table completely fills the screen.

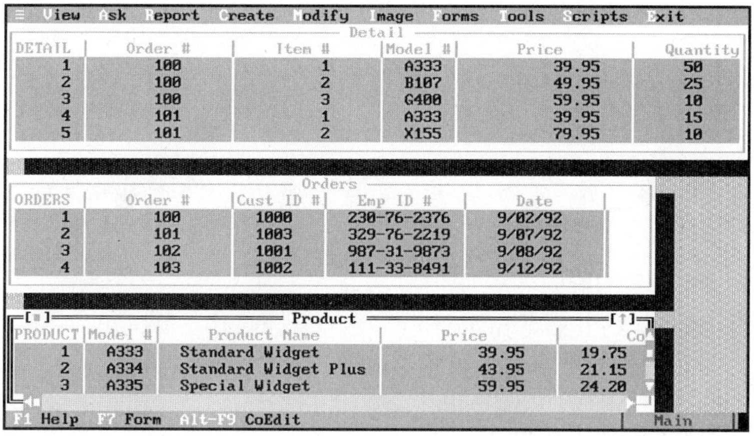

FIG. 3.27

Three tables displayed on-screen after table size has been modified.

Paradox sets a maximum column width for each field type. The data places practical limits on how narrow a column can be, and Paradox allows no column to be less than one character in width. Table 3.2 lists the default widths and the maximum allowable widths for the various data types.

Table 3.2. Paradox Default and Maximum Column Widths

Type	Default width	Maximum width
A or M	The longer of defined field length or field name length, up to a maximum of 73 character-widths	The shorter of field length or screen width
N	The longer of field name or 15 character-widths	The longer of field name or 25 character-widths
$	The longer of field name or 18 character-widths	The longer of field name or 25 character-widths
S	The longer of field name or 6 character-widths	The longer of field name or 6 character-widths
D	The longer of field name or 10 character-widths	The longer of field name or 14 character-widths

Reminder:
Data is not affected by changing Image settings.

If you reduce column width too severely, you affect the way data is displayed. Paradox truncates text and memo fields (shortens them by dropping characters from right to left) on-screen and displays all other types of fields as asterisks (*) when you reduce field width too much. In no case is the actual data stored on disk affected when you change a table's on-screen column width.

To change column width using the mouse, click the column's right border and drag it left or right until the column is the desired width.

To modify column width using the Image menu, access the Image menu and select **C**olumnSize. Use the left- and right-arrow keys to move to the column you want to resize and press Enter. Your screen looks similar to figure 3.28.

Suppose that you want to make the Price column of the Detail table narrower so that the entire Quantity column can be seen. Use the keys listed in table 3.3 to size the column. Press Enter to accept the change or Esc to return to the preceding width. Figure 3.29 shows the results. Unless you use the **K**eepSet option on the Image menu, this new column width applies only to the current session. The next time you display the table, column widths return to the defaults.

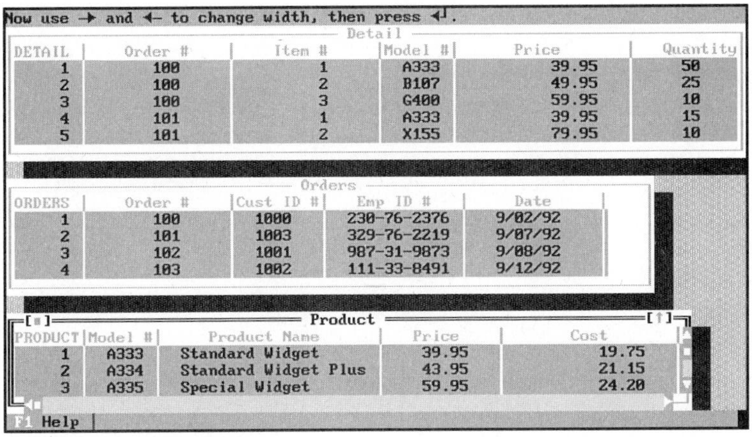

Now use → and ← to change width, then press ↵ .

DETAIL	Order #	Item #	Model #	Price	Quantity
1	100	1	A333	39.95	50
2	100	2	B107	49.95	25
3	100	3	G400	59.95	10
4	101	1	A333	39.95	15
5	101	2	X155	79.95	10

Detail

ORDERS	Order #	Cust ID #	Emp ID #	Date
1	100	1000	230-76-2376	9/02/92
2	101	1003	329-76-2219	9/07/92
3	102	1001	987-31-9873	9/08/92
4	103	1002	111-33-8491	9/12/92

Orders

PRODUCT	Model #	Product Name	Price	Cost
1	A333	Standard Widget	39.95	19.75
2	A334	Standard Widget Plus	43.95	21.15
3	A335	Special Widget	59.95	24.20

Product

F1 Help

FIG. 3.28

Modifying column width in the Detail table.

T I P

You may have a text field on-screen that is not completely visible because of the column size. You can see the entire field by pressing Alt-F5 (Field View) and using the cursor-movement keys to pan right and left.

Image Undo ValCheck DO-IT! Cancel

DETAIL	Order #	Item #	Model #	Price	Quantity	C
1	100	1	A333	39.95	50	
2	100	2	B107	49.95	25	
3	100	3	G400	59.95	10	
4	101	1	A333	39.95	15	
5	101	2	X155	79.95	10	

Detail

ORDERS	Order #	Cust ID #	Emp ID #	Date
1	100	1000	230-76-2376	9/02/92
2	101	1003	329-76-2219	9/07/92
3	102	1001	987-31-9873	9/08/92
4	103	1002	111-33-8491	9/12/92

Orders

PRODUCT	Model #	Product Name	Price	Cost
1	A333	Standard Widget	39.95	19.75
2	A334	Standard Widget Plus	43.95	21.15
3	A335	Special Widget	59.95	24.20

Product

F1 Help F7 Form   Edit

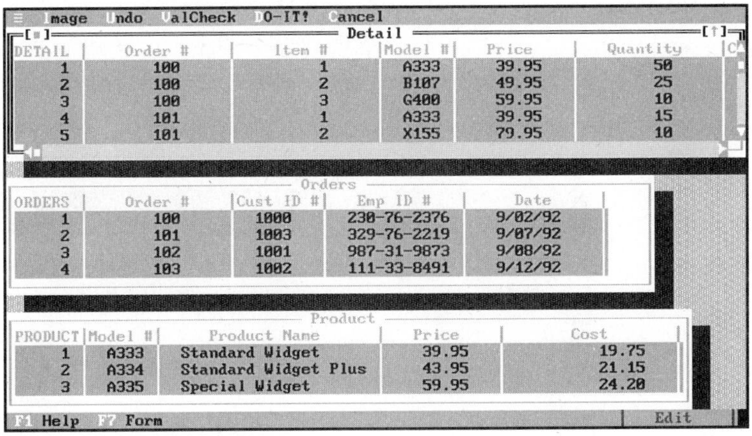

FIG. 3.29

The result of reducing the width of the Price column in the Detail table.

Table 3.3. Paradox ColumnSize Keys

Key	Effect
←	Decrease the column width
→	Increase the column width
Home	Move to minimum width
End	Move to maximum width
Enter	Accept the new column size
Esc	Abort and return to previous column size

Selecting Display Format

The concept of display *format* is a familiar one to seasoned spreadsheet users but may not be to others. Alphanumeric values always are displayed just as you entered them in the table, but Paradox enables you to choose between several display formats for number fields (N and $) and date fields. The data stored in your table never is affected when you change the on-screen format.

To change the format of a field in the active window, access the Image menu (in table or form view) and select **F**ormat. Move the cursor to the column you want to format and press Enter.

The available formats for number fields (N and $) include the following:

Format	Description
General	Displays numbers with as many decimal places as necessary to represent the number, up to a maximum set number of places. The default format for number fields is general format with two decimal places.
Fixed	Displays numbers with a set number of decimal places.
Comma	Separates whole numbers into three-digit groups with commas and a set number of decimal places. This format is the default for currency ($) fields.
Scientific	Displays numbers in scientific notation.

Figure 3.30 shows examples of the four number formats. The same number was entered in all fields of each row to display the effects of the various formats. The column labeled General 2 dec. shows a

number field in general format with two decimal places. The number 1234.567 has been *rounded* to 1234.57 when displayed. The Fixed 3 dec. column is formatted as fixed with three decimal places. The column labeled Comma is formatted in comma format with two decimal places, and the last column, Scientific, illustrates scientific format.

The available formats for dates are as follows:

MM/DD/YY	The default date format
DD-Mon-YY	Sometimes referred to as military format
DD.MM.YY	Often called European format
YY.MM.DD	Reverse European format

Samples of dates in these three formats are shown in figure 3.31.

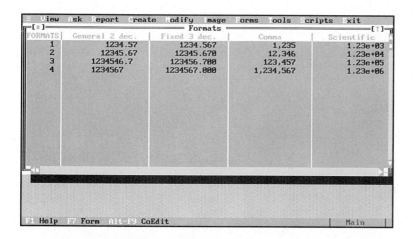

```
 View  sk  eport  reate  odify  mage  orms  ools  cripts  xit
[ ]                        Formats                        [↑]
FORMATS   General 2 dec.  Fixed 3 dec.      Comma      Scientific
   1          1234.57       1234.567          1,235     1.23e+03
   2         12345.67      12345.670         12,346     1.23e+04
   3        1234546.7     123456.700        123,457     1.23e+05
   4        1234567      1234567.000      1,234,567     1.23e+06




F1 Help  F7 Form  Alt-F9 CoEdit                    Main
```

FIG. 3.30

Number format options.

```
 View  sk  eport  reate  odify  mage  orms  ools  cripts  xit
        [ ]                   Formats              [↑]
         MM/DD/YY    DD-Mon-YY    DD.MM.YY    YY.MM.DD
         12/19/89    19-Dec-89    19.12.89    89.12.19
          1/19/90    19-Jan-90    19.01.90    90.01.19
          1/19/1890  19-Jan-1890  19.01.1890  1890.01.19




F1 Help  F7 Form  Alt-F9 CoEdit                    Main
```

FIG. 3.31

Date format options.

Using the Zoom Options

The **Z**oom option on the Image menu provides three shortcut methods for moving around in a large table in table or form view. The Ctrl-Z (Zoom) feature described earlier in this chapter, in the section "Finding a Record with Zoom and Zoom Next," is equivalent to zooming to a value with the menu options.

Zooming to a Field

Using this shortcut, you can move quickly to a particular field in a table. First display the Image menu, and then select **Z**oom, **F**ield. Paradox displays a dialog box with a list of available fields (see fig. 3.32). Use the mouse or the cursor-movement keys to select the field to which you want to go. Paradox jumps the cursor to that field but remains in the same record.

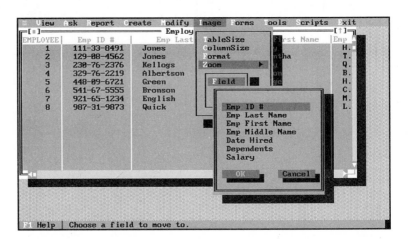

Zooming to a Record

Sometimes you know the record number of a particular row and want to go directly to that record. Access the Image menu and select **Z**oom, **R**ecord. Enter the target record number and press Enter. Paradox jumps the cursor to that record without changing the current field.

Zooming to a Value

Of the **Z**oom options, **Z**oom **V**alue is the most useful. You can use this option to search quickly the entire table for a given field value. You also can use wild-card characters. This feature gives precisely the same result as the Zoom keystroke command, Ctrl-Z.

Display the Image menu and select **Z**oom, **V**alue. Move the cursor to the field you want Paradox to search, preferably a key field, and press Enter. Paradox shows a prompt at the top of the screen, instructing you to Enter the value or pattern to search for. Type the value that Paradox should try to match, and then press Enter. Paradox starts at the top of the table and searches the specified field until finding the first match. The program then moves the cursor to the record that contains the match. If Paradox doesn't find a match, the cursor doesn't leave the record in which you started.

Cue:
The Zoom Value command (Ctrl-Z) is most effective in a key field.

Sometimes you may be searching a field that is not unique, and Paradox may not find the correct record on the first try. The next time you use the **Z**oom, **V**alue option, you don't have to retype the value. You can press Alt-Z (Zoom Next) to repeat the search.

Whether you use the menu method or the Ctrl-Z keystroke command, you don't have to specify exactly how the target value is typed. You can use the following wild-card operators when building a search pattern:

- You can use two dots together (..) to represent any number of characters, including no characters and blank spaces. The following pattern, for example, tells Paradox to search for all words or phrases that begin with *Jo* and are of any length:

  Jo..

- The operator @ takes the place of any single character. The following pattern tells Paradox to search for all values that begin with M and are two characters in length.

  M@

You can combine these wild-card operators in the same search pattern.

Zoom searches are a terrific way to find a record for viewing or editing. Keep in mind that when searching for exact alphanumeric values, Paradox is particular about whether data and search patterns are in the same case. The patterns *Jones* and *JONES* are not equivalent. Zoom searches using each of these patterns find different results.

T I P

When you use a wild card anywhere in the pattern, however, Paradox is no longer so picky. The patterns *jones..*, *JONES..*, and *Jones..* all locate a record with the name *Jones* in the target field. When in doubt, add two dots to the end of your search pattern.

Reordering the Table with OrderTable

By default, Paradox arranges table records in key-field order. You may want to view a table with records arranged in a different order. The **O**rderTable option on the Image menu and the Alt-S (Sort) command enable you to sort the active table on-screen.

T I P   You can perform the commands described in this section only if you have already assigned a key field—also known as the *primary index*—in the current table's structure. Refer to Chapter 2, "Creating Database Tables" for a complete discussion of how and why to assign a key field.

When you want to view records in order by the values in a nonkey field, first position the cursor in the field, and then do one of the following:

- Press Alt-S (Sort).

- Display the Image menu and select **O**rderTable. Position the blinking cursor in the column you want to order and press Enter.

Paradox displays the Indexes dialog box with the current field's name displayed in a text box. Press Enter. The first time you execute this procedure for a particular field in the table, Paradox displays a menu listing the options **C**ancel and **O**K. Select **O**K to cause Paradox to build a secondary index for the current field. A *secondary index* is a file that enables Paradox to quickly sort and search a field that is not the key field (Paradox maintains a *primary index* file for the key field).

After Paradox builds the secondary index file, the program displays the current table in order by the values in the current field.

You learned earlier in this chapter that Paradox performs a **Z**oom, **V**alue (or Ctrl-Z) operation faster if the zoom field is the table's key field—its primary index. If you create a secondary index for a nonkey field, Paradox will use the index whenever you perform a Zoom in the field.

Paradox 4.0 also provides several other ways to create secondary indexes for a table for the purpose of increasing the speed of zooms and data retrieval (data retrieval is introduced in Chapter 4, "Getting Started with Query By Example"). The **M**odify, **I**ndex command provides the most flexibility in creating a secondary index. **M**odify, **I**ndex is covered in Chapter 9. The **T**ools, **Q**uerySpeed command can create a secondary index specifically for the purpose of increasing the speed of a query (data retrieval). **T**ools, **Q**uerySpeed is discussed in Chapter 13, "Using Paradox Tools."

Moving Columns in Table View

One of the basic rules of a relational database is that the order of the fields in the table doesn't matter. You can rearrange field order without affecting the underlying data. This rule is true of Paradox tables. (Note: The order in which fields are listed in table structure is significant if you have defined key fields, but the order of the fields in on-screen windows is not significant.)

Reminder:
The order of fields (columns) doesn't matter.

Paradox provides three ways to move columns on-screen to suit your preferences: by using the mouse, through the Image menu, and by using the Ctrl-R (Rotate) keystroke command.

Repositioning Columns with the Mouse or Move Command

Paradox normally displays columns in the same order that they are listed in the table structure. Figure 3.33, for example, shows the Employee table in the table definition order.

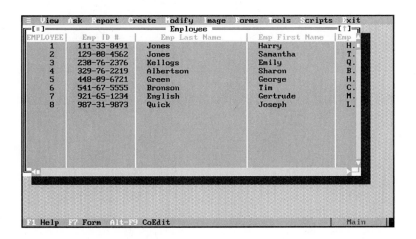

FIG. 3.33

The Employee table in table definition order.

Suppose that you want to see the Salary field listed to the right of the Emp Last Name field. To accomplish this, access the table view Image menu and select **M**ove. Just as with the **Z**oom, **F**ield command, Paradox displays a list of available fields. Select the field you want to move (see fig. 3.34).

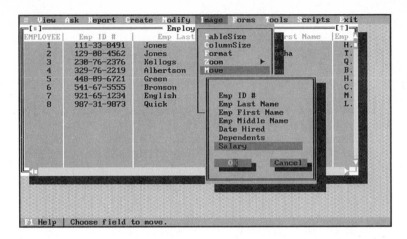

FIG. 3.34

Selecting the Salary field to be moved.

Paradox then instructs you to move the cursor to the new position and press Enter. In this example, place the cursor in the Emp First Name field (the new position for Salary) and press Enter. The result is shown in figure 3.35. Salary is now just to the right of Emp Last Name, and all other fields are pushed one column to the right.

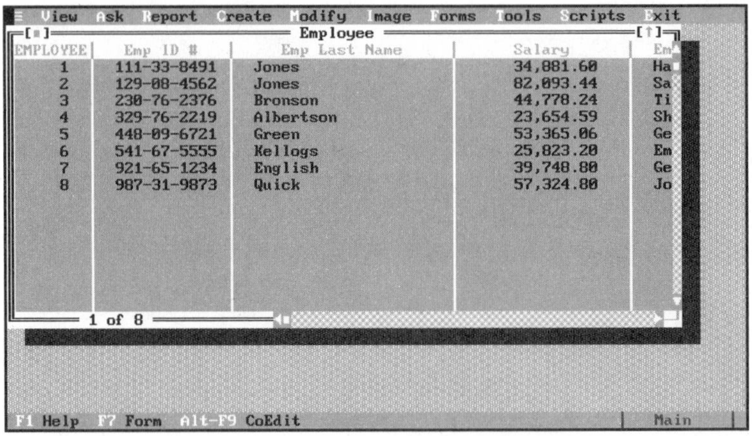

FIG. 3.35

The relocated Salary field.

Repositioning Columns with the Rotate Command

An alternative to the **M**ove option on the Image menu is the Rotate command (see table 1.2 in Chapter 1). This command takes a little practice, but after you get the hang of using the Rotate command, you will find the command tremendously helpful.

To accomplish the same result shown in figure 3.35 with the Rotate command, place the cursor anywhere in the Emp First Name field of the original Employee table, as shown in figure 3.33, and press Ctrl-R (Rotate). The effect of this command is to move the column at the cursor to the far right end of the table. Figure 3.36 shows the result of using this first Rotate command. Emp First Name is gone (moved to the end of the Employee image) and Emp Middle Name has taken its place. To move Salary to the appropriate position, you have to use Ctrl-R repeatedly until Salary comes into view (three more times, in this case).

Cue:

Ctrl-R (Rotate) is the quickest way to rearrange columns.

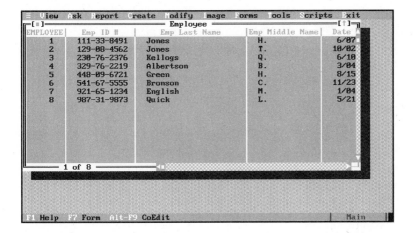

FIG. 3.36

The result of using Rotate.

Using the PickForm Option

The third option on the Image menu in the field and form views is **P**ickForm. This option is used to select a custom-designed form for the table in the active window. Chapter 8 is devoted entirely to the form-design process. Refer to that discussion for detailed information on the **P**ickForm menu command.

Saving Image Settings

The choices on the Image menu are relatively easy to use, and you may want to use them to customize a table or form view on the fly. As you begin to use Paradox in your daily routine, you do not want to worry continually about sizing, moving, or formatting columns every time you use a table. Fortunately, Paradox provides the **K**eepSet option to save image settings.

Cue:
To record image settings, use the Image KeepSet command.

When you finish selecting your image settings, you can record them for future use by selecting **K**eepSet from the Image menu. Paradox records the settings in a file that becomes a member of the table's family. The program displays a message at the bottom of the screen that reads Settings recorded....

This option does not appear on the Image menu in DataEntry mode because you always are working in a temporary table. Saving image settings for a temporary table does not make sense.

FROM HERE...

For Related Information:

▶▶ "Examining the Standard Form," p. 296.

▶▶ "Adding and Using Validity Checks," p. 324.

Using the Paradox Editor

One of the weak links in earlier versions of Paradox was the program's lack of a full-featured editor. Paradox 4.0, however, has added a very capable editor. The sections that remain in this chapter describe how to use the Paradox Editor.

Opening an Editor Window

You can start the Paradox Editor in three ways. The method you use is determined by your purpose in using the Editor:

■ *Memo fields.* When you want to enter or edit data in a memo field (discussed in earlier sections of this chapter), double-click the mouse in the memo field, or move the cursor into the memo field and press Alt-F5 or Ctrl-F (Field View).

■ *ASCII files.* To create or edit an ASCII text file from within Paradox, press Alt-E (Editor) or display the system menu and choose **E**ditor. Paradox displays a pop-up menu listing the options **N**ew and **O**pen. Select **N**ew and type a new file name to open a new file, or choose **O**pen and specify a file name to open an existing file.

■ *Scripts.* To create or edit a script, choose **S**cripts, Editor, New from the Main menu to create a new file or choose **S**cript, Editor, **O**pen to open an existing file. Specify the name of the script in the text box labeled Script. Refer to Chapter 6 for a first look at creating and using Paradox scripts.

Suppose that you restructure the Customer table and add a memo field named Notes. After you define the memo field, you enter data into the field using the Paradox Editor. While editing the table in DataEntry, Edit, or CoEdit mode, move the cursor to the field and double-click the mouse on the field, or press Alt-F5 or Ctrl-F (Field View). Paradox opens an Editor window with the label Customer—>Notes in the title bar, as shown in figure 3.37 (in DataEntry mode the window label would be Entry—>Notes).

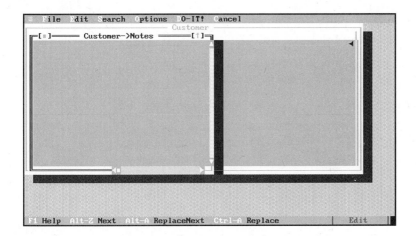

FIG. 3.37

The Editor window.

Adding Text

When you have an Editor window displayed as the current window, you are ready to type text into the field. Type the text as you would on a typewriter or on a typical word processing program. You can type any of the characters on your computer's keyboard, including letters, numbers, and special characters. You can display any ASCII (American Standard Code for Information Interchange) character by holding the Alt key and pressing the corresponding PAL keycode (listed in Appendix C). This procedure enables you to use, for example, the ASCII box-drawing characters to create organizational charts.

When you are typing text, you can use the Tab key. Every time you press Tab, the Editor moves the cursor eight spaces to the right.

Understanding Word Wrap

Do not worry about typing past the right margin in an Editor window. The Editor moves words that break at the right margin to the next line. When you want text formatted in paragraphs, press Enter at the end of every paragraph rather than at the end of every line.

The Editor formats any text to fit within the current window border. The Editor window in figure 3.38, for example, is narrower than the window in figure 3.39, but both display the same text. You may have to scroll vertically to read the entire document, but using the word-wrap feature—even in a narrow window—means that you do not have to scroll horizontally.

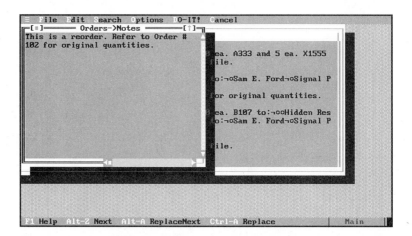

FIG. 3.38

Text displayed in a small Editor window.

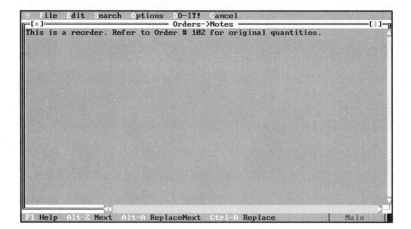

FIG. 3.39

Text displayed in a full-screen Editor window.

To create or edit a document that is wider than the Editor window, turn off the word-wrap feature. For example, if you view a report that you have printed to a file (see the "Controlling Output" section of Chapter 5 for an explanation of how to send a report to a file), the report may look scrambled (see fig. 3.40).

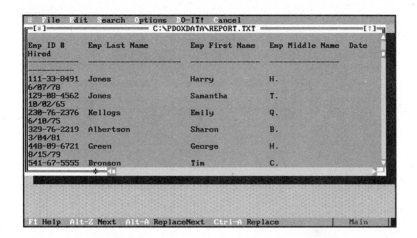

FIG. 3.40

Viewing a report
printed to a file,
REPORT.TXT.

To turn off word wrap, select **O**ptions to display the Options pull-down
menu and select **W**ordWrap, **C**lear. Compare figure 3.41 to figure 3.40.
With word wrap turned off, you can view all the necessary columns for
the report, even though not all the columns fit on-screen. The Editor
does not wrap words back to the left side of the window border. You
can reactivate word wrap by selecting **O**ptions, **W**ordWrap, **S**et.

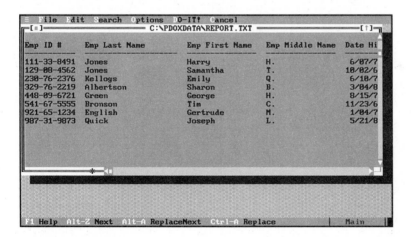

FIG. 3.41

Viewing
REPORT.TXT with
word wrap off.

Using Autoindent

By default, when you are typing in an Editor window and press Enter,
the Editor places the cursor at the left margin of the Editor window.
When you expect to type several indented lines, one after the other,
turn on the autoindent feature. Select **O**ptions, **A**utoIndent, **S**et. When

autoindent is activated, pressing Enter causes the Editor to place the cursor below the first character in the line above.

If you decide you want to deactivate autoindent, select **O**ptions, **A**utoIndent, **C**lear.

Moving Around the Editor Window

When you want to make a change in the Editor window, you first must move the cursor to where the text needs to be edited. The Editor provides several ways to move the cursor around the screen. Table 3.4 lists the complete set of cursor-movement keys available in the Editor.

Table 3.4. Paradox Editor Cursor-Movement Keys

Key	Cursor movement
↓	Down one line
↑	Up one line
→	One character to the right
←	One character to the left
Backspace	Erases character to the left
Ctrl-→	First space the right of the following word
Ctrl-←	First character of the preceding word
Home	Left end of the line containing the cursor.
End	Space to the right of the last word in the line containing the cursor
PgDn	Down one window screen
PgUp	Up one window screen
Ctrl-PgDn	To the beginning of the file
Ctrl-PgUp	To the end of the file
Enter	Down one line below the first character on the left, while moving all subsequent text down one line

You also can use the mouse to move the cursor around the window. Use the left or right button on the mouse to click on the position in which you want the cursor.

Using the mouse and scroll bars is another way to move the cursor quickly around the file. To scroll up or down, use the vertical scroll bar displayed on the right side of each Editor window. When you have toggled off word wrap to create a file wider than one window width, you can scroll the screen left and right by using the horizontal scroll bar displayed at the bottom of the Editor window.

The Editor also provides a menu command to move the cursor directly to a specific line. Select **E**dit and then select **G**oto from the Edit menu. The Editor displays a dialog box containing a text box labeled `Line:`. To jump to a particular line, type the number of this line and select the OK button. The Editor moves the cursor to the target line in the file. You can select the Cancel command button instead to abort the command without moving the cursor.

Cue:
Use the **E**dit, **G**oto command to jump to a particular line in the file.

If you want to know the current location, in terms of column number and row number, select **E**dit, **L**ocation from the Editor menu bar. The Editor displays the current column and row number near the lower left corner of the window border. For example, `10:42` means that the cursor is in the 10th row of the file and the 42nd character (including spaces) from the left end of the line.

Inserting and Deleting Text

When the cursor is located where you want to make a change, you need to be able to insert and/or delete text as necessary. This section describes how to insert and delete characters and entire documents.

The first time you load an Editor window, the Editor is in Insert mode (indicated by the shape of the cursor—an underscore). As you type, the Editor displays the character at the cursor's position and pushes existing characters one space to the right.

If you want to replace the text already on-screen, you can type over existing characters in Overtype mode. To switch from Insert mode to Overtype mode, press the Ins key. The Editor changes the shape of the cursor to a large block.

When you type a character in Overtype mode, the Editor displays the character at the cursor's position, replacing any character already displayed at that position. Pressing Ins again returns to Insert mode.

To delete a character, position the cursor on the character that you want to delete and press Del. Each time you press Del, the Editor deletes one character. The word-wrap feature adjusts the line length.

Using the Clipboard

You may need to use cut-and-paste capabilities when working in an Editor window. To delete more than just a few characters and less than the entire file from the window or to move or copy a portion of the text, you use the Editor's Clipboard, accessed from the main menu.

The Clipboard enables you to delete, copy, and move text as a block within an Editor window and between windows.

The Clipboard is a separate Editor window used in conjunction with another Editor window. The Clipboard acts as a staging area or buffer. For example, when you cut a block of text from an Editor window, the Editor temporarily moves the deleted block to the Clipboard. If you cut a block of text by accident, therefore, you can retrieve the text from the Clipboard. The Clipboard also acts as a buffer for copying and moving text within the Editor and copying text between DOS applications. The Editor enables you to edit the text in the Clipboard. Cutting or copying text to the Clipboard replaces previous Clipboard contents.

Selecting a Text Block

The first step toward cutting, copying, or moving a text block is to highlight or select the block. The Editor provides a number of ways to select a text block. Use one of the following procedures:

■ Position the mouse pointer at one end of the text block. Hold down the left or right mouse button and move the mouse pointer to the other end of the text block. Release the mouse button. Scroll the screen by moving the mouse pointer into the top or bottom window border while continuing to press the left mouse button.

■ Position the cursor at one end of the text block. Hold down the Shift key and use the cursor-movement keys (listed in table 3.4) to position the cursor at the other end of the block. Shift-PgUp selects all text from the cursor to the beginning of the file. Shift-PgDn selects all text from the cursor to the end of the file.

All these methods highlight the characters and blank spaces from the point where you began the selecting to the point where you ended the selecting and from the left to the right side of the file. While the text is selected, you can easily turn off the highlighting by clicking either mouse button or by pressing a cursor-movement key.

> While text is selected, you can quickly erase the selected text by pressing any key other than a cursor-movement key. If you accidentally delete text in this manner, refer to the next section for instructions on how to use the Paste option to recover the deleted text.

T I P

Moving, Copying and Erasing Text

When you want to move selected text, you must cut or remove the block from the original location and place the text in the Clipboard. If you want to place a copy of the selected block in another location in the current file, or in another Editor window, without removing the selected text from the original location, you copy the block to the Clipboard instead of cutting the text.

To cut a selected block to the Clipboard, press Shift-Del or select **E**dit and then choose X**C**ut. The Editor removes the selected text from the Window on-screen and places the text into the Clipboard. Table 3.5 lists Clipboard keystroke commands.

Cue:
To move selected text, cut the block from the original location and place it in the Clipboard.

Table 3.5. Clipboard Keystroke Commands

Key	Function
Shift-arrow key	Selects a block of text in the direction of the arrow key
Del	Erases selected text and does not place erased text in the Clipboard
Shift-Del	Cuts the selected block to the Clipboard
Shift-Ins	Inserts the contents of the Clipboard at the cursor's location
Ctrl-Ins	Copies selected text to the Clipboard

If you want to copy selected text to the Clipboard, press Ctrl-Ins or select **E**dit and choose **C**opy. The Editor places a copy of the selected text into the Clipboard but does not remove the original text.

To erase selected text, without causing the Editor to place the erased text into the Clipboard, either press Del or select **E**dit, **E**rase from the menu bar.

Editing Text in the Clipboard

One of the most convenient features of the Paradox Editor's cut-and-paste facility is that the Editor enables you to edit the contents of the Clipboard. While working in the Clipboard, you can perform the following operations: print the contents of the Clipboard, mark and delete a text block, delete all text, insert an entire file, move the cursor to a specific line in the file, find specified text, and find and replace text.

Before you can edit the Clipboard, you have to open the Clipboard window. Select **E**dit from the Editor main menu and then select **S**howClipboard. The Editor displays the Clipboard window and any text that you have copied or cut to the Clipboard.

While the Clipboard window is the current window, you can move, resize, and zoom it like any other Editor window. You can make any necessary modifications to the text, using the available editing features.

Pasting Text from the Clipboard

After you have cut or copied the subject text to the Clipboard and made any desired additions, deletions, or modifications, you are ready to place or paste the Clipboard's contents into the target destination.

When you want to paste text into an Editor window, move the cursor to the target text destination. The intended destination can be within the same Editor window as the text originated or within a different window. When the cursor is located properly, press Shift-Ins or select **E**dit, **P**aste. The Editor copies the contents of the Clipboard into the target Editor window, beginning at the cursor's position.

NOTE Each time you copy or cut text, the Editor places the text into the Clipboard. The Editor also selects (highlights) the text that it places in the Clipboard window. The Editor abandons any highlighted text that was already in the Clipboard window, replacing it with the newly copied or cut text. When you use the Paste command on the Edit menu, the Editor pastes into the target window all highlighted text from the Clipboard.

If you turn off the highlighting in the Clipboard, however, the program behaves differently. When the Clipboard's content is not highlighted, text you copy or cut from an Editor window is inserted at the cursor in the Clipboard, rather than replacing existing text. Similarly, the Paste command does not copy unhighlighted text from the Clipboard.

Inserting and Writing ASCII Files

One of the great conveniences of a word processor is the ease with which you can incorporate previously finished work into a new file. The Editor enables you to insert entire files into an Editor window.

To insert the entire contents of a file, place the cursor where you want the inserted text to begin. Select **F**ile and choose **I**nsertFile. Type a file name in the File text box or press Enter and select a file from the list of files. The Editor inserts the entire contents of the disk file into the Editor window, beginning at the cursor.

Cue:
To insert a file, place the cursor where you want the inserted text to begin and select **F**ile, **I**nsertFile.

Paradox also enables you to save a portion of the contents of an Editor window under a different file name. Highlight the text you want to save and choose **F**ile, **W**riteblock. Specify the name of the file to which you want the Editor to copy the selected text. Press Enter or select the OK button.

If you specify a file that already exists, the Editor warns you and displays a menu containing the options Cancel and Replace. Choose Replace to cause the Editor to replace the existing file's contents with the selected text. Select Cancel if you don't want to replace the existing file.

Searching the Editor Window

As you work in an Editor window, you may need to find the occurrence of a particular word or phrase. In a long memo field entry, for example, you may want to find the section that discusses Deluxe Widgets. At other times you may want to replace a word or phrase in the file displayed in an Editor window with another word or phrase. If you discover that Ms. Smith's name is actually Ms. Smythe, for example, you can search for and replace all occurrences of Smith. The Editor's Search feature enables you to easily perform both of these tasks—search and replace.

Finding

When you want to find a certain string of characters in a file displayed in an Editor window, select **S**earch and choose **F**ind from the Search menu.

In the Value text box, type the character string for which you want the Editor to search. Press Enter or select the OK button to execute the search.

The Editor begins at the position of the cursor and searches toward the end of the file. If the Editor finds a match, the program highlights the matching string and places the cursor at the first character to the right of the matching string.

To find the next occurrence of the search string, press Alt-Z and click on the word Next in the status line, or choose Search, Next from the menu bar. When the Editor reaches the end of the file without finding another occurrence of the search string, the program displays the message Search value not found.

T I P By default, the Editor's search is not case sensitive. If you want the Editor to look for a character string that matches the case exactly (upper- or lowercase), select Options, CaseSensitive, Set from the Editor's main menu before you start the search operation. To return to the default setting, select Options, CaseSensitive, Clear.

Finding and Replacing

In addition to finding a particular character string in an Editor window file, the Editor enables you to easily find and then replace a search string with another character string. To activate this feature, select Search, Replace. The Editor displays the Find dialog box.

Type the search string in the Value text box and press Enter or select the OK button. The Editor displays another dialog box. Type the character string you want to replace the search string in the Replacement text box and either press Enter or select OK.

The Editor begins at the position of the cursor and searches toward the end of the file. If the Editor finds a match, the program highlights the matching string and places the cursor at the first character to the right of the matching string.

Press Ctrl-A to perform the replacement. Press Alt-Z to skip to the next occurrence of the search string without performing a replacement. Press Alt-A to skip to the next occurrence and immediately perform the replacement. Click the mouse or press a cursor-movement key to abort the search-and-replace operation.

If you want to replace all occurrences of a text string in one step, use the ChangeToEnd option on the Search menu, instead of the Replace command.

Printing from the Editor Window

To print the contents of an Editor window, select **F**ile, **P**rint from the main menu. Paradox sends the contents of the Editor window to the printer connected to your computer's first printer port (LPT1).

Saving Your Work

To save your work and continue editing the current Editor window, select **F**ile to display the File menu and choose **S**ave. The Editor saves the contents of the current window to the file whose name is listed in the window's title bar. You can continue to work in the Editor window.

If you want to both save changes and exit the Editor in one step, press F2 (Do-It!) or select DO-IT! from the Editor's main menu. The Editor saves to disk any changes you have made to the Editor file since the file was last saved.

Closing an Editor Window

As described in the preceding section, press F2 (Do-It!) to save changes to the current Editor file and to exit the Editor.

If you want to exit from the Editor without saving changes, click on the close box. The Editor informs you and asks for confirmation if you are about to abandon changes that have not yet been saved.

For Related Information:

▶▶ "Editing Scripts," p. 229.

▶▶ "Editing a Script," p. 521.

▶▶ "Using the Script Editor," p. 593.

FROM HERE...

Chapter Summary

This chapter introduced you to the fundamentals of entering, editing, and viewing your database. Armed with these techniques and commands, you are ready to start pouring information into your computer.

Placing data into your database and keeping the data current is only half the story. The best part is still to come. In Chapter 4, you begin learning how to use Paradox's unique Query By Example (QBE) method. This simple method of asking questions gives you complete control over even the most complex Paradox database.

Getting Started with Query By Example

T he first three chapters of this book introduce you to many terms that may be new to you. You learn about tables, fields, records, objects, views, and so on. These early chapters enable you to become familiar with the "look" of Paradox and the basics of moving around the program and screen.

This chapter introduces you to the heart of Paradox, known as *Query By Example* (QBE). QBE is the Paradox method of retrieving information from your database. If you have never used a database program before Paradox, you immediately will take a liking to its check mark and example methodology. If you are an experienced database user, you may have a little more trouble getting used to this unique procedure but will be amazed at how easily you can retrieve the information you need.

Chapters 1, 2, and 3 show you how to put information into the computer. In this chapter, you learn how to build Paradox queries so that you can retrieve precisely the data you want. As you read, place your fingers on the keyboard and mouse and try out what you learn. Play around with the tricks and techniques presented, and you probably will discover a few of your own.

Understanding Query By Example

Before you get into the step-by-step details of building Paradox queries, you may be wondering what a query is and why you would want to use Query By Example.

Defining a Query

Reminder:

A query is a specific request for information.

When your boss calls you on the phone and tells you she has to have your department's monthly sales figures for the last six months on her desk by 10:00 a.m., she is making a *query*. Your boss has made a specific request for information.

To do your job properly, your response or *answer* has to be as specific as the request. You have the information your boss wants to see, but you shouldn't produce every number you possibly can—just the sales figures. You also shouldn't give her every sales figure—just the figures for the last six months.

The same information retrieval principles apply when you are working with a computer database, but this time, you are the boss. When you want to see certain information on-screen, you have to request the data specifically; you have to build a query. The computer then responds by displaying its answer. You have to learn how to query any computer database system before the system can become useful to you.

Why Use Query By Example?

Database programs have always provided methods for retrieving data from storage. Learning how to understand fully and use those methods traditionally has been a task for programmers and power users. In the past, asking a question of a database often required knowledge of a cryptic computer database language with rigid syntax and dozens of commands. If you are a programmer or you regularly use terms such as *byte* or *nanosecond*, these database systems may have given you no problem. For most of us, however, a new approach was needed that would enable us to ask complex queries of any database without resorting to programming. Query By Example attempts to fill that need. M. M. Zloof and others at IBM's Research Laboratory in Yorktown Heights, New York, developed the idea. The designers of Paradox, Richard Schwartz and Robert Shostak, made QBE the hub of this powerful program.

Query By Example, in a nutshell, is a two-step process:

1. You request specific data from a database by constructing a *query statement* made up of one or more *query forms*.

2. Paradox responds to your query by producing the requested data in the form of a temporary table named Answer.

The entire QBE drama unfolds in query forms and answer tables. This chapter shows you how to build queries and retrieve information without writing one line of program code.

Displaying a Query Form

To display a query form, select **Ask** from the Main Paradox menu. Specify the name of the Paradox table that contains the information you need. Paradox displays an empty table on-screen in Main mode that looks identical in structure to the table you are querying (see fig. 4.1).

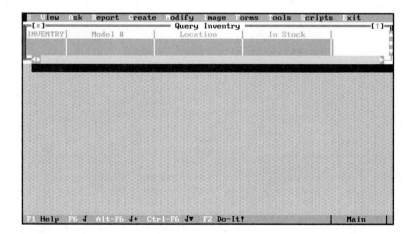

FIG. 4.1

The query form.

Think of this image as an order form used to bring up records from your Paradox table. (The image is not a table and is not stored to disk.) Check off the fields you want to see and provide enough criteria for Paradox to find specific records. Figure 4.2, for example, asks Paradox to look in the Inventry (inventory) table to determine how many of model number B107 are in stock. The details of building such a query form are presented in the next several sections.

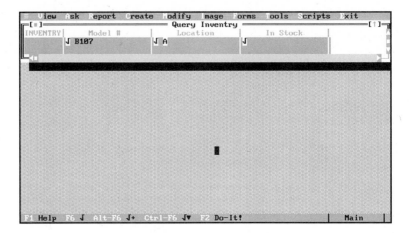

FIG. 4.2

Querying the Inventry table.

NOTE You can use the **QuerySave** command on the Scripts menu to save a query to disk, but a query is not stored automatically to disk.

Reminder:

Rearranging the column order of a query form usually has no effect on column order in the Answer table.

You enter and edit information in a query form while in Main mode in almost the same manner you enter and edit data in a normal table in Edit mode, including the use of field view (Alt-F5 or Ctrl-F). Because a query form is not a table, certain editing options are not supported, including Undo, form view, and most image-manipulation commands. You can rearrange the columns using the **M**ove command from the Image menu or the Ctrl-R (Rotate) keystroke command. Changing the order of the columns in the query form, however, usually has no effect on column order in the Answer table. Columns in Answer are initially in table definition (structure) order. After Paradox produces the table, you can modify its image in all the ways described in Chapter 3.

CAUTION: Pressing F9 (Edit) or Alt-F9 (CoEdit) inadvertently in a query form places you in Edit mode, just as if the form were a table. At that point, pressing F2 (Do-It!) does *not* execute the query but ends the edit session. You then have to press F2 a second time to execute the query. Also, if you are in this mode, pressing F10 (Menu) gives you the Edit menu, not the Main menu. This situation can be confusing.

> **T I P**
>
> Paradox usually displays fields in the Answer table in the same order as in the table definition. In Paradox, you can change this display through the Custom Configuration Program (CCP). Set the query order to Image Order in the Interface Settings dialog box. Be aware, however, that this selection may lead to problems. You may, for example, perform two similar queries on a table, producing two Answer tables with exactly the same fields but in different field order. Paradox does not enable you to add these two tables with the Add command because the program considers them to no longer have compatible table structure. Refer to Appendix B for more details on the CCP and to Chapter 13, "Using Paradox Tools," for a discussion of the Add command.

Queries can consist of multiple query forms in the workspace. Together, all query forms in the workspace make up a query statement. This chapter discusses how to use single-form queries. Chapter 7, "Using Advanced Query By Example and Multiple Tables," explains the more powerful and more complicated multiform query statements.

> **CAUTION:** The fact that you can display more than one query form on-screen can be dangerous. Paradox tries to relate the query forms even if you want them separate. When you query, therefore, always clear the screen first by pressing Alt-F8 (Close All Windows).

For Related Information:

FROM HERE...

▶▶ "Building Multitable Queries," p. 262.

▶▶ "Adding and Subtracting Tables," p. 432.

▶▶ "Controlling the Interface Settings," p. 1001.

Displaying and Clearing the Answer Table

To tell Paradox to execute a query you have constructed, press F2 (Do-It!). Paradox displays the message Processing query... and then

presents the Answer table as a distinct image in the workspace (see
fig. 4.3).

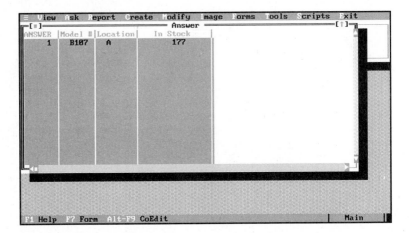

FIG. 4.3

The Answer
table.

The query form and the Answer table are each one window in the Paradox workspace. At any time, you can clear either one from the screen
by making that window active and pressing F8 (Close Active Window).
To clear both windows from the screen, press Alt-F8 (Close All
Windows).

FROM HERE...

For Related Information:

◄◄ "Understanding Temporary Tables," p. 93.

Selecting Fields in Query By Example

When you build a query in Paradox, you have to specify which fields
and which records from a table should be displayed. The basic tool
you use to select fields in Paradox is the *check mark*.

Using the Checkmark Key

The simplest way to include a field in the answer is to mark the field in the query form with F6, the Checkmark key. Move the cursor to each field you want included in the Answer table and press F6 (Checkmark). Paradox places a check mark (the square root symbol in the IBM extended character set) at the left side of the column. Press F2 (Do-It!), and Paradox produces a table that includes all the checked fields. Figure 4.4 shows a simple query form for the Employee table and the resulting Answer table. The fields Emp ID #, Emp Last Name, Emp First Name, and Emp Middle Name in the query form are checked, so they are included in Answer. The Date Hired field contains no check mark and does not appear in the Answer table.

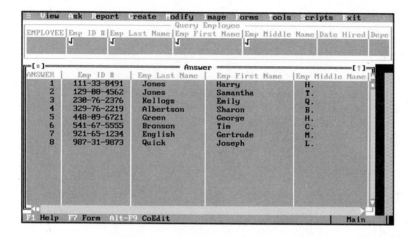

FIG. 4.4

Selecting fields with F6 (Checkmark).

F6 (Checkmark) is a toggle. Press this toggle a second time in a query form field to remove the check mark.

To include all fields of a table in a query, use the following shortcut: position the cursor in the first column of the query form, beneath the table name (the column that contains record numbers when the table is displayed), and press F6 (Checkmark). Paradox checks off all fields in the table. If any fields are already checked, they remain checked, and the rest of the fields are checked. A second press of F6 removes the check marks from all the fields.

Changing the Field Name

With Paradox, you can rename a field during a query so that the field name in the Answer table is different from the field name in the query form and underlying table. Type the word *as* followed by the new field name. For example, you can change the name of the Emp ID # column in the Answer table shown in figure 4.4 to Employee ID Number by typing *as Employee ID Number* in the Emp ID # column of the query form.

Displaying Duplicates

One of the rules of good relational database design is that you have no duplicate records. Paradox prevents you from entering duplicate records into any keyed table. For similar reasons, Paradox usually eliminates duplicate records (records identical to one or more preceding records in the table) from Answer tables.

In figure 4.4, records 1 and 2 are included because they are not exactly the same. Both employees have the same last name, but all the other field values are different. When only the Emp Last Name field is included, however, as in figure 4.5, Paradox automatically eliminates one of the Jones records.

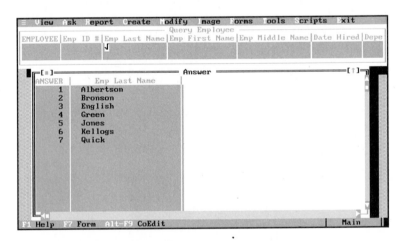

FIG. 4.5

Using F6 (Checkmark) to avoid listing duplicate records.

Paradox provides a way for you to include duplicates in the Answer table. Use Alt-F6 (CheckPlus) rather than F6 (Checkmark) in the first query form field (from left to right), and Paradox includes all records, whether or not they exactly duplicate other records in the table. The same query shown in figure 4.5 is redone in figure 4.6 with Alt-F6 (CheckPlus). Both Jones employees are included in the Answer table.

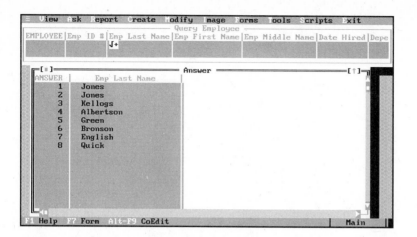

FIG. 4.6

Using Alt-F6 (CheckPlus) to return duplicate values.

For maximum speed, use Alt-F6 (CheckPlus) in the first field to be retrieved by the query. Because Paradox does not have to eliminate duplicates or sort the Answer table, the program displays the Answer table more quickly than usual.

T I P

Sorting the Answer Table in Ascending Order

Paradox stores table records in the order in which you enter the records unless you have defined one or more key fields. Keyed records are stored in order by the key values in each record. When you perform a query, however, Paradox sorts the Answer table in ascending order by the leftmost field (in the table's structure) also included in the query. Ties are broken by using the next field to the right in the table structure included in the query. Record sort order, therefore, is not affected by the order of the fields within the query.

Reminder:
Query field order usually does not affect record sort order.

The query form and Answer table in figure 4.7 show the same group of employees listed in figure 4.4, but this time the Emp ID # field is not included. The order of the columns (fields) in the Answer table is determined by the order of the fields in the table structure, not in the query form (unless the CCP is used to switch to QueryOrder). Even though Emp First Name is listed first in the Query form, this field is second in the Answer table. Because Emp Last Name is the first field of the included fields in the Employee structure, Paradox lists the records in the Answer table in order by Emp Last Name. Because two employees are named Jones, the Emp First Name column establishes which record Paradox lists first.

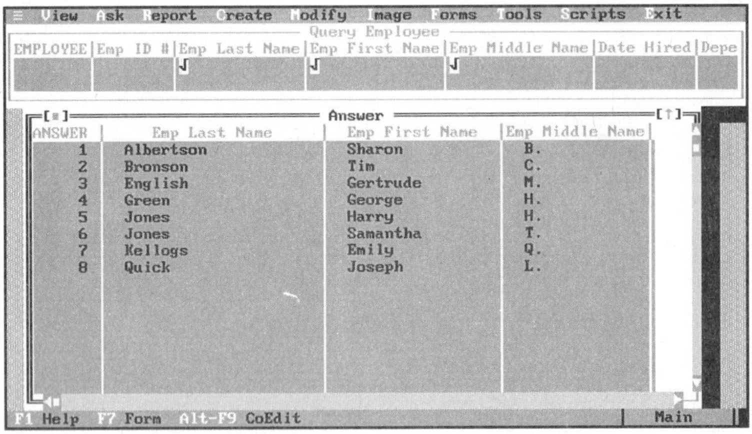

```
≡  View  Ask  Report  Create  Modify  Image  Forms  Tools  Scripts  Exit
                              ─ Query Employee ─
 EMPLOYEE│Emp ID #│Emp Last Name│Emp First Name│Emp Middle Name│Date Hired│Depe
         │        │      √      │      √       │      √        │          │

  ┌─[■]════════════════════════ Answer ═══════════════════[↑]─┐
  │ANSWER │   Emp Last Name   │  Emp First Name  │Emp Middle Name│
  │     1   Albertson          Sharon             B.
  │     2   Bronson            Tim                C.
  │     3   English            Gertrude           M.
  │     4   Green              George             H.
  │     5   Jones              Harry              H.
  │     6   Jones              Samantha           T.
  │     7   Kellogs            Emily              Q.
  │     8   Quick              Joseph             L.

 F1 Help  F7 Form  Alt-F9 CoEdit                              Main
```

FIG. 4.7

Using F6 (Checkmark) to sort in ascending order.

T I P

Rearranging the order of the fields in the query form normally does not affect the Answer table. This statement also is true for the sort order. If you use the Custom Configuration Program to change the QueryOrder setting to ImageOrder, however, moving fields around in the query form with Ctrl-R (Rotate) or the Move command affects the order in which records appear in the Answer table. When Paradox sorts in ImageOrder, the program sorts the Answer table first by the values in the leftmost column, regardless of the position of that field in the source table's structure. By default, Paradox sorts records by the values in the leftmost column in the first source table's structure also included in the query. If you find that you often are using the Sort command to rearrange data in the Answer table, consider using the CCP to make this change to the QueryOrder option.

Sorting the Answer Table in Descending Order

Cue:

Use Ctrl-F6 to sort the Answer table in descending order.

Paradox also provides a method for sorting the Answer table in reverse or *descending* order (as in Z to A, or 9 to 0). Rather than use F6 (Checkmark), use Ctrl-F6 (CheckDescending) to mark the fields.

Paradox places a downward-pointing triangle to the right of the normal check mark symbol to indicate that the records will be sorted in descending order. Paradox still sorts the fields on the left first, however.

Figure 4.8 shows the Emp First Name field in descending order. When the Emp Last Name field is added in figure 4.9 with a normal check mark, the records are ordered first by the Emp Last Name field, and then the ties are broken in descending order by the Emp First Name field. Samantha Jones comes before Harry Jones, but only after following Albertson, Bronson, English, and Green.

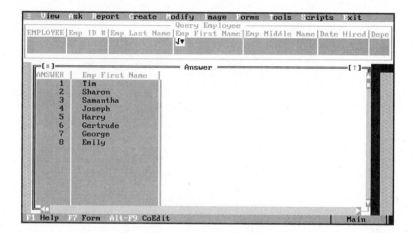

FIG. 4.8

Using Ctrl-F6 (CheckDescending) to sort in descending order.

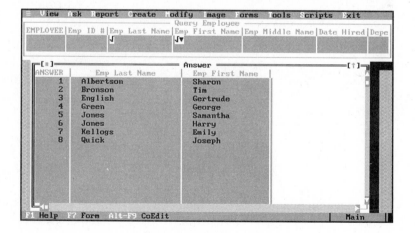

FIG. 4.9

Sorting the second field in descending order.

FROM HERE...

For Related Information:

◄◄ "Reordering the Table with OrderTable," p. 138.

►► "Sorting Tables," p. 346.

Selecting Records in Query By Example

So far, this chapter has shown you how to select the fields that you want Paradox to include in the Answer table. You can use F6 (Checkmark), Alt-F6 (CheckPlus), and Ctrl-F6 (CheckDescending) to select fields in a query. When you press F2 (Do-It!), Paradox displays the field(s) you indicate for every record in the table. This section of the chapter explains how to select particular records for Paradox to include in the Answer table. You learn how to search for records that exactly match examples you give, that match a general pattern you provide, or that fall within a range of values you define.

Finding an Exact Match

Reminder:
The value you can use to retrieve a record is the record's identifying value.

In its simplest form, selecting records in Query By Example involves your filling in values in one or more of the query form fields and Paradox looking for exact matches in the table. When you fill in the field values, you are providing the *example* part of Query By Example. When you tell Paradox to do it (with F2), the program takes your example and performs the query, trying to find records that match the example exactly. In a properly designed database, you can use this simple method to find any record, because every record in every table is unique and can be identified precisely by the value in its key field(s). In this book, the value you can use to retrieve a record is referred to as the record's *identifying value.*

Cue:
Place the identifying value in the single-key field to find a specific record.

To find one of the employees in the Employee table, for example, you can provide the employee's identifying value—the Emp ID #. This field is the single-key field for Employee and is a unique identifier for each record. Start with the empty query form and type the employee's ID number in the appropriate field, as shown in the query form in figure 4.10. Select the fields you want to see by pressing F6 (Checkmark) and then press F2 (Do-It!).

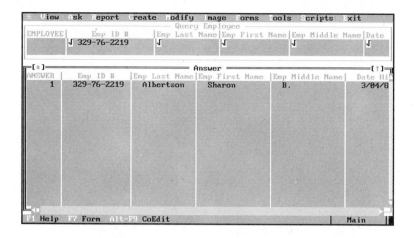

FIG. 4.10

Finding an exact match.

When a table has a multifield key, you have to provide an example in each of the key fields to retrieve just one record successfully. Suppose that you have a Detail table in which each record is identified by combining the Order # field with the Item # field. Together, these fields constitute a unique identifier and have been defined as a multifield key. The query in figure 4.11 indicates that you want to see the second item of order number 103.

Reminder:
When a table has a multifield key, provide an example in each of the key fields.

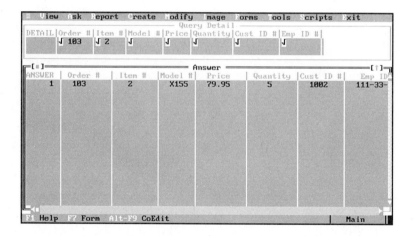

FIG. 4.11

Using multiple fields to find a match.

You often need to see more than just one record at a time, so you also can use Query By Example to retrieve multiple records that match a given set of identifying values or criteria. Suppose that you want to see a list of all order numbers credited to the employee listed in figure 4.10. To ask Paradox to produce that information, you type the employee's

ID number in the Emp ID # field of the Orders table. Even though that field uniquely identifies the employee, each employee can handle more than one order, so the answer to this query includes more than one record (see fig. 4.12).

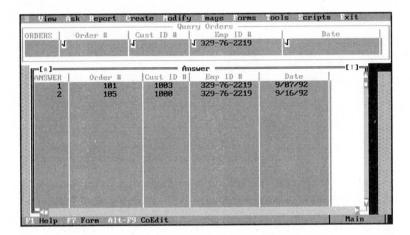

FIG. 4.12

Matching multiple records.

Guidelines for Matching Values

You should keep several rules in mind when building queries that look for exact matches:

- Use precise spelling. (See also the discussion of the LIKE operator in this chapter's section "Making an Educated Guess with the LIKE Operator.")

- Remember that Paradox is case-sensitive. If a value in the table is entered in all caps, search for the value in all caps; if the value is entered in all lowercase, search in all lowercase; and so on. (Refer also to the discussion of patterns and wild cards in the "Matching a Pattern with Wild Cards" section later in this chapter.)

- When searching for a value that includes punctuation, enclose the entire field example in double quotation marks (as in "Clyde W. Davis, Jr."). When the value contains double quotation marks, precede each pair of double quotation marks in the query example with a backslash character (\).

- If the identifying values contain any of Paradox's reserved words or operators, enclose those values in double quotation marks. For example, the word *OR* can be used as an operator in a query (discussed in the "Using Special Query Operators" section, later in this chapter). But OR is also the standard abbreviation for Oregon. If in a query form you don't enclose OR in quotation marks, Paradox assumes that you are trying to use the OR operator.

- When searching numeric fields, do not use whole number separators (the comma is the U.S. convention and the period is the international convention) or the dollar sign. Always search for exactly two decimal places in currency fields. You can search for any number of decimal places in number fields, but at most, two display in the answer.

- Enter date values in any of the following formats: MM/DD/YY, DD-Mon-YY, or DD.MM.YY. The format used in the example does not have to match the format used to enter the date.

For Related Information:

▶▶ "Building Multitable Queries," p. 262.

FROM HERE...

Using Paradox Operators

You may not be sure how the identifying value for a particular record or group of records is spelled. Maybe you cannot remember whether data was typed in uppercase, lowercase, or some combination. Perhaps you want to see a number of records that have nonidentical identifying values but fall into a certain pattern or occur within a certain range of values. Paradox provides tools that can help solve these problems: the LIKE operator, wild-card patterns, and range operators. These tools require that you have at least some idea of what the identifying values you are trying to match look like, but you do not have to ask for an exact match.

Making an Educated Guess with the LIKE Operator

One of the most amazing and useful features of Paradox is its LIKE operator. The purpose of this operator is to locate information in your database based on your best guess as to spelling. Generally, you should use the LIKE operator as a second resort, after failing at least once to find the data using a more specific query.

Reminder:
The LIKE operator locates records based on your best guess as to spelling.

To use the LIKE operator, type the word *like* in front of your best guess. Suppose that you want to see the entire record from the Customer table for a certain freight line, but the only name you can think of is "Alpo Freight Lines." You tried that name, but Paradox returned an empty table, meaning that no such record exists. Figure 4.13 shows the same query with the word *like* added before the original entry. This time Paradox returns a record. The correct company name is "Alpha Freight Lines." This operator does not work if you don't get at least the first letter correct.

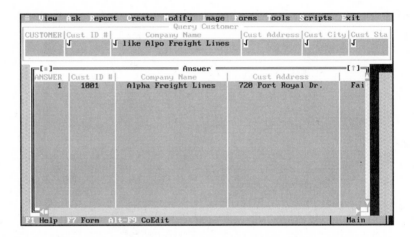

FIG. 4.13

Using the LIKE operator.

Matching a Pattern with Wild Cards

Paradox also enables you to specify *patterns* as search criteria. You can use wild cards in place of specific characters or numbers in your examples. Patterns provide another way to locate records without having to match identifying values exactly. Patterns have a broader usefulness than the LIKE operator because you can more precisely control which records you locate. Paradox provides two wild cards you can use in building patterns: .. and @.

Reminder:
The wild card .. returns any alphanumeric character, number, or date of any length.

When you use two dots or periods side-by-side (..) in an example value, Paradox returns any alphanumeric character, number, or date of any length as a match, including no characters or blank spaces. Used by itself, the .. operator returns *every* record in the table. In fact, you can say that Paradox uses .. as the default entry in every field in Query By Example. The .. operator usually is not used alone but is used to represent a series of characters or numbers in an example value. Figure 4.14 shows a query that returns the Customer record of every company whose name begins with the letter *a*. When you use this operator, the case of any characters in the pattern no longer matters.

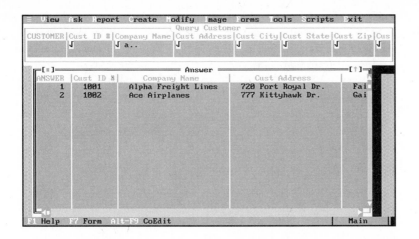

Using the .. wild
card in a pattern.

The other wild card, @, is used to represent any single character. Use
@ when the position of specific characters in the example is important.
To retrieve all company names with the letter *a* as the second letter, for
example, use the pattern @*a*.., as shown in figure 4.15. By contrast, the
pattern @@*a*.. finds names with *a* in the third position.

Reminder:
The wild card @ represents
any single character.

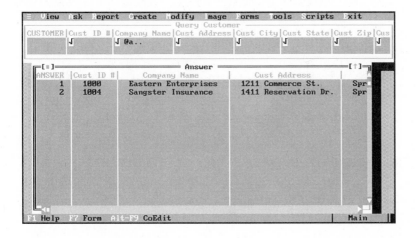

Using the @ wild
card.

The following rules apply to using patterns in Query By Example:

■ You cannot mix operators. You cannot use the LIKE operator with
wild-card patterns in the same query example.

■ Use double quotation marks around characters or words that
have a special meaning to Paradox during query.

■ Patterns in date fields must be in the current screen date format, even if you have used the Format option on the Image menu to change the way a particular date field is viewed. Refer to Appendix B for information on how to change the screen date format using the Data Formats dialog box in the Custom Configuration Program. The default format is mm/dd/yy.

■ Don't use dollar signs or whole number separators with numbers. You should, of course, use the decimal point when appropriate. Because the period also is a part of the .. wild card, enclose the decimal point in double quotation marks to eliminate ambiguity. Always account for exactly two decimal places when building a pattern for currency fields. Patterns for number fields can search for any number of decimal places, but no more than two places are displayed in the Answer table.

Table 4.1 includes a few examples of valid query patterns, showing values retrieved by a query and, in some cases, values not retrieved.

Table 4.1. Examples of Valid Query Patterns

Pattern	Matches	Does not match
Jo..	Jones JOHNSON Jolliet Jo Jo	Mr. Jones
J@@n	Jean John	jeans Johnson
..q..	quick aquatic WMZQ FM	
@q..	aquatic	quick
..th..r	MOTHER path finder Fifth of October	Mother's Day
@@other	brother	mother
12/../91	Matches all dates in December 1991 if the current screen date format is set to MM/DD/YY (the default format unless you change it with the CCP)	

Pattern	Matches	Does not match
21..	21,000 210.45 21.3	.21 2.1
..21	13,018.21 456.021	130,182.1 321.00
3@@@.@@	3,000.00 3,000.01 3,724.15	3,000 3,000.1 3,724.156

T I P

Because the .. wild card renders Paradox insensitive to case, this operator provides an easy way to assure yourself that you will find the information you are looking for even when you cannot remember whether the data was entered in uppercase, lowercase, or a combination. Tack the .. wild card onto the end of the example. Be aware that you may get more than you bargained for, however, because this method makes the search pattern more general.

Finding a Range of Values

Another way to ask Paradox for a group of records is to specify a range of values, which can be a range of numbers, dates, or even alphanumeric characters. Use one or more of the five available range operators listed in table 4.2 to specify the limits of the range.

Reminder:
You also can specify a range of values.

Table 4.2. Range Operators

Operator	Meaning
=	Equal to (optional)
>	Greater than
<	Less than
>=	Greater than or equal to
<=	Less than or equal to

Range operators most often are used with number, currency, and date fields. You may, for example, want to see a list of employees with a salary of less than $25,000. To display records in just that range, type *<25000* in the Salary column, as shown in figure 4.16. Because all salaries are necessarily greater than zero, you don't have to worry about the low end of this range. Paradox shows you the salaries less than $25,000 and greater than $0.

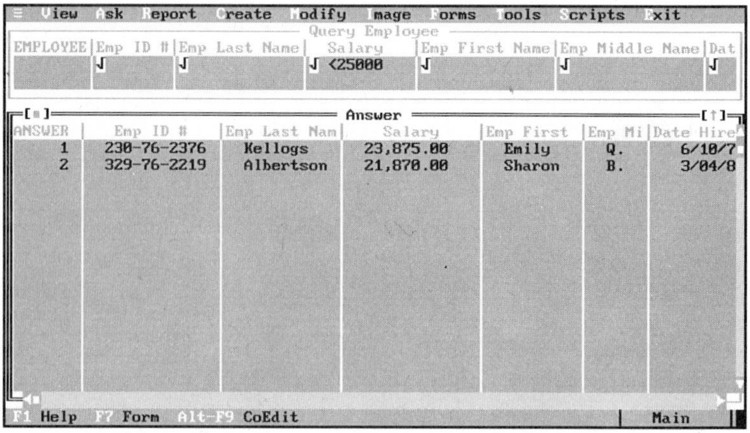

FIG. 4.16

Finding a range of numbers.

Reminder:
You can include multiple conditions in the same query example separated by commas.

A typical use of query ranges is to select records that occur over a certain period of time. To see the orders placed from September 5 to September 20, 1992, you need to specify two conditions. The orders must have been placed on or after 9/5/92 and on or before 9/20/92. Paradox enables you to include multiple conditions in the same query example by separating the conditions with a comma. The complete selection criteria are shown in the query form in figure 4.17. When you include two conditions in the same field, Paradox assumes that both conditions must be met before a particular record can be displayed.

Using Special Query Operators

You can retrieve any record or group of records from your database tables by using one of the methods already covered in this chapter, but Paradox provides a number of other query functions that can help you select records more precisely with a minimum of effort. These operators are listed in table 4.3. The next several sections of this chapter explain the use of these special query operators.

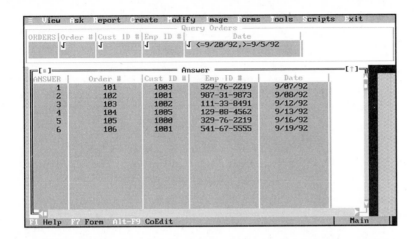

FIG. 4.17

Finding a range
of dates.

Table 4.3. Special Query Operators

Operator	Meaning
TODAY	System date
,	Logical AND condition (when used between conditions in the same query row and field)
OR	Logical OR condition
NOT	No match (not equal to)
BLANK	No data entered

Using the TODAY Operator and Date Arithmetic

All PCs have a built-in system clock. The correct date and time are maintained by a battery, or you have to reset the date and time when you turn on your computer. Paradox gives you access to the current date through the special operator TODAY. Although the TODAY operator is always equal to the current system date, your system clock must be properly set. You can use the TODAY operator in a query the same way you use any date value.

Another feature often used in conjunction with the TODAY operator is *date arithmetic*. This feature enables you to perform calculations on a date, usually addition (+) or subtraction (–). Paradox then arrives at a new date based on these calculations and the program's built-in calendar, which stretches from January 1, 100, through December 31, 9999.

Reminder:
You can access the current date using the TODAY operator.

Using ranges and date arithmetic together, the following query example finds records with dates spanning the last 180 days:

>TODAY180, <=TODAY

All the standard arithmetic operators (+, –, *, /, and ( )) are available for use in date arithmetic. See Chapter 7 for further discussion of performing calculations in Query forms.

Specifying Multiple Conditions—AND versus OR

Reminder:
When you specify examples in multiple fields, Paradox assumes logical AND.

Paradox can handle multiple conditions in the same query example if you separate the conditions with a comma. To identify a record or records in your table precisely, you also may want to enter examples in more than one field. This situation is always true for multifield keyed tables. When you specify examples in multiple fields, Paradox assumes that you want all the fields to be matched at the same time. This condition is the logical AND. For example, because two employees in the Employee table are named Jones, you have to specify first and last names to pick just one of those employees (see fig. 4.18).

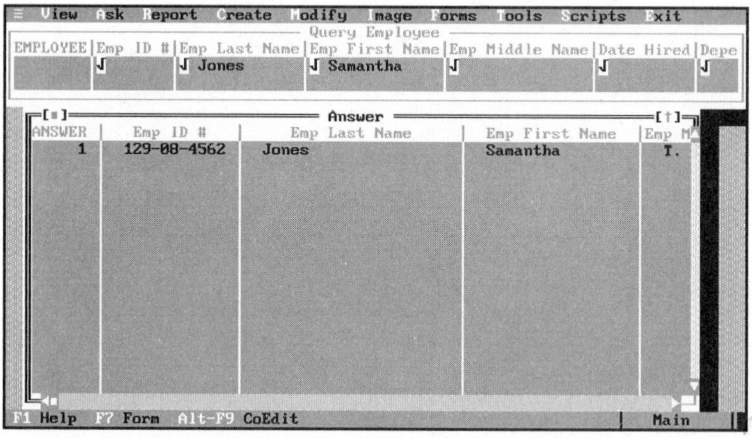

```
≡   View  Ask  Report  Create  Modify  Image  Forms  Tools  Scripts  Exit
                         Query Employee
EMPLOYEE|Emp ID #|Emp Last Name|Emp First Name|Emp Middle Name|Date Hired|Depe
        |√       |√ Jones      |√ Samantha    |√              |√         |√

  [■]                            Answer                          [↑]
 ANSWER |    Emp ID #    |   Emp Last Name  |   Emp First Name  |Emp M
      1 |  129-08-4562   | Jones            | Samantha          |T.




 F1 Help  F7 Form  Alt-F9 CoEdit                          | Main
```

FIG. 4.18

Using multiple fields to find a match (logical AND).

The alternative to logical AND is logical OR. A more common way to express this idea is *either or*. When two conditions are joined by logical OR, the combined condition is met if *either* one *or* the other condition is met. If both conditions are met, the search pattern also considers the entry a match, but matching both conditions is not required.

Cue:
In all versions you can use two rows in a query form to specify logical OR.

Paradox now provides two ways of joining conditions with logical OR. With versions of Paradox before Version 3.0, two rows in a query table are necessary to specify this condition. For example, to determine which orders include either of the two lowest price widgets, model A333 or model B107, you construct the two-row query shown in figure 4.19. You must check the same fields in both rows, and any other multifield conditions must be repeated.

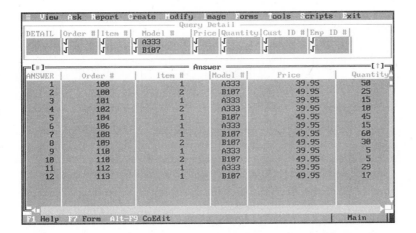

FIG. 4.19

Using the multirow logical OR method.

Paradox 3.0 and later versions have the OR operator. With this feature, you type both conditions in the query field side-by-side, separated only by the word *or*. The query in figure 4.20 duplicates the one in figure 4.19 but uses only one query form line.

Cue:
In Paradox 3.0 and higher you can use the OR operator.

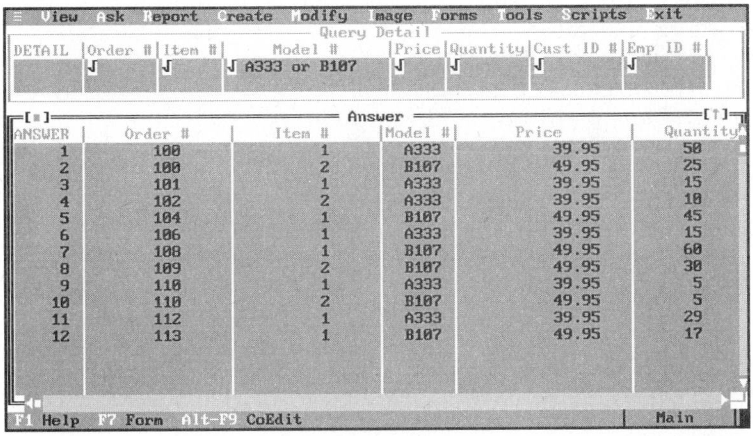

FIG. 4.20

Using the single-row logical OR method.

The multiple-line method is sometimes still the appropriate way to specify a query criterion. Suppose that you are interested in all products in the Product table priced between $40 and $50 (inclusive), but you also want to see any model whose cost is less than $20. The query to retrieve the records you want cannot be constructed all on one line of the query table, even with the OR operator, because the OR operator can be used only within a single field (see fig. 4.21).

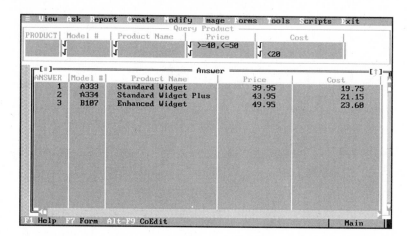

FIG. 4.21

Using the multirow logical OR method.

Finding Unmatching Records with the NOT Operator

You may not be looking for records that match a certain example; you may be looking for records that don't match. You may want to see a list of all orders placed for products other than model G400. Paradox provides the operator NOT, which effectively finds all records that do not match a given value (see fig. 4.22). You can use this operator to reverse the effect of any of the other query operators: LIKE, arithmetic operators, range operators, and patterns. Used as a range operator, NOT means *not equal to*.

Finding Blank Values with the BLANK Operator

The basic Query By Example methodology requires that you provide an example value in a particular field when you want Paradox to retrieve only records that contain that value in the field. Leaving a field blank in the query form means that you don't care what Paradox finds in that field. What if you happen to need records identified by the lack of information in a certain field? You may, for example, want to see all Customer records that have no telephone number listed. If you perform a query and leave all fields blank, Paradox returns all records from the table in the Answer. Use the BLANK operator to indicate that you intend for Paradox to search for records that have no entry in the Cust Phone field (see fig. 4.23). If you type the word *blank* in the query form field, Paradox returns a match only if that field contains no data.

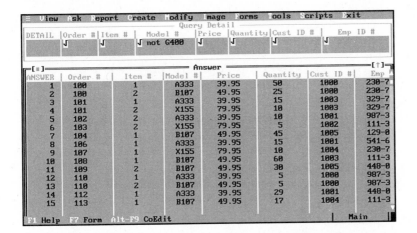

FIG. 4.22

Using the NOT operator.

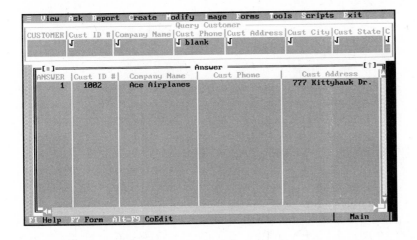

FIG. 4.23

Using the BLANK operator.

For Related Information:

▶▶ "Combining Selection Criteria," p. 266.

FROM HERE...

Saving a Query

When you are first learning QBE, you should experiment freely with many query approaches. That method is the only way to learn the ropes. As you become more proficient, however, you will find yourself using the same queries with certain tables time and again. QBE may be fun, but eliminating repetition is what computers are all about, so Paradox provides a quick and easy way to save any query that you expect you may need to use again.

Cue:
To save a query, use Scripts QuerySave.

To save a query for later use, construct the query as usual, then press F10 (Menu), and select **S**cripts, **Q**uerySave. Paradox prompts you to give the script a name. Type a unique script name and press Enter. (Refer to Chapter 6 for more information on scripts.)

The next time you need to retrieve information meeting these same criteria, select **S**cripts, **P**lay from the Main menu. At the prompt, type the script's name and press Enter or press Enter at the blank line and select the name from a list of available scripts. Either way, Paradox reconstructs the query on-screen but does not execute it. All you need to do is press F2 (Do-It!).

FROM HERE...

For Related Information:

▶▶ "Recording and Playing Scripts," p. 222.

Chapter Summary

This chapter introduced you to Query By Example. QBE is just one part of this powerful program, and if you have looked through the earlier chapters, you should have a good idea of what Paradox is all about. After you have a quick look at the basics of creating reports in Chapter 5 and scripts in Chapter 6, you return to QBE in Chapter 7 for an in-depth look at some of its most powerful features.

Getting Started with Reports

When working with databases, all the data entry, editing, and querying you can muster is worth little if the output doesn't please or inform your audience. Often, the sensible approach is for you to look first at the overall design of the end product and then work backward to determine what data you need to collect and what queries you need to perform to produce that report. This chapter introduces you to the fundamentals of using Paradox report design features so that early in the database design process you can begin to think about how your printed output will look.

Underlying Paradox is the philosophy that a computer program should do as much of the work for you as possible—the ease-of-use side of Paradox. Faithful to this theme, Paradox provides you with instant reports at the touch of a keystroke command, Alt-F7. After a quick overview of the report design process, this chapter explains how to use the Instant Report feature.

True to the other side of Paradox, the program's reporting features provide the capability you expect from a full-featured database program. This chapter introduces you to the basics of creating customized tabular reports with Paradox and presents a number of tools you can use immediately. The discussion lays a foundation for Chapters 10 and 11, which cover more complicated tabular and free-form reports.

This chapter works with only one database table at a time to present Paradox report fundamentals most clearly. Paradox, however, is meant to be used as a relational database, pulling information from many tables to build the output you need. Some of Paradox 4.0's most exciting features involve the creation of multitable reports. Study this chapter first to develop a clear understanding of basic terminology and a sound design approach.

Previewing the Report Design Process

In previous chapters, you learn how to design database tables, enter and edit data, and retrieve particular fields and records from these tables into an Answer table. The Paradox Report Generator provides the means to produce and control the output of data from your database to a printer, to your screen, or to a file.

Understanding Paradox Reports

If you are an experienced database user, you can skip this section. If you are a new user, you may not have a clear understanding of the term *report* in database jargon. Figure 5.1 shows the easiest type of report Paradox creates—the *instant report*. This report is essentially just a version of your database table that you can print, display on-screen, or save to a file. Although reports generally are produced in hard copy, you usually preview the report to screen before printing. Occasionally, you may want to create a text file that you can import into a word processing program for inclusion in a longer document.

Figures 5.2 and 5.3 show two other reports that use various fields from the Employee table shown in figure 5.1. The report in figure 5.2, similar to the instant report, arranges the data in rows and columns like the Paradox table that contains the data. This type of report is referred to as *tabular* style. Figure 5.3 shows a Paradox *free-form* report. When designing this type of report, you can place data in almost any position or order. In this chapter, you learn how to create the instant report, as well as simple tabular reports.

```
5/31/92                    Standard Report              Page    1


Emp ID #        Emp Last Name  Date Hired        Salary
-----------     ---------------  ----------      ----------
111-33-8491     Jones            6/07/78         33,540.00
129-08-4562     Jones           10/02/65         78,936.00
222-39-9999     Brown           10/17/85         35,700.00
230-76-2376     Bronson         11/23/69         43,056.00
311-99-5549     Harrison        11/23/83         44,616.00
329-43-5855     Singer           2/12/88         22,522.50
329-76-2219     Albertson        3/04/81         22,744.80
349-04-9862     Harrell          4/18/79         51,558.00
398-21-2198     Brown           11/29/87         36,575.00
410-44-4232     Plum             8/23/76         44,887.50
448-09-6721     Green            8/15/79         51,312.56
541-67-5555     Kellogs          6/10/75         24,830.00
553-09-3466     French           9/01/88         29,834.75
752-23-3953     Smith           10/13/83         46,280.00
888-52-9058     Harvey           7/17/82         44,935.00
921-65-1234     English          1/04/71         38,220.00
987-31-9873     Quick            5/21/83         55,120.00
994-23-7840     Carson           9/01/88         22,000.00
```

FIG. 5.1

The instant report.

```
Employee Telephone Roster
Current as of   05/31/92                        Page    1

                        Sales Department


                                     Phone Number
                                     ----------------
        Albertson, Sharon B.         (703) 555-2361
        Bronson, Tim C.              (703) 555-7630
        Brown, Bruce R.              (703) 555-4421
        Brown, David E.              (703) 555-9812
        Carson, Susan T.             (703) 555-3434
        English, Gertrude M.         (703) 555-5575
        French, Freda P.             (703) 555-3322
        Green, George H.             (703) 555-9999
        Harrell, Stanley Q.          (703) 555-2351
        Harrison, Steven M.          (703) 555-4432
        Harvey, Christopher P        (703) 555-3298
        Jones, Harry H.              (703) 555-1234
        Jones, Samantha T.           (703) 555-8872
        Kellogs, Emily Q.            (703) 555-3378
        Plum, Hercule P.             (703) 555-2987
        Quick, Joseph L.             (703) 555-1298
        Singer, Sarah S.             (703) 555-8888
        Smith, Angel L.              (703) 555-2198
```

FIG. 5.2

A tabular report.

With Paradox, you also can create reports that draw data from several tables at the same time, called *multitable* reports. Creation of multitable tabular reports is covered in Chapter 10, "Using Tabular Reports," and free-form reports are covered in Chapter 11, "Using Free-Form Reports." Figure 5.4 is an example of an invoice produced by a multitable report specification. Data for this report is drawn from the Detail, Customer, and Employee tables. Although the invoice was produced by a tabular report specification, you also can create a similar report using a free-form style.

```
      Harry H. Jones                    Samantha T. Jones
      1711 Lakeview Dr.                 663 Yuppie Lane
      Burke, VA  22155                  McLean, VA  22101


      Bruce R. Brown                    Tim C. Bronson
      3451 Fox Lane                     9828 Rocky Ridge
      Arlington, VA  22210              Centreville, VA  22020


      Steven M. Harrison                Sarah S. Singer
      3987 Glendale Dr.                 120 S. 2nd, Apt B
      Springfield, VA  22152            Alexandria, VA  22313


      Sharon B. Albertson               Stanley Q. Harrell
      770 Shaw Rd., Apt 23              8999 31st St.
      Arlington, VA  22210              Fairlington, VA  22312


      David E. Brown                    Hercule P. Plum
      16 Hounds Hunt                    239 Belgium Wood Dr.
      Fairfax, VA  22030                Clifton, VA  22140


      George H. Green                   Emily Q. Kellogs
      872B S. Hill St.                  1000 Flake Way
      Mount Vernon, VA  22320           Alexandria, VA  22313


      Freda P. French                   Angel L. Smith
      1299 Houston, Apt G               326 S. Ford St.
      Springfield, VA  22150            Alexandria, VA  22313


      Christopher P. Harvey             Gertrude M. English
      3907 Raleigh Rd.                  1681 School House Rd
      Burke, VA  22155                  Fairfax, VA  22030


      Joseph L. Quick                   Susan T. Carson
      622 Sloth Street                  4252 Burbank St.
      Herndon, VA  22070                Springfield, VA  22152
```

FIG. 5.3

A free-form report (mailing labels).

```
      Order #      100

      Customer:    Eastern Enterprises
                   1211 Commerce St.
                   Springfield, VA 22150

      Salesman:    Tim C. Bronson

      Item #   Model   Product            Qty    Price   Extended Price
      ------   -----   -------            ---    -----   --------------
         1     A333    Standard Widget    50     39.95     1,997.50
         2     B107    Enhanced Widget    25     49.95     1,248.75
         3     G400    Deluxe Widget      10     59.95       599.50
                                                          ============
                                            Total: $      3,845.75
```

FIG. 5.4

A multitable report (an invoice).

Understanding Report Specifications

Reminder:
Each report design is saved as a report specification—up to 15 per table.

To provide maximum flexibility, Paradox gives you many report-writing options. Using the options can be fun, but you don't want to have to redraft the perfect report every time you need it. Paradox provides a way to save a report design as a *report specification*. Each report specification is associated with a particular database table, called the *master table*. You can define up to 15 reports per table. A report is one of the objects in the table's family that is reconciled when the table is restructured.

You may recall a discussion in Chapter 2 about relationships between tables that also used the term *master table*. The concept is the same here. In Chapters 10 and 11, the distinction between the master table and other related tables becomes more significant when you learn how to generate reports from more than one table. The table you select for a report is the table whose data you want to print. This table may be one of the normal tables from your database, or it may be an Answer table generated by a query (when you use the **Ask** command).

T I P

You may want to create a report from the data in an Answer table. Suppose that you want to create a telephone list for a single department of employees, but the table includes four departments. You can use **Ask** to create an Answer table that includes only the specific department.

To use a report that you already designed for another table with the Answer table, you can use the **Copy** command from the Tools menu (see Chapter 13) to copy the report specification from one table to the other. For this procedure to work, however, you have to be careful when you perform the query that creates the Answer table. Make sure that in the query you include all the fields from the original table, even if some of them are not included in the report. Otherwise, Paradox does not enable you to copy the report and informs you that the two tables (the table that owns the report and the new Answer table) have incompatible structures.

Understanding Design Considerations

The type of report you choose—tabular or free-form, single-table or multitable—depends on the nature of your data and the message you want to convey. Your answers to the following questions can help you determine which style of table can best accommodate your data.

Can you visualize the way the report will look? Building a report is always easier if you sketch it on paper first. Better yet, if you are duplicating an existing form, work from that form. You may want to include some real data so that you get a better idea of how the final product will look.

Will your new report replace an existing report or form? When practical, design your report specification to look as much like the current form or report as possible. This consideration has little to do with computer software but much to do with human nature and resistance to change.

Will data be arranged in rows and columns or in groups? A telephone list of your department's employees probably should be a columnar table with each employee's name and phone number on a single row. A report to print mailing labels to those employees should group the data about each employee vertically in several rows (compare figs. 5.2 and 5.3).

Should the information be arranged in a particular order? Usually you do not dump data on the page from your database. Instead, you organize the information in a manner that makes it easier to use or understand. Even a simple list of phone numbers is usually in alphabetical order by each person's last name.

Will records be grouped? A phone book for your entire company also may be grouped by department or division for convenience.

Will summary computations be necessary? When your data includes numeric information, you often need to perform summary calculations. Subtotals, subaverages, and so forth require that the data be appropriately grouped in the report.

Is all the necessary information in one table, or do you have to draw some data from other tables in the database? Paradox can combine data from related tables in two ways: multitable queries (Chapter 7) and multitable reports (Chapters 10 and 11). You have to decide which method you are going to use before you begin to design your report. This factor is important even when choosing the master table for the report. To create a report from multiple tables, the master table must be related directly or linked to each of the other tables, called *lookup* tables.

As you are designing your report, keep in mind the basic report-building capacities of Paradox, summarized in table 5.1.

Table 5.1. Paradox Reporting Capacities

Feature	Capacity
Fields	255
Characters	2,000 per record
Tables	Five linked lookup tables in addition to the master table

Feature	Capacity
Grouping (breaks)	16 levels
Width of page	10 to 2,000 characters
Length of page	2 to 2,000 lines
Width of report	2,000 characters
Length of report	Unlimited

If you cannot decide which report style is best even after answering the questions listed in this section, try the tabular form first. A tabular format is more likely to present your data clearly with a minimum of effort on your part. Don't forget to consider the instant report—it may be all you need.

For Related Information:

▶▶ "Starting the Free-Form Report Designer," p. 381.

FROM HERE...

Using the Instant Report Feature

Before you can try this feature, you already must have created a table and entered data. When you have proceeded at least that far, you are ready to display a report.

Select the **View** command from the Main menu to display the table you want to print. If you are editing the table, you must return to the Main mode before you can produce a report.

Cue:
Return to Main mode before producing a report.

Next use the **Ask** command to select the fields and records you want included in the report. You can skip this step if all the data in the table is to be printed.

Finally, make sure that your printer is turned on and properly connected to your computer. While viewing the table you want to print (the Answer table, if you performed a query), press Alt-F7 (Instant Report).

Cue:
Press Alt-F7 for an instant report.

Paradox prints a standard tabular report that looks similar to figure 5.1. The program prints the data in the same row and column order as displayed and prints a header of field names at the top of each page. This report is not fancy, but this quick print of your data may often be just what you need.

T   I   P

Don't be concerned if your table includes too many columns to print on your printer. Paradox breaks your report into page-size pieces, 80 characters by 66 lines. Before printing, set the left edge of the paper no more than two or three spaces to the left of the 0 mark on your printer's paper guide. Most printers print 10 characters per inch (often called *pica* style) by default. With 8 1/2-inch paper, therefore, you have only 1/2-inch total (5 spaces) to use for left and right margins.

If you don't want your report to be split vertically, use a query to limit the fields included. A good rule of thumb is that the columns will fit on the paper if you can see them all on-screen at the same time.

FROM HERE...

For Related Information:

▶▶ "Controlling the Printer," p. 375.

Getting Started with the Report Generator

The next several sections describe how to create basic tabular reports using the Paradox Report Generator and working with only one table at a time. You already have seen the Employee table in this book several times, beginning with Quick Start 1. For the purposes of this chapter, several fields, including a Department field and Emp Phone field, and a few more employees have been added. The table now includes individuals from four departments: Sales, Administration, Accounting, and Production.

To start designing a report in Report mode, you first must be in the Main mode. From the Main menu, select Report, Design and choose a table. To use the Employee table, for example, you type the name *Employee* and press Enter or press Enter at the blank prompt and then select Employee from the list of available tables.

Naming the Report Specification

After you have chosen the table for the report, Paradox presents a dialog box containing an unusual-looking list of available report specifications (see fig. 5.5).

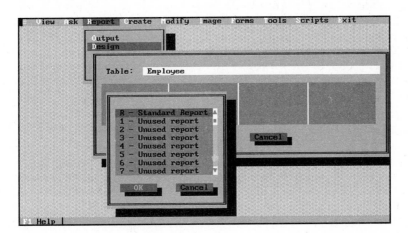

FIG. 5.5

Selecting a report specification.

Paradox can store up to 15 report specifications (*report specs*) as a part of the table's family. Paradox builds the spec named *R*, referred to as the *preferred report* and listed in the menu as the Standard Report. When you press Alt-F7 (Instant Report), you get this report specification. You can modify report spec R, and you can create up to 14 additional specs.

Reminder:
You can have up to 15 report specifications per table.

Select a name (number) for the report. You typically should select a report listed as an Unused Report. If you choose a report name that is already in use, Paradox alerts you and gives you a chance to stop or replace the old specification with your new one.

The next prompt instructs you to enter a report description. This step is an optional but useful feature that serves two purposes:

■ The report description gives you a longer report name. When the menu shown in figure 5.5 is displayed, the description displays just to the right of the report name in the menu. You should enter a few words to help you remember what this report does. If you are building a list of telephone numbers, for example, you may type *Telephone List* in the Report description text box. With 14 other specifications possible, you can easily get them confused if you don't take advantage of this memory aid.

■ The report description becomes a report title that prints at the top of every page. You can modify or remove the title from the report specification if you decide not to use it.

Choosing Report Type

After you enter the report description, press Enter or select OK. The next pop-up menu displayed requires you to choose between the two available report styles, **T**abular and **F**ree-form. The options and menus for the two report types are different from this point. The next several examples in this chapter assume that you are working with a tabular report.

When you choose the **T**abular field type, Paradox displays a window labeled `Report Designer` similar to figure 5.6. The report specification displayed in the Report Designer window is called the standard specification for a tabular report. The next portion of this chapter describes the various components that comprise the specification and then explains the fundamentals of customizing this report definition.

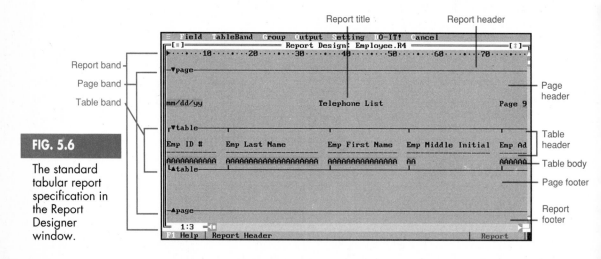

FIG. 5.6

The standard tabular report specification in the Report Designer window.

FROM HERE...

For Related Information:

▶▶ "An Overview of Form Design," p. 294.

▶▶ "Comparing Free-Form Reports to Tabular Reports," p. 383.

▶▶ "Renaming Forms and Reports," p. 429.

Examining the Tabular Report Specification

The *tabular report specification* is a stylized version of how your report will look when printed. When you begin designing the specification, Paradox displays the standard specification, which is almost identical to the preferred specification (report R) used when you press Alt-F7 (Instant Report). The only difference is that the instant report reads Standard Report at the top (see fig. 5.1), and your report spec displays the report description you entered (see fig. 5.6).

The specification, as indicated in figure 5.6, is made up of three vertical *bands*. Each band consists of the following parts:

■ *Report band.* A *report header* and *report footer* comprise the outside layer or band of the report. The header prints only once, at the beginning of the report. The report footer also prints only once, at the end of the report.

■ *Page band.* The next layer is the *page band*, which also contains a *header* and a *footer*. These bands print at the top and bottom of each page, respectively.

■ *Table band.* This area is where most of the action takes place. The table band includes two parts: the *table header* and the *body*. The table header, by default, prints at the top of every page—above the fields and below the page header. Initially, the standard specification places the field names in this header, above the corresponding fields in the body. The body of the report prints once for every record in the table.

The groups as shown in figure 5.6 indicate that Paradox has placed each of the fields from the table into the table band. These letters are *field masks* that show the field type and size. (For more information on field masks, see "Placing Regular Paradox Fields" later in this chapter.) As you move the cursor into one of these masks, Paradox displays the field name in the status line, at the bottom of the screen to the left of the mode indicator.

Reminder:
The body of the report prints once for every record in the table.

These report elements appear in the specification in the same order in which they print. The report header prints first, followed by the page header, the table header, and finally the records from your Paradox table. If you include a page footer, the footer prints at the bottom of each page. In multipage reports, the page header and table header print at the top of every page. After all records have printed, the report footer prints, followed by the last page footer.

Figure 5.7 shows a simple report specification for a phone list with the various report elements labeled so that you can easily find them. The corresponding report, printed to screen, is shown in figure 5.8. Notice the order in which each of these elements has printed (don't be concerned about the order of the data).

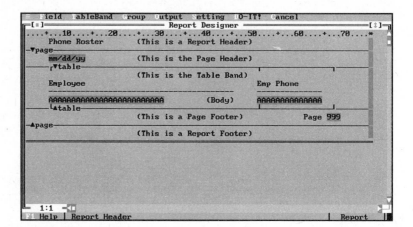

FIG. 5.7

The report elements.

```
Phone Roster        (This is a Report Header)
 06/02/92            (This is the Page Header)
                    (This is the Table Band)
Employee                                           Emp Phone
-----------------------------------------        ---------------
Harry Jones                         (Body)          (703) 555-1234
Samantha Jones                      (Body)          (703) 555-8872
Bruce Brown                         (Body)          (703) 555-4421
Tim Bronson                         (Body)          (703) 555-7630
Steven Harrison                     (Body)          (703) 555-4432
Sarah Singer                        (Body)          (703) 555-8888
Sharon Albertson                    (Body)          (703) 555-2361
Stanley Harrell                     (Body)          (703) 555-2351
David Brown                         (Body)          (703) 555-9812
Hercule Plum                        (Body)          (703) 555-2987
George Green                        (Body)          (703) 555-9999
Emily Kellogs                       (Body)          (703) 555-3378
Freda French                        (Body)          (703) 555-3322
Angel Smith                         (Body)          (703) 555-2198
Christopher Harvey                  (Body)          (703) 555-3298
Gertrude English                    (Body)          (703) 555-5575
Joseph Quick                        (Body)          (703) 555-1298
Susan Carson                        (Body)          (703) 555-3434
                    (This is a Report Footer)



                    (This is a Page Footer)          Page   1
```

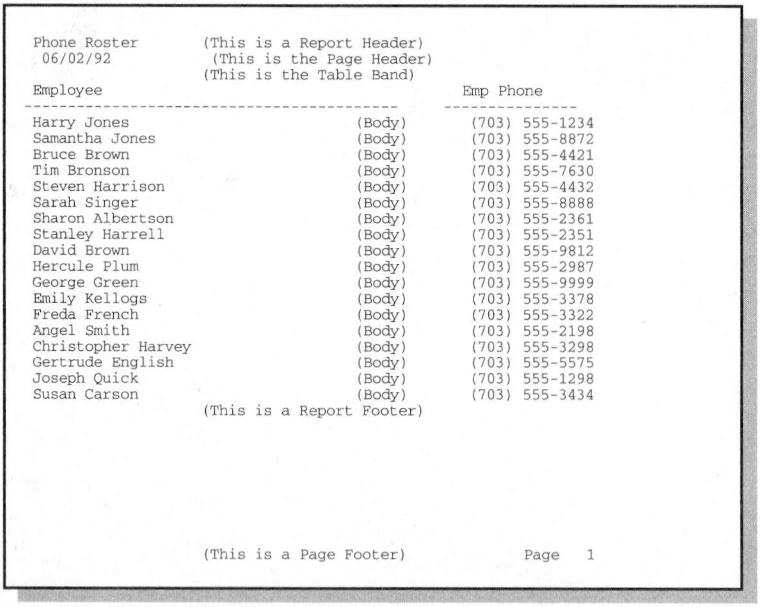

FIG. 5.8

The report produced by the report specification in figure 5.7.

Paradox also enables you to add a fourth type of band: the *group band*. Some database programs call this type of band a *break*. Paradox enables you to have up to 16 group bands in a single report. Inserting a group band causes two things to happen:

■ The data in the body is sorted and grouped according to a field that you specify.

■ You have the option of inserting blank lines and summary calculations at the end of each group of records.

Suppose that you want to print a report of employee salaries, grouped by the four departments of your company. Within each department's grouping, you want to see the employee names in alphabetical order. This report requires two group bands: one for the Department field and one for the Emp Last Name field. The first group band groups the records in the report by the employee's department. You then have the opportunity to subtotal the salaries by department. The second group band places employee names in ascending order for the convenience of the reader, but no further subtotal is needed at this level.

The specification shown in figure 5.9 produces this report, which is depicted in figure 5.10. Chapter 10 discusses the creation of this report in more detail.

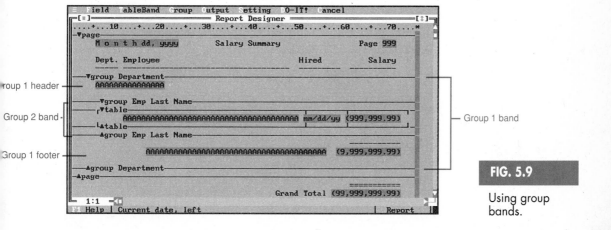

FIG. 5.9

Using group bands.

For Related Information:

▶▶ "Examining the Standard Form," p. 296.

▶▶ "Grouping Records in Tabular Reports," p. 351.

▶▶ "Examining the Standard Specification and the Form Band," p. 382.

FROM HERE...

```
June  3, 1992           Salary Summary              Page 1

Dept. Employee                          Hired        Salary
----- ------------------------------- --------    ----------
Accounting

     David E. Brown                  11/29/87    36,575.00
     Freda P. French                  9/01/88    29,834.75
     Christopher P. Harvey            7/17/82    44,935.00
                                                 ----------
          Total Salary for Accounting Dept.     111,344.75

Administration

     Bruce R. Brown                  10/17/85    35,700.00
     Hercule P. Plum                  8/23/76    44,887.50
     Sarah S. Singer                  2/12/88    22,522.50
                                                 ----------
          Total Salary for Administration Dept. 103,110.00

Production

     Stanley Q. Harrell               4/18/79    51,558.00
     Steven M. Harrison              11/23/83    44,6f16.00
     Angel L. Smith                  10/13/83    46,280.00
                                                 ----------
          Total Salary for Production Dept.     142,454.00

Sales

     Sharon B. Albertson              3/04/81    22,744.80
     Tim C. Bronson                  11/23/69    43,056.00
     Susan T. Carson                  9/01/88    22,000.00
     Gertrude M. English              1/04/71    38,220.00
     George H. Green                  8/15/79    51,312.56
     Harry H. Jones                   6/07/78    33,540.00
     Samantha T. Jones               10/02/65    78,936.00
     Emily Q. Kellogs                 6/10/75    24,830.00
     Joseph L. Quick                  5/21/83    55,120.00
                                                 ----------
          Total Salary for Sales Dept.          369,759.36

                                                 ==========
                                    Grand Total  726,668.11
```

FIG. 5.10

The grouped report.

Using the Keyboard When Designing Reports

Table 1.2 in Chapter 1 describes the special keys available in Paradox. In several situations, including the report design process, Paradox provides full screen-editing capabilities. The cursor-movement keys assume slightly different meanings here than they do elsewhere in the program. Table 5.2 shows the effect of each cursor-movement key on the report design screen.

Table 5.2. Using Cursor-Movement Keys on the Report Design Screen

Key	Moves cursor
Home	To first line
Ctrl-Home	To beginning of line
End	To last line
Ctrl-End	To last character of line
PgUp	Up one screen
PgDn	Down one screen
Left arrow	One character left
Ctrl-left arrow	Left one-half screen
Right arrow	One character right
Ctrl-right arrow	Right one-half screen
Up arrow	Up one line
Down arrow	Down one line
Enter	Down one line

Deleting Lines

As you edit a report specification, you may want to delete an entire line at the same time. To do so, press Ctrl-Y. Paradox deletes from the cursor position to the right side of your report spec. You occasionally may hear an irritating beep when you try this command, indicating that nothing is there to delete. This situation occurs most often when you are attempting to delete a blank line. To delete a blank line, place the cursor at the far left margin; then press Ctrl-Y.

Cue:
Press Ctrl-Y to delete a line.

Displaying a Vertical Ruler

You probably already have noticed that Paradox displays a ruler line along the top of the report spec, just below the status/message lines. This ruler helps you track the size of your report horizontally. A related feature is the *vertical ruler*, which numbers the lines down the left side of the screen. The horizontal ruler is always displayed, but you have to turn on the vertical ruler.

To display line numbers down the left side of the report spec, as shown in figure 5.11, press Ctrl-V. These numbers can be extremely helpful when you are designing a form to meet rigid space requirements, such as printing on a preprinted form.

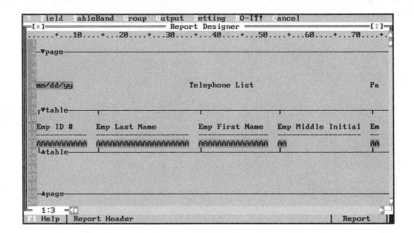

FIG. 5.11

Displaying the vertical ruler.

Using Replace and Insert Modes

Cue:

Press Ins to toggle between Insert and Overwrite modes.

You already have learned that Paradox normally is in Insert mode when you are using the field view to edit existing data. The report design screen is the opposite. This screen always begins in Overwrite mode, which means that existing text is replaced if you type new text over the existing data. To switch to Insert mode, press the Ins key. Paradox changes the shape of the cursor from a large block to an underscore. Press Ins again when you are ready to return to Overwrite mode.

Two major differences exist between Insert and Overwrite modes:

- Paradox usually replaces existing text as you type. In Insert mode, however, the program pushes existing text and spaces to the right as you type.

- In Insert mode, Paradox adds a carriage return each time you press Enter. You use this feature to add new lines to a report.

Inserting Lines

If you already have typed text into any area of the report design screen, follow these guidelines before you decide to add more lines:

- To insert lines above an existing line of text, place the cursor at the beginning (left end) of the line and press Enter.

- To insert a blank line below an existing line of text, place the cursor to the right of the last character on the line (the right end) and press Enter.

For Related Information:

▶▶ "Squeezing Blank Spaces and Lines Out of the Report," p. 384.

FROM HERE...

Adjusting the Page Layout

A tabular report, by definition, prints the data in columns and rows. Using this type of report is much like transferring the table directly from the disk to paper, with the same columns and rows. If all the columns do not fit horizontally within an 80-character width, Paradox splits and prints the report on several *page widths* until all columns have been printed. With this method, Paradox can print tables up to 2,000-characters wide.

Printing the entire Employee table, for example, places fields up through the Emp Address column on the first page width. Then Paradox runs out of space, as figure 5.12 shows. The last few letters of the Emp Address heading do not fit on the page. The next page width is shown in figure 5.13, but even that page does not hold enough room for all the fields. Finally, after printing the third page width (see fig. 5.14), Paradox is finished. You have to bring out the tape or stapler and put the table back together. Obviously, you may not always want to follow this procedure to print a table.

Changing the Page Width

The standard report specification starts with the page width set at 80 characters (unless you have changed the default through the Custom Configuration Program, discussed in Appendix B). On the report design screen, Paradox displays a vertical inverse video bar at the point at which the current page width ends (see fig. 5.15).

```
06/03/92      Telephone List   Page    1


Emp ID #       Emp Last Name    Emp First Name    Emp Middle Initial    Emp Addr
-----------    -------------    --------------    ------------------    --------
111-33-8491    Jones            Harry             H.                    1711 Lak
129-08-4562    Jones            Samantha          T.                    663 Yupp
222-39-9999    Brown            Bruce             R.                    3451 Fox
230-76-2376    Bronson          Tim               C.                    9828 Roc
311-99-5549    Harrison         Steven            M.                    3987 Gle
329-43-5855    Singer           Sarah             S.                    120 S. 2
329-76-2219    Albertson        Sharon            B.                    770 Shaw
349-04-9862    Harrell          Stanley           Q.                    8999 31s
398-21-2198    Brown            David             E.                    16 Hound
410-44-4232    Plum             Hercule           P.                    239 Belg
448-09-6721    Green            George            H.                    872B S.
541-67-5555    Kellogs          Emily             Q.                    1000 Fla
553-09-3466    French           Freda             P.                    1299 Hou
752-23-3953    Smith            Angel             L.                    326 S. F
888-52-9058    Harvey           Christopher       P.                    3907 Ral
921-65-1234    English          Gertrude          M.                    1681 Sc
987-31-9873    Quick            Joseph            L.                    622 Slot
994-23-7840    Carson           Susan             T.                    4252 Bur
```

FIG. 5.12

The first page width.

```
ess            Emp City     Emp State    Emp Zip    Emp Phone          Date Hir
-----------    ---------    ---------    -------    ---------------    ---------
eview Dr.      Burke        VA           22155      (703) 555-1234     6/07/78
ie Lane        McLean       VA           22101      (703) 555-8872     10/02/65
Lane           Arlington    VA           22210      (703) 555-4421     10/17/85
ky Ridge       Centreville  VA           22020      (703) 555-7630     11/23/69
ndale Dr.      Springfield  VA           22152      (703) 555-4432     11/23/83
nd, Apt B      Alexandria   VA           22313      (703) 555-8888     2/12/88
Rd., Apt 23    Arlington    VA           22210      (703) 555-2361     3/04/81
t St.          Fairlington  VA           22312      (703) 555-2351     4/18/79
s Hunt         Fairfax      VA           22030      (703) 555-9812     11/29/87
ium Wood Dr.   Clifton      VA           22140      (703) 555-2987     8/23/76
Hill St.       Mount Vernon VA           22320      (703) 555-9999     8/15/79
ke Way         Alexandria   VA           22313      (703) 555-3378     6/10/75
ston, Apt G    Springfield  VA           22150      (703) 555-3322     9/01/88
ord St.        Alexandria   VA           22313      (703) 555-2198     10/13/83
eigh Rd.       Burke        VA           22155      (703) 555-3298     7/17/82
ool House Rd   Fairfax      VA           22030      (703) 555-5575     1/04/71
h Street       Herndon      VA           22070      (703) 555-1298     5/21/83
bank St.       Springfield  VA           22152      (703) 555-3434     9/01/88
```

FIG. 5.13

The second page width.

```
ed   Dependents   Salary       Department
--   ----------   ----------   -------------
      2           33,540.00    Sales
      1           78,936.00    Sales
      3           35,700.00    Administration
      3           43,056.00    Sales
      4           44,616.00    Production
      1           22,522.50    Administration
      1           22,744.80    Sales
      3           51,558.00    Production
      2           36,575.00    Accounting
      2           44,887.50    Administration
      4           51,312.56    Sales
      0           24,830.00    Sales
      1           29,834.75    Accounting
      2           46,280.00    Production
      4           44,935.00    Accounting
      2           38,220.00    Sales
      3           55,120.00    Sales
      2           22,000.00    Sales
```

FIG. 5.14

The third page width.

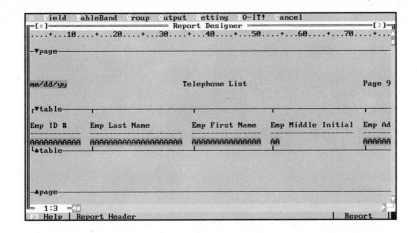

FIG. 5.15

The report
specification with
a page width of
80 characters.

Also notice that the message 1:3 appears in the lower left corner of the
Report Designer window in figure 5.15. This message indicates that this
screen is the first of three page widths. Paradox figures how many 80-
column page widths are required to print all the fields in the table and
establishes that figure as the report width. The report width for the
report spec shown in figure 5.15 is three page widths, or 240 characters.

Assume that you want to create a telephone list from data in the Employee table. You need to include only each employee's name and
phone number, so the information should fit easily within a normal
page width. To leave an inch margin on the left and an inch on the
right, you decide to print the report within a 65-character page width—
(8.5 inches – 2 inches) × 10 characters per inch = 65 characters. To
change the Paradox page width from the default of 80 to the new width
of 65, select **S**etting from the menu bar to display a pull-down menu.
Then select **P**ageLayout, **W**idth. Paradox displays the existing width,
80, and prompts you to enter a new one. Use the Backspace key to
erase the current number, and then type the new page width and press
Enter.

Cue:
To change the Paradox
page width, select **S**etting,
PageLayout, **W**idth.

Paradox responds to the page-width alteration by moving the vertical
inverse video bar to the new margin, column 65 in the example (see
fig. 5.16). The program also recalculates the number of page widths
needed to display the report. The Employee table requires four page
widths at 65 characters per page, as indicated by the 1:4 message in
the lower left corner of figure 5.16.

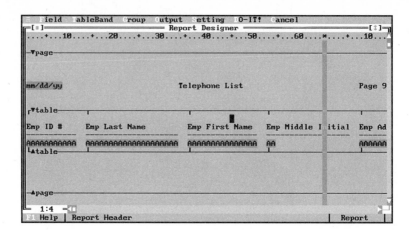

FIG. 5.16

The report
specification with
a page width of
65 characters.

Changing the Page Length

In a Paradox report specification, the page length parameter informs
the program of the number of lines your printer is capable of printing
on each page. If Paradox is misinformed as to page length, the program
will paginate the report incorrectly.

You can alter page length in a manner similar to the way you modify
page width. The default page length is 66 lines per page, which is the
correct page length for most dot-matrix printers (6 lines per inch times
11 inches). Some printers require a different page length. Most laser
printers, for example, will not print on the top 1/2-inch or bottom 1/2-
inch of paper. For these laser printers, therefore, you should set page
length to 60 lines (6 lines per inch times 10 inches).

Cue:
To change the page
length, select **S**etting,
PageLayout, **L**ength.

To change the page length, access the Report menu and select **S**etting,
PageLayout, **L**ength. Backspace over the current setting and enter the
maximum number of lines per page your printer can print.

T I P

If you want to change the top or bottom margin of your report, add
blank lines in the page header or page footer, respectively. Do not
attempt to use the page length parameter to set the top or the bottom margin of your report.

You can tell Paradox to print the report in one continuous page, with
no breaks. Type the letter *c* rather than a number as the page length.
Page headers and page footers do not print.

Reducing and Increasing the Report Width

You seldom need to include all fields from a table in a report, so you may want to reduce the total report width. In the telephone list example, you can reduce the width only after removing unneeded fields (refer to "Inserting and Deleting Fields" later in this chapter).

Paradox is smart enough not to print an empty page if your report width is wider than your report requires. You can leave the report width at the default size with no adverse effects.

> **CAUTION:** Do not reduce the report width until you have removed the unwanted fields from the report spec, and the remaining fields fit within the new report dimensions. Otherwise, Paradox may remove fields from the screen that you intended to keep.

To reduce the report width, first set the page width as you want it and then access the Report menu by pressing F10 (Menu). Select **S**etting, **P**ageLayout, **D**elete, **OK**. Paradox deletes one page width from the total report width each time you repeat this procedure.

Conversely, you can increase the report width one page width at a time by selecting **S**etting, **P**ageLayout, **I**nsert from the Report menu.

Cue:
To change the report width, use **S**etting, **P**ageLayout, **I**nsert or **D**elete.

Changing the Left Margin

By default, Paradox starts printing reports at column 1 on your printer. The left margin is at 0. To change this setting, select **S**etting, **M**argin from the Report menu. Backspace over the current margin setting, type the new one, and press Enter. Keep in mind that this margin setting is only for the left side of the page. The right margin is established by the page size. If you change the left margin, you also may have to adjust page size by the same amount. In the employee telephone list example, changing the left margin to 10 requires that the page size be increased to 75, the original 65 spaces plus 10 (see fig. 5.17).

Cue:
To change the left margin, select **S**etting, **M**argin from the Report menu.

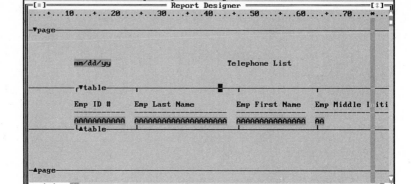

FIG. 5.17

The report specification with a left margin of 10 and a page width of 75.

For Related Information:

▶▶ "Using Headers and Footers," p. 357.

Modifying the Table Band

In Paradox tabular-style reports, all records print within the table band. When you modify the standard specification, you almost always are making adjustments, additions, and deletions to this report component. Because the standard spec initially includes all the fields in the table, you probably need to delete a few fields.

The table band is divided horizontally into columns, just as the underlying table is divided into fields. The boundaries of each column in the table are indicated by small hash marks (see fig. 5.17). The table band also is divided vertically into the table header and the body.

In the standard specification, Paradox places a field name in each column in the table header line, with the corresponding field value in the body below. You can have an empty column, however, and you can even place more than one field value in a single column. Matching the number of columns to the number of fields is usually preferable.

Deleting Columns from the Table Band

To delete a column from the table, select TableBand from the menu bar to display the TableBand menu and choose Erase. Position the cursor within the hash marks of the column you want removed, in the table header or the body, and press Enter. Paradox removes the field—field name and value—and fills the vacant space with any fields remaining on the right. Repeat these steps for each column you want to remove. In the telephone list, for example, you can remove all columns except the four columns that contain Emp Last Name, Emp First Name, Emp Middle Initial, and Emp Phone. Compare figure 5.18 to figure 5.17.

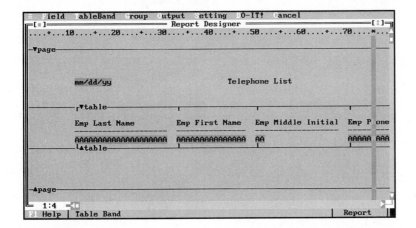

FIG. 5.18

After deleting a column from the table band.

Inserting Columns in the Table Band

Inserting a column is the reverse of deleting one, but Paradox does not choose a field to go in the new column. When you insert a new column, that column is blank. Placing a field in the column requires another step, described in "Inserting and Deleting Fields" later in this chapter.

To insert a new column, select TableBand, Insert. Move the cursor to the position in the table band where you want the new column to go and press Enter. Paradox inserts a column that is 15 spaces wide.

Cue:
To insert a column, use TableBand, Insert.

Resizing a Column in the Table Band

Often you need to change the size of a column to make your report fit within the available space. Figure 5.18, for example, shows that the

Emp Phone field overlaps into the second page width. The obvious solution in this particular example is to reduce the width of the Emp Middle Initial column.

To reduce the width of a column, you first must reduce the size of any field or label that the column contains. Reducing the size of a field is called *reformatting* the field and is discussed in "Inserting and Deleting Fields" later in this chapter. The Emp Middle Initial field already is small enough, but the heading is too big. You don't need this heading anyway, so you can use the Del key or the Backspace key to erase it. After deleting the heading, access the Report menu and select **T**ableBand, **R**esize. Move the cursor to the far end of the column, away from the value (AA in this example) and press Enter. Use the cursor-movement keys to shrink the column and press Enter when you are finished. Figure 5.19 shows the results.

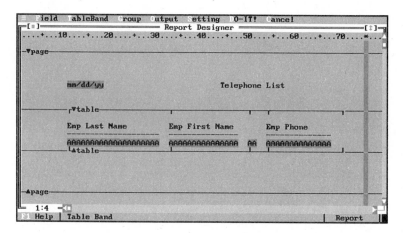

After resizing the Emp Middle Initial column.

Rearranging Columns in the Table Band

The **M**ove option on the TableBand menu works in a manner similar to the corresponding command on the Image menu. To move a column in the table band, access the Report menu and select **T**ableBand, **M**ove. Use the cursor-movement keys to position the cursor in the column that needs to be repositioned and press Enter. Then move the cursor to the new position and press Enter again. Paradox moves the column. The **C**opy command works in the same way, but instead of moving the column, **C**opy makes a duplicate version. The Ctrl-R (Rotate) keystroke command, discussed in Chapter 3, also is available for rearranging columns quickly in the table band. Figure 5.20 shows the result of rearranging the employee name fields so that they are in the order of first, middle, and last.

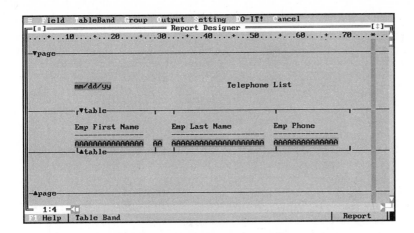

```
≡ Field  TableBand  Group  Output  Setting  DO-IT!  Cancel
┌[■]════════════════ Report Designer ══════════════════[↕]┐
....+...10....+...20....+...30....+...40....+...50....+...60....+...70....*...

 ▼page
    mm/dd/yy                        Telephone List

      ┌▼table
      Emp First Name        Emp Last Name        Emp Phone

      AAAAAAAAAAAAAA  AA  AAAAAAAAAAAAAAAAAAAA  AAAAAAAAAAAAAA
      └▲table

 ▲page

   1:4
 F1 Help | Table Band                              Report
```

FIG. 5.20

Rearranging columns in the table band.

For Related Information:

▶▶ "Creating Mailing Labels," p. 387.

FROM HERE...

Previewing the Report

A previous section of this chapter describes how you can produce a quick and easy report directly from the Main mode by pressing Alt-F7 (Instant Report). This keystroke combination has exactly the same effect during report design. You can use this feature to get a quick look at how your report looks.

Cue:
Use Alt-F7 for a quick printout.

Perhaps a better way to preview a report is on-screen. Access the Report menu and select Output, Screen. Paradox displays a window titled Report Preview containing on-screen a preview of output from the report you are designing. When you have designed the report to your liking, print a test run using Alt-F7 (Instant Report). Figure 5.21 shows the current state of the employee telephone list that has been developed in this chapter.

Cue:
Use Output, Screen for an on-screen preview.

Inserting and Deleting Fields

Even though Paradox places all of a table's fields on the specification for you, in many situations, you need to add or delete fields. The telephone list you are creating, for example, would look better with the employee names squeezed together. Accomplishing this task requires the use of one of the special field types, called a calculated field. The next several sections discuss how to insert regular and calculated Paradox fields, including the calculated date and page number fields.

```
06/04/92            Telephone List            Page    1


Emp First Name            Emp Last Name         Emp Phone
------------------        ----------------      ----------------
Harry          H.         Jones                 (703) 555-1234
Samantha       T.         Jones                 (703) 555-8872
Bruce          R.         Brown                 (703) 555-4421
Tim            C.         Bronson               (703) 555-7630
Steven         M.         Harrison              (703) 555-4432
Sarah          S.         Singer                (703) 555-8888
Sharon         B.         Albertson             (703) 555-2361
Stanley        Q.         Harrell               (703) 555-2351
David          E.         Brown                 (703) 555-9812
Hercule        P.         Plum                  (703) 555-2987
George         H.         Green                 (703) 555-9999
Emily          Q.         Kellogs               (703) 555-3378
Freda          P.         French                (703) 555-3322
Angel          L.         Smith                 (703) 555-2198
Christopher    P.         Harvey                (703) 555-3298
Gertrude       M.         English               (703) 555-5575
Joseph         L.         Quick                 (703) 555-1298
Susan          T.         Carson                (703) 555-3434
```

FIG. 5.21

The telephone list report.

Placing Regular Paradox Fields

To place a field from the table onto the report spec, access the Report menu and select Field, Place, Regular. Then pick the field name from a list provided by Paradox. Move the cursor to the position where you want the field to begin and press Enter. Paradox places a *field mask* on-screen, beginning at the cursor location. The field mask shows you the field type and field size. Table 5.3 lists the default field masks used to represent the various Paradox field types. The length of the mask represents the field length.

Table 5.3. Report Specification Default Field Masks

Field type	Field mask
A (alphanumeric)	AAAAAA
M (memo)	AAAAAA
N (number)	9999999
$ (currency)	(999,999)
D (date)	mm/dd/yy

Erasing Fields

As you work in a report spec, you probably will make a number of false starts until the spec is designed exactly the way you want it. Therefore, you need some way to erase your mistakes, including fields that you may have placed in error.

To erase a field, access the Report menu and select **Field, Erase**. Move the cursor to the field to be removed and press Enter. Note that Paradox does not remove any corresponding labels in the table header. To remove table header text, use the Del or Backspace keys.

Cue:

To erase a field, select **F**ield, **E**rase.

Placing Calculated Fields

A *calculated field* in a report specification is a field whose value is typically derived from other fields in the table. This type of field can be a number or alphanumeric field. Each calculated field is defined by an *expression* consisting of field names, constant values, operators, and PAL expressions (refer to Chapter 15, "An Overview of the Paradox Application Language"; PAL expressions can be used in calculated fields in Paradox 3.5 and later).

Reminder:

A calculated field is derived from other fields in the table or from PAL expressions.

When building an expression, you must enclose field names in brackets ([]) and text constants in double quotation marks (""). You can use the operators listed in table 5.4 when creating calculated fields. To create a calculated field from Price and Quantity, for example, use the following expression:

[Price]*[Quantity]

The * operator in this expression indicates that the value in the first field is multiplied by value in the second field.

Table 5.4. Operators for Calculated Fields

Arithmetic operator	Meaning
+	Add a numeric field or constant or concatenate an alphanumeric field or constant
–	Subtract a numeric field or constant
*	Multiply a numeric field or constant
/	Divide by a numeric field or constant
()	Perform operations within the innermost pair of parentheses first

continues

Table 5.4. Continued

Summary operator	Meaning
Sum	Add the values of a field or expression over a specified group of records
Average	Average values of a field or expression over a specified group of records
Count	Count the number of values in a specified group of records
High	The maximum value in a specified group of records
Low	The minimum value in a specified group of records

T I P   Use the *summary* operators in a header or footer only, usually in a footer. Summary operators are used with groups of records and are discussed more fully in Chapters 10 and 11.

Before you insert a calculated field, you must make sure that you have sufficient space in the report spec for the field. When placing fields in the table band, you may have to increase the size of a column (using the **R**esize command on the TableBand menu). In the employee telephone list example, you may decide to replace the name fields with one calculated field. First, you must remove the existing employee name fields. Figure 5.22 shows the report spec with only two columns remaining—the Emp Phone column and one for the new calculated field. The empty column has been resized to provide room for the full employee names. The remaining label in the table header also has been shortened to Phone.

To insert a calculated field, position the cursor where you want the new field to start. Access the Report and select **F**ield, **P**lace, **C**alculated. Paradox then prompts for an Expression. Type the formula for the new field. Be sure to enclose field names in brackets and text constants in double quotation marks. You can edit this expression in the same manner as any Paradox field, including use of the field view (Alt-F5). The following expression creates an employee name field that includes the three regular fields from the table:

[Emp First Name]+" "+[Emp Middle Initial]+" "+[Emp Last Name]

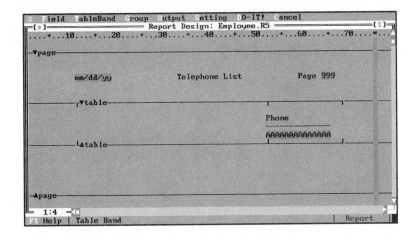

FIG. 5.22

Making room for a calculated field.

When the expression is as you want it, press Enter or select the OK button. Paradox prompts you to move the cursor to the starting position for the new field. If you already have moved the cursor to the proper starting point, press Enter again. Paradox places the field mask in the column in the indicated position. You can use the cursor-movement keys to increase or decrease the size of the field mask. Accept the size by pressing Enter once more, and the field is defined (see fig. 5.23). When the cursor is positioned within the field mask of a calculated field, Paradox displays the formula (the expression) in the status line at the bottom of the screen.

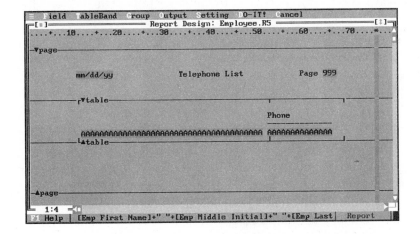

FIG. 5.23

The calculated field.

Notice the double quotation marks around each blank space in the expression for the new employee name field. This formula tells Paradox to leave one space between first name and middle initial and one space between middle initial and last name when printing the report. Figure 5.24 shows how the report looks when printed.

```
        06/04/92              Telephone List           Page   1


                              Phone
                              ---------------
        Harry H. Jones        (703) 555-1234
        Samantha T. Jones     (703) 555-8872
        Bruce R. Brown        (703) 555-4421
        Tim C. Bronson        (703) 555-7630
        Steven M. Harrison    (703) 555-4432
        Sarah S. Singer       (703) 555-8888
        Sharon B. Albertson   (703) 555-2361
        Stanley Q. Harrell    (703) 555-2351
        David E. Brown        (703) 555-9812
        Hercule P. Plum       (703) 555-2987
        George H. Green       (703) 555-9999
        Emily Q. Kellogs      (703) 555-3378
        Freda P. French       (703) 555-3322
        Angel L. Smith        (703) 555-2198
        Christopher P. Harvey (703) 555-3298
        Gertrude M. English   (703) 555-5575
        Joseph L. Quick       (703) 555-1298
        Susan T. Carson       (703) 555-3434
```

FIG. 5.24

The telephone list report with the calculated field.

Placing the Date and Page Fields

You may have noticed that Paradox supplies the system date and the page number at the top of each page when the program prints an instant report (refer to fig. 5.12). These two special fields also are included in the standard specification, under the designations mm/dd/yy and Page 999, respectively (refer to fig. 5.7). With the cursor in the date field, a message at the top of the screen reads Current date. Place the cursor in the page number field, and the message reads Current page number.

T I P Note that the word Page is not part of the field but is a text label (or *literal*) often used in front of the page number field to label it clearly.

You can remove these fields using the **Field, Erase** command from the Report menu and place them anywhere in the report. Usually the page number is in the page header or the page footer.

Suppose that you decide to erase the page number field and move the field into the page footer instead. To place a current page number field or a current date field in the report spec, select **Field**, **Place**, and then choose **Date** or **Page**, as appropriate. Position the cursor where the field should appear and press Enter. Finally, adjust the field size with the left- and right-arrow keys and press Enter again. For a page number field, you probably want to precede the field mask with the word *Page*, as shown in figure 5.25.

Cue:

To place a current page number field or a current date field, select **Field**, **Place** and choose **Date** or **Page**.

```
≡  Field  TableBand  Group  Output  Setting  DO-IT!  Cancel
┌─[■]═════════════ Report Design: Employee.R5 ═════════════[↕]─┐
│....+...10....+...20....+...30....+...40....+...50....+...60....+...70....*...│
│ ┌▼page───────────────────────────────────────────────────────
│
│      mm/dd/yy              Telephone List
│
│      ┌▼table──────────────────────────────────────────────
│                                           ┬                ┬
│                                           Phone
│                                           ─────────────
│      AAAAAAAAAAAAAAAAAAAAAAAAAAAAAAAAAAAAAAAAA AAAAAAAAAAAAAA │
│      └▲table──────────────────────────────────────────────
│                        Page  999
│
│
│ └▲page───────────────────────────────────────────────────────
│   1:4  ═◄┤                                              ►│
├ F1 Help │ Current page number                    │ Report ■
```

FIG. 5.25

Placing the current page number field.

Reformatting Fields

Paradox provides a way to change the size of alphanumeric and numeric fields (indicated on-screen by the size of the field mask) and the format of numeric and date fields.

To increase or reduce the field mask size, access the Report menu and select **Field**, **Reformat**. Move the cursor to the field to be modified and press Enter. For alphanumeric and memo fields, you then use the cursor-movement keys to change field size and press Enter to indicate when you are finished.

Cue:

To change mask size, select **Field**, **Reformat**.

For number fields, Paradox presents the following menu choices:

■ *Digits*. Choose this option to change the size of the mask. Use the cursor-movement keys to adjust the size; then press Enter. The first time you press Enter, Paradox sets the size to the left of the decimal and then asks you to adjust the number of decimal places. Press Enter again when you are finished.

■ *Sign-Convention.* After choosing this option, you must make another choice: between NegativeOnly, **P**arenNegative, and **A**lwaysSign. NegativeOnly, the default for number fields, shows a negative sign in front of negative numbers but no sign in front of positive numbers. The **P**arenNegative choice, the default for currency fields, places parentheses around negative dollar figures. The final option, **A**lwaysSign, shows the plus (+) or minus (–) sign in front of each number, as appropriate.

■ *Commas.* Select this option to add or delete the display of whole number separators.

■ *International.* You use this option to switch whole number separators from commas (U.S.Convention) to periods (International Convention).

To adjust the format of a date field, from the Report menu select **F**ield **R**eformat. Move the cursor to the date field and press Enter. Paradox displays a list of 12 formats:

    1) mm/dd/yy
    2) M o n t h dd, yyyy
    3) mm/dd
    4) mm/yy
    5) dd-Mon-yy
    6) Mon yy
    7) dd-Mon-yyyy
    8) mm/dd/yyyy
    9) dd.mm.yy
    10) dd/mm/yy
    11) yy-mm-dd
    12) yy.mm.dd

Select the format you need. The first format, mm/dd/yy, is the default.

FROM HERE...

For Related Information:

▶▶ "Placing and Erasing Fields on the Form," p. 301.

Using the Report Header

A *header* is that portion of the report that repeats at predetermined intervals, printing above the body. Headers can, and often do, include data from the table but usually only for the purpose of labeling a grouping of data. One Paradox report can have up to 19 different headers: the report header, the page header, the table header, and as many as 16 group headers. With this many choices, keeping them distinguished in your mind is sometimes difficult.

The *report header* is easy to distinguish from other types of headers because the report header prints only once, always at the beginning. A fairly typical use of the report header is to create a title page. You may, for example, want to use the following title page for the telephone list:

> Wonder Widgets of America
> Employee Telephone List

To begin creating this title page, position the cursor in the top line of the report spec screen by pressing the Home key. Your cursor is above the line labeled page and below the horizontal ruler line. A message in the status line tells you that you are working in the report header (see fig. 5.26).

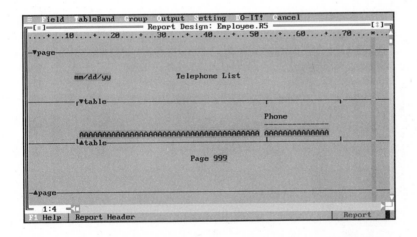

FIG. 5.26

Working in the report header.

First, make some space in which to work by inserting several blank lines. Type the text that you want to appear on the title page. As shown in figure 5.27, a report header does not usually get an entire page. You can insert anywhere in your report a page break that causes Paradox to skip to the next page when the program encounters the break. Type the word *PAGEBREAK* in all caps at the far left of the report specification. The finished report specification, with title page, is shown in figure 5.27. A printout of the report is shown in figure 5.28.

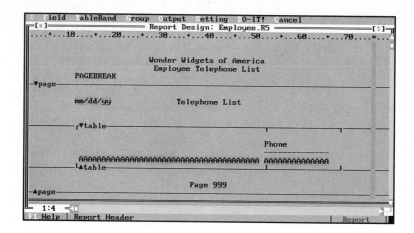

FIG. 5.27

Creating the title page.

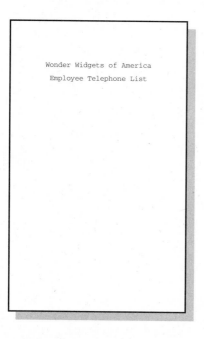

FIG. 5.28

The title page (left) and page 1 (right) of the telephone list report.

For Related Information:

▶▶ "Using Headers and Footers," p. 357.

Saving the Report Specification

After all the work of designing your report, you certainly do not want to have to repeat the procedure all over again the next time you want to use the report design. With Paradox, saving the report specification is easy. Press F2 (Do-It!). The report spec is saved to disk under the name you gave it. This report specification is a member of the family tied to the table for which you created the spec. If you later restructure the table, Paradox reconciles the report, to the extent possible. If, for example, you delete a field from the table structure, Paradox deletes that field from the report.

Cue:

Press F2 (Do-It!) to save the report specification.

Modifying the Report Specification

You may decide that you want to change your report not long after you thought you had finished it. With Paradox, making alterations is simple. You essentially just pick up where you left off.

Access the Paradox Main menu and select **R**eport, **C**hange. Choose the table's name and then select the name of the report you want to change. Press Enter or select OK at the Report Description prompt, and you are back in the report specification, just as you left it. All the features you have learned thus far about designing the report specification still apply. When you are finished making changes, press F2 (Do-It!), and Paradox saves the changes and returns you to the Main mode.

Cue:

To modify a report spec, access the Paradox Main menu and select **R**eport, **C**hange.

Controlling Output

After you design a report specification, you generally print the entire report on paper. Sometimes, however, you may want to print only a portion of the report, or perhaps send a portion to the screen rather than your printer. You may even want to create a file that contains an image of the report. Paradox provides the capability to do each of these things through the Report menus.

Using the Output Menu To Choose the Output Device

In addition to the Alt-F7 (Instant Report) keystroke option, Paradox has three ways to output your report through the Output menu: to printer, to screen, and to file. These choices are the same whether you already are in Report mode and in the middle of designing your report or whether you have saved the specification and are starting from the Main mode.

When starting from the Report mode, access the Report menu and select **O**utput. If you have finished designing your report and are back at the Main mode, access the Main menu and select **R**eport, **O**utput. Your next step is to select a table and a report name. Paradox then displays the following choices:

- *Printer*. This option sends the report to the printer. Choosing **P**rinter is the same as pressing Alt-F7 (Instant Report) while designing or changing the report specification.

- *Screen*. Use this choice to send the report to the screen. Paradox displays the report in the Report Preview window, in Preview mode. You can use cursor-movement keys and the mouse scroll bar to move around within the Report Preview window.

  The Preview mode has its own menu in the menu bar: Goto Search Cancel. Use **G**oto, **P**age to move to a specific page in the report preview, or **G**oto, **G**otoEnd to display the end of the report. Use Ctrl-Z (Zoom) or the **S**earch, **F**ind option to search for specific text in the report. After performing an initial search, you can use Alt-Z (Zoom Next) or the **S**earch, **N**ext option to find the next occurrence. You can close the window using **C**ancel or any of the other standard window closing procedures.

- *File*. This selection prints the report to a file. When prompted, enter a unique file name (perhaps with the extension ASC or TXT to remind you that the file is in ASCII format) and press Enter. This file is an exact image of how the report will look when printed to paper. The file can be used by any other program that can handle plain ASCII files.

Changing the Output Range

You may want to print only a few of the pages of your entire report. Paradox refers to the number of pages as the *output range*. When you need to change the output range, choose **R**eport, **R**angeOutput from the Main menu. Select the proper table, report, and device (**P**rinter,

Screen, or File). Paradox then asks for the beginning page number and suggests the number 1 as the default. Change this number to the number of the first page that should be printed; then press Enter. Next, enter the number of the last page to be printed. Leave this response blank if you want Paradox to print all the way to the end of the report. When you press Enter, Paradox sends the appropriate portion of the report to the chosen device.

For Related Information:

▶▶ "Controlling the Printer," p. 375.

FROM HERE...

Using Reports on a Network

With Paradox, using reports on a network is almost identical to using them on a stand-alone system. When you start to print a report based on a shared table, everything works as usual unless another user happens to be working with the table. In that case, Paradox takes a snapshot of the table during a period when no changes are being made to the table and then runs your report from the snapshot. Using this method, you can print a report on a table even while it is being viewed or edited by another user on the network.

For Related Information:

◀◀ "Creating Tables on a Network," p. 82.

FROM HERE...

Chapter Summary

This chapter is a Paradox report-writing primer, introducing you to the fundamentals of designing, building, and printing reports from your Paradox data. This chapter barely began to show you all the program's reporting features, however. When you feel ready to delve a bit deeper into creating more powerful tabular tables, take a look at Chapter 10. For details about creating custom free-form reports, check out Chapter 11. Before you move on to Part II of this book, "Paradox Power Techniques," read the next chapter to learn how you can use Paradox scripts to automate some of the commands and techniques you already have learned.

Getting Started with Scripts and Keyboard Macros

One of the tasks computers do best is automate repetitive routines. Paradox helps you automate your database-related tasks by enabling you to record your keystrokes for later use. The program stores the recorded keystrokes in *script* files. This chapter describes how to record and play back Paradox scripts and introduces you to the Paradox Script Editor, which you use to modify and enhance your recorded scripts.

After discussing scripts in general, this chapter describes how to create *keyboard macros*, multiple keystrokes that you can execute by pressing a single key or key combination. You learn how to create keyboard macros to make your database usable by nearly anyone, with little or no training.

An Overview of Paradox Scripts

This first portion of this chapter gives you a brief overview of Paradox scripts and answers several general questions you may have about scripts and their uses.

What Are Paradox Scripts?

Many popular PC programs have some capability to record keystrokes. Recorded sets of keystrokes often are called *keyboard macros* because you usually run them by pressing a key or key combination. In Paradox, keyboard macros are just one special use of the more encompassing *scripts* feature.

With Paradox, you can create a script to perform any task that you can do yourself. Scripts can automate those routines that you find yourself having to do over and over. The easiest way to create this type of script is to turn on a keystroke recorder and then press the proper keys for the operation. When the task is complete, turn off the recorder, and Paradox saves the script. The next time you want to perform the same operation, you *play* the script. At your command, Paradox executes every keystroke that you previously recorded.

You also can assign a script to a particular key or key combination, which you then press to play the script. Scripts assigned to keys are keyboard macros.

How Useful Are Paradox Scripts?

The most important use of Paradox scripts is to program entire turn-key, menu-driven, database applications. You create these powerful scripts through the applications generator, the *Paradox Application Workshop (PAW)*, or by typing them in the *Paradox Script Editor*. You can incorporate already recorded scripts into new scripts as you can create them. These types of sophisticated scripts use the commands of the *Paradox Application Language* (PAL). Because scripts that use PAL are essentially programs, Paradox users often use the terms script and program interchangeably.

This chapter, however, concentrates on creating simple scripts used to play back your keystrokes. Refer to Part III of this book for information on how to use Paradox, the Application Workshop, and PAL for application development.

Because scripts can become a part of powerful, customized database applications, many users are reluctant to give scripts a try. You have nothing to lose, however, and much to gain by learning to create Paradox scripts. Even in their simplest form, these tools can increase your speed and accuracy in performing almost any database task. The computer always can press keys faster than you can and never makes typos. As the complexity of your database tasks increases, the value of scripts to reduce repetition increases even faster. Playing a script that automates a multitable query, for example, saves you more keystrokes and effort than does using a script to perform a single-table query.

Scripts certainly save knowledgeable users time and effort. Perhaps even more important, scripts can enable novice users to accomplish tasks they would otherwise not be able to perform. Entering data in form view, for example, is something that most clerical personnel can handle. They may, however, be less comfortable having to execute the commands necessary to display the entry form in the first place. You can record a script to display the form, letting data-entry personnel stick to entering data.

What Kinds of Tasks Can Scripts Perform?

Almost any operation you can perform with Paradox can be assisted or completely automated by a script. You can, for example, easily record the following tasks as scripts:

- Displaying the Customer table in form view and DataEntry mode
- Displaying data from the Orders and Detail tables together for a particular order number
- Printing a report showing employee salaries from the Employee table

Turn on the script recorder and go through the steps one time. After that, you or anyone else can perform the operations by playing the script. You probably can teach even your boss how to do it.

Can You Edit Paradox Scripts?

Using the Paradox Editor, you can modify and enhance your Paradox scripts. This editor is the same editor you use to enter data in a memo field. Refer to Chapter 3 for a detailed discussion of the Paradox Editor.

Through the Editor, you can delete or correct errant keystrokes, make changes necessitated by additions or deletions from your tables, and add the powerful features available through the Paradox Application Language.

How Are Scripts Stored?

Reminder:
Paradox gives all scripts the extension SC.

Each script is a Paradox object and is saved to disk as a separate file. The *instant script* always is saved with the name INSTANT.SC. Paradox gives all scripts the file-name extension SC. You must name other scripts according to the following rules:

- The name can contain up to eight characters (not including the file-name extension).

- You can use letters, numbers, and the following special characters:

  $ # & @ ! % ( ) - _ { } ' ^

- You cannot include spaces.

- You cannot create duplicate names.

Reminder:
Scripts are not a part of any one table's family of objects.

Scripts are not a part of any one table's family of objects. If you modify the structure of a table in a way that causes a script to no longer work properly, Paradox does not reconcile the error. You have to use the Editor to modify the script accordingly. (For more information, see the section "Editing Scripts," later in this chapter.)

FROM HERE...

For Related Information:

▶▶ "PAL Scripts," p. 516.

◀◀ "Saving a Query," p. 180.

Recording and Playing Scripts

You have three ways to record scripts:

- You can use Alt-F3 (Instant Script Record) to create a temporary script to record keystrokes that you expect to use several times in the current session but don't want to save for later use. Paradox automatically names this script INSTANT.

■ You can use the **B**eginRecord command from the Scripts menu. Most scripts are recorded with this method.

■ You can use the **B**eginRecord command from the PAL Menu (Alt-F10 displays the PAL Menu).

■ You can use the Scripts menu's **Q**uerySave command, introduced in Chapter 4, to save a query for future use.

The first two of these methods are covered in the discussions that follow. Refer to Chapter 4, "Getting Started with Query By Example," to review how to save a query with **Q**uerySave.

Recording and Playing an Instant Script

You can begin recording a script instantly by pressing Alt-F3 (Instant Script Record). Paradox places the letter R in the lower right corner of the screen, at the right end of the status bar, to remind you that a script is being recorded. You then execute the keystrokes and commands as usual. When you have finished the operation, stop the instant recorder by pressing Alt-F3 again.

Cue:
To start and stop recording an instant script, press Alt-F3.

> **CAUTION:** Paradox treats the instant script like the program treats temporary tables. Each time you create an instant script, any previous instant script is erased without warning. To save an instant script, use the **R**ename command on the Tools menu to rename the script to some other valid script name. You must rename the script before you start recording another instant script.

Cue:
To play an instant script, press Alt-F4.

Playing an instant script is just as easy as recording the script—press Alt-F4 (Instant Script Play). Every keystroke you make while recording the instant script is played back in sequence but you do not see the results of each keypress. The screen remains unchanged until the script is finished. Then Paradox refreshes your screen.

Use instant scripts to perform tasks that you expect to have to repeat several times within the same session. These tasks may be simple or complicated but keep in mind that this type of script is temporary.

Suppose that you expect to view the Orders table several times during the current Paradox session but you don't want to have to press the necessary keystrokes, and you don't need a permanent script for this purpose. To record an instant script that displays Orders, start the recorder by pressing Alt-F3 (Instant Script Record). When you see the R message at the right end of the status line, execute the following keystrokes to view Orders:

1. Press F10 (Menu) to display the Main menu.
2. Select **V**iew.
3. Press Enter and select the Orders table.

When the Orders table appears on the desktop, turn off the recorder by pressing Alt-F3. Paradox has recorded your keystrokes as the script named INSTANT. Press Alt-F4 (Instant Script Play), and Paradox displays Orders. You do not need to be at the Main menu but you do need to be in Main mode.

Reminder:
Play a script from the mode in which you recorded it.

A script can be played successfully only from the mode in which you recorded the script. If you try to run a script from a different mode, Paradox balks and displays a menu with two options: **C**ancel and **D**ebug.

Figure 6.1, for example, shows the result of pressing Alt-F4 (Instant Script Play) to play the instant script for displaying Orders. Because Paradox is in Edit mode and the script was recorded in Main mode, the script does not run. Instead, you see the **C**ancel and **D**ebug options.

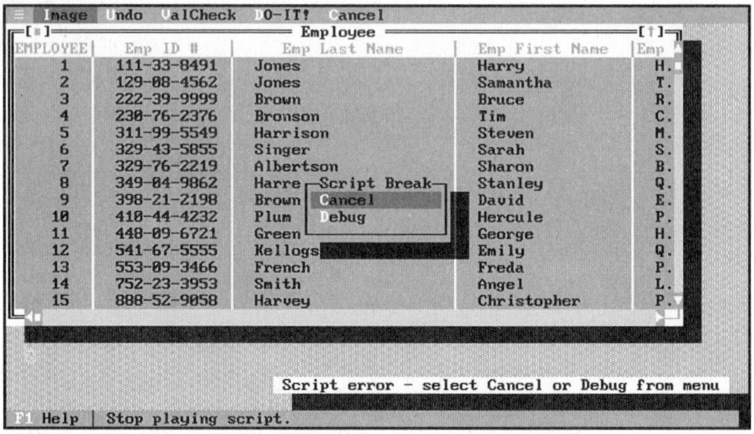

FIG. 6.1

Playing a script from the wrong mode.

To discover why the script does not play, select **D**ebug. Paradox displays the message `Not a possible menu choice` near the lower right corner of the screen and the offending line of the script in an inverse video line at the screen's bottom edge (see fig. 6.2).

In this case, the script contains only one line:

```
{View} {Orders}
```

This line means that you pressed the **V**iew and **O**rders selections on the menu in succession. Because the Edit menu does not include a **V**iew option, however, the script does not run. You have two easy ways to remedy this problem:

■ Cancel Debug by pressing Ctrl-Q. Return to the Main mode and rerun the instant script.

■ Return to the Main mode from Debug—in this case by selecting Cancel, Yes—and continue the script by pressing Ctrl-G.

Return to the Main mode by pressing F2 (Do-It!) and saving your work.

If an error occurs while you are playing an instant script, usually you should choose Cancel. Make sure that you are in the correct mode before trying to play the script again.

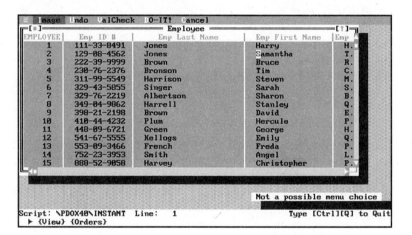

FIG. 6.2

Finding the error with **D**ebug.

Using BeginRecord and End-Record To Record a Script

Paradox provides methods of recording a script from any Paradox mode. To start recording a script from the Main menu, select **S**cripts, **B**eginRecord. Then type a valid script name and press Enter. If you enter a script name that you already have used, Paradox warns you and gives you the option to either cancel the recorder or replace the existing script. As with instant scripts, after Paradox begins to record your keystrokes, the program displays R in the lower right corner of the status line (see fig. 6.3). You can execute keystrokes as usual, and Paradox shadows your every move.

Cue:
To start recording a script from the Main menu, select **S**cripts, **B**eginRecord.

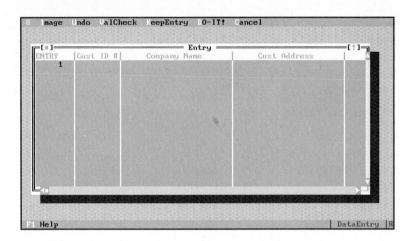

FIG. 6.3

The letter R appears in the status line, indicating that a script is being recorded.

If you need to begin recording in a mode other than the Main mode, use the PAL menu to access the Scripts menu. Press Alt-F10 (PAL Menu) and select **B**eginRecord.

Cue:
To stop recording, select **S**cripts, **E**ndRecord.

To end the recording session from Main mode, access the Main menu and select **S**cripts, End-Record. Paradox saves the script as a file on your working directory and removes the R from the screen. The file has the same name as the script, with the file name extension SC.

As with the **B**eginRecord option, if you are not in Main mode when you need to end the recording, you have to use the PAL menu. In that case, press Alt-F10 (PAL Menu) and then select **E**nd-Record.

Suppose that you want to create a script named CENTRY (for Customer ENTRY) that displays the Customer table in DataEntry mode and form view. Start recording the script by selecting **S**cripts from the Main menu and selecting **B**eginRecord. Type *centry* as the script name and press Enter. Paradox begins recording. To access Customer in Data Entry mode, access the Main menu and select **M**odify, **D**ataEntry, press Enter at the Table: prompt and choose the Customer table. Switch to form view by pressing F7 (Form Toggle). Finally, to maximize the window, press Alt-space bar to display the System menu and select **M**aximize/Restore. Turn off the recorder by pressing Alt-F10 (PAL Menu) and then selecting **E**nd-Record.

You now have a script named CENTRY, which quickly displays a full-screen data entry form for the Customer table in DataEntry mode. The next section describes how to use the **P**lay option to run the script.

Cue:
To stop recording without saving, select **S**cripts, **C**ancel.

You may decide that you have made a mistake while recording the script and want to start over rather than try to fix the script. To stop recording the script without saving it, access the Main menu and select **S**cripts, **C**ancel. If not in Main mode, press Alt-F10 (PAL Menu) to display the PAL menu, and select **C**ancel. Paradox stops the recorder but does not write a script to disk.

Using the Play Option To Run a Script

Just as you can record a script from any Paradox mode, you can play a script from any mode. You must, however, play the script from the same mode in which you began recording.

To play a script from the Main mode, access the Main menu and select **S**cripts, **P**lay. Press Enter at the `Script:` prompt to display a list of available scripts. Select your script and press Enter or select the OK button. Paradox runs the script.

Cue:
To play a script, select **S**cripts, **P**lay from the main menu.

In the CENTRY example discussed in the preceding section, Paradox displays the Customer DataEntry screen when you run the CENTRY script.

Use the PAL menu to start a script from any mode other than Main mode. Press Alt-F10 (PAL Menu), select **P**lay, and choose your script.

Another way to run a script is to use a command line argument when you load Paradox. If you type *PARADOX CENTRY*, Paradox loads and runs the script called CENTRY. The main Paradox screen doesn't come up if you use this technique.

T I P

CAUTION: You can stop a script in midstream by pressing Ctrl-Break, but use this command carefully because it also may cancel other Paradox operations. Suppose that you run a script while editing a table but then decide to stop the script prematurely. You press Ctrl-Break once to halt the script. If you press Ctrl-Break a second time, however, Paradox cancels your edit session without saving any changes or entries that you may have made.

Displaying a Script Step-by-Step

You may not get the results you expect when you play a script. One way to discover the cause is to have Paradox display each step as the script is executed. This option is available for scripts that begin in Main mode only.

Cue:

To display every step, select **S**cripts, **S**howPlay.

Paradox usually displays the final outcome of a script. If you want the program to display the result of every step, access the Main menu and select **S**cripts, **S**howPlay. After you choose a script, Paradox displays another menu, which contains the following options:

- *Fast.* Choose this option to tell Paradox to play the script quickly. This speed is not particularly helpful when you are trying to discover an error but the choice may be preferable if the script is long and you think the problem is near the end of the script.

- *Slow.* This choice plays the script at a pace slow enough that you can keep up easily.

The actual speed of either selection depends on the speed of your computer.

Running a Script Repeatedly

Cue:

To run a script repeatedly, select **S**cripts, **R**epeatPlay.

One of the more interesting options available in Paradox is the **R**epeatPlay choice on the Scripts and PAL menus. To have the program run a script several times in rapid succession, either access the Main menu and select **S**cripts, **R**epeatPlay, or press Alt-F10 (PAL Menu) and select **R**epeatPlay.

Select the script, and Paradox displays the prompt Number of times to repeat:. Type a positive whole number and press Enter. Paradox then executes the script the specified number of times. If you want Paradox to run the script continuously, enter the letter *C* rather than a number in response to the prompt.

This feature is quite useful when making the same change to a particular field in dozens of records. Rather than edit each record, you can record an instant script while correcting the first record and then use the **R**epeatPlay option to make the change to as many records as necessary.

You also can use this repeating feature to print multiple copies of a report. If you have a script that prints the report, use **R**epeatPlay to run the script once for each copy you want. Otherwise, just record an instant script to print one report and then use **R**epeatPlay.

Perhaps the flashiest use of **R**epeatPlay is to create a graphics show on a network. Refer to Chapter 12, "Using Paradox Graphics," for a description of how to use this script feature to display a graph that is updated continuously as network users change the underlying data.

For Related Information:

▶▶ "Using the PAL Debugger," p. 606.

FROM HERE...

Editing Scripts

The Paradox Editor, introduced in Chapter 3, provides a method for editing your scripts. Without this feature, you have to rerecord any macro that requires alterations, even if you need to make only a minor change. This section just touches on the basic features of editing scripts. Part III of this book introduces you to the use of the Editor as a tool for applications development and PAL programming.

Beginning the Editor

To begin the Editor and display a previously recorded script, access the Main menu and select **S**cripts, **E**ditor, **O**pen. Type the name of the script you want to change; or press Enter and select the script name from the list displayed. Paradox displays your script in a window similar to figure 6.4. Notice that Paradox is in Script mode.

Cue:
To begin the Paradox Editor, select **S**cripts, **E**ditor, **O**pen.

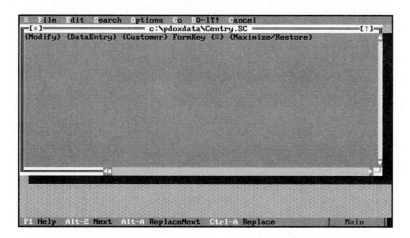

FIG. 6.4

Using the Editor to edit the CENTRY script.

Understanding Special Script Key Codes

When you display a recorded script, you probably can recognize most of the words the script has used to record the keys you pressed. Menu options are enclosed in braces ({ }), and keys and keystroke commands are represented by special code words that duplicate or closely resemble the key names or commands. Table 6.1 lists these special codes.

Table 6.1. Script Codes for Special Keys and Keystroke Commands

Key or Keystroke command	Script code
Home	Home
End	End
PgUp	PgUp
PgDn	PgDn
Left arrow	Left
Right arrow	Right
Up arrow	Up
Down arrow	Down
Ins	Ins
Del	Del
Backspace	Backspace
Esc	Esc
Enter	Enter
Tab	Tab
Shift Tab	ReverseTab
Ctrl-Break	CtrlBreak
Ctrl-Home	CtrlHome
Ctrl-End	CtrlEnd
Ctrl-Left arrow	CtrlLeft
Ctrl-Right arrow	CtrlRight
Ctrl-Backspace	CtrlBackspace
Ctrl-PgUp	CtrlPgUp

Key or Keystroke command	Script code
Ctrl-PgDn	CtrlPgDn
Alt-X	CrossTabKey
Ctrl-D	Ditto
Ctrl-O	DOS
Alt-O	DOSBig
Ctrl-F	FieldView
Alt-K	KeyLookup
Ctrl-L	ReSyncKey
Alt-L	LockKey
Ctrl-R	Rotate
Alt-R	Refresh
Ctrl-U	Undo
Ctrl-V	VertRuler
Ctrl-Y	DeleteLine
Ctrl-Z	Zoom
Alt-Z	ZoomNext
F1	Help
F2	DO_IT!
F3	UpImage
F4	DownImage
F5	Example
F6	Check
F7	FormKey
F8	ClearImage
F9	EditKey
F10	Menu
Alt-F3	InstantRecord
Alt-F4	InstantPlay
Alt-F5	FieldView
Alt-F6	CheckPlus
Alt-F7	InstantReport

continues

Table 6.1. Continued

Key or Keystroke command	Script code
Alt-F8	ClearAll
Alt-F9	CoeditKey
Ctrl-F6	CheckDescending
Ctrl-F7	GraphKey
Shift-F6	GroupBy

Assume that you want to modify the CENTRY script so that it uses CoEdit rather than DataEntry mode to enter new records into Customer. Change the {DataEntry} command in CENTRY to {CoEdit} and add the codes for the End and PgDn keystrokes to the end of the script so that the cursor moves to a blank record at the end of the Customer table. This script is so short that rerecording it is as easy as modifying it. This example, however, demonstrates the same procedure you would use to edit a longer script.

When you are editing a script, you can make it easier to read and follow by moving each command to its own line. In the CENTRY script, for example, first turn on Insert mode by pressing the Ins key. Then place the cursor on the left brace portion ({) of the {DataEntry} command and press Enter. {DataEntry} and the other commands to its right move down to the second line (see fig. 6.5).

After you repeat this procedure for the other two commands, Paradox displays the screen shown in figure 6.6.

Then edit the CENTRY script and create the version shown in figure 6.7. (Replace {DataEntry} with {CoEdit} and add the commands End and PgDn to the end of the script.)

Saving a Script's Changes

Cue:
To save your changes,
press F2 (Do-It!).

As with many other Paradox commands, you can complete the script editing process and save your changes by pressing F2 (Do-It!). Paradox replaces the original script with the newly modified version and then returns you to the Main mode.

Paradox also provides a way to save and test the script. Press F10 (Menu) and select **G**o. Paradox saves and then plays the new script.

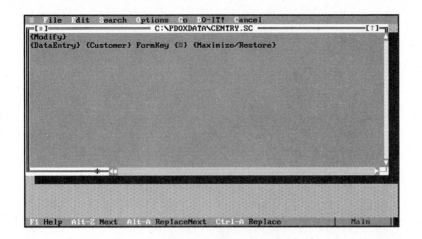

FIG. 6.5

Pressing Enter before the {DataEntry} command.

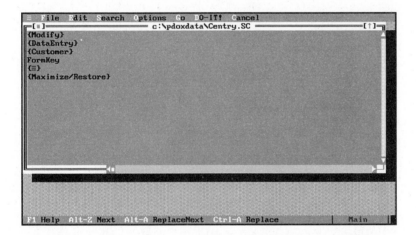

FIG. 6.6

Each command on its own line.

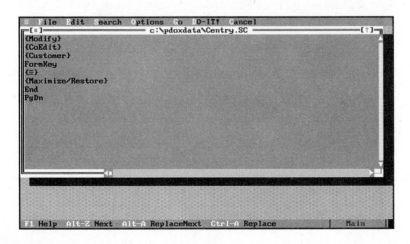

FIG. 6.7

The new version of CENTRY.

Refer to Part III, "Programming Paradox," for further ideas on using the Paradox Editor to write and edit PAL scripts.

FROM HERE...

For Related Information:

▶▶ "Keypress Interactions," p. 539.

▶▶ "Using the Script Editor," p. 593.

Using the INIT Script

Every time you turn on your computer, the operating system (DOS) searches the boot disk for a file named AUTOEXEC.BAT. When DOS can locate this special script-like file, the system executes the AUTOEXEC.BAT file. If DOS cannot find the file, however, the system starts the computer by asking for the current date and time. Most PCs have an AUTOEXEC.BAT file on the root directory of the boot disk. This file usually is used to start a program or display a menu when you turn on the computer. Because you must have a hard disk to use Paradox 4.0, your system undoubtedly has an AUTOEXEC.BAT file that is executed at start-up.

Reminder:
At start-up, Paradox searches for a script file named INIT.SC.

When you start Paradox, rather than look for an AUTOEXEC.BAT file, Paradox searches the start-up directory for a script file named INIT. The Paradox documentation suggests that you place this script file in the directory that contains the Paradox program files. This directory is the appropriate one only if you start Paradox from there. If you use the method suggested in Quick Start 1 and Appendix A to start Paradox from your working directory, create and save the INIT script, just as you would any other script. Paradox saves INIT to the proper start-up directory.

The INIT script usually is used to perform operations that you routinely do every time you start Paradox. The nature of these tasks depends entirely upon the type of work you do with the program. One powerful use of INIT is to assign keyboard macros for use throughout your Paradox session. The next section shows how you can use INIT in this manner.

For Related Information:

▶▶ "Playing a Script," p. 517.

FROM HERE...

Creating Keyboard Macros

A *keyboard macro* is a script assigned to a particular key or key combination. This use of scripts is closest to the kind of macros found in most other popular programs.

You can create keyboard macros in a number of ways. The easiest method is to record the keystrokes for the macro as a normal script. Use whatever valid script name you want. When the script is working properly, use the Script Editor to create another script that contains the following PAL command:

```
SETKEY x PLAY "script_name"
```

Replace *x* with one of the key codes listed in Appendix C of this book and replace *script_name* with the name of the script that you recorded.

When assigning macro keys, follow several common-sense rules: **T I P**

- Do not assign a macro to any commonly used key, such as a single letter or a number.

- Do not assign a macro to a key or key combination already used by Paradox for some special purpose.

- Use mnemonics (memory aids) when assigning macro key names. If your macro's purpose is to add data to the Customer table, for example, use a name such as Ctrl-C for Customer.

Perhaps the best place for SETKEY commands—especially for assigning keyboard macros that you want to use routinely—is the INIT script, discussed in the preceding section. You may want, for example, to assign the CENTRY script to the key combination Ctrl-C. Use the INIT script to set up this assignment so that the Ctrl-C key combination is redefined for the entire Paradox session. Then your data-entry person can press Ctrl-C from anywhere in Main mode to have Paradox immediately display a blank data-entry form. Use the Paradox Editor to place the following command in the INIT script:

```
SETKEY 3 PLAY "CENTRY"
```

The number 3 is the ASCII code for the Ctrl-C key combination. This code is found in Appendix C. Save the new INIT script by pressing F2 (Do-It!). The next time you start Paradox, pressing Ctrl-C displays a CoEdit data-entry screen for Customer like the one shown in figure 6.8.

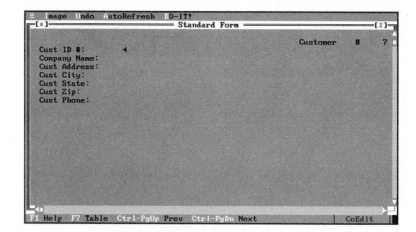

FIG. 6.8

The Customer CoEdit mode data-entry screen.

FROM HERE...

For Related Information:

▶▶ "SETKEY," p. 920.

Using Scripts on a Network

The following rules apply to the use of scripts from a shared network directory:

- Paradox imposes no limitation on how many users can play a particular script at the same time.

- No other user can play or edit a script that you currently are editing.

- No other user can edit a script while you are playing it.

For Related Information:

◄◄ "Creating Tables on a Network," p. 82.

FROM HERE...

Chapter Summary

This is the last chapter in Part I, "Paradox Fundamentals." Now that you have completed this portion of the book, take some time to practice all that you have learned. Create a database or two and play around with data entry, editing, queries, reports, scripts, and macros. Try each feature covered in these first six chapters until you understand clearly how the features work and what they accomplish. Learning any PC program, especially a database management system, is a building process. When you feel confident in your understanding of Paradox fundamentals, move on to Part II, "Paradox Power Techniques."

Paradox Power Techniques

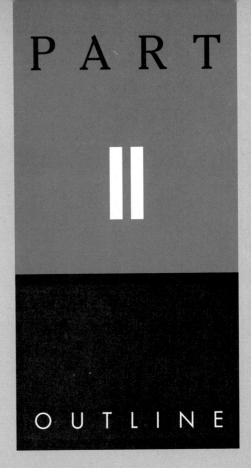

PART

II

OUTLINE

Quick Start 2: Using Advanced Paradox Features

This lesson is the second of two quick starts included in this book. Each quick start is designed to help you get a running start with Paradox. Quick Start 2 is based on the assumption that you have finished Part I of this book or are familiar with the information covered there. Now that you have discovered the ease of working with the fundamental features of Paradox, you are ready to move on to the more powerful capabilities of the program.

In this lesson, you get a taste of the topics presented in Part II—from multitable queries to graphics. After building a few tables, you perform multitable queries to produce a list of orders showing customer names and to find the name of the customer who placed a particular order. Next, you design a data-entry form for the Orders table and add validity checking that prevents you from accidentally entering an invalid customer ID number or a nonexistent employee ID number. You then use your new form to enter several orders into the Orders table. To get a quick glimpse of custom report design, you next create a tabular report that calculates the totals for the orders entered in Orders and Detail. In the last portion of this lesson, you create a graph that compares the numbers of each type of widget your company sold for the month.

You can use one of two approaches to studying this quick start. You can go straight through the quick start and then go to Chapter 7, or you can read this lesson one section at a time, stopping to study the applicable chapter before moving to the next part of the lesson. The various parts of this quick start are progressive, however, so you need to complete the earlier sections before you can do the later ones.

Building the Database

Before you can begin this lesson, you need to have a few tables with which to work. If you have not already done so, build the Employee table described in Quick Start 1. Then use the procedures you learned in Part I of this book to create the following tables. These tables are essentially the same ones that have been used to create the book's screen examples:

Customer field	Type	Orders field	Type
Cust ID #	A4*	Order #	N*
Company Name	A20	Cust ID #	A4
Cust Address	A20	Emp ID #	A11
Cust City	A20	Date	D
Cust State	A2	Notes	M240
Cust Zip	A5		
Cust Phone	A14		

Product field	Type	Detail field	Type
Model #	A4*	Order #	N*
Product Name	A20	Item #	N*
Price	$	Model #	A4
Cost	$	Quantity	N

Use table or form view to enter the following data:

Table QS2.1. Customer Table

Cust ID #	Customer data	Cust ID #	Customer data
1000	Eastern Enterprises 1211 Commerce St. Springfield, VA 22150 (703) 555-2355	1001	Alpha Freight Lines 720 Port Royal Fairfax, VA 22030 (703) 555-8092
1002	Ace Airplanes 777 Kittyhawk Dr. Gaithersburg, MD 20877 (301) 555-2777	1003	Hidden Resorts 6601 Wales Rd. Vienna, VA 22180 (703) 555-9662
1004	Sangster Insurance 1411 Reservation Dr. Springfield, VA 22152 (703) 555-9995	1005	Signal Plumbing 3333 Half Street Oxon Hill, MD 20745 (301) 555-8379

Table QS2.2. Orders Table

Order #	Cust ID #	Emp ID #	Date
100	1000	230-76-2376	9/02/92
101	1003	329-76-2219	9/07/92
102	1001	987-31-9873	9/08/92
103	1002	111-33-8491	9/12/92
104	1005	129-08-4562	9/13/92
105	1000	329-76-2219	9/16/92

Order #	Notes
100	This order was received by FAX.
101	Special shipping instructions:

Ship 10 ea. A333 and 5 ea. X155 to:
    Hidden Resorts 2
    4747 Sharp Rd.
    Ocean City, MD 20640

Ship remaining items to invoice address.

continues

Table QS2.2. Continued

Order #	Notes
102	This is a telephone order. Signature on file.
103	None
104	Special shipping instructions:
	Address to:
	Sam E. Ford
	Signal Plumbing Receiving
	3121 Half Street
	Oxon Hill, MD 20745
105	None

Table QS2.3. Product Table

Model #	Product name	Price	Cost
A333	Standard Widget	39.95	19.75
A334	Standard Widget Plus	43.95	21.15
A335	Special Widget	59.95	24.20
B107	Enhanced Widget	49.95	23.60
C777	Jumbo Widget	55.95	24.66
G400	Deluxe Widget	59.95	25.15
V107	Royal Widget	69.95	27.50
X155	Imperial Widget	79.95	32.50

Detail Table

Order #	Item #	Model #	Quantity
100	1	A333	50
100	2	B107	25

Order #	Item #	Model #	Quantity
100	3	G400	10
101	1	A333	15
101	2	X155	10
102	1	G400	35
102	2	A333	10
103	1	G400	22
103	2	X155	5
104	1	B107	45
105	1	G400	30

Notice the relationships between these files (including the Employee table from Quick Start 1). Using the notation technique described in Chapter 2, you can depict the relationships as shown in the following chart:

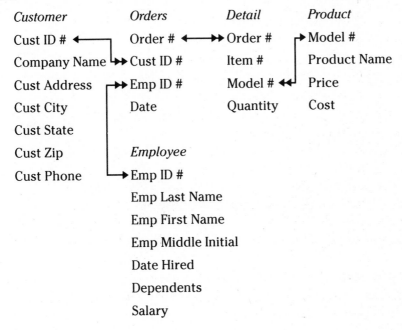

Performing a Multitable Query

Now that you have a database with several tables, you can perform a query to pull information from more than one table. (Chapter 7 covers the topic of multitable queries.) First, do a single-table query on the Orders table to look at the list of all orders. Then query Orders and Customer to try to match the proper company name in the Customer table with each order in the Orders table. Finally, look up only the data for Order #105. Complete the following steps:

1. To list all the orders, select **Ask** from the Main menu. Select the Orders table and use F6 (Check Mark) in the query form to select the Order #, Cust ID #, and Date fields (see fig. QS2.1). Execute the query by pressing F2 (Do-It!). Paradox displays the screen shown in figure QS2.2.

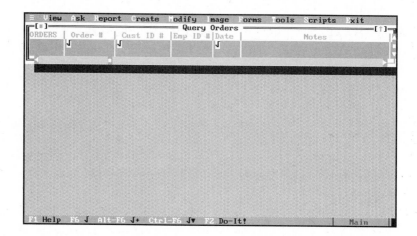

FIG. QS2.1

Building a single-table query.

2. The Answer table does not show the name of the company that placed each order. To add that information, you need to query Customer along with Orders. Clear the Answer table from the desktop by clicking on the window's close box or by making that window active and pressing F8 (Close Active Window). Access the Main menu and select **Ask**. Choose the Customer table. Paradox adds a second query form to the desktop.

3. You need to tell Paradox to use the Cust ID # field as the link between the Customer and Orders tables. You send this message by using *example elements*. Move the cursor to the Cust ID # field of the Customer table, press F5 (Example), and type *abc*. Paradox displays abc in inverse video as the example element in the Cust ID # column of the query form. Also place a check mark in the

Company Name column so that this column is included in the Answer table (see fig. QS2.3).

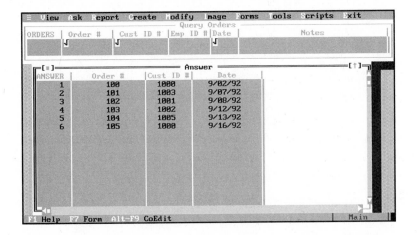

FIG. QS2.2

The Answer table for a single-table query.

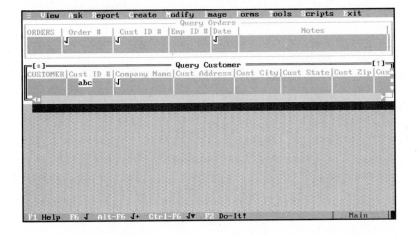

FIG. QS2.3

Building a multitable query.

4. To complete the link between Orders and Customer, you must place a matching example element in the linking field of the Orders table. Press F3 (Up Image) and move to the Cust ID # field. Press F5 (Example), type *abc*, and press Enter. Paradox displays abc in the column in inverse video (see fig. QS2.4). Now press F2 (Do-It!). The resulting Answer table shows the Order #, Cust ID #, Date, and Company Name fields (see fig. QS2.5).

5. Next, you want to see the same information, but for Order #105 only. While displaying the screen shown in figure QS2.5, clear the Answer table's window by clicking the window's close box, or by

pressing F8 (Close Active Window). To perform the query for Order #105 only, move the cursor to the Order # column in the Orders query form, type *105* (do *not* press F5 this time), and press F2 (Do-It!). Paradox displays one row of data, for Order #105 only.

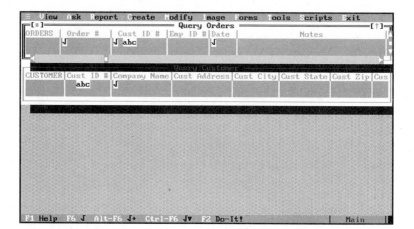

FIG. QS2.4

Example elements linking Orders with Customer through Cust ID #.

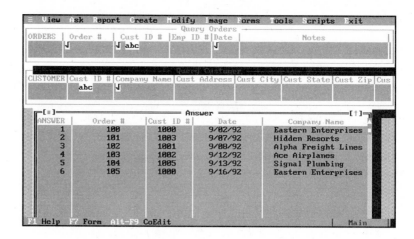

FIG. QS2.5

The Answer table for a multitable query.

Designing an Entry Form

Paradox does a good job of designing a form for each table, but you may want to design a form more to your liking. You also may want to add many of the editing aids that Paradox makes available. In this portion of the lesson, you learn to custom design a form for the Orders table. Chapter 8 covers "Using Advanced Form Techniques" in more detail.

To design a form, follow these steps:

1. Select **F**orms, **D**esign from the Main menu. Select the Orders table, press 1, and press Enter to select form number 1. At the Form description: prompt, type *Orders Entry Form* and press Enter. Paradox displays an empty Form Designer window, the mode indicator Form in the status line, and the message 1,1 1:1 in the lower left corner of the window.

2. As you use the cursor-movement keys to move around the screen, the cursor-position indicator changes. The first number tells you the screen row (1 to 23), and the second number tells you the screen column (1 to 80). The third and fourth numbers indicate the current page number and the total number of pages, respectively. Move the cursor to position <4,28> and type *Master Order Entry Form*. This phrase is a title for the form and does not affect data that goes into the Orders table. Also type the following labels, starting at the positions indicated (see fig. QS2.6):

Order Number:	<7,10>
Date:	<7,45>
Customer Identification Number:	<10,10>
Salesperson's Identification Number:	<13,10>
Notes:	<16,10>

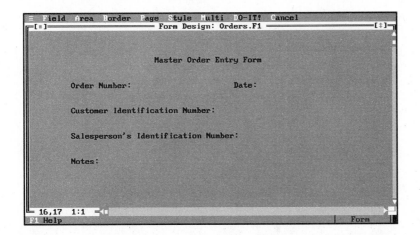

FIG. QS2.6

The title and labels for the Orders table entry form.

3. Place the fields next to the labels. Move the cursor to the right of the Order Number label to position <7,24>, leaving one blank space. Make sure that Paradox is not in Insert mode. To place the Order # field here, access the Main menu and select **F**ield, **P**lace, **R**egular, **O**rder_#. Then press Enter. Paradox displays a dashed line 23 characters long. This line is too long, and the Date label is

partially obliterated. Press the left-arrow key 16 times to shorten the line until exactly seven dashes remain. Press Enter to accept this length for the field. Paradox responds by displaying a solid underscore, seven characters in length, beginning at position <7,24>. Follow a similar procedure to place the remaining fields in the positions indicated:

Field	Starting position	Ending position
Date	<7,51>	<7,61>
Cust ID #	<10,43>	<10,46>
Emp ID #	<13,47>	<13,57>
Notes	<16,17>	<16,67>

4. Now draw a border around the forms, placing the upper left corner at <2,5> and the lower right corner at <18,72>. Start by positioning the cursor at <2,5>. To draw the border, access the menu bar and select **B**order, **P**lace, **S**ingle-line. Then press Enter. Use the cursor-movement keys to move the cursor to position <18,72> and press Enter.

5. When you are finished, your screen should look similar to figure QS2.7. To save the form, press F2 (Do-It!).

FIG. QS2.7

The completed Orders table entry form, with fields and border.

Adding a Validity Check

In this part of Quick Start 2, you add a validity-checking feature to two fields of the form you designed for the Orders table. This feature prevents you from accidentally entering a customer identification number (Cust ID #) or a salesperson's identification number (Emp ID #) that does not already exist in its respective table. The validity check also provides a way of looking up a correct value in the tables. This and many other power-editing features are covered in Chapter 8.

1. To get Paradox to display your new form, select **M**odify, **D**ataEntry from the Main menu and choose the Orders table. Paradox displays an empty record in normal table view. To display the new form, select **I**mage from the Main menu and select **P**ickForm, and then choose **1** - Orders Entry Form. Paradox displays in DataEntry mode the form you designed.

2. Move the cursor to the Cust ID # field in the form (the label says Customer Identification Number) and press F10 (Menu). Then select **V**alCheck, **D**efine. Press Enter to indicate that you want to check the Cust ID # field. From the next menu, choose TableLookup and indicate the Customer table. From the third menu, select JustCurrentField, HelpAndFill. Near the bottom right corner of the screen, Paradox displays the message `Table lookup recorded`.

3. To test your validity check, use the form to enter a record. Type *106* as the order number and *9/18/92* as the date of the order. Then try using *1110* as the customer's identification number. Figure QS2.8 shows the message that Paradox displays.

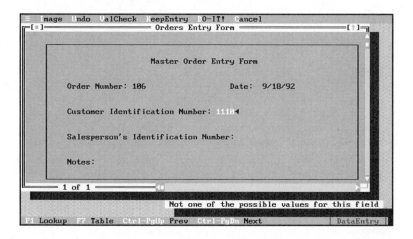

FIG. QS2.8

The result of entering a nonexistent customer ID number.

4. To see a list of available customer identification numbers, press F1. Paradox shows you the Customer table. A message in the status line tells you to `Move to the record you want to select`. Use the down-arrow key to move down to Customer 1001, Alpha

Freight Lines, and press F2. Paradox returns to the Orders entry form and replaces the number you entered in the Cust ID # field with 1001.

5. Move to the Emp ID # field (Salesperson's Identification Number) and add the same validity-checking feature. Press F10 (Menu), select **ValCheck**, **D**efine, and press Enter. From the ValCheck menu, choose **T**ableLookup and select the **E**mployee table. Again choose **J**ustCurrentField, **H**elpAndFill.

6. Use the lookup feature to choose the Emp ID # for Emily Kellogs (541-67-5555).

7. To finish entering this record, move to the Notes field, press Alt-F5 or Ctrl-F (Field View) to display the Entry->Notes window and add the following note:

    This is a reorder. Refer to Order # 102 for original quantities.

    Press F2 (Do-It!) to return to the Orders Entry Form window.

8. Use your form and the F1 and F2 keys (validity-checking options— explained in steps 4 and 5) to enter the following new data into Orders:

Order #	Cust ID #	Emp ID #	Date
107	1004	230-76-2376	9/21/92
108	1003	111-33-8491	9/22/92
109	1005	448-09-6721	9/24/92
110	1000	987-31-9873	9/25/92
111	1002	230-76-2376	9/26/92
112	1001	448-09-6721	9/29/92

Order #	Notes
107	None
108	Special shipping instructions:

Ship 30 ea. B107 to:
    Hidden Resorts 2
    4747 Sharp Rd.
    Ocean City, MD 20640

Ship remaining items to invoice address.

Order #	Notes
109	Special shipping instructions:
	Address to:
	Sam E. Ford Signal Plumbing Receiving 3121 Half Street Oxon Hill, MD 20745
110	None
111	This is a reorder. See order # 103.
112	This is a telephone order. Signature on file.

9. To save the new records, press F2 (Do-It!). Paradox returns to Main mode and displays the Orders table with the new records added.

10. Use any method you know to enter the following records into the Detail table. They represent the detail information behind each of the orders you just entered into the Orders table.

Order #	Item #	Model #	Quantity
106	1	A333	15
106	2	G400	5
107	1	X155	10
108	1	B107	60
109	1	G400	25
110	1	A333	15
110	2	B107	5
111	1	G400	22
112	1	A333	29
113	1	B107	17
113	2	G400	8

Creating Custom Reports

This portion of Quick Start 2 demonstrates using lookup tables, grouping, and summary fields in a Paradox tabular report. This lesson gives you a chance to practice a few of the concepts you learned in Part I of the book and introduces some new ones. You build a tabular report that calculates the total bill for each of the orders by totaling the detail in the Detail table. Creating tabular reports with such features as grouping, multiple tables, and summary fields is discussed fully in Chapter 10. You can find similar coverage of free-form reports in Chapter 11.

Placing Lookup Fields and Grouping Records

One of the fields that you need to calculate the total bill for each order is the Price field, which contains the price of each model sold. This field has to be looked up from the Product table, based on the model number.

You are going to start with the standard tabular report specification for the Detail table and then add the Price field from the Product table.

1. At the Main menu, select **R**eport, **D**esign. Select the Detail table and form 1. Type the description *Summary Fields* and press Enter. Choose the field type **T**abular. Paradox displays the standard report specification.

2. Insert two new columns to the right of the Quantity field in the table band. To insert these columns, move the cursor into the table band, just to the right of the Quantity column. From the Main menu, select TableBand, **I**nsert, and press Enter. Paradox inserts one column. Repeat this procedure for the second column.

3. Place the Price field, looked up from the Product table, in the first new column. To do so, place the cursor in the first new column, in the body of the table band, and select **F**ield, **L**ookup, **L**ink and choose the Product table. Indicate that the Model # field is the link between Detail and Product so that the Price can be looked up.

4. To define the Price field, select **F**ield, **P**lace, **R**egular. Use the cursor-movement keys to move to the option that reads [Product->] and press Enter. Paradox shows the available fields from the Product lookup table: Model #, Product Name, Price, and Cost. Choose

Price. Press Enter to indicate where the field should begin, use the left-arrow key to shorten the field to (9,999), and press Enter. Leave the number of decimal places at two by pressing Enter again.

5. Add the word *Price* and an underline of hyphens to the table band header. Figure QS2.9 shows how the report specification should look at this juncture.

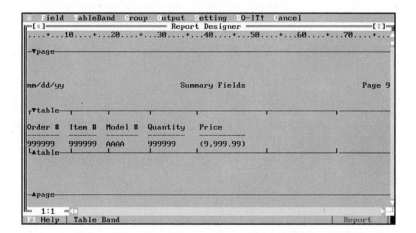

FIG. QS2.9

Adding a lookup field to the report specification.

6. Place a calculated field in the second new column. This new field is the product of Quantity × Price. Price is a looked-up field, so you have to use the special syntax *[lookup_table->fieldname]*, or in this case *[Product->Price]*, in the expression for the calculated field. Position the cursor in the body of the second new column, select **F**ield, **P**lace, **C**alculated, and then type the following expression and press Enter:

    [Quantity]*[Product->Price]

Press Enter a second time to indicate where the field should begin in the column. Use the left-arrow key to adjust field length to (99,999) and press Enter two more times. Place a heading above this calculated field that reads *Ext Price* (for extended price) and type a line of hyphens beneath the heading.

7. Group the records in the report by order number. Place the cursor in the last line of the page header area, just above the table band, and access the menu bar and select **G**roup, **I**nsert, **F**ield, **O**rder_# and press Enter. This step ensures that all records in the Detail table from each order are grouped together. To prevent the order number from being repeated every record, select **S**etting, **G**roupRepeats, **S**uppress.

Placing Summary Fields

Summary fields are often used to create totals and subtotals in reports. Place a summary field in the group footer of your report to get a total for each order and place a summary field in the report footer for a grand total at the end of the report. Both of these summary fields must sum up the calculated product of Quantity × Price.

1. To create the subtotal field, move the cursor into the group footer. Insert a blank line. Move the cursor just below the Ext Price column and create a line of hyphens to indicate a total. Move the cursor to the second line of the group footer, and select Field, Place, Summary, Calculated. Type the same expression you used for the Ext Price calculated field:

   [Quantity]*[Product->Price]

   After you press Enter, Paradox displays a menu. Select Sum, PerGroup to indicate that the results of calculations should be summed and subtotaled for each group (for each Order # value). Press Enter to indicate the starting point of the field and use the cursor-movement keys to adjust its length to (999,999). Press Enter twice.

2. Perform a similar operation in the report footer, just below the new subtotal field. Place a double line (using the equal sign) in the first line of the report footer. Move the cursor below the double line and select Field Place Summary Calculated. Type the following expression and press Enter:

   [Quantity]*[Product->Price]

   Choose Sum Overall. Press Enter to indicate position. Use the left-arrow key to reduce the size of the field to (9,999,999) and press Enter twice. Your screen should appear similar to figure QS2.10.

3. Before saving the report specification, test the specification to the screen by selecting Output, Screen. Paradox sends the report to the screen. Your report should be similar to figure QS2.11. After you have fixed any problems that you discover, save the report specification by pressing F2 (Do-It!). The report then is ready to be sent to the printer.

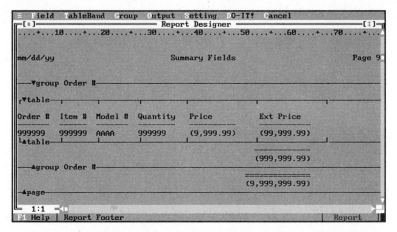

```
≡  Field  TableBand  Group  Output  Setting  DO-IT!  Cancel
┌─[■]══════════════════ Report Designer ═══════════════════[↕]┐
....+...10....+...20....+...30....+...40....+...50....+...60....+...70....+...

mm/dd/yy                      Summary Fields                    Page 9

───▼group Order #──────────────────────────────────────────────
┌─▼table─┬───────┬───────┬──────────┬───────────┬──────────────┐
Order #  Item #  Model #  Quantity   Price        Ext Price
999999   999999  AAAA     999999     (9,999.99)   (99,999.99)
└─▲table─┴───────┴───────┴──────────┴───────────┴──────────────┘
                                                  (999,999.99)
───▲group Order #──────────────────────────────────────────────
                                                 ═════════════
                                                  (9,999,999.99)
───▲page───────────────────────────────────────────────────────
  1:1  ◄
F1 Help | Report Footer                              Report
```

FIG. QS2.10

The completed report specification with lookup field (Price), calculated field (Ext Price), and summary fields.

```
≡  Goto  Search  Cancel
┌─[■]══════════════════ Report Preview ═══════════════════[↕]┐

3/29/92                       Summary Fields                    Page


Order #  Item #  Model #  Quantity   Price        Ext Price
                                      ─────        ─────────
  100        1   A333         50      39.95        1,997.50
             2   B107         25      49.95        1,248.75
             3   G400         10      59.95          599.50
                                                   ─────────
                                                   3,845.75

  101        1   A333         15      39.95          599.25
             2   X155         10      79.95          799.50
                                                   ─────────
                                                   1,398.75
F1 Help                                              Preview
```

FIG. QS2.11

The first page of the Summary Fields report.

Creating Graphs

This section of Quick Start 2 gives you a good idea of how easy Paradox's graphics feature is to use, but keep in mind that Chapter 12 is devoted to Paradox graphics. In this part of the lesson, you use the Detail table and QBE to calculate the number of each model of widget sold and compare the totals in a bar graph.

You need to use a query form to calculate the total number of each type of widget sold and at the same time look up the name of each model from the Product table. Paradox makes this procedure easy.

1. From the Main menu, choose **Ask** and select the Detail table. To place an example element in the Model # field, place the cursor in that field, press F5 (Example), type *123*, and press Enter. Paradox displays the example in inverse video. Move to the Quantity column and type *calc sum as Total*.

2. Add a second query form. Access the Main menu and select **Ask**. Select the Product table. Move the cursor to the Model # column, press F5 (Example), type *123*, and press Enter. Move to the Product Name field and mark this field with a check mark (press F6), and then press Enter. The example elements in the Product and Detail tables correspond, which causes Paradox to match the proper product name with the model number listed in each Detail record. Because only one field is checked, the data is grouped by that field, and the calc-sum field totals the quantities of each model sold. To execute the query, press F2 (Do-It!). Figure QS2.12 shows the results.

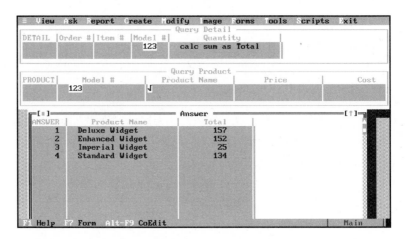

FIG. QS2.12

Using a multitable query to calculate the total number of each model of widget sold.

3. Creating a graph is so easy that you can create one from the Answer table, but the graph looks better if you rename the table first. (By default, Paradox uses the table name as the title of the graph.) To rename the table, access the Main menu with F10 (Menu) and select **Tools**, **Rename**, **Table**. Select the Answer table. Type the new table name *Totals* and press Enter. Because Answer was the active window on the desktop, Paradox changes the name of the Answer table on-screen to Totals. Now you are ready to create the graph.

4. To display a bar graph that compares the total numbers of units sold, you first must place the cursor in the Total column of the Totals table. Next, press Ctrl-F7 (Graph) or access the Main menu

and select Image, **G**raph, **V**iewGraph, **S**creen. Paradox displays the graph shown in figure QS2.13. Press Esc when you finish viewing the graph.

5. To print your graph, make sure that your printer is connected and on-line. Then access the Main menu and select Image, **G**raph, **V**iewGraph, **P**rinter. Paradox prints the graph.

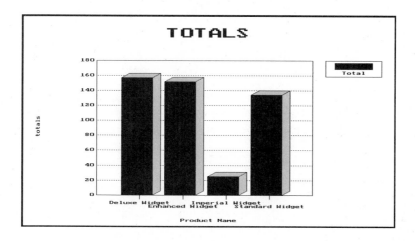

FIG. QS2.13

The graph of the
Totals table.

Quick Start Summary

Quick Start 2 provided an appetizer for the feast of powerful Paradox features that awaits you in Part II. This lesson enabled you to experiment with creating databases, designing an entry form, and creating multitable queries. In Chapter 7, you learn how to use Query By Example to ask complex questions of your database.

Using Advanced Query By Example and Multiple Tables

his chapter is the first in Part II because developing a good understanding of how to use the full power of Paradox Query By
Example (QBE) is important. The degree of your understanding of the
Paradox QBE methodology determines how satisfied you are with the
program and how effective your use of the program will be.

Chapter 4, "Getting Started with Query By Example," introduces you to
QBE fundamentals. By now, you should be able to use the techniques
presented in that chapter to retrieve data from any Paradox table.
Chapter 4, however, covered queries of individual tables only. This
chapter shows you how to use example elements to link multiple query
forms so that you can retrieve information from any number of related
Paradox tables. You learn how to create answers that combine records

from related tables based on common data (called inner joins) and how to combine records even when no match exists (outer joins).

You also discover in this chapter how Paradox provides some of the number-crunching capability of spreadsheets, enabling you to refine raw data into information that shows you the bigger picture. Another aspect of Paradox QBE is the capability to work with sets of data. This chapter teaches you how to use *set operators* in a query to answer questions such as "Which customers have ordered every model of widget in the inventory?" The final portion of this chapter demonstrates how to use Query By Example operators to make changes to the contents of the tables.

As you go through this chapter, apply the concepts you learn to real-life examples. Use the tables you created in Quick Start 2 or create some tables of your own.

Building Multitable Queries

Reminder:
Paradox enables you to work with many database tables at the same time.

As a true relational database management system, Paradox enables you to work with many database tables at the same time. With Paradox QBE, you can combine data from multiple tables in a way that helps you focus on the information you want to find rather than have to worry about command syntax or programming. The QBE techniques used in multitable queries are natural extensions of the methods you already have learned in Chapter 4.

Normalizing a Database

A well-planned relational database is the model of efficiency. Every piece of information is in its place, and no data is duplicated. To accomplish this ideal, however, you usually have to divide (or *normalize*) the database into several relatively small tables. Unfortunately, this structure sometimes can make working with the data a little more confusing.

The sample database that has been used throughout this book has been normalized to eliminate any duplication of information. For each order placed for widgets, only one record exists in the Orders table. The Detail table contains one record for each line item in an order. Customer information is included only once, in the Customer table. The Employee table includes exactly one record for each employee. The Product table includes one record for each model of widget.

Reminder:
In Paradox QBE, you use example elements to link tables.

As you work with this data, however, you routinely need to use or link information from two or more of these normalized tables. You may want to get the name and address of the customer who placed order number 103, for example. This information is split between two tables. The Orders table stores the customer ID number for each order, but the customer's name and address are in the Customer table. The tools that enable you to link these two tables in Paradox are *example elements*.

Linking Tables with Example Elements

To combine or join data from two tables into one Answer table, you construct a *query statement*, made up of two or more query forms. You then place matching example elements in the fields that link the tables. In the Orders/Customer example, the linking field in each table is the Cust ID # field. By placing matching example elements in the Cust ID # field of each query form, you tell Paradox to look for a match in the data when performing the query. The basic techniques presented in Chapter 4 for selecting fields and records for inclusion in the answer still apply.

Reminder:
To combine data from two tables, construct a query statement of two or more query forms.

To place multiple query forms on the desktop, use the **Ask** command several times in succession. The order of the forms on the desktop does not affect which records Paradox includes in the Answer table. The order, however, does affect the order of the columns in the Answer table. Checked fields from the query form placed on the desktop first (the bottommost table in the stack) become the leftmost fields in the Answer table. Fields from the second query form in the stack are added to the Answer table to the right of the first form's columns, and so forth. Because you can rearrange fields later by using the Image menu options and the Ctrl-R (Rotate) command, however, you don't need to be too concerned with the order of your query forms.

> Paradox uses sophisticated artificial intelligence (AI) procedures, called Heuristic Query Optimization, to ensure that every query is executed as quickly as possible. The order of the query forms on the desktop has no effect on this optimization one way or the other. Users of competing PC-based QBE products may find that the order of the query forms on the desktop is surprisingly significant in determining query speed. You don't have to worry about that problem with Paradox.

T I P

One of the options in the Custom Configuration Program enables you to specify that records be sorted during a query in **I**mageOrder rather than the default of **T**ableOrder. With this option set, rearranging column order in query forms does have an effect on the sorted order of the Answer table.

To place an example element in a query form field, press F5 (Example), type a name for the example element, and press Enter. Paradox displays the entry in inverse video. When naming an example element, you can use any alphabetic characters (A through Z, upper- or lowercase) and the numbers 0 through 9. No spaces or other characters are permitted. Figure 7.1 shows an example element, abc, displayed in the Cust ID # field of each query form. The name does not have to match the field type. You can use the example element *123* in an alphanumeric field, therefore, and use *abc* in a numeric field; or you can use a combination of letters and numbers. The example element you use is not determined by the field name or type.

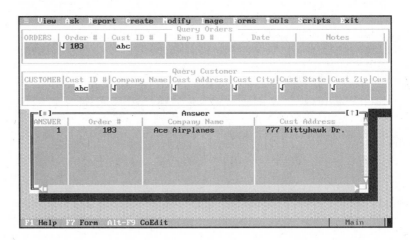

FIG. 7.1

A multitable query showing example elements.

Reminder:
Identical example elements in two query forms define the link.

Placing identical example elements in two query forms defines the link between the two tables. In the example shown in figure 7.1, the example element *abc* asks Paradox to match records from the Customer table with records in Orders where the Cust ID # is a match. You place the number 103 in the Order # field to display the information about that order only. Notice that the customer's ID number is not checked and therefore does not display in the Answer table. Because the Company Name, Cust Address, Cust City, Cust State, and Cust Zip fields contain check marks, those fields are included in the Answer table. (Note that the columns in both query forms in the figure are reduced in width so that they fit on one screen.)

You can link query forms with example elements whether or not you use F6 (CheckMark) to include the link field in the Answer table. If you want the link field in the Answer table, place a check mark in the link field of only one of the query forms. Otherwise, the Answer table will include the field more than once.

T I P

You can join as many as 24 tables through a query (you can have no more than 24 images on the desktop at once). You may want to build on the query shown in figure 7.1, for example, and show which salesperson was responsible for order number 103. To add a third query form to the desktop, access the Main menu and select **A**sk, and then choose another table (in this example, use Employee).

If other query forms that should not be related to your query are on the work area, Paradox attempts to link them. Make sure that you clear all unwanted query forms with F8.

To have the correct Employee record matched with each record in Orders, you use an example element in the Emp ID # field of each table. So that Paradox can distinguish this link from the link between Orders and Customer, you use a different example element name (something other than *abc*).

Move the cursor to the Emp ID # field in the Employee query form, for example, and press F5 (Example). Then type *123* and press Enter. With F6 (CheckMark), mark the fields that you want included. In this example, mark the three fields that make up an employee's name: Emp Last Name, Emp First Name, and Emp Middle Initial. Then move to the Orders query form using the mouse or by pressing F3 (Up Image) twice and add the same example element, *123*, to the Emp ID # field of that form. Finally, perform the query by pressing F2 (Do-It!). Paradox includes the Employee data in the Answer table, as shown in figure 7.2.

To build multitable queries successfully, you must clearly understand the relationships between the various tables in your database. Keep a diagram of your tables handy as you try the query techniques presented in this chapter. (See the tip included in the "Understanding How Tables Are Related" section of Chapter 2.) Such a diagram for the tables queried in figure 7.1 quickly shows you that Cust ID # is the link between Orders and Customer and, therefore, is the field that should contain example elements.

Paradox does not erase the Answer table from the screen when you begin to construct another query. This design enables you to proceed step-by-step in a progression of more and more refined queries until you reach the Answer table for which you are looking.

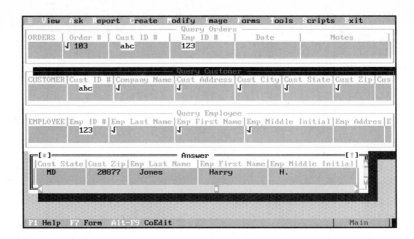

FIG. 7.2

A three-table query.

Don't forget that you can save a query with the **QuerySave** option from the Scripts menu. (For more information, refer to Chapter 6).

Combining Selection Criteria

Chapter 4 introduces you to the concept of combining selection criteria in one query. You can construct single-table queries that find records meeting several criteria at the same time—the logical AND condition. You also can create queries that select records meeting one or more of several criteria—the logical OR condition. Multitable queries expand these ways of combining selection criteria.

Creating AND Conditions

Three rules summarize how you can indicate that multiple query conditions should be met concurrently (the logical AND condition):

■ Multiple conditions placed in the same field of a query form and separated by a comma (,) must be met at the same time for a record to be included in the Answer table.

■ Multiple conditions placed in the same row of a query form must be met concurrently.

■ When rows from different query forms are linked by example elements, Paradox treats the rows as if they are one row from one table, for the purposes of the second rule.

The first two rules are discussed in Chapter 4. The following example demonstrates the third rule. Suppose that you want to determine which customers have purchased more than 20 Deluxe Widgets. To produce the answer to this question, Paradox needs to look at information in four tables. The Detail table contains the model number and quantity of widgets sold in each order. The product name is found in the Product table, referenced by the model number. To know which customer made each purchase, you have to get the customer's ID number from the Orders table and the customer company's name from the Customer table. Information from all these tables is necessary to produce an answer.

To perform this query, you first use **Ask** to display a query form for each of the four tables. The next step is to use example elements to specify linking fields between the related tables. You can, for example, use the words *red*, *blue*, and *green* as example elements. Figure 7.3 shows red as the example element linking the Order # fields in Orders and Detail. The word blue is used to link Cust ID # between Orders and Customer. The example element green in the Model # fields links the Product table to the Detail table.

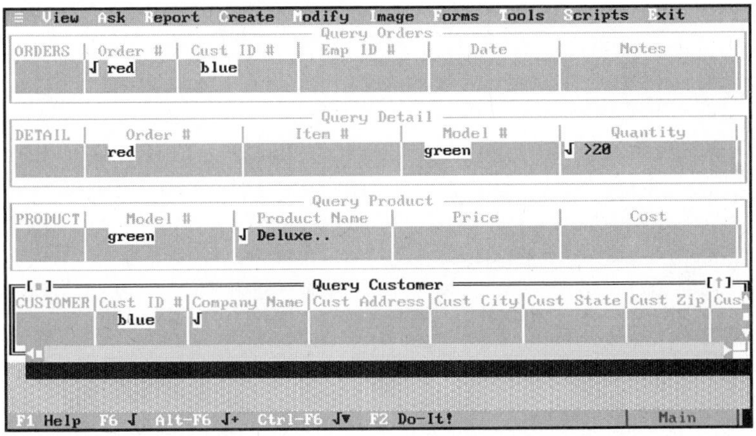

FIG. 7.3

The logical AND condition.

In this example, the Detail table is controlling the action. If you do not specify any conditions before you execute the query, Paradox includes a record in the Answer table for every record in Detail. Detail is on the many-side of one-to-many relationships with the Orders and Product tables. The fields that contain a check mark—Order #, Quantity, Product Name, and Company Name—are the only fields in the Answer table.

To limit the records to just customers who bought Deluxe Widgets, you place the pattern *Deluxe..* (you also can spell out *Deluxe Widget*) in the Product Name field of the Product query form. To limit further the answer to customers who bought more than 20 widgets, use the range *>20* in the Quantity field of the Detail query form, as shown in figure 7.3. When you execute the query with F2 (Do-It!), Paradox retrieves only records that match both conditions, as shown in figure 7.4.

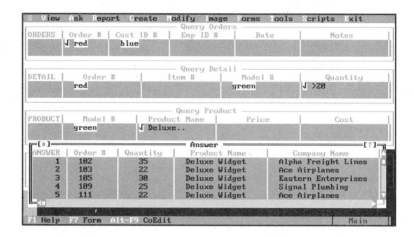

FIG. 7.4

The Answer table.

Creating OR Conditions

You create the OR condition in two ways:

- Separate two or more criteria in the same field and same row with the operator OR.

- Place criteria in separate rows of the same query form. This method is required when alternate conditions are not in the same field. In a single-table query, check marks and any concurrent AND conditions must be repeated in each row. In multiple-table queries, each new row has to be linked again to the other table(s) with different example element(s).

Building this type of query is like building two independent AND conditions and then sticking the results together, especially when you are forced to use multiple rows.

You can build on the preceding example by using the OR operator. Assume that you want to know the names of customers who ordered more than 20 of the Deluxe Widget or the Enhanced Widget. You can accomplish this query by using the OR operator in the Product Name field. The new criterion becomes `Deluxe..` or `Enhanced..` (see fig. 7.5), and the Answer table includes orders for Enhanced Widgets along with the orders for Deluxe Widgets.

Often you cannot express search conditions all in one row. Suppose that you want to know which customers ordered more than 20 Deluxe Widgets or at least 10 Imperial Widgets. You may attempt to construct this query by using the OR operator in the Product Name field, as in figure 7.5, and the OR operator in the Quantity field of the Detail table (>=20 or >=10). This query, however, may give you the wrong answer. This query would erroneously select orders for Deluxe Widgets in the range 10 to 20. The proper query is shown in figure 7.6. As you can see, this new query requires another set of example elements—cyan, gold, and orange—and all check marks must be repeated in the second row. The Answer table, shown in figure 7.7, includes orders for 10 or more Imperial Widgets and 25 or more Deluxe Widgets.

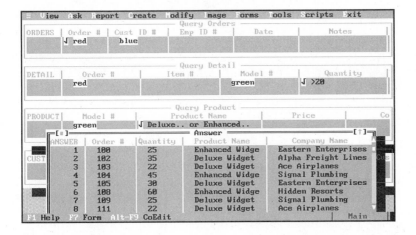

FIG. 7.5

The logical OR condition in a single-row query.

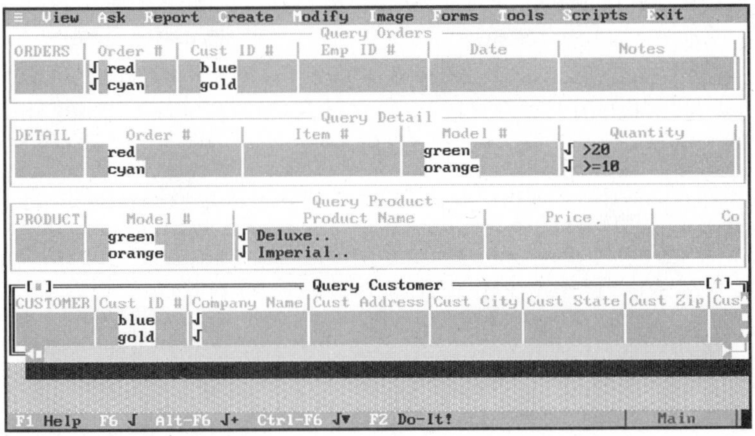

FIG. 7.6

The logical OR condition in multiple rows.

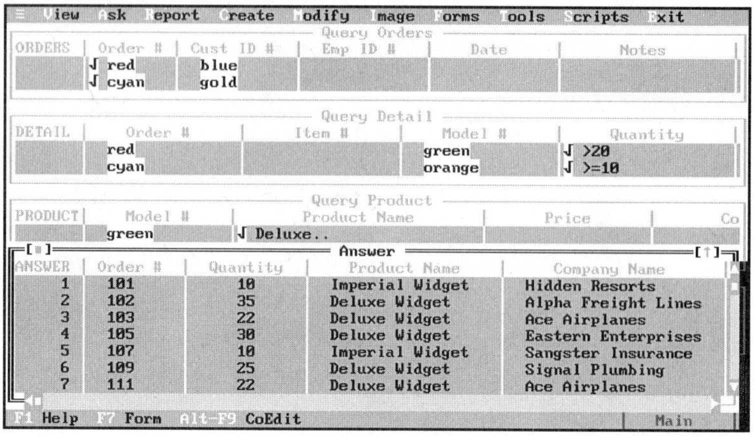

FIG. 7.7

The Answer table for the query in figure 7.6.

T I P   You cannot use the OR operator between example elements.

Creating BOTH Conditions

Reminder:

Using the same example element in more than one row creates a BOTH condition.

Using the same example element in more than one row of the query statement creates a special kind of AND condition—a BOTH condition. Suppose that you want to know whether any of your customers have ordered both Deluxe and Imperial widgets. If you try to use the normal AND query and place the criteria *Deluxe.., Imperial..* in the Product Name field, you get an empty Answer table for the result. The reason is that no record in the Detail table contains both Deluxe and Imperial widgets.

You can accomplish the result you intended, however, by using the same example element in two rows of the Detail query form. Figure 7.8 shows the proper query. Two different example elements, green and orange, are used in the Model # field to link the two rows from the Product table. The same example element, red, is used in the Order # field in both rows of the Detail query form. This setup causes Paradox to create a second Product Name column in the Answer table and returns the name of the customers who have ordered both Deluxe and Imperial widget models (see fig. 7.9). In this case, only one company, Ace Airplanes, has ordered both types of widgets.

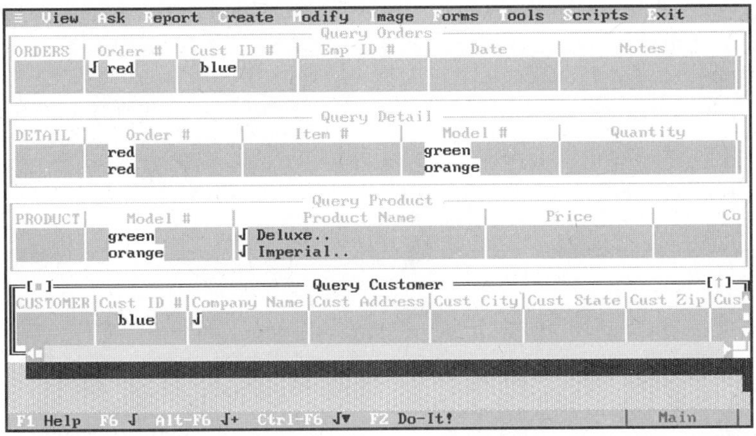

FIG. 7.8

Creating the BOTH condition.

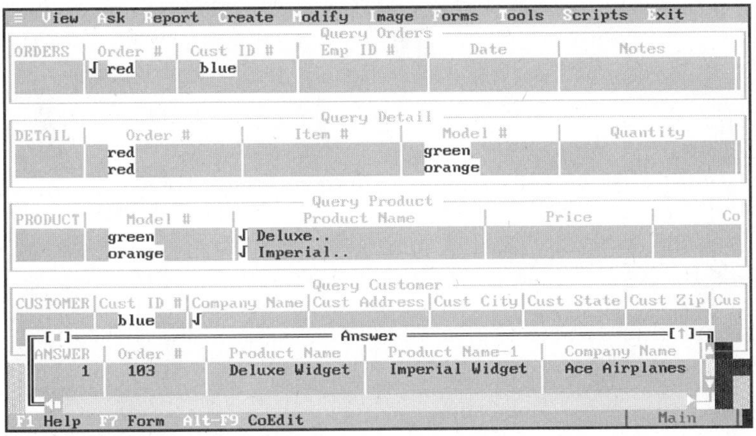

FIG. 7.9

Who ordered both types of widgets?

Using Example Elements To Represent Values

One of the most interesting uses of example elements doesn't necessarily involve multiple tables. Sometimes you want to select records based on a match or comparison with another record in the same table. Suppose that you want to see a list of all employees whose salaries are greater than Tim Bronson's. You can do a query to determine Tim Bronson's salary. You then can enter that salary as an example value in the Salary field and execute another query to find your answer. Using example elements, however, you can perform the operation in only one query.

The first line of this type of query finds the value used for comparison. In figure 7.10, the example element *sal* is placed in the first row of the Salary column to represent the value of Tim Bronson's salary. No check marks are placed in this first row, but *Bronson* and *Tim* are entered in the Emp Last Name and Emp First Name fields, respectively. The second row then compares the salaries of all other employees to the example salary and builds the Answer table accordingly.

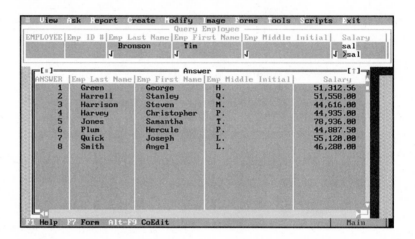

FIG. 7.10

Using example elements to represent values.

Using the Inclusive Link

Reminder:
A query that includes only matching records is an inner join.

All the multitable queries mentioned in this chapter have created Answer tables that include only records in which a match occurs in all linked tables. This type of matching is an *inner join* and is usually the result you need.

In some situations, however, you may want to include even those records that don't produce a match. This type of matching is an *outer join*. Paradox's *inclusion* operator performs an inclusive link as opposed to an exclusive link. This operator is represented by the exclamation point (!) and is typed in the query column immediately after an example element.

Reminder:
A query that includes records that don't match is an outer join.

You may want to produce a list of all the recent orders sold by each of your company's salespeople. The normal inner join produces a complete list only if every salesperson has made a sale. An outer join, however, includes even nonproductive salespeople in the Answer table. Figure 7.11 shows just such a query. Notice that two salespeople have nothing listed in the Order # column.

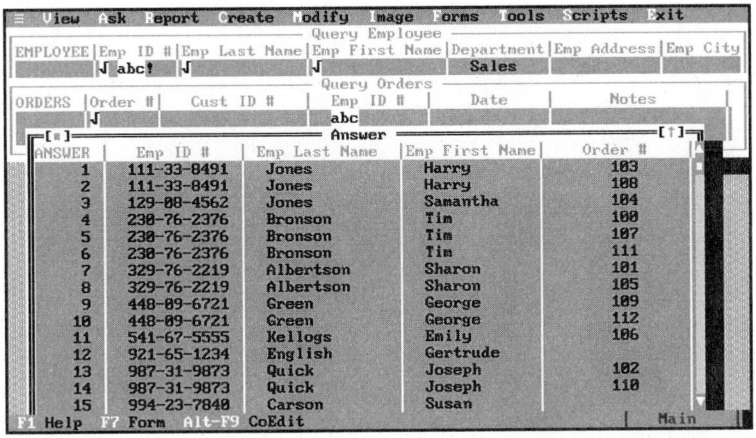

FIG. 7.11

Creating an outer join.

> **CAUTION:** The location of the inclusion operator is crucial to obtaining the result you intend. Make sure that you place the exclamation point (!) in the link field of the table containing the records that should be included, with or without a match. In the example in figure 7.11, if the inclusion operator was placed in the Orders query form, the Answer table would not include salespersons who have made no sales because their ID numbers do not appear in the Orders table.

The outer join shown in figure 7.11 has an inclusion operator in only one query form—the Employee form. This type of query statement is an *asymmetrical outer join*. Another benefit of the inclusion operator is its capability to *union* several tables easily. You can place the inclusion operator on both ends of the query statement, creating a *symmetrical outer join*.

Figure 7.12 shows an example of a query to create the union or symmetrical outer join of the Employee (Sales Department only), Orders, and Customer tables. Notice the exclamation points after every example element. The resulting Answer table is shown in figure 7.13. The Answer table shows employees who haven't made a sale. The Answer table also would show customers who have not recently placed an order, except that every customer has placed at least one order in our limited hypothetical database. This information would not be displayed in a normal inner (exclusive) join, sometimes called an *intersection* of tables.

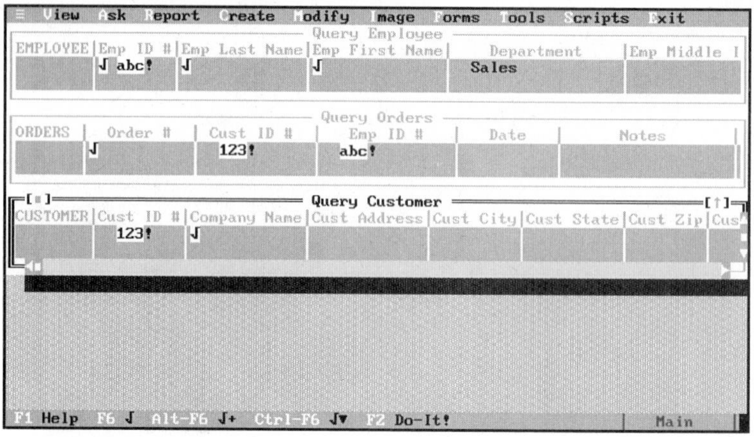

FIG. 7.12

Creating a
symmetrical outer
join.

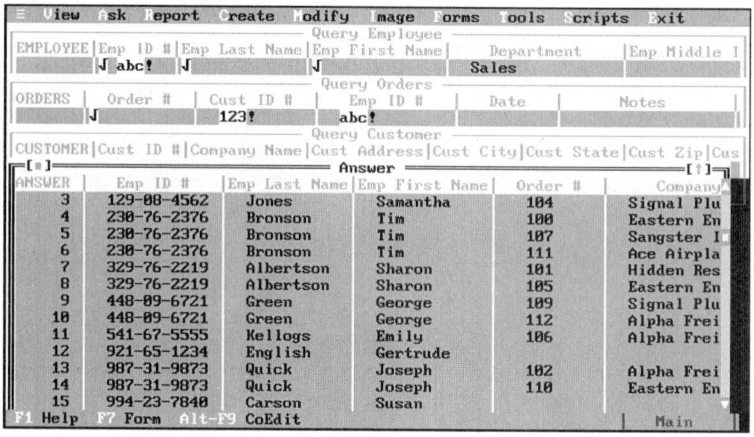

FIG. 7.13

The result of the
outer join.

When creating inclusive links in a query statement, you must follow
three rules:

- Do not mix inclusive and exclusive links in the same pairs of query
  statement rows (in other words, don't use an example element
  with an inclusion operator and an example element without an
  inclusion operator in the same row). Figure 7.12 shows an example of two inclusive links in the same row.

- Subject to the first rule, you can use inclusive and exclusive links
  in the same query statement.

- Use the inclusion operator on a particular example element no
  more than once per row and twice per query statement.

Paradox processes links in the following order: exclusive links, asymmetrical inclusive links, and then symmetrical inclusive links.

Experiment with the inclusion operator. Creating inclusive links between the tables in your database often can reveal information that otherwise would go unnoticed.

For Related Information:

◄◄ "Designing a Database," p. 68.

◄◄ "Using Paradox Operators," p. 169.

FROM HERE...

Performing Calculations in Queries

Many PC users continue to force their database applications into spreadsheets—often because of the relative ease with which spreadsheet programs perform numeric calculations. Spreadsheets are marginal at best when working with real database tasks, such as inputting, editing, retrieving, sorting, and reporting substantial amounts of data. Paradox combines high-powered database functionality with surprisingly flexible number-crunching capability to provide the best of both worlds.

Paradox can perform two general categories of calculations: operations that use numeric or text values from the fields in an individual record and summary calculations that perform calculations over groups of records.

Performing Calculations within a Record

All calculations in Paradox query forms must be preceded with the CALC operator. You can use this operator to combine a value in a Paradox table field with values from other fields in the record, with constant values, or with both. The formula you create is called a *Calc expression*. The following basic rules apply when you are building Calc expressions:

Cue:
Precede all calculations with the CALC operator.

■ Precede all Calc expressions with the CALC operator.

- Place Calc expressions in any column of the query statement, separated from any other entry in the column with a comma.

- Combine numeric and date values with the following arithmetic operators:

  +– * / ( )

- Combine (concatenate) alphanumeric values with the + operator.

- Represent each field value with its own example element.

- Enter constant number values and date values in the same way as in data entry (for example, 1234.7 and 12/31/89).

- Enclose alphanumeric constant values in double quotation marks (for example, "Current Resident").

The CALC operator, like the check mark, causes Paradox to add a field to the Answer table. Paradox gives the new field a name based on the Calc expression used, unless you use the AS operator to rename the field. For more information about using the AS operator, see the "Changing the Field Name" section of Chapter 4, "Getting Started with Query By Example."

Performing Numeric Calculations

The first step in performing numeric calculations is to construct the basic query statement, including any necessary links for multitable queries. Next, you must decide which fields in the query statement you need to use in the calculation. Place a unique example element in each of these fields and place a check mark in the fields if you want them to be included in the Answer table. When all necessary fields are named, you can construct the Calc expression in any column of the query statement.

Figure 7.14 shows how you may build a Calc expression to determine the total price for each row in the Detail table. (*Note:* The figure does not show the entire Answer table.) The *quant* example element represents the quantity ordered, and the *price* example element represents the price of the item. The AS operator added to the end of the expression causes Paradox to name the calculated field *Total Price*. If you don't include this operator, Paradox names the new calculated field *Quantity * Price*.

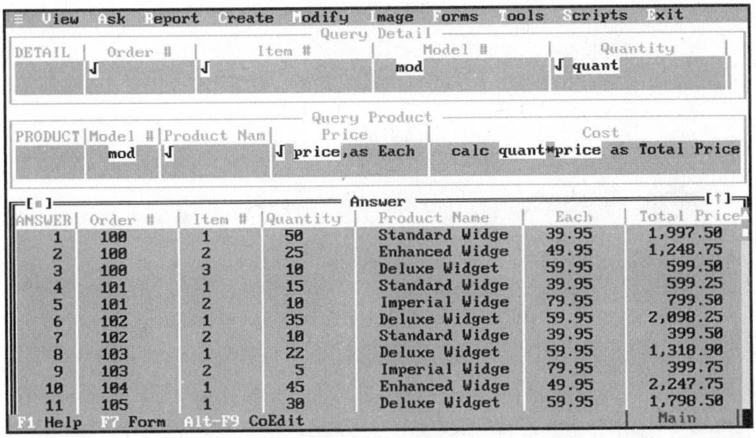

FIG. 7.14

Figuring total prices.

> **T I P**
>
> If you use descriptive example element names, your Calc expressions are easier to build. The example element names shown in figure 7.14, *quant* and *price*, clearly describe the fields they represent, so the Calc expression is easy to understand. You also may find the Calc expression more readable if you construct it in an otherwise unused column.

Combining Alphanumeric Values

The CALC operator also enables you to combine or concatenate alphanumeric values. This feature most often is used to construct names or phrases from available data. As with numeric Calc expressions, you assign a separate example element to each field you want to include in the expression. You can add spaces and punctuation within the expression by enclosing these items in double quotation marks. A typical example of alphanumeric concatenation is constructing a mailing list from your Customer table. You may, for example, assign the example elements *addr*, *city*, *st*, and *zip* to the Cust Address, Cust City, Cust State, and Cust ZIP fields, respectively. You then build the following Calc expression:

Reminder:
The CALC operator also enables you to combine or concatenate alphanumeric values.

    calc addr+", "+city+", "+st+" "+zip

This expression causes Paradox to concatenate the values contained in the various fields into one field. Any trailing spaces at the end of the alphanumeric values are trimmed, so you have to add any necessary spaces or commas as alphanumeric constants within double quotation marks. Figure 7.15 shows the result of this query. The AS operator at the end of the Calc expression is used to give the calculated field the name *Address* in the Answer table.

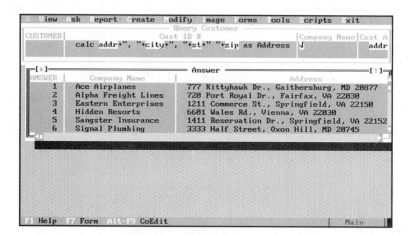

FIG. 7.15

Concatenating alphanumeric values.

Using Summary Operators and Grouping Records

Paradox has several special operators that enable you to perform summary calculations during queries. Rather than operate on values from several fields within a single record, like the operators discussed in the preceding section, these summary operators calculate statistics over several records. Using query summary operators, you can find the sum, average, maximum, minimum, or number of values for groups of records. These summary operators are listed in table 7.1.

Table 7.1. Query Summary Operators

Operator	Meaning	Applicable field types	Default grouping
AVERAGE	Average of values in group	N,$,D,S	All
COUNT	Number of values in group	All	Unique
MAX	Highest value in group	All	Unique

Operator	Meaning	Applicable field types	Default grouping
MIN	Lowest value in group	All	Unique
SUM	Total of values in group	N,$,S	All

The *Default grouping* column in table 7.1 refers to whether duplicate records are ignored by the operation. The SUM and AVERAGE operators generally calculate their statistics over all records in each group; the COUNT, MAX, and MIN operators ignore duplicates within each group. You can specify that the latter operators apply to all records by placing the word *all* in the query column, immediately after the operator.

You also can use these summary operators with range operators (see table 4.2 in Chapter 4) to select a group of records to be included in the Answer table.

The following rules apply to the summary operators when you use them to perform calculations:

■ Precede the summary operator with the CALC operator.

■ Place the summary operator in the column on which the computations should be performed.

■ Place a check mark in the field or fields that you want to determine the grouping. Paradox performs the summary calculation on each group of records that have identical values in the checked fields.

■ Leave blank all other fields in the query form to perform the summary calculation on all records.

The result for each grouping and calculation is a single record in the Answer table, containing all the checked fields and the newly calculated summary field.

You may want to sum up the line item totals calculated in figure 7.14, for example, so that you can have a grand total for each order. Suppose that you change the name of the Answer table in that figure to Dtotals. The Dtotals table then includes the fields Order #, Item #, Quantity, Product Name, Each, and Total Price. To sum the Total Price field for each order, you first place a check mark in the Order # column of the Dtotals query form. This step causes Paradox to group all records with the same Order #. Then you place the expression `calc sum as Order Total` in the Total Price column. When you perform the query by pressing F2 (Do-It!), Paradox adds the values in the Total Price field for each group. The program creates an Answer table consisting of only two fields, Order # and Order Total, with a single record for each different order number (see fig. 7.16).

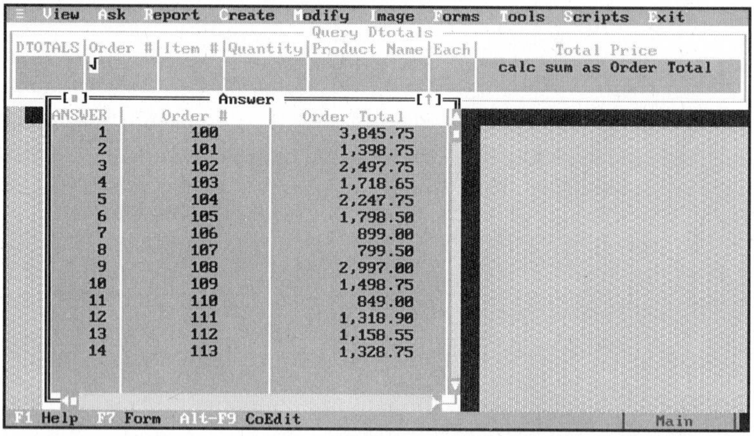

FIG. 7.16

Performing a calculation with a summary operator.

Figure 7.17 shows an example that uses multiple tables and multiple checked fields. This example determines the number of each model of widget sold by each sales representative. This query uses the SUM operator to total the Quantity field for each group of records that has identical employee ID numbers and identical model numbers. Paradox sorts records by the leftmost field first and then by other fields, from left to right.

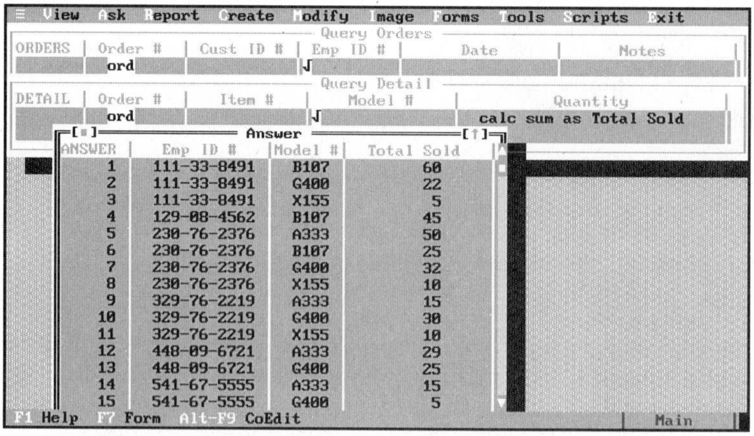

FIG. 7.17

Using multiple tables and multiple checked fields.

Selecting Groups of Records with Summary Operators

Chapter 4 discusses the concept of selecting groups of records with range operators (see table 4.2 for a list of range operators). You also can use the summary operators with range operators to select a group of records. When used this way, the summary operator need not be preceded with CALC.

Assume that you want to know which models of widgets have average orders of more than 15. The Detail table contains the information on how many of each model is ordered, so you need to construct a query on that table. Place a check mark in the Model # column to tell Paradox to sort and group the records by that field and place the expression *average > 15* in the Quantity column. Without the CALC operator, the AVERAGE operator is used for comparison. In this example, Paradox finds all models whose per-order quantity averaged more than 15. You also can include the CALC AVERAGE operator in the same query column if you want to see the actual average number sold in the selected range (see fig. 7.18).

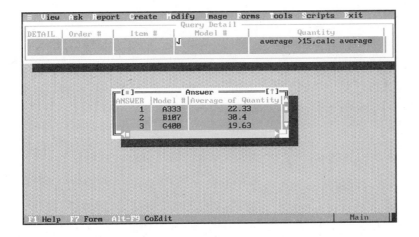

FIG. 7.18

Selecting a group of records with a summary calculation.

For Related Information:

FROM HERE...

▶▶ "Grouping Records in Tabular Reports," p. 351.

▶▶ "Using Summary Operations," p. 367.

Working with Sets of Records

Another category of queries enables you to establish an example group—referred to as a *set*—and then to compare other groups of records to that set. Special operators, listed in table 7.2, enable you to ask questions such as the following:

- Which customers have ordered *only* widgets that have a price greater than $50?

- Which customers have ordered *no* widget more than $50 in price?

- Which customers have ordered *every* type of widget that is more than $50 in price?

- Which customers have ordered *every* widget more than $50 *and only* widgets more than $50 in price?

In these examples, you are comparing the group of orders placed by each customer to the *set* of orders for widgets greater than $50. When a customer's group of orders passes the comparison test, the customer is added to the answer.

Table 7.2. Set Operators

Operator	Meaning
ONLY	The values in the group contain only members of the set.
NO	No value in the group contains a member of the set.
EVERY	The group contains every member of the set.
EXACTLY	The group contains every member of the set and only members of the set

Constructing Set Queries

You must consider the following rules when defining sets:

- Define a *set* with one or more linked query statement forms. Place the word *set* in the table name column of each row that is used to define the set.

■ Do not use check marks or CALC operators in rows that define a set.

■ Use an example element to mark the field in the set that will be used for comparison—the *set comparison field*.

Consider the following guidelines as you define the records that you want to compare to the set:

■ Define the records to be compared to the set by using one or more query forms. You can use multiple query forms or rows of the same query forms that define the set.

■ Do *not* place the word *set* in the table name column of rows that defines these records for comparison.

■ Use an example element to indicate the *comparison field*, which is the field that you want to compare to the set comparison field. Precede this example element with one of the operators listed in table 7.2. Do not place a check mark or CALC operator in this field.

■ Place a check mark (press F6) or a GROUPBY operator (press Shift-F6) in the field that determines how the records should be grouped—the *grouping field*. This field *must* be in the same query form and row as the comparison field. (The GROUPBY operator has the same effect as a check mark in grouping records but does not cause the field to be included in the Answer table.)

Suppose that you want to determine which customers have ordered only widgets that have a price more than $50. The set, or control group, of records is the list of all orders for products in that price range. An order number may appear more than once in this set if several different items priced greater than $50 were ordered at the same time.

You can define this list by constructing query forms from Product and Detail. Product contains the Price field, and Detail contains the orders placed for widgets of all prices. Link these two query forms with an example element (such as *mod*) in the Model # fields and place the range expression *>50* in the Price field of the Product query form. To indicate that this query is a set definition, not a normal query, type *set* in the first column of each form.

The next step is to define the records that Paradox is to compare to the set you have defined. In this example, you want Paradox to compare a list of all the orders of each customer to the comparison set of orders. If any one order from a particular customer does not appear in the comparison set, that customer should not be included in the Answer table. Also, customers with no orders in the comparison set should not be included in the answer. You can create a list of all orders and the corresponding customers by linking the Orders and Customer tables (by typing an example element in the Cust ID # field of each query form). Place a check mark in the Company Name field in the Customer query form, because you are looking for the customer's name.

To complete the process, add matching example elements and a SET operator to the comparison fields and indicate the grouping field. Because you want Paradox to compare order numbers, add the example element *ord* to the Order # field in Detail and then type the set operator ONLY in front of the example element *ord* in the Order # field of the Orders table. Also, place the GROUPBY (Shift-F6) operator in the Cust ID # column of Orders so that the answer is grouped by customer but without displaying the ID numbers. The completed query statement is shown in figure 7.19, and the answer is shown in figure 7.20. Note that the GROUPBY operator displays as a G on-screen.

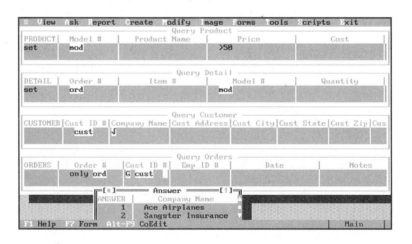

FIG. 7.19

Which customers have ordered only widgets that have prices greater than $50?

FIG. 7.20

The answer to the query in figure 7.19.

> Using Paradox set operators can be confusing. Following the rules presented in this section helps, but you may need to divide the process into manageable steps.
>
> **T I P**

Start by building the set as a normal query. For example, you may build a query to display all orders for products more than $50 in price. Then save and clear this query from the desktop. Next, build a query to define the records you want to compare to the set. In this chapter's example, this query should produce a list of all orders grouped by customer. Save and clear this second query from the screen.

Use the Script Editor to view the first script. Use the **R**ead option on the Editor menu to add the second script at the end of the first and then delete the extra Query and EndQuery lines. Save and play the script. Add the matching comparison field example element and set operator. When the query works as you intended, save it again.

The advantage of this method is that you can see each of the two groups of records separately before trying to compare them. If you do the procedure all in one step, you may not be able to get a clear picture of the data in either group and consequently find yourself spinning your wheels and going nowhere.

Using Summary Operators in Set Queries

The summary operators discussed in the earlier section, "Using Summary Operators and Grouping Records," also work in set queries.

Suppose that you want to know which orders for Enhanced Widgets exceed in number the average order for Standard Widgets. In this example, the comparison set and the records to be compared to the set come from combining the Detail and Product tables. Figure 7.21 shows the two query rows used to create the set query statement.

For Related Information:

▶▶ "Using Summary Operations," p. 367.

FROM HERE...

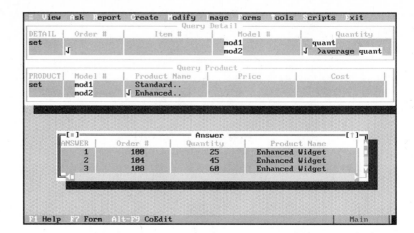

FIG. 7.21

Using a Summary
operator in a set
query.

Changing the Content of Tables with Query Operations

All the queries presented in the preceding sections of this chapter have
no effect on existing tables; all the queries produce a new table, the
Answer table. Unless you choose to make the Answer table permanent
by changing its name, the results of all the queries discussed thus far
are transitory. The query operations listed in table 7.3, however, except
for the FIND operation, act directly and permanently on a table in the
database.

Table 7.3. Query Operations

Operation	Meaning
INSERT	Insert new records
DELETE	Delete selected records
CHANGETO	Replace values in selected records
FIND	Locate selected record

Adding Records with the INSERT operation

Even though the **A**dd option on the Paradox Tools More menu (discussed in Chapter 13) enables you to add records from one table to another, that option is not always effective because it requires that the tables have identical structures. The insert query operation provides a more flexible alternative.

Reminder:
You can use the INSERT operation to add records.

Suppose that a branch office of your company has been moved to the headquarters, and you want to consolidate customer lists. The branch office has been tracking its sales and other data on a spreadsheet, so the customer list is in that format. After using the Paradox Export-Import option on the Tools menu to import the data into the Cust table, the table looks like figure 7.22. (A typical customer list would be much longer.) You need to add the table to the end of your headquarters' customer list.

To use the INSERT operation to add records to a table, you display a query form for the *source* table and a query form for the *destination* table. In this example, the Cust table is the source, and the Customer table is the destination. Place unique example elements in each of the source fields. Type the word *insert* in the leftmost column of the destination query form and then place an example element in each field that has a corresponding field in the source table. You are mapping each field from the source table to a field in the destination table. Do not use any check marks.

When you have entered all the example elements, press F2 (Do-It!). Paradox adds the new records from the source table to the destination table and displays a table named *Inserted* (see fig. 7.23). This table is a temporary one that contains the newly inserted records. If you decide that you added the records in error, you can use the Subtract option on the Tools More menu to subtract the Inserted table from the destination table. As with any temporary table, the Inserted table is overwritten the next time you use it and is erased when you exit Paradox. The source table is not changed by the query operation.

Observe the following guidelines when you perform an insert:

■ Corresponding fields must be the same type.

■ Place a constant value in a field to initialize all new records with this value.

■ Empty fields in the destination query form result in blank fields in the new records.

■ Use expressions to alter or combine the source data as it is being added to the destination table, but do not precede the expression with the CALC operator.

■ When the definition of a destination alphanumeric field is shorter than the source data, the extra data is truncated (cut off).

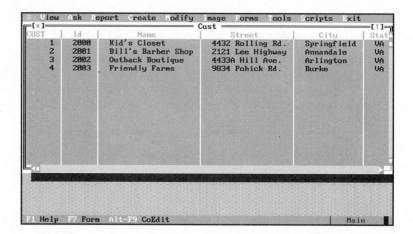

FIG. 7.22

The imported table.

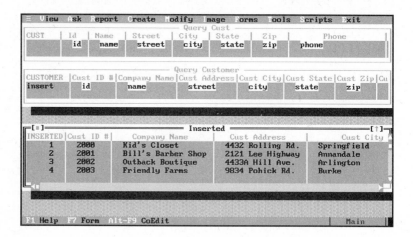

FIG. 7.23

Using the INSERT operation to add records.

Nearly all data eventually becomes obsolete. Paradox offers several methods for discarding unwanted data. You can use Edit or CoEdit mode and delete records one at a time. This approach is probably the best method for removing just a few records. When many records are involved, such as at the beginning of a new fiscal year, you can use Paradox's DELETE operation to delete many records simultaneously.

You can use the DELETE operation during a query to delete any number of records, so long as you provide appropriate selection criteria.

To delete a group of records, display a query form for the target table and type the word *delete* in the left column (beneath the table name). Enter selection criteria in the other fields of the table, being specific enough to select only the records you want to delete, and press F2 (Do-It!). Do not use check marks. Paradox deletes the records from the target table, places them in a temporary table named *Deleted*, and displays the Deleted table at the bottom of the desktop.

You can undo this deletion operation by using the **A**dd option on the Tools More menu (see Chapter 13), if you do so before the temporary Deleted table is overwritten or erased. Two convenient ways to archive these records are to rename the Deleted table to a permanent name and to copy the records to another existing permanent table.

T I P

A good practice is to construct your query first *without* the word *delete* in the table name column. Check mark every column and execute this query, and Paradox displays the records that will be deleted. After you confirm that Paradox will erase the correct records, you can remove the check marks, add the word *delete* to the table name column, and execute the DELETE operation with F2 (Do-It!).

When Paradox deletes records, it does not recover the file space used by the records. To tell Paradox to pack or recover this otherwise wasted space, use the **R**estructure option on the Modify menu. Don't change the structure. Display the screen and press F2 (Do-It!). You also may want to make a backup copy of your table and its family before running the restructure operation, especially when the table is large. This step protects you from data loss that can occur if the computer "hiccups" during the restructuring.

Making Global Changes with the CHANGETO Operation

The CHANGETO operation is the Paradox equivalent of a search-and-replace option for a word processing program. You can make a change to every record in a table, or you can create a specific search criterion that applies the change to selected records.

To use the CHANGETO operation, first use the normal query options to select the records that you want to change. You may, for example, need to apply a 4 percent raise to all employees in the Production and Sales departments, a 4.5 percent raise to the Accounting department, and a 5 percent raise to Administration. Because the Production and Sales departments get the same raise, you can process them on the same row of the query form for the Employee table. Type the criterion *Sales or Production* in the first line of the query form in the Department field. Because each of the other two departments gets different percentage increases, however, you must select those departments in separate rows in the query form. As with INSERT and DELETE, do not use check marks.

To apply a change to a field in a selected record, type the word *changeto*, followed by the new value or expression. To create an expression that calculates a new value, you first type a unique example element in the field. Then type a comma and the word *changeto*, followed by the expression, as shown in figure 7.24.

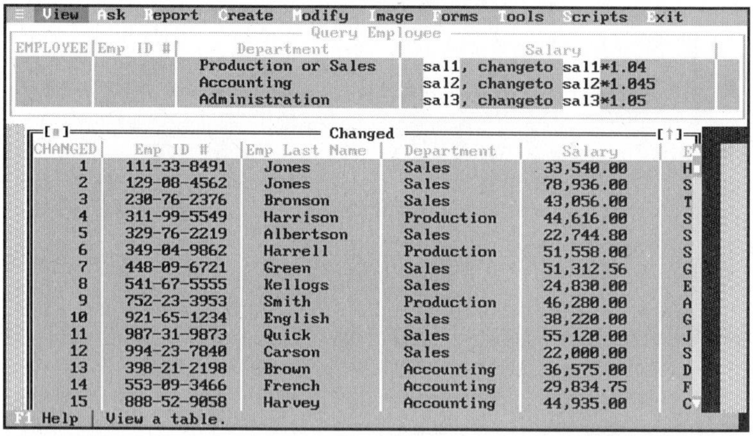

FIG. 7.24

Using the CHANGETO operation.

Performing a query with the CHANGETO operation does not create an Answer table but makes changes directly to the target table. To give you an escape hatch, in case you change your mind about the changes, Paradox temporarily saves the original version of the target table, without changes, in a temporary table named Changed. Paradox displays Changed at the completion of the query. You then can use the **A**dd option on the Tools More menu (see Chapter 13) to merge the records in Changed back into the table if you decide that you changed too much.

Finding Records with the FIND Operation

The FIND operation in a query form serves a purpose similar to the **Z**oom option on the Image menu and the Ctrl-Z (Zoom) keystroke command but provides the added flexibility of Query By Example. To use this operation, type *find* in the left column of the query form. You then can build a search criterion as normal, except that check marks and group operators are not permitted.

Reminder:
The FIND operation serves a purpose similar to Zoom.

When performing a FIND query, Paradox places your cursor in the first record of the target table that meets the criterion. At the same time, the program creates (but does not display) an Answer table containing the selected records, arranged in the order displayed in the target table rather than in sorted order.

Use the FIND operation to view or edit the target table. You may want to check the date of the first order placed by customer Eastern Enterprises with salesman Harry Jones, for example. A normal query would produce an answer table including this information, but you want to view the record for this order in the Orders table. To find this record, you can use the FIND operation. You first display a query form for Orders, then you type the word *find* in the first column (under *Orders*), type *1000* in the Cust ID # column, and type *111-33-8491* in the Emp ID # column. When you press F2 (Do-It!), Paradox moves the cursor to the proper order in Orders. The program also creates an Answer table but does not display the answer on the desktop.

Cue:
Use the FIND operation to view or edit the target value.

For Related Information:

◄◄ "Using the Zoom Options," p. 136.

FROM HERE...

Performing Queries on a Network

Using queries on a network is fairly worry-free. When you place a query form on the desktop, Paradox checks to see whether anyone else already has placed a full lock on the table. If so, you have to wait until the other user is finished before you can do the query. Otherwise, Paradox places a prevent full lock on the table, enabling all other network users complete access to the table.

Reminder:
A prevent full lock is placed on a shared table during a query.

Except for the operations that change the original table (INSERT, DELETE, and CHANGETO), Paradox takes a "snapshot" of the table during a period when no changes are being made and then runs your query from the snapshot. Using this method, you can perform queries on a table even while the table is being viewed or edited by another user on the network.

FROM HERE...

For Related Information:

◄◄ "Creating Tables on a Network," p. 82.

Chapter Summary

Now that you have a firm grasp of Paradox QBE, everything else will be easy. Interactive use of Paradox, as you have discovered, depends heavily on this methodology. In this chapter, you have learned how to use example elements, multiple query forms, and outer joins. You also have learned how to perform several types of calculations and comparisons on table data, including grouped summary calculations and set comparisons. Finally, you learned how to change Paradox tables directly and permanently by using special query operations.

Continue your tour through Paradox by turning to Chapter 8, "Using Advanced Form Techniques." Some of the multitable concepts discussed in this chapter also come into play in that chapter, as you explore how to create multitable and multirecord forms.

Using Advanced Form Techniques

U ntil now, this book has said little about Paradox's form view because you can accomplish almost every Paradox task in a tabular format. The table view, however, is not always the best way to look at data. Because your screen is only 80 characters wide, data is almost always hidden off-screen. By contrast, with form view, you can use the entire screen and often fit all the data from a record on one screen. This chapter explains how to design forms that present data exactly the way you want to see the data on-screen.

This chapter describes how to create calculated fields, borders, multipage forms, and fields that provide automatic word wrap. You can also display portions of the form in inverse video, intense video, blinking text, and custom foreground and background colors.

Some of the most important features of Paradox involve forms. With Paradox, you can enter data into multiple tables from one form without creating a multientry map table (which is still available and is discussed in Chapter 9). You also can create multirecord forms that combine many of the advantages of both views. By combining the features of multitable and multirecord forms, you can design amazingly powerful forms.

An Overview of Form Design

Building forms is similar to building reports. More is involved than just the raw data. In Paradox, you can use forms for entering, editing, and viewing data in one or multiple tables. Whatever the use, someone is going to be looking at the form and trying to use the data that form contains. You should design Paradox forms with the typical user of your database in mind. When you are the only user, your main concerns are probably speed and efficiency. When you build a form for someone else to use, you are usually more concerned with clarity and on-screen prompts.

Introducing Paradox Forms

You can think of a Paradox form as an alternate front end for your database (the other front end being the table view). The form is a structure or positioning that Paradox applies to on-screen data. Forms often include lines, labels, and prompts that surround your data as you enter information into a table but which have no effect on the data.

By default, Paradox displays your data in table view. When you press F7 (Form Toggle), Paradox switches to form view, using the current *preferred form*. For any new table, Paradox builds a standard form named *F* and assigns it as the preferred form. Because you know better than anyone else how you want the screen to look, Paradox enables you to customize forms and use several forms for one table. With Paradox 2.0 and above, you can design up to 15 forms per table, which means that you can create forms for special purposes as well as a customized form for the preferred form.

Paradox uses the standard form for form view unless you do one of the following:

- Alter the design of the standard form F.

- Use the **R**ename option or the **C**opy option on the Tools menu to replace the standard form F with a form you have designed.

- Use the **P**ickForm option on the Image menu to select another form you prefer and then save the settings with the Image menu's **K**eepSet option.

You can use the techniques described in this chapter to modify the standard form. The **R**ename and **C**opy options are discussed in

Chapter 13, "Using Paradox Tools," and the **P**ickform and **K**eepSet options are discussed in Chapter 3, "Entering, Editing, and Viewing Data."

Considering Form Design

Although many of the choices you make in form design involve personal preference, you should ask yourself the following important questions as you plan your form:

- *Who will be using the form?* When you are the only user, you can make your forms lean and mean. If you design forms for novices and infrequent users, include plenty of clear on-screen help and instructions.

- *Can you visualize the way the form will look?* Building the form is always easier if you sketch it on paper first. If you are duplicating an existing paper form, work from that example.

- *Will your new form replace an existing form?* When practical, design your form to look as much like the current form as possible. This approach may go a long way toward quick acceptance of your form.

- *Will computations be necessary?* When your data includes number information, you may want to create fields in the form that perform some calculation on-screen—price times quantity, for example.

- *Will you need to see multiple records in the form at one time?* Often, being able to see previous entries in a table as you enter the next entry (as in table view) is convenient, but you don't want to give up the flexibility and additional features of form view. The Paradox multirecord forms capability gives you the best of both views.

- *Is all the necessary information to go in one table, or will you have to place the data in several tables in the database?* The Paradox form designer can create multitable forms that enable this type of placement, but you have to make sure that your tables are properly defined and keyed. For one-to-many relationships, you can even combine multitable forms with multirecord forms. By combining several multirecord forms into a single multitable form, you can create a "windowing" effect.

As you are designing your form, keep in mind the basic form capacities of Paradox, summarized in table 8.1.

Table 8.1. Form Capacities	
Feature	**Capacity**
Fields	255
Tables	1 master and 9 detail tables
Width	80 characters per line
Length	23 lines per page
Pages (screens)	15 per single-record nonembedded form
	1 per embedded form
	1 per multirecord form
Records	21 per multirecord form
Forms	15 per table

For Related Information:

◄◄ "Enjoying the View," p. 98.

FROM HERE...

Examining the Standard Form

The standard form provides a good example of a completed form. Figure 8.1 shows the standard form for the Customer table. The following indicators help you keep track of the form window:

- *Cursor position indicator.* In the lower left corner of the window for a new form, Paradox displays 1,1, a set of coordinates to represent the current cursor position. As you move the cursor around the screen, the coordinates change. The first number is the *row* position, and the second number is the *column* position. The lower right corner of the screen is coordinate 21,78.

- *Mode indicator.* In the lower right corner of the screen, you see that the desktop is in Form mode. (The mode indicator is discussed in detail in Chapter 1.)

- *Page indicator.* The page indicator, located to the right of the cursor position indicator, shows the page you are working on and the total number of pages in the form. For example, 1:1 means that you are on the first page of a one-page form.

■ *Field identifier.* When you move the cursor into a field, Paradox displays the type and name of the field in the status line and indicates whether the field is a wrapped field. In figure 8.1, the cursor is in the Cust ID # field, a regular field.

The standard form is reminiscent of the table structure screen (in Create mode). The field names are listed vertically on the left side of the screen rather than across the top as in standard table view. The standard form displays up to 19 fields per screen and then adds another page. When you have more than 19 fields, Paradox continues to add pages to the form, 19 fields to each page. Paradox forms can have up to 15 pages (screens), which is more than enough room for the maximum number of 255 fields per table.

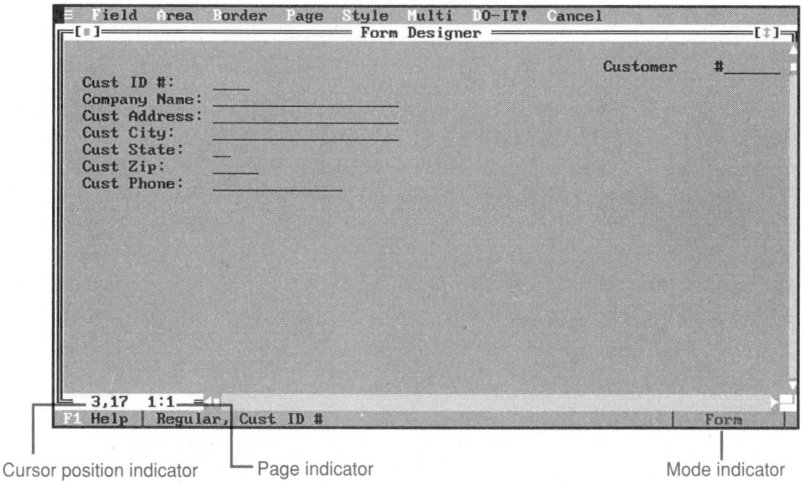

Reminder:
The standard form displays up to 19 fields before adding another page.

```
≡  Field  Area  Border  Page  Style  Multi  DO-IT!  Cancel
 ┌[■]══════════════════ Form Designer ══════════════════[↕]┐
 │                                          Customer    #_____  ▲
 │   Cust ID #:        ____                                      
 │   Company Name:     _____                            
 │   Cust Address:     _____                            
 │   Cust City:        _____                            
 │   Cust State:       __                                       
 │   Cust Zip:         _                                        
 │   Cust Phone:       _____                                
 │                                                              
 │                                                              ▼
 └─ 3,17  1:1 ─◄□──────────────────────────────────────────►
  F1 Help | Regular, Cust ID #                      | Form
```

Cursor position indicator — Page indicator   Mode indicator

FIG. 8.1

The standard form for the Customer table.

The field names that appear on the form are just text used for descriptive purposes, and they have no effect on the actual data you enter when you use the form. These labels are called *literals*. The lines that appear to the right of the literals represent the fields into which you enter data.

Reminder:
Literals have no effect on data.

The built-in standard form demonstrates only a few of the features of Paradox forms. The table name is displayed in inverse video in the upper right corner of the form, and the number symbol (#) followed by a field line is the record-number field.

The standard form is often adequate for small tables, especially if you are the only user who will be working with the data. But for most applications, you should design custom forms.

For Related Information:

◄◄ "Using the PickForm Option," p. 141.

FROM HERE...

Starting the Form Designer

To begin creating a custom form, start from the Main menu and select **F**orms, **D**esign. Then indicate the table for which you want to design a form.

Your next step is to name and describe your custom form. Paradox displays a list of 15 available form names: the letter *F* and the integers from 1 to 14. Form F is listed as the Standard Form. Each of the other 14 forms is initially listed as an Unused form. Remember that each form is a separate object and a member of the table's family of objects.

Click one of the unused form names with the mouse or use the cursor-movement keys to point to your choice and then press Enter. Paradox alerts you if you accidentally choose a form that has been used, giving you a chance to stop or to replace the old form definition with a new one. The first form, F, is the standard form. Because you may want to use the standard form at some other time, use other names for a new form.

After you have selected a name for your form, Paradox instructs you to `Enter a description for the new form`. You can enter any text up to 40 characters in length. (Paradox displays this description to the right of the form name the next time you are selecting a form name from the form name list.) After you type your description and press Enter, Paradox displays a blank window with the title `Form Designer`, as shown in figure 8.2.

After you have saved and tested your form, you may want to make changes. To alter the form, from the Main menu select **F**orms, **C**hange. Indicate first the table and then the name of the form you want to change.

Adding Labels and Prompts to the Form

When you use a form rather than a table, you can add text to the form. In Paradox, the term *literal* is used to refer to words, numbers, or other characters that appear on a form. Literals are not data and have no effect on data entered or edited with the form. You most often use literals to label fields, but you also can add literals as prompts, titles, and any text that you think would be helpful to users of the form.

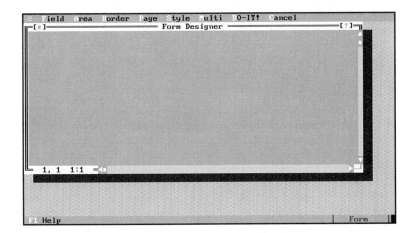

FIG. 8.2

A new form design screen.

Typing Literals

Typing literals on the form window is similar to typing on the report design screen. Review table 1.4 in Chapter 1 for a summary of cursor-movement key operation during form design. Remember that you can insert characters with the Ins key and delete characters with the Del key.

Suppose that you are designing a form for the Employee table to include all fields from the table and a temporary calculated field to display the length of time an employee has been working for the company. Using simple typing techniques, the cursor-movement keys, and the Ins and Del keys, you can type field labels *anywhere* in the window. Remember to leave enough space between labels for the fields. Your screen may look similar to figure 8.3. (***Note:*** The window in figure 8.3 is maximized.)

Moving and Erasing Portions of a Form

The line-delete (Ctrl-Y) feature of the report design screen does not work during form design. Instead, Paradox uses an *area* or block erase method. To erase a portion of the form, access the menu bar and select **Area, Erase.** Paradox prompts you to use the cursor-movement keys to move to a corner of the area to be erased. Do so and press Enter. Next, follow the prompt to move the cursor to the opposite diagonal corner of the area to be erased. To erase a single line, move the cursor to the opposite end of the line and press Enter. Paradox highlights the rectangular area between the starting position and the cursor. When all of the area to be removed is highlighted, press Enter. Paradox erases everything in the highlighted block—literals and fields alike.

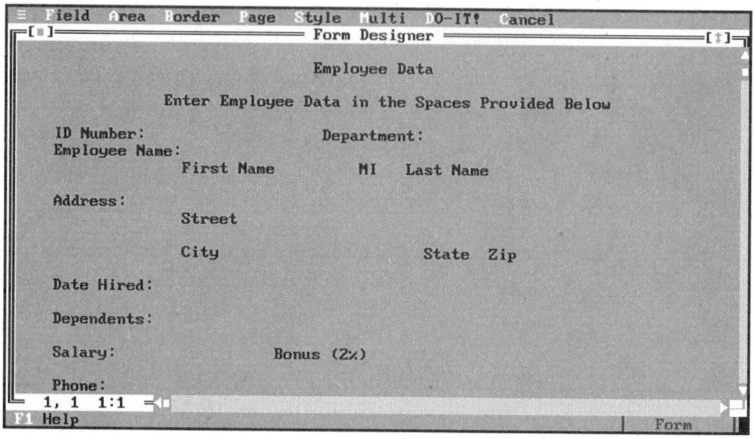

```
≡  Field  Area  Border  Page  Style  Multi  DO-IT!  Cancel
┌[■]══════════════════════ Form Designer ══════════════════════[↕]┐
│                          Employee Data                          │
│                                                                 │
│              Enter Employee Data in the Spaces Provided Below    │
│                                                                 │
│        ID Number:                    Department:                │
│        Employee Name:                                           │
│                       First Name        MI   Last Name          │
│                                                                 │
│        Address:                                                 │
│                    Street                                       │
│                                                                 │
│                    City                       State  Zip        │
│                                                                 │
│        Date Hired:                                              │
│                                                                 │
│        Dependents:                                              │
│                                                                 │
│        Salary:                   Bonus (2%)                     │
│                                                                 │
│        Phone:                                                   │
│═ 1, 1  1:1 ═◄▌                                               ▲  │
│ F1 Help                                            │    Form    ▐│
```

FIG. 8.3

Literals for the
Employee Data
form.

Cue:
To move a block of text,
use **A**rea, **M**ove.

Inserting a blank line in a form is not quite as simple as doing so in a report, but you can *move* an area of the form as a block. Moving a block on the form is almost the same as erasing. Just choose the **M**ove option rather than **E**rase from the Area menu. When you press Enter at the second corner of the block, Paradox doesn't erase the block but prompts you to use the cursor-movement keys to drag the area to its new location. The text and fields in the highlighted area do not move, but the highlighting does. Press Enter when the highlighted rectangle is in the appropriate position. Paradox then moves the contents of the area to the new location.

Paradox prevents you from accidentally overwriting a portion of your form. If you attempt to do so, the program displays the message Area must be placed in a clear space.

You will find yourself using both of these form-editing features often. Suppose that you are working on the form shown in figure 8.3 and decide that you want to put the Emp Phone field (labeled Phone:) just above the Date Hired field rather than at the bottom of the form. You decide to erase the literal Phone:, move down the labels Date Hired:, Dependents:, Salary:, and Bonus (2%):, and retype *Phone:* in the new position. When you are finished, the form looks like figure 8.4.

```
≡  Field  Area  Border  Page  Style  Multi  DO-IT!  Cancel
┌─[■]══════════════════════ Form Designer ═══════════════════[‡]─┐
        Enter Employee Data in the Spaces Provided Below

   ID Number:              Department:
   Employee Name:
                  First Name      MI    Last Name

   Address:
                  Street

                  City                  State  Zip

   Phone:

   Date Hired:

   Dependents:

   Salary:                  Bonus (2%)



═ 22,76   1:1  ═◄
  F1 Help                                          Form
```

FIG. 8.4

The form after labels are rearranged.

For Related Information:

◄◄ "Using the Keyboard When Designing Reports," p. 194.

FROM HERE...

Placing and Erasing Fields on the Form

Ultimately, the purpose of a form is to enter, edit, and view data from one or more tables. Therefore, you must place fields from the tables on the form. These fields are equivalent to the blanks in a fill-in-the-blank form. During data entry, you enter information into these fields, and Paradox places the information in the table. During form design, you do not have to place every field on the form, but for data-entry forms, you usually will.

Not all fields on a form are necessarily even defined in the underlying table(s). All fields in the standard form are those that you defined during the table-creation process. These fields are *regular* fields. When you design your own forms, Paradox enables you also to place *display-only* fields, *calculated* fields, and *record-number* fields.

Reminder:
Fields defined in the table are *regular* fields.

As you design your form, you may find yourself losing track of where you placed fields on-screen. Paradox has a handy feature to help you. To display field names where you place them, access the menu bar and select **S**tyle, **F**ieldnames **S**how. Then, as you follow the procedures de-scribed in the following sections for placing fields in the form, Paradox displays the field names rather than just a string of underscores. Of course, if the field name is longer than the field length, the name ap-pears truncated on-screen.

Placing Regular Fields

Typically, you place each regular field next to some sort of label. Other-wise, when you use the form in form view, you will be unable to tell into which field you are entering data.

Cue:

To place a regular field, select **F**ield, **P**lace, **R**egular.

To place a regular field, access the menu bar and select **F**ield, **P**lace, **R**egular. Paradox displays a list of available fields. Select the name of the appropriate field, position the cursor where the field should begin, and press Enter. (Paradox displays a line of hyphens and prompts you to use the cursor-movement keys to adjust the length of the field.) The line is normally at the maximum defined field length, so you can leave the line as is or use the left-arrow key to decrease the width and then press Enter. Paradox replaces the line of hyphens with a line of under-scores. (***Note:*** With the **S**tyle, **F**ieldnames, **S**how option chosen, the field name also appears.) As you place more fields on the form, Paradox does not enable you to place a field more than once.

Figure 8.5 shows the form for employee data with all regular fields de-fined. When the cursor is on one of the field lines of a regular field, the field identifier indicates the field type *Regular* followed by the field name.

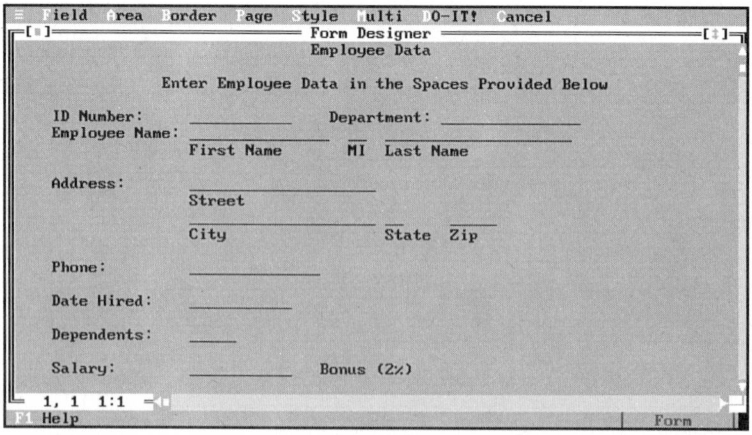

FIG. 8.5

The employee data form with regular fields defined.

Sometimes the maximum field length defined in the table structure is wider than necessary for your data. This situation often occurs with number fields because Paradox allows a maximum of 23 spaces. Your form will look better and use space more efficiently if you shorten these fields to a size just wide enough for the data you intend to enter. Note, however, that you should not make the field length shorter than five spaces for a number field, even when the data needs no more than one space. Paradox needs a space each for a potential minus sign and decimal point and two digits to the right of the decimal.

If you already have entered a literal to the right of where you are placing a field, the dashed line may seem to replace some or all of the literal. Don't despair. Use the left-arrow key to shorten the field width, and the literal reappears.

Placing Display-Only Fields

In some circumstances, you want to display data in a form but not enable a user to change the data. At other times, you may want to display on subsequent pages of a form data that was entered on a previous page. You can fill both of these needs by using *display-only* fields.

A display-only field is like an exhibit in a museum. You can see it, but you cannot touch it. You cannot change the data during data entry or editing. The cursor never moves into a display-only field.

To place a display-only field in a form, access the menu bar and select Field, Place, DisplayOnly. Choose the appropriate field and then use the cursor-movement keys to position the field. Press Enter and adjust field length, just as you do with a regular field. When the field is the correct length, press Enter. When the cursor is resting on a display-only field during form design, the field identifier displays the field type DisplayOnly.

Suppose that the form shown in figure 8.5 was intended for use by employees to keep their personal information up-to-date. You may want to make such sensitive fields as Salary and Date Hired display-only. Neither field should be modifiable by the employee.

Placing Calculated Fields

Because forms often are designed for looking at data, they are frequently good candidates for the inclusion of calculations based on record data. A calculated field in a Paradox form is defined by a formula that depends on the value of one or more regular fields. By changing the value of the regular field(s), you change the value of the calculated field.

To place a calculated field, access the menu bar and select Field, **P**lace, **C**alculated. Then type an expression (a formula) that will produce the result you need. Refer to the discussion in Chapter 5 on "Placing Calculated Fields" for details on how to type a formula for number and alphanumeric fields. The normal arithmetic operators (+, −,*, /, (, and)) are available for use in these formulas, but summary operators are not. After typing the formula, press Enter.

For example, the form in figure 8.5 includes the literal Bonus (2%):. The value of this field for any particular record is determined by multiplying 0.02 (2 percent) by the employee's salary. Therefore, the appropriate expression is as follows:

    [Salary] * .02

When the cursor is in a calculated field, Paradox displays the formula in the status line (see fig. 8.6)

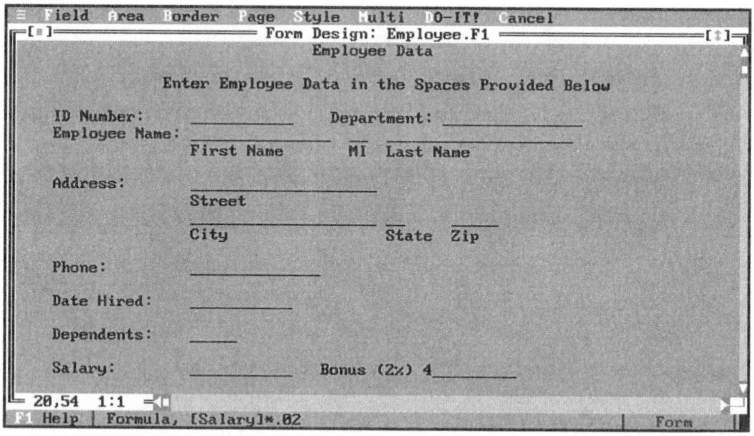

FIG. 8.6

A calculated field.

To change a formula after you have placed a calculated field, use the CalcEdit option. Access the menu bar and select **F**ield, **C**alcEdit. Position the cursor on the calculated field whose formula you want to alter and press Enter. Paradox displays the formula in a dialog box for editing. The current formula is highlighted. You can type a new entry to replace the old one, erase with the Backspace key and retype, or press the left-arrow key and make changes. When the formula is correct, press Enter or click OK.

Placing the Record-Number Field

As you add records to a table, Paradox assigns a record number. Having this number somewhere on your form is handy. To display the record number on the form, access the menu bar and select **F**ield, **P**lace, #Record. Position the cursor where you want the field to begin and press Enter again. Adjust the length if necessary and then press Enter or just press Enter to accept the length.

Erasing and Reformatting Fields on the Form

To remove a field from a form, access the menu bar and select **F**ield, **E**rase. Move the cursor to the field to be removed and press Enter. Paradox erases the field from the form.

If you decide that you initially placed a field with the wrong length, you can easily change the length. Access the menu bar and select Field **Re**format. Move the cursor to the field you need to lengthen or shorten and press Enter. Paradox displays a dashed line. Use the cursor-movement keys to increase or decrease the field length to suit your purposes. Press Enter to accept the new length.

For Related Information:

◄◄ "Inserting and Deleting Fields," p. 77.

FROM HERE...

Enhancing the Form

So far in this chapter, you have seen several of the advantages of custom forms over the standard form. You now know how to place any text you want on the form, how to position the fields where you need them, and how to use display-only and calculated fields. The next few sections describe how Paradox also enables you to create multiline fields with automatic word wrap, place borders around portions of the form, add pages to the form, and add special screen attributes.

Creating Multiline Fields with Word Wrap

A common problem with many database programs is how to allow for lengthy but workable alphanumeric fields. Paradox enables you to use alphanumeric fields with a maximum width of 255 characters, as well as unlimited-length memo fields, but table view and the standard form view enable you to see no more than a screen-width at a time. Using custom forms and Paradox's word-wrap feature, however, you can display long alphanumeric fields and memo fields on multiple lines.

Placing a lengthy field on the form with word wrap is a two-step procedure. First, place the field on the form as usual. The left and right ends of this initial field define the left and right margins of the multiline field.

To invoke the word-wrap feature, access the menu bar and select **F**ield, **W**ordWrap. Use the cursor-movement keys to move to the target field and press Enter. At the Number of lines: prompt, type the number of lines that Paradox should reserve in the form for the field. The only way to tell whether a field is a wrapped field is to place the cursor in the field and look at the field identifier. When the cursor is resting in a word-wrap field, the message in the status line is wrap:n, where n is the number you indicated as the maximum number of lines for the field.

Make sure that you leave enough empty space below a wrapped field for the maximum number of wrapped lines. Otherwise, when you attempt to save the form, Paradox informs you that the form contains insufficient space for the wrapped field, and the program refuses to save the form.

When you use this form for data entry and type text in the word-wrap field, Paradox knows when you type past the right margin of the field. The cursor moves down to the next line. The program also detects spaces between words and does not split a word between two lines, unless the word is bigger than an entire line of the field. Memo fields are still edited in the Paradox Editor (refer to Chapter 3).

Adding and Deleting Borders, Boxes, and Lines

Cue:
To add a border, select
Border, **P**lace.

Often, small things are what make a design look complete. When you are designing forms, you can use borders, boxes, or lines to make your forms look polished and professional. Paradox refers to lines around portions of the screen as *borders*. To add a border, access the menu bar and select **B**order, **P**lace. Then choose among the following options:

■ **S**ingle-line. Produces a single unbroken line

■ **D**ouble-line. Produces a double unbroken line

■ **O**ther. Forms a border from any repeating character you choose (for example, *****)

After you choose the type of border, Paradox prompts you to use the cursor-movement keys to move to a corner of the area that should be surrounded by the border. Then the program instructs you to use the cursor-movement keys to move to the opposite diagonal corner of the form. As you move the cursor, Paradox draws the border on-screen. When the border is positioned the way you intended, press Enter.

Figure 8.7 shows a single-line border around the Employee Data form. You are not limited to one border per form or even one per screen. Use the **B**order option to create as many boxes on the form as you want. This feature also is useful for creating straight vertical or horizontal single lines, double lines, or repeated characters on the form. You create straight lines by moving the cursor vertically or horizontally, but not both ways.

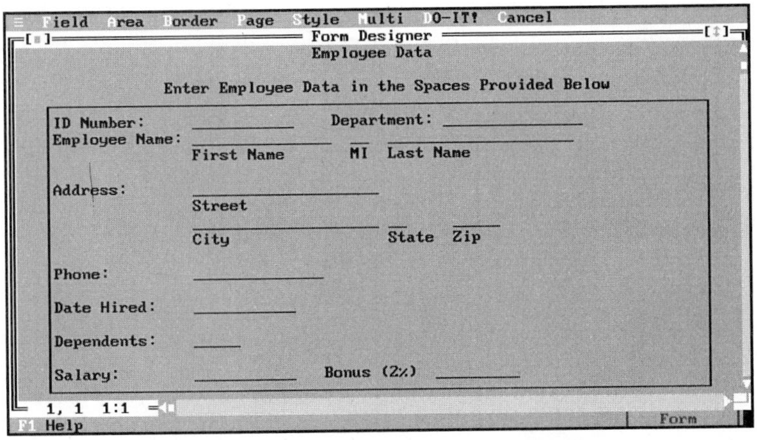

```
 ield  rea  order  age  tyle  ulti  O-IT!  ancel
[ ]                    Form Designer                    [ ]
                       Employee Data

          Enter Employee Data in the Spaces Provided Below

 ID Number:       _____     Department:  _____
 Employee Name: _____
                 First Name     MI  Last Name

 Address:
                 Street  _____
                 City  _____   State  Zip
                                           ___  ___

 Phone:          _____

 Date Hired:     _____

 Dependents:     _____

 Salary:         _____     Bonus (2%)  _____

 1, 1  1:1                                          Form
 F1 Help
```

FIG. 8.7

The employee data form enhanced with a border.

A quick way to move to the other side of the screen is through the back door. To move from the left edge of the screen to the right edge, press the left-arrow key. The cursor wraps around to the right side of the screen. This process works left-to-right, right-to-left, top-to-bottom, and bottom-to-top. The technique is especially helpful when you are highlighting a large portion of the screen for a border or for a block move or erase.

Removing a border is almost the same as adding a border. Access the menu bar and select **B**order, **E**rase. Position the cursor at a corner of

Cue:
To erase a border, select **B**order, **E**rase.

the border, press Enter, move to the diagonally opposite corner, and press Enter again. Paradox erases the border.

Adding and Deleting Pages

Database tables sometimes can grow to encompass a large number of fields. Ideally, you should break up large tables into smaller tables, but that approach may not always make sense. For extremely large tables, you may not be able to fit all the fields on one screen and leave any room for labels and prompts. Unlike in table view, Paradox does not enable you to scroll off the screen while in form view. You can, however, add pages. A page on a Paradox form is just another complete screen.

Cue:
To add a page, select **P**age, **I**nsert.

Paradox forms are by default only one page (one full screen height and width) in size. To add a page, access the menu bar and select **P**age, **I**nsert. You then must choose to add the new page **A**fter or **B**efore the current page. As soon as you add the new page, Paradox places the cursor in that page at coordinate 1,1 so that you can begin designing the page. Use the PgUp and PgDn keys to move between pages. You must place at least one regular field on each page. Paradox does not enable you to save the form until each page has at least one regular field.

Cue:
To delete a page, select **P**age, **D**elete, **O**K.

If you decide that you don't need one of the pages, you can delete the page as easily as you added it. First, position the cursor somewhere on the page to be deleted. Then access the menu bar and select **P**age, **D**elete, **O**K. Paradox removes the page and all its contents from the form.

Customizing Color

Paradox looks best on a color screen. Judicious use of color is an excellent way of accenting input forms and making them more interesting to use. With Paradox, you can apply as many as 128 color combinations to areas of the screen and to any borders you create with the **B**order option.

Cue:
To add color, select **S**tyle, **C**olor.

To add color, access the menu bar and select **S**tyle, **C**olor. Choose to apply the new color combination to an **A**rea of the form or to a **B**order. Then use the cursor-movement keys to move to a corner of the area or border, press Enter, use the cursor-movement keys to move to the diagonally opposite corner, and press Enter again. Paradox displays a color palette in the upper left corner of the screen. Use the arrow keys to move to the background/foreground color combination you prefer and then press Enter. You can use as many different colors on-screen as you want, but try not to get carried away. Use color to enhance the form, not overwhelm it.

When you are using the color palette to select a color combination, sometimes the palette obscures the portion of the screen that you want to color. Press Alt-C to toggle off the palette. Use the arrow keys to cycle through the various color combinations and press Enter to accept the new colors.

Changing Screen Attributes

Paradox provides methods for displaying literals and borders in high-intensity, blinking, or inverse video. These attributes also can be applied to fields. Only the *blink* attribute can be applied with a color. The other attributes discussed in this section are intended for use with monochrome monitors.

To add one of these screen attributes to your form, access the menu bar and select **S**tyle, **M**onochrome. Then choose between **A**rea and **B**order. Move to a corner of the area or border and press Enter; move to the opposite corner and press Enter again. Use the right- and left-arrow keys to switch between these attributes. Each time you press an arrow key, the screen attribute changes in the following order:

Attribute	Description
Normal	Removes all monochrome and color settings
Blink	Literals or borders continuously blink; coexists with other settings
Non-Blink	Removes blinking without changing other settings
Intense	Causes foreground to display in intense video
Reverse	Literals or borders display in inverse video; does not coexist with color settings
Intense-Reverse	Displays in intense foreground and inverse video; does not coexist with color settings

Applying the blink attribute with another screen attribute requires two separate steps. You have to go through the steps once to apply the blink attribute and go through all steps again to add the other desired attribute.

When the area or border displays in the screen attribute you want to use, press Enter. Figure 8.8 shows the form title, Employee Data, in inverse video (the Reverse screen attribute).

```
Field  Area  Border  Page  Style  Multi  DO-IT!  Cancel
[■]                 Form Design: Employee.F1                [↕]
                          Employee Data

              Enter Employee Data in the Spaces Provided Below

    ID Number:  _____    Department:  _____
    Employee Name: _____
                   First Name    MI  Last Name
    Address:  /
              Street
              City                    State  Zip

    Phone:         _____
    Date Hired:    _____
    Dependents:    _____
    Salary:        _____    Bonus (2%)  _____
    1, 1  1:1
F1  Help                                            Form
```

FIG. 8.8

Adding inverse video.

You should routinely assign a color or screen attribute to literals in your forms so that you clearly distinguish them from fields. Otherwise, when you or someone else uses the form, distinguishing data from labels and prompts may be difficult. The easiest way is to assign the color combination you want for the entire form first and then assign a different color to the data fields. On a monochrome screen, for example, you may assign all literals the *intense* attribute.

For Related Information:

▸▸ "Enhancing the Report," p. 371.

Creating a Multirecord Form

Form view offers many aesthetic advantages over table view, but form view seems to have one major disadvantage: you can see only one record on-screen at a time. Paradox enables you, however, to add multirecord capability to forms without forcing you to give up the many positive aspects of using this alternate view.

For example, in the table view of the Customer table, you can see the information from many customers at the same time but cannot see all the fields for one customer (see fig. 8.9). Conversely, the standard form for Customer shows all fields, but only one customer at a time (see fig. 8.10). A multirecord form can give you the best of both worlds.

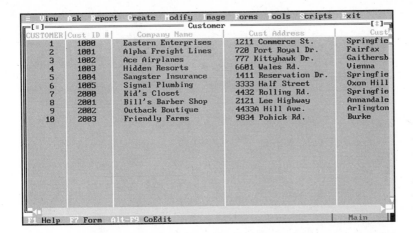

FIG. 8.9

The table view of the Customer table.

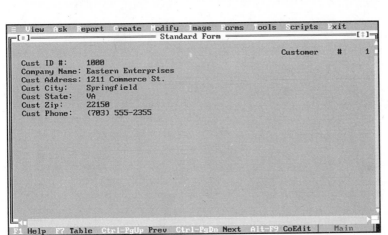

FIG. 8.10

The standard form view of the Customer table.

To create a multirecord form, first place all the appropriate fields for one record. The fields do not have to be all on one line, but you should group them closely together so that you can fit more records on-screen at the same time. Figure 8.11 shows all the fields for the Customer table placed on a form. This first record is the *original record*.

To multiply the original record, access the menu bar and select **M**ulti, **R**ecords, **D**efine. Use the cursor-movement keys to move to a corner of the area that contains the original record and press Enter. Next, use the cursor-movement keys to move to the other diagonal corner and press Enter again. Paradox highlights the entire original record area. Then each time you press the down-arrow key, Paradox adds another copy of the original record. Each time you press the up-arrow key, Paradox

Cue:
To multiply the original record, select **M**ulti, **R**ecords, **D**efine.

removes a copy of the original record. Paradox does not enable you to place more copies than fit completely on-screen. After you have added enough forms, press Enter.

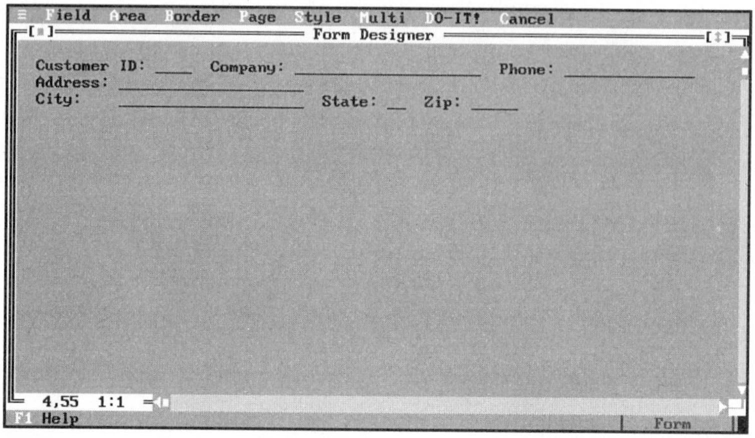

FIG. 8.11

The original record.

Figure 8.12 shows the Customer form description multiplied four more times. Now you can see all fields for five customers at the same time. You also can scroll through the entire table, always viewing five records at a time.

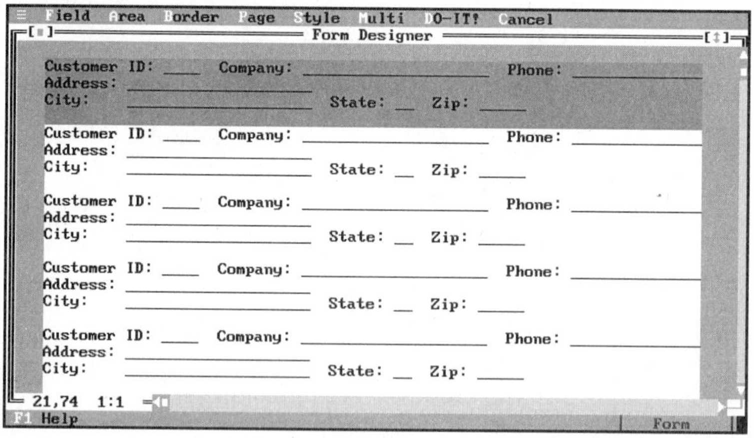

FIG. 8.12

A multirecord form.

Include at least one blank line at the beginning or end of the original record so that you have some space separating each record from the next.

As evident in figure 8.12, Paradox displays the multiple record area of the screen in inverse video (highlighting). To turn off this highlighting, access the menu bar and select **S**tyle, **S**howHighlight, **H**ide. You can turn the highlighting back on by selecting **S**tyle, **S**howHighlight, **S**how.

If you decide to remove the multirecord feature from the form, access the menu bar and select **M**ulti, **R**ecords, **R**emove. Paradox removes all copies of the original form, leaving only the first record.

The multirecord feature becomes extremely useful when coupled with the multitable capability, which is covered in the next section.

For Related Information:

◄◄ "Enjoying the View," p. 98.

FROM HERE...

Creating a Multitable Form

Relational database theory and technology promise power, flexibility, and efficiency, but often at the cost of convenience to the typical user. A properly normalized order-entry database, such as the one used as an example in this book, uses at least five different tables to store information about any one order: Orders, Detail, Product, Customer, and Employee. If a new salesperson sells a new product to a new customer, entries must be made in all five tables to track one order. To help alleviate potential confusion and greatly speed data entry in such situations, Paradox provides multitable forms that enable you to enter data into more than one table.

Understanding Relationships among Tables

Chapter 2 introduces you to the concept of relationships among tables. Because you need to have a good grasp of this concept before you can design multitable forms, you should look at Chapter 2's discussion of table relationships. Paradox enables you to create forms that not only service several tables but also, in certain instances, enforce the relationships among these tables.

When you build a multitable form, one table is designated as the *owner* of the form. The form is a member of the table's *family*. The table that owns the form also is the *master* table. Other tables serviced by the multitable form are *detail* tables.

When you build multitable forms, Paradox recognizes the relationships between pairs of tables, even if you don't. You must have structured the tables properly, however, for the necessary links to be established. The following two rules may help you:

- The unique end of the link is the *one-side*.

- The one-side link field must be keyed and therefore must be the first field in the table's structure.

To keep this section from becoming too complex, multikey fields are not discussed. The basic concepts, however, are the same as for single-key fields.

The tables used as examples in this book have the following relationships:

Tables	Relationship
Orders-to-Detail	One-to-many
Orders-to-Customer	Many-to-one
Orders-to-Employee	Many-to-one
Detail-to-Product	Many-to-one
Orders-to-Product	Many-to-many

In each case, the one-side table structure starts with the link field. The first field in Orders is the Order # field, which is the link to Detail; the first field in Customer is the Cust ID # field, which is the link to Orders; and so forth.

The most difficult relationship to understand is between Orders and Product. Because each order potentially can include more than one product, and each product can be found in more than one order, the tables meet the definition of a many-to-many relationship. To help you avoid having to deal directly with this relationship, you use the Detail table to buffer or link the two tables.

You may want to see information from Product and Orders on-screen at the same time, but Paradox does not enable a two-tier link in multitable forms. One solution to this problem is to restructure Detail to include Product Name, Price, and Cost, but this approach would violate the basic rule of avoiding data duplication. Fortunately, you can use a special feature called *validity checks* to eliminate duplicate entry. Validity checks are discussed in the next chapter.

Multitable forms that use a one-to-one or one-to-many relationship get special editing support, *referential integrity*, from Paradox.

Enforcing Referential Integrity

Referential integrity is much easier to understand than to say. Suppose that a customer places an order for three different kinds of widgets. To record this transaction, you have to add one record to Orders and three records to Detail. If, an hour later, you realize that you used the wrong order number and have to change the number in the Orders table, you also must change the number in each of the Detail records. Otherwise, the link is lost. Similarly, if the customer calls and cancels the order, you cannot just delete the record from the Orders table. You also have to delete the three records from the Detail table. This example describes referential integrity.

The formal referential integrity rule for relational databases states that a detail table cannot contain a link field value that doesn't occur in the master table. You don't want to have records in the Detail table, for example, for an order that is not found in the Orders table. With respect to data entered in tables linked by a one-to-one or a one-to-many relationship, this rule of referential integrity leads to the following two rules:

- Any change to the link field in a master table record must be accompanied by a corresponding change to the link field of each referenced (linked) record in the detail table.

- All referenced (linked) records in the detail table must be removed before a record in the master table can be removed.

When you use multitable forms to enter and edit data in tables with one-to-one or one-to-many relationships, Paradox (Version 3.0 and later) helps you ensure that referential integrity is maintained. When you alter the link field in the master table, Paradox makes an identical change to the link field data in each corresponding detail record. This step enforces the first rule. Paradox enforces the second rule by not enabling you to delete a master record until you remove all corresponding detail records. If you try to delete a master record, you see the message `Can't delete master record while detail records depend on it.`

Understanding the Structure of Multitable Forms

A multitable form is one or more detail forms *embedded* in a master form. You must follow these rules when building multitable forms:

- You can embed up to nine detail forms in a master form.
- The master form can be multipage but cannot be multirecord.
- Each detail/embedded form can be multirecord but not multipage.
- One embedded form cannot contain another embedded form.

Building the Master Form

The first step in building a multitable form is deciding which table is the master table and, therefore, the owner of the master form. Two sometimes competing considerations can help you determine which table should be the master:

- Paradox enables only direct links between master and detail tables. You should try to choose as the master table the table with the most direct links to other tables. For example, the Orders table is linked directly to Customer, Employee, and Detail. Orders is not linked directly to Product, but that table is the only one that cannot be included if you use Orders as the master table.

- Paradox enforces referential integrity in one-to-one and one-to-many relationships. Master-detail tables should fit into one of these categories. In this book's example, Orders and Detail are linked in a one-to-many relationship, but Orders-to-Customer and Orders-to-Employee have the opposite relationship (many-to-one).

Assuming that the purpose of your form is primarily to enter order detail rather than customer or employee data, suppose that you decide to choose Orders as the master table and embed a form only from Detail.

To also show Customer and Employee data, without risking referential integrity, you can embed forms from each of these tables and use only display-only fields in those embedded forms.

When you have a master table, you then design the master form, using the procedures already covered in this chapter. Figure 8.13 shows a form containing the fields from the Orders table.

```
 ≡  Field  Area  Border  Page  Style  Multi  DO-IT!  Cancel
 ┌─[■]════════════════════ Form Designer ═══════════════════[↕]─┐
 │                        Order Entry Form                       │▲
 │                                                               │▓
 │       Order Number: _____        Date: _____           │
 │                                                               │
 │       Customer Indentification Number: ____                   │
 │                                                               │
 │       Salesperson's Identification Number: _____          │
 │                                                               │
 │       Notes: _____             │
 │                                                               │
 │                                                               │
 │                                                               │
 │                                                               │
 │                                                               │
 │                                                               │
 │                                                               │▼
 │  1, 1  1:1  ═◄▪                                          ►═   │
 ═ F1 Help                              │          Form          │▓
```

The master form
for a linked
multitable.

Building the Embedded Forms

The next step is designing the detail form(s). As you design and build each detail form, keep in mind that the form eventually will become a part of the master form.

Consider the following rules when building forms that will be embedded:

- The link field(s) in the detail table must be keyed.

- The link field(s) cannot be placed as a regular field in the embedded form.

- All nonlink fields must be placed in the form so that you can enter data in them. You need to place in the form all key fields that are not part of the link. These key fields are needed to break ties between detail records with identical link values.

- The size of an embedded form is determined by its *natural size*, the size from the top left corner of the form design screen to the diagonally opposite corner that includes all literals and fields. Therefore, the best place to build embedded forms is usually as near to the upper left corner of the screen as possible.

Because Detail can contain multiple records for the same order, you also should make this embedded form multirecord. Figure 8.14 shows a multirecord form for Detail. Notice that the form has no labels. The labels are provided in the master form. For single-record embedded forms, such as this example, you don't want the labels to repeat over and over. You create a minitable view of the embedded table by placing column headings in the master form and placing the multirecord embedded form beneath the headings. The table has only three fields. The Order # field is not included, because that field is the link between Orders and Detail.

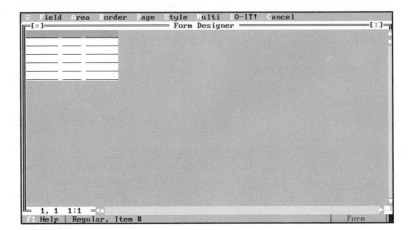

FIG. 8.14

The Detail portion of the linked multitable form.

Embedding the Form

The final step is to embed the detail form into the master form. While in Form mode and while designing or changing the master form, access the menu bar and select **M**ulti, **T**ables, **P**lace, **L**inked. Indicate the detail table and then the detail form (in this example, select the Detail table and the Detail table's multirecord form). Paradox determines the key field(s) that you have not placed on the detail form and asks which field(s) in the master table is (are) the corresponding link(s). In this example, the Order # field is the link.

Paradox then displays a highlighted block in the lower right corner of the screen that is the *natural* size of the detail form. Use the cursor-movement keys to drag this block to the appropriate position and press Enter. Paradox fills in the block with shading. When you move the cursor into this area, Paradox displays a message near the upper right corner of the screen, indicating that this block is an Embedded table. Figure 8.15 shows the completed multitable form, after the form has been embedded and the labels added. When you use a multitable form for data entry, editing, or viewing data, you use F3 (Up Image) and F4 (Down Image) to move between the forms. Figure 8.16 shows the data for order number 100 displayed in the Orders multitable form. The master record from the Orders table and three detail records from the Detail table are displayed on-screen together in the same form.

```
 ≡ Field  Area  Border  Page  Style  Multi  DO-IT!  Cancel
 [■]════════════════════════ Form Designer ════════════════════[↕]
    Order Number: _____        Date: _____

    Customer Indentification Number: ____

    Salesperson's Identification Number: _____

    Notes: _____

                   Item # Model Quantity
                   ────── ───── ────────

 ═ 12,51  1:1  ═◄                                            ◄►
 F1 Help                                          │  Form
```

FIG. 8.15

The completed linked multitable form.

```
 ≡ View  Ask  Report  Create  Modify  Image  Forms  Tools  Scripts  Exit
 [■]════════════════════════ Multitable form ════════════════[↕]
                        Order Entry Form

    Order Number: 100                Date:  9/02/92

    Customer Indentification Number: 1000

    Salesperson's Identification Number: 230-76-2376

    Notes: This order was received via FAX.

                   Item # Model Quantity
                   ────── ───── ────────
                     1    A333   50
                     2    B107   25
                     3    G400   10


 F1 Help  F7 Table  Ctrl-PgUp Prev  Ctrl-PgDn Next  Alt-F9 CoEdit │  Main
```

FIG. 8.16

Using a linked multitable form.

For Related Information:

▶▶ "Entering and Editing Data with Multitable Forms," p. 335.

FROM HERE...

Building and Using Unlinked Forms

Paradox enables you to create a windowing effect with form view by embedding forms without linking them. Unlinked forms are treated as completely unrelated. Therefore, you can use this procedure to combine almost any forms.

To embed an unlinked form, display one of the forms in the form window and access the menu bar. Then select **M**ulti, **T**ables, **P**lace, **U**nlinked. Indicate the appropriate table and form, use the cursor-movement keys to position the highlighted block, and press Enter. Save the form by pressing F2 (Do-It!). Figure 8.17 shows an example of an unlinked multitable form that includes Employee data and Customer data on the same screen. You can switch between tables by pressing F3 (Up Image) and F4 (Down Image).

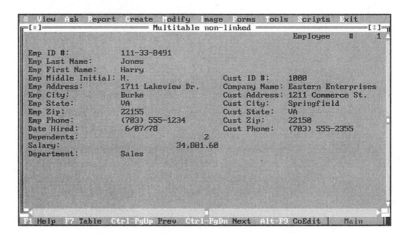

A sample unlinked multitable form

Changing an Existing Form

After you have used a form, you may decide to make changes. To access the form again, you must access the menu bar, select **F**orms, **C**hange, and specify the proper table.

When you start the form designer with the **C**hange option, Paradox displays a list of only the previously defined forms. If you want to enhance the automatic standard form, you can choose F from the form name list.

To enhance the standard form and keep an unaltered version, first copy the standard form definition to one of the other form names, using the **C**opy option from the Tools menu (see Chapter 13). You then can make the appropriate changes to the copy and leave form F intact.

For Related Information:

▶▶ "Copying Paradox Objects," p. 430.

FROM HERE...

Saving a Form

When you have finished defining a form, you save the form by pressing F2 (Do-It!). Paradox saves the form as an object in the table's family of objects.

Using Forms on a Network

When you are designing or changing a form on a network, Paradox places a prevent full lock on the table on which the form is based but places a full lock on the form. You cannot access a form while someone else on the network is using that form. Also, when one user is coediting with a multitable form, all users wanting to edit the table must use the same form.

Cue:
On a network, Paradox places a prevent full lock on the master table.

Chapter Summary

This chapter has explained how to design forms that present data exactly the way you want to see it on-screen. This chapter, however, presents only half the story about entering and editing data. The form is the canvas that users see while adding to or changing data in a database, but Paradox provides a number of important behind-the-scenes edit and entry features that can help maintain valid data. These powerful features are discussed in Chapter 9.

Using Power Entry and Editing Features

This chapter introduces you to some of Paradox's most powerful data-entry and editing capabilities. The greatest database system in the world is no better than the data placed within the system. Paradox provides a number of special data-entry and editing tools *(validity checks)* to assist you in snagging errors before they are buried in your database. This chapter introduces you to these error-prevention features and demonstrates how you can save labor with them.

Expanding on Chapter 8's discussion of forms, this chapter discusses how to use Paradox's multitable forms for DataEntry, Edit, and CoEdit modes and explains how Paradox handles master records, linked fields, and key violations.

This chapter also covers the **MultiEntry** option. The **MultiEntry** feature enables you to enter and edit data in multiple tables. Aspects of **MultiEntry** also are important to **MultiAdd**, covered in Chapter 13. These last two topics are introduced in Part III, "Programming Paradox."

Finally, you learn in this chapter how to use the Paradox **S**ort option to rearrange records.

Adding and Using Validity Checks

Validity checks are a group of features that help you enter data more easily and accurately. Validity checks are accessed from the DataEntry menu or the Edit menu, but once established, they also are effective in CoEdit mode. Validity checks apply in table and form views and help you prevent the entry of invalid data. Paradox always provides a certain amount of validity checking based on the defined structure of a table. Text is never allowed in a number field, for example. The features discussed in this section go beyond this minimal screening.

Several of the validity checks do more than prevent the entry of invalid data. You can use the TableLookup options, for example, to fill in data. When you see how well these features work, you will never want to edit a table without them.

All options discussed in this section are accessed through the **Val**Check choice on the DataEntry or the Edit menu and apply only to the current image. When you add or clear validity checking, the change takes effect immediately. The validity settings that are current when you end an edit session are saved as an object in the table's family for use in future sessions.

Controlling the Range of Acceptable Values

Usually, Paradox enables the entry of any number in a number or currency field and any date in a date field. In most database applications, however, field values usually occur within a fairly narrow range. For example, you may want to limit Salary values in the Employee table to the range $12,000 to $100,000. Paradox provides a group of validity-checking tools that enable you to place limits on acceptable data in number, currency, date, and alphanumeric fields.

Cue:
To establish a minimum value for a field, select **V**alCheck, **D**efine, **L**owValue.

To establish a minimum value for a field, access the menu bar from DataEntry or Edit mode and select **Val**Check, **D**efine. Move the cursor to the target field and press Enter. From a pop-up menu, select

LowValue. For a number or currency field, just type a number and press Enter. When you are placing a minimum on a date field, however, you can type a specific date or the special keyword *today*, which represents the system-supplied date. After you have made your entry, Paradox displays the message `Low value recorded`.

After you establish the minimum, Paradox prevents the entry of data below this value. For example, if you set a low value of 12000 for the Employee Salary field and then try to enter 11000, Paradox refuses to enter the data and displays the error message `Value no less than 12000.00 is expected`. Paradox does not enable the cursor to leave the field. You must erase or correct the error before you can proceed. Refer to this chapter's section on "Using Lookup Tables" for a description of how to construct a list of acceptable values.

You establish a ceiling or maximum acceptable value in the same manner. From DataEntry or Edit mode, access the menu bar and select **V**alCheck, **D**efine. Move the cursor to the target field and press Enter. Then select **H**ighValue. For a number or currency field, type a number and press Enter. Paradox displays the message `High value recorded`. For a date field, you may type a specific date or the keyword *today* and press Enter. As with the low value check, when you set a high value check, Paradox prevents the entry of data that falls beyond that upper limit.

Cue:
To establish a ceiling, select **V**alCheck, **D**efine, **H**ighValue.

Establishing a Default Value

Although in theory every record in your database is unique, in practice much of the information in many records is repetitive. The State field in the Employee table, for example, contains VA in every record. To streamline such repetitions, you can establish a value that the program enters in any field left blank during DataEntry, Edit, or CoEdit.

To assign a default value to a field, access the menu bar from Edit or DataEntry mode and select **V**alCheck, **D**efine. Move the cursor to the target field and press Enter. Then select **D**efault from the pop-up menu. Type the value you want established as the default and press Enter. Paradox displays a message at the bottom of the screen that reads `Default value recorded`.

Cue:
To assign a default value, select **V**alCheck, **D**efine, **D**efault.

For the Emp State field in the Employee table, you may establish VA as the default. Then each time you add a record, you can leave the State field blank and have Paradox fill in the correct value. If a new Employee lives in Maryland, you can override the default by typing *MD* in the State field and pressing Enter.

Using Lookup Tables

Preventing the entry of data outside a given range is helpful but still may not be limiting enough to prevent errors. In many database applications, you should confine acceptable entries for a certain field to a finite set of values. In the Orders table, for example, the Cust ID # field should contain only values that occur in the Cust ID # field in the Customer table. Similarly, entries in the Orders table's Emp ID # field should each have a corresponding value in the Employee table. Paradox enables you to create a list of acceptable values for a given field. The program then compares new entries to the list, which often is referred to as a *lookup table*.

A lookup table is not a special kind of table, just a special way to use a table. In Paradox, you can use any table as a lookup table so long as it meets the following criteria:

- The field containing the validation data must be the first field in the table structure. This field is the *lookup field*.

- The lookup field must have the same data type, but not necessarily the same field name, as the field you want to validate.

- Normally you should key the lookup field, although this step is not a requirement. Do not create more than one key field for the lookup table. Paradox will not permit you use a table as a lookup table if the table has multiple key fields.

The Customer table meets these criteria. Cust ID # can be used as the lookup field to validate entry of customer ID numbers in the Orders table.

Activating a Private Lookup

Sometimes you want to use a lookup table for a particular field but don't want to give users direct access to the list of acceptable values. In Paradox, this type of lookup is a *private lookup*. To activate a private lookup, from Edit or DataEntry mode, access the menu bar and select **V**alCheck, **D**efine. Move the cursor to the target field and press Enter. Then select **T**ableLookup. At the prompt for a table name, type the name of the table containing the validation list or press Enter and choose the table from the list of available tables. Then choose **J**ustCurrentField, **P**rivateLookup. Notice that you don't specify the field to be matched in the other table.

Using Automatic Fill-In

The next logical step after simple data validation is for Paradox to enable you to select your entry from a list of valid data, or a *pick list*. Paradox calls this feature *HelpAndFill*.

To activate a HelpAndFill lookup, from Edit or DataEntry mode, access the menu bar and select **ValCheck, D**efine. Move the cursor to the target field and press Enter. Then select **TableLookup**. Indicate the lookup table and then choose **JustCurrentField, H**elpAndFill. Paradox displays the following message at the bottom of the screen: Table lookup recorded.

Cue:
To create a pick list of valid values, use the **H**elpAndFill command.

When you press F1, Paradox temporarily displays the lookup table on the desktop. Use the down- or up-arrow key to move to the record that contains the entry for which you are looking. Press F2 to select the record and return to the original table, or press Esc to return without selecting a record.

Suppose that you add a HelpAndFill lookup to the Cust ID # field in the Orders table to look up values from the Customer table (the lookup table). Then when you are entering the next order in Orders and come to the Cust ID # field (see fig. 9.1), you don't need a list of valid numbers handy. Press F1, and Paradox displays the Customer table (see fig. 9.2). Move the cursor down to the row for the customer, Sangster Insurance in this example, and press F2. Paradox places the number 1004 into the Cust ID # field in Orders.

Keep in mind that you do not have to use this feature. You can type the valid data on your own.

ORDERS	Order #	Cust ID #	Emp ID #	Date	
1	100	1000	230-76-2376	9/02/92	This order w
2	101	1003	329-76-2219	9/07/92	Special ship
3	102	1001	987-31-9873	9/08/92	This is a te
4	103	1002	111-33-8491	9/12/92	None
5	104	1005	129-88-4562	9/13/92	Special ship
6	105	1000	329-76-2219	9/16/92	None
7	106	1001	541-67-5555	9/19/92	This is a re
8	107	1004	230-76-2376	9/21/92	None
9	108	1003	111-33-8491	9/22/92	Special ship
10	109	1005	448-09-6721	9/24/92	Special ship
11	110	1000	987-31-9873	9/25/92	None
12	111	1002	230-76-2376	9/26/92	This is a re
13	112	1001	448-09-6721	9/29/92	This is a te
14	113	◄			

FIG. 9.1

The Orders table with the cursor in the Cust ID # field.

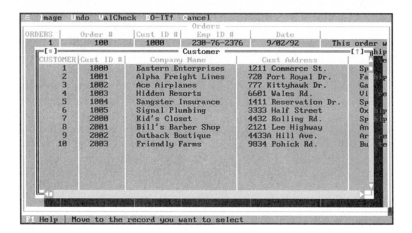

FIG. 9.2

The Customer table, used as a lookup table.

Using Multifield Automatic Fill-In

Paradox can even fill in multiple fields at the same time. You enter data into a field, and Paradox looks up and fills in other fields with corresponding data from another table. For automatic fill-in to be successful, each field to be filled in must have the same name and data type as a field in the lookup table.

Cue:
For multifield automatic fill-in, select **V**alCheck, **D**efine, **T**ableLookup and choose **A**llCorrespondingFields.

To activate a lookup with multifield automatic fill-in, from Edit or DataEntry mode, access the menu bar and select ValCheck, **D**efine. Move the cursor to the target field and press Enter. Then select TableLookup. Indicate the lookup table name and choose AllCorrespondingFields. Finally, choose between FillNoHelp and HelpAndFill. The first option is equivalent to a private lookup. This option checks the data entered for validity and fills in corresponding data when a match is found, but does not enable you to see the lookup table. The HelpAndFill option works the same as with single-field lookup. The next section describes an example that uses multifield lookup.

> **T I P** When you define a lookup with automatic fill-in, you should designate as display-only those fields to receive the looked-up data. This approach helps you maintain data integrity by protecting the looked-up data from alteration.

Also consider the following guidelines when you add a multifield lookup:

- Paradox does not perform validity checks on the data being filled in.

- You cannot use one lookup/fill-in operation to trigger another. Data that is filled in does not immediately cause Paradox to look up data from another lookup table. You need a second step. After the first lookup/fill-in, move the cursor to the second field for which you have defined a lookup. Press Alt-F5 (Field View) and Enter. Paradox performs the second lookup/fill-in.

- Changes to data in the lookup table are not retroactively posted to records in other tables where data was previously filled in.

Solving the Many-to-Many Problem

Chapter 8's section on building multitable forms includes a brief discussion of many-to-many table relationships. The relationship between the Orders table and the Product table is of this type. Because of the difficulties of representing many-to-many relationships in forms and reports, the examples in this book have used the Detail table as a link between Orders and Product. Using the Detail table converts the relationship into reciprocal one-to-many (Orders-to-Detail) and many-to-one (Detail-to-Product) relationships. This relationship is called *one-to-many-to-one*.

After the linkage table is added, you can more easily work with the database. For example, the multitable form developed as an example in Chapter 8 used Orders and Detail. As you work with database applications, you will find that many-to-many relationships are quite common. Conversion to a one-to-many-to-one relationship is the best way to handle these relationships.

Sometimes, however, you want to see information from all three tables in one-to-many-to-one relationships on-screen at the same time. The only way to handle this situation with properly normalized tables, however, is to use the *middle* table—Detail in this example—as the master table for multitable forms and to use the other two tables as embedded detail tables. This design, however, defeats the protective features of Paradox's automatic enforcement of referential integrity. In such a form, the master-to-detail relationships are many-to-one, and Paradox maintains referential integrity only for one-to-many relationships.

You have one way to solve this problem. First, decide which of the two *outside* tables in the relationship (Orders and Product in this example) you want to use as the master table in a form. The multitable form developed in Chapter 8 used Orders as the master table. Next, restructure the middle table to include all the fields from the other outside table that you want to see in the form. For example, you may want to see the

Product Name and Product Price fields on the order-entry form constructed in Chapter 8. You need to restructure Detail to include these fields.

Restructuring the middle table in this way seems to violate the rule that says you should not enter the same data more than once. You may think that every time you sell model A333, for example, you also have to type in the model name, Standard Widget, and the price, $39.95. Fortunately, you can use the TableLookup feature to eliminate the need for this duplication of data entry.

Use the TableLookup, AllCorrespondingFields validity check on the field that links the middle table to the nonmaster outside table. In the example, the Model # field links Detail to Products, so you place a TableLookup, AllCorrespondingFields validity check on this field. Paradox then fills in Product Price and Product Name when you provide the Model # field. To prevent any changes to data after it is looked up, you can make the Product Name and Product Price fields display-only.

You can remake the order-entry form from Chapter 8 to include not only the model number of each product ordered but also its name, price, and even a calculated field showing price times quantity (see fig. 9.3).

While using the multitable form in Edit or DataEntry mode, place the cursor in the Model # column and access the menu bar. Select ValCheck, Define and press Enter. Choose Tablelookup and indicate Products as the lookup table. Choose AllCorrespondingFields and FillNoHelp or HelpAndFill.

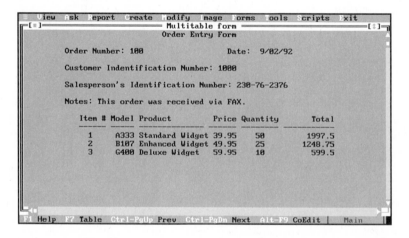

FIG. 9.3

The order-entry form showing data from Orders, Detail, and Product.

Controlling Data Entry through Pictures

One of the most convenient ways to control data entry is referred to as a *picture*. This feature is especially convenient for entering rigidly formatted data. A picture gives you a way to create custom data types.

A picture is a template that defines character-by-character what Paradox should expect to be entered into a field. To add a picture to a field, from Edit or DataEntry mode, access the menu bar and select ValCheck, **D**efine. Move the cursor to the target field and press Enter. Then choose **P**icture. Paradox displays the prompt Enter a PAL picture format (e.g., ###-##-###). Use the codes listed in table 9.1 to type the format of the data for the field; then press Enter. Paradox displays the message Picture specification recorded at the bottom of the screen. The next time you enter data into this field, Paradox uses the picture to check the format of your entry.

Cue:
To add a picture to a field, select **V**alCheck, **D**efine, **P**icture.

Use one of the available codes to represent each of the characters or digits in the permissible entry. For example, you can ensure that a user types a letter in the first position of the Model # field by placing a *?* in the first position of a picture for this field. If you want Paradox to convert the letter to uppercase, you can use an & in the first position instead. To force the user to type a number in the final three positions you can use ###. The complete picture for the Model # field is &###.

Table 9.1. Picture Codes

Code	Meaning
#	Character must be a number digit
?	Character must be a letter (upper- or lowercase)
&	Character must be a letter; Paradox converts the character to uppercase
@	Character can be anything
!	Character can be anything; Paradox converts the character to uppercase
;	The next character is taken literally, where the next character would otherwise be interpreted as a picture code
*n	Repeat the next code n times, where n is a positive integer
[ ]	Any picture code inside the brackets is optional
{ }	Inhibit auto fill-in
,	Character is a separator for a list of alternatives.

NOTE: *Any displayable character that you can type and that is not in this list can be used and will be taken literally.*

The Emp ID # field in the Employee table provides a good illustration of using a picture. The company in this book's example uses an employee's social security number as an identification number. The picture for the Emp ID # field is therefore ###-##-#### (see fig. 9.4).

This picture means that any number is acceptable in the first three positions, but the fourth position must be a hyphen. The fifth and sixth positions must be any number, and the seventh must be a hyphen. Finally, the last four positions must be numbers.

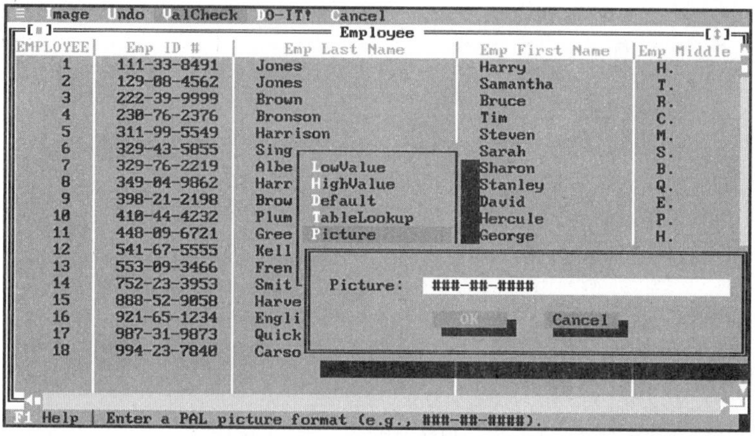

FIG. 9.4

A picture for controlling data input into the Emp ID # field.

```
  Image  Undo  ValCheck  DO-IT!  Cancel
 [=]                       Employee                       [↕]
EMPLOYEE|   Emp ID #   |  Emp Last Name  |  Emp First Name | Emp Middle
    1     111-33-8491    Jones             Harry           H.
    2     129-08-4562    Jones             Samantha        T.
    3     222-39-9999    Brown             Bruce           R.
    4     230-76-2376    Bronson           Tim             C.
    5     311-99-5549    Harrison          Steven          M.
    6     329-43-5855    Sing              Sarah           S.
    7     329-76-2219    Albe  LowValue    Sharon          B.
    8     349-84-9862    Harr  HighValue   Stanley         Q.
    9     398-21-2198    Brow  Default     David           E.
   10     410-44-4232    Plum  TableLookup Hercule         P.
   11     448-89-6721    Gree  Picture     George          H.
   12     541-67-5555    Kell
   13     553-89-3466    Fren
   14     752-23-3953    Smit  Picture:   ###-##-####
   15     888-52-9858    Harve
   16     921-65-1234    Engli             OK        Cancel
   17     987-31-9873    Quick
   18     994-23-7840    Carso

 F1 Help | Enter a PAL picture format (e.g., ###-##-####).
```

T I P   Contrast using a picture to specifying a default value. Paradox uses a default value only if you leave the field blank. A picture value always is used.

Using Automatic Fill-In

Paradox helps even more than may at first be apparent. In the Emp ID # example, as soon as you type the first three digits, Paradox fills in the hyphen. After you type the fifth digit, Paradox fills in the second hyphen. The program automatically fills in literal characters (characters that are not special picture codes). Paradox does not, however, fill in the first character or digit in a field.

Sometimes, you may prefer that fill-in not be automatic, perhaps when the individuals entering data are touch typists and seldom look up at the screen. To inhibit auto fill-in, enclose the literal characters in braces ({ }). For example, you can prevent automatic fill-in of the hyphens in the Emp ID # field by using the picture *###/-/##/-/###*. With this picture, Paradox fills in the hyphen when you press the hyphen key or the space bar. Typing any character other than a hyphen at the fourth and seventh positions results in a beep, but no hyphen.

Using the Repeat Code

Some pictures may contain the same code many times in sequence. An alternate way of expressing such repeating codes is with the asterisk (*) followed by a positive integer. The asterisk instructs Paradox to repeat the code that follows, and the integer tells Paradox how many times to repeat the code. You can, therefore, write the Emp ID # field picture as *3#-*2#-*4#*.

To repeat a series of codes, enclose the codes in braces ({ }). The picture *2{##-}## is equivalent to ##-##-##.

Creating Optional Picture Codes

Pictures are excellent for maintaining data uniformity but occasionally may be too confining. Paradox provides a method for indicating that certain portions of the picture are optional. Enclose the codes within brackets ([ ]). Paradox then uses the portion of the picture within the brackets only if you type a character that matches the portion's first character or if you press the space bar.

Cue:
Enclose optional picture codes in brackets ([ ]).

For example, you may want to provide a picture for a telephone number field that accounts for the possibility of an area code and a three-digit extension but doesn't force the entry of either in every case. The picture for such a field is *[(###)]###-####[/###]*. With this picture, the following phone numbers would be acceptable:

    (222) 333-3333
    452-3449/123
    989-7721
    (703) 555-3321/876

Providing Alternatives

Another useful picture feature is the capability to limit the entry of data to a certain group of alternatives. This feature is similar in effect to the validation feature but more flexible. To provide alternative picture codes, separate the codes with commas. When each alternative includes more than one character, enclose all alternatives in braces ({ }).

Cue:
Separate alternative picture codes with commas.

For example, the metropolitan Washington, D.C., area includes three
area codes: 301, 703, and 202. You can limit phone numbers to numbers
with these three area codes by using the picture *({301,703,202}) ###-*
####. Then when you enter *(3* in the field, Paradox adds *01)* to complete the first alternative. If you type *(7*, Paradox adds *03)*; if the first
characters you type in the field are *(2*, Paradox finishes with *02)*. Paradox does not allow any other area code and beeps if you try to enter
one. After the area code is entered, you can type any exchange and
phone number. Paradox fills in the hyphen. When each alternative includes more than one character, enclose all alternatives in braces ({ }).

T I P   To use the picture statement when two of the list choices start with
the same letter, you can embed the braces. For example, you can use
the following code:

{J{an,uly},March,Apr}

Because January and July start with J, Paradox waits for more
characters.

Specifying a Required Field

Cue:

To specify a required field, use **V**alCheck, **D**efine, **R**equired, **Y**es.

In nearly every database table, at least one field contains essential information. Certainly data should be entered in every key field. Otherwise, you may not be able to identify reliably and retrieve the data in
your table. Paradox provides a validation tool that you can use to force
some type of entry in a given field.

To specify that a certain field must contain some type of entry, access
the menu bar from Edit or DataEntry mode and select **V**alCheck, **D**efine.
Move the cursor to the target field and press Enter. Then choose **R**e-
quired, **Y**es. Paradox displays the message Required status
recorded. If you attempt to leave this field blank, Paradox informs you
that A value must be provided in this field and refuses to leave
the field. You always should add this validity-check option to key fields.

Clearing Validity Checks

Paradox provides a number of ways to clear validity checks. You can
undo or modify most of the options described in the previous sections
by following essentially the same steps used to create the options. For

example, to remove the required status set on a field, access the menu bar and select **ValCheck**, **Define**. Indicate the appropriate field and choose **Required**, **No**.

Another method of removing validity checks is through the **Clear** option. From Edit or DataEntry mode, access the menu bar and select **ValCheck**, **Clear**. You then have two choices: **Field** and **All**.

To clear the validity checks from just one field, select **Field**. Move the cursor to the field whose validity checks you want to remove and press Enter. Paradox removes all validity checks from the field and displays the message `Validity checks removed from field`.

You can clear the validity checks for all fields at the same time by selecting **All**. Paradox then informs you that `All validity checks removed, deleting .VAL file....`

For Related Information:

◄◄ "Creating a Multitable Form," p. 313.

►► "Assigning Field Validity Checks," p. 618.

FROM HERE...

Entering and Editing Data with Multitable Forms

Chapter 8 describes how to build multitable forms. That chapter also introduces the concept of *referential integrity*. This chapter discusses how to use multitable forms for data entry and editing and explains how Paradox handles key violations with multitable forms.

Using DataEntry Mode with Multitable Forms

After you have built a multitable form, you can use the form to enter data in DataEntry mode. From the Main menu, choose **Modify**, **DataEntry** and indicate the name of the master table. Paradox displays a blank record in table view and DataEntry mode. Then access the menu bar, select **Image**, **PickForm**, and choose the appropriate multitable form. Paradox displays the empty form.

T I P

You can assign the multitable form as the preferred form. Rename the form to *F* or use **PickForm** and then **KeepSet** from the Image menu while in Main, Edit, or CoEdit mode. After you do so, you can press F7 (Form Toggle) to display the multitable form. (The **PickForm** and **KeepSet** options on the Image menu are discussed in Chapter 3.)

To make your system even easier to use, assign to a keyboard macro the keystrokes that display your multitable form in a data-entry mode. (For more information on keyboard macros, refer to Chapter 6.)

Entering Data

Cue:

To move between master and detail forms, use F3 and F4.

Enter data in the same manner you do in single-table forms but move between master and detail forms with F3 (Up Image) and F4 (Down Image) (see fig. 9.5). When you finish entering data in one transaction and want to move to the next, make sure that the cursor is back in the master table portion of the form and press PgDn. If you press PgDn in another portion of the form, Paradox just beeps. Press F2 (Do-It!) when you are finished.

```
≡ Image  Undo  ValCheck  KeepEntry  DO-IT!  Cancel
┌─[■]══════════════ Multitable form ══════════════[↕]─┐
│                   Order Entry Form                    │
│                                                       │
│   Order Number: 115              Date: 10/02/92       │
│                                                       │
│   Customer Indentification Number: 2000               │
│                                                       │
│   Salesperson's Identification Number: 329-43-5855    │
│                                                       │
│   Notes: This is a phone order.                       │
│                                                       │
│      Item # Model Product        Price Quantity  Total│
│                                                       │
│         1   G400 Deluxe Widget   59.95   10     599.5 │
│         2   V107 Royal Widget    69.95    5    349.75 │
│         3        ◄                                    │
│                                                       │
└─◄■──────────────────────────────────────────────────┘
 F1 Help                                    │ DataEntry │
```

FIG. 9.5

Data entered into a multitable form.

Paradox places the following restrictions on data entry in *linked* multitable forms:

Reminder:

When entering data in a linked multitable form, Paradox *link locks* the tables.

■ After you start entering data in a linked multitable form, Paradox *link locks* the tables, which prohibits you from entering data in table view during the current DataEntry session. Pressing

F7 (Form Toggle) displays the master table in table view, but you cannot use this view to enter data. If you attempt to enter data in table view, Paradox displays the message `Table being edited using a linked form; make changes using that form.` Paradox requires that you return to the multitable form to continue data entry. Press F7 again and continue.

■ For multitable forms in which the master-to-detail relationship is one-to-many or one-to-one, you must enter a value in the field that links the master table to a detail table before you can enter data in the detail table. This step enters the value in the detail table's link field for each of the records you add to the detail table.

■ For multitable forms in which the master-to-detail relationship is one-to-many or one-to-one, you cannot delete a master record while linked detail records exist. This restriction is to preserve referential integrity. If you decide to delete a transaction while in DataEntry mode, you first must delete the detail records and then the corresponding master record.

Reminder:
You cannot delete a master record while its detail records exist.

Handling Key Violations

In DataEntry mode, Paradox adds data to your tables only at the end of your DataEntry session when you press F2 (Do-It!). If Paradox finds key violations in any of the records at this time, the program places them in several temporary tables named Keyviol, Keyviol1, Keyviol2, and so forth. To inform you of these key violations, the program displays the Keyviol tables along with another temporary table named List. The List table shows which table in your form corresponds to each temporary Keyviol table (see fig. 9.6).

You then can correct the offending records through Edit or CoEdit and use the FormAdd option on the Tools More menu to add the records to their respective tables. (Chapter 13 discusses how to use the FormAdd operation.)

Using DataEntry on a Network

As described in Chapter 3, when you select **DataEntry** on a network, Paradox places a *prevent full lock* on the table. No other network user can set a lock that requires exclusive use of the database. If a *full lock* is already in place on the shared table, Paradox does not enable you to begin a DataEntry session until the other user finishes the operation that required a full lock.

Reminder:
In DataEntry, Paradox places a *prevent full lock* on the table.

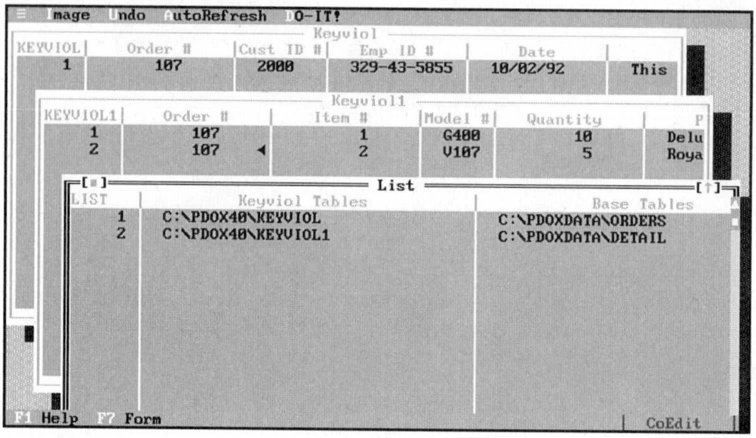

FIG. 9.6

The List, Keyviol1, and Keyviol tables created by key violations in a multitable form.

Using DataEntry with a multitable form on a network is essentially the same as on a stand-alone system. You must have at least entry rights, however, to the master table and each of the detail tables.

Reminder:

When you press F2 (Do-It!), Paradox places a *prevent write lock* on the target table.

In addition, when you attempt to complete your data-entry session with F2 (Do-It!), Paradox places a *prevent write lock* on the target table. No other user can write to the table until your new records have been added to the master table and detail table(s). If another network user already has placed a *write lock* on one of these tables, however, you must wait until the other user is finished or use the **K**eepEntry option on the DataEntry menu. KeepEntry temporarily saves the master and detail Entry tables to disk in a series of temporary tables named Entry, Entry1, Entry2, Entry3, and so forth. The program ends the DataEntry session and returns to the Main mode. No changes are made to the master table or detail table(s). You can later use the FormAdd option from the Tools More menu (discussed in Chapter 13) to add the Entry records to the target tables.

You can rename these Entry tables in the meantime to guard against their being accidentally overwritten or deleted before you can add them to their respective target tables. The FormAdd command, however, is easier to use if you do not rename the Entry tables because the command contains an option for adding data from Entry to target tables (see Chapter 13).

Using Edit Mode with Multitable Forms

You have three ways to begin Edit mode with a multitable form:

■ *The menu method.* From the Main menu, select **M**odify, **E**dit and specify the master table. When the master table is displayed in

Edit mode, use the **P**ickForm option from the Image menu to select the appropriate multitable form. Paradox then displays the multitable form in Edit mode.

■ *Edit key method 1.* Use the **V**iew option on the main menu to view the master record. Then press F9 (Edit) and use the Image menu's **P**ickForm option to select the multitable form.

■ *Edit key method 2.* Use the **V**iew option on the main menu to view the master record. Next, choose the **P**ickForm option from the Image menu to select the multitable form. Finally, press F9 (Edit).

Entering and Editing Data

When you are working with linked tables, the same basic restrictions listed in the preceding discussion of entering data with DataEntry mode also apply to Edit mode.

After you start entering or editing data in a linked multitable form, Paradox *link locks* the tables to prohibit you from entering or editing data in table view during the current Edit session. If you begin changing or adding to a table in table view, Paradox does not enable you to switch to a linked multitable form view to continue editing.

Reminder:

In DataEntry mode, Paradox *link locks* the tables.

If the master-to-detail relationship in the form is one-to-many or one-to-one, you must enter a value in the field that links the master table to a detail table before you can enter data in the detail table. Paradox then enters the value in the detail table's link field for each of the records you add to the detail table. Similarly, if you change a link field value in the master table, all corresponding values in the detail table(s) also are changed.

If the master-to-detail relationship is one-to-many or one-to-one, you cannot delete a master record while linked detail records exist. You first must delete the detail records so that referential integrity is maintained.

CAUTION: Paradox enforces referential integrity only when you use properly linked one-to-one or one-to-many multitable forms. You can intentionally or unintentionally delete a master record without first deleting detail records if you are not using one of these special multitable forms. You therefore create orphan detail records.

Using Edit on a Network

Reminder:
In Edit mode, Paradox places a *full lock* on shared tables.

Paradox places a *full lock* on shared tables when you access these tables in Edit mode. No other user can use the table until you finish your Edit session. Conversely, Paradox does not enable you to use Edit mode on a table already in use by any other user on the network. For both of these reasons, you should use CoEdit rather than Edit when editing shared network tables.

Using CoEdit Mode with Multitable Forms

The same restrictions discussed in the preceding section on Edit mode apply to using CoEdit mode with multitable forms, with one distinction. Paradox does enable you to begin making changes or additions in table view and continue after switching to multitable form view. If you switch back to table view while in the same CoEdit session, you can look, but you cannot do any editing. This limitation protects the internal consistency of your data. Similarly, after you have started coediting with a multitable form, another network user wanting to coedit any of the tables included in the form can do so only by using the same multitable form. Other users can view the data in table view but can make no changes.

Cue:
Press Alt-L to post changes you have made to shared tables.

Before enabling you to toggle to table view, Paradox may prompt you to post explicitly (by pressing Alt-L) any changes you have made. You receive this prompt when you are coediting a shared table and another network user is using the table. Your changes need to be posted to the shared table before you switch to table view. When you start making changes to the record, Paradox places a lock on this record. Pressing Alt-L (lock toggle) releases the automatic lock and posts any changes to the shared table. This step updates the records on which you were working so that other network users can view current records.

When using CoEdit mode with a multitable form on a network, if you place a lock (press Alt-L) on one of the tables (master or detail), Paradox also places a lock on all other tables in the form. You can place a lock only if none of the tables is already locked.

FROM HERE...

For Related Information:

◄◄ "Creating a Multitable Form," p. 313.

◄◄ "Entering Data in DataEntry Mode," p. 99.

◄◄ "Entering and Editing Data in Edit Mode," p. 109.

◄◄ "Entering and Editing Data in CoEdit Mode," p. 119.

Adding Data with the MultiEntry Option

The Paradox **MultiEntry** option gives you the capability to enter data into what appears to be one table and have the information inserted into multiple tables. This capability is not the same as using multitable forms, although for most purposes you can use a multitable form rather than **MultiEntry** to accomplish the same result.

In many ways the MultiEntry feature has been superceded in Paradox 3.0 and later by the multitable form capability, particularly for one-to-many relationships. MultiEntry is still useful, however, for breaking up large tables into smaller, more manageable tables without losing the convenience of single-form data entry.

Using **MultiEntry** requires that you first create a *source* table and a *map* table. The source table is equivalent to the Answer table created by a query but used in reverse. Rather than join tables—the purpose of a query—a source table holds the data to be entered in other tables. You enter data into the source table and then Paradox distributes the data among two or more tables. The purpose of the map table is to specify how the data is to be distributed.

Cue:
To use **M**ultiEntry, first create a source table and a map table.

Creating Source and Map Tables

The first step in using **MultiEntry** is to create the source table and the map table. A normal Paradox table, the source table is made up of fields from two or more target tables. After you have constructed the source table, you can use that table in table view or standard form view and can design custom forms for the source table. This table, however, will never hold data. Instead, the source table is used to funnel data to the target tables.

The map table also is a Paradox table but has only three fields: the Source field, the Target field, and the Target Table field. Each record in the map table determines which target field and table is fed by a particular field in the source table.

To create the source and map tables to allow simultaneous data entry into a particular set of target tables, first create a query with the following properties:

- The query statement must include each of the target tables.

- Every field must contain an example element, a check mark, or both—and nothing else.

■ One and only one field in each group of fields linked by a particular example element should have a check mark.

■ Example elements can be used only once per query form.

Suppose that you have created a new table called Payroll, which includes the fields Emp ID #, Date Hired, Dependents, Salary, and Department. You have moved the last four fields and their data from the Employee table. Emp ID # provides a link between Payroll and Employee. The two tables have a one-to-one relationship. So that you can enter all the employee information from one form, you want to create multientry source and map tables. A query statement to create a source and map table for this example is shown in figure 9.7.

Next, with the query statement on the desktop, access the menu bar and select **M**odify, **M**ultiEntry, **S**etup. Paradox prompts you for the name of a source table. Type a unique name for the source table and press Enter. At the next prompt, type a name for the map table and press Enter again. Paradox then builds the source and map tables based on the query you created. Figure 9.8 shows an example where Emppay is the source, and Empmap is the map table.

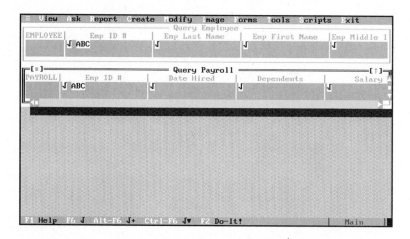

FIG. 9.7

A sample query for use with MultiEntry.

Entering Data

Cue:
To use the source and map tables for data entry, select **M**odify, **M**ultiEntry, **E**ntry.

To use the source and map tables for entering data, select **M**odify, **M**ultiEntry, **E**ntry from the Main menu. Indicate the source table and the map table, and Paradox places you into what appears to be ordinary DataEntry mode (see fig. 9.9).

At this point, you enter data into the Entry table, as you normally do in DataEntry. When you press F2 (Do-It!) to end the session, Paradox uses the map table to determine how to split up the data you entered and place the data in the correct target tables and fields. Figure 9.10 shows the record for Susan Carson entered in both target tables, Employee and Payroll. No records are added to the source table.

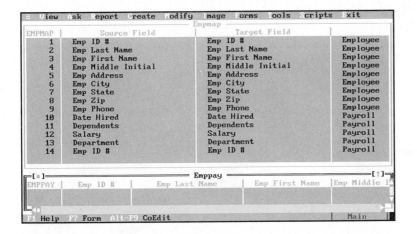

FIG. 9.8

The source and map tables.

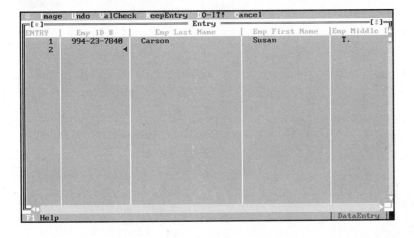

FIG. 9.9

Data entered into the source Entry table with MultiEntry.

After you create the source and map tables, you can still use DataEntry, Edit, or CoEdit mode to add data to each target table separately. If you are not careful, however, you may lose the logical one-to-one relationship with which you started. In the Employee/Payroll example, be sure not to add a record to the Employee table without adding one to Payroll with the same Emp ID #.

You must use caution when you edit the target tables, especially if you are making a change to the link field. Paradox does not provide a

MultiEdit option; if you change the link in one table, you must change the link in all the others, or the link is destroyed. You also must not delete a record from one of the targets without deleting the corresponding record from all the other target tables. You have to maintain referential integrity on your own. Using the multitable forms capability is a much better and safer choice.

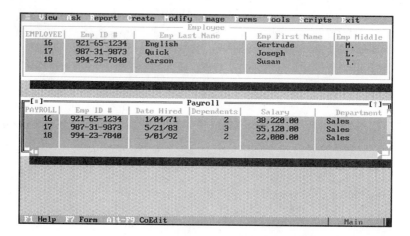

FIG. 9.10

The target tables.

Refer to Chapter 13, "Using Paradox Tools," for a discussion of the **MultiAdd** option on the Tools More menu. That option uses source and map tables created by **MultiEntry Setup** to update records in multiple target tables. Also take a look at Chapter 14, which introduces you to the Paradox Application workshop. The Application workshop uses source and map tables to produce a sort of instant query called a *multitable view*, which makes working with multiple tables easier in applications developed with the Workshop.

Handling Key Violations

The **MultiEntry** feature of Paradox handles key violations a bit differently than does normal DataEntry mode. When you add records through DataEntry mode and duplicate a key value, Paradox places the record containing the duplicate in the Keyviol table. The program follows this procedure without regard to the contents of the nonkey fields in the offending record.

When you enter a record with a duplicate key value during **MultiEntry**, Paradox does not add the record to the Keyviol table if the record is an exact match of an existing record. When every field in the new record matches every field in an existing record, the new record is not considered a key violation. The record also is not added to the target table. Instead, the new record is absorbed into the existing record, enabling you to use **MultiEntry** when a one-to-many relationship exists between target tables. You also would have to do a great deal of redundant typing. For example, if you use **MultiEntry** to enter data into the target tables Orders and Detail and then receive an order for five different widget models, you have to enter the master order data five times.

When a key violation does occur—when nonkey values do not exactly match—Paradox places the record in the temporary table Keyviol. You then need to correct the error, rename the Keyviol table with the **R**ename option from the Tools menu, and use **MultiAdd** to insert the record into the target tables (see Chapter 13).

Using MultiEntry on a Network

When you select **MultiEntry** on a network, Paradox places a *write lock* on the table. Other network users can use the target tables but cannot change their structures or contents. If a full lock or prevent write lock is already in place on one of the shared target tables, Paradox does not enable you to begin the **MultiEntry** session until the other user finishes the operation that required the lock.

Reminder:
In MultiEntry, Paradox places a *write lock* on each shared table.

When you attempt to complete your data-entry session by pressing F2 (Do-It!), Paradox places a *prevent write lock* on each of the target tables. No other user can write to the tables until your Entry table records have been added to the various target tables. You may get a message, however, saying that a file is locked. That message indicates that another user is performing some operation with a shared table and has placed a write lock on the file. You have to wait until the other user is finished or use the **K**eepEntry option on the DataEntry menu. KeepEntry temporarily saves the current Entry table to disk and ends the session, returning to the Main mode workspace. No changes are made to the target tables. You later can use the **MultiAdd** option from the Tools More menu to add the records from Entry to the shared target files.

Cue:
When you press F2 (Do-It!), Paradox places a *prevent write lock* on each shared target table.

For Related Information:

◀◀ "Creating a Multitable Form," p. 313.

▶▶ "Adding and Updating from One Table to Two or More Tables," p. 434.

FROM HERE...

Sorting Tables

Paradox provides several methods for sorting records in your database. For keyed tables, Paradox stores records sorted in ascending order by the key field(s). If you are satisfied with that sort order, you need do nothing but add data to the table. You may decide, however, that you want to see your data in a different order in your report. As mentioned in Chapter 5, Paradox sorts data when you use the group band features. If your table is not keyed or if you want to work with a table that has data stored in a different sorted order, Paradox provides the Sort option on the Modify menu.

Using the Sort Command

To sort a table, access the Main menu and select **M**odify, **S**ort. Then indicate the name of the table you want to sort. When the table is not keyed (has no key fields assigned), Paradox displays the following choices:

- *Same.* Paradox replaces the current contents of the table with the data sorted into the new order.

- *New.* Paradox creates a table to contain the sorted version of the table. When you choose this option, Paradox prompts you for a table name.

For keyed tables, replacing the current table contents doesn't make sense, because the key fields control record order. Paradox asks you for a name for the new sorted table. If you supply a name that already exists, Paradox warns you and gives you a chance to back up and change the name (**C**ancel) or to go ahead and **R**eplace the existing table with the new one.

Next, Paradox displays a Sort Questionnaire that resembles the standard input form for the table. To indicate the order in which records should be sorted, you place numbers to the left of the appropriate field names. By adding the letter *D* after the sort number, you tell Paradox to sort in descending order by the indicated field.

For example, to sort the Customer table in order by Cust State, Cust City, Cust ZIP, and Company Name into a new table named Custsort, the Sort Questionnaire would look similar to figure 9.11. After you have indicated the sort order you want, press F2 (Do-It!). Paradox sorts the records and places them in the table you indicated (see fig. 9.12).

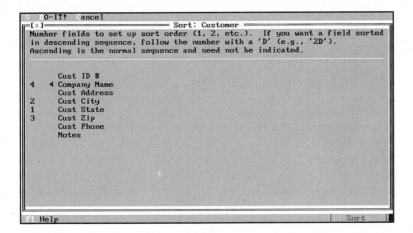

FIG. 9.11

The Sort questionnaire.

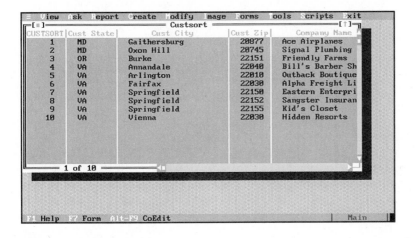

FIG. 9.12

The result of the sort.

NOTE For purposes of illustration, the fields in Custsort have been rotated in figure 9.12 to show all the sort fields on-screen. Paradox does not rearrange the fields during a sort, just the records.

Unless you specify descending order by adding the letter *D* after the sort number, Paradox sorts in ascending order. Ascending order for N, $, and S number fields is from lowest number to highest. For alphanumeric (A) fields, ascending order is in the default alphabetic sort order. (Refer to Chapter 14 of the *Paradox User's Guide* for instructions on changing the way Paradox sorts data.) Ascending order in date fields is from earliest date to latest date.

Using the Index Command

The Sort command enables you to rearrange the order of records, but it is slow. Every time you execute the Sort command, Paradox *physically* rearranges the order of all records in the table and saves the changes to disk. Paradox 4.0's Index command provides a more efficient sorting alternative. Rather than sorting entire records, the Index command creates an index file that stores record pointers that are sorted in a specified order.

If you occasionally search or query a table by one or more nonkey fields, you may want to use the Index command to create a *secondary index* file—a file that enables Paradox to quickly sort and/or search a field that is not the key field. For example, you may want to be able to quickly search the Employee table by Emp Last Name, but you still want to use Emp ID # as the key field.

T I P You can perform the commands described in this section only if you have already assigned a key field—also known as the *primary index*—in the current table's structure. Refer to Chapter 2, "Creating Database Tables," for a complete discussion of how and why to assign a key field.

You can cause Paradox to create a secondary index file in several ways. Chapter 3, "Entering, Editing and Viewing Data" discusses how you can use the OrderTable option on the Image menu or the Alt-S keyboard command to create a secondary index file. Chapter 13 explains how you can use the QuerySpeed command toward the same end. This section discusses how to use the Index command on the Modify menu.

When you want to create a secondary index, access the Main menu and select Modify, Index. Select the name of the table you want to index. Paradox displays the Secondary Index questionnaire, similar to the screen displayed in figure 9.13.

Type an index name. By default, Paradox uses the field name if you create an index based on a single field. If you want to create an Index that is based on multiple fields, you must provide an Index name. You might assign Emp Last Name as the Index Name for the secondary index that will sort Employee by Emp Last Name.

The default value in the Maintained text box is Yes. This setting causes Paradox to update the index file each time you change the contents of the table. Change the setting to No to cause Paradox to update the index file only when necessary to speed up a search or sort. On a large table, the time required to update a secondary index may be significant. By default, Paradox does maintain secondary indexes. Paradox updates the secondary index file every time you add or change data in the table. If you set Maintained to No, however, Paradox updates the index file whenever the secondary index is needed to help Paradox to locate data faster (when you use Ctrl-Z (Zoom) or when you use QBE, for example).

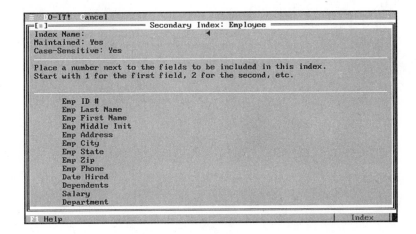

FIG. 9.13

The Secondary Index questionnaire.

By default, Paradox sorts uppercase and lowercase letters together. Press *Y* (or *yes*) in the *Case-Sensitive* field to cause Paradox to sort the file in ASCII order—with all uppercase letters before all lowercase letters.

The remainder of the Secondary Index questionnaire is similar in appearance to the Sort questionnaire (refer to fig. 9.11). To indicate the order in which the index file should be sorted, place numbers to the left of the appropriate field names. For example, to sort the index file in order by Emp Last Name, place the number 1 to the left of the Emp Last Name row. After you have indicated the sort order you want, press F2 (Do-It!). Paradox generates the secondary index.

Paradox does not immediately sort the records on-screen in the new order. To display records in the index-file order, move the cursor to the field on which you want the table sorted and press Alt-S. Paradox displays a dialog box containing a text box and two buttons. The text box displays the name(s) of the secondary index files based on the current field. Select an index file and press Enter or select the OK button. Paradox uses the secondary index file to quickly display the table in order by the values in the current field (see fig. 9.14).

```
≡  View  Ask  Report  Create  Modify  Image  Forms  Tools  Scripts  Exit
┌─[■]────────────────────────── Employee ──────────────────────[↕]─┐
│EMPLOYEE│   Emp ID #    │   Emp Last Name   │  Emp First Name  │Emp Middle│
│     1  │ 329-76-2219   │ Albertson         │ Sharon           │ B.       │
│     2  │ 230-76-2376   │ Bronson           │ Tim              │ C.       │
│     3  │ 222-39-9999   │ Brown             │ Bruce            │ R.       │
│     4  │ 398-21-2198   │ Brown             │ David            │ E.       │
│     5  │ 994-23-7840   │ Carson            │ Susan            │ T.       │
│     6  │ 921-65-1234   │ English           │ Gertrude         │ M.       │
│     7  │ 553-09-3466   │ French            │ Freda            │ P.       │
│     8  │ 448-09-6721   │ Green             │ George           │ H.       │
│     9  │ 349-04-9862   │ Harrell           │ Stanley          │ Q.       │
│    10  │ 311-99-5549   │ Harrison          │ Steven           │ M.       │
│    11  │ 888-52-9058   │ Harvey            │ Christopher      │ P.       │
│    12  │ 111-33-8491   │ Jones             │ Harry            │ H.       │
│    13  │ 129-08-4562   │ Jones             │ Samantha         │ T.       │
│    14  │ 541-67-5555   │ Kellogs           │ Emily            │ Q.       │
│    15  │ 410-44-4232   │ Plum              │ Hercule          │ P.       │
│    16  │ 987-31-9873   │ Quick             │ Joseph           │ L.       │
│    17  │ 329-43-5855   │ Singer            │ Sarah            │ S.       │
│    18  │ 752-23-3953   │ Smith             │ Angel            │ L.       │
└──────────────────────────────────────────────────────────────────┘
  F1 Help  F7 Form  Alt-F9 CoEdit                          Main
```

FIG. 9.14

The Employee table, sorted using the Emp Last Name secondary index.

For Related Information:

◄◄ "Assigning Key Fields," p. 77.

◄◄ "Reordering the Table with OrderTable," p. 138.

►► "Speeding Up Queries with QuerySpeed," p. 442.

Chapter Summary

This chapter introduced you to some of Paradox's most powerful data-entry and editing capabilities: validity checks; the use of multitable forms for DataEntry, Edit, and CoEdit modes; the MultiEntry feature; and the Paradox Sort and Index options. Through the use of these features and those you learned in previous chapters, you should be able to massage your database into shape.

You are ready to turn to the topic of reports. The next chapter revisits tabular reports, discussed first in Chapter 5. Chapter 10 shows you everything you need to know to create beautiful printouts of your data in tabular format. Chapter 11 then turns to creation of the most flexible type of report, the free-form report.

Using Tabular Reports

F or most database applications, the primary purpose of collecting data is to be able to produce a document, schedule, invoice, list, or some other type of report. Multitable queries and forms are great, but you need to be able to control precisely how your data is printed. Chapter 5, "Getting Started with Reports," introduces you to the fundamentals of creating reports with Paradox. This chapter takes up where Chapter 5 leaves off, covering all the finer points of creating tabular reports. Chapter 11 finishes the report-design story with a discussion of free-form reports.

Grouping Records in Tabular Reports

In Chapter 5, you learn the basics of how to use group bands to group records in tabular reports and place records in sorted order. This part of Chapter 10 covers creating group bands, creating multiple levels of group bands, removing group bands, and regrouping bands.

Creating a Group Band

Data often sends a clearer message when organized in some meaningful way. Paradox enables you to group records in several ways by creating group bands. The program also establishes the location of a header and a footer for each grouping that you define.

Often the primary purpose of grouping records with group bands is to compute summary statistics at the end of each group. Creating summary fields and calculations is discussed fully later in this chapter. Another reason for creating a group is to insert blank lines at appropriate places to enhance readability. After you define a group, you easily can ensure that at least one blank line accompanies each group by placing a blank line in the group header or footer.

Cue:
To place a group band, select **G**roup, **I**nsert.

To place a group band in the report specification, access the menu bar and select **G**roup, **I**nsert. You then must choose among these three options: **F**ield, **R**ange, and **N**umberRecords.

Grouping by Field

Select the **F**ield grouping choice from the Group Insert menu to group records that have the same value in a particular field. When you make this selection from the Group Insert menu, Paradox presents the list of available fields, including fields from lookup tables.

For example, you may want to group salaries from the Employee table by the Department field. If you choose Department as the name of the field on which to group, Paradox prints all employees from the same department one after another in a group, before proceeding to the next department. The entire report is sorted by the Department field in ascending order so that the Accounting department and the Administration department print before Production and Sales. (*Note:* You don't have to include in the report the field that establishes the group—in this case the Department field.)

After you have chosen the field, position the cursor above the table band and below any page header that you may have established and press Enter. Paradox marks the top edge of the group band header with a horizontal line, a downward-pointing triangle, the word group, and the name of the field (see fig. 10.1).

The bottom edge of the group header is determined by the top edge of the table band (or the next group header—see the section on "Creating Levels of Grouping"). The bottom edge of the group footer line begins with an upward-pointing triangle, the word group, and the field name. The top of the group footer is marked by the bottom of the table band (or the bottom of another group footer).

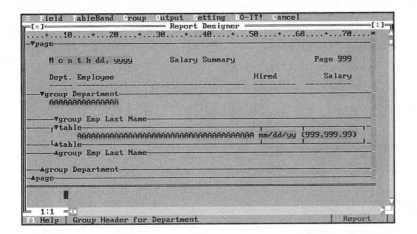

```
≡  Field  TableBand  Group  Output  Setting  DO-IT!  Cancel
┌─[■]══════════════════ Report Designer ══════════════════[↕]─┐
....+...10....+...20....+...30....+...40....+...50....+...60....+...70....*
─▼page──────────────────────────────────────────────────────────────────
    M o n t h dd, yyyy      Salary Summary           Page 999

    Dept. Employee                      Hired           Salary
  ──────────────────────────────────     ─────────      ──────────
    ─▼group Department───────────────────────────────────────────
      AAAAAAAAAAAAAAA

    ────▼group Emp Last Name──────────────────────────────────
    ┌─▼table──────────────────────────────────────────────────
    │    AAAAAAAAAAAAAAAAAAAAAAAAAAAAAAAAAAAAAAAAA  mm/dd/yy  (999,999.99)
    └─▲table──────────────────────────────────────────────────
    ────▲group Emp Last Name──────────────────────────────────

    ─▲group Department───────────────────────────────────────────
─▲page──────────────────────────────────────────────────────────────────
    ▌
── 1:1 ═◄▮                                                     ►═
  F1 Help │ Group Header for Department                │  Report │
```

FIG. 10.1

Inserting group bands to group by the Department and Emp Last Name fields.

T I P

You may want to place the field that determines the group in the group header rather than in the table band. Then, the value that all the group records have in common prints only once. Figure 10.1, for example, shows the Department field placed in the group header for that field.

You also can group records that have the same value in a particular field by using the **GroupRepeats** option. Access the menu bar and select **S**ettings, **G**roupRepeats, **S**uppress. When you use this feature, you can leave the field in the table band, and Paradox prints only the first occurrence of each different value.

Cue:
Use **S**ettings, **G**roupRepeats, **S**uppress to print only the first occurrence.

Grouping by Range

Choose the **R**ange option from the Group Insert menu to group records whose values in a particular field fall into a certain range. The sort order of the records is no different from when you group by field only. The position of the header or footer, however, does differ.

Cue:
Choose the Range option to group records in a certain range.

Paradox first asks the Name of the field to group on. After you specify the field, you must indicate the range. Your response depends on the type of field you selected, as follows:

- When you select an alphanumeric field, Paradox prompts for the number of initial characters in a range. You need to specify the number of initial characters in the field that must be the same for the field to be included in a grouping. For example, you may want all the products with model numbers beginning with a particular letter to be grouped. Type *1* in response to the prompt.

■ For numeric fields, Paradox asks for the size of a range. To group employee records that fall within each $1,000 range ($0 to $999, $1,000 to $1,999, $2,000 to $2,999, and so on), you specify the number *1000*.

■ If you select a date field, Paradox presents the following choices: **D**ay, **W**eek, **M**onth, and **Y**ear. Select the increment of time you want Paradox to use for grouping records. For example, you may want to group employees by the year they were hired.

After you select the field for grouping and specify the range, position the cursor where the header should start and press Enter. Paradox displays the header indicator and, below the table band, the footer indicator.

Grouping a Set Number of Records

Cue:
To group a set number of records, choose the **N**umberRecords option from the Group Insert menu.

Sometimes you just want to group a certain number of records, usually to make the report easier to read. For example, you may find the data easier to read and comprehend if Paradox inserts a blank line every five records. Choose the **N**umberRecords option from the Group Insert menu, and Paradox prompts you to enter the number of records that should be included in each group. Position the cursor where the group header should be placed and press Enter. Paradox inserts the group header marker at the cursor and inserts the footer marker below the table band. Paradox includes a blank line in the header and footer, leaving two blank lines between groups of records. If you want only one line, delete one by pressing Ctrl-Y.

FROM HERE...

For Related Information:

◄◄ "Examining the Tabular Report Specification," p. 191.

◄◄ "Using Summary Operators and Grouping Records," p. 278.

◄◄ "Sorting Tables ," p. 346.

Creating Levels of Grouping

Chapter 5 mentions that Paradox enables you to create up to 16 levels of grouping, sometimes called *breaks*, in a tabular report. Multiple group bands assume an order of priority determined by their positions in the report specification. The first group band listed in the report specification is given the highest priority and is the *principal sort.* Paradox sorts the master table records in the order first by the principal sort field, and then breaks any ties by looking to the other sort bands, in order.

Reminder:
The first group band listed in the report specification is the principal sort.

The report specification shown in figure 10.1 has the Department field as the principal sort. If this field were the only group band, the records would be grouped by department, and the records for each department would be printed in the order in which they were entered into the Employee table (the master table). When you add the second group band (Emp Last Name), Paradox sorts the employee records within each department in ascending order by employees' last names. Figure 10.2 shows the report generated by this specification.

```
June 13, 1992            Salary Summary                Page   1

Dept. Employee                          Hired        Salary
----- ------------------------          ---------    ----------
Accounting

      Brown, David E.                   11/29/87     36,575.00
      French, Freda P.                   9/01/88     29,834.75
      Harvey, Christopher P.             7/17/82     44,935.00
                                                     ----------
           Total Salary for Accounting Dept.        111,344.75

Administration

      Brown, Bruce R.                   10/17/85     35,700.00
      Plum, Hercule P.                   8/23/76     44,887.50
      Singer, Sarah S.                   2/12/88     22,522.50
                                                     ----------
           Total Salary for Administration Dept.    103,110.00

Production

      Harrell, Stanley Q.                4/18/79     51,558.00
      Harrison, Steven M.               11/23/83     44,616.00
      Smith, Angel L.                   10/13/83     46,280.00
                                                     ----------
           Total Salary for Production Dept.         142,454.00

Sales

      Albertson, Sharon B.               3/04/81     22,744.80
      Bronson, Tim C.                   11/23/69     43,056.00
      Carson, Susan T.                   9/01/88     22,000.00
      English, Gertrude M.               1/04/71     38,220.00
      Green, George H.                   8/15/79     51,312.56
      Jones, Harry H.                    6/07/78     33,540.00
      Jones, Samantha T.               10/02/65     78,936.00
      Kellogs, Emily Q.                  6/10/75     24,830.00
      Quick, Joseph L.                   5/21/83     55,120.00
```

FIG. 10.2

The salary summary report.

| T   I   P | You can combine the effects of the Field, **R**ange, and **N**umber Records grouping options. For example, even though you group records by department with the Field option, you can limit each grouping to five records by following the Field option; you also can limit each grouping to five records by following the Field group band immediately with a NumberRecords group band, indicating five as the number of records per group. The count starts over for each department. Create no more than one header and footer for this pair of group bands. |

Removing a Group Band

Cue:
To remove a group band,
select **G**roup, **D**elete.

Sometimes you need to remove a group band from the report specification. Beware, however, that if you do, you also remove all fields placed in the group header or footer. To remove a group band, access the menu bar and select **G**roup **D**elete. Move the cursor to the group band you want deleted (anywhere in the group band will do) and press Enter. Then confirm the deletion with **OK**.

> **CAUTION:** Paradox removes the group band and all its contents.

Regrouping a Group Band

When you design your report, you may realize late in the game that you used the wrong field for a group band, or you may decide that you want to create a range grouping rather than a grouping by just the field. Suppose that you already have placed several fields and literals in the header and footer for this group, and you don't want to have to remove and redefine the group band from scratch. Paradox provides the **R**egroup option for this reason.

Cue:
To select a different grouping, select **G**roup, **R**egroup.

To select a different group field or grouping type, access the menu bar and select **G**roup, **R**egroup. Use the cursor-movement keys to move the cursor to the group band that you want to regroup and press Enter. Choose the correct grouping type and group field. Paradox redefines the group without deleting any existing literals or fields in the group header or footer.

For Related Information:

◄◄ "Modifying the Table Band," p. 202.

FROM HERE...

Using Headers and Footers

As explained in Chapter 5, a header in a Paradox report prints above the body (the fields in the table band), and a footer prints below the body. Paradox enables you to create many different headers and footers for your tabular report—as many as 19 distinct headers and 18 footers.

Using Report, Page, and Table Headers and Footers

Chapter 5 introduces you to the basic properties of report, page, and table headers and footers. The following paragraphs summarize that discussion:

- The report header prints once at the beginning of the report. The report footer prints once at the end of the report (before the last page footer).

- The page header prints at the top of each page, and the page footer prints at the bottom of each page.

- The table header prints at the top of each page, below the page header (see the "Creating a Group of Tables or a Table of Groups" section later in this chapter).

Using Group Headers and Footers

Group bands also have their own headers and footers. A group header prints above each grouping of records, and the footer prints below the grouping. You typically locate summary computations in the footer. Group headers and footers print in the order listed in the report specification. The following rules define when group headers and footers print:

- All group headers print at the beginning of the report, in the order listed in the report specification.

- All group footers print at the end of the report, in the order listed in the report specification.

- Each group footer prints when its record-grouping condition is met and when a higher level footer prints.

- Each group header prints just after its corresponding group footer prints, except at the end of the report.

- Group headers print at the bottom of the page when a page break occurs in a lower level footer (see the "Inserting a Page Break" section later in this chapter).

- Group headers print at the top of a page, below the page and table header, if the group spills over to that page. You can suppress this spillover header by pressing F10 (Menu) and selecting **G**roup **H**eadings. Move the cursor to the group band, press Enter, and choose **G**roup. Paradox then prints the header only at the beginning of the group, not at the top of a spillover page.

Cue:

To suppress header spillover select **G**roup, **H**eadings Group.

Figures 10.3 and 10.4 should help you gain an understanding of the print order of headers and footers. Figure 10.3 shows a report specification with group headers and footers labeled, and figure 10.4 shows the resulting report.

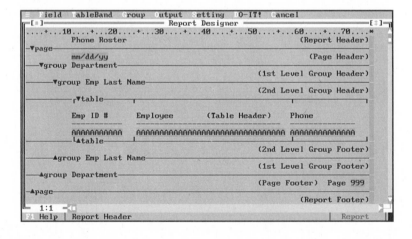

FIG. 10.3

A sample report specification with multilevel groups.

```
Phone Roster                            (Report Header)
6/14/92                                 (Page Header)
Dept. Employee          (Table Header)  Phone
----- --------------------------------  ----------------
Accounting                              (1st Level Group Header)
                                        (2nd Level Group Header)
       David E. Brown        (Body)     (703) 555-9812
                                        (2nd Level Group Footer)
                                        (2nd Level Group Header)
       Freda P. French       (Body)     (703) 555-3322
                                        (2nd Level Group Footer)
                                        (2nd Level Group Header)
       Christopher P. Harvey  (Body)    (703) 555-3298
                                        (2nd Level Group Footer)
                                        (1st Level Group Footer)
Administration                          (1st Level Group Header)
                                        (2nd Level Group Header)
       Bruce R. Brown         (Body)    (703) 555-4421
                                        (2nd Level Group Footer)
                                        (2nd Level Group Header)
       Hercule P. Plum        (Body)    (703) 555-2987
                                        (2nd Level Group Footer)
                                        (2nd Level Group Header)
       Sarah S. Singer        (Body)    (703) 555-8888
                                        (2nd Level Group Footer)
                                        (1st Level Group Footer)
Production                              (1st Level Group Header)
                                        (2nd Level Group Header)
       Stanley Q. Harrell     (Body)    (703) 555-2351
                                        (2nd Level Group Footer)
                                        (2nd Level Group Header)
       Steven M. Harrison     (Body)    (703) 555-4432
                                        (2nd Level Group Footer)
                                        (1st Level Group Footer)
Sales                                   (1st Level Group Header)
                                        (2nd Level Group Header)
       Sharon B. Albertson    (Body)    (703) 555-2361
                                        (2nd Level Group Footer)
                                        (2nd Level Group Header)
       Tim C. Bronson         (Body)    (703) 555-7630
                                        (2nd Level Group Footer)
                                        (2nd Level Group Header)
       Susan T. Carson        (Body)    (703) 555-3434
                                        (2nd Level Group Footer)
                                        (2nd Level Group Header)
       Gertrude M. English    (Body)    (703) 555-5575
                                        (2nd Level Group Footer)
                                        (2nd Level Group Header)
       George H. Green        (Body)    (703) 555-9999
                                        (2nd Level Group Footer)
                                        (2nd Level Group Header)
       Harry H. Jones         (Body)    (703) 555-1234
       Samantha T. Jones      (Body)    (703) 555-8872
                                        (2nd Level Group Footer)
                                        (2nd Level Group Header)
       Emily Q. Kellogs       (Body)    (703) 555-3378
                                        (2nd Level Group Footer)
                                        (2nd Level Group Header)
       Joseph L. Quick        (Body)    (703) 555-1298
                                        (2nd Level Group Footer)
                                        (1st Level Group Footer)
                                        (Report Footer)




                      (Page Footer)   Page   1
```

FIG. 10.4

The report generated by the report specification in figure 10.3.

Inserting a Page Break

The term *page break* often is used by word processing and other types of computer programs to mean "send a signal to the printer to eject the current page and start printing on a new page." Controlling the page breaks can be one of the simplest and yet sometimes most frustrating things about printing reports with multiple group bands.

Cue:

To insert a page break, type *PAGEBREAK*.

As explained in Chapter 5, you can use the Length option on the PageLayout menu to set the page length for your report. Paradox then uses this number to determine where page breaks should occur. Forcing a page break when a particular group changes, however, is a common practice. To cause Paradox to insert a page break when a group changes, type *PAGEBREAK* (in all uppercase letters) at the far left in the group's footer.

CAUTION: Typing *PAGEBREAK* in a footer causes the headers of higher level groups to print at the end of the page before the page break. Use PAGEBREAK only in the highest level footer (see fig. 10.5); or, if you use PAGEBREAK in a lower level footer, make sure that you leave higher level headers blank.

Suppose that you want salary summaries for each department to be printed as separate pages. To accomplish this task, type *PAGEBREAK* in the footer for the Department group band, as shown in figure 10.5.

```
≡  Field  TableBand  Group  Output  Setting  DO-IT!  Cancel
┌[■]════════════════════ Report Designer ════════════════[↕]┐
....+...10....+...20....+...30....+...40....+...50....+...60....+...70....*
─▼page─────────────────────────────────────────────────────

      M o n t h dd, yyyy          Salary Summary          Page 999

      Dept. Employee                           Hired          Salary

   ─▼group Department─────────────────────────────────────────
    AAAAAAAAAAAAAAAA
                                                               )
      ─▼group Emp Last Name─────────────────────────────────
      ┌▼table─────────────────────────────────────────────
        AAAAAAAAAAAAAAAAAAAAAAAAAAAAAAAAAAAAAAAAAAAAA  mm/dd/yy  (999,999.99)
      └▲table─────────────────────────────────────────────
        ─▲group Emp Last Name───────────────────────────────
         PAGEBREAK
        ─▲group Department───────────────────────────────────
 ─▲page──────────────────────────────────────────────────────

   1:1  ◄■                                                    ─■─
 F1 Help │ Group Footer for Department              │  Report
```

FIG. 10.5

Using
PAGEBREAK.

For Related Information:

◄◄ "Using the Report Header," p. 212.

FROM HERE...

Creating Reports from Multiple Tables

Just as you can create forms and queries from multiple tables, you also can create multitable reports. This feature gives you a great deal of flexibility in how you design your database. Multitable reports enable you to divide your database into smaller, more manageable tables—*normalization*—without losing the capability of creating reports based on any part of your data.

When you are working with several tables at the same time, a good understanding of table-to-table relationships helps. The terms *one-to-many*, *one-to-one*, *many-to-one*, and so on, are defined in Chapter 2 and reviewed in Chapter 8. If they are not familiar to you, turn to these earlier discussions for a review before you proceed.

Choosing the Master Table

When you create multitable Paradox forms, you refer to the table that "owns" the form as the *master* table. The same is true with multitable reports. The first major step in designing a multitable report is to decide which table should be the master table. Your report becomes an object in the master table's family.

The tables linked into a multitable form are *detail tables*. In report design, linked tables are *lookup tables*.

Master and lookup tables must meet the following specifications before you can use them for multitable reports:

■ Each lookup table must be keyed. Every key field in a lookup table must have a corresponding field in the master table that has the same data type and will be used to link the tables logically. These linking fields in the master table do not have to be key fields.

■ All lookup tables must be linked *directly* to the master table. A field looked up from one lookup table cannot be used to generate another lookup.

■ The master-to-lookup relationship must be one-to-one or many-to-one. One-to-many and many-to-many relationships are not allowed.

■ You should select as the master table the table that has the links to most other tables.

■ The master table records determine the contents of the report body. The body portion of the table band prints exactly one time for each record in the master table.

Suppose that you want to print an invoice for each customer based on the data in the Orders and Detail tables. Assume that the structure of the tables in your database is as follows (**Note:** the Order # field in the Orders table and both the Order # and Item # fields in the Detail table are key fields):

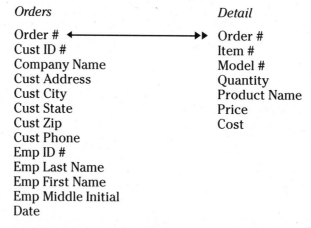

Orders	Detail
Order # ◄──────────►	Order #
Cust ID #	Item #
Company Name	Model #
Cust Address	Quantity
Cust City	Product Name
Cust State	Price
Cust Zip	Cost
Cust Phone	
Emp ID #	
Emp Last Name	
Emp First Name	
Emp Middle Initial	
Date	

These tables are derived from the ones used as examples in previous chapters. During data entry, you look up the Product information you need for a report and place that information in the Detail table by using the **T**ableLookup option on the ValCheck menu (see Chapter 9 for more information on **T**ableLookup). Similarly, customer and employee data is looked up from the Customer and Employee tables and stored in Orders. Orders and Detail are linked by the Order # field. Both tables meet the first four rules for creating multitable reports, but only the Detail table contains the information that should print as the body of the report. Detail, therefore, is the master table for a report to print an invoice.

T I P

When you want to create a report from tables that have a one-to-many relationship, you always use the many-side table as the master table. This approach is exactly the reverse of multitable forms in which the one-side table usually is the master table.

Beginning the Design of a Multitable Report

After you determine the identity of the master table for the report, begin designing a report for this table. Follow the procedures outlined in Chapter 5 to start the Paradox Report Generator for tabular reports.

After you have the standard specification on-screen, arrange the regular fields from the master table where you want them. For an invoice, you may delete the Order # field from the table band and place that field in a group band header that groups the records by the order number, as shown in figure 10.6.

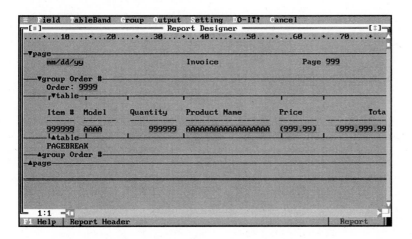

FIG. 10.6

Grouping by order number in the invoice report.

Before you can place fields from a lookup table into the report, you must link the lookup table to the report specification.

Linking a Lookup Table

Cue:
To link a lookup table to the report specification, select **F**ield, **L**ookup, **L**ink.

To link a lookup table to the report specification, access the menu bar and select Field, Lookup, Link. Then indicate the name of the lookup table. After you identify the lookup table, Paradox examines the lookup table structure and determines which field in the lookup table is to be used to match the key field in the lookup table. (*Note:* If the lookup table has a multifield key, Paradox asks for a matching master table field for each of the key fields.) In the invoice example, Order # is the name of the field in Detail used to match the key field in Orders.

After you specify the link field(s), Paradox links the lookup table to the report specification, and the lookup table's fields are available for use.

Unlinking and Relinking a Lookup Table

When you design a report, you may change your mind about using a particular lookup table, or you may realize that you used the correct lookup table but the wrong link field. Paradox provides the Unlink and Relink options to help you correct either of these two errors.

Cue:
To unlink a lookup table, select **F**ield, **L**ookup, **U**nlink.

To unlink a lookup table, access the menu bar and select Field, Lookup, Unlink. Select the name of the lookup table from the displayed list. Paradox requires that you confirm the operation by selecting OK. Paradox then unlinks the lookup table from the report specification and removes any of the table's fields that you already may have placed.

When you discover that you made a mistake when specifying a link field but don't want to remove the link, use the Relink option. Access the menu bar and select Field, Lookup, Relink. Select the name of the lookup table whose link is mismatched. Then choose the correct link field from the list of master table fields. Assuming that you already placed looked-up fields on the report specification before discovering that the link field was wrong, this Relink option saves you the trouble of having to place these fields again.

Placing a Field from a Lookup Table

Cue:
To place a linked field, select **F**ield, **P**lace, **R**egular; then choose the lookup table and the linked field.

The fields from the master table usually are referred to as regular fields. After a lookup table is linked to the report specification for purposes of report design, the lookup table's fields also are considered regular fields. To place a linked field on the report specification, access the menu bar and select Field, Place, Regular. Paradox displays the list of regular fields. In addition to the master table's fields, Paradox displays the name of the lookup table and the pointer symbol enclosed in brackets (see fig. 10.7).

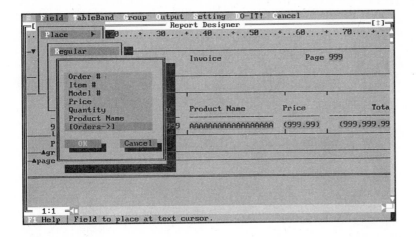

FIG. 10.7

The list of regular
fields, including
the lookup table
name.

Move the highlight to the lookup table name and press Enter. Paradox
displays a new list of field names—this time the fields from the lookup
table. The remaining steps are the same as with any regular field: select
the field you want to place, indicate the proper position, and adjust
field width.

When the cursor is resting on a field from a lookup table, the field identifier in the upper right corner of the screen reminds you of the table
name and field name. The Company Name field from the Orders table,
for example, is denoted by the following:

    [Orders->Company Name]

Creating Calculated Fields

Because they are treated as regular fields, you can use fields from
lookup tables in calculated fields. When you type the field name, include table and field names in the following format:

Reminder:
You can use lookup fields in
calculated fields.

    [*table name–>field name*]

For example, the formula to create a field that concatenates the Orders
fields Cust City, Cust State, and Cust Zip appears as follows:

    [Orders–>Cust City]+", "+[Orders–>Cust State]+" "+[Orders–>Cust Zip]

Remember that you must enclose alphanumeric constants in double
quotation marks. Figure 10.8 shows the invoice report specification
with regular fields and calculated fields from the Orders table placed in
the group header area.

The calculated field containing the customer's name is the field to the right of Customer:. The formula for this field is shown at the bottom of the screen. The next field in the address block is the customer's street address. The third line is the calculated field whose formula was listed previously.

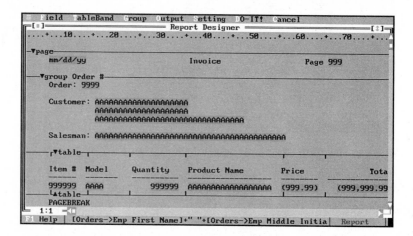

FIG. 10.8

Placing a lookup calculated field.

Creating a Group of Tables or a Table of Groups

Usually, Paradox prints the table header at the top of each page, just below the page header, even if multiple group headers print below the table header on a single page. Figure 10.9 shows this default format, which is called a *table of groups*.

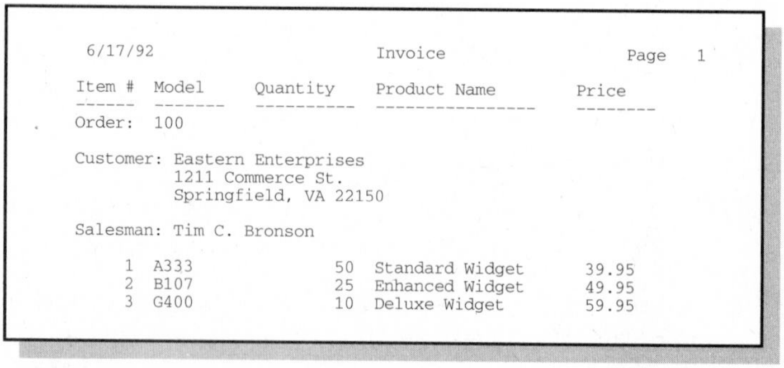

FIG. 10.9

Displaying the invoice report in the default format: a table of groups.

In Paradox, you can cause the table header to print beneath the group headers, creating a *group of tables* rather than a *table of groups*. Access the menu bar and select **S**etting, **F**ormat, **G**roupOfTables. Paradox displays the message Settings changed at the bottom of the screen. Figure 10.10 shows the result of this operation. Note that the table header prints beneath the group header.

Cue:
To create a group of tables, select **S**etting, **F**ormat, **G**roupOfTables.

```
   6/17/92                  Invoice              Page   1

   Order:  100

   Customer: Eastern Enterprises
             1211 Commerce St.
             Springfield, VA 22150

   Salesman: Tim C. Bronson

   Item #   Model   Quantity      Product Name        Price
   ------   -----   ----------    ----------------    ---------
        1   A333           50     Standard Widget     39.95
        2   B107           25     Enhanced Widget     49.95
        3   G400           10     Deluxe Widget       59.95
```

FIG. 10.10

After choosing **S**etting, **F**ormat **G**roupofTables.

For Related Information:

◀◀ "Creating a Multitable Form," p. 313.

◀◀ "Placing Calculated Fields," p. 207.

FROM HERE...

Using Summary Operations

Frequently, the purpose for grouping records with group bands is to perform summary computations on the groups. Paradox provides several ways to place summary fields on the report specification.

Placing Summary Fields

When you have a numeric field (N, $, or S) in one of the tables of a report, you can create *summary fields* that compute certain statistics—using the sum, average, maximum, minimum, and count operators—on the values found in that field. For date fields, you can compute average, count, maximum, and minimum. For alphanumeric fields, you can

Reminder:
Summary fields compute statistics-sum, average, maximum, minimum, and count.

choose between the count, high, and low operators. These computations are done across multiple records rather than on a single record. Calculated fields, by contrast, perform their computations on field values within the same record.

You can place a summary field anywhere in the report specification, but placing the field in a footer, below the field that is summarized, usually makes the most sense. Note, however, that the summarized field does not have to appear in the report specification.

To place a summary field, access the menu bar and select **F**ield, **P**lace, **S**ummary, **R**egular. Select the field to summarize; then choose one of the available statistics. Paradox presents the choices **P**erGroup and **O**verAll. When placing the summary field in a group footer, choose the first option, **P**erGroup. When you are placing the field in the report footer, select **O**verAll to summarize the field for every record in the body of the report. Then position the cursor where you want the summary field to be placed, press Enter, and adjust the field width. Paradox places the summary field in the report specification. When the cursor rests on the field mask for the summary field, the field indicator displays a message that tells you the field name, the summary operation, and whether the field is per group or overall.

Returning again to the salary summary example, suppose that you want to see a total salary for each department. You therefore need to place in the footer for the Department group a summary field that computes the sum of the salary fields. Figures 10.11 and 10.12 show the report specification and the output.

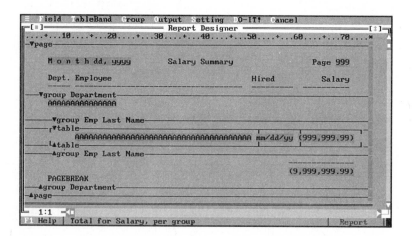

FIG. 10.11

Adding a summary field to total the salaries for each group.

```
June 16, 1992           Salary Summary           Page    1

Dept. Employee                         Hired        Salary
----- ---------------------           ----------   ----------
Accounting

     Brown, David E.                  11/29/87    36,575.00
     French, Freda P.                  9/01/88    29,834.75
     Harvey, Christopher P.            7/17/82    44,935.00
                                                  -----------
           Total Salary for Accounting Dept.     111,344.75
```

FIG. 10.12

The report generated by figure 10.11.

Placing Summary Calculated Fields

In addition to summarizing regular fields, you can place *summary calculated* fields to summarize calculations. Again, you most often place these summary calculations in a footer below a corresponding calculated field. The calculation being summarized, however, does not have to appear in the report specification.

To place a summary calculated field, access the menu bar and select **F**ield, **P**lace, **S**ummary, **C**alculated. Type the expression of the calculation to be summarized and then choose one of the available statistics. Choose between **P**erGroup and **O**verAll, and position and size the field.

Cue:
To place a summary calculated field, select **F**ield, **P**lace, **S**ummary, **C**alculated.

In the invoice report specification, for example, you need to calculate Quantity times Price for each item, and then total the calculations for each order. Figure 10.13 shows the report specification after a calculated field that computes [Quantity]*[Price] is placed in the table band. A summary field is placed in the group footer to total this same calculation for all fields in each group. Figure 10.14 contains the resulting report.

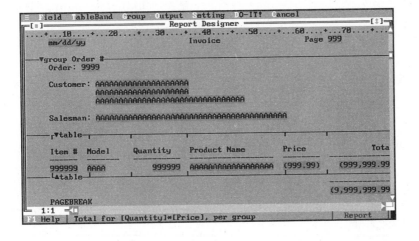

FIG. 10.13

Creating a summary calculated field for totaling the orders.

```
6/17/92                    Invoice               Page   1

Order:  100

Customer: Eastern Enterprises
          1211 Commerce St.
          Springfield, VA 22150

Salesman: Tim C. Bronson


Item #  Model    Quantity     Product Name      Price         Total
------  -------  ----------   ----------------  --------    -----------
   1    A333          50      Standard Widget   39.95         1,997.50
   2    B107          25      Enhanced Widget   49.95         1,248.75
   3    G400          10      Deluxe Widget     59.95           599.50
                                                            -----------
                                                              3,845.75
```

FIG. 10.14

The report generated by figure 10.13.

Placing Calculated Summary Fields

A third type of summary field is the *calculated summary* field. The calculated summary field is a more flexible alternative to the other two types of summary field.

Cue:

To apply sum, average, count, high, or low to a group, add a comma and the word group.

To duplicate the effect of the regular summary field, you can create a calculated field that uses one of the following operators on a single regular field: sum, average, count, high, or low. (Calculated fields are discussed in Chapter 5.) You can apply these operators to a field or to any valid expression. Enclose the argument for the operation in parentheses. To apply the calculation to a group, add a comma and the word *group* within the parentheses. In the salary summary example, you can total the Salary field with the following expression:

    sum([Salary],group)

You can duplicate the summary/calculated field that computes the invoice total with the following expression:

    sum([Quantity]*[Price],group)

This type of field is more flexible than the other two types of summary fields, because this field enables you to combine several summary operations and to combine normal calculations with summary operations.

You can, for example, add to the invoice a tax field that calculates a 4.5 percent tax and a grand total that adds the tax to the total of quantity times price. The expression for the tax is as follows:

    sum([Quantity]*[Price],group)*0.045

For the grand total, the expression is as follows:

    sum([Quantity]*[Price],group)*1.045

Figure 10.15 shows the invoice report with these two calculated summary fields added.

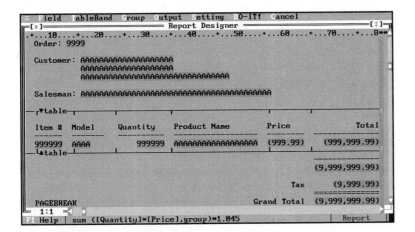

FIG. 10.15

Creating a calculated summary field for figuring tax and a grand total.

For Related Information:

◄◄ "Using Summary Operators and Grouping Records," p. 278.

◄◄ "Placing Calculated Fields," p. 207.

FROM HERE...

Enhancing the Report

Paradox provides a number of features that help enhance the appearance of your report. You can number the records in a report; place more than one field horizontally or vertically within a table band field; cause data within a report field to be left-justified, right-justified, or centered; and word-wrap text within a field.

Numbering Records in the Report

You may decide that your report would be easier to understand if the records were numbered. To add record numbers to the report, access the menu bar and select Field, Place, #Record. Then choose between Overall and Per-Group. Position the cursor where the field should be

Cue:
To add record numbers to the report, select Field Place #Record.

placed and press Enter. Select **O**verall to number records consecutively from the beginning to the end of the report. Choose **P**er-Group to number records consecutively, starting with 1 at the beginning of each group.

You may want to number the employees in each department in the salary summary report. If you place the #Record field at the left end of the table band and choose the Per-Group option, Paradox numbers the employees. You have to remove the Emp Last Name group band, however, or the count starts over when the Emp Last Name field changes (see fig. 10.16). (The #Record field is represented by 999 at the left end of the table band.) While the cursor is on this field, Paradox displays the message, `Current record number, per group` in the status line, at the bottom of the screen.

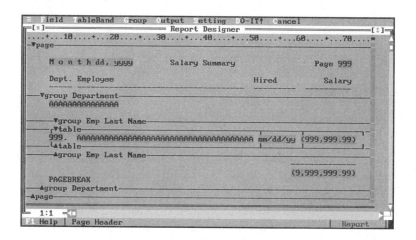

FIG. 10.16

Numbering
records.

Creating Multifield Columns

You already have seen that when you begin a new tabular report specification, Paradox creates a four-row table band. The first, second, and third rows make up the table header, and the fourth row is the report body. You are free to delete the table band's header rows, as in figure 10.16, and you can even delete the body row if all you need are summary computations that can be placed in group and report footers. (Chapter 5 explains how to insert and delete columns from the table band.)

In addition to deleting rows from the table band, you can insert new rows. This capability gives you the option of placing more than one field vertically in a table band column. (You also can place multiple fields horizontally in the same column, but you have no reason to insert multiple fields that way, because you easily can insert more columns.)

To insert a new row in the table band, turn on the Insert mode (press the Ins key), move the cursor to the bottom table band boundary line, and press Enter. Paradox inserts a blank line. Now you can place fields in this second body row. The two body rows together print once for each record in the master table.

Cue:
To insert a row, turn on Insert mode and press Enter.

Looking again at the employee phone list report, you may decide that you want to have each employee's address in the phone list, just below the employee's name. Figure 10.17 shows the phone list report specification with a second body row that contains a calculated field consisting of the Emp Address, Emp City, and Emp State fields. The resulting report is shown in figure 10.18.

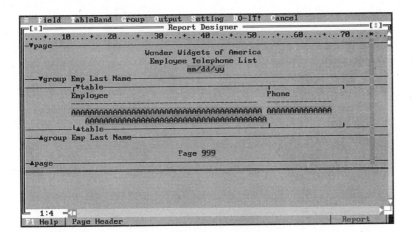

FIG. 10.17

Adding another row to the table band.

Altering Field Justification

Another fine-tuning adjustment you can perform on a report specification is *field justification*. When the value of a field in a Paradox tabular report is shorter than the field mask, Paradox has the choice of printing the value *left-justified* (on the left side of the available space), *right-justified* (on the right side of the space), or *centered*. You usually do not have to assign justification. By default, fields are justified as follows:

- Numeric fields are right-justified.
- Alphanumeric fields are left-justified.
- Date fields are right-justified.

To change the justification of a field, access the menu bar and select **Field Justify**. Then move the cursor to the mask of the field to be affected and press Enter. Finally, choose the alignment you want to use: **Left**, **Center**, **Right**, or **Default**.

Cue:
To change the justification, select Field, Justify.

```
                        Wonder Widgets of America
                        Employee Telephone List
                                6/16/92
          Employee                                    Phone
          ----------------------------------------    ----------------
          Sharon B. Albertson                         (703) 555-2361
             770 Shaw Rd., Apt 23, Arlington, VA
          Tim C. Bronson                              (703) 555-7630
             9828 Rocky Ridge, Centreville, VA
          Bruce R. Brown                              (703) 555-4421
             3451 Fox Lane, Arlington, VA
          David E. Brown                              (703) 555-9812
             16 Hounds Hunt, Fairfax, VA
          Susan T. Carson                             (703) 555-3434
             4252 Burbank St., Springfield, VA
          Gertrude M. English                         (703) 555-5575
             1681 School House Rd, Fairfax, VA
          Freda P. French                             (703) 555-3322
             1299 Houston, Apt G, Springfield, VA
          George H. Green                             (703) 555-9999
             872B S. Hill St., Mount Vernon, VA
          Stanley Q. Harrell                          (703) 555-2351
             8999 31st St., Fairlington, VA
          Steven M. Harrison                          (703) 555-4432
             3987 Glendale Dr., Springfield, VA
          Christopher P. Harvey                       (703) 555-3298
             3907 Raleigh Rd., Burke, VA
          Harry H. Jones                              (703) 555-1234
             1711 Lakeview Dr., Burke, VA
          Samantha T. Jones                           (703) 555-8872
             663 Yuppie Lane, McLean, VA
          Emily Q. Kellogs                            (703) 555-3378
             1000 Flake Way, Alexandria, VA
          Hercule P. Plum                             (703) 555-2987
             239 Belgium Wood Dr., Clifton, VA
          Joseph L. Quick                             (703) 555-1298
             622 Sloth Street, Herndon, VA
          Sarah S. Singer                             (703) 555-8888
             120 S. 2nd, Apt B, Alexandria, VA



                              Page    1
```

FIG. 10.18

The resulting report.

Creating Word-Wrap Fields

When you are designing a report, one of the practical limitations that you should be aware of is paper size. When you are limited to 8 1/2-inch-wide paper, you need to make sure that your report fits within that space. Paradox provides several options that affect the horizontal space used by your report. One of these options enables you to create alphanumeric fields that continue onto subsequent lines when necessary. This *automatic word wrap* feature is the counterpart to the word-wrap feature in Paradox forms, discussed in Chapter 8.

Cue:
To add word-wrap to an alphanumeric field, select **F**ield, **W**ordWrap.

Usually you want to add the word-wrap feature to a field when one line of the report may not be enough space for all the data. To add the word-wrap feature to an alphanumeric field, access the menu bar and select **F**ield, **W**ordWrap. Position the cursor on the target field and press Enter. Paradox prompts you to enter the Number of Lines. The number you enter here establishes the maximum number of lines per record Paradox will use to print data for this field. You can specify any positive whole number from 1 to 255. Type the number and press Enter. Paradox displays the message Word wrap value recorded.

Using this feature, you can reduce the horizontal space needed to display the Product Name field in the invoice report. The report that results after word wrap is added to the Product Name field is shown in figure 10.19.

```
 6/17/92                  Invoice             Page   1

 Order:  100

 Customer: Eastern Enterprises
           1211 Commerce St.
           Springfield, VA 22150

 Salesman: Tim C. Bronson


 Item #  Model   Quantity    Product Name    Price        Total
 ------  -----   --------    ------------    ------     --------
      1  A333          50    Standard        39.95      1,997.50
                             Widget
      2  B107          25    Enhanced        49.95      1,248.75
                             Widget
      3  G400          10    Deluxe Widget   59.95        599.50
                                                       ----------
                                                       3,845.75

                                             Tax         173.06
                                                       ==========
                                   Grand Total          4,018.81
```

FIG. 10.19

Using the word-wrap feature.

For Related Information:

◄◄ "Enhancing the Form," p. 305.

FROM HERE...

Controlling the Printer

Ultimately, a report is useful to you only if you can create a permanent copy in the form of a printout. Therefore, you need to be able to use Paradox to set up your printer. Paradox enables you to control such things as the printer port to which the report is sent, a setup string to send to the printer before printing, and custom setup strings to be sent during the printout.

Choosing a Printer Port

Cue:
To select another printer port, select **S**etting, **S**etup, **C**ustom.

By default, Paradox assumes that your report should print to the first parallel printer port, LPT1. If you never want to print to this port, you should use the Custom Configuration Program to change this default setting. To select another printer port for just the current session, access the menu bar and select **S**etting, **S**etup, **C**ustom. Choose from among the following ports: LPT1, LPT2, LPT3, COM1, COM2, and AUX. You may have to consult the user's manual for your computer to determine the appropriate port designation.

After you choose the port, Paradox prompts you to supply a setup string. The next section discusses the meaning of this message. If you don't want to make any changes, press Enter at the current setup string.

Controlling Printouts with the Setup String

In addition to making an assumption about the printer port, Paradox also assumes that you are printing on an IBM Graphics compatible printer in the normal character size and quality. By default, Paradox sends ASCII text to the printer, preceded by no special printer setup string. Often this setup is adequate, but for special purposes or for wide reports you may want to add a setup string that causes your printer to switch to another type size and character spacing.

Cue:
To choose a predefined setup string, select the **S**etting, **S**etup, **P**redefined.

You have two ways to change the setup string. You can choose one of a number of predefined setup strings, or you can create your own string. To choose a predefined setup string, access the menu bar and select **S**etting, **S**etup, **P**redefined. Then choose from among the predefined printer setup strings, which are listed in table 10.1. Choose the setup option that most closely matches your printer. In this list, the description Small means compressed print.

Table 10.1. Predefined Printer Setup Strings

Printer	Predefined setup string
Standard Printer	(none)
Small-IBMgraphics	\027\000\015
Reg-IBMgraphics	\027W\000\018
Small-Epson-MX/FX	\015

Printer	Predefined setup string
Small-Oki-92/93	\015
Small-Oki-82/83	\029
Small-Oki-192	\029
HPLaserJet	\027E
HP-Portrait-66lines	\027E\027&17.27C
HP-Landscape-Normal	\027E\027&l1O
HP-Compressed	\027E\027(s16.66H
HP-LandscpCompressed	\027E\027&l1O\027(s16.66H
Intl-IBMcompatible	\027\054
Intl-IBMcondensed	\027\054\015

To specify the setup string or to edit an existing setup string, access the menu bar and select **S**etting, **S**etup, **C**ustom. Select the proper port, and then specify the setup string for your printer. You need to consult your printer manual for the appropriate setup code. These codes often are referred to as *escape codes* because they begin with the ASCII code for the Esc key. In constructing these codes, follow two rules:

Cue:
To specify a custom setup string, select **S**etting, **S**etup, **C**ustom.

■ Enter printable characters literally.

■ For nonprintable characters, use the ASCII equivalent code preceded by the backslash (\). For example, the ASCII code for the Esc key is 027. Any setup string using the Esc key must include the string \027. You can find the ASCII codes in Appendix C of the *PAL User's Guide*, included with your Paradox documentation.

Press Enter when you are finished typing the new setup string. Paradox saves the change with the settings for this table.

Enhancing Specific Portions of Text

A third way to specify a setup string is to include the string as a field in the report. With this method, you can specify any number of setup codes in a report. For example, you can print headers in wide print but have the remainder of the report printed in normal text mode. To use this feature, place a setup string in a calculated field to the left of where the special print attribute should start. (***Note:*** These features do not cause text on-screen to show up in a different font or print size. Only the printout is affected.)

Overriding the Print Settings

Paradox usually uses the print settings stored with the report specification to print the report. You may want to print a report with a different setup string (for example, to print in compressed type) or send the report to a different printer port, but you do not want to change permanently the print settings in the report specification. Paradox provides the SetPrinter option on the Report menu for that purpose.

To override the print settings stored with a report specification, before printing the report, select **R**eport, **S**etPrinter, **O**verride from the Main menu.

Paradox displays the following choices:

- ■ *PrinterPort.* Use this option to choose a different printer port. The choices are LPT1, LPT2, LPT3, COM1, COM2, and AUX.

- ■ *Setup.* Select this option to enter a new setup string.

- ■ *EndOfPage.* Choose this option to specify that the form-feed character should be used at the end of a page instead of a series of line feeds. This option may enhance the performance of certain laser printers.

To reset the printer settings so that Paradox uses the settings stored with report specifications, from the Main menu select **R**eport, **S**etPrinter, **R**egular. Reports printed after this command use the print settings stored with the report specification.

FROM HERE...

For Related Information:

◄◄ "Controlling Output," p. 215.

►► "Creating a REPORT PRINT Action," p. 490.

Chapter Summary

In this chapter, you learned all the ins and outs of designing tabular reports, including grouping data; using group headers and footers; creating multi-table reports; using summary operations to create summary, summary calculated, and calculated summary fields; enhancing your reports by numbering records, adding rows, and wrapping fields; and controlling your printer so that you can produce your reports. Turn now to Chapter 11 to complete your report-writing knowledge by learning about free-form reports.

Using Free-Form Reports

I n Chapter 5, you learn report-writing fundamentals. In Chapter 10, you learn how to create more elaborate tabular reports. The third chapter about generating reports with Paradox, Chapter 11, shows you how to get the most out of the flexible Paradox free-form Report Designer.

Starting the Free-Form Report Designer

You begin a free-form report design session like you do a tabular report design session, as follows:

1. From the Paradox Main menu, select **R**eport, **D**esign.

2. Specify the table for which you are designing the report and choose a report name.

3. Fill in a description for the report. Paradox uses this description as a title in the page header of the free-form report. You also can erase or change the description during report design.

4. Choose **F**ree-form.

Paradox displays the free-form standard report specification for the table with which you are working (see fig. 11.1).

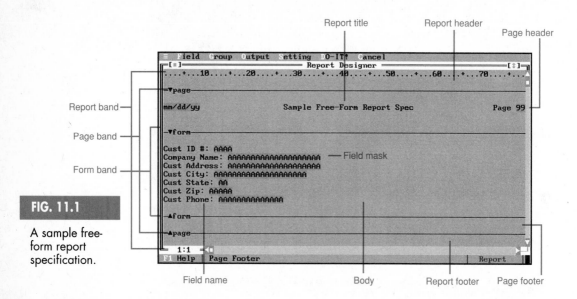

FIG. 11.1

A sample free-form report specification.

For Related Information:

◄◄ "Getting Started with the Report Generator," p. 188.

Examining the Standard Specification and the Form Band

The most obvious difference between a free-form report specification and a tabular report specification is the *form band* (see fig. 11.1). In free-form report specifications, the form band replaces the table band in tabular report specifications.

The form band looks like the standard input form F created by Paradox. The program places each field of the associated table in a separate line of the form band, preceded by the field's name as a literal. Think of the form band as a column of a tabular report specification stretched out vertically.

When you finish designing the form, press F2 (Do-It!) to save the form to disk. If you decide that you want to make changes to the specification, the steps are the same as described in Chapters 5 and 10.

For Related Information:

◄◄ "Examining the Tabular Report Specification," p. 191.

FROM HERE...

Comparing Free-Form Reports to Tabular Reports

Most of what you have learned about report design also applies to designing free-form report specifications, including linking tables to create multitable reports. This chapter presents features unique to free-form design. The differences between free-form report specifications and tabular report specifications are as follows:

- *Field placement.* Fields placed in the form band are not limited to vertical columns as are fields in the table band of tabular reports. You can place regular, calculated, and looked-up fields anywhere in the form band.

- *Literal placement.* In free-form report specifications, you can type literals anywhere in the form band as if the band were a word processing screen. Each literal in the table band of a tabular report is associated with a particular field, must be placed above the field, and cannot straddle the boundary between table band columns.

- *Word and line squeeze.* In tabular report specifications, you create calculated fields to eliminate excess spaces between fields (for example, [Cust First Name]+" "+[Cust Last Name]). When you use the Free-Form Report Designer, Paradox provides an easier way of squeezing unwanted spaces out of the form band. The program also enables you to squeeze excess blank lines out of the form band portion of the report.

- *Mailing labels.* The Paradox Free-Form Report Designer has a built-in mailing label feature. You design the layout for one label, and Paradox handles the behind-the-scenes work necessary to print multiple labels in one row. The tabular report specification format can handle only 1-across mailing labels.

■ *Report Width.* The starting report width for a new free-form report specification is 80 spaces. Usually, the starting report width for a tabular report is larger because the report has to be wide enough to accommodate all fields horizontally. The maximum report width for both types of report specifications is 2,000 spaces.

These differences make free-form reports ideal for generating mailing labels and short form letters.

T I P   Even with the special free-form design features, Paradox is not a match for most dedicated word processing and mail-merge programs for creating long mail-merge documents. Paradox's full-screen editing features are limited when compared to other programs. If your document is more than a page or two long, consider using the Export feature on the Tools, ExportImport menu to create a database file that can be used by your word processor or mail-merge program (discussed in Chapter 13). Most of these programs can import or directly use one of the file formats that Paradox produces—1-2-3, dBASE, PFS, or ASCII.

Squeezing Blank Spaces and Lines Out of the Report

Reminder:
The field squeeze option tells Paradox to delete excess spaces and to leave one space between fields.

A common problem in report design is eliminating unwanted spaces between words. When you place field masks side by side and the data for the leftmost field does not fill the allocated space, unneeded blank spaces are left before the next field's value prints. Chapters 5 and 10 demonstrate how to solve the problem with calculated fields, but that method is cumbersome and requires you to type formulas to concatenate fields. You need a method to tell Paradox to delete excess spaces and to leave one space between fields. Paradox provides an option in free-form report design called *field squeeze*.

You also may want Paradox to delete blank lines from the form band. When you create mailing labels, for example, you do not want blank lines in the middle of a label. If some records have blank fields, however, blank lines can result.

Using Field Squeeze

To eliminate—*squeeze out*—extra spaces from between fields in the form band, access the menu bar and make the following selections: **S**etting, **R**emoveBlanks, **F**ieldSqueeze, **Y**es. Paradox displays the message `Settings changed`.

Figure 11.2 shows a free-form report specification for a letter to customers. (***Note:*** This report is for the table Cust2, the Customer table with additional fields Title, Cust First Name, Cust Middle Initial, and Cust Last Name.) Compare the report output in figures 11.3 and 11.4. The first letter is the report output in the default condition. Paradox leaves blank spaces in the address block and in the body of the letter. Figure 11.4 is the same letter with the **F**ieldSqueeze option chosen. Notice that the extra spaces are gone.

Cue:
To eliminate extra spaces, select **S**etting, **R**emoveBlanks, **F**ieldSqueeze, **Y**es.

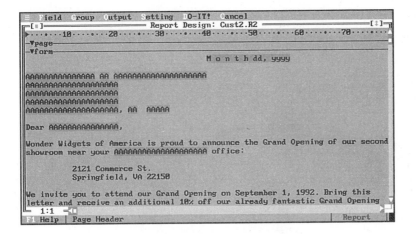

FIG. 11.2

The free-form report specification for a form letter to customers.

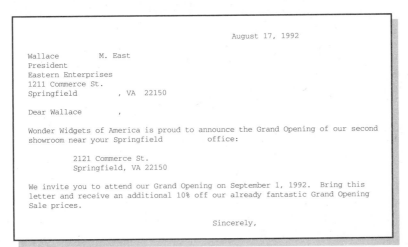

FIG. 11.3

The customer form letter before activating **F**ieldSqueeze.

```
                                        August 17, 1992
Wallace M. East
President
Eastern Enterprises
1211 Commerce St.
Springfield, VA  22150

Dear Wallace,

Wonder Widgets of America is proud to announce the Grand Opening of our second
showroom near your Springfield office:

            2121 Commerce St.
            Springfield, VA 22150

We invite you to attend our Grand Opening on September 1, 1992.  Bring this
letter and receive an additional 10% off our already fantastic Grand Opening
Sale prices.

                              Sincerely,
```

FIG. 11.4

The Customer form letter after activating **F**ieldSqueeze.

Using Line Squeeze

Cue:

To delete excess lines, select **S**etting, **R**emoveBlanks, **L**ineSqueeze, **Y**es.

Similar to the problem of excess spaces, you sometimes need to get rid of blank lines. Some of your customers may not have a title. Normally, the letter leaves a blank line in that position, as shown in figure 11.5. To delete excess lines, access the menu bar and make the following selections: **S**etting, **R**emoveBlanks, **L**ineSqueeze, **Y**es.

Paradox gives you two choices:

- ■ *Fixed.* Choose this option when you are using continuous forms (page length C) and must account for every line. Paradox moves unneeded blank lines to the end of the form band, and total line count is not affected. Use this choice when building mailing labels.

- ■ *Variable.* Select this option when you want to use every available line and do not need all forms to be the same length. Paradox deletes unwanted blank lines but does not move them to the end of the form band.

Figure 11.5 shows a blank line in the address block because the customer does not have a title. After selecting the LineSqueeze option, the same letter prints without the extra line (see fig. 11.6).

FROM HERE...

For Related Information:

◀◀ "Enhancing the Report," p. 371.

```
                          August 17, 1992

Henry H. Harrison

Henry's Hair Hut
7112 Commerce St
Springfield, VA  22150

Dear Henry,

Wonder Widgets of America is proud to announce the Grand Opening of our second
showroom near your Springfield office:

          2121 Commerce St.
          Springfield, VA 22150

We invite you to attend our Grand Opening on September 1, 1992.  Bring this
letter and receive an additional 10% off our already fantastic Grand Opening
Sale prices.

                              Sincerely,
```

FIG. 11.5

The customer
form letter
without
LineSqueeze.

```
                          August 17, 1992
Henry H. Harrison
Henry's Hair Hut
7112 Commerce St
Springfield, VA  22150

Dear Henry,

Wonder Widgets of America is proud to announce the Grand Opening of our second
showroom near your Springfield office:

          2121 Commerce St.
          Springfield, VA 22150

We invite you to attend our Grand Opening on September 1, 1992.  Bring this
letter and receive an additional 10% off our already fantastic Grand Opening
Sale prices.

                              Sincerely,
```

FIG. 11.6

The customer
form letter with
LineSqueeze.

Creating Mailing Labels

Virtually every business needs to generate mailing labels. For some
companies, producing mailing labels is their business. With many programs, however, getting your data printed properly onto labels is not
easy. True to its advertising campaign slogan, "Power Without Pain,"
Paradox makes swift work of mailing labels.

Designing a 1-Across Mailing Label Report

Designing a form to print mailing labels one to a row (1-across mailing labels) is simple. Complete the following steps:

1. Access the free-form design screen and delete all header and footer lines. You do all your work in the form band.

2. Toggle on the vertical ruler (Ctrl-V) to help you count lines.

3. Measure the size of a label in inches from the top edge of one label to the top edge of the next label. (Labels are usually 1 inch or 1 1/2 inches.)

4. Multiply the length by 6 to convert the measurement to printer lines. (Single spacing is 6 lines vertically per inch.)

5. Adjust the size of the form band on-screen, adding or deleting lines as necessary, until the same number of lines are available as on the label. Don't count the lines taken up by the page header and form header markers.

6. Measure a label horizontally, also in inches.

7. Multiply the label width by 10 if you are printing in a pica format (10 characters per inch), by 12 if you are printing in an elite format, or by 15 if you are printing in compressed type.

8. Set the page width to this number.

9. Set the page length to continuous (page length C).

10. When you line up the printer, make sure that the print head is where you want to begin printing. With all header lines removed, Paradox does not roll up a line before printing.

11. Place the fields in the form band as you want them to print but do not use the last line of the form band. Leave this line blank to account for the vertical space between labels. Use only the first page width.

12. Invoke the FieldSqueeze and LineSqueeze Fixed options to eliminate unneeded spaces and lines when Paradox prints the labels.

Figure 11.7 shows a report specification to print 1-inch, 1-across mailing labels. FieldSqueeze and LineSqueeze are activated. The report generated by this form is shown in figure 11.8.

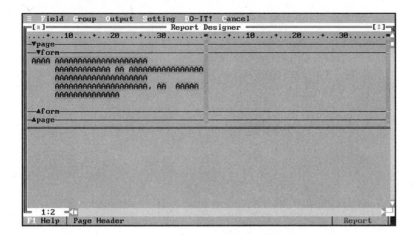

FIG. 11.7

A free-form report specification to print mailing labels.

Designing a Report for N-Across Mailing Labels

Single-column labels are great for use with a tractor-fed printer but are not as useful with a friction-fed printer and are practically useless with a laser printer. In the latter two situations, you use mailing labels with more than one label in a row. Fortunately, Paradox makes creation of labels for these forms as easy as for 1-across labels.

To create *n*-across labels, where *n* is the number of labels per row, follow the instructions in the preceding section for 1-across labels. Set the page width by the distance from the left edge of one label to the left edge of the next label.

You also need to activate the **Labels** feature of Paradox. Access the menu bar and select the following: **Setting, Labels, Yes.** Paradox responds by displaying the message Label status has been recorded.

Cue:
To create n-across labels, activate the **L**abels feature.

Make sure that exactly *n* page widths are available. If, for example, you have 3-across forms, make sure that you have a total of three page widths (refer to the Chapter 5 section on "Changing the Page Width"). Paradox uses the number of page widths to determine how many labels across should be printed.

You can, for example, cause the report specification in figure 11.7 to print 2-across labels by activating the **Labels** feature. Notice that the report-width indicator in the top right corner of figure 11.7 already indicates two page widths. The resulting labels are shown in figure 11.9.

```
Wallace M. East
President
Eastern Enterprises
1211 Commerce St.
Springfield, VA  22150

Alfred H. Long
Chief Buyer
Alpha Freight Lines
720 Port Royal
Fairfax, VA  22030

Charlie Y. Eager
Ace Airplanes
777 Kittyhawk Dr.
Gaithersburg, MD  20877

Rex T. Comfort
Manager
Hidden Resorts
6601 Wales Rd.
Vienna, VA  22180

Robert M. Sangster
Agent
Sangster Insurance
1411 Reservation Dr.
Springfield, VA  22152

Sarah G. Moores
Signal Plumbing
3333 Half Street
Oxon Hill, MD  20745

Henry H. Harrison
Henry's Hair Hut
7112 Commerce St
Springfield, VA  22150

Francis P. Jones
Chief Teller
2nd Savings & Loan
2229 Hillcrest Dr.
Arlington, VA  22210

Sarah L. Smiley
Manager
Big Top Lanes
13 Baker St.
Alexandria, VA  22213

William B. Bailey
Chicken Chef Supreme
3227 Feathers Rd
Burke, VA  22159

Benjamin Q. Harris
2411 St. Peters Blvd
Arlington, VA  22210
```

FIG. 11.8

1-across mailing labels.

```
Wallace M. East              Alfred H. Long
President                    Chief Buyer
Eastern Enterprises          Alpha Freight Lines
1211 Commerce St.            720 Port Royal
Springfield, VA  22150       Fairfax, VA  22030

Charlie Y. Eager             Rex T. Comfort
Ace Airplanes                Manager
777 Kittyhawk Dr.            Hidden Resorts
Gaithersburg, MD  20877      6601 Wales Rd.
                             Vienna, VA  22180

Robert M. Sangster           Sarah G. Moores
Agent                        Signal Plumbing
Sangster Insurance           3333 Half Street
1411 Reservation Dr.         Oxon Hill, MD  20745
Springfield, VA  22152

Henry H. Harrison            Francis P. Jones
Henry's Hair Hut             Chief Teller
7112 Commerce St             2nd Savings & Loan
Springfield, VA  22150       2229 Hillcrest Dr.
                             Arlington, VA  22210

Sarah L. Smiley              William B. Bailey
Manager                      Chicken Chef Supreme
Big Top Lanes                3227 Feathers Rd
13 Baker St.                 Burke, VA  22159
Alexandria, VA  22213

Benjamin Q. Harris
2411 St. Peters Blvd
Arlington, VA  22210
```

FIG. 11.9

2-across mailing labels.

TIP

Use group bands to sort labels. If, for example, you want to sort the customer labels by ZIP code, add a group band that groups records on the field Cust Zip. After you add the group band, be sure to delete the blank lines in the group header and group footer, or these lines will throw off the line count.

For Related Information:

◀◀ "Creating Levels of Grouping," p. 355.

FROM HERE...

Chapter Summary

You have explored the many options provided by the Paradox Report Designer. Chapter 5 showed you report writing fundamentals. Chapter 10 explored the creation of reports from multiple tables, using grouping summary fields. This chapter presented the special features of free-form report design, including mailing labels. Continue to explore Paradox on your own, using this book as a reference and backup should you run into something you don't remember.

You have not heard the complete Paradox story. A major feature of Paradox is its graphics facility. Presenting complex data in a picture is often the best way. Now that you have a good understanding of the standard reporting features of Paradox, creating graphs to bring your data to life is a snap. Turn to Chapter 12 to find out how easy graphics can be when an excellent program does most of the work for you.

Using Paradox Graphics

P aradox is the only high-end PC database application to offer an integrated graphics capability. Like other portions of the program, the graphics function is faithful to the Paradox philosophy of providing powerful and easy-to-use features. Creating a graph is so easy that the process may become your favorite part of working with Paradox.

An Overview of Paradox Graphics

Paradox makes creating an impressive graph simple. Two keystroke combinations can transform your mundane data into an impressive graph. Alt-X creates a cross-tabulated version of your data (see fig. 12.1). Ctrl-F7 (Graph) transforms the cross-tabulated table into a stacked bar graph with a title, labels, and legends (see fig. 12.2). Paradox also enables you to modify this standard graph, produced by Ctrl-F7, to create simple bar graphs, rotated bar graphs, 3-D bar graphs, line graphs, marker graphs, combined line and marker graphs, area graphs, X-Y graphs, and pie graphs. This section describes the graph types and the terminology you need to understand Paradox graphics.

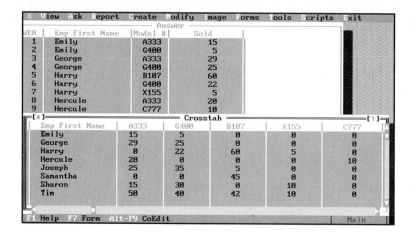

FIG. 12.1

The Crosstab command.

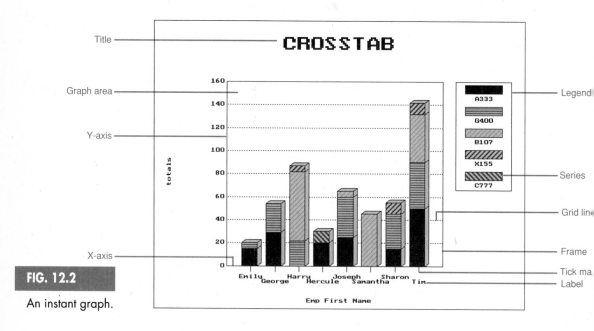

FIG. 12.2

An instant graph.

Understanding Graph Elements

Business graphics programs have their own set of terminology. As you go through this chapter, you learn how to use and modify the following *graph elements*:

■ *Graph area.* The large rectangular area containing bars, lines, markers, or a pie graph. All data is graphed in the graph area.

■ *Axes*. All Paradox graphs except pie graphs have a horizontal line along the bottom edge called the *x-axis* and a vertical line along the left side called the *y-axis*.

■ *Frame*. The rectangle surrounding the graph area

■ *Series*. Paradox enables you to show trends by indicating that several pieces of data belong in a set or category and should be graphed to show this relationship. Each of these groups of data is a *series*. Each of the five shadings in figure 12.2 depicts a data series. Paradox enables up to six data series per graph in all types except pie graphs. You can use up to nine series for a pie graph.

■ *Tick marks; grid lines*. Each axis is divided into segments of equal length by *tick marks* or *grid lines*. Tick marks are short line segments, and grid lines extend across the entire width or height of the graph area.

■ *Scale*. The distance, in units, between tick marks. The y-axis in figure 12.2 is divided into 20-unit segments. The *scale*, therefore, is 20.

■ *Labels*. Words or other characters along the x-axis. Labels are used to describe the data graphed at the corresponding tick mark. The names Emily, George, Harry, Hercule, Joseph, Samantha, Sharon, and Tim are the labels in the graph shown in figure 12.2.

■ *Titles*. Words or other characters above the graph area, below the x-axis labels or along the y-axis

■ *Legends*. Paradox uses various *colored lines*, *shading*, and *marker shapes* to depict multiple data series in the same graph. The legend provides the key to identifying the proper series with each shading, line color, or marker. Figure 12.2 shows the legend as a rectangular box to the right of the graph area, and a model number is assigned to each shading used in the graph.

Examining the Graph Types

With Paradox, you can create 10 types of graphs from your data. To decide which type can best present your message, you must be aware of the choices. The examples that follow illustrate the available graph types. The actual steps you take to select one of the graph types for your data are explained later in the chapter.

Stacked Bar Graphs

Assuming that you have more than one series to graph, Paradox builds a *stacked bar graph* as the default graph. The graph in figure 12.2 is a stacked bar graph. Each series is represented as a different shading, and the height of each shaded portion of a bar represents one value in the series. The total height of the stacked bar shows the cumulative total of values from all series. This type of graph is good for comparing values that comprise a portion of a larger number you want to see. Figure 12.2 depicts the number of widgets of each type sold and the total widgets of all types sold by each of the eight salespeople.

Simple Bar Graph, 3-D Bars

A *simple bar graph* shows multiple series in a different way. Instead of stacking the respective bars from each series as in figure 12.2, Paradox places the bars side by side. Figure 12.3 shows the same data as a simple bar graph. Because all the bars begin at zero, determining which salesperson has sold the most of a particular model is easier. With a simple bar graph, however, you can no longer easily compare the total sales of the salesperson. You can add the illusion of depth by creating a 3-D bar graph, like the one in figure 12.4.

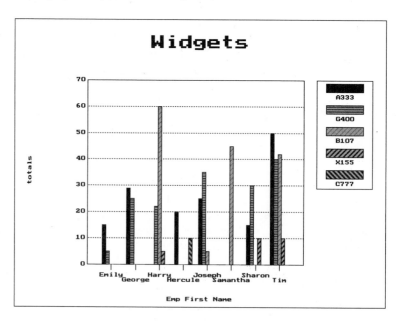

FIG. 12.3

A simple bar graph with multiple data series.

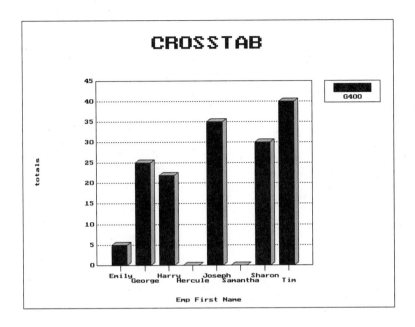

FIG. 12.4

A 3-D bar graph
with one data
series.

Rotated Bar Graph

Another option is to create a *rotated bar graph* by turning the bars on
their sides. Figure 12.5 shows the same data as figure 12.4, but the bars
are turned.

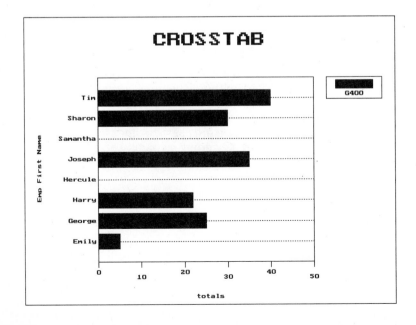

FIG. 12.5

A rotated bar
graph.

Line Graph, Marker Graph, Combined Lines, and Markers

A *line graph* is constructed with straight line segments connecting points. Each point represents one value in a series. All the points in the series are connected to form a continuous line. Figure 12.6 shows one series and therefore one line, but you can depict up to six series and have up to six lines per graph. Line graphs usually are used to show trends over time.

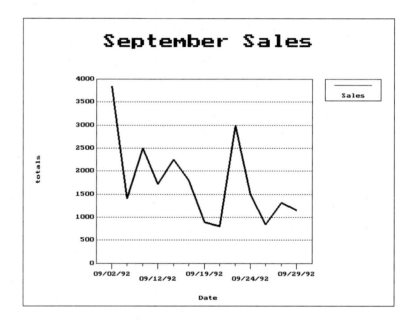

A marker graph is a line graph without the lines. The points representing series data values are denoted by markers, and lines are not used to connect the points. You can, however, combine lines and markers, which sometimes makes distinguishing several lines in the same graph easier. Figure 12.7 shows a marker graph depicting sales of widget models on dates in September. The same data is graphed in figure 12.8 using a combined marker and line graph.

X-Y Graph

X-Y graphs are line graphs that compare one series of numeric data with another series. The classic example of this type of graph is used by economists to show that as prices go up, demand declines. Figure 12.9 shows an X-Y graph.

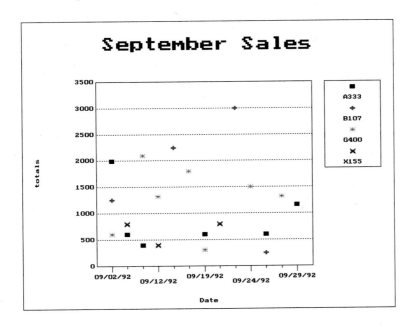

FIG. 12.7

A marker graph.

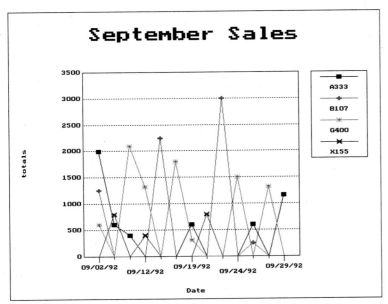

FIG. 12.8

Combined lines and markers.

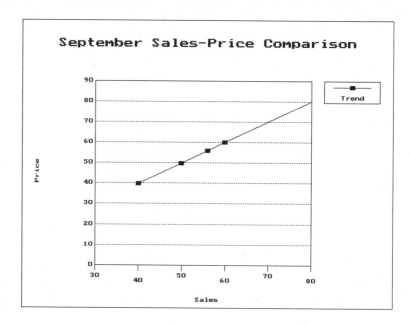

FIG. 12.9

An X-Y graph.

Pie Graph

Paradox also generates *pie graphs*. Each piece or slice of the pie represents a value series. Each series is shaded and colored (on a color monitor) differently. You can have up to nine series (slices) in a Paradox pie graph. One enhancement, shown in figure 12.10, can make one or more slices explode from the pie.

Area Graphs

Cue:
Area graphs can show cumulative totals and trends.

Another type of graph that can show cumulative totals, like stacked bar graphs, and trends, like line graphs, are *area graphs*. This type of graph is a stacked line graph. Figure 12.11 shows the contribution of the various models of widgets to the total sales on various dates in September. The top line of the area graph shows the cumulative total of all the series' values for each date.

For Related Information:

FROM HERE...   ◀◀ "Understanding Paradox Objects," p. 65.

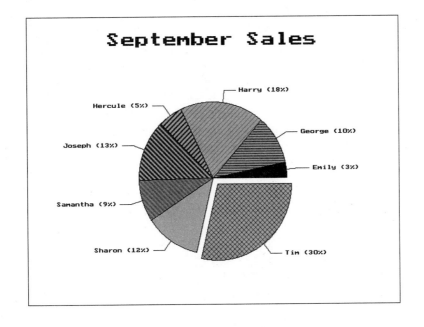

FIG. 12.10

A pie graph.

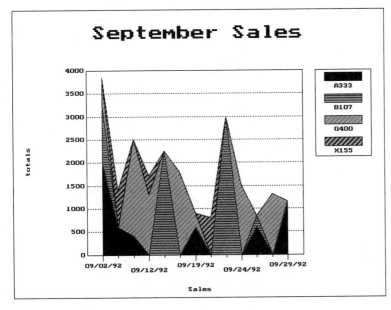

FIG. 12.11

An area graph.

The Basics of Paradox Graphics

The terminology and graph types described in the preceding portion of this chapter are not unique to Paradox. Now that you have the necessary background, you are ready to learn the particulars of Paradox graphics.

The graphics-creating capability of Paradox builds on everything you have learned about using the program so far:

■ *Table*. All graphs are generated based on data found in a Paradox table.

■ *Paradox object*. A graph specification is a Paradox object that, like a form or report specification, can be saved and reused.

■ *Query by example*. You need a good understanding of query by example to successfully build the graph you want.

■ *Instant graph*. Just as Paradox provides ready-made input forms and report specifications, the program also provides default graph settings that can be applied with a keystroke combination.

■ *Full range of enhancements*. Paradox gives you instant graphs and provides a wide variety of enhancements.

To successfully tap the power of Paradox graphics, you have to understand how to set up a Paradox table for graphing. Paradox expects to find the data to be graphed in a certain position in the table. The program also uses data from the table to determine axis labels, legend labels, and graph titles. Paradox refers to the conversion from table to graph as *transformation*. The first step in learning Paradox graphics is learning transformation rules.

Understanding Transformation Rules

Paradox can create a graph only if you provide the following information in the table:

Reminder:
A graph series must be numeric.

■ *Series*. A series (group of data for graphing) must be a column in the table. A series also must be numeric. Paradox cannot produce a graph from alphanumeric or date fields. For a pie graph, one series column provides all the data and cannot be longer than nine rows. You can have a maximum of six series columns when generating other graph types.

■ *X-axis data.* The data for the x-axis also must be a column in the table. X-axis data for X-Y graphs must be numeric. For all other graphs, x-axis data is used as labels and can be any data type.

You must provide each of these elements as separate columns in the current Paradox table. Because the maximum number of series columns is six, the minimum number of series is one. Because all graphs must have x-axis data, a table used for generating a graph should have from two to seven columns. Although you can create graphs from tables with more than seven columns, a maximum of seven columns is used for graphing. To make the discussion as clear as possible, this chapter shows how to create tables containing only essential columns.

Reminder:
A table used for generating a graph should have from two to seven columns.

Regarding the data you include in the table for graphing, Paradox makes the following assumptions about x-axis data:

■ For keyed tables, the least significant (rightmost) key field becomes the x-axis data because the least significant key field always breaks the last tie to prevent duplicate records in the table. The value of this field in each record should be a good identifier for that record and is used to label the data for that record along the x-axis.

■ In nonkeyed tables, the first (leftmost) non-numeric column (field) in the table becomes the x-axis data. Paradox displays one tick mark and one label along the x-axis for every row in the table. This column's field name becomes the *x-axis title.*

> **T I P**
>
> You usually build a graph from an nonkeyed Answer table. You can easily *rotate* (Ctrl-R) the fields until the appropriate x-axis label field is the first one on the left.

Paradox also makes the following assumptions about series elements:

■ The position of the cursor determines the first data series. Paradox assumes that the column containing your cursor is the first series of data. Each value in the column (field) becomes a value to be graphed.

■ Series fields must be numeric. Paradox treats the next five numeric columns as additional series columns.

■ Paradox uses the field names of these series columns in the legend to label the corresponding shading, line, or marker. Paradox assigns the name Totals as the *y-axis title.*

Paradox also assigns the table name as the graph's main title.

The other settings used by Paradox to create the standard graph are the *default graph settings*. These settings are analogous to the standard Paradox report specification. The settings are used to produce the standard graph and can be fully modified, saved, and used again.

Examining the Default Graph Settings

Reminder:
The first time you press Ctrl-F7, Paradox uses the default graph settings to create a graph from the current table.

Just as Paradox has a standard form and report specification, the program also has a standard graph specification. The first time you press Ctrl-F7 (Graph), Paradox uses the default graph settings to create a graph from the data in the current table on the workspace. Unlike the standard report specification and the standard form, the standard graph specification is not a format that you can view on-screen. This specification is a group of default settings Paradox applies to the data in the current table to generate a graph. The default graph settings are just the starting point. Making changes to these settings is the subject of "Enhancing the Graph" later in this chapter. That section also explains how to save a modified specification to a file and how to load the settings later for application to the same or another table.

Table 12.1 lists the main default graph settings. Table 12.2 lists the settings that determine color and shading patterns applied to graphs, including the colors and patterns applied when you build pie graphs. You also can use the Custom Configuration Program (CCP), discussed in Appendix B, to make permanent changes to these settings.

Table 12.1. Default Graph Settings

Setting	Default value
Graph Type	Stacked Bar
Override Types	None
Output Device	Screen
Scaling	Automatic
Main Title (1)	Current table name
Main Title (1) size	Autosize
Main Title (1) font	Default
Main Title (2)	Blank
Main Title (2) size	Autosize

Setting	Default value
Main Title (2) font	Default
X-axis Title	Field name of x-axis column
X-axis Title size	Autosize
Y-axis Title	Totals
Y-axis Title size	Autosize
Legend Labels	Series field names
Interior Labels	None
Axis scaling	Automatic
Low (X and Y)	0
High (X and Y)	0
Increment (X and Y)	0
Format (X and Y)	Fixed
Decimal Places (X and Y)	0
Minor Ticks (X and Y)	0
Alternate Ticks?	Yes
Display Axis Scaling?	Yes
Grid Line	1 (horizontal dotted line)
Grid Color	B (dark blue)
Frame Graph?	Yes
Frame Color	B (dark blue)

Table 12.2. Colors and Patterns—Default Graph Settings

Setting	Color	Pattern
Background	H (light gray)	
Main title (1)	B (dark blue)	
Main title (2)	B (dark blue)	
X-axis title	B (dark blue)	
Y-axis title	B (dark blue)	

continues

Table 12.2. Continued

Setting	Color	Pattern
1st Series/ 1st pie slice	B (dark blue)	B (filled)
2nd Series/ 2nd pie slice	C (green)	C (------)
3rd Series/ 3rd pie slice	D (cyan)	D (Lt ///)
4th Series/ 4th pie slice	E (red)	E (Hvy ///)
5th Series/ 5th pie slice	F (magenta)	F (Lt \\\)
6th Series/ 6th pie slice	G (brown)	G (Hvy \\\)
7th pie slice	H (light gray)	H(++++++)
8th pie slice	I (dark gray)	I (crosshatch)
9th pie slice	J (light blue)	J (hatch)

The next two sections describe how to create a graph using these default settings.

Creating an Instant Graph

The trick to learning Paradox graphics quickly is to keep graphs simple, to use a minimum of columns (fields), and to develop a routine. The following two sections describe simple routines that work well and use the instant graph feature. This section describes how to create a simple bar graph in two steps; the next section demonstrates how to use a *crosstab* feature to create a stacked bar graph in three steps. When you master these methods, you should be ready to learn how to create other types of Paradox graphs and to apply many other enhancements.

Step 1: Use Query By Example To Prepare a Table with Two Columns

Cue:
You can use Ctrl-R to place the columns in the right position.

To make learning and understanding the process easier, reduce the number of columns you are working with to two. You probably need to use Query By Example, and you may need to draw data from multiple tables. The first column is the x-axis data, and the second column is the data series that must be numeric. You can use Rotate (Ctrl-R) to place the columns in the right position, if necessary. After the two-column table is created and columns are in the proper positions, you are ready to create the graph.

Step 2: Position the Cursor in the Second Field and Press Ctrl-F7 (Graph)

To create a graph from a table, place the cursor in the data series column, the second column, and press Ctrl-F7 (Graph).

Suppose that you want to compare the widget sales of six salespeople. With the Orders and Detail tables, you use QBE to create a table containing each salesperson's name in the first column and the total quantity of widgets sold in the second column (see fig. 12.12). In the graph, you want to see the names displayed along the x-axis and the calculated field Sold displayed as bars in the graph area.

To create a graph from this table, place the cursor in the Sold column and press Ctrl-F7 (Graph). Paradox displays the bar graph shown in figure 12.13. The names from the first column in Answer are now the labels along the x-axis. Values from the field Sold are depicted by the eight bars.

This two-step method always works but shows only one series of data at a time. The next section explains how to use the Crosstab function to create a stacked bar graph that shows up to six series of data.

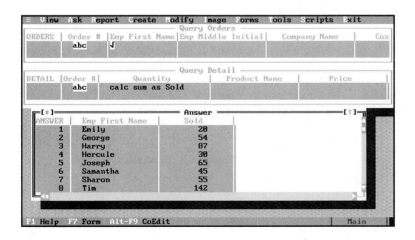

FIG. 12.12

A query to determine the number of widgets sold by each salesperson.

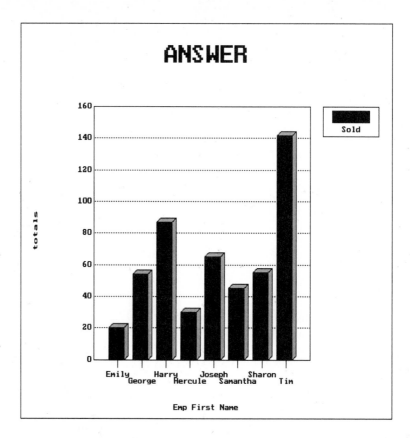

The default graph of the Answer table in figure 12.12.

Using Crosstab

You often want to compare several series of data with one another. For example, you may want to see the total widgets sold by each salesperson broken out by model—a separate data series for each model of widget that shows the number sold by each salesperson. You can compare these series in a bar graph. By default, Paradox graphs multiple series in a stacked bar graph.

Cue:

Put x-axis data in column 1 and numeric data in columns 2 to 7.

To create an instant stacked bar graph, you need a table with the x-axis data in the first column and from two to six additional columns, each containing a numeric data series. In the widget example, you need the Emp First Name column, as in the Answer table, and you need a separate column for each model of widget that has been sold.

Your database usually is not structured so that you can easily extract more than one series column. A normalized database has the data you want to compare in one column. (Designing a normalized database is discussed in the "Designing a Database" section of Chapter 2.) You can, for example, use a query to generate an Answer table showing the number of each model of widget sold by each salesperson (see fig. 12.14). The data you want broken out into separate columns—one for each model of widget that one of the sales representatives has sold—is contained in the Sold column. To solve this problem, Paradox includes the *crosstab* feature. Crosstab breaks the data series out for you.

Step 1: Use Query By Example To Prepare a Table with Three Columns

To use the crosstab feature, you need a table with at least three columns. Assume that you have exactly three columns arranged so that the x-axis data column is first; the column with the series categories is second; and the numeric column is third. The Answer table in figure 12.14 shows this arrangement.

Reminder:
To use crosstab, you need at least three columns.

Step 2: Use Crosstab

After you have built the three-column table, move the cursor to the first column and press Alt-X (Crosstab). Paradox displays a new table called Crosstab. The first column of Crosstab contains the same values as the source table, except that the duplicates are removed. The values in the second column of the source table are now field names for the second and subsequent columns of the Answer table. These columns represent the data series to be graphed. The data from the original third column is broken out to the appropriate series column in the Answer table. The effect is to place the data from the third column of the source table into a matrix or spreadsheet structure in the Answer table.

Cue:
To perform crosstab, move the cursor to the first column and press Alt-X.

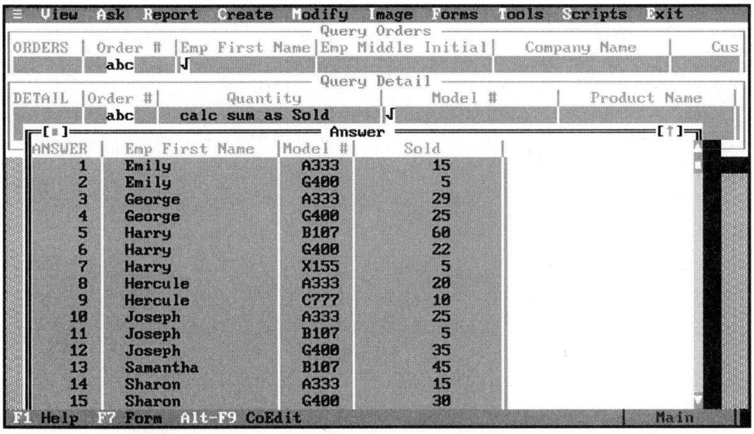

FIG. 12.14

A query to determine the number of each model of widgets sold by each salesperson.

Figure 12.15 shows the result of performing Crosstab on the Answer table from figure 12.14. Each of the widget models has its own column. The data from the Sold column in Answer is distributed among five columns in Crosstab.

T I P

For instructional purposes, this explanation oversimplifies Crosstab, which actually performs a summation function while distributing data to the appropriate data series column. In the example, the summation already is performed in the query shown in figure 12.14 so that you don't notice that Crosstab also performs a summation. You obtain the same result even if the calc expression in the Quantity field (in the query in fig. 12.14) is replaced with a check mark.

Crosstab also is available on the Graph menu. Instead of pressing Alt-X, you can access the menu bar and select **Image Graph Crosstab**.

Paradox displays a menu containing the following statistical computations:

     1) Sum **2)** Min **3)** Max **4)** Count

Select **1)**_Sum from the menu to perform the same operation as Alt-X. Position the cursor in the x-axis data column and press Enter. Position the cursor in the series label column and press Enter again. Move the cursor to the data column and press Enter a third time. The other choices perform the respective computation as data is cross-tabulated.

Step 3: Display the Graph

When you perform the Crosstab, the table is ready to graph. To display a stacked bar graph, move the cursor to the first series column and press Ctrl-F7 (Graph). Figure 12.16 shows the graph based on the data in the Crosstab table shown in figure 12.15. Compare this graph to the graph in figure 12.13. The two graphs are the same, but the latter shows sales broken down by model as well as total sales.

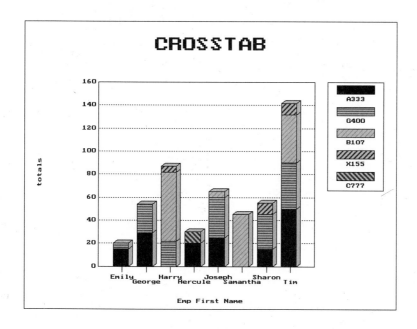

```
≡  View  Ask  Report  Create  Modify  Image  Forms  Tools  Scripts  Exit
┌──────────────────────── Query Orders ────────────────────────────────
│ORDERS │ Order # │Emp First Name│Emp Middle Initial│  Company Name   │ Cus
│       │  abc    │              │                  │                 │
├──────────────────────── Query Detail ────────────────────────────────
│DETAIL │Order #│    Quantity    │        Model #      │   Product Name  │
┌─[#]═══════════════════════ Crosstab ═══════════════════════════[↑↓]┐
│CROSSTAB│Emp First Name│ A333  │ G400  │  B107  │  X155  │  C777        │
│    1   │   Emily      │  15   │   5   │   0    │   0    │   0          │
│    2   │   George     │  29   │  25   │   0    │   0    │   0          │
│    3   │   Harry      │   0   │  22   │  60    │   5    │   0          │
│    4   │   Hercule    │  20   │   0   │   0    │   0    │  10          │
│    5   │   Joseph     │  25   │  35   │   5    │   0    │   0          │
│    6   │   Samantha   │   0   │   0   │  45    │   0    │   0          │
│    7   │   Sharon     │  15   │  30   │   0    │  10    │   0          │
│    8   │   Tim        │  50   │  40   │  42    │  10    │   0          │
└──────────────────────────────────────────────────────────────────────
F1 Help   F7 Form   Alt-F9 CoEdit                            Main
```

FIG. 12.15

Using the Crosstab command.

FIG. 12.16

The default graph of the Crosstab table in figure 12.15.

T I P

An easy way to obtain a presentable graph without doing much more work is to rename the Crosstab table (**R**ename is covered in Chapter 13). For example, you may rename the Crosstab table shown in figure 12.15 to Widgets. When you press Ctrl-F7 (Graph), Paradox uses the graph title Widgets, instead of Crosstab.

FROM HERE...

For Related Information:

◀◀ "Assigning Key Fields," p. 77.

◀◀ "Understanding Query By Example," p. 156.

◀◀ "Using the Instant Report Feature," p. 187.

Enhancing the Graph

Paradox provides a significant number of enhancements that you can apply to your graph. In addition to the graph types already described, Paradox enables you to combine certain graph types, and you can customize all the settings listed in tables 12.1 and 12.2. These settings include the content, size, and font of all titles; labels; legends; scaling; tick marks; grid lines and color; frame color; markers; line color; area and bar color; and shading patterns.

Starting Graph Mode

Cue:
To access Graph mode, select Image, **G**raph, **M**odify.

All enhancements are chosen or modified from Graph mode. To access Graph mode, access the menu bar and select Image, **G**raph, **M**odify. Paradox starts Graph mode and displays the Graph Type form. To access the Main Graph menu, access the menu bar. Paradox displays the following menu in the menu bar:

Type Overall Series Pies ViewGraph DO-IT Cancel

Altering the default settings with this menu is explained in the following discussions. After you make the desired change, press F2 (Do-It!) to change the setting temporarily from the default value.

Saving the Graph Specification

Cue:
To save an altered graph specification, select **I**mage, **G**raph, **S**ave.

Any changes you make to the default settings are effective only for the current Paradox session unless you save the changes to the file. To save an altered graph specification select Image, **G**raph, **S**ave from the Paradox Main menu.

Type a name, following the same file naming rules described in the "Defining Table Structure" section of Chapter 2, and press Enter. Paradox saves the graph specification to a disk file, giving the file the file-name extension .G. You can, for example, save the settings for your widget graph under the name Widget. Paradox saves the graph settings in a disk file named WIDGET.G.

Loading a Graph Specification

Later, during the same or another Paradox session, you can load a saved graph specification. At the Paradox Main menu, select Image, Graph, Load. Specify the name of the graph specification. Paradox replaces the default setting with the specifications loaded from disk.

Cue:
To load a graph spec, select Image, **G**raph, **L**oad.

Graph specifications are not necessarily identified with one table. After you modify the default settings or load a previously established specification, the new settings apply to any table you make current and graph with Ctrl-F7 (Graph).

T I P

Resetting the Graph Specification

After you make changes to the graph specification, or load a previously saved graph specification, you may decide that you need to return to the default settings. You need to reset the specification. Access the Main menu and select Image, Graph, Reset, OK.

Paradox clears all modifications to the default sets and returns to the Main mode.

Selecting Graph Type

To change the graph type, access the menu bar and select Image, Graph, Modify.

Paradox displays Graph mode and the Customize Graph Type form (see fig. 12.17). Choose from among the graph types listed on the right side of the form by pressing the highlighted letter that appears in parentheses.

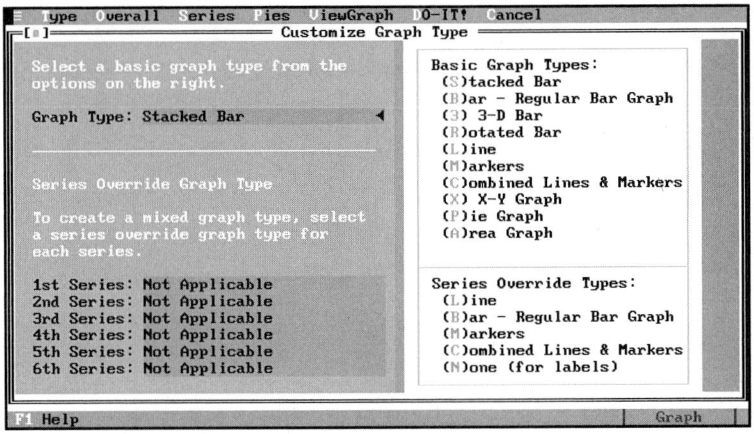

FIG. 12.17

The Customize
Graph Type
form.

The bottom portion of this form provides the *Series Override* option
that enables you to mix any combination of the following graph types:

Line
Bar—Regular Bar Graph
Markers
Combined line and marker
None (for labels)

Move the cursor down to any one or more of the series lines and
choose the desired override graph type. The chosen series is graphed
with the override graph type, rather than the basic type chosen in the
top half of the Graph Type form. Notice in figure 12.17 that because the
graph type is Stacked Bar, series override is Not Applicable.

Customizing Graph Elements

Cue:

To access Graph mode,
select **I**mage, **G**raph,
Modify.

Paradox Graph mode enables you to enhance the appearance of your
graph by modifying the graph's titles, colors, fill patterns, scaling, label
format, tick marks, grid lines, legends, and internal series labels. These
modifications are made to the standard graph specification and do not
affect the series data. To access Graph mode, access the menu bar and
select **I**mage, **G**raph, **M**odify.

When Paradox displays the Customize Graph Type form, the Main
Graph menu appears at the top of the screen. You can look at the graph
with the current settings at any time by pressing Ctrl-F7 (Graph). When
the graph is displayed on-screen, press any key to return to the same
Graph Mode screen.

When you finish making changes, press F2 (Do-It!). Paradox returns to the Main mode.

> Don't forget to save the graph specification to disk if you may want to use the specification in a later Paradox session. From the Main menu, access the menu bar and select **I**mage, **G**raph, **S**ave.
>
> **T I P**

NOTE Paradox does not save the specification to disk when you press F2 (Do-It!). This feature is inconsistent with form and report design but enables you to use one graph specification with more than one table.

Changing Overall Settings

Paradox divides graph elements into groups according to their scope. Because one group of graph elements applies generally to the entire graph, Paradox refers to the elements as *overall* settings. The overall settings include titles, color, scale, label format, and grids. To alter any of these settings, press **O**verall from the Main Graph menu.

Cue:
To change titles, color, scale, label format, or grids, select **O**verall.

Paradox lists the following options:

Titles
Colors
Axes
Grids
PrinterLayout
Device
Wait

Each of these choices displays an options form on which you record the desired changes to the graph specifications. The discussions that follow introduce you to five of these options. **P**rinterLayout and **D**evice are discussed in "Creating Other Output" later in this chapter.

When you complete your changes to an options form and want to go to another one, access the menu bar to select another options form. When you finish making all changes, press F2 (Do-It!). You also can cancel any changes made to the graph specification by selecting **C**ancel from the menu bar. Either way, Paradox returns to the Main mode.

While you are customizing the graph specification, you can view the graph by pressing Ctrl-F7 (Graph). Pressing any key returns you to the same Graph Mode screen.

Customizing Titles

When you choose the Titles option on the Overall menu, Paradox displays the Customize Graph Titles form. This form enables you to alter the main graph title or the axes titles.

Reminder:
Paradox graphs can have two main title lines.

Paradox graphs can have two main title lines centered above the graph area. The default setting uses the table name as the first line of the main title. Use the Customize Graph Titles form to change, add, or delete either line of the main title.

You also can use this form to choose among 11 fonts for the main title: default, bold, triplex, sans serif, small, simplex, triplex script, script, euro style, complex, and gothic.

By default, Paradox assigns font size to titles. Use the Customize Graph Titles form to choose small, medium, or large font size.

The Customize Graph Titles form also contains a section for modifying the content and size of the x-axis and y-axis titles. By default, Paradox uses Totals for the y-axis title and the field name of the x-axis column as the x-axis title. Any entries made in this portion of the Customize Graph Titles form override the default titles.

Customizing Colors

Select Colors, Screen from the Overall menu to access the Customize Graph Colors form. Use this form to alter the default color settings for screen display (with a color monitor) or color printing (with a color printer). You can choose from up to seven colors for the background and from 16 colors for the graph frame, grid, titles, and series data. Pie slice colors are not set on this menu. (Setting pie slice colors is discussed in "Customizing Pie Settings" later in this chapter.)

Customizing Axes

The Axes selection on the Overall menu displays the Customize Graph Axes form. Use this form to adjust y-axis and x-axis scaling.

By default, Paradox sets the low end of the scale to zero and the high end to the increment above the highest series value. Paradox also assigns the increment between tick marks. To override the defaults, select Manual as the Set Axis Scaling option and fill in the Low, High, Increment lines on the Customize Graph Axes form.

For the x-axis (except X-Y graphs), Paradox displays one tick mark and a label for each value in the x-axis data column. Fill in the Minor Ticks line to suppress some of the x-axis labels. Typing 1 in this line suppresses every other x-axis label; a 2 suppresses two out of every three labels, and so on. Alternate Ticks places x-axis labels on alternating levels so that the labels are less likely to overlap.

Paradox abbreviates y-axis tick mark values when the high end of the scale reaches 10,000. For example, the tick mark label 20,000 is abbreviated as 20 to keep from cluttering the image with zeros. The Display Axis Scaling line in this form determines whether Paradox displays the scaling factor beneath the y-axis title (for example, Paradox displays the word thousands to indicate that the y-axis label 20 means 20 thousand). Don't get this option confused with the Set Axis Scaling option.

Reminder:
Paradox abbreviates y-axis tick marks when the high end of the scale reaches 10,000.

Customizing Grids

Choosing the **G**rids option from the Overall menu displays the Customize Grid and Frames form. Use this form to select one of six grid line choices and to change the grid display color. You also can turn off the grid by changing grid color to the same as the background color.

Also use this form to toggle the graph frame and set the graph frame color. The color option duplicates an option on the Customize Graph Colors form.

Setting the Wait Duration

By default, Paradox displays your graph until you press a key. With the **W**ait option on the Overall menu, you can alter this setting so that the graph displays for a certain amount of time, and then returns to the workspace. Select **W**ait, **D**uration.

Type a number that represents the number of seconds the graph should display and press Enter. The next time you display a graph, the new wait period takes effect. Paradox returns the screen to the desktop.

To return the wait feature to the default conditions, select **W**ait, **K**eystroke.

Customizing Series Settings

Another group of settings is the Series group. These graph settings affect the display of the numeric data portion of the graph—the series. Through the series settings, you can customize the legends that describe each series on the graph, label the data inside the graph area, assign different marker shapes, assign different fill patterns, and access the Customize Graph Colors form.

To modify one of the series settings, access the menu bar from the Graph mode and select **S**eries.

Paradox displays the following menu:

> **LegendsAndLabels**
> **MarkersAndFills**
> **Colors**

The next two sections discuss **LegendsAndLabels** and **MarkersAndFills**. **Colors**, however, takes you to the same Customize Graph Colors form discussed in the preceding description of the Overall graph settings and is not covered again in this section.

Customizing Legends and Labels

The **LegendsAndLabels** option on the Series menu displays the Customize Series Legends and Labels form. This form has spaces for up to six series legends. Paradox uses the field name of each series column as a label for the series in the graph's legend. Fill in the appropriate line to override the default.

Paradox also provides a method for labeling your graph. The default graph specification does not include any labels that show the exact value of a series. Having the underlying data printed on the graph, however, can be helpful. The Customize Series Legends and Labels form provides the following label placement alternatives: center, above, below, right, left, none (to reset).

Customizing Markers and Fills

Choose **MarkersAndFills** from the Series menu to make changes to the fill pattern of a series element or the marker symbols used in marker graphs. You can assign any of the fill patterns or marker symbols listed in table 12.3.

Table 12.3. Fill Patterns and Marker Symbols

Code	Fill pattern	Marker symbol
A	Empty	Filled square
B	Filled	Plus sign
C	Dashed line	Eight-point star
D	Light ///	Empty square
E	Heavy ///	X
F	Light \\\	Dollar sign
G	Heavy \\\	Filled triangle
H	++++++	Hourglass
I	Crosshatch	Six-point star
J	Hatch	Box with X inside
K	Light dots	Shadowed cross
L	Heavy dots	Vertical line
M	(None)	Horizontal line

Customizing Pie Settings

Pie graphs have their own Customize Pie Graph form. From the Main Graph menu, choose **P**ies to display this form. You can set the format for pie slice labels, set colors and fill patterns, and explode pie slices.

Reminder:
Pie graphs have their own Customize Pie Graph form.

The default label for each pie slice is the series value. For example, if a pie slice represents 65 widgets sold, 65 is the label. Paradox also enables you to label slices showing the percentage that each slice represents of the whole, to label slices as currency, or to suppress labels.

Paradox provides the same fill pattern choices shown in table 12.3. All 16 colors also are available for you to assign to any of the nine possible pie slices.

You also use this form to explode a pie slice. By default, no slices are exploded. To explode a slice, type *y* in the Explode Slice column to the right of the slice number.

FROM HERE...

For Related Information:

◄◄ "Enhancing the Report," p. 371.

Creating Other Output

So far, this chapter has dealt with displaying your graph on-screen. Paradox also can print the graph on a graphics-capable printer or plotter and can save the graph to a file on disk.

Printing or Plotting a Graph

Before you can print or plot your graph, you have to use the Custom Configuration Program (see Appendix B) to define your printer or plotter driver as one of the four available printer setups. You also need to make this setup *current* and make sure that the printer layout is the way you want it.

Selecting a Printer or Plotter

Cue:
To choose a different printer, select **O**verall, **D**evice, **P**rinter.

By default, the printer or plotter you define, using the CCP, as Printer 1 is the current printer, but you may have more than one printer or plotter attached to your system. To choose a different printer, access the Main Graph menu and select **O**verall, **D**evice, **P**rinter.

Choose one of the four printer/plotter setups. This setup becomes the current printer or plotter for the Paradox session until you select another one, **R**eset the graph specification settings or quit Paradox.

Customizing the Printer Layout

Cue:
To customize printer settings, select **O**verall, **P**rinterLayout.

The default settings for printer layout are listed in table 12.4. If these settings match the layout you intend to use to print your graph, you are ready to send the graph to the printer or plotter. To customize one or more of these settings, select **O**verall and **P**rinterLayout from the Main Graph menu. Paradox displays the Customize Graph Layout for Printing form.

Table 12.4. Printer Layout Settings

Setting	Default Value
Units	Inches
Left Margin	0
Top Margin	0
Graph Height	0 (page size)
Graph Width	0 (page size)
Orientation	Landscape
Break Page	No
Plotter Speed	0

Use this form to change the unit of measurement (inches or centimeters), left margin, top margin, graph height, and graph width. You also can choose whether the graph should print in landscape orientation (horizontal) or portrait orientation (vertical). Although the default width and height are set at 0, Paradox assumes that you are using an 8 1/2-by-11-inch page. To change the graph size, type appropriate numbers into these lines on the form.

Printing several graphs on one page is possible. For example, to print two graphs in portrait orientation on the same page, use Graph Height and Graph Width to reduce the graph size to a width of 8 inches and a height of 5 1/2 inches. Also make sure that the orientation is set to Portrait and the Break Page line contains an entry of No. After printing the first graph, Paradox does not eject the page, enabling you to print the second graph on the same page. The Plotter Speed option on this form enables you to choose plotter speed.

Reminder:
Paradox enables you to print several graphs on a single page.

When you finish customizing these printer/plotter layout settings, press F2 (Do-It!).

Sending the Graph to the Printer or Plotter

After making sure that the correct printer/plotter is current and adjusting the printer layout options, you are ready to print or plot your graph. Make sure that the printer or plotter is on, properly connected to your computer, and loaded with paper. When using a plotter, the pens must be mounted in their holders with the caps off. From the Main Graph menu, select ViewGraph, **P**rinter.

Paradox sends your graph to the chosen printer or plotter.

Sending the Graph to a File

Instead of sending your graph to a printer or plotter, you may want to save the graph image (instead of the graph specification) to a disk file.

Reminder:
Paradox enables you to save the graph image to a file.

Before sending output to the file, select a file format. The default format matches the current printer (often called a *print image*). Paradox sends to the file the output needed to generate the graph on your printer/plotter. Paradox also enables you to save your graph in Encapsulated PostScript (EPS) format or 1-2-3 (PIC) format. To choose one of these formats, select **O**verall, **D**evice, **F**ile, from the Main Graph menu.

Choose **C**urrentPrinter, **E**PS, or **P**IC. EPS files can be used with other graphics programs and for desktop publishing.

When you are sure that you have chosen the correct file format, you are ready to send the graph to the disk. Select **V**iewGraph, **F**ile from the Main Graph menu.

Type a unique file name and press Enter. Paradox generates the file in the format you have chosen. Files formatted for your printer or plotter have the extension GRF.

T I P

You can print a file formatted for your printer or plotter from DOS with the COPY command. You don't have to use the same computer, but you must be printing to the same type of printer or plotter. For example, if you name the file BARGRAPH, Paradox provides the extension GRF. To print the file, type *copy bargraph.grf prn*.

If the printer or plotter you want to use is not connected to the first parallel printer port, replace *PRN* with the appropriate port name (for example, LPT2). Do not use the DOS PRINT command.

You also should be aware that the default print image format creates large files (often in excess of 500K). EPS and PIC formats are much more efficient.

FROM HERE...

For Related Information:

◄◄ "Controlling the Printer," p. 375.

Using Graphics on a Network

Using Paradox graphics on a network with shared files usually is the same as with private files. To view a graph, you must have the data to be graphed in the current image. When you view a shared table or perform a query using a shared table, Paradox places a prevent full lock on the table. If another network user already has placed a full lock on a table that you need to use, you cannot generate the graph until that user is finished. After you generate the Answer or Crosstab table that is the actual basis of the graph, you are working with a private file.

Paradox takes some special steps to make network use of graphics efficient and enables you to create a continuously updating graph that reflects changes being made by multiple users of shared tables.

Using Crosstab on a Network

Similar to a query, the Crosstab function has to look at the data in a table but doesn't make any changes to that data. When you perform Crosstab on a shared table, Paradox places a prevent full lock on the shared table. Paradox then takes a snapshot of the shared table, releases the prevent full lock, and processes the command. If another user is making a change to the table when you execute the Crosstab command, Paradox tries to take the snapshot until the other user releases the record. You see a message as this process takes place. You can press Ctrl-Break to abort the Crosstab if you don't want to wait.

Using Autoregraph

One of the most impressive feats you can perform with Paradox graphics is referred to in the Paradox documentation as *autoregraph*. This operation uses the **R**epeatPlay option on the Scripts menu to continually redraw your graph. Autoregraph is effective only on a network where other network users are making changes to the data on which the graph is based.

The purpose of autoregraph is to see changes to shared data reflected in the graph as the changes are made. Autoregraph can be useful in sensitive business applications such as stock or commodities trading. Price or quantity updates of the underlying data, or both, are reflected in the graph, perhaps making trends easier to spot.

The first step is to design your graph. When you can manually produce the desired picture of your data, you are ready to make the graph automatic by completing the following steps:

1. Make sure that the proper graph specification is current. Load the specification from disk if necessary. Set the wait duration to the same number of seconds as the current Autorefresh setting. (The **A**utorefresh choice on the **T**ools, **N**et menu is discussed in Chapter 13.)

2. Clear all windows from the desktop.

3. Start recording a script by selecting **S**cripts, **B**eginRecord from the Main menu.

   Type a unique script name and press Enter.

4. Perform all the keystrokes necessary to display your graph, including any queries or crosstabs.

5. Clear all images with Alt-F8 (Clear All).

6. Stop recording the script by selecting **S**cripts, **E**nd-Record

7. Play the script by selecting **S**cripts, **R**epeatPlay from the Main menu.

8. Specify the script. When prompted for the number of times to repeat the script, type *c* and press Enter. The graph is refreshed at approximately the same time that the data is refreshed and reflects the most current data.

FROM HERE...

For Related Information:

◀◀ "Using Reports on a Network," p. 217.

Chapter Summary

The graphics capability of Paradox is a significant tool for quickly and easily analyzing your Paradox database. This chapter introduced the tools available in the Paradox graphics module and demonstrated the easiest way to get started at building informative graphs from tables. You can learn to enhance your graphs to their fullest potential. Graphics products are designed for experimentation. If your graph doesn't look right at first, play around with the graph options until you are satisfied.

Using Paradox Tools

References to the Tools menu are scattered throughout this book. Probably, you have turned to this chapter before finishing all the chapters that precede it. Like any good toolbox, the Paradox Tools menu contains tools for many purposes. You never know when the toolbox may come in handy. Just the same, some of the tools are so specialized that you may never need to use them.

This chapter is near the end of the book because it covers a broad range of topics. The Paradox Tools menu includes tools that supply information about your database; exchange files with other programs; rename, copy, and delete Paradox objects; add and subtract tables; speed up queries; provide password protection; provide access to the operating system; and enable you to lock, unlock, and prevent locking of shared tables on a network. Some of these features are mentioned briefly in other chapters, in the context in which they may be used, but each is explained again in this chapter for your convenience.

The Tools menu has so many options that the Tools pull-down menu is split into two parts. To access the Paradox Tools menu, select **T**ools from the Paradox Main menu. Paradox displays the following menu:

> **R**ename
> **Q**uerySpeedup
> **E**xportImport
> **C**opy

Delete
Info
Net
More

The last choice, **More**, displays a second pull-down menu:

Add
MultiAdd
FormAdd
Subtract
Empty
Protect
Directory
ToDOS

For clarity, this chapter refers to the first menu as the Tools menu, and to the second menu as the Tools, More menu.

Obtaining Information about Your Database

Working with Paradox, you may encounter many situations in which you need an answer to questions like the following:

- How did I define the Cust ID # field—as a numeric field or an alphanumeric field?

- What was the name of the table I created the day before yesterday—Detail or Details?

- How many reports have I defined for the Employee table?

- Who else on the network is working in Paradox right now?

- What are the current locks on the Orders table?

You can obtain the answers to each of these questions by using the **Info** option on the Tools menu. Consistent with virtually all other procedures in Paradox, all answers are provided in the form of a temporary table that can be queried, renamed, and printed. From the Tools menu, select **Info**; Paradox displays the following choices:

- *Structure*. Choose this option and specify the table name to list quickly the structure of a table in the temporary table Struct.

- *Inventory*. Choose this option to show the following menu:

    Tables
    Scripts
    Files

Choose **T**ables to build a list of all tables in the current directory or another specified directory (see fig. 13.1). Paradox displays the temporary table list. This list shows table names and the dates on which they were last modified. Temporary tables always have today's date because they are deleted at the end of each session. Choose **S**cripts to produce a list table of scripts in the current or specified directory. When you choose **F**iles, Paradox asks for a DOS pattern. Press Enter to list all the files in the current directory, or specify a valid DOS search pattern (including path) to produce a list table of files from a different directory. The **F**iles option provides a convenient way to produce a catalog of all the files on your disk.

Cue:

Choose **T**ools, **I**nfo, Inventory, **T**ables to build a list of all tables in the current or specified directory.

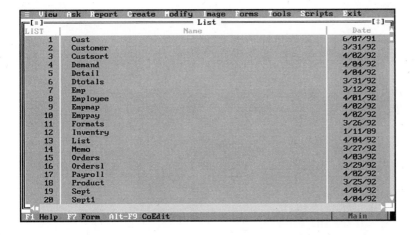

FIG. 13.1

An inventory of all tables in the current directory.

- *Family*. Choose this option and specify a table. Paradox displays a list of all the members of the table's family of objects as a temporary table named Family (see fig. 13.2).

- The next two options on the Tools, Info menu, **W**ho and Lo**c**k, are discussed in "Using Tools on a Network" later in this chapter.

- *TableIndex*. Choose this last option on the Tools, Info menu to list the available secondary index files for a particular table.

For Related Information:

◄◄ "Understanding Paradox Objects," p. 65.

◄◄ "Defining Table Structure," p. 72.

◄◄ "How are Scripts Stored?" p. 222.

FROM HERE...

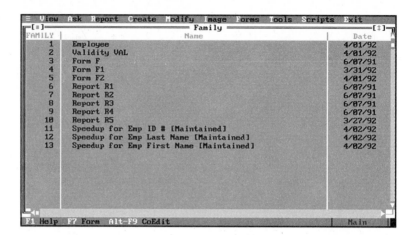

```
≡  View  Ask  Report  Create  Modify  Image  Forms  Tools  Scripts  Exit
┌[■]══════════════════════════ Family ═══════════════════════[↕]┐
│FAMILY │                        Name                        │    Date  │
│      1│ Employee                                           │  4/01/92 │
│      2│ Validity VAL                                       │  4/01/92 │
│      3│ Form F                                             │  6/07/91 │
│      4│ Form F1                                            │  3/31/92 │
│      5│ Form F2                                            │  4/01/92 │
│      6│ Report R1                                          │  6/07/91 │
│      7│ Report R2                                          │  6/07/91 │
│      8│ Report R3                                          │  6/07/91 │
│      9│ Report R4                                          │  6/07/91 │
│     10│ Report R5                                          │  3/27/92 │
│     11│ Speedup for Emp ID # [Maintained]                 │  4/02/92 │
│     12│ Speedup for Emp Last Name [Maintained]            │  4/02/92 │
│     13│ Speedup for Emp First Name [Maintained]           │  4/02/92 │
│                                                                     │
 F1 Help  F7 Form  Alt-F9 CoEdit                            Main
```

FIG. 13.2

The Family table.

Renaming Paradox Objects

Paradox makes liberal use of temporary tables. Queries create the Answer table; DataEntry creates the Entry table; key violations create the Keyviol table; and the Info option discussed in the preceding section creates several different temporary tables. The potential problem with temporary tables is that their contents are not safe until you copy the data to another table or give the temporary table a new name. Changing the names of temporary tables is the most common use of the **Re**name option on the Tools menu, although you also can rename scripts, graphs, forms, and reports.

Renaming a Table

Cue:
To rename a table, select
Tools, **R**ename, **T**able.

To rename a table, temporary or otherwise, select Tools, **R**ename, **T**able from the Main menu. At the first prompt, specify the name of the table whose name is to be changed. At the next prompt, type a new table name and press Enter. Make sure that you do not use one of the following temporary table names:

Answer	Changed
Crosstab	Deleted
Entry	Family
Inserted	Keyviol
List	Password
Problems	Struct

Paradox renames the table and all family members with the new name.

Renaming Forms and Reports

In Paradox, the names of forms and reports are not really significant, with two major exceptions: the standard form F is the default preferred form, invoked by pressing F7 (Form Toggle); the standard report specification R is selected by default by pressing Alt-F7 (Instant Report). As suggested in previous chapters, you may want to create your own customized form and report specification to replace the default choices. One method of accomplishing the replacement is through the **R**ename command.

To rename a form, select **T**ools, **R**ename, **F**orm from the Main menu. Specify the table that contains the form. To help you, Paradox displays a list of defined forms. Select the one to be renamed and then select the new name. Paradox warns you if the new name you type is already in use. Then you must decide whether to **C**ancel the operation or **R**eplace the existing form.

Cue:
To rename a form, select
Tools **R**ename **F**orm.

Changing the name of a report is accomplished in a similar way.

Renaming Scripts and Graphs

Paradox scripts and graphs are stored as files outside of a table's family of objects. Because scripts and graph specifications can be used with more than one table, they have their own name and are not automatically renamed when you rename the table.

The Instant script, recorded when you press Alt-F3 (Instant Script Record), is similar to a temporary table. If you think that you may want to use the Instant script again, you must rename the temporary script before saving.

Paradox does not create temporary graph specifications, but you may want to change the name of a graph specification to reflect its content more clearly or to use the name for a different graph.

To change the name of a script file, select **T**ools, **R**ename, **S**cript from the Main menu. Specify the name of the script, type the new name, and press Enter. If you select a name that already exists, Paradox gives you a choice of canceling the **R**ename operation or replacing the existing script.

Follow a similar procedure to rename a graph specification.

FROM HERE...

For Related Information:

◄◄ "Renaming Tables," p. 92.

◄◄ "Naming the Report Specification," p. 189.

◄◄ "Starting the Form Designer," p. 298.

◄◄ "How are Scripts Stored?" p. 222.

Copying Paradox Objects

The Copy option on the Tools menu enables you to make copies of Paradox tables, forms, reports, scripts, graphs, and a family of objects with the parent table.

Copying Tables

Cue:
Always use the **C**opy option to make a backup of a table.

When you copy a table, you copy the table and its entire family. Therefore, you always should use the Copy option to make a backup of a table. In one step, you copy the table and its forms, reports, indexes, validity checks, and settings. As long as you copy to a different disk or directory, you can even use the same name for the copy.

Cue:
To copy a table, select **T**ools, **C**opy, **T**able.

To copy a table, select Tools, Copy, Table from the Main menu. At the prompt for the table name, indicate the name of the table to be copied, and at the prompt for the new name, type the name of the new table. Paradox informs you if a table by the same name already exists and gives you a chance to cancel or proceed with the copying process.

Copying Forms and Reports

The procedures for copying forms and reports are nearly identical. To copy a Paradox form, select Tools, Copy, Form from the Main menu. Then choose between the following menu options:

■ *SameTable*. Select this choice to copy the form in the same family of objects. When prompted, specify the table containing the form, the form to be copied, and a name for the copy.

■ *DifferentTable*. Choose this option to copy the form to a different table. For this option to work, both tables must have identical structures. If they do not, Paradox displays a message stating that the tables do not have the same field names or field types. When prompted, supply the name of the source table, the destination table, and the name of the form.

Follow similar steps to copy a report specification. The most likely situation for copying a report occurs when you want to use an existing report specification to print an Answer table. The Answer table must have a structure identical to the source table.

Copying Just a Table's Family

Although separate options exist for copying forms and reports, you may want to copy an entire family of objects from one table to another, especially if you have chosen validity checks for use with forms or have several forms or reports to copy. The JustFamily option copies all objects, including validity checks and image settings. The JustFamily option copies a table's family of objects without copying the table. The target table must already exist, however, and must have a structure identical to the source table.

Reminder:
The JustFamily option copies all objects.

To copy a family of objects without copying the table to which the family belongs, select **T**ools, **C**opy, JustFamily from the Main menu. Specify the source table and the target table. Then choose **R**eplace to indicate that any existing family objects should be replaced.

Cue:
To copy a family of objects, select **T**ools, **C**opy, JustFamily.

You are most likely to use the JustFamily option to add forms, reports, validity checks, and settings to a table just extracted from another table through a query operation. You may, for example, decide to create a separate telephone list for the Sales department. To do this, you first use QBE to create an Answer table containing only employees from the Sales department. Next, you use the **R**ename **T**able option to change Answer to Sales. Finally, you use the JustFamily option to copy all forms, reports, and so forth to the Sales table. Not only do you have the telephone list report available, you also have any other reports and all forms, validity checks, and other settings.

T   I   P

Copying Scripts and Graphs

The steps for copying scripts and graphs are nearly identical to the steps for renaming these objects, except that you select **C**opy instead of **R**ename from the **T**ools menu. Refer to "Renaming Scripts and Graphs," earlier in this chapter, for detailed instructions.

FROM HERE...

For Related Information:

◄◄ "Understanding Query By Example," p. 156.

◄◄ "Modifying the Report Specification," p. 215.

Deleting Objects and Emptying a Table

The **D**elete choice on the Tools menu provides options to delete tables, forms, reports, scripts, secondary index files, image settings, validity checks, and graphs. These operations are self-explanatory, but because they are irreversible, they should be used with caution.

> **CAUTION:** Use all the **D**elete options with caution, but be particularly sure that you really want to delete a table before selecting that option. Deleting a table also deletes its family of objects.

The Empty option on the Tools, More menu provides a method of deleting all records from a table without deleting the table's structure or family. To use this option, select **T**ools, **M**ore, **E**mpty from the Main menu and specify the table to be emptied. Paradox requires that you confirm the deletion with **O**K.

Adding and Subtracting Tables

Several options on the Tools, More menu enable you to add and update data from table to table. One option enables you to use one table to specify deletions in another table, and another option adds or updates data from one table to two or more tables at once.

T I P

Empty provides an alternative to using the Copy option to copy JustFamily to a new table. Instead, you can use Empty to delete the existing records and Add (see "Adding and Subtracting Tables" in this chapter) to add the records from the new table to the emptied table. One advantage of the Empty-Add method is that key-field assignments are maintained; they are lost in the Copy-JustFamily method.

For example, you may use QBE on the Employee table to create an Answer table containing only employees from the Sales department. Answer tables do not have key fields, and using the Copy/JustFamily tool does not create the key fields. To use the Empty method, you first make a copy of the Employee table (using the Copy/Table options from the Tools menu), perhaps with the name Sales. Then use Empty to remove all records from Sales. Finally use Add from the Tools, More menu to add the Sales department employees to the Sales table. The Emp ID # field in Sales is still the key field, and Paradox stores records in order by that field.

Adding and Updating Records from One Table to Another

Unlike the Copy and Rename operations, the Add option can handle tables without identical structures. To add one table to another using Add, however, the two tables must have the same number of fields, in the same order, and with compatible field types (number field matched to number field, alphanumeric matched to alphanumeric, and date matched to date).

Reminder:
The **A**dd option can handle tables without identical structures.

To add one table to another, select Tools, More, Add from the Main menu. Specify the source table and the target table. If the target table is not keyed, Paradox adds the new records to the end of the table. If the table is keyed, you must choose between the following menu options:

Cue:
To add one table to another, select **T**ools, **M**ore, **A**dd.

■ *NewEntries*. Choose this option if the records being added do not yet exist in the target table. When Paradox performs the Add operation, any key violations are placed in the Keyviol table. This choice essentially is a mass DataEntry session.

■ *Update*. When some or all of the records you are adding may already exist in the target table, use the Update option. This selection acts much like an Edit session. Old field values where key values match new records are replaced by new field values. Where no matching record already exists, the new record is merged into the target table in key-field order. The original values of any existing records that have been updated are placed in a temporary table named Changed so that you easily can determine what changes have been made.

T I P	Database users commonly distribute to satellite offices portions of a master database. A problem that is just as common is how to later reconcile the master database with any changes made by the various satellite offices to their portion of the database. The Add, Update option provides a possible solution.

Adding and Updating from One Table to Two or More Tables

The **MultiAdd** option on the Tools, More menu is the counterpart to the MultiEntry feature. To use **MultiAdd**, you first must have created a source table and a map table using the **MultiEntry S**etup option from the Modify menu (refer to Chapter 9).

Cue:
To add data from one table to two or more tables, select **T**ools, **M**ore, **M**ultiAdd.

To add data from one table to two or more tables, select **T**ools, **M**ore, **MultiAdd** from the Main menu. Specify the source table (created by **MultiEntry S**etup) and the map table. Paradox displays the following options from which you must select:

■ *NewEntries.* Choose this option when you want to add the new records to the tables, rather than update records that already exist in the target tables. As with MultiEntry, Paradox places in Keyviol tables key violations that occur during the MultiAdd operation. A new record that exactly duplicates, in every field, an existing record is not considered a key violation, but also is not added to the table. Such an exact duplicate is absorbed into the existing record. When a key violation does occur, correct the error and use **MultiAdd** to insert the record into the target tables.

T I P	You must rename the Keyviol table using the **R**ename option before Paradox enables you to add the corrected records with **MultiAdd**.

■ *Update*. Select this option to use the source table to update the target tables. For nonkeyed target tables, records are added to the end of the table. For keyed target tables, records with no match are merged in key order; records matching the key fields are used to update values in the matching records in the target tables. A Changed table is not created, as opposed to a changeto query that creates a temporary Changed table (see Chapter 7).

Using a Multitable Form To Add or Update Multiple Tables

Sometimes, you may want to consolidate data from several sources into one set of tables. When several of the target tables are logically related—one-to-one, one-to-many—you should use all available tools to ensure referential integrity. The **FormAdd** option on the Tools, More menu is the batch-processing equivalent of using a multitable form during DataEntry. FormAdd is analogous to **MultiAdd** but needs no map table because the multitable form *is* the map.

To use **FormAdd** to add to or update one set of related tables from a corresponding set of related tables, the following must be true:

■ Each of the source tables has a structure compatible with its corresponding target table: fields in the same order, same number of key fields, and compatible field types (numeric fields match numeric fields, alphanumeric fields match alphanumeric fields, and date fields match date fields).

■ A multitable form exists that contains all the fields of the target tables.

The next sections describe several scenarios for using **FormAdd**.

Adding Multiple Entry Tables

When you use DataEntry to add records to your database through a multitable form, Paradox builds a series of Entry tables with the names Entry, Entry1, Entry2, and so on, depending on the number of tables linked in the multitable form. When you press F2 (Do-It!) to complete DataEntry, Paradox attempts to add the data from these Entry tables to the target tables, using the multitable form as a map. If Paradox is successful, you can forget about the Entry tables.

Reminder:
When you use a multitable form in DataEntry, Paradox builds a series of Entry tables.

Two eventualities can prevent successful addition of all the new records to the target tables:

- ■ *KeepEntry.* On a network, another user may have locked one of your target tables. In this case, Paradox informs you that the table is locked. You may choose to wait for the other user to finish or choose the **KeepEntry** option from the DataEntry menu. (See Chapter 9 for a discussion of entering records from multitable forms.) **KeepEntry** makes sure that all the new records are in the Entry tables, clears the form from the screen, and returns to Main mode.

- ■ *Key violations.* A key violation in adding records to one or more of the target tables causes Paradox to build a set of Keyviol tables: Keyviol, Keyviol1, Keyviol2, and so forth. These tables contain the offending records. Paradox also does not immediately erase the Entry tables. (Remember that Keyviol tables and Entry tables are *temporary.*) When such a key violation occurs, Paradox builds the Keyviol tables, adds nonoffending records to these tables, adds nonoffending records to the target tables, and returns you to Main mode.

In either of these two cases, you must add records to the target tables in a batch, instead of one at a time. In the first situation, you add the Entry tables; in the second situation, you add the corrected records that caused key violations. You probably want to use the Entry tables in both cases as source tables for a **FormAdd** operation.

T I P

Paradox balks at adding Keyviol tables using FormAdd because the program doesn't maintain key fields in the Keyviol tables. Instead of using these tables, correct the key violations in the Entry tables, and then use FormAdd. Ignore the second set of Keyviol tables, if applicable (unless you make a mistake correcting the first violations—the second set of tables appears when some of the new records are successfully added during the first try with DataEntry).

Cue:
To add Entry tables to target tables, select **T**ools, **M**ore, **F**ormAdd.

To add Entry tables to existing compatible target tables, select Tools, More, FormAdd from the Main menu. Specify the name of the master target table at the first prompt and choose the multientry form from the next prompt. Then select EntryTables from the menu that Paradox displays. Paradox locates the Entry tables and adds the new records to the target tables.

Adding to or Updating Multiple Tables Using AnyTables

When you are not adding Entry tables, you must take a few more steps to use FormAdd. From the Main menu, select Tools, More, FormAdd. Specify the target master table at the first prompt and multitable form at the next prompt. Then, select AnyTables from the menu. Paradox provides the following menu options from which you can choose:

- *NewEntries*. When all the source records are new or exact duplicates of existing records, choose this option. Paradox places key violations in the Keyviol tables. (Contrary to the Paradox documentation, exact duplicates are not ignored. See also the following tip.)

- *Update*. Select this option to use the source tables to update the target tables. Because you always should use keyed tables, records with no match are merged in key order, and records that match the key fields are used to update values in the matching records in the target tables. Changed tables *are* created for detail tables (contrary to a statement in the Paradox documentation). Paradox names these tables Changed1, Changed2, and so forth, and displays a List table that maps each Changed table to its corresponding detail table. If you are adding records to target tables that are not keyed, the records are added to the end of the table.

Regardless of whether you choose NewEntries or Update, you must choose source tables that match the target tables included in the multitable form, starting with the master table. Paradox prompts you for the correct number of tables based on the number of tables used in the multitable form. When you select the last source table, Paradox performs the FormAdd operation.

Reminder:
Choose source tables that match the target tables included in the multitable form.

Subtracting Tables

Occasionally, you will compile a table that contains a list of records that should be deleted from another table. You may have just updated your product line, for example, adding new models and deleting slow sellers. You can go through the Products table and delete each obsolete model, but an easier method is to compile a list of the model numbers and use the Subtract option on the Tools, More menu to delete all the obsolete models at the same time.

To use this option, select Tools, More, Subtract from the Main menu. Specify the name of the table that includes the records to be deleted. Then specify the target table. The structures of the source and target tables must be compatible, although not necessarily identical. The way Paradox handles the deletions depends on whether or not the tables are keyed:

- When the tables are keyed, Paradox deletes any records in the target table that match the key field or fields of the source table. You can leave blank all source fields except key fields and still delete the obsolete records.

- If tables are not keyed, Paradox deletes only the target-table records that are exact matches of source-table records.

FROM HERE...

For Related Information:

◄◄ "Understanding Query By Example," p. 156.

◄◄ "Making Global Changes with the CHANGETO Operation," p. 289.

◄◄ "Creating a Multitable Form," p. 313.

◄◄ "Adding Data with the MultiEntry Option," p. 341.

Exporting and Importing Tables

If life were perfect, everyone in the world would use Paradox for database applications and you would not have to worry about other file formats. Because life is never perfect, Paradox provides a number of tools that enable you to export to and import from file formats used by other programs.

Exporting Paradox Tables

Cue:

To export a table, select **T**ools, **E**xportImport, **E**xport.

Occasionally, you must use data contained in a Paradox table with another program. Translating the data from the file format used by Paradox to that of the other program is referred to as *exporting* the file. To export a Paradox table, select **T**ools, **E**xportImport, **E**xport from the Main menu. Paradox presents a list of the formats to which you can export the Paradox table. Choose the appropriate format:

- *Quattro*. Use this option to create a Quattro spreadsheet; then choose **1**)_Quattro_Release_1.X or **2**)_Quattro_Pro, depending on the version of Quattro to be used.

- *1-2-3.* Select this option to create a Lotus 1-2-3 spreadsheet. Then choose **1**)_1-2-3_Release_1A or **2**)_1-2-3_Release_2, depending on the version of 1-2-3 to be used.

- *Symphony.* Choose this format to create a Symphony spreadsheet. Select **1**)_Symphony_Release_1.0 or **2**)_Symphony_Release_1.1, depending on the version of Symphony to be used.

- *dBASE.* To create a dBASE file, choose this option. Then select **1**)_dBase_II, **2**)_dBase_III, or **3**)_dBASE_IV depending on the version of dBASE to be used.

- *PFS.* This selection creates a file in a format compatible with PFS:File or IBM Filing Assistant.

- *Reflex.* Select this format to export the table as a Reflex database file. Then select **1**)_Reflex_Release_1.0, **2**)_Reflex_Release_1.1, or **3**)_Reflex_Release_2.0, depending on the version of Reflex to be used.

- *VisiCalc.* Select this option to create a file for use by any program that can use a DIF file.

- *ASCII.* Use this option to convert the table into an ASCII file. Then choose **D**elimited (fields are separated by commas; records are on separate lines) or **T**ext (use only with a table containing exactly one field where the field is an alphanumeric field).

After selecting the export format, specify the name of the Paradox table to export and the name of the target table. You can use the same name for the target table because Paradox adds a different extension, depending on the export format chosen. Paradox converts the source data to the selected format. Table 13.1 lists how Paradox converts data types during Export.

Importing Data from Other Formats

One of the rules of thumb stated early in this book is never to enter data more than once. An even better rule, when you can, is never to enter data at all—let someone else do it for you. If anyone ever offers you data created in the format of another program, take it. More likely than not, Paradox can *import* (bring in) the file.

To import data from another file format, select **T**ools, **E**xportImport, **I**mport from the Main menu. Choose the appropriate file format (the same choices listed in the preceding section, "Exporting Paradox Tables," are presented, except for ASCII files, which are described in the next paragraph). Then specify the file to be imported, including the

Cue:
To import data, select **T**ools, **E**xportImport, **I**mport.

DOS path if the file is not in your working directory. Finally, type a name for the new Paradox table. Paradox converts the data to a Paradox table, following the conversion rules listed in table 13.1.

Table 13.1. Paradox Export/Import Data Type Conversion

Format	Export target data type	Paradox data type	Import source data type
Quattro, 1-2-3, or Symphony	Labels	Alphanumeric (A)	Labels
	Numbers	Numeric (N)	Numbers
	Numbers (2 decimals in currency format)	Currency ($)	Numbers (2 decimals in currency format)
	Numbers (formatted as dates)	Date	Numbers (formatted as dates)
dBASE	Character	Alphanumeric (A)	Character
	Number	Numeric (N)	Number (19 digits, 14 whole, 4 decimal)
	Number (2 decimals)	Currency ($)	Number (2 decimals)
	Date (dBASE III) or Character (dBASE II)	Date	Date (dBASE III)
	Number (5 digits)	Short (S)	
	Character (dBASE II, III)	Memo	Memo (dBASE III Plus or IV)
	Memo (dBASE III Plus or IV)		
	Character	Alphanumeric (A) (length 1)	Logical
PFS	Character string	Alphanumeric (A)	Contains any nonnumeric character
	Character string	Numeric (N)	All numeric characters
	Character string	Currency ($)	All numeric and 2 decimals

Format	Export target data type	Paradox data type	Import source data type
	Character string	Date (D)	All values in yy/mm/dd or mm/dd/yy format
	Character string	Alphanumeric (A) (length 255)	Attachment pages
Reflex	Text	Alphanumeric (A)	Text
		Alphanumeric (A)	Repeating text
	Numeric	Numeric (N)	Numeric
	Numeric	Currency (formatted as currency)	Numeric (formatted as currency or financial)
	Integer	Short (S)	Integer
	Date (formatted as mm/dd/yy)	Date	Date
Visicalc	Text	Alphanumeric (A)	Text
	Numbers	Numeric (N)	Numbers
	Numbers (2 decimals)	Currency	Numbers (2 decimals)
	Text (formatted as mm/dd/yy)	Date	Text (formatted as mm/dd/yy)

You can import ASCII files into a new table created by Paradox, or you can add the ASCII data to an existing Paradox table. To Import an ASCII file into a Paradox table, select **Tools ExportImport Import Ascii** from the Main menu. Then choose from the following options:

■ *Delimited.* Choose this option when the ASCII file is stored as comma delimited (the CCP program discussed in Appendix B enables you to configure Paradox so that the program uses some other delimiting character, if necessary) and you want Paradox to create a file automatically.

■ *AppendDelimited.* Make this choice to add an ASCII file to an existing Paradox file. This option works in the same fashion as the **Add** choice on the Tools, More menu. Refer to the "Adding and Updating Records from One Table to Another" section of this chapter for details. Contrary to the Paradox documentation, this feature does not create a Changed table.

After you have selected the **Delimited** or **AppendDelimited** option, specify, at the first prompt, the source file name (including the path if the file is not in the current directory) and the name of the target table at the second prompt.

FROM HERE...

For Related Information:

◄◄ "Designing a Database," p. 68.

Speeding Up Queries with QuerySpeed

Reminder:
Paradox finds the fastest route to your data.

A consistent complaint that daily users of database products have is that data retrieval is too slow. One of the hallmarks of Paradox is the use of artificial intelligence (AI) routines that find the fastest possible route to your data. With Paradox you seldom have to worry about query speed.

This book encourages the creation of at least one key field (*primary index*, see the "Assigning Key Fields" section in Chapter 2) per table. Several reasons for the use of key fields in Paradox exist, and one of the reasons is to help speed up queries. Because Paradox always stores tables in order by key fields, and because queries often are done by key field, you get the fastest query response possible.

Situations arise when you routinely use a query that may benefit in terms of speed by maintenance of an index on a field other than key fields. Such an index is a *secondary index*. You can have Paradox create a secondary index file in several ways. Chapter 3, "Entering, Editing, and Viewing Data," discusses how you can use the **O**rderTable option on the Image menu or the Alt-S keyboard command to create a secondary index file. Chapter 9 explains how to use the Index command on the Modify menu to create a secondary index. This section describes how to use the QuerySpeed command toward the same end.

To try to speed up a query, first construct the query statement on the desktop and then select **T**ools, **Q**uerySpeed from the Main menu. Paradox displays the message Processing query speedup. Often, however, Paradox is using the fastest search method already and displays the message No speedup possible. Paradox does not build a secondary index, which increases program overhead, unless the secondary index can increase the speed of the search.

For Related Information:

◄◄ "Reordering the Table with OrderTable," p. 138.

◄◄ "Using the Index Command," p. 348.

FROM HERE...

Protecting Your Files

One of the inherent weaknesses of the DOS operating system is a lack of system-level file protection. DOS provides no utility for securing your programs or data against tampering by other users. The only protection you can place on a file with DOS is the read-only attribute (DOS 3.2 and later), and that only prevents accidental modifications or deletions. Anyone with access to the disk that contains the file can remove the attribute and delete the file.

The Paradox **P**rotect tool on the Tools, More menu significantly improves your ability to protect data from unauthorized access. With this feature, you can add sophisticated password protection to tables and scripts, and Paradox-specific, read-only protection to tables.

Adding Password Protection to a Paradox Table

Paradox enables you to claim *ownership* of a Paradox table by adding a password. The original password placed on a table is the *owner* password (also called the *master* password). Placing an owner password on a file does the following:

■ *Encryption*. Adding a password encrypts the table and all its family members so that they no longer can be used without the password.

■ *Ownership*. Knowledge of the owner password enables you to assign multiple *auxiliary passwords* that grant limited access to the table or its family of objects.

Assign the same password to all related tables for the following reasons:

■ *Convenience*. Entering the password once during a Paradox session grants you access to all tables with the same password.

■ *MultiTable Forms*. Paradox does not prompt you for a password for detail tables embedded in a multitable form. Unless one password accesses the master table and all detail tables, Paradox displays the message `Insufficient rights for Detail table` when you try to use a multitable form.

■ *Memory* (yours, not the computer's). Remembering one password is easier than remembering several for a single database.

Cue:
To assign an owner password, select **T**ools, **M**ore, **P**rotect, **P**assword, **T**able.

To assign an owner password, select **T**ools, **M**ore, **P**rotect, **P**assword, **T**able from the Main menu. At the first prompt, specify the table you want to protect. At the `Password` prompt, enter a password of up to 15 characters, including numbers and spaces, and press Enter. Paradox prompts you to enter the password again, to confirm the original entry. Use a word that you can remember, or write the password down where you can find it. Remember also whether you used upper- or lowercase letters in your password. For example, Paradox views safeword and SAFEWORD as two different passwords. If you forget the password, you cannot use the table or any of its objects.

T I P

As an added precaution against forgetting your password, assign yourself an *auxiliary password* with **A**ll rights. Refer to the next section, "Assigning Table Rights, Family Rights, and Field Rights," for more information. You then have to forget both passwords to be completely locked out of the table.

After confirming that the password was entered properly the second time, Paradox enters Password mode and displays the *auxiliary password form* (see fig. 13.3). Using this form, you can assign table rights or family rights to other users as discussed in the following section. This form is actually a special data-input form for a table named Password. You can press F7 (Form Toggle) to see the Password table in table view.

When you finish adding auxiliary passwords, press F2 (Do-It!) to complete definition of the passwords. Paradox displays the message `Encrypting...` and converts the target table and all family members into an encrypted format. After a table and its family of objects is encrypted, you can access them only with the proper password.

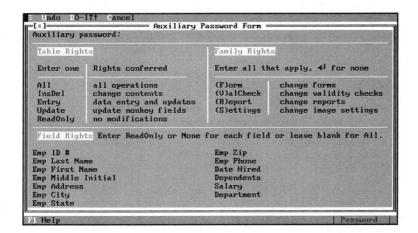

FIG. 13.3

The auxiliary
password form.

Assigning Table Rights, Family Rights, and Field Rights

When you are the only user of your database, you already have all rights to use, modify, and delete the table and all its family members, whether or not you add personal protection. When others need to use some or all of the tables in your database, however, such as in an office environment or on a network, you may want to grant each of the users a level of access consistent with their needs. You assign certain access rights to auxiliary passwords and provide the passwords only to those users who need the corresponding level of access.

For each auxiliary password, you can grant any one of the following table rights by making a choice in the Table Rights section of the auxiliary password form:

- *All.* This right is equivalent to ownership, but because the user obtains access with an auxiliary password, not the owner (master) password, he or she doesn't have access to other tables unlocked by the owner password.

- *InsDel.* The user has Entry rights and can change the content of all fields, insert and delete records, and change key fields.

- *Entry.* The user has Update rights and can enter records into the table using DataEntry or Add.

- *Update.* The user can view the table and make changes to nonkey fields but cannot insert or delete records or make any changes to key fields.

- *ReadOnly*. The user who knows (and uses) the auxiliary password can view the table but cannot make changes or deletions.

Grant each auxiliary password any combination of the following rights, with respect to the family of objects belonging to the protected table, through the Family Rights section of the auxiliary password form. Type the first letter of each choice, and Paradox displays the letters you type to the right of the `Family Rights` label on the auxiliary password form:

- *(F)orm*. The user who knows (and uses) the auxiliary password can design, change, and delete forms in the protected table's family.

- *(V)alCheck*. The user can assign, change, or delete validity checks for members of the protected family.

- *(R)eport*. The user can design, change, and delete report specifications in the protected family.

- *(S)ettings*. The user can add, change, and delete image settings.

You can even control access to specific fields with the Field Rights section of the auxiliary password form (choose only one):

- *ReadOnly*. The user can view but not change the protected field values.

- *None*. The user can neither see nor alter the values in the field.

- *(blank)*. All field rights, including the right to view and change any value in the field, are granted.

After you have assigned all the desired access rights to the auxiliary password, press PgDn to display new forms for additional auxiliary passwords or press F2 (Do-It!) to indicate that you are finished.

When you are working on the auxiliary password form, Paradox presents the following Password Mode menu:

> **Undo   Help   D**O**-IT!   Cancel**

These options work exactly like their namesakes in Edit mode. You also can press Ctrl-U (Undo) to back out of changes made to the Password table, one transaction at a time.

Assigning Passwords to Scripts

The purpose and effect of assigning a password to a Paradox script is different from that of password-protecting a table. Tables can contain sensitive or valuable information that needs to be protected from unauthorized access, but a script is just a program. The reason for protecting a script is not to prevent the use of it, but to prevent anyone from changing the script.

To add a password to a script, select **T**ools, **M**ore, **P**rotect, **P**assword, **S**cript from the Main menu. Specify the name of the target script. Type the desired password and press Enter and type the password again and press Enter for confirmation. Paradox displays the message Encrypting.... You do not have to supply the password to play the script, just to edit or debug it.

Cue:
To add a script password, select **T**ools, **M**ore, **P**rotect, **P**assword, **S**cript.

Changing and Removing Passwords

Occasions almost certainly will arise when you need to remove or change a password. To delete or make changes to a password, select **T**ools, **M**ore, **P**rotect, **P**assword from the Main menu and then choose **T**able or **S**cript, depending on the entity for which you want to change the password.

For a table password, specify the name of the protected table. If you have not already accessed this table during the current session, you must enter the current password. Then choose **M**aster or **A**uxiliary. Choosing **M**aster enables you to enter a new password. To delete the current password, just press Enter. When you delete the owner (master) password, Paradox displays the message Decrypting... as the program unprotects the indicated table. Choosing **A**uxiliary, on the other hand, displays the Password table in the auxiliary password form and enables you to make changes.

For a script password, specify the script name and enter the current password. To change the password, type the new one and press Enter. To remove the password without replacing it, press Enter at the prompt for the new password.

Clearing Passwords

For your convenience, Paradox does not require you to enter your password every time you redisplay a protected table in a given session. If you walk away from your computer for a short time without exiting Paradox, however, someone else may access the protected files you opened.

To prevent this from occurring, before you leave the computer, select **T**ools, **M**ore, **P**rotect, **C**learPasswords from the Main menu. Paradox clears everything from the desktop and displays the message All passwords cleared. This process does not remove the passwords but

Cue:
Select **T**ools, **M**ore, **P**rotect, **C**learPasswords to clear the desktop and active passwords.

resets the protection feature so that anyone trying to access the table must know the proper passwords. When you return to the computer and start to use the protected table again, you must enter the password again.

Using the Write-Protect Option

The Paradox write-protect feature (for tables only) is similar in concept to the DOS read-only attribute or the write-protect notch on a floppy disk (or the write-protect slide on a 3 1/2-inch disk). This feature is only effective in Paradox, however; the feature does not prevent access, alterations, or deletions from DOS.

Cue:
To add the write-protect feature, select **T**ools, **M**ore, **P**rotect, **W**rite-protect.

To add the Paradox write-protect feature to a table, select **T**ools, **M**ore, **P**rotect, **W**rite-protect from the Main menu. Specify the name of the table to be protected. Then choose **S**et. This feature provides protection against accidental changes and deletions from within Paradox but does not prevent unauthorized access to your data. While a table is write-protected, Paradox does not enable you to edit or delete records in the table.

To remove Paradox write-protection, select **T**ools, **M**ore, **P**rotect, **W**rite-protect from the Main menu. Specify the name of the protected table. Then choose **C**lear.

FROM HERE...

For Related Information:

◄◄ "Creating Tables on a Network," p. 82.

◄◄ "Adding Password Protection and Claiming Table Ownership on a Network," p. 94.

◄◄ "Using the Index Command," p. 348.

Changing the Working Directory

The DOS directory that contains your database is the *working directory*. Appendix A, "Paradox 4.0 Installation and Start-Up," explains how to start Paradox from the working directory. When you use that procedure, Paradox reads and saves tables to the working directory. The **D**irectory option on the **T**ools, **M**ore menu provides a method of changing the working directory after you begin Paradox.

To change the working directory, select **T**ools, **M**ore, **D**irectory from the Main menu. Backspace over the current working directory name and type a new directory name. Press Enter, and then select **O**K.

Cue:
To change the working directory, select **T**ools, **M**ore, **D**irectory.

> **CAUTION:** This operation not only changes the directory but also clears any images on the desktop and deletes all temporary tables. Make sure that you rename any temporary tables that you want to save before executing this option.

For Related Information:

▶▶ "Starting Paradox 4.0," p. 991.

▶▶ "Controlling the Interface Settings," p. 1001.

FROM HERE...

Accessing the Operating System

Paradox provides three methods of accessing DOS without exiting Paradox. Two are equivalent. From the Main menu, you can select **T**ools, **M**ore, **T**oDOS. Paradox displays the following warning:

```
WARNING! Do not delete or edit Paradox objects or load
RAM-resident programs. To return to Paradox, type exit.
```

Paradox saves the current Paradox state, loads a DOS shell, and displays the DOS prompt. Paradox still occupies about 420K of memory, so keep this memory restriction in mind when you perform any DOS operations.

The keystroke command Ctrl-O (DOS) is equivalent to the **T**oDOS menu option.

At times, the preceding options do not leave you enough DOS memory to execute the desired operation. In such cases, use the keystroke Alt-O (DOS Big). With this option, Paradox uses only about 100K of memory, but because it saves the Paradox environment temporarily to disk, this option is slower than the other options.

Reminder:
Alt-O (DOS Big) uses only 100K of DOS memory.

When you access DOS using any of these methods, observe the following precautions:

- Do not delete, rename, or change any Paradox system files or objects. If you do, Paradox may not be able to resume when you try to exit DOS.

- Do not load additional RAM-resident programs. Paradox needs all the memory it released to DOS.

- Do not use the DOS PRINT or MODE commands.

- If you change disks or directories while accessing DOS, return to the original disk or directory before exiting the DOS session.

- Terminate the DOS session by typing *exit* on a DOS command line.

These guidelines help ensure that you don't corrupt your database when performing a DOS operation.

Using Tools on a Network

All the tools discussed thus far in this chapter also can be used on a network. The password and access rights features in particular are even better suited for use on a network than on a single-user system. A few special considerations apply when some of the tools are used on a network, and Paradox has several tools of interest only to network users.

Special Considerations

When you use Paradox tools on shared objects on a network, you have to keep in mind the locks that Paradox places on these objects. Locks are described in "Creating Tables on a Network" in Chapter 2. Table 13.2 lists the locks placed on source and target objects as you work with the various tools discussed in this chapter.

Assigning a User Name

Many networks enable you to establish a user name that identifies you to other network users for such things as electronic mail. Paradox uses this name, if it exists. Paradox also has its own facility for assigning user names. The Paradox user name overrides any other name you may be assigned on the network, but only during the Paradox session. You can use this feature even if your network does not directly support user names.

Table 13.2. Locks Placed When Using Tools on a Network

Tool	Type of Lock
Add	Write lock on source, prevent write lock on target
Copy	
Table	Write lock on source, full lock on target
JustFamily	Write lock on source, full lock on target
Form, Report	Write lock on source, full lock on target, prevent full lock on table
Script, Graph	Write lock on source, full lock on target
Delete	
Table	Full lock on table and its family
Form Report	Full lock on target object and prevent full lock on table
Script, Graph	Full lock on target object
QuerySpeedup	Same as the query (see Chapter 7)
Empty	Full lock on table
Export	Write lock on source table
FormAdd	Prevent full lock on all source tables until Do-It!; Update causes write lock on source and target tables; NewEntries causes write lock on sources and prevent write lock on all target tables
Import	Full lock on target table
Info	
Structure	Prevent full lock on table
Family	Write lock on table and family
MultiAdd	Write lock on source and map tables, prevent write lock on all target tables
Protect	Full lock on table or script
Subtract	Full lock on both tables

You should encourage all network users of Paradox to establish user names because the names help you determine who is using and locking shared resources. When you attempt to use a table but are prevented because the table is locked, Paradox can give you the name of the user who locked the table only if a user name is assigned.

Reminder:
Paradox displays the user name when a table is locked.

Cue:

To assign a user name, select **T**ools, **N**et, **U**serName.

To assign a user name, select **Tools**, **Net**, **UserName** from the Main menu. Type your new user name (up to 15 characters, no spaces) and press Enter. Confirm the new name by selecting **OK**. Paradox displays a message indicating your new user name. This new name is in effect for the current Paradox session only.

A more permanent way to assign a user name is available through the Custom Configuration Program. Refer to Appendix B for details.

T I P When using Paradox on a large network, include each user's telephone number (or extension) as a part of the user's name. Although most networks provide a method of communicating through the network, it may be more convenient just to pick up the phone and call the user who has locked you out of a table you need.

Assigning a Private Directory

Reminder:

When using Paradox on a network, you need a working and private directory.

When you use Paradox on a network, you must have a *working directory* and a *private directory*. Because the purpose of using Paradox on a network is to share files, your working directory obviously cannot be accessible only to you, but you should have a place for all temporary objects created by Paradox that is not accessible to other network users. You also can place permanent objects you don't want to share with other users into the private directory.

Cue:

To assign a private directory, select **T**ools, **N**et, **S**etPrivate.

To assign or reassign a private directory during a Paradox session, select **Tools**, **Net**, **SetPrivate** from the Main menu. Type the complete path for the private directory and press Enter. Then confirm the change by selecting **OK**.

CAUTION: Changing the private directory during a Paradox session clears the desktop and deletes all temporary objects. Be sure that you have renamed any temporary objects that you want to save for future use.

As with your user name, it probably is easiest to assign your Paradox private directory permanently through the CCP (refer to Appendix B).

Because you must have a private directory when you use Paradox in a network environment, Paradox attempts to assign one if you don't have one. By default, Paradox looks first to the directory from which you started Paradox on your local hard disk. For workstations without a C drive, Paradox tries to use the network directory from which you started Paradox. If this network directory is shared, Paradox displays the message `Can't start Paradox: can't get private directory.`

T I P

If your workstation has its own hard disk, assign the private directory to this hard disk. This procedure gives Paradox the quickest access, and by definition, other users have no need to access this disk.

On a workstation with no local storage, check with your network administrator for assistance in creating a directory on the network accessible only by you. Use that directory as your Paradox private directory.

Placing Explicit Locks and Prevent Locks on Paradox Objects

As explained throughout this book, Paradox places locks and prevent locks on Paradox objects as you use them. The specific type of lock or prevent lock is based on the type of operation you perform. Paradox tries to provide all users the maximum level of concurrent access to shared tables and objects consistent with the current needs of individual users.

Reminder:
Paradox places locks and prevent locks on Paradox objects.

Situations may arise when the automatic locks and prevent locks that Paradox applies are not sufficient protection. In such cases, Paradox enables you to place explicit locks and prevent locks on objects as well.

To place an explicit lock on a Paradox object, select **T**ools, **N**et, **L**ock from the Main menu. Then choose one of the following options:

Cue:
To place an explicit lock, select **T**ools, **N**et, **L**ock.

- *FullLock*. Choose this option to gain exclusive access to a table and its family of objects.

- *WriteLock*. Select this option to prevent other users from changing the structure or content of a table and its family of objects while still enabling users to manipulate the table and other objects in other ways.

After choosing the type of lock you want to impose on the table, specify the name of the table to be affected and choose **S**et. Paradox displays the message `Full lock set` or `Write lock set`. When you finish using the table, don't forget to clear the lock immediately, using the same keystrokes, **Tools**, **Net**, **Lock**, **FullLock/WriteLock**, and choosing **Clear** at the end. Paradox then displays the message `Full lock cleared` or `Write lock cleared`.

Cue:

To place an explicit prevent lock, select **T**ools, **N**et, **P**reventLock.

To place an explicit prevent lock, select **Tools**, **Net**, **PreventLock** from the Main menu. Then choose one of the following options:

- Select **FullLock** to prevent other network users from placing a full lock on the table and its family of objects.

- The **WriteLock** choice prevents other network users from placing a write lock or a full lock on the table and its family.

- Choose **DirLock** to place a directory lock on an entire directory. This action is the same as placing a full lock on each table in the directory—limiting other users to read-only access to all Paradox objects in the directory. When you select **DirLock**, Paradox displays a dialog box that contains the name of the current working directory. If you want to lock a different directory, type the name of the directory. Press Enter or select OK to complete the operation.

T I P   Placing a directory lock on a shared working directory can cause Paradox to process queries and other object-related operations more quickly because the program uses disk-caching rather than continually writing all changed objects to disk.

After choosing the type of prevent lock, specify the target table and choose **Set**. As with explicit locks, don't forget to explicitly **Clear** each prevent lock you assign.

Table 13.3 shows which locks and prevent locks can be applied to a table at the same time by several network users.

Table 13.3. Locks and Prevent Locks That May Coexist on a Table

	Full Lock	Write Lock	Prevent Write Lock	Prevent Full Lock
Full Lock				
Write Lock		X		X
Prevent Write Lock			X	X
Prevent Full Lock		X	X	X

Regulating AutoRefresh

As explained earlier in this book, Paradox keeps all current network users of a shared table up-to-date by continually refreshing the screens with changes being made by other users. The default interval for screen refreshes is three seconds. If this interval is not appropriate for your current needs, you can change it. To do so, select Tools, Net, AutoRefresh from the Main menu. Backspace over any existing number and type a new number between 1 and 3600. The number you type represents a particular number of seconds. Leave the interval blank to disable AutoRefresh.

Reminder:
The default interval for screen refreshes is three seconds.

Gathering Network Information

When you intend to use a feature of Paradox that needs to place a lock on a shared table, you may want to determine first what locks are already in place on the table. Even if the table is not currently locked, you may want to see who else is using Paradox on the network. This may tell you whether to expect another user to compete with you for use of the table. The Info choice on the Tools menu gives you all this information.

To see a list of locks in place on a table, and who placed them, select Tools, Info, Lock from the Main menu. Specify the target table. If any locks are currently in place on the table, Paradox displays a temporary List table containing the locks placed and the user name (if available) of the individual who placed each lock.

Cue:
To see a list of locks and who placed them, select Tools, Info, Lock.

To see a list of network users currently using Paradox, select Tools, Info, Who from the Main menu. Paradox displays the list of users in a temporary List table.

For Related Information:

◄◄ "Creating Tables on a Network," p. 82.

◄◄ "Using DataEntry Mode on a Network," p. 107.

◄◄ "Using Edit Mode on a Network," p. 118.

◄◄ "Using CoEdit Mode on a Network," p. 125.

◄◄ "Using Reports on a Network," p. 217.

◄◄ "Using Scripts on a Network," p. 236.

◄◄ "Performing Queries on a Network," p. 291.

◄◄ "Using Forms on a Network," p. 321.

◄◄ "Using Graphics on a Network," p. 423.

FROM HERE...

Chapter Summary

This chapter has helped you examine the tools Paradox provides for accomplishing such tasks as exchanging files with other programs; renaming, copying, and deleting Paradox objects; adding and subtracting tables; speeding up queries; adding password protection; accessing the operating system; and locking and preventing locking of shared tables on a network. With this chapter, you have completed your tour of the interactive features of Paradox. You can still learn more about this seemingly boundless program. Turn now to Part III of this book, "Programming Paradox," for an introduction to the use of the Paradox applications generator called the Application Workshop and an overview of the Paradox Application Language (PAL).

PART

III

Programming Paradox

OUTLINE

Using the Application Workshop

This chapter introduces Paradox's new Application Workshop, a powerful package used to generate entire applications. (The Application Workshop replaces the Personal Programmer from earlier versions of Paradox.) After you develop a menu structure, or hierarchy, and attach an action to each menu selection, the Application Workshop generates a series of scripts necessary to run your application.

This chapter describes the Application Workshop as a tool you can use to develop Paradox applications. The discussion covers most of the menu selections available to the user. Because the Application Workshop is so big and powerful, this chapter focuses on the options offered by the Application Workshop only—and not by Paradox. To get the most out of this chapter, you need to have a good understanding of the topics covered in the previous chapters.

Chapter 6, "Getting Started with Scripts and Keyboard Macros," introduced you to simple Paradox Application Language (PAL) scripts you can create by recording keystrokes. The PAL scripts control your application by performing some or all of the following actions:

- Displaying a splash screen
- Performing password and table rights checking
- Displaying menu selections
- Prompting for user input
- Executing queries
- Displaying forms
- Performing edits
- Updating tables
- Printing reports
- Displaying context-sensitive help screens

The Paradox Application Workshop is a powerful, easy-to-use, menu-driven system that enables you to create complex PAL programs without having to become an expert in the Paradox Application Language. If you want to learn more about PAL, see Chapter 15, "An Overview of the Paradox Application Language," and Chapter 16, "Using the Paradox Application Language."

Recommendations for Using the Application Workshop

Before getting involved in the technical aspects of using the Application Workshop, this section gives you some recommendations on how to use this tool. Following these recommendations will save you valuable time and energy and will make your programming efforts with the Application Workshop more productive. Using these recommendations also will make easier changing or maintaining your application later.

Designing the Application

Before you begin to develop an application with the Application Workshop, first carefully plan all of its desired features.

Design your application thoroughly on paper, making sure that the following design elements have been thought through adequately:

■ *Menu structure.* Also referred to as the *menu hierarchy.* You create the menu structure by choosing names for each of the menu choices in your application and by grouping the user's choices functionally. The Paradox menu structure, for example, groups all table, form, and report copying actions under the menu choice **T**ools, **C**opy.

■ *Tables.* Decide the structure and relationships of all the tables your application will use. Be sure that the structure and design of the tables are adequate for your application.

Deciding how the tables will be manipulated by your application is very important. The Application Workshop will ask you to choose an action—such as edit, query, or report—and then pick a table (or tables) that the action will affect.

You need to determine ahead of time whether a table will be modified in Edit or CoEdit mode or used only for viewing. (Actions in the Application Workshop are discussed later in this chapter.)

When designing tables, also plan the actions to be performed on them.

T I P

■ *Forms.* Decide when and under what circumstances each form will be used; then determine what fields, including calculated fields, will appear on the forms. Be sure to give special thought to forms used for multitable or multirecord views. Don't forget to include the embedded forms.

■ *Multitable views.* Determine the content of the source and map tables used in multitable views and DataEntry sessions.

■ *Queries.* Plan all the queries that your application will make. Be sure to include in your plan which fields will be checked, what the matching criteria, if any, for a field will be, and what linking examples will be used in multitable queries.

During the planning stage, you can record your queries using **S**cripts, **R**ecord or save them using **S**cripts, **Q**uerySave (refer to Chapter 6, "Getting Started with Scripts and Keyboard Macros"). Later, when you are using the Application Workshop, you can enter the query manually or attach your recorded script.

■ *Settings and Validity checks.* Decide the appearance of table images, which fields will need validity checks, and what each validity check should consist of—pictures, defaults, ranges, and so on.

■ *Reports.* Decide when and under what circumstances each report will be used. Then determine what fields, including calculated fields, will appear on the reports. Be sure to give special thought to multitable reports.

■ *Help screens.* With the Application Workshop, you can attach a help screen to each menu selection and to some objects. You also can cross-reference various help screens with each other, creating a help system similar to that used for Paradox itself.

As you design your application, note the areas that might need a help screen and decide what the content of the help screen should be. In many cases, your own design notes about how your application functions can be adapted to help text for the user.

Paradox and the Application Workshop are flexible and can accommodate change readily but they are not as flexible as an eraser. The benefits of designing on paper first become more apparent when you have to change a large application. Planning well on paper helps save you the frustration of false starts and having to redo your previous work.

Occasionally, you need to build an application using tables, forms, and reports that you have created previously and used interactively. Even though you are familiar with these existing objects and know what actions you want, formally planning how you will connect these objects with menus and actions in the Application Workshop still is worthwhile.

Using Paradox To Create Objects

When you have completed your design on paper, use Paradox to create all the objects your application needs. Test each object as you create it. Make sure that validity checks and calculated fields work correctly, that forms and image settings produce the correct appearance and function, and that reports are satisfactory.

Make sure that your planned queries produce the expected results. Setting up a query action in the Application Workshop involves filling in a query form exactly like using the **A**sk command from the Paradox Main menu. If you choose to record your queries ahead of time, you need to attach the recorded query as a script to be played instead of as a query action. You can record your queries using **S**cripts, **R**ecord or **S**cripts, **Q**uerySave.

Although some of the items your application needs can be created or modified in the Application Workshop, creating and testing them in

Paradox usually is much more convenient. The Application Workshop's strength is in pulling objects together into an application, not in creating them.

Use Paradox to create the following objects:

- Tables

- Forms

- Multitable forms

- Multirecord forms

- Source and map tables (using multientry multitable views)

- Queries (optional)

- Settings and validity checks

- Reports

- Multitable reports

Pulling Elements Together with the Application Workshop

After you have designed, created, and tested the objects that your application needs, you are ready to use the Application Workshop to pull all the parts together.

First, you start the Application Workshop and assemble the menu structure you decided on during your design process. Next, define all the actions for your application and the objects on which they act. Finally, attach the actions to their respective menu selections. You also may define and attach each action as the menu selection is created.

For Related Information:

FROM HERE...

◄◄ "Understanding Query By Example," p. 156.

◄◄ "Previewing the Report Design Process," p. 182.

◄◄ "An Overview of Form Design," p. 294.

►► "The PAL Programming Paradigm," p. 508.

Starting the Application Workshop

The Application Workshop is integrated in Paradox Version 4.0. This means that you do not have to leave Paradox to use the Application Workshop.

To start the Application Workshop, press Alt-Space (System Menu), or click the ≡ symbol. Now choose Utilities from the System Menu. Another submenu appears; choose Workshop (Application Workshop). The Application Workshop now loads. First, the Application Workshop splash screen (greeting) appears. After a moment the Main menu screen appears (see fig. 14.1). The Application Workshop now is ready for you to create a new application or change an existing one.

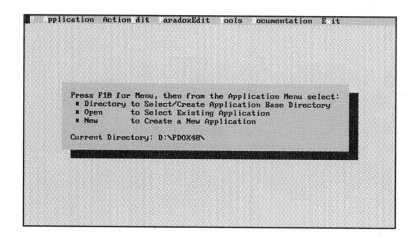

FIG. 14.1

The Application Workshop main menu.

Using the Application Workshop Menu System

Before discussing the specific steps involved in creating or modifying an application, this section provides a brief overview of the menu system available in the Application Workshop.

Like Paradox, the Application Workshop contains a series of menus and submenus. To use the Application Workshop, you make choices from the menus and then fill in the dialog boxes that appear. Some of the information you provide will be short; other selections require you to fill out several dialog boxes.

When you have finished defining all of your application's menus and actions and have attached the actions to their appropriate menu selections, you may test or finish your application. Testing your application enables you to run the application without leaving the Application Workshop. Testing generates the scripts for your application, but the scripts are not kept.

Finishing your application makes sure that all the supporting files your application uses, such as Application Workshop procedure libraries, are copied into the application's directory. The main script for the application then is generated permanently. (Refer to Chapter 15, "An Overview of the Paradox Application Language," for more information on procedure libraries.)

If you change your application after it has been finished, the main script is not updated unless you perform the finishing operation again.

Besides providing menu explanations at the bottom of the screen, the Application Workshop provides on-line help. Press F1 to invoke the Application Workshop's help screens. Make selections on the Application Workshop menus as you do in Paradox, by using the arrow keys to move the highlight bar over the desired selection or by using the mouse to click on the desired selection. Much of the information that the Application Workshop needs to create your application is obtained from dialog boxes you fill out. Like much of Paradox's operations, using the Application Workshop is straightforward and fairly intuitive.

For Related Information:

◄◄ "Using Paradox Menus and Prompts," p. 39.

▶▶ "Procedures and Procedure Libraries," p. 551.

FROM HERE...

Creating an Application

The following sections explain the various steps you take to create an application in the Application Workshop.

Just as each Paradox database should be placed in its own directory, you should create a separate directory for each application you generate with the Application Workshop. This keeps the files from different applications from becoming intermingled and confused and enables you to distribute your application more easily to other users. If you have created your application in its own directory, then you need to copy only the contents of that directory (and its subdirectories) in order to move your application.

If you are generating an application to handle activities with an existing database, you can build the new application in the same directory as your data tables.

Cue:
Create a separate directory for each application you want to generate.

Use DOS commands to create the subdirectory for your application, and then change to the new application's subdirectory and start Paradox, or just start Paradox. After Paradox is running, you can use the **Tools, More, Directory** menu selections to change the current working directory to the directory for the new application. Activate the System Menu by pressing Alt-space bar or clicking on the ≡ symbol. Choose **Utilities** and then **workshop** to start the Application Workshop.

Getting Started

If the current directory is not set to the application directory, select **Application Directory.**

To create a new application, select **Application, New.** The Application Workshop presents you with a dialog box asking you to confirm your choice to create a new application. Press Enter or click OK, and the New Application dialog box appears. The following paragraphs describe how to complete the dialog box (see fig. 14.2).

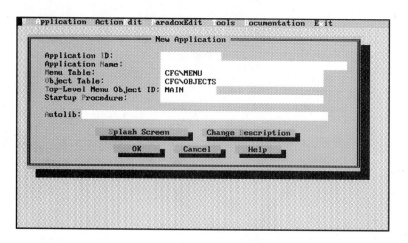

FIG. 14.2

New Application dialog box.

The first field in the dialog box is for the Application ID. This is an eight-letter (maximum) name that will be used by the Application Workshop in naming files belonging to the application. The Application ID name may not contain spaces and must be a legal DOS file name (without an extension). When you have entered the Application ID, press Tab to move to the next field or click on the next field to make it active.

The next field is the Application Name. This name is shown at the bottom of the screen while you are working on the application. This name also is used as a splash screen (greeting) if you do not explicitly create one. You have up to 80 characters and may enter any text you want.

The next two fields ask for the names of the directories in which the menu and object tables are stored. These tables, created by the Application Workshop, contain information about your application's menus and objects. Although you may change the directory names, you probably should use the default names for these directories. If the directories do not exist, the Application Workshop creates them.

The Top-Level Menu Object ID field is the name by which the main, outermost menu of your application will be known. The default (MAIN) for this field usually is best.

In the StartUp Procedure field, you may enter the name of a procedure to be played before the application is played. In most cases, you leave this field blank.

The field labeled *Autolib* usually should remain blank. If you intend to attach PAL procedures you have written to this application, then enter the name(s) of the libraries that contain the procedures to be attached. Refer to Chapter 15, "An Overview of the Paradox Application Language," and Chapter 19, "PAL Command and Function Reference," for more information on procedures, procedure libraries, and the autolib global variable.

An application displays the splash screen, or greeting screen, while it is starting up. When you start Paradox, for example, it shows a splash screen with your name, company name, and Paradox serial number. Your application may have its own splash screen. Creating a splash screen is optional. If you do not create a splash screen, the Application Workshop uses the text that you entered for the Application Name as a splash screen.

To create a splash screen for your application, choose the Splash Screen button. The Application Workshop then starts an Editor session for the new Splash Screen. Compose your splash screen and, when you are satisfied, select **DO-IT!** from the Editor menu. If you change your mind about creating the splash screen, choose **C**ancel, **Y**es from the Editor menu. When you close the Editor window, you return to the New Application dialog box.

Documenting your applications as much as possible is always wise. Although the Application Workshop offers some documentation tools that are very useful, a basic description of what the application is intended to do is quite helpful. Spend the time to make these comments and descriptions today, and you will thank yourself when you want to make changes in your application six months from now.

Choose the Change Description button to enter a description of your application. Include enough information that someone who has never seen it before can get an idea of the application's purpose. An Editor session opens, and you can enter the application's description. When you are done entering the description, select **D**O-IT! from the Editor menu. If you change your mind about entering the description, choose **C**ancel, **Y**es from the Editor menu. When you close the Editor window, you return to the New Application dialog box.

To use the Application Workshop's help system, choose the **H**elp button. If you want to abandon this application, choose **C**ancel—none of your work will be saved.

Cue:

Select **A**pplication **N**ew from the Main menu to create a new application.

When you are satisfied with your entries in the dialog box, choose OK. The Application Workshop displays a blank menu bar two lines below its own menu. You start building your application's menus here. The next section describes the menu building process.

Creating the Application's Main Menu

Figure 14.3 shows the screen used while defining the application's menus and submenus. In the illustration, a few menu items already have been created. When the menu is completely empty, only the <New> choice will show.

This section describes how to create menu entries on the Main menu and how to create submenus. The easiest method usually is to create the entire menu structure for your application—effectively transcribing the structure that you previously designed on paper—and attach actions to the menu items later.

Actions are attached to menu choices when the menu is created or by editing a previously defined menu selection. The next section in this chapter, "Creating Actions," explains how to attach actions to your menu choices. When a menu choice has no action attached to it, the status message at the bottom left corner of the screen reads No Action Defined.

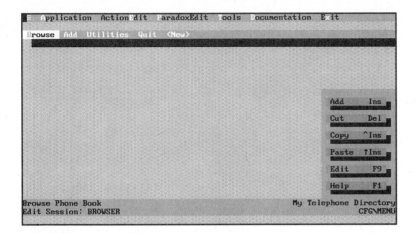

FIG. 14.3

Defining the
Main menu.

When you create the Main menu for your application, don't forget to
include a menu choice that exits from your application. You must provide a menu selection for the user to leave your application manually.

Repeat the instructions in this section as many times as necessary until
all of your Main menu choices have been created. To complete your
menu structure and attach actions to the menus, follow the instructions below in "Menu Definition Leading to a Submenu" and "Menu Definition Leading to an Action."

Reminder:
Don't forget to provide a
way for the user to leave
your application.

To create a new selection on your application's Main Menu, double-
click on the <New> choice on the application menu bar. You also can
create a new menu item by using the arrow keys to move the highlight
bar over the <New> choice and pressing Enter or by pressing **Ins**.

The Application Workshop then presents you with the Menu Insert
submenu. To create a menu item that leads to a submenu, choose
SubMenu. To create a menu item that leads directly to an action,
choose Action. The Menu Definition dialog box appears. This dialog
box's appearance varies depending on whether you choose SubMenu
or Action. The next two sections describe creating each of these types
of menu item. Attaching an action is covered later in this chapter's
section titled "Creating Actions."

Menu Definition Leading to a Submenu

To create a menu item leading to a submenu, choose SubMenu from the
menu that appears after choosing <New> from the application's menu
bar. The Menu Definition dialog box appears (see fig. 14.4). First, enter
the keyword for the new menu selection. This keyword is the name of

the menu choice. *Tools*, for example, is the keyword for the Paradox menu selection that leads to a submenu of utility commands.

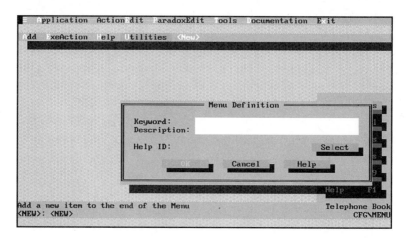

Menu Definition dialog box for SubMenu.

Fill in the Description field next. This field is the menu selection's description, which is displayed in the explanation line at the bottom of the screen when your application is played. These descriptions are like the descriptions provided when the cursor is placed on the Application Workshop menu selections.

The final information area of the Menu Definition dialog box is the Help ID. The Help ID is the name of the help screen that will be used with this menu selection. By specifying a help screen, you make it possible for your application to have context-sensitive help. The Help ID field itself is a display-only field. To create or select a help screen for this menu choice, choose the Select button. Refer to "Creating a HELP DIS-PLAY Action," later in this chapter, for information on how to use the Help Selection dialog box.

If you need help, choose the Help button to gain access to the Application Workshop's help system. If you decide not to continue with this menu selection, choose Cancel. Your work on this menu selection will be lost.

When you are satisfied with the configuration of this menu selection, choose OK. The Menu Definition dialog box closes, and your new menu appears on the application menu bar.

Menu Definition Leading to an Action

To create a menu item leading to an action, choose Action from the menu that appears after choosing <New> from the application's menu bar. The Menu Definition dialog box appears (see fig. 14.5). First, enter the keyword for the new menu selection. This keyword is the name of the menu choice. *Ask*, for example, is the keyword for the Paradox menu selection that leads directly to the action of making a query.

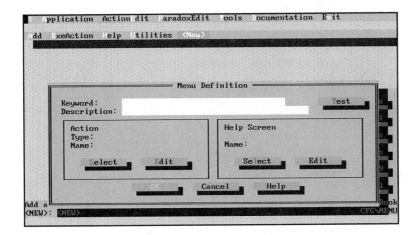

FIG. 14.5

Menu Definition dialog box for Action.

The next field to fill in is the Description field. This description of the menu selection will be displayed in the explanation line at the bottom of the screen, just like the descriptions provided when the cursor is placed on the Application Workshop menu selections.

In the lower left of the Menu Definition dialog box is an area for specifying an action. Following the recommendation made earlier, fill in your entire menu structure now and attach actions to the menu selections later. Specifying actions is covered in the "Creating Actions" section of this chapter. To define the action now, choose the **S**elect button in the Action part of the dialog box. Follow the instructions for the specific action you want to catch in the "Creating Actions" section of this chapter. Any menu selections that lead to an action that has not been defined yet will be indicated with a message at the bottom left corner of the screen.

The next information area of the Menu Definition dialog box is the Help ID. The Help ID is the name of the help screen that will be used with this menu selection. By specifying a help screen, you make it possible for your application to have context-sensitive help. To create or select a help screen for this menu choice, choose the **S**elect button in the Help part of the Menu Definition dialog box. Refer to the section "Creating a HELP DISPLAY Action," later in this chapter, for information on how to use the Help Selection dialog box.

To test your menu selection, choose the Test button in the upper right area of the Menu Definition dialog box. This command causes the Application Workshop to test the command attached to the menu selection.

If you need help, choose the Help button to gain access to the Application Workshop's help system. If you decide not to continue with this menu selection, choose Cancel. Your work on this menu selection will be lost.

When you are satisfied with the configuration of this menu selection, choose OK. The Menu Definition dialog box closes, and your new menu appears on the application menu bar.

Creating a Submenu

You must create a submenu for each Main menu item you created to lead to a submenu. Click your menu choice or use the arrow keys to highlight your menu choice and press Enter. A pull-down menu appears, containing only one choice, the item <New>. To create the submenu, press Enter or double-click the <New> choice in the pull-down menu. A pop-up menu with three choices will appear: Action, SubMenu, and Separator.

If the menu selection you are creating will lead directly to an action, choose Action and then follow the instructions given earlier in the section "Menu Definition Leading to an Action." Defining actions is discussed in the next section, "Creating Actions."

If the new menu selection leads to another submenu, choose SubMenu and then follow the instructions given earlier in the section "Menu Definition Leading to a Submenu."

The third choice is Separator. This choice inserts a horizontal bar in the pull-down menu to which you are adding. Use the separator to group commands visually or to set off commands listed on the pull-down menu. The way the Directory choice on the Application Workshop's Application Menu is set off from the other choices on the menu shows how the separator is used.

After you have made your choice and filled out the appropriate dialog boxes, the Application Workshop returns you to a view of your application's Main menu.

Creating Actions

The Application Workshop provides a variety of pre-defined *action objects* that you may choose to use in your application. Table 14.1

shows a list of the action objects and a brief description of what each object does. In the same way that a window on the screen is treated as an object with certain properties (a given number of location, height and width, and a title), the Application Workshop treats actions as objects that can be assigned certain properties. An OK/Cancel action object has properties such as the number of buttons in the dialog, text to display, and a title.

Table 14.1. Application Workshop Action Objects

Action object	Description
EDIT SESSION	Edits or CoEdits tables, using selected forms
EXECUTE PAL	Executes a Paradox Application Language Expression
EXIT PARADOX	Exits the application and Paradox, returning to DOS
HELP DISPLAY	Displays a help screen
MULTIPLE ACTIONS	Defines a series of action objects to be performed together and allows several actions with one command
OK/CANCEL	Creates a dialog box to present a message or have the user make yes/no choices
PLAY A SCRIPT	Plays a previously created script
PROC (EXECPROC)	Executes a previously created procedure from a library
QUERY	Queries a selected table or group of tables
QUIT TO PARADOX	Exits the application and returns to Paradox main mode
REPORT PRINT	Sends a selected report to the printer, screen, or file

You basically have two ways to create a new action object: You can create the action from the ActionEdit menu, or you can create the action from the Menu Definition dialog box.

Creating an Action from the ActionEdit Menu

To define an action from the ActionEdit menu, select ActionEdit and then the menu choice corresponding to one of the action object types listed in the table 14.1. Before you select ActionEdit, be sure that you have an application open; the application's main menu shows on the Application Workshop workspace when it is open.

Follow these steps to create the action object from the ActionEdit menu:

1. Choose ActionEdit.

   A submenu listing most of the action objects in table 14.1 appears.

2. Select the action object type you want to create from the menu by highlighting the desired action type and pressing Enter.

   An Edit dialog box containing a list of objects of the selected type opens.

   If this is the first action object of this type for this application, the list is empty; otherwise it shows the action objects of this type already defined. If you choose PRINT REPORT, for example, then all report action sessions defined for this application are listed in the dialog box.

3. Choose the **New** button to create a new object of the selected type and refer to the instructions for that type.

Creating an Action from the Menu Definition Dialog Box

You also can define an action while you are creating or editing a menu selection that leads directly to an action. The Menu Definition dialog box has an area for information about its action. The Menu Definition dialog box is displayed when a menu is created. The Menu Definition dialog box also is displayed by placing the highlight on a menu choice in your application that leads to an action and choosing Edit. Menu selections in your application that lead to actions, but do not yet have an action attached to them, are indicated by the phrase "No action defined" in the lower left corner of the screen. Menu selections with undefined actions may also be found by generating an Action Detail report from the Documentation menu of the Application Workshop. The Documentation feature is described later in the section titled "Using Tools."

To create the action objects from the Menu Definition dialog box, follow these steps:

1. Choose the **Select** button in the Action area to attach an action, or choose the **Edit** button to modify the currently attached action.

To create a new action and attach it to the menu selection, choose the **S**elect button.

The list of object types appears.

2. Choose one of the object action types by placing the highlight bar over it and choosing the OK button.

   An Edit dialog box showing a list of objects of the selected type appears. If this is the first action object of this type for this application, the list is empty; otherwise it shows all action objects of this type already defined for this application.

3. Choose the New button to create a new object of the selected type and refer to the instructions for each type, presented later in this chapter.

Creating an EDIT SESSION Action

You use an edit session to modify the data in a table or group of tables. The edit session may involve changing the information stored in one or more fields or records, deleting records, or using **D**ataEntry or Multi-Entry to update a table or group of tables.

After you create a new action and select EDIT SESSION as the action type, the New Edit Session dialog box appears. Enter the name for this edit session in the single field of the dialog box. Choose a meaningful name. An edit session to add records to an address database, for example, might be called ADD NEW ADDRESS. Choose OK after entering the edit session's name.

Now the Edit Session dialog box appears (see fig. 14.6). Because you are creating a new edit session, the pick list of tables on the workspace is empty and shows only the selection <New Table>. Choose the **A**dd button to open the Table Information dialog box. Enter the name of the table or choose the Table Select button to get a pick list of tables available in the current directory. Select a table by entering its name or pressing Tab to activate the pick list. Highlight the desired table and press Enter or choose OK.

After you have selected the table, you are returned to the Table Information dialog box (see fig. 14.7). Choose in which modes the table should be available, as follows:

■ If the edit session being created allows records to be inserted, check Insert.

■ If the edit session allows records to be deleted, check Delete.

■ If the table is to be edited, check Edit.

■ If the table is to be updated with a DataEntry session, check Update.

■ If the table is to be displayed for viewing without an edit of some kind being active, check View.

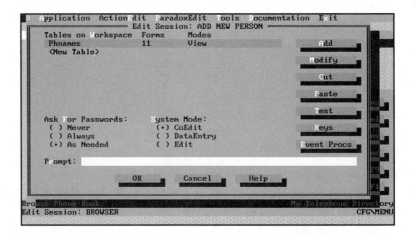

FIG. 14.6

The Edit Session dialog box.

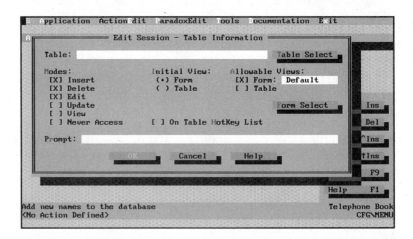

FIG. 14.7

Table Information dialog box.

These modes may be checked in any combination. Unchecked modes are not available in this edit session for this table. If you do not check Delete, for example, then a user cannot delete records from the table when using this edit session object.

Next, use the options in the Initial View information area of the Table Information dialog box to select whether the table will be in table view or form view when it is first placed on the workspace. Use the Allowable Views information area to select what views of the table will be permitted. Check **Table** if the table will be placed in **Table View**; check **Form** if the table will be viewed in **Form View**.

If you check the **Form** box to allow **Form View**, then you must select the form to use. Choose the **Form Select** button to see the table's list of forms. Choose the desired form from the pick list by highlighting it and choosing OK.

Repeat the table selection steps until you have selected all tables that this edit session will act on. When the Table Information dialog is filled in to your satisfaction, choose OK. You are returned to the Edit Sessions dialog box, which gives you the following options. Continue your Edit Session definition by choosing values for the remaining options.

■ *Choosing the Passwords mode.* Set the option in the Passwords information area of the Edit Sessions dialog box. These options control when the application generated by the Application Workshop will ask for passwords. The default, As Needed, usually is appropriate.

■ *Choosing the System mode.* These options control the mode in which the edit session will occur: CoEdit, DataEntry, or Edit. The default, CoEdit, usually is appropriate.

■ *Choosing a Prompt.* If you want a prompt to show at the bottom of the screen when the table(s) for this edit session are placed on the workspace, indicate so in the Prompt field of the dialog box.

■ *Testing the Edit Session.* Choosing the **Test** button lets you test the operation of your new edit session. The table (or tables) you have selected are displayed, and you can interact with them just as the user of your application will.

■ *Changing the table order.* The tables for this edit session are placed on the workspace in the order that they appear in the Tables on Workspace list. To change their order, highlight the table you want to move. Use the **Cut** button to remove the table from the list. Now move the highlight bar to the desired location and choose the **Paste** button. The table is inserted into the list.

■ *Removing a table from the Edit Session.* If you want to remove a table from the "Tables on Workspace" list completely, **Cut** it from the list as described earlier but do not **Paste** it.

■ *Modifying a table's properties in the Edit Session.* To modify the permitted views, forms, or other information about a table that already is on the workspace for this edit session, select the desired table and choose **M**odify. When the Table Information dialog appears, fill it out or change its settings, using the directions given earlier.

■ *Attaching procedures to Keys and Events.* Two of the remaining options in the Edit Session dialog box, **K**eys and **E**vent Procs, represent advanced features of the Application Workshop and are too complex to discuss in depth here. The next paragraphs give you an overview of their function; refer to the *Application Workshop Guide* (supplied with Paradox) for full details.

Use the **K**eys button to assign a specific action or procedure to be executed when a particular keystroke is made while this Edit Session is active. This action is similar to assigning a macro to a keystroke. (Refer to Chapter 6, "Getting Started With Scripts and Keyboard Macros," and Chapter 15, "An Overview of the Paradox Application Language," for information on procedures.)

When you choose the **K**eys button, a Key Procs dialog box is shown. This dialog box contains a list of all keystrokes that can be detected by Paradox. The keystrokes beginning with a minus sign (–) are extended keystrokes. Refer to Appendix C, "PAL Keycodes and Extended Codes," for more information on the keystrokes and the codes that they produce.

You may give a keystroke one of the pre-defined actions ($Edit, $Finished, $Disabled, $Beep, or $Notyet) by highlighting the keystroke in the list and choosing the corresponding button. These predefined actions will, respectively, begin editing, finish the action, disable the key, beep when the key is pressed, or display the message You can't do that yet.

If you want to have a procedure executed whenever a particular key is pressed, highlight the keystroke in the list and enter the name of the procedure in the Current Key Proc entry field. Note that the procedure chosen must be one that you have written previously and stored in a library.

Use the All Keys Proc field to enter the name of a procedure that you want executed when *any* key is pressed.

When you are satisfied with your selections in the Session Key Procs dialog box, choose OK. To use the Application Workshop's Help system, choose the **H**elp button.

NOTE If you attach a procedure to a keystroke, the library containing the procedure must be specified in the Autolib field when you created the application. Refer to the directions in the earlier section, "Getting Started," for filling in the New Application dialog box.

Use the **Event Procs** button to assign a specific action or procedure to be executed when a particular event occurs. As its name implies, an *event* literally is "something that happens." (See Chapter 15, "An Overview of the Paradox Application Language," for a more comprehensive definition of events.)

After you choose the **Event Procs** button, the Application Workshop opens the Session Event Procs dialog box. This dialog box contains a list of events and a field in which you enter the name of the procedure you want executed when that event occurs. Most of the events listed in the Session Event Procs dialog box are caused by movement of the cursor. Other events are caused by editing or posting a record.

NOTE If you attach a procedure to an event, you must specify the library containing the procedure in the Autolib field when you create the application. Refer to the directions in the earlier section, "Getting Started," for filling in the New Application dialog box.

Entering a procedure name in the field for an event causes the procedure to be executed every time that event occurs. If you want a procedure executed every time this edit session begins, enter its name in the StartUp field. Similarly, enter in the ShutDown field the name of a procedure to be executed every time this edit session ends.

If you enter the name of a procedure called StartFieldView for the Arrive Field event, then your StartFieldView procedure is executed every time the cursor enters any field of any table in this edit session.

If you want key violation tables that might be produced by the edit session to be renamed and placed in your private directory (as established on a network), then put an *X* in the check-box labeled Rename Key Viol Tables.

When you are satisfied with your selections in the Session Event Procs dialog, choose OK. To use the Application Workshop's Help system, choose the **Help** button.

When you are finished with the Edit Session dialog box, choose OK to save the edit session or choose Cancel to discard it. You then return to your application's main menu and the Application Workshop main menu.

Creating an EXECUTE PAL Action

The EXECUTE PAL action executes a Paradox Applications Language expression. The EXECUTE PAL action is very similar to using the MiniScript or Value options available on the PAL Menu. (Refer to Chapters 15, 17, and 19 for more information on the PAL Menu and commands.)

To create a new EXECUTE PAL action, follow the instructions in the section "Creating the Action from the ActionEdit Menu" or the instructions in the section "Creating the Action from the Menu Definition Dialog Box". Select EXECUTE PAL as the action type. A New Execute Pal dialog box appears with a single field in which you must enter the name for this execute PAL action. Choose OK when you have entered the action's name.

The Application Workshop then opens a Script Editor session. Enter the text of the PAL expression that you want to have executed. The expression must be syntactically correct for the Paradox Applications Language. (Refer to Chapters 15, 17, and 19 for information on syntax, expressions, the Script Editor, and PAL commands available.) When you enter the PAL expression in the editor, you may use any of the editor menu commands that normally would be available in a Script Editor session.

When you are finished entering your PAL expression, choose DO-IT! from the Editor menu. The Editor window closes, and you are asked to confirm that the expression should be saved. If this Edit Session dialog was started from the ActionEdit menu, you return to your application's main menu and the Application Workshop main menu. If the Edit Session dialog was started from a Menu Definition dialog box, you return to the Menu Definition dialog box.

Creating an EXIT PARADOX Action

The EXIT PARADOX action causes your application to stop running and Paradox to exit back to the DOS command line. Use this action when you want your application to return the user to DOS.

The Application Workshop main menu has a menu choice called Exit, which has a submenu giving you the option of exiting to either DOS or Paradox. To give your user a similar option, attach the EXIT PARADOX action to the submenu that returns to Paradox.

This action object does not appear on the ActionEdit menu. You must attach this type of object by using the Menu Definition dialog box. The Menu Selection dialog box is opened when a new menu selection is created, or when an existing menu selection is edited. To edit a menu selection, use the arrow keys or the mouse to highlight the menu selection to edit, and then choose Edit. Refer to the method described at the beginning of this section for attaching an object directly to a menu selection in order to create an EXIT PARADOX action object.

When you select EXIT PARADOX from the list of action objects, the Application Workshop does not need any more information, and the action is attached immediately to the menu selection. Choose OK on the Menu Definition dialog box to save the new action. You return to the Application Workshop main menu and the display of your application's Main menu.

Creating a HELP DISPLAY Action

You have two ways to create help screens for your application:

- Create and attach a help screen directly to a menu choice.

- Create a separate action object to provide a help screen.

The first method of creating a help screen is accomplished from the Menu Definition dialog box. The Menu Definition dialog box is opened when a new menu choice is created, or when an existing menu selection is edited. To edit a menu selection, use the arrow keys or the mouse to highlight the menu selection to edit, and then choose Edit. You also can create or edit a help screen by using the ActionEdit menu. Help objects created with either method may be attached or removed from any menu selection later, whether the menu selection leads to another menu or to an action.

To create a new HELP DISPLAY action, follow the instructions in the section "Creating the Action from the ActionEdit Menu" or the instructions in the section "Creating the Action from the Menu Definition Dialog Box." Select HELP DISPLAY as the action type. The New Help Display dialog box appears. This dialog box has a single field in which you must enter the name for this help text action. Choose OK when you have entered the help action's name.

The Application Workshop now opens the Help Screen dialog box (see fig. 14.8). This dialog box is divided into the following two primary information areas.

At the top of the dialog box is a display-only field that displays the text of the help action being defined.

In the lower left corner is a list of cross-references that shows all of the help screens that are cross-referenced with this one. Titles of cross-referenced help screens are shown as menu selections at the top of the screen.

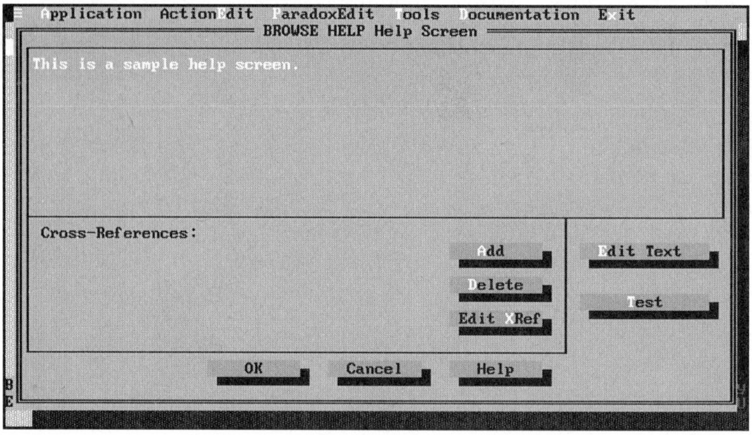

FIG. 14.8

The Help Screen
dialog box.

Cross-references in the help system enable your application's user to look up related topics on other help screens. This way, you give your application a help system similar to the help systems used in the Application Workshop and in Paradox.

To enter or change the text for your help screen, choose **Edit Text**. An Editor session is opened. Enter the text you want this help screen to contain. When you are satisfied with the text for the help screen, save your changes and end the Editor session by choosing **DO-IT!** from the Editor menu. You are returned to the Help Screen dialog box.

To add cross-references to this help screen, choose the **Add** button in the Cross-Reference information area of the Help Screen dialog box. The Adding Cross-References dialog box appears.

The first field in this dialog box is the cross-reference title. Enter the text that will show at the top of the screen as the menu selection leading to the cross-reference screen.

The second field in the Adding Cross-References dialog box is for the name of the help screen you are cross-referencing. To select the cross-reference help screen from a pick list, choose the Select button.

Another dialog box is shown with a list of help screens already defined for this application, or an empty list if no help screens are defined. If the list is empty, you cannot add a cross-reference yet; finish this help screen and then create its cross-references.

Choose OK after you enter the name and title of the cross-reference help screen, returning you to the Help Screen dialog box.

You may edit a cross-reference by placing the highlight bar in the cross-reference list and then choosing the Edit **XRef** button. The current help text is saved, and a new Help Screen dialog box for the cross-reference is opened.

To delete a cross-reference, choose the item in the cross-reference list you want to remove from the list and choose the **D**elete button.

Use the **T**est option to test the appearance and cross-references of your help screen.

When the help text and the cross-references are satisfactory, choose OK. The Help Screen dialog box closes. If you started the Help Screen definition from the Menu Definition dialog box, you are returned to the Menu Definition; otherwise you return to the Application Workshop main menu and the display of your application's Main menu.

Creating an OK/CANCEL Action

The OK/CANCEL action creates a dialog box with one or two push-buttons. You define the message that the dialog box displays and the labels of the buttons. Use the OK/CANCEL action the following two ways:

- To create yes/no confirmation for activities that the user might select in your application. (Asking the user to confirm actions that have irrevocable results, such as deleting files or subtracting records, always is a good idea.)

- To provide single-button informational messages in your application.

To create a new OK/CANCEL action, follow the instructions in the section titled "Creating an Action from the ActionEdit Menu" or the section titled "Creating an Action from the Menu Definition Dialog Box" and select OK/CANCEL as the action type. The New OK/Cancel dialog box opens, with a single field in which you must enter the name for this action. Enter the name and then choose OK. The Application Workshop now opens an OK/Cancel Object dialog box, shown in figure 14.9.

Complete the definition of the OK/Cancel Object by performing the following tasks:

- *Giving the OK/Cancel a title.* Enter the title of the new OK/Cancel action in the Title field. This title is displayed across the top of the dialog box as the window title.

- *Specifying the message.* To have the OK/Cancel action dialog box display a message, enter the message in the Text to Display fields. Four lines are provided for this text; each line is a separate field. If this OK/Cancel action will be used to confirm the deletion of a record, the Text to Display fields may be filled-in as shown in figure 14.9.

■ *Displaying an expression.* You can use the OK/Cancel action to display the result of a PAL expression. Enter the PAL expression you want to have displayed in the Expression to Display field; leave it blank for no expression. (Refer to Chapters 15 and 19 for more information on expressions and their elements.)

■ *Selecting the OK/Cancel buttons and labels.* To control the number of buttons displayed by the new OK/Cancel action, fill in (or clear) the check boxes for OK **B**utton and **C**ancel Button. If you want both buttons to appear in the dialog box created by the OK/Cancel action, put an *X* in both boxes. If you select only the OK **B**utton, the OK/Cancel action you are creating will signal OK to any following actions. If you select only the **C**ancel button, the OK/Cancel action will signal Cancel to any following actions.

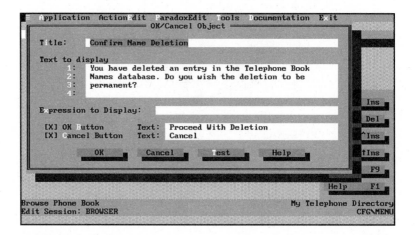

FIG. 14.9

The OK/Cancel Object dialog box.

The final step in defining an OK/Cancel action is to decide what labels the buttons will have. You use the two text fields to the right of the check boxes to choose which buttons will be included in the OK/Cancel action. Each text field contains the text label for the button. If the default labels (OK and Cancel, respectively) are not adequate, enter any text in the corresponding field to change the button's label.

■ *Testing the OK/Cancel action.* Use the **T**est button to see how your OK/Cancel action will appear to your application's user.

■ *Closing the OK/Cancel dialog box.* When you are satisfied with the behavior of your OK/Cancel action, choose OK to save it. The OK/Cancel Object dialog box closes. If you opened the OK/Cancel dialog box from the Menu Definition dialog box, you return to the Menu Definition dialog box; otherwise you return to the Application Workshop main menu and the display of your application's Main menu.

Creating a PLAY A SCRIPT Action

The PLAY A SCRIPT action causes your application to play a previously written or recorded script. Use this action when you want to play a subroutine script—like a query recorded with **S**cripts, **Q**uerySave—or a script that you have written yourself. (Refer to Chapters 6 and 15 for more information about scripts.)

This action object does not appear on the ActionEdit menu. To create a PLAY A SCRIPT action object, you must attach the object from the Menu Definition dialog box. The Menu Definition dialog box is opened when a new menu choice is created, or when an existing menu selection is edited. To edit a menu selection, use the arrow keys or the mouse to highlight the menu selection to edit, and then choose Edit.

When you select PLAY A SCRIPT from the list of action objects, the Select Script dialog box appears, containing an entry field and pick list (see fig. 14.10).

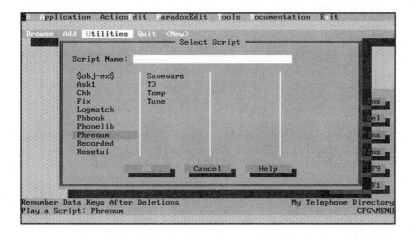

FIG. 14.10

Select Script dialog box.

To select and attach a script, enter the name of the script to be played or press Tab to activate the pick list and then choose the script from the pick list. Choose the OK button. The Select Script dialog box is closed, the script is attached to the menu, and you are returned to the Menu Definition dialog box.

Choose OK on the Menu Definition dialog box to save the new action and return to the Application Workshop Main menu and the display of your application's Main menu.

Creating a PROC (EXECPROC) Action

The PROC (EXECPROC) action causes your application to execute a procedure that was placed previously in a procedure library. Use this action object when you want to execute a subroutine procedure.

In order for the Application Workshop to execute your procedure, the procedure library that contains the procedure must be specified in the Autolib field when you create your application. The procedure, which is executed with the PROC (EXECPROC) action, also must meet the requirements of a procedure used with the PAL command EXECPROC, described in Chapter 19. (For more information on procedures, procedure libraries, and the autolib global variable, see Chapters 15 and 19.)

This action object does not appear on the ActionEdit menu. To create a PROC (EXECPROC) action object, you must attach the action from the Menu Definition dialog box. The Menu Definition dialog box is opened when a new menu choice is created, or when an existing menu selection is edited. To edit a menu selection, use the arrow keys or the mouse to highlight the menu selection to edit, and then choose Edit.

When you select PROC (EXECPROC) from the list of action objects, the Application Workshop presents you with a dialog box containing a single entry field. Enter the name of the procedure to be executed and choose the OK button. The Procedure dialog box is closed, the PROC (EXECPROC) procedure is attached to the menu, and you are returned to the Menu Definition dialog box. Choose OK on the Menu Definition dialog box to save the new action and return to the Application Workshop Main menu and the display of your application's Main menu.

Creating a QUERY Action

A QUERY action executes a Paradox query and then optionally performs one of several standardized activities with the results table from the query.

To create a new QUERY action, follow the instructions in the section titled "Creating an Action from the Menu Definition Dialog Box" or the instructions in the "Creating an Action from the ActionEdit Menu" section. Select QUERY as the action type. The New Query dialog box opens with a single field in which you must enter the name for this query action. Choose OK when you have entered the query action's name.

The Application Workshop now opens the Query By Example (QBE) dialog box. At the top of this dialog box is a list of tables to be queried (see fig. 14.11). You must enter at least one table in this list. To select the table or tables for this query action, choose the QBE button. When you choose **Q**BE, the Application Workshop workspace is cleared, and a special QBE menu is displayed. Create your query using commands from this menu (see fig 14.12). When you have completed your query, choose **D**one from the QBE menu.

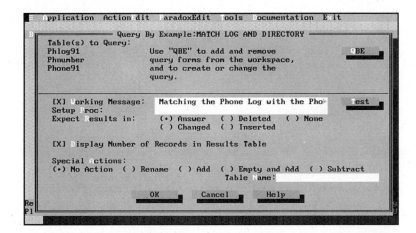

FIG. 14.11

Query By Example dialog box.

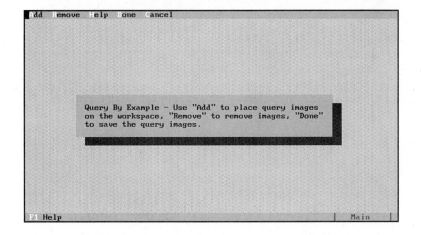

FIG. 14.12

The QBE Menu

To place the first query on the workspace, choose **A**dd from the QBE menu. A dialog box to select the table to be queried is opened. Enter the name of the table or press Tab to activate the pick list. When you have selected a table, the Select Table dialog box closes, opening a query form exactly like that used in the Paradox **A**sk command. Fill in the query form, using check marks, matching criteria, and examples just as you would when constructing a query in Paradox. Use the **A**dd menu selection as many times as necessary to place the query forms for a multitable query.

Use the QBE menu to perform the following tasks:

■ To remove one or all of the query forms from the workspace, use the **R**emove menu choice.

■ To remove a single query form, make it the current image by using the F3 (UpImage) and F4 (DownImage keys), and then choose **Re**move **C**urrent.

■ To remove all the query forms and start over, choose **R**emove **A**ll.

■ To get the Application Workshop's on-line help for creating a query action, choose **H**elp.

■ To abandon the definition of your query, choose **C**ancel.

When the query is set up the way you want it, choose **D**one **S**ave from the QBE menu. The QBE menu and workspace close, returning you to the Query By Example dialog box and the following options:

■ *Choosing the Working Message.* Because some queries—especially multitable queries—can take a long time, you may want to have your query action display a message while the query is being made. Place an *X* in the **W**orking Message check box to have the message displayed. Now enter the text of the working message in the **W**orking Message entry field.

■ *Defining the Setup Procedure.* If you have a procedure already written and stored in a procedure library that you want to have executed every time this query is run, enter its name in the Setup **P**roc field. Any procedure name entered here must have the library in which it is contained also listed in the Autolib field (filled in when the application is created). Refer to Chapters 15 and 19 for more information on procedures, procedure libraries, and the autolib global variable.

■ *Choosing the Results table.* Now use the Expect **R**esults In options to select where the results of the query are to be expected. By choosing the corresponding option, you indicate whether you expect your query action to result in an Answer table, a Deleted table, a Changed table, an Inserted table, or None.

■ *Giving the User a Choice.* Put an *X* in the check box labeled **D**isplay Number of Records in Results Table if you want this query action to display a dialog box showing the number of records in the results table. The dialog box that your query action displays as a result of checking this option contains an OK and a Cancel button and asks the user whether or not to continue. If your application's user presses Cancel, the remainder of this query action is stopped.

Using the **D**isplay Number of Records in Results Table option is most useful when this query action will be part of a Multi-Action object or when you have defined a Special Action to take place after the query is complete.

■ *Selecting special actions for after the query.* The final step in defining your query action is to select which, if any, special actions will take place when the query is completed. Use the options in the Special **A**ctions area of the QBE dialog described below. The default action is No Action, which leaves the query's results table (for example, answer or changed) untouched. Eventually, the results table will be removed or replaced as other activities occur, and it will be deleted when Paradox is shut down or the working directory is changed.

To have the table resulting from your query renamed, select Rename in the Special Actions area, and enter the new name for the table in the Table **N**ame field.

To have the results table added to another table, select Add in the Special Actions area, and enter the name of the table that the results will be added to in the Table **N**ame field.

To subtract the results table from the table named in the Table **N**ame field, select the Subtract option in the Special Actions area.

The Special Actions option labeled Empty and Add selects a twofold action. First, the table whose name is entered in the Table **N**ame field is emptied (without confirmation). The results table then is added to the table just emptied. This option has the effect of replacing the contents of the table named in the Table Name field with the contents of the results table.

When the query produces satisfactory results, choose OK. The QBE dialog box closes. If the QBE dialog box was started from a Menu Definition dialog box, you are returned to the Menu Definition dialog box; otherwise, you return to the Application Workshop main menu and the display of your application's Main menu.

Creating a QUIT TO PARADOX Action

The QUIT TO PARADOX action causes your application to stop running and returns the user to Paradox Main mode. Use this action when you want your user to be able to remain in Paradox after leaving your application. When you choose E**x**it from the Application Workshop main menu, a submenu opens, giving you the choice of exiting to DOS or exiting to Paradox. For your application to give a user a similar choice, you would use the QUIT TO PARADOX action as the menu choice to return to Paradox.

This action object does not appear on the ActionEdit menu. To create a QUIT TO PARADOX action object, you must attach the action from the Menu Definition dialog box. The Menu Definition dialog box is opened when a new menu choice is created, or when an existing menu selection is edited. To edit a menu selection, use the arrow keys or the mouse to highlight the menu selection to edit, and then choose Edit.

When you select QUIT TO PARADOX from the list of action objects, the Application Workshop does not need any more information, and the action is attached to the menu selection immediately. Choose OK on the Menu Definition dialog box to save the new action and return to the Application Workshop Main menu and the display of your application's Main menu.

Creating a REPORT PRINT Action

The REPORT PRINT action causes a Paradox report to be generated.

To create a new REPORT PRINT action, follow the instructions in the section "Creating the Action from the ActionEdit Menu" or the instructions in the section "Creating the Action from the Menu Definition Dialog Box". Select REPORT PRINT as the action type. A New Report Print dialog box appears with a single field in which you must enter the name for this report action. Choose OK when you have entered the report action's name.

The Report Print dialog box now appears (see fig. 14.13).

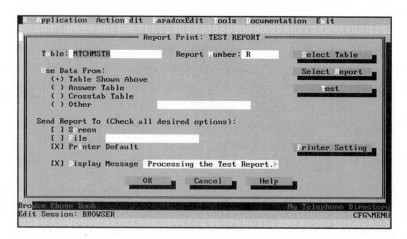

Fig. 14.13

The Report Print dialog box.

■ *Selecting the source of the Report specification.* The first field in the Report Print dialog box is the **Ta**ble field. Enter the name of the table that will supply the report form used to generate the report. Choose the **S**elect Table button to open a dialog box containing a pick list of tables. After selecting the table that will supply the report specification, enter the report number in the Report **Num**ber field. Choose the Select **R**eport button to open a dialog box containing a pick list of reports for the table in the **Ta**ble field.

■ *Selecting the data source for the Report.* Now use the following options under **U**se Data From to select the source of data for this report action. The default, Table Shown Above, prints the report using data from the table named in the Table field. The Answer Table option causes the report form to be copied to the answer table before the report is generated. Crosstab Table also causes the report to be copied to the Crosstab table before the report is generated. The Other option copies the report form to another table. The report is generated using the data in the other table. If you select Other, you also must enter the name of the table that the report will be copied to in the provided field.

■ *Selecting the Report destination.* Fill in the check boxes in the Send Report To area of the dialog box. These check boxes control the possible destinations for the report generated by this action. You must check at least one destination. If you select more than one destination, your application displays a dialog box asking the user to choose the final destination of the report.

■ *Selecting the Display Message.* Report generations can be relatively lengthy, so you may want to display a message to the user. Put an *X* in the check box labeled **D**isplay Message and then enter your message in the provided field.

■ *Testing the Report.* Use the **T**est button to test your report action and make sure that the report prints correctly.

■ *Closing the Report Print Dialog Box.* When the report action is satisfactory, choose OK. The Report Print dialog box closes. If the Report Print dialog was opened from a Menu Definition dialog box, you return to the Menu Definition dialog box; otherwise you return to the Application Workshop main menu and the display of your application's Main menu.

Creating a MULTIPLE ACTIONS Action

The MULTIPLE ACTIONS action object enables several actions to be performed one after the other. Your application then can accomplish several actions with one menu selection.

To create a new MULTIPLE ACTIONS action, follow the instructions in the section "Creating an Action from the ActionEdit Menu" or the instructions in the section "Creating an Action from the Menu Definition Dialog Box". Select MULTIPLE ACTIONS as the action type. You are presented with a New Multiple Actions dialog box with a single field in which you must enter the name for this multiple action. Choose OK when you have entered the multiple action's name.

The Application Workshop now opens the Multi-Action dialog box (see fig. 14.14). This dialog box contains a list of the actions that have been defined for this multi-action. If no actions have been added to this multi-action, then only the prompt <New Action Item> appears in the list.

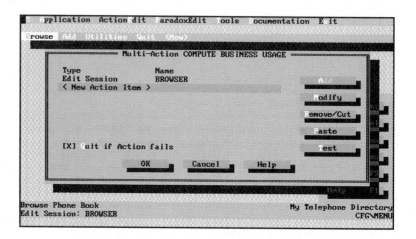

FIG. 14.14

Multi-Action
dialog box.

Complete the Multi-Action dialog box by performing the following tasks:

- *Adding an action to the Multi-Action.* To add an action to the list, choose the **A**dd button. A dialog box containing the list of object types opens. Choose an action type from the list; another dialog box opens, listing all action objects of the selected type that have been defined for this application. Choose one of the actions from the list or choose <New> to create a new action object.

  Use the appropriate directions earlier in this section if you decide to create a new action object. When you have completed selecting or creating the action object, the Multi-Action dialog box returns. Repeat this step as often as necessary to add all of the desired actions to the action list, and then go on to the remaining steps.

■ *Choose whether to continue after an action fails.* Place an *X* in the check box labeled **Q**uit If Action Fails to have this multi-action stop when one of the actions it performs fails. Clear this check box if you want this multi-action to continue even if one of its actions fails.

■ *Modifying an action in the Multi-Action.* Highlight the action in the action list that you want to modify and then choose the **M**odify button. A pick-list dialog listing the types of action objects open. Select the action object to add. A dialog box for editing the selected action opens. The exact appearance of the dialog box depends on the type of action being edited. Use the instructions earlier in this section for defining the selected type of action object. If you choose an Edit Session, then follow the instructions for "Creating an EDIT SESSION Action." When you close the edit dialog for the action, the Multi-Action dialog box returns.

■ *Changing the action order or removing an action.* The actions on the action list are performed in the order in which they appear on the list. To change the order of actions on the list, select the action you want to move by highlighting it. Choose the **R**emove/Cut button, move the highlight bar to the new location for the action, and choose **P**aste. To remove an action from the action list, highlight the action to be removed and choose the **R**emove/Cut button.

■ *Testing the Multi-Action.* Choose the **T**est button to test your multi-action. All actions in the list will be performed.

■ *Closing the Multi-Action dialog.* When the behavior of the multi-action is satisfactory, choose the OK button. The Multi-Action dialog closes. If the Multi-Action dialog was opened from a Menu Definition dialog box, you return to the Menu Definition. Otherwise, you return to the Application Workshop main menu and the display of your application's Main menu.

For Related Information:

◀◀ "Entering and Editing Data in Edit Mode," p. 109.

◀◀ "Displaying and Clearing the Answer Table," p. 159.

◀◀ "Controlling Output," p. 215.

◀◀ "Recording and Playing Scripts," p. 222.

▶▶ "Procedures and Procedure Libraries," p. 551.

FROM HERE...

Modifying an Application

As you are developing and perfecting your application, you will need to modify some of the actions and menus. If you thoroughly planned your application, serious changes are kept to a minimum. Modifying an application consists of editing the properties of the menus and action objects already defined or creating new menu, submenu, and action objects.

- If you are adding to your application, follow the directions in "Creating an Application" for creating the desired menu or action objects.

- If you are changing existing menu and action objects, proceed with the discussion that follows.

The next section describes how to access and open the dialog boxes controlling the various objects that make up your application. For detailed information in filling out these dialog boxes—especially the action object dialog boxes—refer to the descriptions for each dialog box in "Creating an Application," earlier in this chapter.

Opening the Application

Before you can modify your application, you must open it. If the Application Workshop is not running, follow the instructions for starting the Application Workshop in the section "Starting the Application Workshop," earlier in this chapter. Make sure that the current directory for the Application Workshop is the same directory that contains your application. If not, change the directory by choosing **Application Direc**tory and entering the name of the subdirectory that contains the application you want to change.

To open the application, choose **Application Open**. The Application Selection dialog box, with a pick list of applications in the current directory, appears. Note that the dialog box displays the first few lines of the Application Description—entered when you created the application—for the application that is highlighted. Place the highlight bar on the application that you want to open and press Enter or click OK.

Editing the Application Definition

The application definition—the first set of information that you fill out when you create an application—includes the application ID, its name, description, autolib settings, and splash screen.

You can edit an application's definition as you are opening the application by choosing **A**pplication, **O**pen, placing the highlight bar over the application you want to edit, and then choosing the Edit button. You also can edit an application's definition by opening the application and then choosing **A**pplication, **E**dit. In either case, the Edit Application dialog box appears. For instructions on filling in the Edit Application dialog box, refer to the earlier section of this chapter, "Creating an Application."

Modifying a Menu or Submenu and Attaching an Action

To modify a menu or submenu, follow these steps:

1. Open the application. The top-level (usually called Main) menu appears.

2. Highlight the menu selection you want to change.

3. If you are changing an entry on a submenu, make selections on your application's menu system until the highlight bar is over the submenu you want to change.

4. When the correct menu or submenu item is highlighted, press F9 (Edit) or choose the Edit button; the Menu Definition dialog box appears.

   The specific appearance of the Menu Definition dialog box varies, depending on whether the menu object you are changing is a submenu or an action.

For instructions on filling in the Menu Definition dialog box, refer to the earlier section of this chapter, "Creating a Submenu."

NOTE   If you want to attach an action to a menu or submenu selection, the menu object must have been defined originally as leading to an action.

If you want to attach an action to a menu object that is defined as leading to a submenu, you must delete the menu selection and re-create it.

If you are attaching an action to a menu object that was originally defined as leading to an object, simply select the menu object and open the Menu Definition dialog box. Then follow the directions for attaching an action described in the section of this chapter titled "Menu Definition Leading to an Action."

Changing or Adding a Splash Screen

To create or change an application's splash screen, you must edit the application's definition and select the Splash Screen button in the Edit Application dialog box. Follow the instructions in this chapter titled "Opening the Application" and "Editing the Application's Definition."

Finishing Your Application

When your application has been fully developed and tested, you probably will want to finish it. In the Application Workshop, finishing your application means that the application is converted to a *closed application*. All Application Workshop libraries and support files are copied into your application's disk directory, and all scripts necessary to run your application are generated. Your application now is self-sufficient (hence *closed*) and may be run without assistance from the Application Workshop.

You can make changes in your application after it has been finished, but you must perform again the finishing operation to update your application's scripts.

To finish your application, open it and select **A**pplication **F**inish from the Application Workshop menu. The Application Workshop will finish your application.

Playing Your Application

You can play your application in three ways. You may play the application from the Application Workshop, from within Paradox, or from the DOS command line.

While testing and debugging your application, you usually will play it from within the Application Workshop. Open your application and select **A**pplication **T**est from the Application Workshop menu. Your application will play.

After you have perfected the operation of your application, you should finish it. To finish your application, follow the instructions in the preceding section of this chapter. Only finished applications can be played from within Paradox or from DOS.

To play your application from within Paradox, be sure that the current working directory is the directory containing your application. Select

Scripts, Play. Enter your application's ID as the script name and press Enter or choose OK. (The application ID is the eight-letter ID that you chose when you created your application.) Your application will play.

To play your application from DOS, first use DOS commands to change to the directory that contains your application. Type *paradox* at the DOS prompt, followed by your application ID, and then press Enter. If your application's ID is *myapp*, for example, you would run the application from DOS by typing the following command and pressing Enter.

    paradox myapp

For Related Information:

◄◄ "Recording and Playing Scripts," p. 222.

FROM HERE...

Using Tools

The Application Workshop's tool box includes utilities necessary to manage the action objects and regular Paradox objects used by your applications. The Tools menu selections enable you to copy, rename, or delete actions, tables, forms, reports, and scripts as follows:

- To delete the item, choose the Delete button.

- To rename the item, choose the Rename button. You will be prompted for the item's new name.

- To copy the item, choose the Copy button. You will be prompted for a name for the copy of the item.

To copy an entire application, see the next section in this chapter, "Copying an Application."

To copy, rename, or delete an action. Open the application and choose **T**ools, **A**ctionObjects from the Application Workshop menu. The Action Object Tools dialog box appears. This dialog box contains a pick list of all action objects defined for this application. Select an action object highlighting the desired action.

To copy a table's family or to copy, rename, or delete a table. Open the application and choose **T**ools, **T**ables from the Application Workshop menu. The Table Tools dialog box appears. Select a table by entering the table name in the entry field or by highlighting the desired table in the pick list. When copying the table, when you are prompted for a name for the copy of the table, choose the Family button to copy the table's family. You then are prompted to enter the name of the table to which the selected table's family should be copied.

To copy a form. Open the application and choose **Tools**, **Forms** from the Application Workshop menu. The Form Tools dialog box appears. Select a form by entering the form name in the entry field or by highlighting the desired form in the pick list. When copying a form, after you choose the Copy button you are prompted for a name for the copy of the form and requested to indicate whether you are copying it to the same table.

To copy a report. Open the application and choose **Tools**, **Reports** from the Application Workshop menu. Select a report from the Report Tools dialog box by entering the report name in the entry field or by highlighting the desired report in the pick list. When copying the report, name the copy and specify whether or not you are copying it to the same table.

To copy a script. Open the application and choose **Tools**, **Scripts** from the Application Workshop menu. The Script Tools dialog box opens. Select a script by entering the script name in the entry field or by highlighting the desired script in the pick list.

FROM HERE...

For Related Information:

◀◀ "Copying Paradox Objects," p. 430.

Copying an Application

To copy an application, you must copy the entire contents of the application's directory and all its subdirectories. The best way to accomplish this task is to use the DOS command XCOPY with the /S parameter (copy all subdirectories). For full details on using the XCOPY command, refer to your DOS manual. If your application was stored in a directory called *mydir*, for example, and you wanted to copy it to a directory called *newdir*, you would use the following command at the DOS prompt:

```
XCOPY \pdox40\mydir \*.* \newdir /s
```

For Related Information:

◄◄ "Copying Paradox Objects," p. 430.

FROM HERE...

Deleting an Application

To delete an application, use DOS commands to empty all of your application directory's subdirectories. Next, use DOS commands to remove the subdirectories and delete all files in your application directory. Then remove the application directory. Refer to your DOS manual for more information on deleting files and subdirectories.

> **CAUTION:** Be sure that you are not discarding vital data when you delete an application.

For Related Information:

◄◄ "Deleting Objects and Emptying a Table," p. 432.

FROM HERE...

Documenting an Application

The Application Workshop provides several types of automatically produced documentation for an application. Start by opening the application you want to document, if it is not already open.

Documenting an application's menu structure can be very useful. Use this documentation to ensure that the menu structure of your application is the same as the menu structure of your design. The menu structure documentation also is useful in tracking down any menu selections that remain unassigned.

Choose **D**ocumentation, **M**enu Tree from the Application Workshop main menu. You are asked whether you want the documentation result sent to a file, the screen, or to the printer. After you select the destination, a diagram of your application's menu structure is drawn and sent to the output device selected.

To produce a detailed description of every action object defined for your application, choose **D**ocumentation, **A**ction Detail. You are asked whether you want the action detail listing sent to a file, the screen, or to the printer.

To make a cross-reference listing of all of the Paradox objects and Application Workshop objects, choose **D**ocumentation, **C**ross Reference. You will be asked whether you want the action detail listing sent to a file, the screen, or to the printer.

Exiting from the Application Workshop

To leave the Application Workshop and return to DOS, choose E**x**it from the Application Workshop's Main menu. A pull-down submenu appears. Choose To **P**aradox to return to the Paradox Main menu; choose To **D**OS to return to the DOS command line.

Version Compatibility

The Application Workshop cannot run or modify applications created with the Personal Programmer supplied with prior versions of Paradox. To convert your old Personal Programmer applications, follow these steps:

1. Make a backup copy of your old application. Be sure to include all of the tables, scripts, forms, and so on that your old application uses.

2. Using the version of the Personal Programmer that your old application was created with, print out a listing of the application's menu structure.

3. Using the menu structure printout, use the Application Workshop to create an identical menu structure. Then create action objects for each of the Paradox objects from the old application and attach them to the menu structure.

Chapter Summary

After completing this chapter, you should be familiar with the Application Workshop as a tool to generate the Paradox Application Language (PAL) scripts needed to control an application. You are familiar with the menu selections and the capabilities of the Application Workshop. You now have at your command the fundamentals necessary to develop complex applications.

Chapter 15 presents an overview of the Paradox Application Language (PAL) and discusses the fundamental definitions of the PAL language and its basic elements. Using the knowledge in the next chapter, you will be able to provide customized actions and some fine-tuning for your applications created with the Application Workshop.

An Overview of the Paradox Application Language

This chapter provides an overview of the capabilities of the Paradox Application Language (PAL), a complete database application development environment. In this chapter, you learn the basic features of this programming language and environment. The next chapter provides help with more advanced programming tasks. In Chapter 17, "Using the Script Editor and PAL Debugger," you learn how to use some of the built-in programming facilities, such as the Paradox Editor for scripts and the PAL Debugger.

Like programming with any high-level programming language, programming with PAL is far too complex for its capabilities to be covered in just one or two chapters. This chapter and the next two help you get started with PAL but cannot make you a PAL expert.

Use this chapter to get a basic understanding of PAL's philosophy and features. Use Chapters 16 and 17 to learn the basic ways you can create, run, modify, and debug (correct errors in) PAL programs and to discover more of the wide array of PAL commands and expressions available. Chapter 18, "Creating PAL Applications," shows you how an entire application is put together. Refer to Chapter 19, "PAL Command and Function Reference," to learn the syntax and use of individual PAL commands and functions.

Even if you are an experienced programmer—especially if you do not have experience with object- and window-oriented programming—you may want to skim this and the following chapters. They provide a quick review of PAL's features and the fundamentals of using the built-in editor and the debugging facility. For more details on all features discussed in this chapter, refer to the *PAL Programmer's Guide*, distributed with Paradox.

What is PAL?

Reminder:
PAL is a high-level database
programming language.

PAL is a high-level database programming language you can use to create structured programs with a standardized user interface. The Application Workshop uses this language to create menu-driven applications. By modifying programs created by the Application Workshop or by writing programs completely on your own, you can develop database applications of almost unlimited power and complexity. The Application Workshop described in Chapter 14 is written with PAL.

The Paradox Application Language is not a beginning programmer's tool. If you are a seasoned programmer, the structure and commands should be easy for you to understand. If you are a novice at programming, take time to learn some basic programming concepts before trying to develop an application with PAL.

After you have gained some general expertise, you can advance your knowledge by reading Que's *Paradox 4 Developer's Guide* by Dana Greaves, Jenifer Lindsay, and Matthew Harris.

Understanding PAL Scripts

PAL programs are scripts. Chapter 6, "Getting Started with Scripts and Keyboard Macros," introduced you to scripts and demonstrated how to record keystrokes into a script that you can play again later. In that chapter, you also learned how to use the SETKEY command to create keyboard macros from PAL scripts.

Applications generated by the Application Workshop (discussed in Chapter 14, "Using the Application Workshop") also are PAL scripts. These menu-driven applications provide an idea of the capability of the PAL programming language. PAL commands enable you to perform any task that you can perform interactively in Paradox. Therefore, you can create database applications completely customized to your exact specifications.

Reminder:
PAL programs are called scripts.

PAL scripts are stored on disk as ASCII (American Standard Code for Information Interchange) files. Each script file name must have SC as the file extension. Each script consists of a series of PAL commands used to manipulate Paradox *objects*—tables, forms, and reports—to obtain input from the user and make decisions based on a variety of factors.

Reminder:
Script files have the SC extension.

Paradox reads the lines of the script from the disk file, parses each line, and then interprets each command. Each command is separated from the line containing it and is checked for correct *syntax*. Syntax is the special order in which the PAL commands and their accompanying data must be arranged and punctuated. After the parsing operation is complete, Paradox writes a new file which contains the parsed commands. The new file of preparsed commands is given the same name as the script source file, but with an extension of SC2. The preparsed file is now read into memory, and PAL carries out (executes) each command in sequence, after evaluating all expressions in the command. The commands are interpreted and executed from top to bottom and from left to right, just as you read a book.

When the same script is used again, PAL will load and execute the pre-parsed commands in the SC2 file. This two-pass process improves the performance of PAL by skipping the parsing and syntax-checking operation when it is not necessary. PAL will perform the parsing and syntax-checking operations only if the original script file has been changed since the SC2 file was last generated, or if the SC2 file is missing.

You do not need special commands to start or end a PAL script. Paradox begins executing commands at the top and quits when it runs out of commands to execute.

You can use special *program control* commands to alter this top-to-bottom program flow and create more powerful and more structured programs. These commands enable your script to make decisions or repeat actions under various conditions, giving your application flexibility as well as power. The flow control commands are described in the section "Language Elements," later in this chapter.

Comparing PAL to Other Languages

The PAL programming language is similar in many ways to traditional programming languages like C or Pascal and to modern implementations of BASIC (such as QuickBASIC). Some examples of these similarities follows:

- *Placement of Commands.* PAL is a free-form programming language. Lines in a script can be up to 132 characters long. You can start a command anywhere on a line. You can indent commands to enhance code readability—a highly recommended practice. You can place as many PAL commands on one line as you want— up to the line length limit. You can split one command onto several lines—as long as you do not divide a keyword, variable name, or data value onto more than one line. You can use upper- or lowercase letters when you type PAL commands or the names of your own variables, arrays, or procedures. PAL is not case-sensitive. You can internally document or explain the operation of a script. (This internal documentation is referred to as a *comment*.) You can use blank lines to make the script easier to read; they do not affect how a script operates. Paradox ignores any text typed to the right of a semicolon (;), except when the semicolon is contained in text enclosed by double quotation marks ("ice cream; cake; cookies").

- *Modularization.* PAL enables you to *modularize* your programs. A design technique for producing complex programs (scripts), modularization basically involves breaking a program into several small, easily manageable pieces. Each piece, or module, of the program contains the instructions to perform its own particular job. Each module will invoke (or be invoked by) the other modules in the program when it is time for them to perform their respective tasks. Scripts played from another script are *subroutines*. A script may use any number of other scripts or procedures. With modularization, several scripts can share the same modules, making your programming efforts more productive.

- *Structure.* You can create *structured* programs—scripts that are internally modularized—by using PAL program control commands. PAL provides structures for branching (decision making) and looping (repeating actions a predetermined number of times or until certain conditions are met or ended).

- *Procedures.* Another method of modularizing a program, procedures also make your programs and programming more efficient. Using a procedure is similar to playing another script as a subroutine. The difference is that a script resides on disk as an ASCII file, whereas a procedure resides in RAM in an interpreted format. If a subroutine script is used more than once in a program, Paradox has to read the subroutine script from the disk each time the script is used. A procedure, however, is read from the disk only once, usually at the beginning of the script, and then stored in RAM. When the procedure is used, Paradox doesn't need to read the commands from the disk again; your script executes that much faster.

Another way procedures make your programming more efficient is that they can be stored in *procedure libraries* and read into RAM singly or in a group. Procedures in a library can be available to all of your scripts, as if they are built-in PAL commands or functions. The Paradox memory manager also can swap library procedures into and out of memory as needed. Procedures read from a library allow the Paradox memory manager to make more effective use of the available RAM. Procedures help keep you from having to write the program instructions (*code*) for the same task more than once. This enables you to keep each of your scripts shorter, easier to understand, and easier to maintain. In effect, you have the un-limited ability to create custom commands to perform nearly any database-related operation.

■ *Functions.* PAL has an extensive list of built-in formulas, collec-tively referred to as *functions*. These functions include the most common mathematical, trigonometric, and statistical formulas. Functions enable you to perform simple and complex computa-tions and manipulations with any type of data that can be entered in Paradox, including text, numbers, dates, and time. Functions also provide information about the status of various aspects of Paradox.

■ Most high-level languages allow the programmer to create new functions, called *user-defined* functions. Paradox procedures may be used to return a value and can be used to create the equivalent of a user-defined function.

In spite of all these similarities, PAL is not exactly like every other pro-gramming language. For example, PAL has some special data types, such as dynamic arrays and memos. Some aspects of PAL data input and display may be different from what you expect. Unlike other programming languages, PAL is very closely associated with the inter-active environment of Paradox. Think of your PAL script as being an invisible user, making choices and giving commands just as you would at the keyboard.

You need to have a thorough knowledge of the Paradox features and capabilities you are going to control with your script. The more you know about Paradox, the better you can use PAL's features and capa-bilities successfully and efficiently.

One of the best ways to become proficient with a new programming language is to roll up your sleeves and write programs. This chapter and the next help you get started. Use these chapters (along with references in Chapter 19) as springboards into the *PAL Programmer's Guide* (provided with Paradox). Then you will be on your way to creating powerful database applications with PAL.

T I P   Be familiar with Paradox before using PAL.

Experienced PAL programmers and developers also may want to take a look at *Paradox 4 Developer's Guide*, by Dana Greaves, Jenifer Lindsay, and Matthew Harris, also published by Que, for a detailed analysis of how to efficiently develop winning PAL applications.

FROM HERE...

For Related Information:

◀◀ "An Overview of Paradox Scripts," p. 220.

◀◀ "Recommendations for Using the Application Workshop," p. 460.

The PAL Programming Paradigm

A *paradigm* is defined as "a pattern, example, or model." Paradox, along with many other contemporary software products, uses the idea of a *desktop* as its model. If you have already used Paradox (or other products such as MS Windows), you are acquainted with this paradigm. If not, you should read the previous chapters of this book and spend some time using Paradox before attempting to write your own scripts. Because PAL is so highly integrated with Paradox, PAL scripts also use this paradigm.

Data is shown in *windows* on the screen, as if each window were a piece of paper on a real desk. Several windows can be shown at one time, just like you might have many references open on your desk. These windows also can be moved and arranged to overlap, be side-by-side, and so on, just like real objects on a desk. Another part of the model that Paradox shares is the concept of making choices from menus or selecting objects (such as windows) by using a mouse or the keyboard to "point and shoot."

The third element of the Paradox model is the way it interacts with you, the user, by carrying on a dialog in a dialog box. When the program needs you to enter data, modify the way a command is carried out, or make some other decision, it presents you with a dialog box. This box may contain fields for entering text, boxes to check, or buttons to choose.

Because this paradigm for user interfaces is consistent and easy to use, it is becoming increasingly widespread throughout the software industry. Gone are the "bad old days" when you had to learn a different way of giving commands to each different program you used. Now, what you know about using one program helps you use another program. This method of creating user interfaces is sometimes referred to as *Common User Access*, or *CUA*.

Although this model of interaction and data presentation is simple and intuitive for the end-user, it is somewhat more complex from the programmer's point of view. If you are an experienced programmer, be aware that writing programs for a CUA type of environment is substantially different from traditional programming methods. Before you begin, you need a good sense of the "look and feel" of operating with windows, pop-up menus, pull-down menus, and dialog boxes.

This section discusses the elements of the CUA paradigm from the programmer's point of view. Chapter 16 covers the commands and gives examples for creating and manipulating these elements.

Windows

If you have used Paradox at all, you already are familiar with how windows look and behave on-screen. Windows are used to provide a canvas on which to display input from the user or output from the application. You also use windows to provide a *view* of an object (such as a table). In programming terminology, the windows used by Paradox are a *class* of objects and have the following properties in common:

- All windows have a location (indicated by the row and column coordinates of the top left corner) and a size.
- Each window has a unique identifying number, known as the *window handle*.

Many windows also share other properties. These properties are optional, and a window may have them in any combination, or none.

- A window may have a title and a frame.
- You may be able to move the entire window to a different spot on-screen, resize the window, or close it.

■ A window may have *scroll bars* at the right edge and at the bottom of the window. These scroll bars enable you to view an object that is larger than the area displayed by the window.

Each scroll bar has an arrow at either end, which the user may select with the mouse to move (scroll) the view of the object up or down or to the left or right.

The scroll bar will have a *slider* or box pictured on each scroll bar to show the position of the current view relative to the overall size of the object in the window.

When you have the cursor positioned in the first field of the first row of a table, for example, the sliders are at the top and extreme left of their respective scroll bars. If you have positioned the cursor at the last record of the table and in the last field, the sliders show at the bottom and extreme right of their respective scroll bars.

Paradox automatically places the scroll bars and moves the sliders for you. You simply specify how much the view of the object moves when the window is scrolled. Paradox also handles most of the work involved in placing and resizing any windows; your script need only specify the initial location and size of a window.

Paradox has a variety of commands to handle resizing, closing, or changing the attributes (color, frame style, and so on) of a window. The section titled "An Overview of PAL Commands and Functions by Category" in Chapter 19 has a list of window-related commands.

Theoretically, an unlimited number of windows may be open on the Paradox desktop. Your PAL script can control all the features of a window that you can control with your mouse or keyboard. It also can control some things that cannot always be controlled with a mouse or keyboard—such as the amount of movement generated by the scrolling arrows or a window's title or frame style.

Before your script can control a window or place data in a window, it must know which window is to be manipulated, especially if more than one window is on the desktop.

Cue:
Windows are identified by their handles.

Windows are controlled from your script by means of their window handles. Each window that is opened on the screen is given a unique number that is not used again, even if the window later is closed. This number, automatically assigned by Paradox, is the *window handle*. Windows are created (opened) either implicitly or explicitly.

Some PAL commands (such as VIEW) automatically open a window; these window handles must be obtained manually. Other commands, like WINDOW CREATE, directly open a window and immediately assign the window handle to a variable. In either case, you must record and keep track of the window handle for later use. The handle is used to select that specific window for subsequent actions.

PAL provides all the commands and functions necessary to get window handles, establish a window's size and appearance, and place output to or get input from a window.

Dialog Boxes

A dialog box is a special kind of window. Dialog boxes may not be closed or resized, although they usually can be moved. Used to get information from the user, a dialog box contains one or more *controls*.

The currently selected control is shown with a highlight. To select a control, point and click with the mouse or use the Tab key to move the highlight from control to control. Controls may be disabled. The label or legend of a disabled control usually shows as *grayed*, which is a low-intensity version of the same color of the enabled control.

The dialog box often presents an informational message only, or asks for confirmation of a command that has irrevocable effects, such as deleting a file or replacing a report form.

Your script must keep track of what controls currently are active and available and must explicitly *gray* or restore controls when their status changes, using commands like REFRESHDIALOG and RESYNCDIALOG. Other controls you must build yourself by combining one or more of the basic controls. Paradox enables you to create a dialog box and certain controls with a single SHOWDIALOG command. An existing dialog can be partially or completely changed by using the NEWDIALOGSPEC command.

A dialog box always should have at least one control. Although you probably are familiar with all of the dialog box controls, the following section discusses the formal names and properties of the controls as supported by PAL.

Push Button

The most common type of control is the *push button*, a rectangular region of the dialog box labeled and shaded to resemble a physical button. Push buttons are used to issue a command or indicate an action of some sort. The indicated command is carried out immediately; often, the action initiated by pushing the button includes closing the dialog box. Most dialog boxes, for example, contain an OK button.

Clicking (or pressing) this button typically indicates that you are satisfied with your entries and selections of other controls in the dialog box. The dialog box then closes, and the application continues with the specified actions.

You create a push button with a single keyword option in the SHOWDIALOG command. The location, label, and other information about the push button are listed after the keyword. Each push button control returns a predefined value in an associated variable.

Radio Button

Another type of button is the *radio button*. In the Paradox environment, a radio button is shown as a circular area enclosed by rounded parentheses. A label indicating the meaning of the choice appears next to the button.

Reminder:
Radio buttons are used when only one of several choices can be made.

Radio buttons are used in groups when at least two choices are available and the choices are mutually exclusive. When a radio button is selected, the circle next to the label is filled in with a diamond-shaped *bullet* character. If another option in the same group is chosen, the new selection replaces the preceding one.

An example of radio buttons may be found when setting the video monitor in the Custom Configuration Program. Because the various video modes are mutually exclusive (the monitor cannot be monochrome and color at the same time), the choice of monitor is shown and selected with a radio button.

You use a single keyword option in the SHOWDIALOG command to create a group of radio buttons. The location of the group, its labels, and other information are listed after the keyword. Each radio button group returns a predefined value in an associated variable.

Check-Box

Just like on a paper form, a *check-box* is used to indicate that a particular item is chosen. If the check-box contains an X, the choice is selected. A check-box consists of a text label explaining the meaning of the choice and a pair of square brackets that form a box.

You use check-boxes to control modes or options, which may be on or off. A check-box, for example, might be used to indicate whether printed output should be made in draft mode.

Check-boxes are similar to radio buttons but represent choices that do not conflict with each other or that indicate an on/off condition. In word-processing, you can have text that is both bold and italic; check-boxes therefore are used to select various font attributes.

An example of check-boxes used in Paradox is found in the Custom Configuration Program. When making the video settings, a check-box is used to indicate whether Snow Prevention is to be used and which types of values (numbers and currency) use a special display color when negative. In the case of Snow Prevention, the feature is either on or off, so a check-box is used. In the case of negative values, no conflict occurs if both numbers and currency are displayed with special colors when they are negative, so a check-box is used for each selection.

Reminder:
Check-boxes indicate a yes/no selection.

You create a group of check-boxes with a single keyword option in the SHOWDIALOG command. The location of the group, its labels, and other information are listed after the keyword. Each check-box group returns predefined values in an associated group of variables.

Pick List

A *pick list* is exactly what its name implies—a list from which you pick items. This type of control also is sometimes called a *list box*. A list is shown in a rectangular area on-screen; you may pick only one item from the list.

Reminder:
A pick list is used to select one item from a list.

When the control is active, the selected item in the list is shown by the combined presence of a highlight bar and the cursor. When the control is inactive, the selected item is shown with an emphasized color or other video attribute.

Use a pick list to show choices in a list that changes length, such as files in a directory or the contents of a dynamic array. If your list has so many choices that using check-boxes or radio buttons would take up too much room on the screen, use a pick list. If all items in a pick list cannot appear in the space allowed for the list on the screen, a scroll bar appears alongside the pick list.

You can use the Paradox pick list control to show lists based on the contents of a fixed or dynamic array or on the tables or files in a given subdirectory. Each pick list control stores a value into an associated variable and is created as part of a dialog box by using a single keyword. The specific keyword varies, depending on the type of pick list used. One of the keywords, such as PICKARRAY or PICKTABLE, is used with a list of the pick list's specifications.

Entry Field

Applications always need to get text information from the user. A *single-line entry field* is used to obtain table, script, or other file names. This control is shown in the dialog as a rectangular box with an accompanying explanatory label. The length of the single-line entry field varies, depending on the type of information being gathered.

A script you write might use a single-line entry field to get dates, telephone numbers, or other short text items to be used in filling out a query or on which to base a locate or zoom command.

The *multiple-line entry field*, a variation of the single-line entry field, allows entering larger amounts of text in the form of multiple lines. The multiple-line entry field may be simply a rectangular area of the dialog box, which accommodates a few lines of text, or it may have scroll bars and be capable of receiving large amounts of text.

Each entry field stores the text entered by the user into an associated variable. The text-entry field is created with a single keyword option used at the same time that your script creates the dialog box. Entry fields also may use Paradox picture statements to format the user's text. (See Chapter 9, "Using Power Entry and Editing Features," for a description of using pictures.)

Combination Box

Each time you select a table using the **View** command, you are using a *combination box*. You may type the table name or have Paradox display a list of tables. A combination box control combines an entry field with a pick list. In general, if you leave the combination box's entry field blank, then the pick list is activated.

All the other controls discussed here can be created using a single keyword option that is part of the Paradox SHOWDIALOG command. The two parts of a combination box, however, must be explicitly created and coordinated by your script. You must create the entry field and list box separately, manually checking to see if the entry field is blank.

Events

Reminder:
An event is something happening, like a mouse click or movement, or key presses at the keyboard.

An essential feature of the CUA type of interface used by Paradox is that such programs are *event-driven*. An *event* is, literally, "something that happens." In a computer program, some of the things that happen are as follows:

- Movements of the mouse

- A key pressed at the keyboard

- Internal activities of the computer (such as a clock tic)

- Internal activities of the program (such as a subroutine signaling the closing of a window)

Event-driven programs typically must trap (record) events as they occur and store them in a queue (list) to be acted upon later. This list of events often is referred to as the *event queue* or *message queue.*

An event-driven program typically consists of a series of *looping structures*. The program first checks to see if there is an event to process and then uses a *decision structure* to determine what action is to be taken in response to the event. If the event is the selection of a menu item, for example, then your script branches to the activity specified by the menu choice.

Sometimes, you may want your program to ignore certain events, such as a user closing a window that contains a data-entry form that is not filled out completely. Your PAL script can block the event produced when the user issues a close command.

PAL provides all the machinery for trapping, blocking, and processing events as high-level commands.

PAL categorizes events into four areas:

- Mouse events are produced by button presses or movements of the mouse.

- Key events are produced when keys are pressed on the keyboard.

- A message event occurs when a user performs an action, such as closing or resizing a window or making a menu selection.

- The idle event is the final event category that Paradox recognizes. Your computer generates an idle event internally whenever no other events have occurred and a fixed interval has passed. The length of time between idle events depends on your computer's speed.

For Related Information:

◄◄ "Using Paradox Menus and Prompts," p. 39.

◄◄ "An Overview of Paradox Scripts," p. 220.

▶▶ "Creating Menus," p. 565.

▶▶ "Handling Windows," p. 577.

FROM HERE...

PAL Scripts

As stated previously, a PAL script is a series of Paradox commands stored in an ASCII file. All script files must have the extension SC. You have several options when creating, changing, or playing your scripts. This section describes some of those options.

Creating a PAL Script

You can create PAL scripts in several ways:

■ You can use the **B**eginRecord command on the Scripts menu or the PAL menu to record your menu selections and other keystrokes. This method is discussed in Chapter 6, "Getting Started with Scripts and Keyboard Macros."

Recorded scripts can be included in scripts that you write from scratch, or attached to applications created with the Application Workshop. Modifying a recorded script to use variables instead of literal names and values can make a recorded script much more powerful and flexible.

■ You can use the Application Workshop to generate scripts that make up an entire menu-driven application, as described in Chapter 14, "Using the Application Workshop."

You also can modify scripts finished with the Application Workshop by using the Paradox Editor or a suitable ASCII editor. (See this chapter's section on "Editing a Script.")

■ You can use the **Q**uerySave option on the Scripts menu to create a special type of script that builds a query statement, as discussed in Chapter 4's section on "Saving a Query."

Reminder:
Your script must provide the
DO-IT! command for queries
created with QuerySave.

Like scripts generated by the Application Workshop, a query saved as a script can be modified with the Paradox Editor. Remember: If you use a query created with **Q**uerySave, your script still must provide the **D**O-IT! command (equivalent to pressing F2).

Be careful if you decide to edit a query saved with the **Q**uerySave option. The syntax of scripts created by the **Q**uerySave option is different from that of other PAL commands. Unlike building a query interactively in Main mode, Paradox cannot help you with the construction of the query.

For the best method to correct a script saved with the **Q**uerySave option, first play the existing script and then modify the query.

Use the techniques described in Chapters 4, "Getting Started with Query By Example," and Chapter 7, "Using Advanced Query By Example and Multiple Tables."

After the query produces the results you want, save it again by using **Query**Save with the same script name, thus replacing the old version. You then can use the **R**ead option in the Paradox Editor to add the corrected query to your program.

You also can use PAL keypress interaction commands, such as {ASK}, and PAL workspace manipulation commands, such as CHECK and MOVETO, to build a query in a script. These commands use more common PAL command syntax and are easier to modify with an editor. Keypress interaction commands and workspace manipulation commands are described later in this chapter. Refer to Chapter 19 for a description of how to use each command.

■ You can write a script from scratch by using the Paradox Editor or any suitable ASCII editor. (See this chapter's sections on "Using the Paradox Editor for Scripts" and "Attaching an Alternate Editor.") The available PAL commands are introduced in this and the next few chapters and are explained in detail in the *PAL Programmer's Guide* and the *PAL Reference* that accompany the Paradox program.

If you are not already an ace programmer, you may want to give the Application Workshop first crack at creating your script.

If the task you want to program is fairly simple, you may want to try recording as much of it as possible with **S**cripts, **B**eginRecord. You then can join together or modify the recorded scripts to meet your application's needs.

If you are an experienced programmer, look at the code generated by the Application Workshop and then decide whether you prefer to start from there and add enhancements, or write your script from scratch.

Playing a Script

After you have created a script, executing or running it is referred to as *playing* the script. You can play a script within Paradox or from the DOS prompt. If your script has a problem while it is running—such as an unrecognized command or a missing file—a *script error* occurs. An error message is displayed, and the PAL Debugger becomes active. You can try to solve the problem or cancel the script. For more information about using the Debugger, see Chapter 17, "Using the Script Editor and PAL Debugger."

Playing a Script within Paradox

To play a script from within Paradox, you first must make certain that Paradox can find the script. This usually is done by setting the Paradox current working directory to the directory containing the script to be played. To make the directory containing the script current, use DOS commands to change to the appropriate directory and then start Paradox. You also can start Paradox first and then use the **T**ools, **M**ore, **D**irectory command to change to the appropriate directory.

You can start a script in a directory other than the current one by typing in the full DOS path along with the script name. Changing the directory usually is much easier.

After setting the directory, you can play your script from the Paradox Main menu or from any Paradox mode. To play your script from the Paradox Main menu, follow these steps:

1. Choose **S**cripts, **P**lay; an untitled dialog box opens (see fig. 15.1).

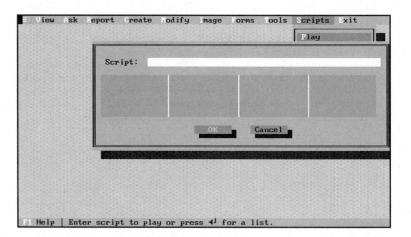

FIG. 15.1

Playing a script
from the Paradox
Main menu.

2. Type the script name in the text entry field or press Enter while the entry field is blank to see a pick list of scripts in the current directory.

3. After you enter the script name or highlight the desired script in the pick list, press Enter again or click the OK button. Paradox plays the script.

To play your script from any Paradox mode, follow these steps:

1. Press Alt-F10 (PAL Menu) and choose **P**lay.

    As with **S**cripts, **P**lay, an untitled dialog box opens (see fig. 15.2).

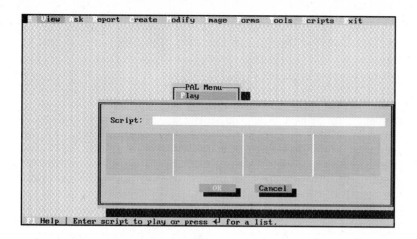

FIG. 15.2

Playing a script
from the PAL
menu.

2. Type the script name in the text entry field or press Enter while
   the entry field is blank to see a pick list of scripts in the current
   directory.

3. After you type the script name or highlight the desired script in
   the pick list, press Enter again or click the OK option. Paradox
   plays the script.

To play a script more than once, follow these steps:

1. Choose **R**epeatPlay from the **S**cripts menu or the PAL Menu
   (Alt-F10).

   As with the previous two methods, a dialog box opens.

2. Select the script to play; a second dialog box is presented
   (see fig. 15.3)

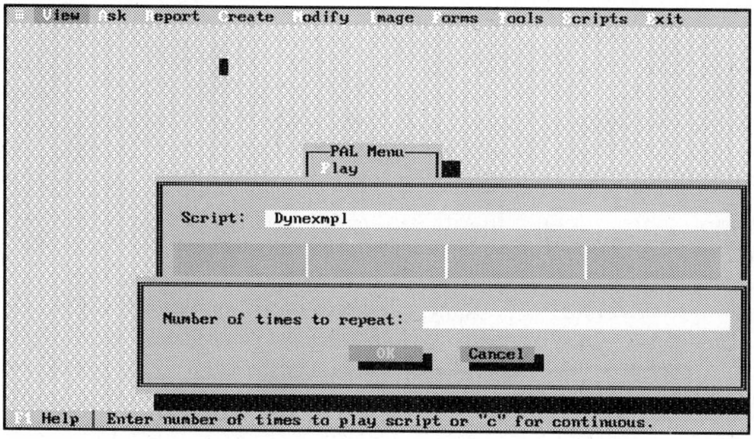

FIG. 15.3

Repeating a
script.

3. Type a number in the entry field to specify the number of times that you want Paradox to play the script.

or

Enter the letter *C* to indicate that Paradox should play the script continuously.

4. Press Enter, or click the OK button.

5. Paradox plays the script for the specified number of times.

6. If you request continuous play, you must stop the script by pressing Ctrl-Break and then choosing **Cancel** from the resulting Error menu.

Playing a Script from DOS

To play a script from DOS, follow these steps:

1. Refer to Appendix A, "Paradox 4.0 Installation and Start-Up," for instructions on setting the DOS path so that it includes the directory containing the Paradox system files.

2. Use DOS to change to the directory that contains the script you want to play.

3. Type *paradox* followed by a space and the script name.

4. Press Enter. Paradox starts and plays the script.

Cue:
To play a script from DOS, specify its name on the command line.

To play a script called MYSCRIPT from DOS, for example, first use DOS commands to change to the directory containing MYSCRIPT. Next, type *paradox myscript* and press Enter.

Playing a Script from Another Script

Creating large applications as a series of small, more easily manageable scripts can be very advantageous. The program development technique of creating the program in self-contained modules is referred to as *modularization*.

To support program modularization, PAL enables you to play a script from another script. Calling a script from another script is sometimes called *nesting scripts* or *calling subroutines*. PAL scripts can be nested for as many levels as necessary. The first script calls a second script; the second script calls a third; and so on.

The PAL command for playing a script is PLAY. A script containing a command such as *play "myscript"* will play the script named MYSCRIPT.

When the called script has executed all of the commands in it or has ended due to a RETURN command, the script that called it resumes executing at the command after the PLAY command.

Cue:
To play a script from another script, use the PLAY command.

Playing a Script on Start-Up

Whenever Paradox is started from the DOS command line, it looks for a script called INIT in the default working directory (usually \PDOX40). If the INIT script is present, Paradox plays that script before it plays any script present on the command line. (This is the method of playing a script described earlier in "Playing a Script from DOS.") This enables you to have all of your Paradox sessions automatically start with the same script. The INIT script often is used to set passwords, enter a user name on a network, compile private directories, and so on.

Cue:
The INIT script is played every time Paradox starts.

Editing a Script

After a script has been created, you may need to edit or change it at different times for different reasons.

If the script was created by recording keystrokes, you may want to change one or two keystrokes without recording the entire script over again, or you may want to modify the script to use variables. If you are writing a script from scratch, you surely need to edit the script as you go through the debugging process.

Paradox provides a built-in editor, the Paradox Editor, that you can use to create and edit PAL scripts.

If for some reason the Paradox Editor is insufficient, or you simply prefer another editor, Paradox enables you to use another editor besides the built-in editor. You can *attach* your editor in place of Paradox's. (Of course, any editor or other DOS program can be run by using the **Tools**, **More**, **ToDOS** or the Ctrl-O command and executing it at the DOS command line.)

Using the Paradox Editor for Scripts

The Paradox Editor creates files in straight ASCII text, without any special formatting characters. When you edit files with the SC extension, Paradox uses the special Script Editor menu. You probably are already familiar with the Paradox Editor because it is the same editor used to edit Memo fields.

One difference exists, however, between the Paradox Editor for memo fields and the Paradox Editor for scripts. The Paradox Editor menu for scripts includes one more choice on its menu than the Editor for Memo fields (see fig. 15.4). This is the **G**o command, which causes Paradox to play the script that is currently loaded in the Editor. If any changes have been made to the script, the script is saved before it is played.

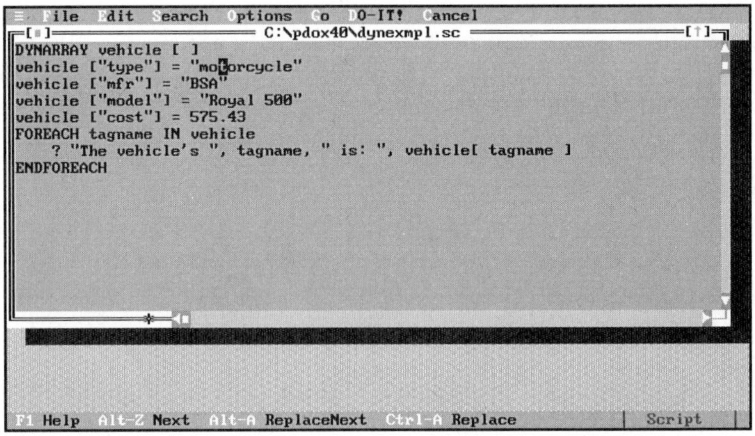

```
≡  File  Edit  Search  Options  Go  DO-IT!  Cancel
┌─[■]════════════════ C:\pdox40\dynexmpl.sc ═══════════════[↑]┐
│DYNARRAY vehicle [ ]
│vehicle ["type"] = "motorcycle"
│vehicle ["mfr"] = "BSA"
│vehicle ["model"] = "Royal 500"
│vehicle ["cost"] = 575.43
│FOREACH tagname IN vehicle
│    ? "The vehicle's ", tagname, " is: ", vehicle[ tagname ]
│ENDFOREACH

 F1 Help  Alt-Z Next  Alt-A ReplaceNext  Ctrl-A Replace        Script
```

FIG. 15.4

The Paradox
Script Editor.

Paradox automatically chooses which Editor menu to use. If you start an Editor session by using the **S**cripts, **E**dit menu choice or Ctrl-E, and then specify a file with the SC extension, Paradox uses the Editor menu for scripts. When the Paradox Editor is being used to edit a script, it is referred to as the Script Editor.

To use the Script Editor, follow these steps:

1. To start the Script Editor from the Paradox Main menu, choose **S**cripts, **E**ditor, or press Ctrl-E and enter a file name ending with SC.

2. To start the Script Editor while you are in the PAL Debugger, press Ctrl-E to edit the script you are debugging.

3. Select **N**ew to begin a new script or **E**dit to edit an existing script.

4. Next, specify the script name in the dialog box that is presented. Like any other file name in Paradox, your script name must adhere to DOS naming conventions.

For more information on using the Paradox Editor and PAL Debugger, see Chapter 17, "Using the Script Editor and PAL Debugger."

Attaching an Alternate Editor

If you don't care for the built-in Script Editor, you can use an alternate editor to develop or modify your scripts. You can use any editor as long as it does not attach special non-ASCII formatting codes to the files it edits.

To attach your own editor to Paradox, use the Custom Configuration Program and follow these steps:

1. From the system menu, select **U**tilities, **C**ustom, **P**AL. A dialog box appears.

2. Use the mouse or the Tab key to move the cursor to the entry field labeled Script Editor.

3. Enter the name of your own ASCII editor. You do not need to include the EXE or COM file extension.

4. The next field enables you to specify an alternate editor for the Blob Editor. The Blob Editor is the editor used for memo fields.

   You can change this editor as well as the Script Editor. If you do not change this field, Paradox continues to use the built-in editor for memo fields and other file editing.

Attaching your editor to Paradox means that you do not have to leave Paradox in order to use it, and it will be invoked whenever the Paradox Script Editor would be. Attaching your editor also enables you to edit protected (encrypted) scripts just as you can with the built-in script editor. (You cannot edit an encrypted script outside of Paradox.)

Be aware, however, that the Paradox clipboard is not available to your attached editor and that the PAL script commands for manipulating Editor Sessions will not work. Only the built-in editor can be invoked with the Ctrl-E command.

For Related Information:

◀◀ "Using the Paradox Editor," p. 142.

◀◀ "Recording and Playing Scripts," p. 222.

▶▶ "Using the Script Editor," p. 593.

▶▶ "Creating Sample Application Scripts," p. 652.

FROM HERE...

Language Elements

This section introduces you to the building blocks of PAL. First, some terms are defined, and then the different elements that make up the Paradox Application Language are explained. You need some familiarity with this material in order to understand the discussion in the next chapter, where you learn the fundamentals of constructing the windows and dialog boxes already described.

Expressions

An *expression* is a value or group of values expressing a single quantity. An expression is said to *evaluate to* (result in) a single quantity or value. The expression *2+2*, for example, evaluates to *4*. Expressions are made up of any one or more of the following building blocks:

> Constants
> Blank values
> Variables
> Arrays
> Array elements
> Operators
> Field specifiers
> Functions

All expressions result in a single value of a single data type. Expressions also may evaluate as *blank*. Some examples of expressions include the following:

Expression	Description
2	Consists of one value and evaluates to the number 2
"2"	Contains one value and evaluates to the character 2
"To" + "day"	Evaluates as the single string "Today"
c * (p/100)	Results in a number obtained by multiplying the contents of variable *c* by the dividend of variable *p* divided by the constant 100
ISTABLE("phone")	Uses a PAL function and results in a logical value indicating the existence of a table called *phone*
a >= 5	Results in a logical value, in this case indicating whether the contents of variable *a* are greater than or equal to the constant number value of 5

Note in the preceding examples that the number 2 is not the same as the alphanumeric character "2".

Expressions can be used to fill in the required *arguments* and *parameters* of the built-in PAL commands and functions. Many PAL commands require that you provide certain information before the program can perform its intended operation. The VIEW command by itself is incomplete, for example, and would cause your script to stop running. Your script must provide the name of a table to be viewed in the Paradox workspace before this command can have any effect.

Each piece of information you must provide to a command is a *parameter* of the command. Many PAL commands require you to provide more than one parameter. Similarly, many PAL functions require additional information.

Reminder:
A parameter is a piece of information you provide to a command.

Each piece of information that you must provide to a function is an *argument* of the function. In the following statement, the expression "mytable" is the argument to the function ISTABLE, which tests to see if a table exists.

```
ISTABLE( "mytable" )
```

Data Types

An expression always evaluates to a result with one of the data types that Paradox supports. In Chapter 2, "Creating Database Tables," you became acquainted with the seven standard Paradox field types: alphanumeric, binary, currency, date, memo, number, and short number. In addition to supporting these standard data types, PAL adds four more data types: logical, fixed array, dynamic array, and procedure. These new data types are valid in PAL expressions only and cannot be used as data types for fields in a table.

Table 15.1 shows all of the data types supported by PAL, and their limits. For more information on fixed and dynamic arrays, refer to the section on arrays later in this chapter.

Table 15.1. PAL Data Types		
Data type	**Symbol**	**Description**
Alphanumeric	A	Text (string) information, which may contain any ASCII character and varies in length from 0 to 255 characters

continues

Table 15.1. Continued

Data type	Symbol	Description
Memo	M	Text (string) information, which may contain any ASCII character and varies in length from 0 to 64 million characters
Array, Dynamic	DY	A dynamic array
Array, Fixed	AY	A fixed array
Currency	$	Number ranging from $\pm 10^{-307}$ to $\pm 10^{308}$
Date	D	Date ranging from 1/1/100 to 12/31/9999
Logical	L	Either True or False, this type is also called *Boolean*
Number	N	Number ranging from $\pm 10^{-307}$ to $\pm 10^{308}$
Short Number	S	Integer ranging from –32767 to +32767

Note that whenever the term *integer* is used, it means a whole number only, with no decimal or fractional part. Do not try to store numbers (or expression results) with decimal places in short number fields or variables.

The type of an alphanumeric expression is determined by its size. If the string is 255 characters or less in length, then it is an *A* (alphanumeric) type. If the string is larger than 255 characters, it is the *M* (Memo) type.

Some data types are compatible with each other. Most numeric, currency, and short number data types can be intermingled in the same expression. Other data types are not compatible. Alphanumeric types—either A or M types—are not compatible with any of the numeric types.

Knowing the data types of expressions is fairly important because expressions that result in or contain incompatible data types produce a script error. If your script tries to store incompatible data types directly into the fields of a table, a script error also results. In some circumstances, Paradox can convert an expression's result into the needed or expected data type, but Paradox cannot evaluate an expression composed of incompatible data types.

The following expression, for example, is not valid because it attempts to combine a string expression with a numeric expression.

```
"512" + 256
```

If your script contains an expression like the one above, Paradox generates a script error and your script stops playing.

Either of the following modifications to the previous expression is valid, although they produce very different results:

```
"512" + "256"    Evaluates to the string "512256"

512 + 256        Evaluates to the number 768
```

Use the TYPE function to determine the type of an expression or variable. PAL also provides a variety of tools for converting information of one data type to another, such as strings into dates, numbers into strings, and so on. Refer to Chapter 19, "PAL Command and Function Reference," for more specific details.

The PAL menu contains an option that enables you to calculate interactively the value of any PAL expression. From any mode in Paradox, press Alt-F10 (PAL Menu) and choose **V**alue. Paradox shows you a dialog box with an entry field labeled Expression:. Type any valid PAL expression (up to the maximum of 175 characters) and press Enter or click OK. The expression can be as simple as a numeric formula, such as 3*225, or a complex expression using any of the expression elements discussed in the following sections. After you press Enter, Paradox evaluates the expression and displays its value in the message window at the lower right corner of the screen.

Constants

A *constant* is a value in an expression that does not change. In the expression examples given previously, the character "2", the strings "To" and "day", and the numbers 2 and 100 all are constant values. These are sometimes referred to as *literal constants* because the literal value is written directly into the expression. The constant can be changed only by editing the script.

A constant may be any of the data types supported by PAL, except fixed arrays, dynamic arrays, binary field values, and memo values. You may use alphanumeric (string) constants, date constants, numeric constants, and so on. This section describes the rules you should follow when writing constants for each data type.

When writing string constants, observe the following rules:

■ A *string constant* must be enclosed in double quotation marks ("").
The following example is not legal in PAL, because it doesn't have
quotation marks.

```
This is not a string constant
```

■ A blank string constant is indicated by two quotation marks together with nothing between them: "".

■ A string constant must be all on the same line. This next example
is not a valid string constant because it is split across two different lines.

```
"This is
not valid"
```

If either of the above examples was encountered in a script, PAL would
produce a script error, and the script would stop running.

The following example is a legitimate string constant:

```
"This is a string"
```

Sometimes you need to include a character in a string for which there
is no key on the keyboard—such as a Greek letter or a line-drawing
character. Or you may need to include a character that already has a
definite meaning—like the " symbol. PAL provides a special character
sequence for overcoming this difficulty. This character sequence is
referred to as a *backslash sequence* because it always is written starting
with a backslash (\) character. Backslash sequences are a special type
of string constant.

Use the following guidelines when using backslash sequences:

■ Use the backslash sequence in string expressions to indicate a
portion that is intended to be enclosed in quotes. If printed or
displayed on-screen, the expression

```
"The book said, \"Do it this way.\""
```

evaluates to the following phrase:

```
The book said, "Do it this way."
```

The character combination \" tells PAL that the " symbol does not
signal the end of the string, but should be included in it.

■ The backslash sequence also is used to include the backslash
character itself in the string. This is especially important when
specifying DOS path names because the DOS path separator character is the backslash (\) symbol. Consider the following example:

```
"C:\\PDOX40\\"
```

The above string expression evaluates to the DOS path:

```
C:\PDOX40\
```

■ Use the other predefined backslash sequences to insert tab characters, start a new line, and so on. These predefined backslash sequences are most useful when sending data to the printer, or into a file. (Refer to the discussion of the PRINT command in Chapter 19 for more information on how to do this.)

■ The backslash sequences must always be part of a string expression, or, if used alone, must be enclosed in quotes to form a string expression.

Table 15.2 lists all the predefined backslash sequences available in PAL.

Table 15.2. Backslash Constants

Sequence	Meaning	Equivalent keystroke or control
\\	Backslash	\
\"	Quote mark	"
\f	Form feed	Ctrl-L; ejects printer page to top of next page
\n	New line	Ctrl-J or Enter; moves cursor/ print-head to next line
\r	Carriage return	Ctrl-M; moves cursor/print-head to start of current line
\t	Tab	Ctrl-I or Tab; moves cursor/ print-head to next tab stop

Table 15.2 shows only the predefined backslash sequences. To include other characters in a string expression (for example, the Greek letter alpha, or α), you create your own backslash sequences. Use the backslash character followed by a three-digit number representing the IBM ASCII code number of the character. You may use any of the 256 characters included in the IBM extended ASCII character set. The IBM extended ASCII code number for the Greek letter alpha (α), for example, is 224. Using this example, the constant string expression

```
"\224 is just Greek to me."
```

would evaluate to the following phrase:

```
α is just Greek to me.
```

Use the following rules and guidelines when using ASCII code numbers:

■ When using the ASCII code number, you must always use all three digits; if the code number is 12, for example, you must write it in the backslash sequence as *012*.

■ Be aware that some of the ASCII characters with very low or very high numbers do not print or display. Some of the low-numbered characters have special meanings. These low-numbered characters—referred to as *control characters*—affect the position of the cursor or print-head in the same way as the "\n", "\f", "\t", and "\r" backslash sequences.

If you intend to control the printhead or cursor position—for example, by starting a new line—the best technique is to use the predefined backslash sequences from Table 15.2.

The next group of rules and guidelines are for writing numeric constants. Numeric constants are used for number, short number, or currency values.

■ A *numeric constant* must consist of the number characters 0 through 9 only. A numeric constant may optionally begin with a minus sign (–) or contain a decimal point. You also may use scientific notation. No other symbols or characters are allowed in a numeric constant. The following examples are valid numeric constants:

```
12
-14.3
6.6E+2
```

The last example uses scientific notation, and means 6.6×10^2, or 660.

■ Do not use dollar signs or whole-number separators in numeric constants. The values $656 and 6,560 are not valid PAL numeric expressions.

■ Use the PAL function BLANKNUM to insert a blank numeric value in an expression. PAL distinguishes between the numeric value 0 (zero) and a blank numeric expression.

Use the following guidelines for date constants:

■ Date constants can be written in any of the date formats used by Paradox (mm/dd/yyyy, dd-Mon-yyyy, dd.mm.yyyy, or yy.mm.dd). Some examples of valid date constants are

```
2/28/92
28-Feb-1992
2.28.92
92.2.28
```

- Do not use quotation marks when you write a date constant; otherwise, you are writing a string constant, not a date constant.

- When writing date constants, do not include any spaces around the separators. The following expression is a valid PAL expression, but is not a date constant:

    2 / 28 / 92

    PAL interprets the slash (/) character as being the division operator, and the expression evaluates to the number value .0007763975155.

- When the date is in this century, only the last two digits of the year portion are necessary.

- If you need to represent a blank date, use the PAL function BLANKDATE.

The final set of guidelines below are for logical constants:

- There are only two valid *logical constants*, the values *true* or *false*. Your script must always use these two words to express the desired logical value as a constant. If your script prints or displays a logical expression, PAL automatically converts it to one of the strings "True" or "False", whichever is appropriate.

- When you write logical constants in your script, you must spell the word out in full. Do not use quotation marks.

- Use PAL's FORMAT function to change the strings that PAL displays from "True/False" to "On/Off" or "Yes/No". Using the FORMAT function this way will help make your application's messages more intelligible to the end-user.

Variables

A *variable* is a name given by you, the programmer, to an area of the computer's memory that is used to store data of any type. A variable can be thought of as a pigeon-hole in which any single item of data can be placed and saved for later use. The variable's name is the identifying label for that pigeon-hole. The contents of the pigeon-hole (the value of the variable) can change but the name of the variable remains the same. PAL variables may contain any of the data types listed previously in table 15.1. PAL variables get or change their type depending on which type of data is stored in them.

PAL variables are used much the way variables in algebraic equations are used. They represent a quantity that is not known exactly at the time an expression is written but will be present and available when the expression is evaluated.

Whenever a variable name appears in an expression, the value currently stored in the memory location that the variable refers to is inserted into the expression. If the variable *a* contains the number *2*, then the expression *a* + *2* evaluates to *4*. If the variable *a* contains the number *4* instead, then the same expression *(a + 2)* evaluates to *6*.

A variable is created, and has memory allocated to it, the first time it is used—usually the first time a data value is stored in it. Storing a data value in a variable is called *assigning the variable* or *making an assignment*. An assignment to a variable is made by using the assignment command, represented by the equal sign (=). The following line is an example of assignment.

```
myvar = 5
```

The statement above stores (assigns) the value (quantity) 5 in the memory location specified by the variable named *myvar*. The new value replaces whatever (if anything) was stored in *myvar*, and the previous contents are lost. If the script has never used the variable *myvar* before, then it is created.

Although the two operations use the same symbol, do not confuse the assignment command with the equal sign used to test for equality. The following statement is not the same assignment that occurs in the previous example but is a logical expression that will evaluate as either true or false, depending on whether *myvar* contains the number 5.

```
(myvar = 5)
```

If this second expression occurred in a script after the assignment made above, then it would evaluate true because *myvar* still contains 5.

Reminder:
Variable names must begin with a letter and cannot contain spaces.

A variable name must begin with a letter and may not contain any spaces. After the first letter, the variable name may consist of any combination of digits, letters, or the period (.), dollar sign ($), exclamation mark (!), or underscore (_) symbols, up to 132 characters in length. Some examples of valid variable names are

```
myvar
taxrate
new_item
Line12
week.day
pay$
done!
```

The following statements are not valid variables:

new item	Not valid because it contains a space character
$pay	Does not begin with a letter
1stLine	Does not begin with a letter

week/day   Contains an invalid character for a variable name, the slash character would be interpreted as a division operation

When you choose names for your variables, try to make them as descriptive as possible. Do not create variable names that duplicate the names of PAL commands, functions, or keywords.

Arrays

An *array* is a special kind of variable used to store a group of data items together. Each data item in the array is an *element* of the array. Each element of the array can store one value. Unlike other variable types, your script must explicitly create an array before it can be used.

PAL uses two different types of array: *fixed arrays* and *dynamic arrays*. A fixed array contains an unchanging number of elements. The number of elements in a dynamic array can change from time to time—hence the name *dynamic*. The elements of both types of arrays are referred to by using a *subscript*. For a fixed array, the subscript always is a number or a numeric expression; for a dynamic array, the subscript is a string or string expression (called a *tag*).

Elements in an array may be of any data type (except array), and the elements do not have to all be of the same data type. Array names must follow the same rules and guidelines as variable names. (See the preceding section on variables.)

Before they can be used, fixed arrays must be *dimensioned*—sometimes also referred to as *declaring* the array. The PAL command ARRAY is used to dimension a fixed array, establishing both its name and its size. The ARRAY command is followed by the array name and then a numeric expression enclosed in square brackets.

The value of the numeric expression indicates the fixed number of elements in the array. A fixed array can have a maximum of 15,000 elements, and your script may have as many fixed arrays as you like (limited by available memory). Some examples of valid array declarations are

```
ARRAY mystuff [12]
ARRAY flexlist [part1 + part2]
```

The first example creates an array with 12 elements. The second example assumes that the variables *part1* and *part2* are both numeric and have had values assigned to them. The actual number of elements in the fixed array is equal to the sum of the two variables.

The various elements of a fixed array are made available by subscripting the array with a numeric expression. The individual array elements may be used or manipulated in any way that is valid for their particular data type. Using the array *mystuff* dimensioned in the example above, you can subscript its elements in the following ways:

```
mystuff [1]
mystuff [n]
mystuff [x +1]
```

Because a record in a Paradox table is a group of fields, fixed arrays often are used to store and manipulate entire records at the same time. PAL includes special commands to copy records to and from fixed arrays. Refer to Chapter 19 for more information on the ARRAY command.

In most cases, dynamic arrays must be declared before they can be used, although a few PAL commands that use dynamic arrays will create the array if it does not exist. Because dynamic arrays change their size, gaining or losing elements as necessary, you do not need to specify the array's size when declaring it.

To declare a dynamic array, use the DYNARRAY command, followed by the array name and then a pair of square brackets. Your script may have as many dynamic arrays as you like, limited by available memory. Some examples of valid dynamic array declarations follow:

```
DYNARRAY winstats [ ]
DYNARRAY vehicle [ ]
```

The first example creates a dynamic array called *winstats*; the second example creates a dynamic array named *vehicle*.

The various elements of a dynamic array are made available by subscripting the array with a string expression called a *tag*. The subscript reference uses the form `arrayname[index_expression]`, where *index_expression* is any PAL expression. The tag *index_expression* automatically is converted to an uppercase string with a maximum length of 176 characters. The tag is the label used to refer to the dynamic array element.

A newly created dynamic array has no elements. The individual array elements are created when a value is assigned to them for the first time. Elements in a dynamic array may be used or manipulated in any way that is valid for their particular data type. Using the dynamic array *vehicle* declared in the example above, you create elements in the array with statements like the following:

```
vehicle ["type"] = "motorcycle"
vehicle ["mfr"] = "BSA"
vehicle ["model"] = "Royal 500"
vehicle ["cost"] = 575.43
```

The above examples create not only the elements in the array but also the tags that subscript the array. Refer to Chapter 19 for more information on dynamic arrays and the DYNARRAY command.

Field Specifiers

All of the data in Paradox tables is stored in fields. Because scripts usually need to manipulate Paradox table data, PAL provides a way for PAL expressions to refer to and include Paradox tables and fields. PAL provides a variety of *field specifiers* in order to provide several ways of referring to the needed data fields. Field specifiers may be used in expressions just like a variable, or to indicate a specific field in order to make an assignment to that field.

Field specifiers are used to refer to a field displayed in a table or query form on the Paradox workspace. [Employee–>Emp City], for example, represents the Emp City field in the current record of the Employee table on the Paradox workspace. [Employee(Q)–>Emp City] refers to the same field but in a query form for the Employee table on the workspace. In the following example, the name of the city *Carmel* is assigned to the Emp City field in the current record of the Employee table on the Paradox workspace.

```
[Employee->Emp City] = "Carmel"
```

Note that if Paradox is not in Edit or CoEdit mode, the above example produces a script error. Table 15.3 lists the field specifier formats available for use in PAL commands.

Table 15.3. Field Specifiers

Format	Meaning
[]	Current field in current image
[#]	Current record number in current image
[fieldname]	Field fieldname in current image
[tablename–>]	Current field in tablename
[tablename–>fieldname]	Field fieldname in current record of table tablename
[tablename(n)–>]	Current field in the nth image of table tablename
[tablename(n)–>fieldname]	Field fieldname in the nth image of table tablename
[tablename(Q)–>]	Current field in query image of table tablename
[tablename(Q)–>fieldname]	Field fieldname in query image of table tablename

When Paradox evaluates an expression that contains a reference to a field from a particular table, the value for that field is taken from the current record in the specified table. The current field is defined as the field containing the cursor in the current record of the current image. For other images on the workspace, the current field and record are the last field and record that contained the cursor.

Functions

PAL functions are built-in formulas that operate on expressions and generate values. A function always *returns* a value, which is inserted into your script at the point where the function is called. Functions are used to provide a value in an expression.

PAL functions look much like PAL commands but have a distinctly different purpose. In a PAL script, a PAL command controls the actions of Paradox but a PAL function produces (returns) a value that can be used in a PAL expression.

Just as several categories of PAL commands exist, PAL functions fall into several groups according to the type of operation or calculation they perform. Functions are used to perform tasks such as the following:

- Convert text strings (alphanumeric values) to other data types.

- Convert other data types to text strings, or return information about text strings.

- Format numbers or other data types for display.

- Manipulate or generate date values.

- Perform trigonometric, logarithmic, statistical, financial, and other calculations.

- Enable you to gather information about files, tables, disk drives, the PAL canvas, the Paradox workspace, and the current modes and status of Paradox itself.

For more detailed information about the functions that are available and their uses, refer to Chapter 19.

You also may create your own functions by using the RETURN command followed by an expression to make your procedure return a value. Procedures that use the RETURN command in this way can be used just like the built-in functions to insert values into PAL expressions. These sometimes are referred to as *user-defined* functions. For more information on using the RETURN command, see the section on procedures later in this chapter and in Chapter 19.

Operators and Comparisons

Just as you can use operators in Paradox to combine data and perform calculations in queries, forms, and reports, you can use operators to combine or compare data and to perform calculations or other manipulations in PAL expressions.

When you use an operator in an expression, the data items—whether variables, fields, array elements, or constants—that the operator acts on are called the *operands*. In the expression *2 + 3*, for example, the numbers *2* and *3* are the operands.

The operands in an expression must be of compatible types. Table 15.4 lists each available operator, the compatible types of operands, and the operator's effect.

Table 15.4. PAL Operators

Operator	Operand type	Effect
+	A	Concatenation (connection) of strings
+	N, S, $	Arithmetic addition
−	N, S, $	Arithmetic subtraction
*	N, S, $	Arithmetic multiplication
/	N, S, $	Arithmetic division
+	D	Addition of integers to dates
−	D	Subtraction of integers or dates from dates
AND	L (Logical)	Logical AND
OR	L (Logical)	Logical OR
NOT	L (Logical)	Logical NOT
=	A, D, L, N, S, $	Comparison: equal to
<>	A, D, L, N, S, $	Comparison: not equal to
<	A, D, L, N, S, $	Comparison: less than
<=	A, D, L, N, S, $	Comparison: less than or equal to
>	A, D, L, N, S, $	Comparison: greater than
>=	A, D, L, N, S, $	Comparison: greater than or equal to

After reviewing the table, look at these examples of operators used in expressions and the results of the expressions:

Operator	Results
`"To" + "day"`	Results in the string "Today"
`7 + 1/1/80`	Results in the date 1/8/80
`47.3 * taxrate`	Multiply contents of variable taxrate by 47.3; the result is numeric
`(1-2) * (3+3)`	Results in the number –6; parentheses change order of evaluation
`1 - 2 * 3 + 3`	Results in the number –2; order of evaluation uses operator precedence
`12/25/92 - 4/15/92`	Results in the number 254, the number of days between the dates
`grosspay < tax_min`	Results in logical value; true if grosspay is less than tax_min, false otherwise
`axis.z = 27.05`	Assigns the value 27.05 to the variable named axis.z
`(axis.z = 23.9)`	Results in a logical value, true if axis.z is equal to 23.9, false otherwise

The logical and comparison operators are used in PAL scripts most often to establish the criterion for making a decision (branching) or to formulate a description of the conditions under which a group of commands will be repeated (looping). Decision structures and looping structures are discussed later in this chapter.

When you include more than one operator in an expression, Paradox evaluates operations in the order of precedence, listed in table 15.5. You can use parentheses, however, to control explicitly the order of operation (see the fourth and fifth examples above). Operations in the innermost parentheses are calculated first. Operations of the same level of precedence and/or the same level of parentheses are evaluated from left to right.

Table 15.5. Order of Precedence of PAL Operators

Precedence	Operators	Description
1	( )	Parentheses
2	* /	Multiplication, division
3	+ −	Arithmetic addition and subtraction
4	= <> < <= > >=	Comparison operators
5	NOT	Logical negation
6	AND	Logical AND
7	OR	Logical OR

Keypress Interaction, Mouse Interaction, and Menu Commands

Earlier in this chapter, a comment suggested that you think of your PAL script as being a sort of invisible user. This invisible user, of course, must be able to enter keystrokes and make menu choices in order to make use of Paradox. PAL provides commands to *emulate* (imitate) specific key presses, mouse operations, and menu choices. Many script commands are direct equivalents of single-key commands that a user can enter at the keyboard. Other commands represent a series of menu selections in an abbreviated form.

Keypress Interactions

PAL *keypress interaction* commands enable you to replicate the effects of pressing keys during an interactive Paradox session. Paradox uses this type of command to record your keystrokes when you create a script with the **B**eginRecord option, as described in Chapter 6, "Getting Started With Scripts and Keyboard Macros."

Commands that represent menu selections are placed in curly braces, as in {Modify} and {Edit}. Cursor-movement selections are represented by commands such as DOWN and LEFT. Function keys are represented by PAL commands such as CHECK (F6), EXAMPLE (F5), and DO_IT! (F2).

Table 6.2 in Chapter 6 provides a complete list of keypress interaction commands that correspond to Paradox function key and special keystroke commands. Additional references for keypress interaction commands may be found in Chapter 19.

You can use this type of PAL command to reproduce any series of operations you can perform at the keyboard, including query operations. *Query images*—scripts created by the **Query**Save option described in Chapter 4, "Getting Started with Query By Example"—fall into this category of PAL commands.

PAL provides several methods of handling keypress interactions that represent text entered by the user. If the text is entered in response to a prompt, the text entered by the user is enclosed in curly braces as if it were a menu selection.

```
MENU {View} {employee}
```

This example places the table named *employee* on the workspace. The next example places a Query for a table named *address* on the workspace and fills in a text string in the first field of the Query form.

```
MENU {Ask} {Address} Right "Dokes"
```

Note that, because the table name is given in response to a Paradox prompt, it is enclosed in curly braces only, as if it were a menu selection. Next, the PAL equivalent of the right-arrow key is used to move the cursor one field to the right (assumed to be an alphanumeric field). Then the script fills in the constant expression to be searched for. Because this text is being placed on the workspace, it must be enclosed in quotation marks. Paradox will fill in the text just as if you typed it yourself.

Abbreviated Menu Commands

An *abbreviated menu* command represents a menu option or series of options that can replace several keypress interaction commands. A script that uses keypress interaction commands to rename the Answer table to Emptemp includes the following commands:

```
MENU {Tools} {Rename} {Table} {Answer} {Emptemp}
```

The following abbreviated menu command accomplishes the same result:

```
RENAME "answer" "Emptemp"
```

This second form is more compact and gives you some advantages over the version written with keypress interactions. The second form is easier to type but also is easier to read and understand later. A good programming practice is to use this more compact structure whenever feasible. Refer to Chapter 19 for a list of abbreviated menu commands.

Decision Structures

The simplest type of script—although not necessarily the shortest—is that created when you use the **S**cripts, **B**eginRecord or the **S**cripts, **Q**uerySave menu commands. A script created in this fashion runs straight through, from start to finish, executing commands exactly as you originally performed them. This script is powerful, enabling you to perform a series of complex tasks repetitively or set up a complex query with little effort.

A recorded script, however, lacks the capability to make decisions and carry out different actions under different circumstances. If the Answer table resulting from a query is empty, for example, there is no point in continuing with any further processing of that Answer table (like generating a report). In such circumstances, the script should print a message explaining the situation and then terminate.

Decisions do not always involve reacting to problems. If you want your script to present a menu to the user, then it must be able to choose (or *branch to*) a course of action corresponding to the user's menu choice. Your script cannot, of course, really "make a decision" the same way that a human being can. It can, however, choose predefined courses of action based on simple conditions and make relatively complex decisions by combining smaller decisions.

Decision structures—sometimes also referred to as *flow control, program control,* or *conditional branching structures*—usually are made up of several related keywords combined with variable expressions. The program control command IF, for example, always is used with the THEN and ENDIF keywords and often with the optional ELSE keyword.

The following discussion gives you a look at how PAL uses commands and keywords together in making decision structures. For more information, refer to Chapter 19, "PAL Command and Function Reference," and to the *PAL Programmer's Guide*, supplied with Paradox.

IF..ELSE..ENDIF

The most basic of the decision structures provided by PAL is the IF..THEN/IF..THEN..ELSE statement. The IF..THEN..ELSE structure gives a script the capability to decide if a single action should be carried out or to decide between two different actions, based on the occurrence of a given condition. Consider the following example:

```
IF temperature > 100 THEN
    MESSAGE "Too hot!"
ENDIF
SLEEP 3000
MESSAGE ""
```

This is a single-branch example of the IF..THEN..ELSE statement. For the statement to be correct, it must begin with the *reserved word* IF. (A reserved word is part of PAL and cannot be used for your own variable or procedure names.) The next part of the statement must be a Logical (Boolean) expression describing the condition on which the decision is based. Only when the logical expression evaluates true is the branch executed.

The branch consists of all commands in between the reserved word THEN and the ENDIF. None, one, or several commands may be enclosed by the THEN and the ENDIF. After the commands in the branch finish executing, the script resumes execution at the first command after the ENDIF.

In the example above, whenever the number stored in the variable *temperature* is larger than 100 (that is, a value of at least 101), the message Too hot! is displayed. Execution continues on to the SLEEP command, which delays for three seconds. Finally, the message area is cleared by displaying a blank string.

The following example is of a two-branch IF..THEN..ELSE statement:

```
IF temperature > 100 THEN
    MESSAGE "Too hot!"
ELSE
    MESSAGE "Stay cool."
ENDIF
SLEEP 3000
MESSAGE ""
```

Like the single-branch variation, the two-branch IF..THEN..ELSE statement begins with the reserved word IF, which is followed by a logical expression. In this case, if the expression evaluates to true, all of the commands between the THEN and the ELSE are executed. If the expression is false, then all of the commands between the ELSE and the ENDIF are executed. The IF..THEN..ELSE statement chooses one or the other branch, but never both at the same time.

When the executing branch is finished, the script resumes execution at the first command after the ENDIF. Each branch may have none, one, or several commands in it. In the example above, whenever the number stored in the variable *temperature* is larger than 100, the message Too hot! is displayed, and execution continues with the SLEEP command. Whenever the condition is not true, the message Stay cool. is displayed, and execution still continues with the SLEEP command.

For more complex decision-making requirements, you can place an IF..THEN..ELSE statement inside another IF..THEN..ELSE statement (called *nesting*):

```
IF temperature > 100 THEN
    MESSAGE "Too hot!"
ELSE
    IF temperature > 50 THEN
        MESSAGE "Stay cool."
    ELSE
        MESSAGE "Too cold!"
    ENDIF
ENDIF
SLEEP 3000
MESSAGE ""
```

Based on the value contained in the variable *temperature*, the above example will display one of three messages:

Too hot! when the value is 101 or above.

Stay cool. when the value is between 100 and 51.

Too cold! when the value is 50 or below.

The above example of nested IF..THEN..ELSE statements easily makes a three-way decision, but what if five, eight, or ten choices need to be made? Although IF..THEN..ELSE statements can be nested many levels, following the course of the decision branches being made becomes progressively more difficult. Deeply nested IF..THEN..ELSE statements can be almost impossible to follow. Fortunately, an alternative structure, the SWITCH statement, can be used when a large number of decisions must be made.

SWITCH..CASE..ENDSWITCH

The SWITCH statement is the decision structure used when there are many branches to choose from. SWITCH operates much as multiple independent IF statements do but is a bit easier to follow. The SWITCH command is used with multiple CASE statements, where each CASE statement tests for the occurrence of a different condition. Only one of the CASE branches will be executed. A CASE branch may contain none, one, or several commands.

Use the reserved word ENDSWITCH to indicate the end of the SWITCH statement. You can use an OTHERWISE statement to specify what command(s) should be executed if none of the CASE conditions is met. If none of the CASE conditions is met and you do not use the OTHERWISE option, the script resumes execution at the first command after the ENDSWITCH:

```
SWITCH
    CASE temperature > 100 :
        MESSAGE "Too hot!"
    CASE temperature > 75 :
        MESSAGE "Pretty warm"
    CASE temperature > 50  :
        MESSAGE "Okay"
    CASE temperature > 30 :
        MESSAGE "Pretty cold"
    OTHERWISE :
        MESSAGE "Too cold!"
ENDSWITCH
SLEEP 3000
MESSAGE " "
```

Reminder:

SWITCH often is combined with the SHOWMENU, SHOWPOPUP, and SHOWPULLDOWN commands.

SWITCH often is combined with commands like SHOWMENU, SHOWPOPUP, SHOWPULLDOWN, WAIT, and other commands that report menu selections or keypresses. This kind of construction enables your script to control its own execution interactively.

An example of SWITCH used in conjunction with a SHOWMENU command appears below. The SHOWMENU command is used to display a pop-up menu in the center of the screen. In the example, each menu selection name is a string expression (usually a string constant) and is followed by a colon. Placed after the colon is another string expression (also usually a string constant) that explains or describes the menu selection.

When the script in the example is executed, a box containing a pick list displaying the menu choices **B**enefits, **E**mployee, **S**alary, and **L**eave appears at the center of the screen. The string expression that describes the highlighted menu choice appears in the bottom line of the screen display. The final line of the SHOWMENU command is the TO statement.

After the user selects one of the menu choices, the name of the choice is stored in the variable after the reserved word TO. The SWITCH statement then is used to test the user's selection and branch accordingly.

```
SHOWMENU
    "Benefits" : "Add, change, display, print benefit info",
    "Employee" : "Add, change, display, print employee info",
    "Salary" : "Add, change, display, print salary info",
    "Leave" : "Leave the application"
    TO response
SWITCH
    CASE response = "Benefits" :
        PLAY "Exben"
    CASE response = "Employee" :
        PLAY "Exemp"
    CASE response = "Salary" :
        PLAY "Exsal"
    CASE response = "Leave" :
        QUIT
ENDSWITCH
```

If the user selects **B**enefits, Paradox plays the Exben script. If the user selects **E**mployee, Paradox plays the Exemp script, and so on. The last menu option, **L**eave, causes the script to QUIT, stopping execution of the script and returning the user to Paradox.

IIF—Immediate If

The final branching structure provided by PAL is a special shorthand version of the IF..THEN..ELSE statement, the *immediate IF* function IIF. The IIF can be used only to make a two-branch decision that selects one of two values based on a condition. The selected value is returned as the function's result.

Use the IIF in expressions or in an assignment statement to a variable. The example used previously to illustrate the two-branch variation of the IF..THEN..ELSE statement can be rewritten to use the IIF and would look like this:

```
MESSAGE IIF( temperature > 100, "Too hot!", "Stay cool." )
SLEEP 3000
MESSAGE ""
```

The IIF function uses three arguments. From left to right, they are the condition being tested, the value to return if the condition is true, and the value to be returned if the condition is false. In the preceding example, the condition being tested is whether or not the number stored in the variable *temperature* is greater than 100. If the number is greater than 100, the string expression `"Too hot!"` is returned; if the condition is not true, then the string expression `"Stay cool."` is returned. In either case, the result returned by IIF is inserted into the MESSAGE command as its parameter (the expression to be displayed). For this type of choice, the IIF is much more compact and powerful than the full IF..THEN..ELSE statement. Unlike the other PAL decision structures, the IIF statement also may be used in calculated fields on reports and forms.

Loop Structures

Often, you need to execute a certain group of commands repetitively for a fixed number of times or until a certain condition is met. Most scripts will show a menu repeatedly, for example, until the user makes the menu selection that quits or leaves the current script module. PAL provides several *loop structures* you can use to accomplish this type of task.

FOR..ENDFOR

The FOR statement often is referred to as a *fixed loop* because, with few exceptions, it executes the commands contained in it a set number of times. The FOR loop often is used when all the elements of a fixed array or of a record must be manipulated. You can use the FOR loop to count up or down in any increment through any range of numbers. The following example shows a simple example of a FOR loop.

```
VIEW "mytable"
FOR count FROM 1 TO NRECORDS( "mytable" )
    IF ISBLANK( [last-name] ) THEN
        MESSAGE "The last name field of record number",
            count, " is blank!"
    ENDIF
    SKIP                ; moves to next record
ENDFOR
```

This example shows the basic syntax features of the FOR loop. It begins with the reserved word FOR and is followed by a variable name. The variable holds the value of the count while the FOR loop is executing. If it does not exist when the FOR loop starts, it is created automatically.

Next is the reserved word FROM, which tells PAL that the following expression is the starting value of the count. The next item is the reserved word TO, which indicates that the expression following it is the ending value for the count. Both of the expressions specified by the

FROM and TO keywords must be numeric. None, one, or several commands may follow.

All the commands up to the ENDFOR will be executed repeatedly until the value of the count is greater than the value specified for the ending limit. When the FOR loop is completed, the script's execution continues with the first command after the ENDFOR keyword.

In the preceding example, the variable used to hold the count is called *count*. The starting limit (FROM) is specified by the numeric constant 1. The ending limit is specified by a numeric expression containing the PAL function NRECORDS, which returns the number of records in the table named *mytable*. After the table *mytable* is placed on the workspace, the FOR loop causes the enclosed IF statement to be executed for as many times as there are records in the table. In each record, the [last-name] field is tested by using the PAL function ISBLANK, which returns a logical value of true if the argument is blank. If any [last-name] field is found to be blank, then a message giving the record number is printed at the lower right corner of the screen.

A FOR loop may use any increment while counting. If no increment is specified, as in the preceding example, the variable used for the count is increased by one each time the FOR loop executes. The following example counts from 2 to 50 by twos:

```
FOR x FROM 2 TO 50 STEP 2
    ? x
ENDFOR
```

The STEP keyword specifies the size of the increment, in this case 2. A FOR loop also can count down from one value to a lower one. To do this, use the STEP keyword and a negative value for the amount of the step. The next example prints the numbers from 27 to 3, counting down by threes:

```
FOR x FROM 27 TO 3 STEP -3
    ? x
ENDFOR
```

FOR loops also may be nested inside each other. Consider the next example:

```
FOR line  FROM  1 TO 10
    FOR Column FROM 1 TO 10
        ?? "*"
    ENDFOR
    ?                          ; start a new line
ENDFOR
```

The outermost FOR loop in the above script executes 10 times. The commands that it executes are another FOR loop and the ? command.

The inner FOR loop prints ten asterisks (*), one right after another, and the ? command moves the cursor to a new line so that the following pattern is displayed:

```
* * * * * * * * * *
* * * * * * * * * *
* * * * * * * * * *
* * * * * * * * * *
* * * * * * * * * *
* * * * * * * * * *
* * * * * * * * * *
* * * * * * * * * *
* * * * * * * * * *
* * * * * * * * * *
```

This FOR loop shows how a fixed array might be processed:

```
FOR arryindex FROM 1 TO ARRAYSIZE( MyArray )
    ? "Element ", arryindex, " is of type ", TYPE( MyArray[arryindex] )
    ? "The element contains: ", MyArray[arryindex]
ENDFOR
```

This example uses the PAL function ARRAYSIZE to determine the upper limit of the count. The value of the counting variable, *arryindex*, is used to subscript the array. The two display commands inside the FOR loop will execute for as many elements as there are in the array. The first display command uses the TYPE function to get the element's type for display. The second display statement simply displays the contents of the currently subscripted element.

If necessary, a FOR loop may be prevented from executing the full number of times by setting the counting variable to a value greater than the upper limit or by using the QUITLOOP command. (Refer to Chapter 19 for more information.)

FOREACH..ENDFOREACH

The FOREACH statement, a special version of the FOR statement, is used for manipulating dynamic arrays only. Unlike a fixed array, the elements in a dynamic array are subscripted with string expressions (tags), and the elements are not in any given order. An ordinary FOR loop cannot be used with a dynamic array. The FOREACH loop, however, makes manipulating a dynamic array easy. Recalling one of the examples used in the previous discussion of dynamic arrays, the following example illustrates how to produce the FOREACH loop:

```
DYNARRAY vehicle [ ]
vehicle["type"] = "motorcycle"
vehicle["mfr"] = "BSA"
vehicle["model"] = "Royal 500"
vehicle["cost"] = 575.43
FOREACH tagname IN vehicle
    ? "The vehicle's ", tagname, " is: ", vehicle[tagname]
ENDFOREACH
```

This example declares a dynamic array *vehicle* and then creates and assigns some elements to the dynamic array. The FOREACH loop begins with the reserved word FOREACH and is followed by a variable name that is used to hold the various tags of the dynamic array. Next is the reserved word IN, followed by the name of the dynamic array that is to be manipulated. All of the commands up to the ENDFOREACH will be executed repeatedly until all tags of the dynamic array have been handled.

When the FOREACH loop is complete, the script will continue execution with the first command after the ENDFOREACH keyword. The preceding example will produce output somewhat like this (the exact order of the lines may vary):

```
The vehicle's COST is: 575.43
The vehicle's MODEL is: Royal 500
The vehicle's MFR is: BSA
The vehicle's TYPE is: motorcycle
```

The only way to determine if a dynamic array has a particular tag is to use the FOREACH loop. Like the FOR loop, the FOREACH loop may be stopped before it has gone through every dynamic array tag by using the QUITLOOP command.

WHILE..ENDWHILE

The WHILE loop executes one or more commands repeatedly for as long as a given condition is true. The WHILE loop may execute the commands it encloses once or several times. If the condition of the WHILE loop is false when it is first tested, the commands in the WHILE loop will not be executed at all. Often, you will use the WHILE loop to show a menu repeatedly until your application's user makes the choice to leave the menu. The following example shows this kind of use and illustrates the correct syntax for the loop:

```
response = ""
WHILE response <> "Leave"
    SHOWMENU
        "Benefits" : "Add, change, display, print benefit info",
         Employee" : "Add, change, display, print employee info",
        "Salary" : "Add, change, display, print salary info",
        "Leave" : "Leave the application"
        TO response
    SWITCH
        CASE response = "Benefits" :
            PLAY "Exben"
        CASE response = "Employee" :
            PLAY "Exemp"
        CASE response = "Salary" :
            PLAY "Exsal"
    ENDSWITCH
ENDWHILE
```

The WHILE loop begins with the reserved word WHILE, followed by a logical expression describing the condition under which the loop should continue to execute. All commands between the logical expression and the keyword ENDWHILE will be executed repeatedly for as long as the logical expression evaluates to true.

The logical expression is evaluated immediately before the commands in the loop are executed and then every time the loop is executed. When the ENDWHILE keyword is encountered, script execution goes back to the WHILE (the top of the loop), and the condition is tested.

In this example, setting the variable *response* to a blank string ensures that the loop will execute at least once. The loop begins, and the specified condition is that the *response* variable's contents not be equal to the menu choice *"Leave"*. The SHOWMENU command is used to display a menu, and the SWITCH statement is used to select a script branch that corresponds to the action chosen from the menu. After each menu choice is completed, the script's execution goes to the top of the WHILE loop and tests the condition. As long as the *response* variable is not equal to *"Leave"*, the menu is shown again.

When the user chooses *"Leave"* from the menu, the loop condition is now false (the *response* variable now is equal to *"Leave"*), and the loop stops executing.

SCAN..ENDSCAN

The SCAN loop acts on records in a table. Like the FOR..ENDFOR loop, commands enclosed in a SCAN loop are executed a fixed number of times. By default, the SCAN statement acts on all records in a table. Use the optional SCAN FOR syntax to act on records matching only certain criteria. The table used with the SCAN loop must be on the workspace and be the current image. Consider the following example:

```
VIEW "employee"
SCAN
     ? [EmpName]
ENDSCAN
```

This fragment first uses the VIEW command (a PAL menu command) to place the Employee table on the workspace, making it current. The SCAN loop begins with the reserved word SCAN. All the commands between the SCAN keyword and the ENDSCAN keyword will be executed for each record in the table. This example merely displays the contents of the EmpName field for every record in the table.

The next example shows how the SCAN FOR option might be used.

```
EDIT "address"
SCAN FOR [zipcode] = "94609"
     [state] = "CA"
     [city] = "Oakland"
ENDSCAN
```

First, the EDIT command is used to place the "address" table on the workspace in edit mode and make it the current image.

The SCAN FOR uses a logical expression to select only the records in which the value stored in the zipcode field is equal to the string expression "94609". The assignments to the state and city fields are made for every record in the table for which the expression [zipcode] = "94609" is true.

Procedures and Procedure Libraries

As you learn to program with PAL, you will notice that many of your scripts include similar series of PAL commands. Sometimes a single PAL script performs identical or nearly identical steps in more than one portion of the script.

To avoid writing the same instructions over and over, and to make your scripts more efficient and flexible, you may choose to modularize your program. Modularization is described earlier in this chapter.

Because the PLAY command provides a method for one script to run another script, one way to modularize scripts is to create a second script that includes only the commands that are duplicated in your original script or several scripts. You then use the PLAY command to

Reminder:
A script called by another script is a subroutine.

run the new subroutine script at the appropriate times from the original script or scripts. This process creates programs that are efficient and easy to follow and debug.

The extensive use of scripts as subroutines, however, can result in an unmanageable directory full of script files—a situation that will confuse your programming efforts. Also, subroutine scripts must be read from the disk each time they are played. The disk access will slow your application. If there are many subroutine scripts, your application may become noticeably slower.

For these reasons, PAL provides facilities to create procedures and procedure libraries. A *procedure* provides a way of encapsulating a group of commands so that they may be stored in RAM in interpreted format. A *procedure library* provides a way to store the same procedures in a disk file in interpreted format. A significant amount of disk access and parsing time can be saved by storing often-used subroutines in this way.

Procedures loaded from a procedure library also can be automatically swapped in and out of memory by the Paradox memory manager, allowing your application to make better use of the memory available.

Procedures

A PAL *procedure* is used much like a subroutine script in that it enables you to modularize your program, writing code in manageable blocks and avoiding repetition. You can write a script that contains one or several procedures so that your disk is not cluttered with more files than necessary.

Reminder:
When you play a script that contains a procedure, Paradox loads the procedure into RAM, where it remains.

Procedures are quicker in operation than subroutine scripts. When you play a script that directly contains procedures, Paradox loads the procedures into RAM. When loaded, the procedures remain in RAM for the remainder of the current Paradox session, unless explicitly removed with the RELEASE PROCS command. You can use any of the loaded procedures anywhere in any script during the current Paradox session (or until you clear the procedure from memory). Paradox does not have to read the procedure script again.

Each procedure is given a name so that PAL can know which procedure you want to use. Procedure names must be made according to the same rules as names for variables (refer to the section "Variables" earlier in this chapter).

To create a procedure or to convert a script into a procedure, use the PROC command, followed by the procedure's name. The PAL commands that are to be part of the new procedure are placed after the procedure name. The keyword ENDPROC is placed after the last command in the procedure to signal PAL that the end of the procedure has been reached. The example from the preceding section on the WHILE looping command is presented below, defined as a procedure named *EmployeeModule*.

```
PROC EmployeeModule()
    response = ""
    WHILE response <> "Leave"
        SHOWMENU
            "Benefits" : "Add, change, display, print benefit info",
            "Employee" : "Add, change, display, print employee info",
            "Salary" : "Add, change, display, print salary info",
            "Leave" : "Leave the application"
            TO response
        SWITCH
            CASE response = "Benefits" :
                PLAY "Exben"
            CASE response = "Employee" :
                PLAY "Exemp"
            CASE response = "Salary" :
                PLAY "Exsal"
        ENDSWITCH
    ENDWHILE
ENDPROC  ; end of EmployeeModule
```

After this procedure has been loaded into memory, it is available to your scripts just like any of the built-in PAL commands. To use the procedure defined above, your script would contain the following command:

```
EmployeeModule()
```

The parentheses are required. The example above shows the essential elements of a procedure's syntax. The procedure begins with the reserved word PROC, followed by the procedure's name.

The next required item is the *parameter list*, which is enclosed in parentheses. The parameter list is the method by which a procedure explicitly shares data with the script or procedure that called it. Although the example above does not have any parameters, the parentheses still are required. (Notice that the parameter list, even if it is empty, also must be given when the procedure is called.)

The commands that form the *body* of the procedure come next, followed by the ENDPROC keyword, which signals the end of the procedure.

Procedures also can be used to return a value, like the built-in PAL functions. The next example shows a procedure that returns a value and uses a single parameter:

```
PROC  Confirm_Yes( c_action )
    SHOWMENU
        "Yes" : "Go ahead, " + c_action,
        "No"  : "No, don't " + c_action
        Default "No" To cy_chc
    SWITCH
        CASE cy_chc = "Yes" : return true
        OTHERWISE : return false
    ENDSWITCH
ENDPROC  ;  Confirm_Yes
```

This is an ideal example of how a general-purpose procedure can save a great deal of programming work. It is always a good idea to write your application so that it obtains confirmation from the user before performing an action that has irrevocable effects—like deleting a table or a record. The procedure in the example obtains this kind of confirmation and returns the user's choice as a logical value. The procedure receives, as a parameter, a string expression. A menu is shown, and the string expression is included in the menu choice explanations displayed at the bottom of the screen. The menu asks the user to choose "Yes" to go ahead with the action described by the string in the parameter or "No" to cancel it. The RETURN command is used to return a value—in this case, a logical true or false. Use this type of general-purpose procedure to avoid writing specific yes/no tests over and over again. A call to the Confirm_Yes procedure might look like this:

```
IF Confirm_Yes( "delete the table" ) THEN
    DELETE "mytable"
ENDIF
```

Refer to Chapter 19 and the *PAL User's Reference* for more information on procedures.

To enhance efficiency further, Paradox gives you the ability to create *closed procedures*. Closed procedures are completely self-contained procedures that can take special advantage of PAL's automatic memory-management features. To use closed procedures, you must observe a number of special restrictions. For example, closed procedures can be called only from a procedure library. Refer to the *PAL Programmer's Guide* for more information on when and how to use this type of procedure.

Libraries

PAL procedure libraries give you additional flexibility. Procedure libraries contain one or more procedures that Paradox already has interpreted into parsed format. Paradox can load and use preparsed procedures more quickly than procedures that must be interpreted after being read from their ASCII files. Other benefits include the following:

- *Memory management.* Because procedures defined directly in a script remain loaded in RAM throughout the remainder of the current Paradox session, they are continuously consuming memory space. When a large application with large procedures or many variables and arrays is playing, all of the available RAM may become used up. If your application uses up all of the available memory, Paradox will print an error message, and your application will stop running. If unneeded procedures are removed from memory, then more room in RAM can be made for new procedures or variables. If the procedures were loaded in memory by being directly defined in a script that was played, then procedures must be explicitly removed from memory by using the RELEASE PROCS command. If they are needed again later, then the script defining them must be played again.

  If a procedure is loaded into memory from a library, then Paradox automatically swaps the procedure into and out of memory, as necessary. Use procedure libraries to let Paradox manage memory for you.

- *Consolidation of procedures.* Even if you develop an application in small modules, you can use procedure libraries to put all the modules together as a library of procedures (up to a maximum of 640 procedures in each library). You then use a single script— often called a *driver* script—to load and orchestrate the various modules.

  A program that otherwise would consist of many scripts—and therefore many files—can be reduced to a library file and a driver script file, at the same time increasing its performance.

- *Keyboard macros.* Procedure libraries are ideal for holding keyboard macros (discussed in Chapter 6, "Getting Started with Scripts and Keyboard Macros"). At the beginning of each Paradox session, you load the procedure from the library that contains all the macros you have developed. You then can operate the macros as quickly as if they were a part of the Paradox program.

A library is created by using a single command—CREATELIB—that creates the library file and gives it a specific name. Be careful when creating libraries, however, because CREATELIB will overwrite (replace) any existing library with the same name. Follow these steps to create a library and place procedures in it:

1. Play one or more scripts containing procedure definitions.

2. Use the CREATELIB command to create the library, if it does not already exist.

3. Use the WRITELIB command to place the procedures into the library file.

The next example uses the previous Confirm_Yes procedure to show how a library is created and a procedure placed in it. The procedure definition is unchanged from the previous example. It is followed by the CREATELIB command, which creates a library named GenLib. If a library named GenLib already exists, it is replaced with the newly created library. Next, the WRITELIB command is used to place the Confirm_Yes procedure into the library named GenLib.

```
PROC  Confirm_Yes( c_action )
    SHOWMENU
        "Yes" : "Go ahead, " + c_action,
        "No"  : "No, don't " + c_action
        Default "No" To cy_chc
    SWITCH
        CASE cy_chc = "Yes" : return true
        OTHERWISE : return false
    ENDSWITCH
ENDPROC  ;   Confirm_Yes
CREATELIB "GenLib"
WRITELIB "GenLib" Confirm_Yes
```

PAL also provides functions for obtaining a list of the procedures stored in a library and for finding out which version of Paradox was used to create the library.

Procedure libraries created with previous versions of Paradox must be converted to the version 4.0 format before they can be used. PAL provides a CONVERT command to do exactly that. Please refer to Chapter 19 for more information about libraries and library commands.

Variable Scope

As discussed earlier in this chapter, Paradox creates a variable the first time you assign a data value to be stored in it. After the variable is created, it continues to exist for the remainder of the current Paradox session. When created in this way, a variable can be accessed and modified by any script or procedure. This kind of variable is called a *global variable* because its scope (the level at which it is available) is global (includes the entire script, its procedures, subroutine scripts, and their procedures).

Using global variables has some advantages, but it also has significant disadvantages. In large applications, a certain amount of memory may be taken up with unused and unneeded variable information, thus reducing the amount of memory available for active procedures and data.

To preserve the maximum memory available for your application and data, use the RELEASE VARS command at the end of a PAL script or procedure. You also can use this command at any point in a script when you know that the variable will not be used again. Use the ALL option of the RELEASE VARS command if you don't want any of the global variables and their current values carried over to the next script executed during the current Paradox session.

Having numerous global variables poses a more serious problem from the programmer's point of view. The more global variables stored in memory, the easier it is to use the wrong one accidentally. A common practice, for example, is to give loop counting variables names like *count*—a quite reasonable name that makes the script easier for a reader to understand. Assume that, using *count* as a controlling variable, the loop calls another procedure or subscript that also uses a variable named *count*. Only one variable with a given name can be available at any scope level. In this situation, both loops use the same counting variable; thus the script cannot work properly.

A better programming practice, therefore, is to use parameters to pass information to your procedures and to limit the scope of variables in your scripts. This enables your script to take advantage of Paradox's memory management features automatically and to make your scripts easier to debug and maintain.

You can limit the use of a particular variable to a specific procedure by defining the variable as *private*. When a procedure stops executing, all of its private variables are released from memory, assisting with memory-management. Note, however, that when a procedure calls another procedure or plays a subroutine script, its private variables are still in memory and are available to the called procedures and scripts. Use the PRIVATE keyword in the procedure definition, right after the procedure's parameter list. The EmployeeModule and the Confirm_Yes procedures, modified to use private variables, are shown in the following example.

Cue:
Use the PRIVATE keyword to define a private variable.

```
PROC EmployeeModule()
  PRIVATE response
    response = ""
    WHILE response <> "Leave"
        SHOWMENU
            "Benefits" : "Add, change, display, print benefit info",
            "Employee" : "Add, change, display, print employee info"
            "Salary" : "Add, change, display, print salary info",
            "Leave" : "Leave the application"
            TO response
        SWITCH
            CASE response = "Benefits" :
                PLAY "Exben"
            CASE response = "Employee" :
                PLAY "Exemp"
            CASE response = "Salary" :
                PLAY "Exsal"
        ENDSWITCH
    ENDWHILE
ENDPROC   ; end of EmployeeModule

PROC  Confirm_Yes( c_action )
  PRIVATE cy_chc
    SHOWMENU
        "Yes" : "Go ahead, " + c_action,
        "No"  : "No, don't " + c_action
        Default "No" To cy_chc
    SWITCH
        CASE cy_chc = "Yes" : return true
        OTHERWISE : return false
    ENDSWITCH
ENDPROC   ;  Confirm_Yes
```

In the EmployeeModule procedure, the *response* variable was made private. When this procedure is not executing, this variable is not needed. Note that the *response* variable would be available to the Exben, Exemp, and Exsal scripts, according to the above scope rules. Similarly, the *cy_chc* variable in Confirm_Yes was made private. The Confirm_Yes procedure does not call any other procedures or scripts. Thus, the *cy_chc* variable is not available to any other procedure or script.

For Related Information:

▶▶ "Queries with Variable Criteria," p. 563.

▶▶ "Building WAIT Sessions," p. 581.

▶▶ "Creating Sample Application Scripts," p. 652.

FROM HERE...

Chapter Summary

This chapter presented an overview of the major features of PAL and introduced you to the basic building blocks that enable you to create sophisticated, relational database applications. You learned important definitions and characteristics of scripts and the PAL programming language—including expressions, variables, arrays, decision and loop structures, and procedures. You now have some of the tools to get started writing your own PAL scripts and the foundation for the material in the next chapter.

Even without programming, Paradox is a powerful database program. As you learn to use the Paradox Application Language, you will become aware of its true, practically unlimited potential. Refer to Chapter 19, "PAL Command and Function Reference," for proper syntax when using PAL commands and functions. Chapter 18 shows a complete sample application.

Using the Paradox Application Language

The preceding chapter introduces you to the fundamentals of the Paradox Application Language (PAL) and gives you an overview of the programming paradigm behind Paradox and PAL. The chapter also familiarizes you with the more traditional and basic PAL language elements. This chapter discusses building entire PAL applications and focuses on creating menus and user interaction. If you have not read Chapter 15, "An Overview of the Paradox Application Language," read it now because it contains information essential to understanding this chapter.

Recommendations for Using PAL

If you have not read the section "Recommendations for Using the Application Workshop" in Chapter 14, read it before proceeding with this chapter. Thorough planning for using the Application Workshop is important, but it's even more important when you are writing programs from scratch.

Many programmers give in to the temptation to write programs "off the tops of their heads." Even short programs you create this way tend to waste time and energy; you have to write and rewrite to correct oversights and omissions. Programs written on the spur of the moment tend to be poorly organized and difficult to maintain. They also tend to be "fragile" (break down often). Spending time now with pencil and paper can save much frustration later.

Making a design on paper doesn't mean that you have to produce reams of flow charts. A simple outline of your application, a diagram of your menu structure, and the submenus or actions to which each menu choice leads are adequate. In outline format, describe each task (action) your script carries out. As you plan the actions, note any conditions that must be established as prerequisites for the action (for example, placing tables on the workspace). Refer to the discussion in Chapter 14, "Using the Application Workshop," for a checklist of considerations for planning your script application. If your script will run in a multiuser environment, plan the time and method for locking and unlocking records and tables. You also should plan how to handle errors when you cannot apply locks.

As with the Application Workshop, use Paradox to create the tables, forms, report specifications, and other objects your application uses *before* you begin writing your script. You then can test various script modules as you write them and be more confident that your completed application works correctly.

Let Paradox objects accomplish as much of the work as possible. Make full use of validity checks, forms, reports, and so on. You often create script modules by recording Paradox menu activities or by saving queries. (Refer to Chapter 6, "Getting Started with Scripts and Keyboard Macros," for more information.)

Write your script in modules. Begin by creating your application's main menu, and write each submenu as a separate script. As you perfect each script module or subroutine, convert it to a procedure and store it in a procedure library (refer to Chapter 15, "An Overview of the Paradox Application Language").

For Related Information:

◄◄ "Procedures and Procedure Libraries," p. 551.

◄◄ "Recommendations for Using the Application Workshop," p. 460.

FROM HERE...

Queries with Variable Criteria

The Paradox system of Query by Example is flexible, easy to use, and powerful. A recorded query made by recording individual keystrokes using **S**cripts, **B**eginRecord or by using **S**cripts, **Q**uerySave is less flexible, however, than the interactive queries. Recorded queries always use the same table with the same criteria. A query may use matching a given date, for example, as a search criterion. The recorded query produces results for only the date you use when recording the script. If you need to repeat this query for a series of dates, the recorded script doesn't meet your needs. Yet this repetitive searching is the sort of task you probably want to script or program. The answer to the problem is to make variable some or all of the query criteria so that your script can fill in the query.

Paradox provides two methods of creating variable queries. Only the second method enables the query to be made on different tables.

The first method begins by using the **S**cripts, **Q**uerySave commands to set up and record a query (refer to Chapter 6, "Getting Started with Scripts and Keyboard Macros"). Carefully edit the resulting script. To make search criterion variable, replace the literal criterion in the recorded query with a PAL variable name preceded with a tilde (~) character. This variable you put in the recorded script is called a *tilde variable*, and it tells PAL to insert the contents of the variable in the query form at that point. When you make multitable queries interactively, you press F5 (Example) to connect tables in your query. Notice that the examples in your recorded query all begin with an underscore (_). The underscore tells PAL to use the text after the underscore as a linking example. For this reason, don't use tilde variable names containing underscores.

Include the edited query in a script that assigns a value to the PAL variable, places the query on the workspace, and performs the query. The example below shows an edited query recorded with **S**cripts, **Q**uerySave. The answer table this query produces includes every field of every record dated January 2, 1992, in the Phone92 table. (Note that the blank lines after the keyword Query and before the keyword Endquery are required.)

```
Query

Phone92  ¦       Date       ¦  Areacode  ¦   Number   ¦  Amount    ¦
         ¦ CheckPlus 1/2/92  ¦  CheckPlus ¦  CheckPlus ¦  CheckPlus ¦
         ¦                   ¦            ¦            ¦            ¦

Endquery
```

The next example performs the same query but uses a tilde variable to establish the date. Note that you assign a value to the variable *before* you place the query. Note also that you add the DO_IT! command to the query because this command isn't included when you save queries with **S**cripts **Q**uerySave.

```
matchdate = 1/2/92
Query

Phone92  ¦       Date       ¦  Areacode  ¦   Number   ¦  Amount    ¦
         ¦ CheckPlus ~matchdate ¦  CheckPlus ¦  CheckPlus ¦  CheckPlus ¦
         ¦                   ¦            ¦            ¦            ¦

Endquery
DO_IT!
```

In a real working script, the preceding query is made into a procedure or subroutine script, and the matchdate variable is assigned a variety of dates.

The second method to allow a recorded script to use variable criteria uses a query recorded as a series of keystrokes using **S**cripts **B**eginRecord. Carefully edit the script. You replace each table name or search criterion in the recorded query with a combination of three things. First, insert the TYPEIN command. The TYPEIN command causes PAL to insert a string expression as if it were typed at the keyboard. Next, insert a PAL variable containing a string expression. The variable you insert provides the string entered by the TYPEIN command. Third, insert the ENTER command. The ENTER command simulates a user pressing the Enter key on the keyboard. Following this method produces a query that is performed with variable criteria on more than one table. The following example shows a script created with **S**cripts, **B**eginRecord and performs the same query as the preceding two examples.

```
    Menu {Ask} {phone92} CheckPlus Right  " 1/2/92" Do_It!
```

The next example performs the same query but uses variables and the TYPEIN command. Note that you assign values to the variables *before* you use them in the query. Also note that a string, not the date value, represents the date.

```
qtable = "phone92"
matchdate = "1/2/92"
Menu {Ask} TYPEIN qtable ENTER CheckPlus Right TYPEIN matchdate Do_It!
```

Use the preceding example in a subroutine script or procedure to ask different queries of different tables. All the tables must have the same structure.

For Related Information:

◄◄ "Saving a Query," p. 180.

◄◄ "Recording and Playing Scripts," p. 222.

◄◄ "Procedures and Procedure Libraries," p. 551.

FROM HERE...

Creating Menus

The simplest way to present choices to your script's user is with menus. You're already familiar with the pull-down and pop-up menus Paradox uses. PAL provides commands to create similar menus and to create menus based on the contents of a disk directory or specially constructed arrays. The following sections describe how to create these menu types.

Creating Pull-Down Menus

The Paradox Main menu is an example of a pull-down menu. A bar across the top of the screen displays the primary menu choices. These selections lead directly to performing an action or lead to a submenu. If the selection leads to a submenu, a vertical list of the submenu choices "pulls down," and the user makes a final selection from the submenu. Submenus also can lead to other submenus. You create all of the primary menu choices and submenus with a single PAL command—SHOWPULLDOWN.

A menu created with SHOWPULLDOWN behaves like the Paradox Main menu. As long as the pull-down menu definition is in effect, the user can access the menu by pressing F10 or by clicking the menu bar. You can select **A**sk from the Paradox menu, for example, to display a query form. While the query form is still on the workspace, you can select any other Paradox menu item. You don't have to finish filling out the query before doing something else.

Use the PAL command SHOWPULLDOWN to create pull-down menus in your scripts. The SHOWPULLDOWN command begins the menu definition. You tell PAL the menu definition is complete by using the ENDMENU keyword at the end of your definition. The menu definition consists of a primary menu selection list, a descriptive prompt, and a *tag*. The tag is a string expression used by PAL to identify the menu selection chosen by a user. A menu selection list (after the primary selection leading to the submenu) defines a submenu. The keywords SUBMENU at the beginning and ENDSUBMENU at the end enclose the submenu definition. These keywords tell PAL that the definitions between compose a submenu. You can nest SUBMENU..ENDSUBMENU definitions to create submenus that lead to other submenus.

After you create a pull-down menu, it replaces the Paradox menu and remains displayed on-screen until a CLEARPULLDOWN command is used to explicitly remove your pull-down menu. The script user activates the pull-down menu the same way you activate the Paradox menu: press F10 (Menu) or click on the menu bar. The menu remains active until the user makes a selection, presses Esc, or clicks any place off the menu area.

The pull-down menu doesn't make your script wait for the user to make a selection. When PAL encounters the menu definition in a script, PAL displays the menu and continues executing the remainder of the script. The script can continue performing or processing other tasks until the user activates the menu. Your script must include a looping structure (usually a WHILE loop) that samples the event queue. Otherwise, your script ends before the user gets a chance to make a selection.

The pull-down menu doesn't directly return the user's selection. PAL handles the menu selection as a message event. (Refer to Chapter 15, "An Overview of the Paradox Application Language," for a definition of events and their types.) To determine a user's selection from your pull-down menu, you must use the GETEVENT command. This command initializes a dynamic array with event information; the dynamic array usually contains three elements. As with every event array, you subscript an element as "TYPE"; this element contains the string "MESSAGE", indicating that the event is a message event. Message event arrays also contain an element you subscript as "MESSAGE", which contains the actual message. For a selection from a pull-down menu, the message is "MENUSELECT." This information tells you that the message event is a menu selection and that the dynamic array contains at least one more element: the "MENUTAG" element. This element contains the string you specify as the menu selection's tag. Your script uses a SWITCH statement to branch to the appropriate subroutine script or procedure to carry out the selected action.

The following example shows the major features of the SHOWPULLDOWN command syntax. The script creates a pull-down menu and loops infinitely, processing events until the user selects Exit from the menu.

Define the pull-down menu. The keyword SHOWPULLDOWN tells PAL that a pull-down menu definition is beginning. For each menu selection you define, you must supply at least three pieces of information: the keyword the menu bar displays, the string that appears at the bottom of the screen as the menu choice prompt, and the menu selection's tag. This last item is the string PAL places in the "MENUTAG" element of the dynamic array created when GETEVENT is used to sample the event queue.

```
SHOWPULLDOWN
   "Browse" : "Browse the Phone Book Entries" : "Browse",
   "Add"    : "Add Names, Numbers, and Addresses" : "AddNode"
      SUBMENU
         "Name" : "Add a New Name" : "AddName",
         "N~u~mber" : "Add a Phone Number to Existing Name" : "AddNumber",
         "Address" : "Add an Address to Existing Name" : "AddAddress"
      ENDSUBMENU,
   "Utilities" : "Print, Renumber, or Index Phone Book" : "UtilNode"
      SUBMENU
         "Print" : "Print the Phone Book" : "PrintBook",
         SEPARATOR,
         "Renumber" : "Renumber the Phone Book Keys" : "PackBook",
         "Index" : "Create Maintained Indexes" : "Index"
      ENDSUBMENU,
   "Exit" : "Exit this application" : "Exit"
ENDMENU

WHILE TRUE <> FALSE
   GETEVENT TO MenuEvent
   WHILE (MenuEvent["TYPE"] <> "MESSAGE")   ; disregard all events except messages
      GETEVENT TO MenuEvent
   ENDWHILE

   IF MenuEvent["MESSAGE"] = "MENUSELECT" THEN
      MenuItemChosen = MenuEvent["MENUTAG"]   ; preserve the menu selection
   ELSE
      MenuItemChosen = ""   ; make sure nothing happens in the SWITCH
   ENDIF

   SWITCH
      CASE MenuItemChosen = "Browse" :
         MESSAGE "User Chose Browse Operation"   ; script or procedure called here
         SLEEP 2000 MESSAGE ""
      CASE MenuItemChosen = "AddName" :
         MESSAGE "User Chose Adding a Name"   ; script or procedure called here
```

```
      SLEEP 2000 MESSAGE ""
    CASE MenuItemChosen = "AddNumber" :
      MESSAGE "User Chose Adding a Number"  ; script or procedure called here
      SLEEP 2000 MESSAGE ""
    CASE MenuItemChosen = "AddAddress" :
      MESSAGE "User Chose Adding an Address"  ; script or procedure called here
      SLEEP 2000 MESSAGE ""
    CASE MenuItemChosen = "PrintBook" :
      MESSAGE "User Chose to Print the Phone Book"
      SLEEP 2000 MESSAGE ""
    CASE MenuItemChosen = "PackBook" :
      MESSAGE "User Chose to Renumber the Phone Book"
      SLEEP 2000 MESSAGE ""
    CASE MenuItemChosen = "Index" :
      MESSAGE "User Chose to create an Index"
      SLEEP 2000 MESSAGE ""
    CASE MenuItemChosen = "Exit" :
      MESSAGE "User Chose to Exit Application"
      SLEEP 2000 MESSAGE ""
      CLEARPULLDOWN
      QUIT
  ENDSWITCH
ENDWHILE ; true does not equal false
```

In the preceding example, the first line after the SHOWPULLDOWN keyword defines a menu choice with no submenu. The menu keyword "Browse" appears in the leftmost position of the pull-down menu bar. In the menu definition, "Browse" is separated from its prompt string by a colon (:). The next string in the definition is the prompt string, "Browse the Phone Book Entries", which appears at the bottom of the screen as an explanation of this menu choice. The last string in the definition, also separated by a colon, is the menu tag. When your script's user makes this menu selection, PAL places the tag string in the "MENUTAG" element of the dynamic array created when GETEVENT samples the event queue. The final part of this menu selection definition is the comma (,). A menu selection definition must end with a comma if it is followed by another menu selection definition.

The second line after the SHOWPULLDOWN command defines a menu selection leading to a submenu. This selection's keyword is "Add," and the prompt is "Add Names, Numbers, and Addresses." The menu tag for this selection is "AddNode"; although your script doesn't use this tag, the tag still is required. This menu selection opens a pull-down submenu with three choices. The SUBMENU keyword indicates the beginning of a submenu definition. All the information between the SUBMENU keyword and the ENDSUBMENU keyword is part of the submenu's definition.

Each menu selection inside the submenu follows the same format as the menu selection definitions on the main bar of the pull-down menu. A keyword is listed, followed by a prompt (explanation) string, and finally by a tag. The first line after the first SUBMENU keyword defines a menu selection called "Name." The prompt string "Add a New Name" displays at the bottom of the screen. When your script's user makes this menu selection, PAL places the tag "AddName" in the "MENUTAG" element of the dynamic array created when GETEVENT samples the event queue.

The second line of this submenu needs some special explanation. You may have noticed that all of the Paradox menu selections have a high-lighted letter in their names. When the menu is active, you can press the highlighted letter to make the menu selection instead of using the mouse or the arrow keys. The menus you create for your scripts be-have in a similar fashion. PAL highlights a menu selection's first letter by default. This default usually is adequate because having the high-lighted letter as a mnemonic for the selection is desirable. Sometimes, as in the example, two menu selections begin with the same letter. To have a unique letter for each selection, you sometimes need to indicate the letter you want to highlight. Enclose the letter you want to highlight with a pair of tilde (~) characters. In the example, the letter *u* is high-lighted in the "N~u~mber" menu selection.

The third menu selection that appears on the pull-down menu bar is the "Utilities" selection. This menu selection also leads to a submenu. The definition for the "Utilities" submenu uses a separator line to group, or set off visually, the choices appearing on the submenu. The first selection the submenu displays is the "Print" choice. A name, a prompt string, and a tag string, as required, define this choice. The special keyword SEPARATOR follows the "Print" choice. This keyword indicates that when the submenu is displayed, PAL should place a hori-zontal line in the submenu at this point. This line divides the submenu into two distinct areas. You can use as many separator lines as you want.

The example defines the final menu item (the "Exit" selection) and ends the pull-down menu definition with the ENDMENU keyword. Note that a comma separates each menu selection definition, and that the menu selection definitions for submenus are also separated from each other with commas.

PAL displays the pull-down menu's bar across the top of the screen at this point, replacing the Paradox menu. PAL does not wait, but contin-ues executing the remaining commands in the script. In the example, the command after the menu definition starts a WHILE loop, which executes an infinite number of times (True never equals False). Assum-ing that the example script represents your application's top level, you want this WHILE loop to run forever, gathering and processing events, until the user explicitly signals the desire to leave your application. In this example, the user chooses Exit from your pull-down menu to end the script. Without the infinite WHILE loop, PAL executes the rest of the commands in the script until the end of the script is reached; the user never has an opportunity to make a choice from the menu.

The first action that occurs inside the infinite WHILE loop is a GETEVENT command. This command initializes a dynamic array with information about the current event in the event queue. Immediately after the GETEVENT command is another WHILE loop. The inner WHILE loop repeats the GETEVENT command until a message event occurs. As soon as a message event occurs, the event-testing loop stops executing, and an IF..THEN..ELSE statement determines whether the message event is the result of a menu selection. If the event is a menu event, the script assigns to the variable *MenuItemChosen* the current value of the menu tag in the menu selection message event; otherwise, the script sets the variable to have a blank string value.

The final action the example performs is a SWITCH statement that chooses which procedure or script to branch to, depending on the menu selection made by the user. The example has only MESSAGE statements for each branch of the SWITCH. (The MESSAGE command displays a message in the lower right area of the screen). In an actual application, replace the MESSAGE commands with procedure calls or a PLAY command that names a subroutine script to carry out the task selected by the user. When the subroutine script or procedure is done executing, this script continues executing at the beginning of the infinite WHILE loop. Events are sampled until a message event occurs. When another message event occurs it is evaluated by the IF..THEN..ELSE statement, and the SWITCH statement executes again.

The example script repeats the event sampling and evaluation process until explicitly stopped. When the user selects "Exit," the script ends by using the QUIT command, which returns the user to Paradox. Note that you must use the CLEARPULLDOWN command to remove the pull-down menu before the script ends.

Figure 16.1 shows the pull-down menu created with the example script; the "Add" submenu is pulled down. The example in this section is a complete script. To see how it behaves, type it into the Paradox Script Editor, and select **G**o from the Script Editor menu. (Refer to Chapter 17, "Using the Script Editor and PAL Debugger," for more information on using the Script Editor.)

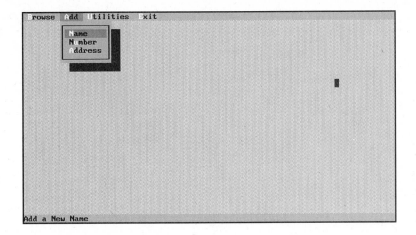

FIG. 16.1

The sample pull-down menu.

The preceding example illustrates the basic steps for creating and using a pull-down menu. SHOWPULLDOWN menu options and variations exist that are not described here. For a description of these items, refer to Chapter 19, "PAL Command and Function Reference," and to the *PAL Reference* supplied with Paradox.

Creating Pop-Up Menus

A pop-up menu is a rectangular box that appears on-screen and vertically lists the menu choices. An example of a Paradox pop-up menu is the PAL Menu (press Alt-F10). Pop-up menus can have choices that lead to other submenus.

You create a pop-up menu in your script with the SHOWPOPUP command. This command places a titled pop-up menu at specified coordinates on-screen and waits until the user makes a choice.

The following example creates the same menu as the preceding pull-down menu example but presents the menu as a pop-up menu. In practice, you usually don't use a pop-up menu as the main menu for an application. You use the pop-up menu in smaller programs or subroutine procedures and scripts.

```
SHOWPOPUP "Phone Book" @ 5, 10
   "Browse" : "Browse the Phone Book Entries" : "Browse",
   "Add"    : "Add Names, Numbers, and Addresses" : "AddNode"
     SUBMENU
       "Name" : "Add a New Name" : "AddName",
       "N~u~mber" : "Add a Phone Number to Existing Name" : "AddNumber",
       "Address" : "Add an Address to Existing Name" : "AddAddress"
```

```
      ENDSUBMENU,
    "Utilities" : "Print Phone Book, Renumber Entries, Create Indexes" :
  "UtilNode"
      SUBMENU
        "Print" : "Print the Phone Book" : "PrintBook",
        SEPARATOR,
        "Renumber" : "Renumber the Phone Book Keys" : "PackBook",
        "Index" : "Create Maintained Indexes" : "Index"
      ENDSUBMENU,
    "Exit" : "Exit this application" : "Exit"
ENDMENU
TO MenuItemChosen

SWITCH
  CASE MenuItemChosen = "Browse" :
    MESSAGE "User Chose Browse Operation"  ; script or procedure called her
    SLEEP 2000 MESSAGE ""
  CASE MenuItemChosen = "AddName" :
    MESSAGE "User Chose Adding a Name"  ; script or procedure called here
    SLEEP 2000 MESSAGE ""
  CASE MenuItemChosen = "AddNumber" :
    MESSAGE "User Chose Adding a Number"  ; script or procedure called here
    SLEEP 2000 MESSAGE ""
  CASE MenuItemChosen = "AddAddress" :
    MESSAGE "User Chose Adding an Address"  ; script or procedure called he
    SLEEP 2000 MESSAGE ""
  CASE MenuItemChosen = "PrintBook" :
    MESSAGE "User Chose to Print the Phone Book"
    SLEEP 2000 MESSAGE ""
  CASE MenuItemChosen = "PackBook" :
    MESSAGE "User Chose to Renumber the Phone Book"
    SLEEP 2000 MESSAGE ""
  CASE MenuItemChosen = "Index" :
    MESSAGE "User Chose to create an Index"
    SLEEP 2000 MESSAGE ""
  CASE MenuItemChosen = "Exit" :
    MESSAGE "User Chose to Exit Application"
    SLEEP 2000 MESSAGE ""
    QUIT
ENDSWITCH
```

The example script begins with the keyword SHOWPOPUP, indicating the beginning of a pop-up menu definition. Everything between the SHOWPOPUP keyword and the ENDMENU keyword is part of the menu definition. A string expression for the menu's title immediately follows the SHOWPOPUP keyword. The example uses a literal string, but you can use any valid PAL string expression. The information after the title string tells PAL where to place the menu. Row and column coordinates follow the @ symbol. PAL places the pop-up menu's top left corner at the specified coordinates. You also can have PAL center the pop-up menu in the middle of the screen by using the CENTERED keyword instead of the @ symbol.

Now, define the menu selections. You define each menu selection on the pop-up menu the same way you define selections for a pull-down menu. Format the selection definition with the menu selection's name appearing first, followed by the selection's prompt string, and finally by the menu selection's tag string. A colon separates each part of the definition.

You define submenus on the pop-up menu the same way you define submenus for a pull-down menu. Place the keyword SUBMENU immediately after the menu selection definition leading to the submenu you're defining, and use the keyword ENDSUBMENU to end the submenu definition. You also use the tilde (~) here to change the highlighted letter in the menu selection's name.

The pop-up menu waits, suspending your script's execution until the user makes a selection. PAL stores the tag string corresponding to the user's selection in the variable listed after the TO keyword at the end of the menu definition. If your script's user chooses the "Browse" selection from the pop-up menu in the example, PAL assigns the string "Browse" to the MenuItemChosen variable.

To be complete, the example includes a SWITCH statement to branch to the appropriate action the user's selection determines.

Figure 16.2 shows the pop-up menu created by the example script; the "Utilities" submenu is also shown.

The example script in this section illustrates the basic steps for creating and using a pop-up menu. Paradox provides other options and variations for the SHOWPOPUP menu. For a description of these additional items, refer to Chapter 19, "PAL Command and Function Reference," and to the *PAL Reference* supplied with Paradox.

Using SHOWARRAY

The SHOWARRAY command creates a special pop-up menu at the center of the screen. The menu created with the SHOWARRAY command shows as a pick list inside a dialog box. The dialog box is untitled, and contains only OK and Cancel buttons. SHOWARRAY uses a pair of fixed arrays to specify the choices shown in the pick list and the prompts shown at the bottom of the screen.

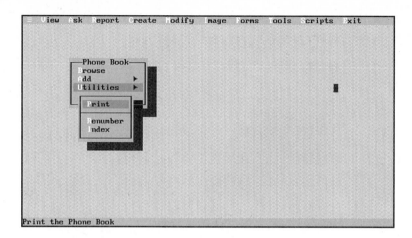

FIG. 16.2

The sample pop-up menu.

Use the SHOWARRAY command to construct menus from the contents of fields in a table, a cumulation of the user's input, or any other source of information you can store as a string in a fixed array. When PAL displays a pick list menu constructed with SHOWARRAY, your script will wait for the user to make a selection before continuing.

The following example declares two fixed arrays and assigns values to their elements. You don't have to perform the array declaration and initialization immediately before the SHOWARRAY command, but you must declare the arrays and assign values to their elements before you use them in the SHOWARRAY command.

```
ARRAY MList[4]                  ; array for list of menu choices
ARRAY MPrompt[4]                ; array for list of corresponding prompts
MList[1] = "Browse"
MPrompt[1] = "Browse the Phone Book Entries"
MList[2] = "Add"
MPrompt[2] = "Add Names, Numbers, and Addresses"
MList[3] = "Utilities"
MPrompt[3] = "Print Phone Book, Renumber Entries, Create Indexes"
MList[4] = " Exit"
MPrompt[4] = "Exit this application"

SHOWARRAY MList MPrompt
   DEFAULT MList[2]
   TO MenuItemChosen

SWITCH
   CASE MenuItemChosen = "Browse" :
     MESSAGE "User Chose Browse Operation"  ; script or procedure called he
     SLEEP 2000 MESSAGE ""
   CASE MenuItemChosen = "Add" :
```

```
      MESSAGE "User Chose Add Operation"  ; script or procedure called here
      SLEEP 2000 MESSAGE ""
    CASE MenuItemChosen = "Utilities" :
      MESSAGE "User Chose Utilities Operation"
      SLEEP 2000 MESSAGE ""
    CASE MenuItemChosen = " Exit" :
      MESSAGE "User Chose to Exit Application"
      SLEEP 2000 MESSAGE ""
      QUIT
ENDSWITCH
```

In the preceding example, you start the definition of the pick list dialog box with the keyword SHOWARRAY. Immediately after the keyword SHOWARRAY, you place the name of the fixed array containing the strings which PAL uses for the menu choices. Next, you place the name of the fixed array containing the strings that PAL displays at the bottom of the screen to explain the menu choices. Now you place the optional keyword DEFAULT after the array names. The DEFAULT keyword causes PAL to place the highlight bar over a particular menu selection as the default choice. If you don't use the DEFAULT keyword, PAL places the highlight bar over the first item in the list of menu selections. In this example, the second element in the array of choices is the default setting: the "Add" choice. After specifying the default choice, you place the keyword TO. The TO keyword is required; it tells PAL to store the user's menu choice in the variable named *MenuItemChosen*.

Unlike the previously introduced methods of creating menus, SHOWARRAY doesn't require you to define a tag for the choices. When the user makes a selection, PAL places a string expression equal to the name of the menu selection into the variable specified by the TO keyword. In this example, if the user chooses "Browse" from the menu, PAL assigns the string "Browse" to the variable named *MenuItemChosen*.

The SHOWARRAY command displays the menu as a pick list inside a dialog box. The dialog box has two push buttons—an "OK" button and a "Cancel" button. Your script's user selects a choice by moving the highlight bar over the desired item in the pick list, and then pressing Enter, or clicking the "OK" button. When your script's user makes a selection, PAL sets the global variable RetVal to True, and then assigns the menu choice string to the variable specified by the TO keyword. Your script's user can cancel the menu by selecting the "Cancel" button. When the "Cancel" button is selected, PAL sets the global variable RetVal to False and assigns the string "Esc" to the variable specified by the TO keyword. Refer to Chapter 19 for more information about the RetVal global variable.

The definition of the SHOWARRAY menu is complete after you specify the TO variable. The example includes a SWITCH statement that branches to call the appropriate subroutines to process the choice. To see how this example behaves, use the Script Editor to enter this example and play it. Figure 16.3 shows the dialog box created by the SHOWARRAY example.

The example in this section illustrates the basic steps for creating and using a menu created with SHOWARRAY. This chapter doesn't discuss all of the options and variations for the SHOWARRAY command. For a description of these other items, refer to Chapter 19, "PAL Command and Function Reference," and to the *PAL Reference* supplied with Paradox.

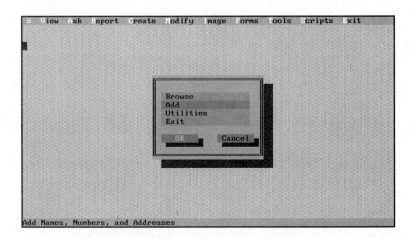

FIG. 16.3

The dialog box created by the SHOWARRAY example.

FROM HERE...

For Related Information:

◄◄ "Using Paradox Menus and Prompts," p. 39.

◄◄ "Creating the Application's Main Menu," p. 468.

◄◄ "The PAL Programming Paradigm," p. 508.

▶▶ "Viewing the Main Menu," p. 626.

Handling Windows

Chapter 15, "An Overview of the Paradox Application Language," introduces you to a definition of windows and window handles. If you haven't read that chapter, read it now. The following discussion mentions several of the PAL commands that you use to manipulate windows. Some of the commands are explained or shown in examples in this section. Too many commands exist, however, to describe in detail here. For full information on the syntax and use of the commands and functions this section mentions, refer to Chapter 19, "PAL Command and Function Reference," and the *PAL Reference* supplied with Paradox.

As you manipulate windows in your scripts, remember to record the window handle of each window as it is opened. Keep in mind that commands such as VIEW and EDIT, both of which place tables on the workspace, implicitly create a window. Immediately record the window handle after using PAL commands that place objects on the workspace. Record the handle by using the WINDOW HANDLE command or the GETWINDOW function. The following example shows one way of recording the handle:

```
VIEW "Phone92"
WINDOW HANDLE CURRENT TO winhandle
```

The first line in the example places a table on the workspace. Paradox automatically opens a window to display the table. Viewing the table also makes it the current image so that you can record immediately the current window handle and know that later the handle refers to the view of the "Phone92" table.

When a window is closed, its window handle becomes invalid. Paradox doesn't use that window handle again during this Paradox session. Using an invalid window handle in one of the PAL commands affecting windows results in a script error. To prevent a script error, use the ISWINDOW function to check that a window is open. This function returns a value of True if the window is open and False if it's not. Use the WINDOW LIST command to obtain a list of the currently valid window handles.

Working with Canvases and Images

The windows on the Paradox workspace display two kinds of objects. The first category of objects is every Paradox object. Placing a table on the workspace, opening a Report or Form Designer session, and so on, produces a Paradox object displayed in a window. These Paradox objects are *images* on the workspace. The PAL canvas is the second category of objects displayed in a window. Windows you create your-self (using the WINDOW CREATE command) contain PAL canvases. A *canvas* is a special type of object. When your script prints output to the screen, the output goes to a canvas.

The current window may be a canvas or an image window. Only the current window has its display updated by Paradox, and only if that window's echo state is on.

The current image may not be the current window. For example, if you place a table on the workspace and then open a window to display a message, the current image is not the current window. The table you placed on the workspace is still the current image, but the canvas win-dow you just opened is the current window. Actions performed by your script, or your script's user, that change the appearance of the current image—like a PgDn keystroke or command— still affect the current image. The change to the current image is not shown on the screen display right away, because the table image is not in the current win-dow. The changes in the current image's display will be shown on the screen whenever the current image again becomes the current window.

In the desktop analogy, the windows on-screen are like pieces of paper on a desktop that can be placed on top of each other like real pieces of paper. Windows on the workspace may be placed by your application, your application's user, or Paradox. The order of the windows on-screen is called the *z-order* of the windows because it's the order of windows going in the z-axis (3rd dimensional) direction out of the screen toward you (or "up" from the "desktop"). Windows on the screen are usually discussed in terms of their z-order. A window's posi-tion in the z-order is usually more important than the window's sequen-tial order of screen placement. The current window, by definition, is at the top of the z-order. As different windows are made current, their z-order diverges from the sequential order in which the windows were placed.

The z-order contains three layers. The bottom layer is the desktop layer which consists of the Paradox desktop and Paradox menu. Para-dox objects and canvas windows appear on the desktop layer. The next layer, the echo layer, doesn't have visible components of its own. The echo layer controls the display of the desktop layer under it and con-tained by it. Your script controls the echo layer by using the ECHO command. When the echo is off (the default when a script starts play-ing), the desktop display is frozen and doesn't change until your script turns the echo on or stops playing. When the echo is turned on, changes to the desktop appear as they occur. To turn on the system echo, use the ECHO NORMAL, ECHO FAST, or ECHO SLOW commands. Unless you're debugging a script and need to have the image display change slowly, use ECHO NORMAL. You can turn off the system echo by using the ECHO OFF command. The system echo is always on when a WAIT command is in effect.

The top layer in the z-order is the application layer. This is the layer in which your script's pull-down menus, pop-up menus, dialog boxes, and the message bar appear. This layer is always visible, regardless of whether the echo is on or off. Even if the echo is off, a pop-up menu still appears because it's in the application layer.

You can use the control provided by the echo layer to compose complex displays without the user seeing the results of each step in creating the display. Turn off the echo and compose the display. Your output is placed on its canvas "behind the scenes." Now turn on the echo. Your screen fully appears.

Each window also has a local echo control. This control is an attribute of the window and is controlled by using the WINDOW ECHO command and by supplying a valid window handle. You also must supply a logical expression to indicate whether the echo should be turned on or off. The first line in the following example shows how to turn on a local window echo. The second line shows how to turn off a local window echo.

```
WINDOW ECHO mywin True

WINDOW ECHO mywin False
```

Another way that your script may control a window's echo attribute is by using a dynamic array and the WINDOW SETATTRIBUTES command. Using this technique, your script first initializes the dynamic array using WINDOW GETATTRIBUTES, sets the echo attribute to true, and then uses the WINDOW SETATTRIBUTES command. Using the WINDOW ECHO command, however, usually is easier.

Setting the Current Window

By now, you know about windows and window handles. You also know how to get and save a window handle when Paradox creates the window or when your script creates the window using WINDOW CREATE. As mentioned earlier, your screen output will go only to the current window. One reason you've been cautioned to preserve each window handle is so that you can select any given window as the current window.

Use the WINDOW SELECT command and a valid window handle to make a window the current window. Use the SETCANVAS command and a valid window handle to make a canvas window the current window.

If you have procedures or subroutine scripts that create or change the current window, you should save the current window when the procedure or script begins and restore it when the procedure or script finishes. The following example shows a procedure declaration and a sample call to the procedure. The procedure uses the GETCANVAS command to preserve the current canvas window handle. As the procedure executes, it opens another canvas window and makes it current. As a final step, the procedure restores the current canvas before returning.

```
PROC watch()
PRIVATE x
  x = GETCANVAS()
  WINDOW CREATE @10,26 WIDTH 34 HEIGHT 5 to canvaswindow
  @1,4 ?? "Watch out for that tree!"
  SLEEP 5000
  WINDOW CLOSE
  SETCANVAS x
ENDPROC

echo normal  ; turn echo on so the display changes show
watch()
```

Moving, Resizing, and Closing Windows

PAL provides simple commands for moving, resizing, and closing windows.

A window's location is determined by the screen coordinates of its top left corner. When your script moves a window, you must specify the new window location with a set of row and column coordinates. Your script uses the WINDOW MOVE command to move a window. You supply a valid window handle and a set of coordinates. In the following example, *mywin* is a variable containing a valid window handle. The command in the example moves the window so that its top left corner is at row 5, column 12.

```
WINDOW MOVE mywin TO 5, 12
```

A window's size is measured in rows and columns. Your script uses the WINDOW RESIZE or the WINDOW MAXIMIZE commands to change a window's size. Like when you choose Maximize from the System Menu, using the WINDOW MAXIMIZE command in a script performs a toggle. If the window already is maximized (as large as possible) when PAL executes the WINDOW MAXIMIZE command, then PAL makes the window smaller. When PAL makes the window smaller as a result of the WINDOW MAXIMIZE command, the window is usually returned to its starting size. If the window is already smaller than the full screen when PAL executes the WINDOW MAXIMIZE command, then PAL makes the window as large as possible.

Use the WINDOW RESIZE command in your script to control the size of a window more explicitly than WINDOW MAXIMIZE. When PAL executes the WINDOW RESIZE command, the window size is always changed to the size specified by the WINDOW RESIZE command. The following example shows a script using the WINDOW RESIZE command. The variable name mywin contains a valid window handle. When the command in the example is executed, PAL changes the size of the window specified by the window handle from its current size to be 5 rows high and 20 columns wide.

```
WINDOW RESIZE mywin 5, 20
```

To close a window, your script uses the WINDOW CLOSE command. Only the current window can be closed. Your script cannot close a window that contains a table in Edit or CoEdit mode. When the WINDOW CLOSE command is executed, PAL closes the current window and sets the global variable RetVal to True. If PAL cannot close the current window for some reason, PAL will set the global variable RetVal to False. Refer to Chapter 19, "PAL Command and Function Reference," for more information on the global variable *RetVal*.

For Related Information:

◀◀ "Understanding Windows," p. 47.

◀◀ "Windows," p. 509.

FROM HERE...

Building WAIT Sessions

A WAIT session is almost essential to script-controlled data entry in Paradox. Use the WAIT command to simplify browsing data tables for viewing or editing and gain the benefit of having Paradox accomplish most of the work for you.

The WAIT command does exactly what its name says: waits. Depending on which form of the command you use, WAIT waits for one or more specified keystrokes or one or more specified events. Using the WAIT command in your script locks the user into one field, one record, one table, or the entire workspace until the specified keystrokes or events occur. While the WAIT command is in effect, your script's user has a limited interaction with the WAIT object (field, record, table, or workspace). The user, however, is locked into the current activity (viewing or editing) until one of the specified keystrokes or events occur.

To use the WAIT command, your script must place at least one table on the workspace and select the desired view. If your script intends to let the user modify the table, your script places the table in Edit or CoEdit mode. The last step before beginning the WAIT command is to place the cursor in an appropriate location for the type of WAIT session being set up. If you're going to confine the user to one field, you must place the cursor in that field before starting the WAIT. If you're going to confine the user to one record, you must place the cursor in that record. If you're limiting the user to one table, make sure that table is the current image before starting the WAIT.

You don't have to worry about the echo state of the canvas when you use the WAIT command. In fact, regardless of the state of the local or system echo, a table being used in a WAIT session always appears so that the user can interact with it.

The user's interaction with a field or table is limited. Only the movement and regular typing keys are active. While the WAIT is in effect, PAL disables all of the function keys (unless one or more of them are specified as one of the keys being waited for). The examples of the WAIT command shown later in this section use the keyword TABLE. The TABLE option gives the user freedom of the entire table. Another option you may use with the WAIT command is the RECORD option. This option causes the WAIT command to limit the user to one record in the table. The user can move the cursor from field to field but cannot move out of the record. The third option available is the FIELD option. This option limits the user to one field. The last option that you use with the WAIT command is the WORKSPACE option. The WORKSPACE option limits the user to whatever images are on the workspace when the WAIT begins. You also use the WORKSPACE option to limit the user's interaction to an Editor session, Report Designer, or Form Designer session.

The following example uses the first form of the WAIT command and waits for a list of specified keystrokes. When you list the keystrokes to wait for, you must use the PAL key equivalent strings. In this form, PAL returns the value of the pressed key (from the list of keystrokes) by setting the global variable *RetVal*. Refer to Chapter 19, "PAL Command and Function Reference," for more information about global variables and *RetVal*.

```
VIEW " Customer"
EDITKEY
WHILE (True)
  WAIT TABLE
    PROMPT "Press Ctrl-U to Undo last transaction; Press F2 when done."
  UNTIL "Down", "Up", "Undo", "Do_It!"
  SWITCH
    CASE RetVal = "Down":
      EDITLOG INDEX
      EDITLOG MARK
      DOWN
    CASE RetVal = "Up":
      EDITLOG INDEX
      EDITLOG MARK
      UP
    CASE RetVal = "Undo":
      EDITLOG REVERT
    CASE RetVal = "Do_It!":
      DO_IT!
      WINDOW CLOSE
      QUITLOOP
  ENDSWITCH
ENDWHILE
```

The preceding example uses the WAIT command to look for several different keystrokes. When the user presses one of these keys, the script uses the SWITCH control structure to take an appropriate action. First, the script places the "Customer" table on the workspace and then puts the table in Edit mode. The script then starts an infinite WHILE loop so that the actions in the loop continue until the user makes an explicit command to stop. The WAIT command starts immediately inside the WHILE loop. The TABLE keyword indicates that the user can move freely throughout the entire table. The optional PROMPT keyword follows the TABLE keyword. The optional PROMPT keyword causes the string expression after it to appear in the prompt line at the bottom of the screen. Next, place the UNTIL keyword and follow it with the list of keystrokes that the WAIT command will wait for. The WAIT command in the preceding example ends when any of the following keys are pressed: up-arrow, down-arrow, Ctrl-U (Undo), or F2 (Do-It!).

The next example uses the second form of the WAIT command. The second form of the WAIT command waits for a list of specific events, instead of keystrokes. When one of the specified events occurs, PAL executes the WAIT procedure. The WAIT procedure contains the PAL commands that you want executed when one of the events specified by the WAIT command occurs. Because the second form of the WAIT command waits for events, it is called an event-driven WAIT.

The next example shows how you construct an event-driven WAIT session. The first part of the script is a procedure definition for the WAIT procedure. A WAIT procedure must always have three parameters. PAL calls your WAIT procedure and sets the actual value of the parameters when one of the events that you listed occurs. The first parameter that PAL passes to the WAIT procedure is a string expression containing the name of the type of event that occurred. The second parameter that PAL passes to the WAIT procedure is a dynamic array structured to contain information about the event that occurred. The third parameter that PAL passes to the WAIT procedure is the cycle number for the event that occurred. When you write the WAIT procedure, you will use the event type information, and the dynamic array describing the event, to determine what action your script will take. You don't usually use the cycle number.

The WAIT procedure defined in this example first uses the information in the dynamic array parameter that PAL passed to it to test if this is a keystroke event. Next the script uses a SWITCH statement to choose appropriate actions based on the key that the user pressed. Notice in the example that each branch of the SWITCH statement ends with a RETURN statement. The RETURN statement ends the execution of commands in the WAIT procedure. The RETURN statement also causes the WAIT procedure to return a value. PAL examines this returned value at the end of the WAIT procedure and uses the value to determine whether the WAIT command should be ended. If the WAIT procedure returns 0, PAL will continue with the WAIT; PAL also passes the event on to be processed by Paradox. If the WAIT procedure returns a value of 1, PAL will continue the WAIT, but does not allow Paradox to process the event. If the WAIT procedure returns a value of 2, then PAL will end the WAIT command.

You start the definition of an event-driven WAIT by placing the keyword WAIT in your script. Next, you use one of the keywords FIELD, RECORD, TABLE, or WORKSPACE to define the type of WAIT session you are defining. This is the same as the WAIT form already discussed.

After you specify the type of WAIT, you must place the keyword PROC, followed by the name of your WAIT procedure. Notice that you must enclose the name of your WAIT procedure in quotation marks, and that you do not include the parentheses. The WAIT procedure in the example is named mywaitproc.

Now you list all of the events for which you want PAL to invoke your WAIT procedure. The script example below uses the keyword ALL to indicate that PAL should invoke the WAIT procedure for any event. Refer to Chapter 19, "Command and Function Reference," for a list of the other keywords that you use to specify events.

The script places the "Customer" table on the workspace, and then puts the table in Edit mode. The WAIT command begins next. The script's user is allowed to freely edit the entire "Customer" table. Any event that may occur now will cause PAL to execute the WAIT procedure named mywaitproc.

```
PROC mywaitproc( EventType, EventRecord, CNumber )
  IF EventRecord["TYPE"] = "KEY" THEN
    SWITCH
      CASE EventRecord["KEYCODE"] = "Down" :
        EDITLOG INDEX
        EDITLOG MARK
        RETURN 0
      CASE EventRecord["KEYCODE"] = "Up" :
        EDITLOG INDEX
        EDITLOG MARK
        RETURN 0
      CASE EventRecord["KEYCODE"] = "Undo" :
        EDITLOG REVERT
        RETURN 0
      CASE EventRecord["KEYCODE"] = ASC("Do_It!") :
        DO_IT!
        RETURN 2  ; return code of 2 means end the WAIT
    ENDSWITCH
  ENDIF
RETURN 0  ; return code of 0 lets PAL process event, and continue WAIT
ENDPROC
VIEW "Customer"
EDITKEY
PROMPT "Press Ctrl-U to Undo last transaction; Press F2 when done."
WAIT TABLE
  PROC "mywaitproc" ALL
ENDWAIT
CLEARALL  ; remove all images from workspace
```

Paradox uses several other options and variations of the WAIT command, particularly the ones involving the different event types that are trapped with the second form of the command. Because these options are too complex to discuss here, refer to Chapter 19, "PAL Command and Function Reference," and to the *PAL Reference* supplied with Paradox.

For Related Information:

▶▶ "The RentalWaitForm( ) Procedure," p. 665.

▶▶ "The RentalWaitProc( ) Procedure," p. 666.

FROM HERE...

Working with Dialog Boxes

By now, you've had some experience using and filling out dialog boxes. Chapter 15 gives you a description and a definition of dialog boxes and dialog box controls. Because of the number and versatility of the available dialog box controls, this section cannot cover them all in detail. This section, however, does get you started with creating dialog boxes in your scripts. This section also describes the construction of a dialog box incorporating some of the most common controls. First, a dialog box with only two buttons is constructed, and then each control will be added and explained.

While the dialog box is being constructed, notice that some controls— for example, check boxes—must have an initial value assigned before the dialog box begins.

Defining Control Elements

Before you can begin defining the control elements in a dialog box, you must define some information about the dialog box itself. You can see from the example in the next section that the dialog box command begins with the keyword SHOWDIALOG. This indicates the beginning of a dialog box definition. Everything between the SHOWDIALOG and the ENDDIALOG keywords is part of the dialog box definition. The first part of the definition you must provide is a valid string expression that will be used as the dialog box's title. The name of the dialog box created by the example script is "Sample Dialog."

The next information you must provide is the location of the dialog box. Remember that the dialog box is a variety of windows, and the row and column coordinates of its upper left corner specify its location. The final items you must define for the dialog box are its height and width, measured in rows and columns. Control elements make up the rest of the dialog box definition.

Working with Push Buttons

The following example creates a dialog box with two push buttons: an OK button and a Cancel button. Push buttons return a value in a variable. The example begins by setting the button variable *BtnVal* to a blank string value.

The push button definition begins with the keyword PUSHBUTTON. The @ symbol indicates the row and column coordinates at which the button is placed. The coordinates are relative to the window, and the top left corner of the window is row 0 and column 0. Next, specify the push button's width (a push button's height is always one line, so you do not need to specify the height). After specifying the button's width, a string expression is used to provide the button's label. The button's width should be about two characters greater than the width of its label.

The first button the example defines uses an optional keyword, CANCEL. This keyword tells PAL that the button in the dialog box will be a Cancel button. If this button is pressed, the dialog box will be canceled.

The next option is the required keyword, VALUE. The string expression following this keyword is the value that will be assigned the variable indicated by the keyword TO. This button assigns the string value "No File" to the *BtnVal* variable. The required keyword TAG follows the VALUE expression. The TAG keyword indicates a string expression that will be used as the button's identification for certain types of event processing.

The second button uses another optional keyword in its definition: OK. This tells PAL that when this button is pressed, the dialog should be accepted. Like the first definition, the push button's location and width are specified first. Another important optional keyword is being used in the definition of this second button: DEFAULT. DEFAULT tells PAL that when the user presses Enter, it's the same as pressing this button, no matter what control is selected. The second button example puts the value "Good File" in the variable *BtnVal* when this button is pressed, and the dialog will be accepted.

```
BtnVal = ""   ; used to store the button value

SHOWDIALOG "Sample Dialog"
   @ 5,5 HEIGHT 15 WIDTH 70
   PUSHBUTTON @ 1,10 WIDTH 10 "Cancel"
     CANCEL VALUE "No File" TAG "quit" TO BtnVal
   PUSHBUTTON @ 1,20 WIDTH 10 "OK"
     OK DEFAULT VALUE "Good File" TAG "Selected File" TO BtnVal
ENDDIALOG
```

Working with Pick Lists

PAL provides several ready-made pick list controls. These controls enable you to create pick lists showing the contents of arrays or disk directories as the body of the list. Only one type of pick list appears here. You define the other pick lists in a similar way. Use the PICKTABLE control to create a pick list of tables in the current directory. Use PICKARRAY and PICKDYNARRAY to create pick lists based on the contents of arrays.

You will now add a PICKFILE pick list control to the dialog box. This control creates and displays a pick list showing files in the current directory. Use a DOS path and wild cards to determine which files will be shown in the pick list. (Refer to your DOS manual for information regarding directory paths and the DOS wild-card characters for file names.)

The PICKFILE control was inserted just ahead of the push button definitions. The pick list definition begins with the keyword PICKFILE. As with all the other dialog box controls, the next information you must supply in the pick list definition is the row and column coordinates of the pick list. The upper left corner of the pick list will be placed at these coordinates. Next, the pick list's height, width, and number of columns are specified.

After supplying the physical dimensions of the pick list, a string expression for the DOS path is required. Only files that match this expression's file specifications will appear in the pick list. Now you must provide a string expression to be used as the tag for the pick list. The final part of the PICKFILE pick list definition is the required keyword TO, followed by the variable name to which the selected file name will be assigned. In the example, when the dialog is accepted, the highlighted file name in the pick list is assigned to the variable *SelFile*.

Note some other additions to the dialog box besides the PICKFILE definition. A print line was inserted after the height and width definitions for the dialog box. This line prints the text "Pick list of Files" inside the dialog box at the specified row and column coordinates. This kind of a print line is a *canvas element* in the dialog box. In the example, the canvas element is used to print a legend over the pick list.

```
SelFile = ""   ; used to store the file selected from picklist
BtnVal = ""    ; used to store the button value

SHOWDIALOG "Sample Dialog"
  @ 5,5 HEIGHT 15 WIDTH 70
  @ 3,5 ?? "Pick list of Files"
  PICKFILE @ 4,5 HEIGHT 8 WIDTH 20 COLUMNS 1
    "D:\\PDOX40\\*.*" TAG "Files in the directory" TO SelFile
  PUSHBUTTON @ 1,10 WIDTH 10 "Cancel"
    CANCEL VALUE "No File" TAG "quit" TO BtnVal
  PUSHBUTTON @ 1,20 WIDTH 10 "OK"
    OK DEFAULT VALUE "Good File" TAG "Selected File" TO BtnVal
ENDDIALOG
```

Working with Check Boxes

The next control you will add to the dialog box is a bank of check boxes. Because each element of a bank of check boxes supplies a value, a large number of variables are needed to contain them. An efficient way of handling this kind of storage is to use a fixed array. Each array element corresponds to one element in the bank of check boxes. For example, a bank of check boxes with two elements will be added; therefore, an array with two elements is declared. Note also that the array's elements are initialized. For check boxes to work correctly, the elements must be initialized ahead of time.

The check box definition begins with the keyword CHECKBOXES. The row and column coordinates of the check-box bank are supplied. Next, the height and width of the check-box bank are defined. Like the other controls, the check-box control also must define a TAG string.

The rest of the check-box definition is simple. A label is listed, followed by the keyword TO, and the name of a variable. Each variable in this part of the definition must be unique. These variables are used to store the status of the check box at the time the dialog is accepted. The variable will be assigned True if the box is checked and False if it is not.

```
ARRAY ChkBox[2]    ; used to store the check-box results
ChkBox[1] = True     ; set up starting values for dialog.
ChkBox[2] = False
SelFile = ""   ; used to store the file selected from picklist
BtnVal = ""    ; used to store the button value

SHOWDIALOG "Sample Dialog"
   @ 5,5 HEIGHT 15 WIDTH 70
   @ 3,5 ?? "Pick list of Files"
   PICKFILE @ 4,5 HEIGHT 8 WIDTH 20 COLUMNS 1
     "D:\\PDOX40\\*.*" TAG "Files in the directory" TO SelFile
   PUSHBUTTON @ 1,10 WIDTH 10 "Cancel"
     CANCEL VALUE "No File" TAG "quit" TO BtnVal
   PUSHBUTTON @ 1,20 WIDTH 10 "OK"
     OK DEFAULT VALUE "Good File" TAG "Selected File" TO BtnVal
   CHECKBOXES @ 1, 45 HEIGHT 2 WIDTH 20 TAG "CheckTest"
     "Test Box 1" TO ChkBox[1],
     "Test Box 2" TO ChkBox[2]
ENDDIALOG
```

Working with Radio Buttons

The next control you will add to the dialog box is a group of radio buttons. Radio buttons return only one value: an integer. The lowest value the radio button returns is one, and the highest value equals the number of radio buttons in the group. Note that the radio button variable is initialized. For radio buttons to work correctly, the variable must have a value assigned to it ahead of time.

The radio button definition begins with the keyword RADIOBUTTONS. The row and column coordinates of the radio button are supplied. Next, the height and width of the radio button group is defined. Like the other controls, the radio button control also must define a TAG string.

The rest of the radio button definition is even simpler than a check box. A series of labels is listed, followed by the keyword TO and the name of the variable. The variable is used to store the number of the radio button that was selected at the time the dialog was accepted. The variable will be assigned the number of the radio button element, numbering the element labels from left to right. In the following example, if the "Low" radio button is selected, the variable *RadBtn* will have the number 3 stored in it.

```
ARRAY ChkBox[2]    ; used to store the check-box results
ChkBox[1] = True    ; set up starting values for dialog.
ChkBox[2] = False
SelFile = ""   ; used to store the file selected from picklist
BtnVal = ""    ; used to store the button value
RadBtn = 1    ; used to store the radio button values

SHOWDIALOG "Sample Dialog"
  @ 5,5 HEIGHT 15 WIDTH 70
  @ 3,5 ?? "Pick list of Files"
  PICKFILE @ 4,5 HEIGHT 8 WIDTH 20 COLUMNS 1
    "D:\\PDOX40\\*.*" TAG "Files in the directory" TO SelFile
  PUSHBUTTON @ 1,10 WIDTH 10 "Cancel"
    CANCEL VALUE "No File" TAG "quit" TO BtnVal
  PUSHBUTTON @ 1,20 WIDTH 10 "OK"
    OK DEFAULT VALUE "Good File" TAG "Selected File" TO BtnVal
  CHECKBOXES @ 1, 45 HEIGHT 2 WIDTH 20 TAG "CheckTest"
    "Test Box 1" TO ChkBox[1],
    "Test Box 2" TO ChkBox[2]
  RADIOBUTTONS @ 5, 45 HEIGHT 3 WIDTH 20
    "High", "Medium", "Low" TAG "RadioTest" TO RadBtn
ENDDIALOG
```

Working with Accept Fields

The last control definition in this section is the ACCEPT control. This control creates an entry field (as described in Chapter 15). Creating this control is as straightforward as creating the other controls.

The control definition begins with the required keyword ACCEPT and the row and column coordinates at which the text entry field will be located. Next, the width of the entry field is defined. Note that the width of the entry field and the size of the accepted text are defined in different ways and are not necessarily the same. A string expression that indicates the data type to be entered in the field follows the width definition. The example uses the string "A20" to indicate that this entry field is alphanumeric and can accept a maximum of 20 characters. Any valid Paradox data type can be used here, such as "D" for dates, "N" for numbers, "$" for currency, and so on. You also can specify any valid Paradox picture statement (not shown in example). Refer to the description of the ACCEPT command in Chapter 19 for more information about the available options.

After specifying the data being accepted in this field, the mandatory TAG string expression is supplied. The final portion of the ACCEPT field definition is the required word TO and the variable name that will store the value entered into the field.

At the same time you add the ACCEPT field, add another canvas element. The command @ 10, 30 ?? "Enter Some Text Below:" displays a prompt string over the entry field just created with the ACCEPT keyword.

```
      ARRAY ChkBox[2]    ; used to store the check-box results
      ChkBox[1] = True    ; set up starting values for dialog.
      ChkBox[2] = False
      SelFile = ""   ; used to store the file selected from picklist
      BtnVal = ""    ; used to store the button value
      RadBtn = 1    ; used to store the radio button values
      Entry = "Default Text"    ; stores the field entry results.

      SHOWDIALOG "Sample Dialog"
        @ 5,5 HEIGHT 15 WIDTH 70
        @ 3,5 ?? "Pick list of Files"
        @ 10, 30 ?? "Enter Some Text Below:"
        PICKFILE @ 4,5 HEIGHT 8 WIDTH 20 COLUMNS 1
          "D:\\PDOX40\\*.*" TAG "Files in the directory" TO SelFile
        PUSHBUTTON @ 1,10 WIDTH 10 "Cancel"
          CANCEL VALUE "No File" TAG "quit" TO BtnVal
        PUSHBUTTON @ 1,20 WIDTH 10 "OK"
          OK DEFAULT VALUE "Good File" TAG "Selected File" TO BtnVal
        CHECKBOXES @ 1, 45 HEIGHT 2 WIDTH 20 TAG "CheckTest"
          "Test Box 1" TO ChkBox[1],
          "Test Box 2" TO ChkBox[2]
        RADIOBUTTONS @ 5, 45 HEIGHT 3 WIDTH 20
          "High", "Medium", "Low" TAG "RadioTest" TO RadBtn
        ACCEPT @ 11, 30 WIDTH 20 "A20" TAG "EntryTest" TO Entry
      ENDDIALOG
```

Refer to Figure 16.4 to see what the dialog box created with the preceding example looks like. To see how this dialog box behaves, type it into the Script Editor, save the script, and play it.

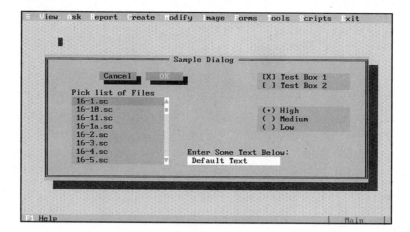

FIG. 16.4

The sample
dialog box.

For Related Information:

◀◀ "Using Paradox Menus and Prompts," p. 39.

▶▶ "Interacting with the User," p. 620.

Chapter Summary

In this chapter, you added to your knowledge of PAL. The chapter gave you some tips and cautions on planning your scripts ahead of time in order to save time and avoid frustration. You also gained some practical knowledge on using PAL menu commands to interact with the user. You learned more about how scripts display information on-screen and how to select and control windows. This chapter introduced you to some methods for creating a WAIT session, and you learned how to construct a dialog box.

Study the examples in this chapter and the sample application in the next chapter and use them as models. With your new knowledge and some practice, you are on your way to becoming a PAL expert.

Using the Script Editor and PAL Debugger

This chapter focuses on the application development tools Paradox provides. Use this chapter to review using the Paradox Editor and to learn how a script can control an Editor session. The Script Editor enables you to create or modify script files and provides features that make your editing sessions more productive. The second half of this chapter gets you started with the PAL Debugger, which examines and tests your script operation. When an error serious enough to make your script stop playing occurs, the Debugger displays a message describing the error, pinpointing its location in your script.

Using the Script Editor

The Paradox Script Editor is a built-in editor that creates and edits PAL scripts. This is essentially the same text editor used to edit Memo fields and ASCII files. (An ASCII file contains only the IBM ASCII codes, with no special formatting information.) Because the Script Editor's operation virtually is identical to that of the Memo Editor, this section provides only a summary of the Editor's overall operation. The emphasis of this section is divided between the features that distinguish the Script Editor from the Memo Editor, and the way PAL commands can control portions of the Editor's operation.

The Script Editor is a variation of the general Editor. The Script Editor is distinguished by the presence of the **G**o command on the menu (discussed later) and by its connection with the PAL Debugger (discussed in the following section). If the **G**o menu appears, you are editing a script. As mentioned in Chapter 15, "An Overview of the Paradox Application Language," all script files must end with the SC file extension. Paradox assumes that any file ending with SC is a script. To avoid confusion, don't use this extension for files that are not PAL scripts.

You can control from a script many of the Editor functions described in this section by using PAL keypress interaction and menu-equivalent commands. With these commands, your script can begin, control, and end editor sessions for memo fields, other scripts, or any ASCII text file. Refer to Chapter 19, "PAL Command and Function Reference," for specific information on each of these commands.

One use for a script that controls an Editor session is to create a keyboard macro for use in the editor. Chapter 6, "Getting Started with Scripts and Keyboard Macros," explains how to attach scripts to the keyboard as macros. If you write an application that closely controls a user's interaction while editing a table, you may want your script to exercise control over the Editor. A script can open the Memo Editor and then position the cursor after the last character in the memo, ready for more input. The script also can open the Memo Editor and position the cursor at a particular word or phrase. Many other times, automating an editor session may be desirable. If you have a table with memo fields, and you need to search for certain words or phrases in memo entries and replace them with another word or phrase, you can expedite the job by writing a script that does this for you. You can create a script that automatically fills in memo fields.

Sometimes, you may need to generate reports too complex for the Report Designer. A script can use an automated Editor session to generate the report. An application also can write form letters or other customized literature in an automated editor session. Using the Editor to bring in an ASCII file containing text used in automatically generated documents makes your script more flexible because you don't have to write text directly into the body of the script. If the text changes, just change the file; you don't have to change your script.

Accessing the Editor

You can start the Script Editor in almost any mode of Paradox, but usually you start it from the Main menu or while in the PAL Debugger.

You can start the Script Editor in the following ways:

■ *Alt-E.* This is the keystroke command you use to start an Editor session. Depending on the file extension you use when you select the file to edit, Paradox chooses to start the Script Editor or the Memo Editor. After you press Alt-E, a menu appears. Choose **O**pen to edit an existing file, or choose **N**ew to create a new file. Next, a file selection dialog box appears. All script file names must end with an SC extension. If you select **O**pen from the editor's starting menu and the file name you enter ends with an SC extension, Paradox uses the Script Editor. (You also can activate the pick list by pressing Enter when the file name entry field is blank; all of the files in the directory appear.) If you select the **N**ew command to create a new script, you must include the SC extension when you enter the file name. If you use a different extension (or no extension), Paradox does not use the Script Editor but uses the usual Memo Editor instead. Invoking the Script Editor usually is easier with one of the other two methods.

> **Reminder:**
> Script files end with the SC extension.

■ *Scripts Menu.* To start the Script Editor from the Paradox Main menu, choose **S**cripts and then choose **E**ditor from the resulting submenu. You then see the Editor submenu. Select **N**ew to begin a new script, or select **O**pen to edit an existing script. If you are creating a new script, type the new script name and press Enter. If you are editing an existing script, type in the script name and press Enter. To activate the pick list, press Enter when the entry field is empty; only the script files in the current directory appear. When you start the Script Editor from the menu this way, it assumes the SC file extension. Whether you choose **O**pen or **N**ew, don't use any extension when you enter the script file name.

> **Cue:**
> To start the Script Editor, choose **S**cripts from the Main Menu, and then choose Editor.

■ *Debugger.* If the Debugger is active, press Alt-F10 (PAL Menu) and select **E**ditor to edit the script you are debugging. Pressing Ctrl-E also starts the Script Editor while the Debugger is active. The debugger is active if your script stops due to an error, if you start the Debugger from the PAL Menu, or if you stop your script with the Ctrl-Break command. (For more information on the Debugger, see "Using the PAL Debugger" later in this chapter.)

When choosing a name for a script, you can use as many as eight characters, including letters, numbers, and the following special characters:

$ # & @ ! % ( ) - _ { } ' ^

Your script name cannot include space characters and must be a valid DOS file name. If you are creating a new script and you choose a name that duplicates an existing script, the new script replaces the old one. Paradox asks you for confirmation.

You can start an Editor session from a PAL script by using the EDITOR NEW or the EDITOR OPEN commands. You can use both of these commands in any context that the Ctrl-E or Alt-E command is available. If you use the EDITOR NEW command with an existing file, however, it replaces the file without confirmation. If you try to use the EDITOR OPEN command to open a nonexistent file, you get a script error.

Using the Editor Menu

Press F10 to activate the Script Editor menu. When editing scripts, the editor menus shows the additional selection **Go**. This special version of the editor is referred to as the "Scripts Editor," even though the Go menu is its only difference from the standard Paradox Editor. PAL can control each of the Script Editor menu commands. The menu in the Scripts Editor displays the choices shown in figure 17.1.

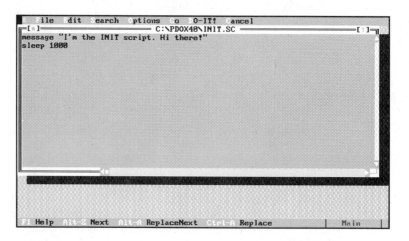

FIG. 17.1

The Scripts Editor Menu.

≡ (System Menu)

This is the System Menu symbol; it contains all of the usual system commands. The System Menu can always be invoked from a script by using the ALTSPACE command. For more information on the System Menu, refer to Chapter 1, "Navigating Paradox."

File Menu

Select the **F**ile menu to perform additional file-related operations. A submenu with the following choices opens: **N**ew, **O**pen, **S**ave, **I**nsertFile, **W**riteBlock, and **P**rint.

■ *New*. Use this menu choice to create a new file. You can create any new ASCII file this way. Paradox does not assume that you are creating a new script, so be sure to include the SC extension when you enter the file name. The menu-equivalent command for this is the EDITOR NEW command described earlier.

■ *Open*. Use this menu choice to edit an existing file, including an ASCII file. Again, Paradox does not assume that you want to edit a script; if you use the pick list, *all* the files in the current directory are displayed. The menu-equivalent command for this is the EDITOR OPEN command described earlier in "Accessing the Editor."

■ *Save*. This menu choice causes *only* the contents of the current window to be saved. This command is very useful to save your script (or other Editor) file without ending or leaving the current editor session. In earlier versions of Paradox, the only way to save an edited script file was to use the **DO-IT!** command and leave the editor. Now, you can use the File, **S**ave command. (Use keypress equivalent commands to perform this operation.)

■ *CopyToFile*. This menu choice enables you to save the file you are currently editing under another name. The file is copied to another file name. Use keypress equivalent commands to perform this operation.

Cue:
Use **F**ile, **S**ave to save your script without leaving the Editor.

■ *InsertFile*. With this menu choice, you can insert any ASCII file from the disk into the script currently being edited. The file is inserted at the current cursor location in the Editor. This option is extremely useful when you are inserting a script created with **Q**uerySave into another script, or if you are gathering several procedures into one file to create a procedure library. After you select **I**nsertFile, a dialog box with an entry field for the file name appears. Enter the name of the file (including its extension) you want to insert, or press Enter when the entry field is blank to activate the pick list. The InsertFile command assumes that you may want to read any file into your script, and the pick list shows all of the files in the current directory. The file you insert with **I**nsertFile must be an ASCII file.

To accomplish the same task in PAL, you must use a combination of PAL commands. First, use the FILEREAD command to load the contents of the file to be inserted into a variable. Then use the EDITOR INSERT command to place the variable contents into the editor session. Be sure that an editor session is open and that it's the current window before attempting this operation.

■ *WriteBlock*. This menu choice writes the currently selected text in the editor to a disk file. See the later section, "Using Special Keys in the Editor," for a description of selecting. This command is most useful when dividing a large script into smaller scripts, or when isolating parts of a script to be converted into procedures. After choosing **W**riteBlock, a dialog box appears, and you are prompted to enter a file name. You can enter any valid DOS file name, with or without an extension. To have the selected block written to disk as a script file, you must specify the SC extension. If you enter a duplicate file name, Paradox asks you for confirmation before replacing the old file. The file you create with the **W**riteBlock command is an ASCII file, with no special formatting characters. To accomplish the same task in PAL, you must use a combination of PAL commands. First, use PAL keypress interaction commands, or the EDITOR SELECT command, to select a text block. Next, use the EDITOR EXTRACT command to copy the selected text block into a variable. Finally, use the FILEWRITE command to write the contents of the variable to a disk file. If the file already exists, it will be replaced without confirmation.

■ *Print*. Select this option to send a copy of the script to your printer. You can obtain the same result by pressing Alt-F7 (Instant Report). To adjust the length of the printed pages, use the Custom Configuration Program (CCP) and change the Report Page Length setting. Appendix B, "Configuring Paradox," discusses how to use the CCP. Use PAL keypress interactions to select CCP in a script.

Edit Menu

With the **E**dit menu, you can access the editor commands affecting "selected" text and the Clipboard. See the later section, "Using Special Keys in the Editor," for a description of selecting and the Clipboard.

When you choose the **E**dit command, a submenu appears with the following options: **X**Cut, **C**opy, **P**aste, **E**rase, **G**oto, **L**ocation, and **S**howClipboard.

■ *XCut*. This menu selection "cuts" (deletes) the selected text from the Editor and places the text on the Clipboard. In a PAL script, you first use keypress interaction commands or the EDITOR SELECT command to select text, and then use the CLIPCUT menu-equivalent command.

■ *Copy*. This selection copies the selected text (without changing it) and places the text on the Clipboard. In a PAL script, you first select text by using keypress interaction commands or the EDITOR SELECT command. You then use the CLIPCOPY menu-equivalent command.

- *Paste*. This menu selection places the contents of the Clipboard into the current Editor session at the cursor position. If a block of text is selected in the Editor, the pasted text replaces the selected text. In a PAL script, you first position the cursor by using key-press interaction commands or the EDITOR GOTO command. Then use the CLIPPASTE menu-equivalent command.

- *Erase*. This menu selection deletes selected text without placing it on the Clipboard. In a PAL script, you must emulate this command by using keypress interaction commands.

- *Goto*. This menu choice prompts you for a line number and then positions the cursor on that line. You can use this command to quickly move from place to place in a large script. PAL's equivalent command is the EDITOR GOTO command. This command, however, has two forms: EDITOR GOTO LINE duplicates the action of the **G**oto menu selection, and EDITOR GOTO POSITION moves the cursor to a specified character position in the file.

- *Location*. This selection shows the current cursor position's line and column number at the bottom left corner of the window. Use PAL keypress interaction commands to duplicate this menu selection. Your script can obtain information about the cursor's position by using the EDITOR INFO command. This command creates and initializes a dynamic array. Each element of the dynamic array contains information about the editor. One element in the array contains the current cursor location's line number.

- *ShowClipboard*. This selection opens an Editor session for the Clipboard. Use PAL keypress interaction commands to duplicate this menu selection.

Search

The **S**earch menu provides access to various editor searching tools. You can use these menu selections to search for a given word or phrase, or to replace a given word or phrase with another. When you choose the **S**earch command, a submenu with the following options appears: **F**ind, **N**ext, **R**eplace, and **C**hangeToEnd.

- *Find*. Use this menu selection to find a particular string or pattern. When you select this option, a dialog box appears, prompting you for the text string or pattern to find. You can use any of the Paradox wild-card patterns: **..** and **@**. (Refer to Chapter 4, "Getting Started with Query By Example," for more information on the Paradox wild cards.) The Editor searches forward from the current cursor position to the end of the editor text. The cursor stops at the first string it finds that matches the specified pattern or string, and marks the pattern or string as selected text. If the program doesn't find a match, a message displays in the message area at the bottom right corner of the screen. A script can perform the same search using the EDITOR FIND command and specifying the text or pattern to search for as a parameter.

- *Next*. This menu choice repeats the search operation previously set up using the **F**ind selection. The PAL command EDITOR FINDNEXT enables your script to invoke this choice.

- *Replace*. This menu selection, like the **F**ind choice, presents a dialog box and prompts you for the text or pattern to be found. Enter the search pattern or string. Like the **F**ind choice, you can use any of the Paradox wild-card patterns. After you fill in the search string (the "target"), a second dialog box appears and prompts you for the text that replaces the target string. The Editor searches from the current cursor location to the end of the file in the Editor. The new text replaces the first string that matches the target and leaves the cursor at the end of the new string. Select the replacement text at the end of the **R**eplace operation. A PAL script invokes this action by using the EDITOR REPLACE command and supplying the search string and replacement string as parameters.

- *ChangeToEnd*. This menu choice performs essentially the same job as the **R**eplace selection. The **C**hangeToEnd choice, however, replaces *all* occurrences of the target with the replacement text. This type of operation often is referred to as a "global find-and-replace." The Editor begins searching at the current cursor location and moves through the file until it reaches the end. Every time the Editor finds a pattern matching the target, it replaces the pattern with the new text. Use keypress interaction commands to make this menu choice from your script.

Options

The **O**ptions menu provides control over how the Editor displays lines and moves the cursor when the Tab key is pressed. This menu also provides some control over how searches (selected from the **S**earch menu) are conducted. When you choose the **O**ptions menu, a submenu displays the following choices: **A**utoIndent, **W**ordWrap, and **C**aseSensitive.

- *AutoIndent*. Use this menu choice to turn the autoindent feature on and off. Autoindent is most helpful when writing scripts. A good programming practice is to format the text in a script so that each procedure, loop structure, SWITCH, or IF..THEN..ELSE structure clearly shows the statements it encloses with different indentation levels. Following this practice makes your scripts easier to understand and consequently easier to maintain and debug. All the examples in this book use this style of script formatting. The autoindent feature in the editor makes it easier to write your script using an indent style. When autoindent is on and you press Enter to start a new line in the Editor, the cursor position on the new line is indented automatically to the same level as the previous line. In other words, the cursor on the new line aligns itself with the first character on the previous line. After choosing AutoIndent, another submenu appears. Choose **S**et to turn on the autoindent feature or **C**lear to turn the autoindent off. Your PAL script can get information about the autoindent status by using the EDITOR INFO command. If your script needs to change this control, you must use keypress interaction commands.

■ *WordWrap.* Select this menu choice to turn the word-wrap feature on or off. This feature is not usually very useful for script writing; therefore, you may want to turn it off. Remember that when an Editor window is on-screen, it's only showing a view of the file being edited (whether or not the file is a script file). You have two choices for displaying file lines longer than the window's width. The first choice is not to show the part of the line extending past the window's right edge. This means that the whole line is not visible, and you must scroll the window right or left to view the entire line. The second choice is to reformat a line too long to fit in the window into a number of shorter lines that do fit. This is called *word-wrap* because the words in the line are "wrapped" (continued) on the next line(s). After making the **W**ordWrap menu selection, another submenu appears. Choose **S**et to turn the wordwrap feature on, or choose **C**lear to turn wordwrap off. Your PAL script can get information about the wordwrap status by using the EDITOR INFO command. If your script needs to change this control, you must use keypress interaction commands.

■ *CaseSensitive.* This final choice affects how searches made from the **S**earch menu are carried out. Case-sensitive refers to whether or not a distinction exists between upper- and lowercase letters. If you use a case-sensitive comparison, the two words *test* and *Test* are not the same. If you search for the word *test* with case-sensitivity on, *Test* is not found. After making the **C**aseSensitive menu selection, another submenu appears. Choose **S**et to turn case-sensitive searching on, or choose **C**lear to turn it off.

The PAL commands for editor searches (EDITOR FIND, EDITOR FINDNEXT, and EDITOR REPLACE) don't use the case-sensitivity setting this menu selection controls. These searches are case-sensitive unless the Paradox .. wild-card pattern is appended to the string expression used to specify the target.

Go

This addition to the usual Paradox Editor menu is distinctive to the Scripts Editor. Use this menu choice to save the script to disk, end the Script Editor session, and play the script. This option has the same effect as pressing F2 (Do-It!) and playing the script through the Scripts Play option on the Main menu. The Go method saves you several keystrokes.

DO-IT!

Choose this option to save the script to disk, end the Script Editor session, and return to Main mode. You can achieve the same result by pressing F2 (Do-It!).

Cancel

Use this option only to end the Script Editor session without saving any entries or changes made since starting the session. Paradox closes the current editor window only.

Using Special Keys in the Editor

A script can emulate almost all the keystroke commands used to control the Paradox Editor. In most cases, a direct equivalent command exists; when it doesn't, use keypress interaction and keypress equivalent commands.

Cursor Movement

Table 17.1 lists the keystrokes controlling cursor movement in the Editor and their PAL equivalents. The cursor also can be positioned under the control of a script by using the EDITOR GOTO command.

Table 17.1. Cursor-Movement Keys in the Editor

Key	PAL equivalent	Moves cursor
Home	HOME	To first character of current line
End	END	To last character of current line
PgUp	PGUP	Up number of lines window is high
PgDn	PGDN	Down number of lines window is high
Left arrow	LEFT	One character left
Right arrow	RIGHT	One character right
Up arrow	UP	Up one line
Down arrow	DOWN	Down one line
Ctrl-PgUp	CTRLPGUP	First character of text in Editor
Ctrl-PgDn	CTRLPGDN	Last character of text in Editor
Ctrl-left arrow	CTRLLEFT	Left one word
Ctrl-right arrow	CTRLRIGHT	Right one word

Special Keystroke Commands

Table 17.2 lists special keystroke commands used in the Editor. Most of the keystroke commands in the table are special key-combination commands that are shortcuts to Editor menu selections. Some commands don't have exact PAL equivalents. For these commands, use the menu commands enclosed in curly braces. For example, to make the editor show the current cursor location (Alt-W), use the following command sequence:

    Menu {Edit} {Location}

Table 17.2. Special Keystroke Commands in the Editor

Command	PAL equivalent	Effect
Ins	INS	Change Insert/Overwrite toggle
Del	DEL	Deletes character at cursor or, if selected text, deletes it

continues

Table 17.2. Continued

Command	PAL equivalent	Effect
Ctrl-A	EDITOR REPLACE	Replace, same as **S**earch **R**eplace
Alt-A	REPLACENEXT	Replace next, same as **S**earch **N**ext, after a Replace has been performed
Alt-W	(none)	Same as **E**dit **L**ocation
Ctrl-Y	DELETELINE	Deletes current line
Ctrl-Z	EDITOR FIND	Zoom, same as **S**earch **F**ind
Alt-Z	EDITOR FINDNEXT	Zoom Next, same as **S**earch **N**ext, after a Find has been performed

Text Selection and Clipboard Commands

Using selected text in combination with the Clipboard provides an easy and powerful means of manipulating large or small portions of text in an Editor window, and also makes copying or transferring text from one Editor window to another very simple.

Selected text is shown with highlighted, or inverse, video. Selected text can be one character, a word, a group of words, an entire line, or several lines. Selected text sometimes is referred to as a *marked block* of text. Selecting text is often the first step in a more complex manipulation. You select a text block to make its deletion easier, to replace it with other text, or to copy it.

Text is selected by holding down the Shift key and using one of the direction keys. As the cursor moves, it selects the text it moves through. Table 17.3 lists the keys that control text selection. To have your script select text in an Editor session, use the EDITOR SELECT command.

You use the Clipboard much like a real clipboard you may have on your desk. To use text from one file in a different file, or to duplicate text elsewhere in the same file, make a copy of the information on your Clipboard, and later paste (insert) the information where needed. At other times, you may want to completely remove (cut) the information out of its current location, and place the information somewhere else. In this case, cut the text out of your file, place the text on your Clipboard, and later paste the text into another place in the same or different file.

When text is pasted from the Clipboard, only text that is selected in the Clipboard is pasted. When text is placed on the Clipboard, the new text replaces the selected text on the Clipboard. Text pasted into an editor session will replace the selected text (if any).

Table 17.3 lists the keys that control Clipboard operations. Basically, you can perform only three operations with the Clipboard: Cut (**Edit XCut**), Copy (**Edit Copy**), and Paste (**Edit Paste**). These operations can be performed by a PAL script using CLIPCUT, CLIPCOPY, and CLIPPASTE.

Table 17.3. Text Selection and Clipboard Keys in the Editor

Command	Effect
Ctrl-Ins	Copies selected text to Clipboard, same as **Edit Copy**
Shift-Ins	Paste (insert) contents of Clipboard, same as **Edit Paste**
Shift-Del	Cuts selected text from Editor to Clipboard, same as **Edit XCut**
Shift Left Arrow	Selects one character to left of cursor, and moves cursor left
Shift Right Arrow	Selects one character to right of cursor, and moves cursor right
Shift-Ctrl Left Arrow	Selects one word to left, and move cursor
Shift-Ctrl Right Arrow	Selects one word to right, and move cursor
Shift-Home	Selects text from cursor location to the beginning of current line
Shift-End	Selects text from cursor location to the end of the current line
Shift Up Arrow	Selects one line up, and move cursor
Shift Down Arrow	Selects one line down, and move cursor
Shift-PgUp	Selects up the number of lines in the window height, moves cursor same amount
Shift-PgDn	Selects down the number of lines in the window height, moves cursor same amount
Shift-Ctrl PgUp	Selects from cursor to first character in Editor text, and moves cursor
Shift-Ctrl PgDn	Selects from cursor to last character in Editor text, and moves cursor

For Related Information:

◄◄ "Using the Paradox Editor," p. 142.

◄◄ "Editing Scripts," p. 229.

◄◄ "Editing a Script," p. 521.

FROM HERE...

Using the PAL Debugger

Paradox provides an excellent interactive tool for finding errors in your PAL scripts. The PAL Debugger tests scripts during the development process or locates application errors or problems. This tool helps you locate syntax errors, run errors, and logic errors.

Syntax errors occur when PAL commands are not constructed properly. Examples include misspelled commands, missing punctuation, too many or too few parameters, or parameter expressions that evaluate to a data type other than that expected by the command. Resolve syntax errors by correcting the command syntax and playing the script again.

Run errors occur when the commands are constructed properly but are used in an improper manner. An example of a run error is a variable used in a command before the variable is assigned a value, or inappropriate commands used for the current context or Paradox mode. Run errors usually are resolved by modifying the script to correct the problem. If the error is the result of a variable used before it's assigned a value (as in the previous example), the script is modified to assign a value to the variable.

Even though a command is constructed and used properly, *logic errors* occur when the program logic is faulty. These errors usually involve situations such as using the wrong variable, making field assignments in the wrong image, or choosing the wrong branch in a SWITCH statement. The basic symptom of a logic error occurs when a script seems to run correctly, but produces improper results. Improper results can be noticed in a mathematical computation that produces the wrong answer, an expected change in a table that does not appear, and so on. Resolving logic errors can be quite difficult because the programmer must be able to determine the exact point the script goes awry. The PAL Debugger provides significant help through its step, trace, and value commands (explained later).

Syntax errors usually are detected by the PAL parsing and interpreting process. Run errors usually are detected when PAL attempts to execute the command. Both types of errors result in a script error. When a script error occurs, PAL stops the script and automatically invokes the Debugger. The script line on which the error occurs appears at the bottom of the screen, along with a message describing the nature of the error.

Logic errors can be detected only by the user because they don't involve anything technically wrong with the script, but represent a reasoning flaw embodied by the script.

In addition to the Debugger's error and problem resolving capabilities, the Debugger can be used to determine where in the script calling sequence the current line is, show the values contained in variables or arrays (and save them in a file), and return from nested scripts or procedures. *Calling sequence* is the term used to describe a line's current position in a series of nested scripts or procedure.

Accessing the Debugger

You can invoke the Debugger in one of four ways. The first three methods are effective only if a script is already running. The last method can play and debug any script.

- ■ If Paradox encounters a syntax or run error while playing a script, the program presents the Script Error menu containing the choices **C**ancel and **D**ebug. Choose **C**ancel to cancel the script and return to Paradox; choose **D**ebug to start the Debugger. The Debugger starts debugging the script at the line that caused the error.

- ■ Insert a DEBUG command in the script. The Debugger begins debugging the script at the line following the DEBUG command, which is useful when tracking down a logic error or some kinds of run errors, especially if you are debugging a large script or application. Insert the DEBUG command in the script before the problem area. You then can play the script. Let the script run through all the parts you know are trouble-free, starting the Debugger at the problem point. This is helpful if you need to check the variable or array element value before a run error occurs.

- ■ Press Ctrl-Break during script execution and choose **D**ebug from the displayed menu. The Debugger starts debugging the script at the next line to be executed.

Reminder:
The Debugger is started automatically after a script error.

■ Press Alt-F10 (PAL Menu) and choose **D**ebug from the PAL menu. A dialog box appears, and you are prompted to enter the script name to debug. Enter the script name (don't use an extension), or when the file name entry field is empty, press Enter to activate the pick list. The Debugger starts debugging the selected script at the first line.

When you invoke the Debugger, it does not completely take over the screen. Instead, the Debugger uses the last line of the screen to display the line currently being executed. This line is called the *script line* (see fig. 17.2). Because one script line can contain several commands, the Debugger indicates the next command to be executed by displaying a triangular-shaped pointer.

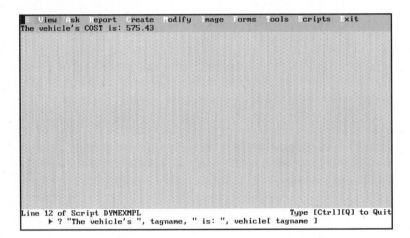

FIG. 17.2

Debugger screen
showing the
script line.

The *status line*, the next to last line on-screen, displays the script's name and the current line number. Because scripts can play other scripts, the displayed script name in the status line may not be the same as the originally executed script.

If you are debugging a procedure in a library, Paradox tries to find the script that defines the procedure. If the Debugger is unable to find the script, it cannot show the script commands in the procedure. If you try to trace a procedure with an unavailable source, the Debugger displays an error message to this effect and terminates.

When a script error occurs, the Debugger is started. The Debugger displays an error message describing the apparent error condition, so you can try to determine the source of the problem.

Using the Debugger Menu

While using the Debugger, you can access several options through the Debugger menu. Press Alt-F10 to see the PAL Debugger Menu. The Debugger menu is similar to the PAL Menu but offers more choices (see fig. 17.3). The Debugger menu shows the following options: **V**alue, **S**tep, **T**race, **N**ext, **G**o, **M**iniScript, **W**here?, **Q**uit, **P**op, **E**ditor.

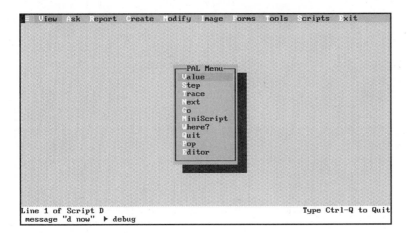

FIG. 17.3

The PAL Debugger menu.

Value

Choose **V**alue to calculate an expression or variable's value. You usually use this command to determine whether a particular variable or array element has the proper value when a run error causes a script to stop. After you choose **V**alue, the Debugger asks you for an expression. To find a variable's value, type the variable name and press Enter. To find an array's element, type the array name and appropriate subscript or tag. The Debugger displays the value in the message window at the lower right corner of the screen.

You also can use the **V**alue option to calculate any expression's value. This is useful when a run error stops your script, but all the variables and array elements appear to have the correct value. Then the problem most likely is due to an expression not evaluating to the expected result. Refer to Chapter 15, "An Overview of the Paradox Application Language," for more information on expressions.

Step

Choose Step to execute the current command (indicated by the pointer in the script line) and move to the next command. This option enables you to go through the script and examine each command's effect one step at a time. This option is the same as Ctrl-S (Step) and cannot be used after a syntax error.

The Step option "steps over" subroutine calls. The subroutine (a nested script or procedure) executes, but the Debugger does not follow the subroutine command-by-command; the subroutine is treated like one of the built-in PAL commands or functions. Use Step to save a lot of debugging time when a subroutine or procedure works properly, and you don't need to go through its individual commands. Note how the Step option differs from the Trace option described in the next section.

The Step option often is used in conjunction with the DEBUG command (mentioned earlier and described in Chapter 19, "PAL Command and Function Reference"). Place the DEBUG command in your script before the problem area. When DEBUG executes, it stops the script and enters the Debugger. Use the Step option to watch the script execute.

Trace

Cue:

Use **S**tep to "step over" subroutines and **T**race to "trace into" them.

Choose the Trace option to execute the current command (at the pointer) and move to the next command. This option, along with Step, enables you to go through the script, tracing the effect of each command. This option is the same as Ctrl-T (Trace) and cannot be used after a syntax error.

The Trace option "traces into" subroutine calls. As the subroutine, the Debugger moves into the subroutine and shows you each command. Use Trace when you are not sure where an error is and you need to see all the commands in a subroutine script or procedure.

The Trace option, like the Step option, is often used in conjunction with the DEBUG command.

Next

The Next option skips the current command and advances the pointer to the next command in the debugging script. This option is the same as Ctrl-N (Next) and cannot be used after a syntax error. Use Next while debugging to skip over a script command causing a run error.

Go

Choose **G**o to continue playing the script, starting with the current command. This option is the same as Ctrl-G (Go) and cannot be used after a syntax error. After you use **G**o, the script plays continuously until it reaches a programmed end-point, another error, or another DEBUG command.

MiniScript

Use the **M**iniScript option to create a one-line script up to 175 characters long. When you finish typing the "miniscript," press Enter, or click OK. The miniscript becomes the current script line, and the first command in the miniscript becomes the current command. To play the miniscript, press Ctrl-G (Go) to start continuous play or Ctrl-S (Step) to step through the miniscript one command at a time. The Debugger **M**iniScript option's behavior is different from the **M**iniScript found on the PAL menu when the Debugger is not active. That **M**iniScript plays immediately instead of becoming the current line.

Miniscripts often are used during debugging to correct situations that produce a run error. Some run errors (such as using a PAL command in the wrong context, making an invalid menu selection, attempting an operation with an image not on the workspace, and so on) can be "patched" with a miniscript. When one of these types of run error occurs, use the **M**iniScript option to correct the problem. Then use the **N**ext menu selection to skip over the command producing the error. Now you can use the **S**tep, **T**race, or **G**o options to continue debugging or playing the script without having to start over. Remember to make appropriate permanent corrections to the script later. An error in the miniscript causes processing to halt and displays the Script Error menu. Choose **D**ebug to debug the miniscript.

Where?

Select the **W**here? option to see the current script level (or procedure level) in the current calling sequence. *Calling sequence* describes a line's current position in a series of nested scripts or procedures. The calling sequence is sometimes referred to as the *call chain*. This option is the same as Ctrl-W (Where).

Use this option when you are debugging a multilevel, nested script. The **W**here? selection shows the sequence of scripts or procedures that reached the script (or procedure) containing the current command. As mentioned in Chapter 15, "An Overview of the Paradox Application

Language," you can modularize large scripts by breaking the application into smaller, more easily manageable scripts and procedures. This practice results in a script that calls (plays) one or more other scripts, each of which, in turn, can call other scripts. The **W**here? option becomes very important when debugging a modularized application. A subroutine script's successful execution often depends on conditions established in the script that called the subroutine, or possibly another script or procedure higher in the calling chain. If a script subroutine produces a run error, even though it appears to be correct, the source of the error can lie in one of the scripts that called it. The only way, then, to find the error's source is to examine the established (or disestablished) script and procedure conditions played before the error becomes noticeable.

When you choose the **W**here? option, the Debugger displays an image on-screen that looks like several stacked pages. The page at the bottom of the stack is the Debugger; the second page from the bottom is the script containing the current command. Each successive page going up through the stack is the next highest nesting level. The page at the top of the stack is the script you played originally.

Quit

Choose the **Q**uit option to quit the Debugger and cancel the script's playing (at all levels). This option is the same as Ctrl-Q (Quit).

Pop

Use the **P**op option to cancel only the current script level and return to the script that called the current script. This option is the same as Ctrl-P (Pop). When debugging a script not played by another script, choosing **P**op has the same effect as choosing **Q**uit. Because **M**iniScript and **V**alue work by playing short scripts, you can use **P**op to get out of an erroneous **M**iniScript or **V**alue operation.

Editor

Select **E**ditor when you want to fix the script rather than skip the erroneous command or try a quick miniscript patch. This command leaves the Debugger and opens a Script Editor session. The script being debugged loads into the Editor and places the cursor at the command indicated by the pointer in the Debugger's script line. When you make the necessary corrections and want to replay the script, select **G**o from the Editor menu.

If you attach an alternate editor (refer to Chapter 15, "An Overview of the Paradox Application Language"), that editor starts instead of the Script Editor. Press Ctrl-G (Go) when you return from your editor to Paradox.

Reminder:
Press Ctrl-G when you return from an alternate editor.

Using Special Keys in the Debugger

Table 17.4 lists the keystroke commands available in the Debugger.

Table 17.4. Special Keystroke Commands in the Debugger

Key	Name	Effect
Alt-F10	PAL menu	Shows Debugger menu
Ctrl-E	Edit	Starts Script Editor
Ctrl-G	Go	Resumes script play
Ctrl-N	Next	Skips current command; moves to next command
Ctrl-P	Pop	Pops up to the calling script (if any), or quit (if script is not called by another script)
Ctrl-Q	Quit	Exits Debugger
Ctrl-S	Step	Steps (and executes) the current command
Ctrl-T	Trace	Traces (and executes) current command or procedure
Ctrl-W	Where	Shows current nesting level

For Related Information:

▶▶ "Testing and Debugging the Application," p. 623.

FROM HERE...

Chapter Summary

In this chapter, you reviewed the Paradox Editor's operations and learned how the Script Editor differs from the Memo Editor. As each Editor operation was reviewed, you were given a brief description of the PAL commands or techniques for controlling all or portions of an Editor session.

The second part of this chapter showed you how to start the PAL Debugger and described the available Debugger commands. As each Debugger command was explained, you were given a short description of debugging techniques to apply with that command.

Now that you are familiar with the fundamentals of PAL (presented in Chapters 15 and 16), the Script Editor, and the PAL Debugger, you are ready to examine the sample PAL application presented in Chapter 18. As you build PAL applications of your own, don't forget to refer to Chapter 19, "PAL Command and Function Reference," for complete command and function syntax as well as many helpful examples.

Creating PAL Applications

This chapter builds on what you have learned in previous chapters and takes you through the steps necessary to create a fully functional PAL application. You learn how to create a video store application complete with pop-up menus, dialog boxes, hot keys, and windows.

This chapter begins with an overview of the application development cycle. As you read through this section, keep in mind the applications you want to build. Then follow along with the development of the sample application provided.

The video store application teaches you how to build applications in PAL, demonstrating many powerful features of the language. Throughout the chapter, you also find tips on how you can continue to develop the sample application to add more features. For beginning programmers, the program code is described in language that is easy to understand; for experienced programmers, the application highlights many of the new features introduced in Paradox 4.0.

Developing Applications

The application development cycle is an iterative process. When you start designing an application, you probably have a firm grasp of what is required and a rough idea of how to implement various features. As you begin implementing your system, however, you may find that it does not work entirely as expected. Users experience this same change in expectations. As they begin to see the interface and output of the application, they revise their idea of what the application should do. For an application to be successful, you must allow time for revision and refinement, but you must know where to draw the line. Without the constraints of time and money, the development process could continue indefinitely.

As you develop an application, new information introduced during the development cycle changes the system requirements, forcing you to reconsider even the most fundamental components of the application. You should plan to invest time early in the process to eliminate as many unknowns as possible.

As you gain experience designing and implementing applications in PAL, you discover how valuable the end user is to you. You will most likely find yourself going back and forth between the user and the emerging program, continually refining the definition of the system. Don't be discouraged when your first solution doesn't meet all the customer's needs—even if the customer is you! In general, the development cycle is as follows:

- Define application requirements
- Design and create a database
- Assign field validity checks
- Create forms used by the application
- Create reports used by the application
- Develop a strategy for user interaction
- Write code to support your strategy
- Test and debug the application
- Deliver the application

Defining Application Requirements

Designing a PAL application begins with careful planning. Decide early in the process the system requirements, getting as much input from the current system users as possible. Find out how the current system operates, and identify the problem(s) you are attempting to solve. Determine whether the application needs to be a multi- or single-user application.

You also need to answer a variety of questions: What security level is required? What are the equipment limitations? Will you be expected to maintain a large database on a computer without a hard drive? Are the users confident in using computer applications? Will they need on-line help for even the most basic operations, or will a less complicated help system suffice? Answering these questions early in the development cycle can save you many hours of rewriting code later. The more you know about the problem, the more effective you will be at engineering a solution.

Consider the basic needs for the video store application:

- Maintain video inventory.
- Maintain a customer list.
- Invoice customers.

The sample application presented in this chapter covers these basic needs. Other requirements such as employee record keeping, overhead accounting, and complicated business reports are certainly within the capability of PAL but beyond the scope of this sample application. Discussions of auxiliary possibilities are sprinkled throughout the chapter.

Designing a Database

Armed with the information you have gathered about the application requirements, you can begin designing the tables your application will rely on. Chapter 2, "Creating Database Tables," introduces you to rules for creating related tables. The tables you create should relate to each other naturally as one to one, one to many, many to one, many to many, and in some cases no relation. Together with other Paradox objects such as forms, reports, graphs, validity checks, and so forth, tables are the foundation of your application.

Before writing one line of PAL code, you need to design a reliable database, complete with the Paradox objects required by your application. Test the reliability of your database by designing forms and reports, making sure that you can present all the information needed in the forms and reports you create. If you need review, study the rules regarding key fields described in Chapter 2 and the discussion of multitable forms and reports in Chapters 8 and 10. The tables, forms, and reports used in the sample application are described in detail later in this chapter.

Assigning Field Validity Checks

Validity checks in Paradox are powerful methods for controlling input to your database. Chapter 9, "Using Power Entry and Editing Features," introduces you to working with validity checks and controlling input through the ValCheck menu options. Validity checks are fundamental to any application.

You should define validity checks interactively within Paradox for each table in the application in order to avoid unnecessary programming. Imagine the difficulty of ensuring that users enter a value contained in a separate table. TableLookup from the ValCheck menu accomplishes this task and more in one easy step without requiring a single line of PAL code.

As you read this section and follow the sample application, you see how important the different validity checks are to the video store application. A new feature in Paradox 4.0 even enables you to control placement of the cursor after certain validity checks have been fulfilled.

Creating Forms for Your Application

After your database tables are in place, you can begin designing the supplementary objects that help you input data and obtain the desired output from your application. These supplementary objects include the forms, reports, or graphs eventually used by your application.

Most of the interaction with the application is through forms or a combination of forms and menus. You can think of forms as the primary *input* objects of your application. Pop-up windows, dialog boxes, and other PAL facilities are very helpful in collecting information from users, but forms are the primary tools your application uses to effect changes to your database. When designing forms for the application, consider how the user will interact with the form. Consider the order in which information is to be entered and whether the cursor must be repositioned after each carriage return, or whether it naturally moves to the next most important field. Although PAL enables you to control the user's every move, a well-designed form can save you programming time.

In addition to regular and display-only fields, calculated fields can add depth and flexibility to forms. You can even use global variables in calculated fields, which enables you to change the forms display output. For example, you could enter the variable name SubTotal in a calculated field, then change the variable's value under script control. When the value of SubTotal changes, that value is reflected on the form as well. You'll see examples of this technique in the sample application later in this chapter.

A forms visual design is also very important. Use attributes, color, borders, and other symbols to distinguish input fields from display-only fields. Recurring visual hints train the eye to recognize quickly that input is required. You can also type text directly on a form to help the user interact with the form. Fields that you expect the user to enter data into should be marked with descriptive text. For instance, the [First Name] and [Last Name] fields placed on an invoice form could be identified with text such as "Customer Name (First/Last):".

Creating Reports for Your Application

Designing reports specifically for your application requires the same process as designing reports for interactive use. In the same way that a form serves as primary input to your application, reports serve as primary *output* from your application. After identifying the data you need to report on, design the reports you need to fulfill the requirements. Reports you design during this phase of the development cycle are output based on user input.

You can create PAL programs to get input from the user regarding report specifications. Users select reports from menus, choose options in a dialog box, or type the name of the report. You need to enable users to decide whether the report should be directed to the screen or to a compatible printer. Finally, you want PAL to step in to check the status of the printer or other device before printing.

The sample application enables the user to print an invoice at the end of the rental transaction. The application uses a typical tabular report specification described later in this chapter.

Interacting with the User

The major responsibility of any application is to ensure database accuracy. The application also serves as a *user interface*, which consists of objects such as messages, prompts, dialog boxes, menus, and sounds. The user interface enables the user to control program flow within the bounds of the application.

When you design an application, consider the tasks the user needs to accomplish and decide how the application should look and "feel" to the end user. When designing menus to enable the user to move through the application, for example, determine which menu items users will use most often. Then structure your menus with those items first on the list, creating pull-down or pop-up menus as appropriate.

The sample application presented in this chapter uses several techniques to illustrate a variety of PAL features. You learn how to create pull-down and pop-up menus, dialog boxes, splash screens, and more. You also learn when such PAL facilities are appropriate.

Your application should inform the user of what is happening at each stage of the program. Tasks initiated as a result of user interaction usually take place in the background, hidden from the user's view. PAL has several excellent facilities to provide immediate feedback to users. The sample application makes use of these techniques and provides a detailed description of each method used.

Among the simplest ways to provide feedback are messages, canvas text, and literal text in forms. Messages can inform the user that a particular task, such as a complicated query, will take a long time; alert the user of an invalid entry; and provide other useful feedback to the user. Although often overlooked as a way to display important information, literal text on forms in a specific part of your application can display tips on how to move within the form, tell the user what is expected next, or indicate which fields have lookup help available.

Other built-in PAL facilities include dialog boxes and prompts included with menus and wait sessions. For example, the syntax of all Menu commands enables you to display a prompt at the bottom of the screen when a menu item is highlighted. Prompts used in this way inform the user immediately of the result of selecting a particular menu item. You can design a dialog box to accept a password before making changes to a table or to get confirmation before executing a critical task. You can, for example, ask for confirmation before deleting a record, cancelling an operation, or leaving the application.

Take every opportunity to make the user aware of what is happening. Providing feedback throughout every stage of the application can help the user make informed decisions while working with your application, decreasing the number of errors. Prompts and messages keep the user well informed and are useful in debugging your application.

Writing Modular Code

After reading the first part of this book and spending time interactively with Paradox, you should have a thorough understanding of how Paradox functions. A strong knowledge of Paradox is crucial to your ability to design efficient PAL applications.

Collecting related tasks into modules makes your application more manageable. Imagine the difficulty you would have finding information in this book if it were not divided into chapters and sections. Writing one very large script would be a similar nightmare. Organizing the code in your application not only makes it more readable but also can dramatically improve the performance of your application. Procedures, procedure libraries, auto-loading libraries, and modular queries are some of the built-in features PAL makes available to enhance your application's organization and performance.

Using procedures and procedure libraries in your applications is an excellent way to structure and reuse your code. Remember, if a procedure can be called from a library, you may execute it from anywhere in your application.

When you construct a procedure that accepts one or more parameters, you are *parameterizing* the procedure. Suppose that you have a procedure that locates a value in the first field of a particular table and then switches to form view to display the entire record. Such a procedure may look like the following:

```
PROC ShowRecord()
    VIEW "Members"     ; view the members table
    RIGHT              ; move to the first field in the table
    LOCATE 3451        ; find the number 3451
    FORMKEY            ; switch to form view
ENDPROC
```

To execute this procedure, you simply use the procedure call:

```
ShowRecord()
```

This procedure locates the value 3451 in the first field in the Members table. To find a different value, you must define a new procedure that locates that value. By parameterizing the procedure, however, you can use it in any number of situations.

A parameterized version of the same procedure follows:

```
PROC ShowRecord(TableName, FieldName, SearchVal)
    VIEW TableName     ; view the table name passed to the procedure
    MOVETO FieldName   ; move to the first field in the table
    LOCATE SearchVal   ; find the value passed to the procedure
    FORMKEY            ; switch to form view
ENDPROC
```

You use the following syntax to call the second form of the procedure:

```
ShowRecord("Tapes", "Video ID", 34511)
```

Now the procedure can search for any value in any field of any table. Notice that this procedure call includes the parameters that may be used within the procedure. Also note that neither procedure checks whether the record has been found before switching to form view. An actual procedure generally checks whether the value was found before continuing.

Look for opportunities to parameterize procedures whenever possible. The sample application provides examples of parameterization, and Chapter 15, "An Overview of the Paradox Application Language," explains how to use procedures and procedure libraries.

Modular queries are another good programming tool. Paradox enables you to create queries interactively and save them to scripts to replay later. Before you integrate queries into your application, create the queries the application will use. You then can test the query on existing tables to ensure that it performs as expected before implementing it into your application. You can attach queries to menus, dialog boxes, or other tools your application makes available for interaction. PAL also enables you to use variables in queries to further parameterize them. The queries in the sample application can help you learn how to use these techniques effectively. Refer to Chapter 4 for details on query design basics and for instructions on saving a query.

Create libraries for storing parsed procedures, which you can call whenever you need them. If you're unsure how to create procedures and procedure libraries, refer to Chapter 15 "An Overview of the Paradox Application Language," for more information. For enhanced organization, and in some cases improved performance, you should create more than one library and include the library names on the auto loading path. The video store application uses two libraries: VidMain.lib and VidUtil.lib. Later in this chapter, you learn how libraries work when called to memory automatically.

Testing and Debugging the Application

The testing phase, like much of the development cycle, is an iterative process. By the time you are ready to do exhaustive testing, you will already have begun the testing process. While you create sections of the application, you will undoubtedly test the code and functionality of each section as it's completed. For example, you will have entered sample data while building the database or assigning validity checks, and you will have used the debugger countless times when running partially completed portions of the application.

The first step in fully testing your system is to generate test data. Create several records of test data for your database so that you know what to expect when certain data is input through the application. If your application uses calculations, first perform the calculations manually to verify the correct result. Then examine the database interactively after each test run to make sure that the results match your expectations.

Don't limit database evaluation to incorrect data, however. Look for unwanted or missing records, as your application may delete or add records erroneously. Run reports from within the application to ensure correctness, again comparing the results with data you know to be correct. PAL code that produces incorrect output, or that generates unwanted records in a database, can be difficult to detect with the PAL debugger. Verifying the actual results of the application against expected results, therefore, is extremely important.

After you have established that the sample data entry is behaving properly, you need to test the application for the unexpected actions that users invariably attempt. Test every conceivable keystroke and mouse action to locate errors in the system. End users have an uncanny knack for finding obscure bugs that you have missed in your testing cycle. These bugs are usually the most frustrating to exterminate because your own thorough testing process failed to detect them.

If the application is intended to run in a multiuser environment, you need to perform tests on a network identical to the one to be used. Don't test the application on a Novell network if it will be used on a Banyan Vines network. Using a different network version also may cause you to miss bugs. Set up test conditions that lock users out of tables your application uses. Lock one or more tables, and see how the application responds.

You also should perform some of the longest operations offered in your application—perhaps that slow multitable report—to observe how other stations perform. You may find that the entire application is slowed severely by disk intensive tasks, and you may decide to add informational messages that appear when a workstation is putting unusual demands on network resources. You may not consider these problems bugs in the classic sense, but they may be if your users reboot because "It wasn't doing anything!"

Delivering the Application

After you have performed all the necessary tests, received favorable initial evaluations from users, and the application is running smoothly, you are ready to deliver the application.

Training your end users to interact with every stage of the application is an important part of delivering the application. You may use sample data, such as the data you used to generate tests, as an aid in teaching the users how to work with the application. Prepare user guides if possible, complete with a quick reference, so that they can answer their own questions when you move on to your next project.

Run your replacement system concurrently with the old system for a certain period of time so that you can recover precious data should the unthinkable occur. Although your system should outperform the old one, you may discover that your system is less efficient in some areas or that some features are unnecessary. If you identify an unneeded feature, eliminate it from the application. Unused features can be misleading to users and can be a significant drain on your resources.

Consider providing bug report forms for the end users to complete. Filling out a formal report may help the user identify exactly what happened at the time of failure, helping you locate the bug more easily and effectively.

Using the Sample Application

The sample application provided in this chapter simulates a typical video store. It is a fully functional application that demonstrates many features of the Paradox Application Language. This section introduces its features and describes how a user interacts with the application. As you read through this section, think of the application you want to build and determine whether you can borrow some of the features described here.

From the user's perspective, the Video Store Application includes the following features:

- User-friendly interface

- Inventory tracking

- Member list maintenance

- Customer invoice generation

- System information at a glance

From the programmer's point of view, the Video Store Application includes the following features:

- Procedures and libraries

- SHOWPULLDOWN menus

- SHOWPOPUP menus

- SHOWDIALOGBOX dialog boxes

- WAIT sessions with event handling through wait procedures

- Other event handling

- Standard programming constructs such as loops and array variables

Starting the Video Store Application

To run the video store application, the user simply plays the *top level script* (sometimes called the *driver script*). RunVideo is the top level script for the video store application. Paradox enables the user to play scripts in two ways:

- From within Paradox, choose **S**cripts, **P**lay from the Main menu, and then type *RunVideo*.

- From the DOS prompt or in a batch file, use the following:

      c:\>*Paradox RunVideo*

    Starting Paradox from the DOS prompt in this way assumes that the Paradox directory is on the DOS path and that the Paradox default directory points to your applications directory.

After the RunVideo script is played, the first thing the user sees is a *splash screen* that displays limited information about the system and notifies the user that the application is loading (see fig. 18.1). This splash screen is designed so that blinking dots follow the message Loading application, indicating that something is happening. (Nothing is more confusing to users than a blank screen).

Viewing the Main Menu

After the application loads, the Main menu displays as a pop-up menu
in the center of the screen (see fig. 18.2). The user navigates through
the application from this point. As you read about the choices the user
has available, you will see that some menu selections appear in reverse
video, indicating that the application does not support these features.
These items have been disabled intentionally; they appear on the Main
menu to show additional features that a video store application could
include.

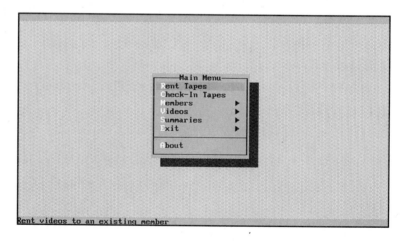

All the menus in the application behave like Paradox menus:

- The first letter in each menu item is highlighted, defining it as a *hot key*. Ideally, you create menus in which each item starts with a unique letter in order to eliminate ambiguity among menu choices.

- Arrows to the right of menu choices indicate submenus.

- The prompt in the lower left corner of the screen describes the action the menu item takes when selected.

- Disabled menu items appear in reverse video.

- Menu items can be selected with the mouse or keyboard.

- Pressing Esc "backs out" of a submenu to its parent menu.

The following sections briefly describe the available Main menu choices.

Rent Tapes

Rent Tapes enables clerks to rent videos to members. A member identification number is requested, and a form records the videos rented to the member. The Rent Tapes session immediately notifies the user whether the account contains any special notes or whether any late fees are due. Before ending the transaction, the user may print an invoice or cancel the entire transaction. The rental transaction is discussed in detail later in this chapter.

Check-In Tapes

Check-In Tapes enables the user to check in any number of previously rented tapes. The application requests a video identification number, then displays the title of the video and updates the database. When the user checks in a video, the application automatically calculates late charges, if any. The application gives the user the opportunity to accept immediate payment, thereby clearing late charges from the account. If the application user does not receive payment for late charges immediately, late charges appear when the member attempts to rent another video. This portion of the application is discussed in detail later in this chapter.

Members

In figure 18.2, four of the Main menu selections have submenus, as indicated by the arrow to the right of the menu item. When the user selects one of these options, such as **M**embers, another menu appears with additional choices. Figure 18.3 shows that two additional choices, **N**ew Member and **D**elete Member, are available under the Members menu. From this menu, the user can edit information on an existing member, delete a member, or add a new member.

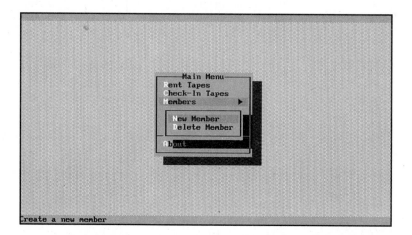

FIG. 18.3

The Members menu.

Videos

Videos, like **M**embers, enables the user to add or delete tapes from inventory. These features are not available in the sample application and therefore are displayed in reverse video. Later in this chapter you see that adding and deleting videos from inventory is much like adding and deleting members.

Summaries

Summaries gives the user the capability to print or display predesigned reports (see fig. 18.4). The user may report on late fees, inventory information, or account and video histories. For the purpose of this sample application, many of these features are not implemented; only the menu structure is in place. To implement the features indicated by the menu, you could design reports that satisfy these selections and attach the appropriate code to support them. Later in this chapter, you see what reports you may want to add.

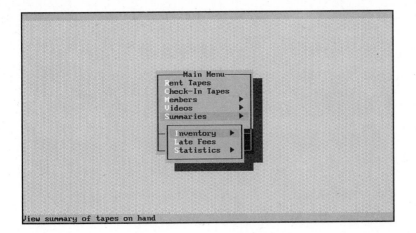

FIG. 18.4

The Summaries menu.

About

About presents the user with a dialog box that provides information regarding the application as well as basic system information such as available memory, date, and time (see fig 18.5). The About dialog box remains on-screen until the user clicks the OK button. OK clears the dialog box from the screen and returns the user to the Main menu.

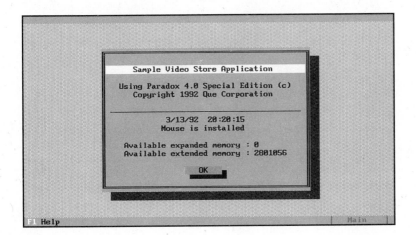

FIG. 18.5

The About dialog box.

Exit

The user selects Exit to leave the application. A submenu confirming the selection appears just as in Paradox interactive mode (see fig. 18.6).

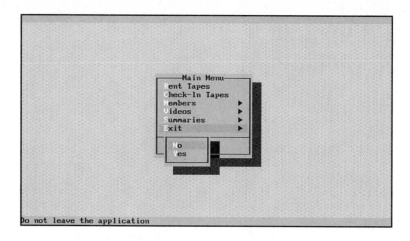

FIG. 18.6

The Exit menu.

If the user happens to press Esc while the Main menu is displayed, another dialog box asks the user to confirm (see fig. 18.7).

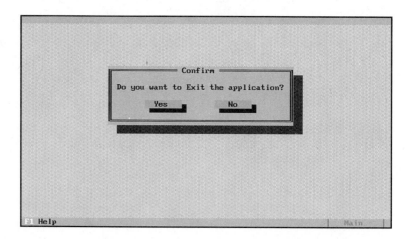

FIG. 18.7

The Confirm Exit
dialog box.

Renting Videos

When renting videos to an existing member, the user is expected to follow these steps:

1. Select **R**ent Tapes from the Main menu.

2. Provide member account number.

3. Enter video identification number for each tape rented.

4. Choose **P**rint from the pull-down menu.

5. Require member to sign invoice.

6. Collect payment for current fees and late fees.

When the user selects **R**ent Tapes from the Main menu, the application immediately requires a member account number before continuing (see fig. 18.8). If an invalid number is entered, the application warns the user and allows another entry. The user may cancel this operation and return to the Main menu at any time by selecting the Cancel button or pressing Esc.

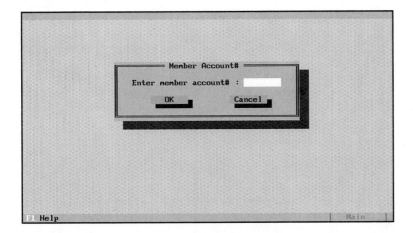

FIG. 18.8

Entering a member account number.

When a valid entry is accepted, the message `Please wait...` appears on-screen for a few seconds followed by a rental transaction image. If notes exist, a window with the notes appears and waits for the user to respond (see fig. 18.9). The message in the lower right corner of the screen instructs the user to begin typing to make changes to the field. The prompt in the lower left corner tells the user to press F2 to save changes to the notes, or Esc to cancel changes; in both cases, the window closes. The user can move or resize the notes using standard Paradox keys (Ctrl-F5) or the mouse.

After the notes window is cleared, the user can begin the rental transaction. The user merely types in the video number, presses Enter, and the Video Title, Date Out, Due Date, and Fee fields are filled in automatically. The Current Charges, Sales Tax, and Invoice Total fields also are calculated and displayed. If any late fees are pending, they too are displayed. Figure 18.10 shows the rental transaction image after one video number has been entered. Notice that all fields are filled, the totals are accurately calculated, and a late fee is pending.

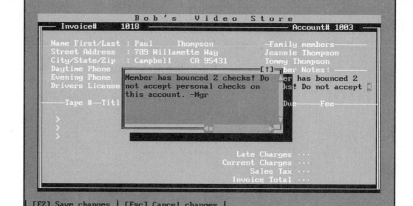

FIG. 18.9

Account notes
displayed
during rental
transaction.

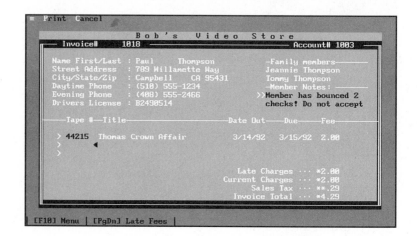

FIG. 18.10

Rental transaction
image after
entering video
number.

The [PgDn] Late Fees prompt in the lower left corner indicates that
late fees can be viewed in more detail by pressing PgDn (see fig. 18.11).
If the user tries to modify any fields while viewing late fee details—by
pressing Backspace, for example—the message Field cannot be
modified appears in the lower right of the screen. The only key available at this point in the application is the PgUp key. The prompt in the
lower left of the screen indicates that the user can press PgUp to return
to the rental transaction. Notice also that all of the menu items are
shown in reverse video when late fee details are displayed.

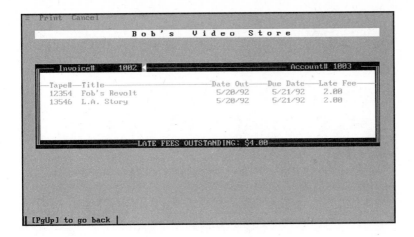

FIG. 18.11

Viewing late fee
details.

Using the Rental Pull-Down Menu

Interacting with the pull-down menu within the rental transaction session is just like interacting with any other menu. The F10 key changes focus from the workspace to the menu bar, and pressing Enter or clicking with the mouse selects the menu item. The Rental pull-down menu consists of three choices: the System menu icon (≡), **P**rint, and **C**ancel.

The system icon displays application-specific information and system information. This menu selection produces the same dialog box as **A**bout from the Main menu, but it displays over the rental transaction image (see figure 18.12).

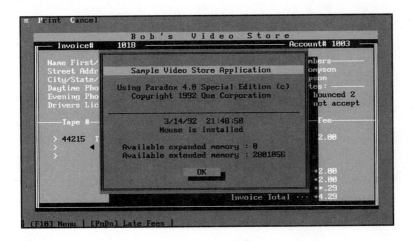

FIG. 18.12

System informa-
tion displayed
over the rental
transaction
image.

The **P**rint option completes the current transaction, checks the printer status, and prints the invoice for the customer to sign. If the printer is not ready, the pop-up menu shown in figure 18.13 notifies the user and provides options to retry or cancel.

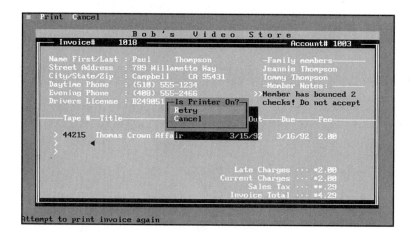

FIG. 18.13

Pop-up menu that displays when printer is not ready.

The user may select **R**etry to attempt to print the invoice again or Cancel to cancel the print job. If the user selects **C**ancel, a dialog box serves as confirmation before cancelling the print job (see fig 18.14). After the application determines that the device is ready for output, the invoice is sent to the printer and the Main menu displays again. Figure 18.15 shows an example of the printed video store invoice.

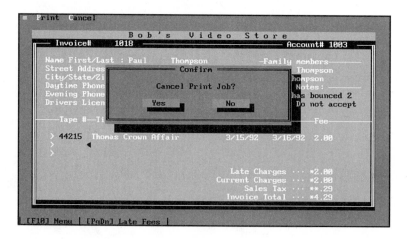

FIG. 18.14

Confirmation dialog box when attempting to cancel a print job.

```
──────────   B o b ' s   V i d e o   S t o r e   ──────────

  (408) 555-9876                              123 Brooklyn Ave
  11am-11pm Daily        Customer Invoice     Campbell CA 95001
                          Member :  1003



  Paul    Thompson                        Invoice: 1018
  789 Willamette Way                      Date :  3/15/92
  Campbell      CA 95431                  Time :  2:54 pm
  Day Phone (510) 555-1234
  Eve Phone (408) 555-2466


  Video#  Movie Title                     Due Date   Fee
  ───     ─────────────────────────       ───────    ───

  44215   Thomas Crown Affair             3/16/92    2.00

  ──────────────────────────────────────────────────────

                                  Late Charges   *2.00
                               Current Charges   *2.00
  Please return tapes rewound!        Sales Tax  **.44
                                  Invoice Total   *4.44



  ──────────────────────    ──────────────
     Customer Signature          Phone



          ***  Thank You For Your Business  ***
```

Sample customer invoice.

If the user selects Cancel instead of selecting Print from the pull-down menu, a submenu appears requesting confirmation (**Yes/No**). **Yes** cancels the entire rental transaction and returns to the Main menu; **No** returns the user to the rental transaction session (see fig. 18.16).

Returning Videos

The sample application provides an easy check-in process. When a member returns tapes to the store, the user merely selects Check-in Tapes from the main menu. The application displays a dialog box for the user to enter a video identification number. When the user types in the video number, a message indicates that the database has been updated (see fig. 18.17).

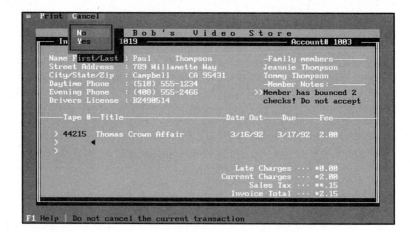

FIG. 18.16

The Cancel pull-down menu.

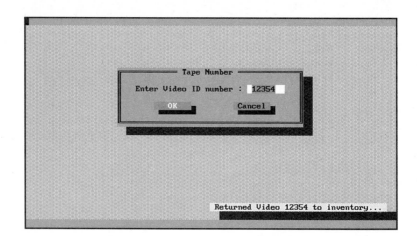

FIG. 18.17

Dialog box for returning videos.

The user may enter any number of video numbers, one at a time, through this dialog box. After a number of videos have been returned to inventory, the user may press the dialog's Cancel button, or press Esc to return to the main menu. Because videos may be returned through the store's night drop, applicable late fees are only calculated and entered into the database. When a customer rents another video, the application displays appropriate late fee charges, which the customer can pay at that time. See "Renting Videos" earlier in this chapter for details.

Creating Sample Application Objects

This section describes all the tables, forms, reports, and validity checks used by the sample application. You learn how the tables are structured, how the forms and reports are designed, and on what validity checks the application relies.

You should recognize the forms and reports described in this section from the preceding section, which introduced you to the application from a user's perspective.

Sample Application Tables

The sample application stores information in a database consisting of six tables. This list describes the contents of each table. Refer to Table 18.1 through Table 18.5 for the structure of the tables.

- *Members.* Contains identifying information on video store customers. Table 18.1 shows the Members table structure.

- *Tapes.* Contains a description of each video in inventory (see table 18.2).

- *Invoice.* Stores information that defines a rental transaction (see table 18.3).

- *LineItem.* Stores detailed information for each member transaction (see table 18.4).

- *PrevBal.* Holds information about the previous balance for each member. This table is a temporary holding bay until the previous balance is resolved (see table 18.5).

- *DummyRpt.* Stores a report specification only. The application copies DummyRpt's report specification to an Answer table to print a customer invoice. The DummyRpt table never holds any data. (see table 18.6).

Table 18.1. Structure of the Members Table

Field no.	Field name	Field type
1	Account#	N*
2	Last Name	A12
3	First Name	A8
4	CDL	A8
5	Street	A25
6	City	A15
7	State	A2
8	Zip	A10
9	Eve Telephone	A14
10	Day Telephone	A14
11	Authorized users	M25
12	Notes	M15

Table 18.2. Structure of the Tapes Table

Field no.	Field name	Field type
1	Video ID	N*
2	Category	A15
3	Title	A35
4	Rate Code	A1
5	Fee	$
6	Comments	M10

Table 18.3. Structure of the Invoice Table

Field no.	Field name	Field type
1	Invoice#	N*
2	Account#	N
3	Late Fees	$
4	Current Fees	$
5	Tax	$
6	Invoice Total	$

Table 18.4. Structure of the LineItem Table

Field no.	Field name	Field type
1	Invoice#	N*
2	Video ID	N*
3	Title	A35
4	Date Out	D
5	Due Date	D
6	Fee	$

Table 18.5. Structure of the PrevBal Table

Field no.	Field name	Field type
1	Invoice#	N*
2	Video ID	N*
3	Title	A35
4	Due Date	D
5	Date Out	D
6	Date In	D
7	Late Fee	$
8	Fee Per Day	$

Table 18.6. Structure of the DummyRpt Table

Field no.	Field name	Field type
1	Invoice#	N
2	Account#	N
3	Tax	$
4	First Name	A12
5	Last Name	A8
6	Street	A25
7	City	A15
8	State	A2
9	Zip	A10
10	Day Telephone	A14
11	Eve Telephone	A14
12	Video ID	N
13	Title	A35
14	Due Date	D
15	Fee	$

Tables used by the video store application have the following relationships to one another:

Invoice table<———*one-to-many*—>>LineItem table

Invoice table<———*one-to-many*—>>PrevBal table

Invoice table<———*one-to-one*———>Members table

LineItem table<———*one-to-one*———>Tapes table

The sample application uses several validity checks to ensure that the user enters information correctly. All of the valchecks created for the sample application were created with the ValCheck menu in Edit mode. If you're unsure how to assign validity checks in Paradox, read Chapter 9, "Using Power Entry and Editing Features".

Table 18.7 describes each of the picture specifications used in the sample application. Refer to Chapter 9 for a complete explanation of the symbols used in each picture.

Table 18.7. Sample Application Picture Specifications

Picture	Purpose
[![?][*]]	Capitalize first letter of every word
CA	Accept only the string "CA"
#####[-####]	Zip code with optional four-digit extension
(###) ###-####	Telephone with area code

The Members table uses the most validity checks of all the tables in the Sample database. Table 18.8 describes each validity check created for the Members table. Notice that the State field has both Picture and Default validity checks.

Table 18.8. Validity Checks for Members Table

Field name	ValCheck	Value
First Name	Picture	*[![*?][*]]
Last Name	Picture	*[![*?][*]]
CDL	Required	
Street	Picture	*[![*?][*]]
City	Picture	*[![*?][*]]
State	Picture	CA
State	Default	CA
Zip	Picture	######[-####]
Eve Telephone	Picture	(###) ###-####
Day Telephone	Picture	(###) ###-####

The LineItem table uses a lookup table to verify that the video tape number entered actually exists in inventory. Table 18.9 describes the validity checks used in the LineItem table. Notice that the FillNoHelp option is enabled so that the user cannot press F1 during data entry.

Table 18.9. LineItem Table Validity Checks

Field name	ValCheck	Value
VideoID	TableLookup	Tapes AllCorrespondingFields FillNoHelp

The PrevBal table also uses a lookup table to verify video identification numbers that the user enters. See Table 18.10 for the PrevBal validity checks.

Table 18.10. PrevBal Table Validity Checks

Field name	ValCheck	Value
VideoID	TableLookup	Tapes AllCorrespondingFields FillNoHelp

The only validity check the Tapes table uses is a Picture to force the first letter of each word to a capital. Table 18.11 shows the validity checks for the Tapes table.

Table 18.11. Tapes Table Validity Checks

Field name	ValCheck	Value
Title	Picture	*[![*?][*]]

Sample Application Forms

Table 18.12 introduces the forms the sample application provides for user interaction. Detailed discussions of each table follow.

Table 18.12. Sample Application Forms

Table name	Tables embedded	Pages	Purpose in application
Invoice	Members	2	Processes rental transactions
	LineItem PrevBal		
Members	None	1	Adds and deletes members

Page One of the Master Invoice Form

Form 1 (Invoice.F1) of the Invoice table is a two-page, multitable form the application uses when the user rents videos to members. The form is designed with the Invoice table as master and the Members, LineItem, and PrevBal tables as embedded detail forms. Figure 18.18 shows the first of two pages of the master invoice form, in form design mode. Two detail tables are placed on page one: Members and LineItem. Table 18.13 describes each field on page one of the master form.

Table 18.13. Descriptions of Fields Placed on Form 1, Page 1 of the Invoice Table

Field#	Name	Type of field	Calculation
1	Invoice#	Display only	n/a
2	Account#	Regular	n/a
3	n/a	Calculated	Format("W6.2,E*", LateCharge)
4	n/a	Calculated	Format("W6.2,E*", SubTotal)

continues

Table 18.13. Continued

Field#	Name	Type of field	Calculation
5	n/a	Calculated	Format("W6.2,E*", Round((SubTotal+ LateCharge)*.0725,3))
6	n/a	Calculated	Format("W6.2,E*", Round((SubTotal+ LateCharge)*1.0725,3))

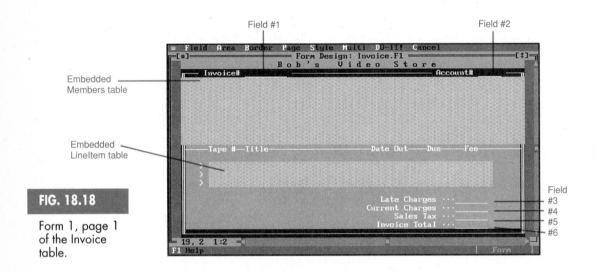

FIG. 18.18

Form 1, page 1 of the Invoice table.

The calculated fields on this form include formatted variables. Remember from earlier chapters that many PAL functions can be used in forms and reports. The FORMAT function is used often in forms and reports to change the appearance of calculated or display-only fields. Later in this chapter, you learn how the application manages the variables used in this form.

The Embedded Members Form

Form 1 of the Members table (Members.F1) is a single table, single record form, designed to be embedded into form 1 of the Invoice table. Figure 18.19 shows the form in form design mode. Notice that borders on the left and right are placed to fit nicely in the master form. Table 18.14 describes the fields placed on the members detail form 1.

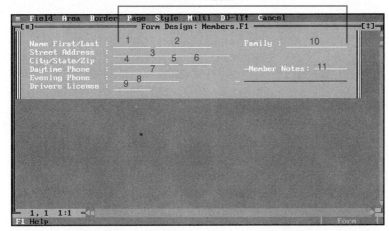

FIG. 18.19

The embedded
Members form 1.

Table 18.14. Field Descriptions of the Members Detail Form 1

Field#	Name	Type of field
1	First Name	Display only
2	Last Name	Display only
3	Street	Display only
4	City	Display only
5	State	Display only
6	Zip	Display only
7	Daytime Phone	Display only
8	Evening Phone	Display only
9	CDL	Display only
10	Authorized Users	Display only: word-wrapped 2 lines
11	Notes	Regular: word-wrapped 2 lines

The Embedded LineItem Form

Form 1 of the LineItem table (LineItem.F1) is designed as an embedded
form for the master Invoice form. This embedded form accepts video

identification numbers directly into the only regular field, Video ID. (The term *regular field* indicates that the field can be edited directly in form view.) The other fields on the form are display-only fields and cannot be edited directly. Figure 18.20 shows the LineItem table's form 1 in Design mode. Table 18.15 describes the fields placed on the LineItem table form 1.

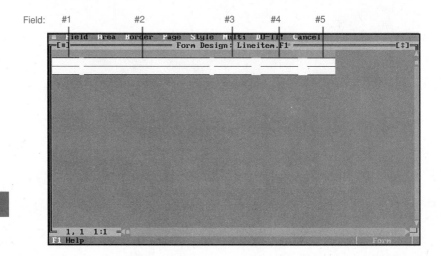

FIG. 18.20

The embedded
LineItem form 1.

Table 18.15. Field Descriptions of the Embedded LineItem Table Form 1

Field#	Name	Type of field
1	Video ID	Regular
2	Title	Display Only
3	Date Out	Display Only
4	Due Date	Display Only
5	Fee	Display Only

Page Two of the Master Invoice Form

The application uses page two of the Master Invoice form to display late charge details, shown in form design mode in figure 18.21. Like the first page, page two also has an embedded form: PrevBal form 1. Information about the video number, title, date rented, date due, and late fees is displayed on this page. Table 18.16 describes its placed fields.

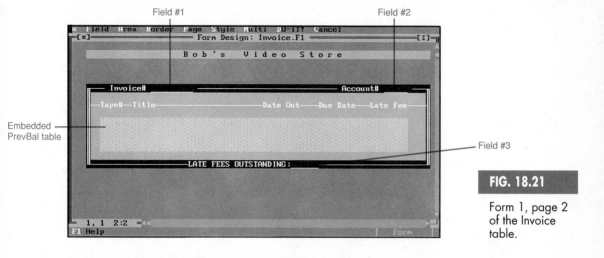

FIG. 18.21

Form 1, page 2 of the Invoice table.

Table 18.16. Field Descriptions of Page 2, Form 1 of the Invoice Table

Field#	Name	Type of field	Calculation
1	Invoice#	Regular	n/a
2	Account#	Display Only	n/a
3	n/a	Calculated	Format("W6.2, E$", LateCharge)

The Embedded PrevBal Form

The PrevBal detail form, which the application uses to display late charge details, is placed on page two of the master Invoice form. Figure 18.22 shows the detail form in form design mode, and Table 18.17 describes each of the fields.

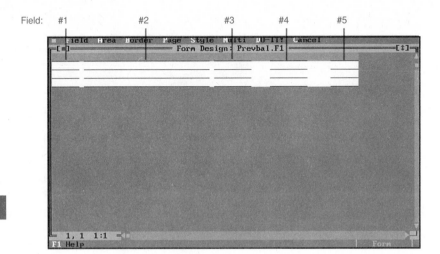

FIG. 18.22

The embedded
PrevBal form.

Table 18.17. Field Descriptions of the Embedded PrevBal Table Form 1

Field#	Name	Type of field
1	Video ID	Regular
2	Title	Regular
3	Due Date	Regular
4	Date In	Regular
5	Late Fee	Regular

Other fields not noted in table 18.16 are placed as regular fields.

The Single Table Members Form

The Members table has two forms designed for use in the sample application. The first form (Members.F1) is a detail form embedded into the master Invoice form, discussed earlier in this chapter. The second form (Members.F2) is a simple single table form used to add or delete member accounts from the database (see fig. 18.23). Table 18.18 describes the fields placed on this form.

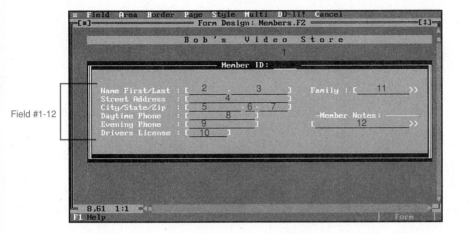

FIG. 18.23

The single table
Members form.

Table 18.18. Field Descriptions of the Members Single Table Form 2

Field#	Name	Type of field
1	Member ID	Display only
2	First Name	Regular
3	Last Name	Regular
4	Street	Regular
5	City	Regular
6	State	Regular
7	Zip	Regular
8	Daytime Phone	Regular
9	Evening Phone	Regular
10	CDL	Regular
11	Authorized Users	Regular: word-wrapped 3 lines
12	Notes	Regular: word-wrapped 3 lines

Sample Application Reports

The sample application enables the user to print an invoice for the
customer's signature after completing a rental transaction. The printed

invoice comes from a report specification designed not for the Invoice table as you might expect, but for the DummyRpt table. The DummyRpt table, as discussed earlier, is a table that never contains any records; it's only purpose is to hold a report specification that the application uses to print a customer invoice.

When the user chooses Print from the rental transaction menu, the application runs a predesigned query, then copies the report specification from the DummyRpt table to the temporary Answer table. After the application has copied the report to the Answer table, the report is sent to the printer. This process is discussed in more detail later in this chapter.

The report designed for the DummyRpt table is a typical tabular report specification, shown in figures 18.24 and 18.25. Figure 18.23 shows the top portion of the report specification.

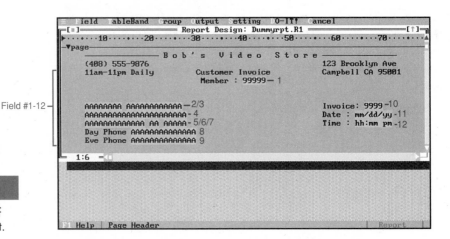

FIG. 18.24

Top portion of the DummyRpt.

As you can see from figure 18.24, much of the report's design is made up of text and other characters typed directly on the report specification. Although you cannot place a border from the report design menus, you can use ASCII characters to create them yourself. The top of the report specification features a single line border on either side of the store name. To create a bordered effect like this, enter the ASCII character 196 directly on the report by holding the Alt key down and typing 196. When you release the Alt key, a single line border appears at the current cursor position.

Instead of repeating these keystrokes for a long border, you can use an instant script to make your job easier. Press the Alt-F3 key combination to begin the instant script recorder, then enter a few border characters as described above. Now press Alt-F3 to end the instant script recorder, and press Alt-F4 to play the instant script. Every time you press Alt-F4, several single line border characters appear at the current cursor location. For more information on recording instant scripts, read Chapter 6, "Getting Started with Scripts and Keyboard Macros".

The top portion of the report specification consists mostly of customer related information, placed as regular fields. Table 18.19 describes each of the fields placed on the top of the report specification.

Table 18.19. Report Specification for DummyRpt Table (Top half)		
Field#	**Name**	**Type of field**
1	Account#	Regular
2	First Name	Regular
3	Last Name	Regular
4	Street	Regular
5	City	Regular
6	State	Regular
7	Zip	Regular
8	Day Telephone	Regular
9	Eve Telephone	Regular
10	Invoice#	Regular
11	"Date"	Current date
12	"Time"	Current time

The lower portion of the report specification displays detail and summary information. Each video that the customer rents appears in the table band, and all summary information is calculated by placing summary fields on the report. Figure 18.25 shows the lower portion of the report specification, and Table 18.20 describes each of the fields.

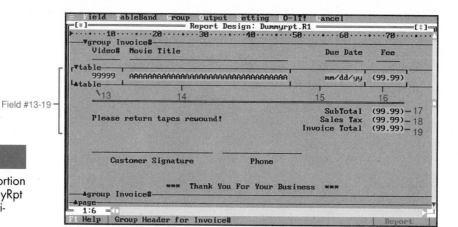

FIG. 18.25

The lower portion of the DummyRpt report specification.

Table 18.20. Report Specification for DummyRpt Table (Lower half)

Field#	Name	Type of field
13	Video ID	Regular
14	Title	Regular
15	Due Date	Regular
16	Fee	Regular
17	Sub Total	Summary-Total for Fee, per group
18	Sales Tax	Summary-Total for Tax, per group
19	Invoice Total	Summary Calculated-[Tax]+[Fee], per group

Creating Sample Application Scripts

This section describes all of the PAL code written for the video store application. Here you find the details of how the application actually makes use of the objects described in the preceding section, including all the program code; a thorough description for every script, procedure, and library; and tips on how you can improve the sample application.

The sample application consists of three scripts. RunVideo.sc is the top level, or driver script, that gets the application going. VidMain.sc defines procedures that are central to the application and writes each procedure to a library named VidMain.lib. VidUtil.sc defines those procedures that can be categorized as utility procedures—usually small procedures that perform one or two tasks. VidUtil.sc writes each of its procedures to a library named VidUtil.lib

As you read through the following sections, refer to the code frequently to help you understand the specifics of each section of code. Notice that all of the scripts and procedure definitions are prefaced with a description section inserted in the form of comments. Comments also are placed strategically near PAL commands to make the code more readable.

You may think that the comments in the sample application are strictly for your benefit, but your own code should contain a similar volume of comments. Including comments in your scripts is not a requirement, but it is good programming practice. Don't be a miser when it comes to writing comments in your code; write plenty of clear, concise comments, and you will thank yourself (or someone else will) when you need to make changes later.

The RunVideo.sc Script

The RunVideo.sc script is the application's top level, driver script; the user must play this script to start the application. It initializes the environment, creates libraries if necessary, and invokes the first procedure in the application.

RunVideo makes sure that the workspace is cleared and that all variables and procedures are cleared from memory before enabling the user to interact with the application. Always initialize the system in the driver script to ensure that the application begins with a clean slate. The computer that is running your application also may be used for other applications (Paradox or otherwise), and you need to clean up after them to reserve system resources for your application.

Consider the RunVideo.sc script task by task. The script first releases all variables and procedures from memory, then returns Paradox to main mode (if it is not there already) and clears the workspace of any image or non-image windows. The first time the user plays RunVideo.sc, the application's libraries may not exist, so the script makes sure that both libraries are rebuilt. The script then assigns the global variable AutoLib. Paradox and PAL use the AutoLib system variable as a search path for procedures. Any procedures called from now on search the VidMain and VidUtil libraries for the procedure code.

After RunVideo.sc makes sure that the necessary libraries exist, it clears the Paradox menus and calls a procedure named AppIntro( ). AppIntro is merely a window that displays basic information about the application. (You probably remember seeing this splash screen earlier in this chapter.) You see how the AppIntro( ) procedure works a little later.

Next, the driver script places the Invoice table on the workspace and moves it out of sight. If the Invoice table is empty, the script cannot switch to form view because form view is available in main mode when the table is empty. (If you have not heeded earlier warnings to learn Paradox before writing PAL code, you may be surprised to learn that this script would fail if it didn't take this aspect of Paradox into consideration.) The script uses the ISEMPTY( ) function before attempting to switch to form view in order to avoid an error.

If the table is not empty, the script switches to the multitable form used for rental transactions, stores its window handle, and moves it off the screen.

Because windows move around on the workspace instantaneously, the top level script places these images on the workspace as part of its initiation process and then hides them until the application needs them. You can create windows off-screen and move them into the visible workspace quickly, when your application needs them.

While this processing is taking place, the user sees only the splash screen. After the workspace is set up, the splash screen is removed, and the Main menu displays.

```
;******************************************************************************
; script name   : RunVideo.sc
; purpose       : driver script for sample video store application
; library       : None
; procedures    : None
; procs called  : AppIntro()
;                 MaxWindow()
;                 MainMenu()
;
;******************************************************************************

RELEASE VARS ALL                    ; release variables
RELEASE PROCS ALL                   ; and procedures

RESET

ALTSPACE {Desktop} {Empty}          ; remove all windows from the workspace
ECHO NORMAL                         ; briefly show changes to the workspace
```

```
ECHO OFF

IF NOT ISFILE(SDIR() + "VidUtil.lib") OR        ; check to see if video
   NOT ISFILE(SDIR() + "VidMain.lib")           ; store libraries exist
   THEN
      MESSAGE "Rebuilding sample libraries, please wait..."
      RUN NOREFRESH "Del VidUtil.lib"           ; delete both libraries
      RUN NOREFRESH "Del VidMain.lib"           ; if one is missing
      CREATELIB "VidUtil"                        ; re-create both libraries
      CREATELIB "VidMain"
      PLAY "VidUtil"                             ; play the script with
      PLAY "VidMain"                             ; utility and main procs
      MESSAGE "All libraries have been rebuilt..."
      SLEEP 1000
      MESSAGE ""                                 ; clear message
ENDIF

AutoLib = "VidMain,VidUtil"         ; automatically look in these libraries

SHOWPULLDOWN                         ; clear Paradox menus from top of screen
ENDMENU
PROMPT ""
ECHO NORMAL
ECHO OFF
AppIntro()                           ; display information screen while
                                     ; application is loading

DYNARRAY MenuProcs[]                         ; define a dynamic array
MenuProcs["RentTapes"]     = "RentTapes"     ; these tag names are used
MenuProcs["ReturnTapes"]   = "ReturnTapes"   ; in MainMenu() proc
MenuProcs["AddMbr"]        = "AddMbr"        ; the values of array elements
MenuProcs["DelMbr"]        = "DelMbr"        ; evaluate to procedure names
MenuProcs["LeaveApp"]      = "LeaveApp"
MenuProcs["AppInfo"]       = "ShowAboutBox"

VIEW "Invoice"                          ; place Invoice table on workspace
WINDOW HANDLE IMAGE 1 TO InvoiceTab     ; get table window handle
WINDOW MOVE InvoiceTab TO 1000,0        ; hide table window off screen

IF NOT ISEMPTY("Invoice")               ; if the table is empty, we won't
                                        ; be able to switch to form view
   THEN PICKFORM 1                      ; if not, switch to multi-table form
        WINDOW HANDLE FORM TO RentalForm ; get form window handle
        MaxWindow(RentalForm)           ; customize form window attributes
        WINDOW MOVE RentalForm TO 1000,0 ; hide form window off screen
   ELSE SLEEP 2000
```

```
    ENDIF

    WINDOW SELECT InfoWindow          ; go to the information window
    WINDOW CLOSE                      ; and close it

      ; Now the environment has been initialized, and the application
      ; can take over. The procedure MainMenu() is called inside
      ; a continuous loop, so that the application will continue
      ; to execute until the user explicitly exits.

    WHILE True
      MainMenu()
    ENDWHILE
```

The VidMain.sc Script

This section describes the VidMain.sc script, which defines eight procedures that make up the core of the sample application.

Comments that appear above each procedure declaration describe the purpose of the procedure. The comments include the names of the procedures that call the procedure and the names of procedures that the procedure executes.

Table 18.21 lists the procedures that VidMain.sc defines and writes to the VidMain.lib library.

Table 18.21. Contents of the VidMain Library (Source Script VidMain.sc)

Procedure name	Major purpose
MainMenu()	Constructs the top level pop-up menu
RentTapes()	Determines what special actions should take place before initiating rental transaction procedures
RentalMenu()	Constructs the pull-down menu used when renting videos
RentalWaitForm()	Sets up the workspace to enable users to rent videos
RentalWaitProc()	Handles interaction with the WAIT session created with RentTapes() procedure

Procedure name	Major purpose
AddMbr( )	Sets up the workspace to enable users to add new members to the database
AddMbrWaitProc( )	Handles interaction with the WAIT session created with AddMbr( ) procedure
DelMbr( )	Enables users to delete members from the database
RetTapesDLogProc( )	Dialog procedure designed specifically for the dialog box defined in the ReturnTapes( ) procedure. Updates late fee information in the PrevBal table.
ReturnTapes( )	Defines a dialog box used to return video tapes to inventory

Structure of the VidMain.sc Script

VidMain.sc defines each procedure (reads it into memory), adds it to a single library, and releases the procedure from memory.

Each procedure begins with several lines of comments that serve as a description of the procedure. Also included in the header comments is a list of the procedures called from the following procedure and a list of its possible return values. After the procedure is read into memory, it is written to a library named VidMain.lib and then released from memory. As you can see, this process is repeated for each procedure in the script.

VidMain.sc declares a variable called LibName near the top of the script. LibName holds the string value "VidMain", which is the library in which all procedures in this script are written. Following each procedure definition, the statement WRITELIB LibName <procedure name> writes the procedure to the VidMain.lib library. (<procedure name> is replaced by the appropriate procedure name.) The value of the LibName variable is retained only while the script is playing and is released at the end of the script.

By assigning the library name you intend to use in a particular script, you can easily change the library name by changing the value of the variable.

The VidMain.sc script begins with script header information in the form of comments and an assignment to the LibName variable.

```
; ************************************************************
; script name : VidMain.sc
; purpose     : defines main procedures used in the sample
;                 video store application
; library     : VidMain.lib
; procedures  : RentalMenu()     : displays pull-down menu
;               MainMenu()       : displays main menu (pop-up)
;               AddMbrWaitProc() : manages Wait when adding members
;               AddMbr()         : sets up Wait for adding members
;               DelMbr()         : manages Wait when deleting members
;               RentTapes()      : initializes workspace before renting
;               RentalWaitProc() : manages Wait when renting videos
;               RentalWaitForm() : sets up Wait when renting  videos
;               RetTapesDlogProc(): dialog procedure for ReturnTapes()
;               ReturnTapes()    : lets user return tapes to inventory
;************************************************************
LibName = "VidMain"        ; assign variable used exclusively for
                           ; this script
;************************************************************
;           Beginning of VidMain procedure definitions
;************************************************************
```

The MainMenu() Procedure

The first defined in the VidMain.sc script is MainMenu(). MainMenu() displays a pop-up menu that the application uses for its top-level, or main menu. The user navigates through the application, beginning with the main menu. All the application's actions are initiated from this top-level menu. After displaying the pull-down menu, MainMenu() takes appropriate action based on the user's menu selection.

MainMenu()'s first task is to clear the Paradox menus from the top of the screen. Because PAL does not have an explicit command for this purpose, MainMenu() uses a simple trick to clear the menus: it uses the SHOWPULLDOWN command immediately followed by the terminating keyword ENDMENU. This sequence places an empty pull-down menu over the Paradox menus, thereby hiding them from view. After hiding the Paradox menus, MainMenu() displays its own pop-up menu in the center of the screen.

The syntax of the SHOWPOPUP command is fairly straightforward (refer to the command reference for details). The structure begins with a SHOWPOPUP command and ends with an ENDMENU command. The body of the SHOWPOPUP structure consists of a menu item with an associated prompt followed by a tag name. The menu item string creates a menu command on the pop-up. The prompt associated with the menu item displays in the lower left corner of the screen; it describes the action that results when the menu choice is selected.

You can think of the pop-up menu tag as the name tag for the menu choice. When the user makes a selection from the menu, the SHOWPOPUP construct assigns the variable designated by the TO keyword, following ENDMENU. Your procedure can evaluate the variable to determine which item the user selected and take appropriate action.

Remember that the dynamic array MenuProcs[] was defined in the application's driver script, and procedure names were assigned to the array elements. When the user selects a menu item, MainMenu() compares the tag name of the menu selection to the dynamic array elements. If the dynamic array MenuProcs[] has an element with the same name as the menu tag, MainMenu() issues an EXECPROC command to execute the procedure with the same name. For this technique to work properly, you must be sure to match all the procedure names with the dynamic array elements and with the menu tags. Menu tags that don't correspond to the dynamic array elements are ignored, and MainMenu() terminates without taking action.

```
; .................................................
; procedure    : MainMenu()
; purpose      : displays the main menu and takes
;                action based on user selection
; returns      : None
; calls procs  : RentTapes()
;                ReturnTapes()
;                AddMbr()
;                DelMbr()
;                LeaveApp()
;                AppInfo()
;                ConfirmBox()
; .................................................

PROC MainMenu()
  PRIVATE MenuSelect                   ; limit scope of variable to this proc

    SHOWPOPUP "Main Menu" CENTERED
      "Rent Tapes"     : "Rent videos to an existing member" : "RentTapes",
      "Check-In Tapes" : "Process tapes returned by members" : "ReturnTapes",
      "Members"        : "Delete or Add members"             : "MbrMenu"
        SUBMENU
          "New Member"    : "Create a new member"            : "AddMbr",
          "Delete Member" : "Delete an existing member" : "DelMbr"
```

```
        ENDSUBMENU,
     "Videos" : "Add or Delete videos from inventory" : "TapeMenu"
       SUBMENU
         "Add Videos"    : "Add videos to inventory" :
            DISABLE "AddTape",
         "Delete Videos" : "Delete videos from inventory" :
            DISABLE "DelTape",
         "Browse List"   : "Review entire video inventory" :
            DISABLE "ViewTape"
       ENDSUBMENU,
     "Summaries" : "Inventory, Late Fees, and Statistics" : "Summaries"
       SUBMENU
         "Inventory"  : "View inventory summary" : "TapeSum"
           SUBMENU
             "Tapes on hand" : "Show list of tapes currently in store" :
                DISABLE "TapesIn",
             "Tapes out"     : "Show list of tapes currently rented":
                DISABLE "TapesOut"
           ENDSUBMENU,
         "Late Fees"  : "View accounts owing late fees"      : "LateSum",
         "Statistics" : "View history of accounts and tapes" : "Stats"
           SUBMENU
             "Account History" : "Summarize history of an account" :
                DISABLE "AcctHist",
             "Tape History"    : "Summarize history of tapes" :
                DISABLE "TapeHist"
           ENDSUBMENU
       ENDSUBMENU,
     "Exit" : "Leave the application" : "ExitMenu"
       SUBMENU
         "No"  : "Do not leave the application" : "DontQuit",
         "Yes" : "Leave the application"        : "LeaveApp"
       ENDSUBMENU,
     SEPARATOR,
     "About" : "Display system information" : "AppInfo"
 ENDMENU

 TO MenuSelect              ; assign variable with choice the menu selection

 IF MenuSelect = "Esc"
   THEN Answer = ConfirmBox("Do you want to leave application?","","")
        IF Answer = True
          THEN LeaveApp()
        ENDIF
 ENDIF
```

```
IF ISASSIGNED(MenuProcs[MenuSelect])
   THEN EXECPROC MenuProcs[MenuSelect] ; execute the procedure with the
   ENDIF                                ; same name as the menu tag name

ENDPROC                     ; end of MainMenu() procedure definition

WRITELIB libname MainMenu   ; write procedure to library
RELEASE PROCS MainMenu      ; release procedure from memory
```

The RentTapes( ) Procedure

RentTapes( ) sets up the workspace for renting videos to members. It automatically assigns a new number for the customer invoice, displays important notes regarding the customer account, and sets up a WAIT session.

The procedure first prompts the user for a member identification number by calling GetAcctID( ). When the user enters a valid member number, the procedure switches to the multitable form if the form is not already on the workspace. Remember that in the application driver script, the table may have been empty and therefore could not switch to the form. If necessary, RentTapes( ) enters coedit mode before attempting to open the form.

The procedure assigns both key fields, Invoice# and Account#, and issues the RESYNCKEY to synchronize the detail forms to the master. Again, knowing how Paradox operates in interactive mode is essential. The procedure uses an IIF( ) function to assign a new, unique invoice number, sequentially numbered starting at 1001, and enters the member identification number entered by the user.

RentTapes( ) checks whether the master table's Memo field contains any notes; if so, RentTapes( ) issues the FIELDVIEW command and then customizes the appearance of the normal Memo field box with a call to TameMemoBox( ).

TameMemoBox( ) customizes the attributes of the Memo field window, placing it in a nested WAIT FIELD session. The user may interact with the Memo field window to add or delete text or to move or resize the window. All the normal Paradox keys and mouse actions are permitted. TameMemoBox( ) is described in more detail later in this chapter.

```
      ;
      ...........................................................
      ; procedure   : RentTapes()
      ; purpose     : manages the rental trasaction session
      ; global vars : LateCharge, SubTotal, AcctID
```

```
; returns      :
; calls procs : GetAcctID()
;               TameMemoBox()
;               RentalMenu()
;               RentalWaitForm()
; .....................................................

PROC RentTapes()

  AcctID = GetAcctID()                          ; calls GetAcctID() procedure
                                                ; and assigns AcctID global
                                                ; variable with a number, or
                                                ; False if user cancelled

  IF AcctID = False
    THEN RETURN        ; False                  ; return False to calling proc
  ENDIF
  MESSAGE "Please wait..."                       ; subsequent workspace
                                                ; manipulation may take a few
                                                ; seconds - notify the user

      ; the toplevel, or driver script placed the Invoice table on the
      ; workspace. If the table was empty, the script was not able to
      ; switch to formview while in Main mode. If this was the case,
      ; this section will put the table into coedit mode, switch to
      ; the multi-table form (the RentalForm window), call a
      ; utility procedure to set attributes for the form window, and
      ; move it in to place. If the RentalForm has already been opened
      ; the window merely is moved in to position, and placed in coedit
      ; mode.

  IF ISASSIGNED(RentalForm)                     ; if the RentalForm window is open
    THEN WINDOW MOVE RentalForm TO 1,0          ; move it in to place
         COEDITKEY                              ; switch to coedit mode
         WINDOW SELECT RentalForm               ; make RentalForm the current window
         END CTRLPGDN                           ; open a new blank record
    ELSE COEDITKEY                              ; otherwise switch to coedit first
         WINDOW SELECT InvoiceTab
         PICKFORM 1                             ; open multi-table form
         WINDOW HANDLE FORM TO RentalForm       ; get handle for the form
         MaxWindow(RentalForm)                  ; apply attributes to form window
  ENDIF

      ; once the form is in coedit mode, assign the primary and secondary
      ; key field values. [Invoice#] field is assigned a consecutive
      ; value starting from 1001 with the IIF() function. [Account#] field
      ; is assigned with a value the user assigned through the GetAcctID()
      ; procedure, and is now the value of the AcctID variable.
```

```
InvoiceNum = IIF(ISEMPTY("Invoice"), 1001,
                         (CMAX("Invoice","Invoice#") + 1))
[Invoice#] = InvoiceNum
[Account#] = AcctID

MOVETO [PrevBal->Late Fee]              ; go to page 2 of master form
LateCharge = IMAGECSUM()                ; assign variable with total
                                        ; late fees

RESYNCKEY                               ; sync the multi-table form after
                                        ; new key field values are entered

IF NOT ISBLANK([Members->Notes])        ; check for Member table notes
   THEN MOVETO [Members->Notes]
        FIELDVIEW                       ; open up memo field
        TameMemoBox(GETWINDOW())        ; make the memo field window
                                        ; pretty, and place user in wait
ENDIF                                   ; field - see proc for details

MOVETO [LineItem->VIDEO ID]             ; move to field where user will
                                        ; enter the rented video number

MESSAGE ""
RentalMenu()                            ; call proc to display menu
RentalWaitForm()                        ; call proc to place user in
                                        ; wait session

ENDPROC                                 ; end of procedure definition

WRITELIB libname RentTapes              ; write procedure to library
RELEASE PROCS RentTapes                 ; release procedure from memory
```

The RentalMenu( ) Procedure

The RentalMenu( ) procedure displays a pull-down menu while the
rental transaction form (Invoice.F1) is on the workspace. RentalMenu( )
produces a pull-down menu with three items. Notice that it does not
take action based on the user's selection. The action each menu item
takes is dictated by the calling procedure RentalWaitProc( ).
RentalWaitProc( ) decides what to do when the user selects an item
from the pull-down menu

The RentalMenu( ) procedure builds a pull-down menu because it is
displayed simultaneously with the multitable form. This enables the
user to have the form in full view while providing access to the menu at
all times. Pop-up menus generally are used with an empty workspace,

whereas pull-down menus are reserved for times when other images or windows appear on-screen.

The SHOWPULLDOWN syntax is similar to SHOWPOPUP, in that each menu item is composed of a literal menu item, a prompt string, and a tag name. SHOWPULLDOWN offers more flexibility within event-driven WAIT sessions, primarily because of the different ways you can evaluate the tag name. Refer to the RentalWaitProc( ) procedure description to see how the tags generated by RentalMenu( ) are evaluated.

Generally, RentTapes( ) is called when the user selects **R**ent Tapes from the Main menu. RentalMenu( ) constructs the pull-down menu, RentalWaitForm( ) issues a WAIT WORKSPACE, and RentalWaitProc( ) handles events generated when the user moves around on the form or selects a menu. These four procedures work together to enable the user to rent videos to customers.

```
; .............................................................
; procedure   : RentalMenu()
; purpose     : displays a pull-down menu used
;               during a rental transaction - this proc
;               only displays the menu; it does not
;               evaluate menu choices
; returns     : None
; calls procs : None
; .............................................................

PROC RentalMenu()
  PRIVATE MenuSelection, EventList

  SHOWPULLDOWN
     "≡"      : "Display system information"                   : "AppInfo",
     "Print"  : "Send invoice to printer, and end session" : "PrintInv",
     "Cancel" : "Cancel the current transaction"              : "CancelMenu"
        SUBMENU
          "No"  : "Do not cancel the current transaction" : "NoCancel",
          "Yes" : "Cancel the current transaction"        : "CancelRent"
        ENDSUBMENU
  ENDMENU

ENDPROC

WRITELIB libname RentalMenu        ; write RentalMenu() to the library
RELEASE PROCS RentalMenu           ; and release it from memory
```

The RentalWaitForm( ) Procedure

RentalWaitForm( ) places the workspace in a WAIT WORKSPACE session to enable the user to rent videos to customers. Like most WAIT sessions in the sample application, this WAIT is event-driven and therefore requires a Wait Procedure to handle events. This one defines RentalWaitProc( ) as its Wait Procedure that manages interaction with the workspace. When the WAIT session is broken (the Wait Procedure returns the value 2), the commands following the ENDWAIT keyword execute to end the coedit session and move the form image off-screen.

```
; ..............................................................
; procedure   : RentalWaitForm()
; purpose     : places the multi-table form and workspace
;               in a wait session
; returns     : none
; calls procs : RentalWaitProc()
; ..............................................................

PROC RentalWaitForm()

  PROMPT "¦ [F10] Menu ¦ [PgDn] Late Fees ¦"
  WAIT WORKSPACE                        ; let user interact with workspace
    PROC "RentalWaitProc"               ; procedure called automatically,

    KEY "PgDn", "Esc", "Del",           ; when any of these specific keys
        "DOS", "DOSBIG"                 ; are pressed,
    MESSAGE "MENUSELECT"                ; when user chooses a menu item,
    TRIGGER "DEPARTROW"                 ; or when user leaves a record
  ENDWAIT
  SHOWPULLDOWN ENDMENU
  PROMPT ""

    ; the following commands execute only when the procedure
    ; returns a 2 value - the wait session has now ended

  WINDOW MOVE RentalForm TO 1000,0      ; move invoice form off screen
  ECHO NORMAL                           ; show change in workspace
  ECHO OFF                              ; then hide further workspace changes
  MESSAGE ""
  RELEASE VARS SubTotal, LateCharge     ; get rid of unneeded variables

ENDPROC                                 ; end of procedure definition

WRITELIB libname RentalWaitForm         ; write procedure to library
RELEASE PROCS RentalWaitForm            ; release procedure from memory
```

The RentalWaitProc( ) Procedure

The RentalWaitProc( ) procedure is the largest single procedure in the application; it is used by the event-driven WAIT created in RentalWaitForm( ). RentalWaitProc( ) is responsible for handling interaction with the multitable form and the pull-down menu and also manages variables embedded directly on the form.

The RentalWaitProc( ) procedure is complex in that it uses one large SWITCH..CASE statement to evaluate the events passed to it. Each event must be handled uniquely, and therefore is evaluated separately in the SWITCH..CASE statement. Because of its complexity, the structure of the procedure is outlined below:

```
SWITCH

    CASE <<conditions>> :
        IF <<conditions>>
            THEN <<do something>>
            ELSE
                IF <<conditions>>
                    THEN <do something>>
                ENDIF
        ENDIF

    CASE <<condition>> :
        SWITCH
            CASE <<condition>> : <<do something>>
            CASE <<condition>> : <<do something>>
            CASE <<condition>> :
                IF<<condition>>
                    THEN <<do something>>
                    ELSE <<do something>>
                ENDIF
            OTHERWISE : <<do something>>
        ENDSWITCH

    CASE <<condition>> :
        SWITCH
            CASE <<condition>> :
                IF <<condition>>
                    THEN <<do something>>
                ENDIF
            CASE <<condition>> : <<do something>>
            CASE <<condition>> : <<do something>>
            OTHERWISE : <<do something>>
        ENDSWITCH

    OTHERWISE:
        <<do something>>

ENDSWITCH
```

As you can see, the procedure tests for many different conditions and reacts differently to each condition or set of conditions. The procedure sometimes uses nested SWITCH..CASE to evaluate a series of similar conditions. When the user presses a key in the event list, for example, the Wait Procedure first determines that the event that occurred was a "KEY" event by evaluating the EventRecord["TYPE"] element. Then the procedure determines which key was pressed by evaluating the EventRecord["KEYCODE"] element. The RentalWaitProc() procedure uses a nested SWITCH..CASE statement in this situation to evaluate this type of condition.

```
; ...............................................................
; procedure   : RentalWaitProc(EventType,    = type of event that triggered
;                                               call to this procedure
;                               EventRecord,  = dynamic array that describes
;                                               the details of the event
;                               CycleNumber)  = trigger cycle number
; purpose     : this is the wait procedure for the wait session defined
;               in RentalWaitForm() - it manages the wait session while
;               the user interacts with the multi-table form and menus
; returns     : a number: 0 - used to process the events in the event cycle
;                         1 - used to break the event cycle but not the wait
;                         2 - breaks the trigger cycle, and the wait
; calls procs : TameMemoBox()
;               PrintInvoice()
;               ShowAboutBox()
;               BadKeyTone()
; ...............................................................

PROC RentalWaitProc(EventType, EventRecord, CycleNumber)

   SWITCH
     CASE EventType = "DEPARTROW" AND        ; if user leaves a record in
          UPPER(TABLE()) = "LINEITEM" :      ; the LineItem detail table
       IF ISBLANK([Video ID])
         THEN DEL                            ; delete blank record
              RETURN 1                       ; break the trigger cycle
         ELSE
           IF ISBLANK([Date Out])
             THEN [Date Out] = TODAY()       ; make field assignments
                  [Due Date] = TODAY() + 1

             ; assign global variable SubTotal increment SubTotal each
             ; time the user adds a video to the LineItem table

                  SubTotal = IIF(NOT ISASSIGNED(SubTotal),
                             [Fee], SubTotal + [Fee])
```

```
                    ; once SubTotal variable is assigned, the form will display
                    ; totals, etc. through calculated fields

          ENDIF
          RETURN 0                           ; process the event and proceed
                                             ; to next - do not break wait
      ENDIF

    CASE EventRecord["TYPE"] = "KEY" :       ; if user pressed a key specified
                                             ; in the wait event list
      SWITCH

        CASE EventRecord["KEYCODE"] = ASC("PgDn") :
                                             ; when user presses PgDn

            ; [Invoice#] is the only "regular" field on page 2 of the
            ; form. Using MOVETO instead of PgDn here lets the user
            ; use PgDn from anywhere in the multi-table, multi-record form
          MOVETO [Invoice->Invoice#]
          IMAGERIGHTS READONLY               ; don't let user change anything
          PROMPT "_ [PgUp] to go back _"
          NEWWAITSPEC KEY "PgUp", "Esc", "DOS", "DOSBIG"
          MENUDISABLE "AppInfo"
          MENUDISABLE "PrintInv"
          MENUDISABLE "CancelMenu"
          RETURN 1

        CASE EventRecord["KEYCODE"] = ASC("PgUp") :
          NEWWAITSPEC  KEY "PgDn", "Esc", "Del", "DOS", "DOSBIG"
          MESSAGE "MENUSELECT"
          TRIGGER "DEPARTROW"
          PROMPT "_ [F10] Menu _ [PgDn] Late Fees _"
          IMAGERIGHTS                        ; then allow changes to fields
          MOVETO [LineItem->Video ID]        ; move back to page 1
          MENUENABLE "AppInfo"
          MENUENABLE "PrintInv"
          MENUENABLE "CancelMenu"
          RETURN 1                           ; break trigger cycle, not wait

                                             ; block the Esc key
        CASE EventRecord["KEYCODE"] = ASC("Esc") :
          BadKeyTone()                       ; sound tones
          MESSAGE "Escape key not valid in this context"
          SLEEP 1500
          MESSAGE ""
          RETURN 1                           ; break trigger cycle - not wait
```

```
              ; only process the Del key when cursor is currently
              ; in multi-record detail (when user wants to delete
              ; a video from the rented list)
      CASE EventRecord["KEYCODE"] = ASC("Del") :
        IF UPPER(FIELD()) = "VIDEO ID" AND
           NOT ISBLANK([Fee])
          THEN
              ; when user deletes a record, the global variable SubTotal
              ; must be reassigned to reflect changes to workspace
            SubTotal = IIF(NOT ISASSIGNED(SubTotal),
                           [Fee], SubTotal - [Fee])
              RETURN 0                    ; process next event
          ELSE BadKeyTone()
              MESSAGE "Delete key not valid in this context"
              SLEEP 1500
              MESSAGE ""
              RETURN 1
        ENDIF

              ; if any events other keys listed in the event list
              ; are pressed, sound tones, deny the current event,
              ; and break the event cycle
      OTHERWISE : BadKeyTone()
                  RETURN 1
    ENDSWITCH

              ; when the user chooses an item from the menu, this
              ; procedure will be called, and EventRecord["TYPE"]
              ; will be assigned "MESSAGE". EventRecord["MENUTAG"]
              ; will be assigned with the tag of the showpulldown
              ; menu selection. The following switch..case structure
              ; evaluates the tag name, and takes appropriate action.

  CASE EventRecord["TYPE"] = "MESSAGE" :
    SWITCH
              ; if user chooses to print the invoice (tagnamed PrnInv),
              ; this section assigns values to summary fields in the
              ; Invoice table. Then it assumes any late fees will be paid,
              ; and deletes them from the PrevBal table on pg 2 of the form
      CASE EventRecord["MENUTAG"] = "PrintInv" :
        MESSAGE "Completing rental transaction..."

        MOVETO "Invoice"
        REPLACEFIELDS [Late Fees] LateCharge,
                      [Current Fees] SubTotal
                      [Tax] = (([Late Fees] + [Current Fees]) * .0725)
                      [Invoice Total] = (LateCharge + SubTotal + [Tax])
```

```
      MOVETO "LineItem"
      SCAN
        COPYTOARRAY Transfer
        MOVETO "PrevBal"
        INS
        REPLACEFIELDS [Video ID] Transfer["Video ID"],
                      [Date Out] Transfer["Date Out"],
                      [Due Date] Transfer["Due Date"],
                      [Fee Per Day] Transfer["Fee"]
        MOVETO "LineItem"
      ENDSCAN
      DO_IT!                               ; end coedit session
      MESSAGE ""
      PrintInvoice(AcctID)                 ; call another procedure to
                                           ; print the invoice
    WINDOW SELECT RentalForm
    RETURN 2

        ; if the user selects Cancel (tagnamed Cancel), the next
        ; section deletes detail records in the LineItem table,
        ; then deletes the Invoice table record, and returns
        ; 2 to break the wait construct
    CASE EventRecord["MENUTAG"] = "CancelRent" :
      MESSAGE "Cancelling current transaction..."
      MOVETO "LineItem"
      FOR Count FROM 1 TO NIMAGERECORDS() + 1
        DEL                                ; delete each detail record
      ENDFOR
      DEL
      MOVETO [Invoice->Account#]           ; to master table
      DEL                                  ; delete the master record
      DO_IT!                               ; end coedit session
      RETURN 2                             ; break the wait

        ; if the system icon "≡" (tagnamed AppInfo) is selected
        ; from the menu, simply call the procedure to display
        ; information about the application
    CASE EventRecord["MENUTAG"] = "AppInfo" :
      ShowAboutBox()
      RETURN 1

        ; the following OTHERWISE statement will break the event
        ; cycle and return to the wait. Menu selections which are
        ; not specifically handled earlier will simply be ignored.
    OTHERWISE : RETURN 1
```

```
      ENDSWITCH

              ; this OTHERWISE statement will trap for other unwanted
              ; events not specifically handled earlier.
      OTHERWISE : BadKeyTone()
                  RETURN 1
    ENDSWITCH

  ENDPROC                           ; end procedure definition

  WRITELIB LibName RentalWaitProc   ; write procedure to library
  RELEASE PROCS RentalWaitProc      ; release procedure from memory
```

The AddMbr( ) Procedure

The AddMbr( ) procedure enables the user to add members to the
video store database. This procedure places the Members table on the
workspace, switches to a single table form (Members.F2), and opens a
new blank record. AddMbr( ) automatically creates a new member identification number, displays a simple pull-down menu, and puts the
workspace in a WAIT RECORD state.

The WAIT construct is an event-driven wait that defines
AddMemberWaitProc( ) as the procedure called when one of the events
in the event list occurs. When the wait procedure returns the number 2,
commands following the ENDWAIT keyword end coedit mode (DO_IT!),
and the image is cleared from the workspace.

Notice that after the image is removed from the workspace
(CLEARIMAGE), the command ECHO NORMAL immediately followed by
ECHO OFF is used to show the user the empty workspace. In this situation, you can think of ECHO NORMAL and ECHO OFF as showing the
user a snapshot of the workspace.

```
  ; ...............................................
  ; procedure    : AddMbr()
  ; purpose      : procedure handles a wait session where
  ;                user may add a new member to database
  ; returns      : None
  ; calls procs  : MaxWindow()
  ;                AddMbrWaitProc()
  ; ...............................................
```

```
PROC AddMbr()

    MESSAGE "Loading new member information..."
    COEDIT "Members"                          ; put Members single table
    PICKFORM 2                                ; form on workspace in coedit

    WINDOW HANDLE FORM TO MemberForm          ; get form window handle
    MAXWINDOW(MemberForm)                     ; customize window attributes
    END PGDN                                  ; open new record

    ; assign the key field with a sequential number, starting with 1001
    [Account#] = IIF(ISEMPTY(TABLE()), 1001,
                   (CMAX("Members", "Account#") + 1))

    IMAGERIGHTS   UPDATE                        ; user cannot change key field
    MOVETO [First Name]                         ; position cursor on first field

    SHOWPULLDOWN                                ; build a pull-down [style] menu
       "≡"      : "Display system information"        : "AppInfo",
       "DO-IT!" : "Add member and return to main menu" : "Do-it",
       "Cancel" : "Cancel entry session"             : "CancelMenu"
          SUBMENU
            "No"  : "Continue adding member information"     : "NoCancel",
            "Yes" : "Cancel entries, and return to main menu" : "Cancel"
          ENDSUBMENU
    ENDMENU

    MESSAGE ""                              ; clear message when menu appears

    PROMPT "_ [F2] Do-It! _ [F10] Menu _ Enter new member information"
    WAIT RECORD                             ; allow user to interact with
                                            ; current record
      PROC "AddMbrWaitProc"                 ; procedure that is called
                                            ; on any of the following events
      KEY "DOS", "DOSBIG", "F2", "DEL"      ; when one of these keys are pressed
      MESSAGE "MENUSELECT"                  ; when user chooses a menu item
      TRIGGER "DEPARTFIELD", "ARRIVEFIELD"  ; when cursor changes fields
    ENDWAIT
    SHOWPULLDOWN ENDMENU
    PROMPT ""
    ECHO NORMAL ECHO OFF

    ; the following commands executed only when the wait procedure
    ; returns a 2 - the wait session has now ended
    DO_IT!                     ; end coedit mode
    CLEARIMAGE                 ; remove members table from workspace
    ECHO NORMAL                ; show user an empty workspace
    ECHO OFF                   ; don't show subsequent workspace actions
```

```
ENDPROC                  ; end of procedure definition
WRITELIB libname AddMbr  ; write procedure to library
RELEASE PROCS AddMbr     ; release procedure from memory
```

The AddMemberWaitProc() Procedure

AddMemberWaitProc() is the wait procedure used exclusively for the wait session generated by the AddMember() procedure. Its primary purpose is to control interaction with the form placed on the workspace and the pull-down menu left on the workspace by the AddMember() procedure. The structure of the AddMemberWaitProc() procedure is that of a SWITCH..CASE statement.

The procedure evaluates the events that trigger a call to the wait procedure and takes appropriate action. Remember from earlier chapters that formal parameters (EventType, EventRecord, CycleNumber) are required syntax for an event-driven WAIT. The wait construct passes three values to its wait procedure whether or not they are used. You therefore must include three formal parameters in the procedure definition. The names of the formal parameters are insignificant; you can give them any name, as long as you have three parameters.

The AddMemberWaitProc() evaluates the formal parameters EventType and EventRecord, disregarding CycleNumber. When you write a Wait Procedure for your application, keep in mind that it is called only when one of the events in WAIT's event list occurs. A bit later you see that AddMemberWaitProc() is called only when the user takes one of the following actions:

■ Presses one of the following keys:

Ctrl-O
Alt-O
[F2]
Del

■ Selects an item from the pull-down menu

■ Leaves a field

■ Arrives on another field

The wait procedure need not trap for any other conditions.

Wait procedures must return a number 0, 1, or 2. The wait construct uses this value to determine what action to take. The value 0 returns to the WAIT and processes the event as usual. The value 1 interrupts the current event cycle and returns to the WAIT without processing the event. When the Wait Procedure returns the value 2, the event cycle is immediately interrupted, or broken. The WAIT session ends, and

control is returned to the commands following the keyword ENDWAIT.
Commands following ENDWAIT execute, and the script or procedure
continues normally.

You can think of an event-driven WAIT session as an inherent loop. The
WAIT construct sets up conditions of the WAIT, the procedure is called
when a specified event occurs, and the workspace is left in a WAIT until
the procedure returns the value 2.

```
; ..................................................................
; procedure   : AddMbrWaitProc(EventType    = the event that triggered
;                                               this procedure
;                              EventRecord,  = dynamic array holding
;                                               description of event
;                              CycleNumber)  = trigger cycle number
; purpose     : this is a wait procedure defined specifically for the
;                 wait session used when adding members to database
; returns     : a number: 0 processes the events in the event cycle,
;                            and does not break the wait session
;                          1 does not process the events in the event cycle,
;                            and does not break the wait session
;                          2 does not process the events in the event cycle,
;                            and breaks out of the wait session
; calls procs : TameMemoBox()
;               BadKeyTone()
;               ShowAboutBox()
; ..................................................................

PROC AddMbrWaitProc(EventType, EventRecord, CycleNumber)

   SWITCH
     CASE EventType = "DEPARTFIELD" :       ; when cursor leaves a field
       RETURN 0                             ; process it

     CASE EventType = "ARRIVEFIELD" :       ; when cursor arrives on a field
       IF SEARCH("M", FIELDTYPE()) > 0      ; if field is a memo field
         THEN FIELDVIEW                     ; open it - like [Ctrl-F]
              TameMemoBox(GETWINDOW())      ; customize window attributes
              RETURN 1                      ; break trigger cycle
         ELSE RETURN 0                      ; if not a memo field process event
       ENDIF                                ; normally

     CASE EventRecord["TYPE"] = "KEY" :     ; trap for KEY events
       SWITCH
         CASE EventRecord["KEYCODE"] = ASC("F2") :      ; [F2] key?
           RETURN 2                                     ; then break wait
         CASE EventRecord["KEYCODE"] = ASC("Del") :     ; Del key?
```

```
        BadKeyTone()                                    ; make sounds
        MESSAGE "Use [Ctrl-Backspace] to erase field"   ; give user a hint
        SLEEP 1500                                      ; pause to read message
        MESSAGE ""                                      ; clear message
        RETURN 1                                        ; don't process Del key
      OTHERWISE :                                       ; if any other keypress
        RETURN 0                                        ; process it normally
    ENDSWITCH

  CASE EventRecord["TYPE"] = "MESSAGE" :
    SWITCH
      CASE EventRecord["MENUTAG"] = "AppInfo" :     ; system icon selected?
        ShowAboutBox()                              ; proc shows About box
        RETURN 1                                    ; don't process the event
      CASE EventRecord["MENUTAG"] = "Do-it" :       ; Do-it menu selected?
        RETURN 2                                    ; break wait session
      CASE EventRecord["MENUTAG"] = "CancelRent" :  ; Cancel menu selected?
        DEL                                         ; delete the record
        RETURN 2                                    ; break wait session
    ENDSWITCH
  OTHERWISE : RETURN 0    ; any other trigger event causes the procedure
                          ; to process the event normally
  ENDSWITCH

ENDPROC                                 ; end of procedure definition

WRITELIB libname AddMbrWaitProc   ; write procedure to library
RELEASE PROCS AddMbrWaitProc      ; release procedure from memory
```

The ReturnTapes( ) Procedure

The ReturnTapes( ) procedure displays a dialog box that accepts a video tape identification number. ReturnTapes( ) is executed when the user selects Check-in Tapes from the application's main menu.

The dialog that ReturnTapes( ) creates employs a dialog procedure to actually update the database with returned tapes (see RetTapesDlogProc( )). The primary function of the ReturnTapes is to place the PrevBal table on the workspace in CoEdit mode, and display the dialog box. When the dialog procedure is finished updating the database, ReturnTapes( ) ends the CoEdit session, closes the PrevBal table, and terminates.

The dialog box that ReturnTapes( ) creates is very similar to the dialog box that the GetAcctID( ) procedure creates. The major difference, besides different variable assignments, is that ReturnTapes does not use

the LOOKUP option for its ACCEPT statement. Remember that the
LOOKUP option verifies entry from the first key field of the specified
table. In this case, you want the user to enter a value that exists in the
second field (Video ID) of the PrevBal table, so you must perform a
manual table lookup. See the description of RetTapesDlogProc( ) for
details of how to perform a table lookup manually.

Note that the dialog box definition specifies that its dialog procedure is
executed only on the ACCEPT trigger. This means that the dialog procedure executes when the user presses the OK pushbutton. Because the
OK pushbutton has been defined as the DEFAULT pushbutton, the OK
pushbutton is also pushed when the user presses Enter after typing the
video number.

If the user presses the Cancel pushbutton, or presses Esc on the keyboard, the dialog procedure is not executed, and ReturnTapes( ) terminates, and returns to the MainMenu( ) procedure.

```
; ................................................................
; procedure    : ReturnTapes()
; purpose      : returns tapes to inventory
; returns      : always True
; calls procs  : RetTapesDlogProc  ; the dialog procedure
; ................................................................

PROC ReturnTapes()
  PRIVATE TapeID, ButtonVal, PrevBalWindow

  COEDIT "PrevBal"
  PrevBalWindow = GETWINDOW()
  TapeID = BLANKNUM()              ; initialize the type-in box control variab
                                   ; define a dialog box to get Tape ID#
  SHOWDIALOG "Tape Number"; @6,20 HEIGHT 7 WIDTH 40
    PROC "RetTapesDlogProc"
    TRIGGER "ACCEPT"
    @6,20 HEIGHT 7 WIDTH 40
    @1,3 ?? "Enter Video ID number :"  ; write text inside the dialog box
    ACCEPT @1,27 WIDTH 8                ; create an accept type-in box
      "N"
      PICTURE "#####"
      TAG "AcceptTag"
      TO TapeID
    PUSHBUTTON @3,6 WIDTH 10            ; place an accept pushbutton
      "OK"
      OK
      DEFAULT
      VALUE True
```

```
      TAG "OKButton"
      TO ButtonVal
    PUSHBUTTON @3,23 WIDTH 10        ; place a cancel pushbutton
      "Cancel"
      CANCEL
      VALUE False
      TAG "CancelTag"
      TO ButtonVal
  ENDDIALOG                          ; end of dialog definition

  DO_IT!                             ; end CoEdit mode
  WINDOW SELECT PrevBalWindow        ; select the PrevBal table
  WINDOW CLOSE                       ; and close it
  MESSAGE ""
  RETURN True

                                     ; entered number or False if
ENDPROC                              ; user canceled


WRITELIB Libname ReturnTapes         ; write the procedure to library
RELEASE PROCS ReturnTapes            ; and release from memory
```

The RetTapesDlogProc( ) Procedure

The RetTapesDlogProc( ) procedure is designed to control the dialog
box created in the ReturnTapes( ) procedure. Its primary purpose is to
update fields in the PrevBal table. The RetTapesDlogProc( ) procedure
enters the current date into the Date In field and enters a late fee in the
Late Fee field. If the returned video is not late, RetTapesDlogProc( )
enters zero into the Late Fee field.

The first thing RetTapesDlogProc( ) does is verify that the user's entry
matches one of the values in the Video ID field of the PrevBal table.
This is accomplished with the following two lines of code:

```
MOVETO [Video ID]

LOCATE INDEXORDER TapeID
```

These lines move the cursor to the Video ID field and attempt to locate
the value of the TapeID variable. The TapeID variable was assigned in
the ReturnTapes( ) procedure and corresponds to the number the user
entered. If LOCATE INDEXORDER finds the value, the system variable
Retval is set to True; if not, Retval is set False.

Next, RetTapesDlogProc( ) evaluates the value of Retval to determine
whether the user's entry matches one of the values in the Video ID
field. If the value doesn't match, the MESSAGE command informs the
user of the invalid entry.

If the value does exist in the Video ID field, RetTapesDlogProc( ) enters the current date into the Date In field and determines if the video is late. RetTapesDlogProc( ) always enters a value into the Late Fee field. If the video has been returned later than the due date (the Due Date field), the procedure calculates the fee based on the number of days the video is late and the daily late fee.

As mentioned previously, RetTapesDlogProc( ) executes when the user accepts the dialog box. By the time this dialog procedure executes, the ReturnTapes( ) procedure has already placed the PrevBal table on the workspace in CoEdit mode. Therefore, RetTapesDlogProc( ) is safe to make field assignments in the table.

```
; .................................................
; procedure    : RetTapesDlogProc(EventType,      ; not used
;                                  TagValue,       ; not used
;                                  EventValue,     ; not used
;                                  ElementValue)   ; not used
; purpose      : Dialog procedure for ReturnTapes() proc
;                returns tapes to inventory
; returns      : False to dialog proc defined in ReturnTapes()
; calls procs  : None
; .................................................

PROC RetTapesDlogProc(EventType, TagValue, EventValue, ElementValue)
  PRIVATE DaysLate,      ; limit scope of variables to this proc
          LateFee

                         ; proc is called only when user presses OK
    MOVETO [Video ID]
    LOCATE INDEXORDER TapeID
    IF NOT Retval
      THEN MESSAGE "Not one of the possible values for this field"
    ELSE
      MESSAGE "Returned Video ", TapeID, " to inventory..."
      DaysLate = TODAY() - [Due Date]
      LateFee = IIF(DaysLate > 0, ([Fee Per Day] * DaysLate), 0)
      REPLACEFIELDS [Date In] TODAY(),
                    [Late Fee] LateFee
    ENDIF
    SELECTCONTROL "AcceptTag"
    RETURN False
ENDPROC

WRITELIB Libname RetTapesDlogProc
RELEASE PROCS RetTapesDlogProc
```

The DelMbr() Procedure

Whereas the AddMbr() procedure enables the user to add members to the video store database, the DelMbr() procedure deletes members. This time, however, the user doesn't edit a new record. First, DelMbr() uses the GetAcctID() procedure (described later) to prompt the user for an identification number. Then the procedure places the Members table on the workspace in coedit mode and searches for the member number with a LOCATE INDEXORDER command.

Note that the number the user enters is always found in the Members table because GetAcctID uses the Members table as a lookup table. Normally, when a procedure uses any form of LOCATE or LOCATE INDEXORDER, it should check whether the value was indeed found before continuing. LOCATE commands set the system variable Retval to True if the value is found and to False if the value is not found.

After the member identification number is found, the procedure switches to a single table form (Members.F2) to show the user the member information, then asks the user to confirm.

The DelMbr() procedure deletes the record if the user confirms, clearing the image from the workspace. If the delete is not confirmed, the record is not deleted, and the image is removed from the workspace.

```
; ............................................
; procedure   : DelMbr()
; purpose     : allows user to delete a member from database
; returns     : True if member is deleted
;               False if not
; calls procs : GetAcctID(),
;               MaxWindow(),
;               ConfirmBox()
; ............................................

PROC DelMbr()
  PRIVATE AcctID, MemberForm, Confirmed    ; limit scope of variables
                                           ; to this procedure

  AcctID = GetAcctID()                     ; call procedure to get account
                                           ; number from user, and assign
                                           ; the result to a variable
  IF AcctID = False                        ; it's possible the user
                                           ; cancelled the GetAcctID()
                                           ; dialog box - which would
                                           ; return false
    THEN RETURN False                      ; if so, return False to caller
  ENDIF
```

```
MESSAGE "Searching for member# ", AcctID
COEDIT "Members"                          ; place Members table on workspace
MOVETO [Account#]
LOCATE INDEXORDER AcctID                  ; locate the account number
                                          ; since the GetAcctID() procedure
                                          ; uses a ValCheck for entries,
                                          ; we know that the locate will
                                          ; always find the record
PICKFORM 2                                ; switch to the single table form
WINDOW HANDLE FORM TO MemberForm          ; get form window handle
MAXWINDOW(MemberForm)                     ; customize the window attributes
ECHO NORMAL                               ; show the user the form
ECHO OFF                                  ; don't show subsequent actions
MESSAGE ""                                ; clear message
Confirmed =
   ConfirmBox("Delete account# " +        ; display a confirmation dialog
           STRVAL(AcctID) + "?",14,19)    ; at low center of screen, and
                                          ; assign True (if Yes button)
                                          ; or False (if no button) to
                                          ; variable "Confirmed"

   IF Confirmed                           ; if user pressed the "Yes" button (ConfirmBox)
      THEN DEL                            ; then go ahead and delete the record
   ENDIF

   DO_IT!                                 ; end coedit mode
   CLEARIMAGE                             ; remove the Members table from the workspace
   ECHO NORMAL                            ; show user the empty workspace
   ECHO OFF                               ; don't show subsequent workspace actions
   RETURN Confirmed                       ; return True if member was deleted,
                                          ; False if not

ENDPROC                                   ; end of procedure definition

WRITELIB libname DelMbr                   ; write procedure to library
RELEASE PROCS DelMbr                      ; release procedure from memory
```

VidMain.sc Script End

After all of the procedures defined in the VidMain.sc script have been
written to the library, the LibName variable is released from memory so
that it does not conflict with a variable of the same name elsewhere.
The LibName variable is not used in the application; it is only used
when the VidMain.sc script (or the VidUtil.sc script) is played. After the
libraries are built, the variable is not used again.

```
;****************************************************************
;                  End of VidMain procedure definitions
;****************************************************************
;
RELEASE VARS LibName        ; release LibName variable from memory
```

The VidUtil.sc Script

This section describes the VidUtil.sc script and each procedure that it defines and adds to the VidUtil.lib library. The sample application uses the VidUtil.lib library to store procedures categorized as utilities to the application (hence the name of the script and library).

The VidUtil.sc is like the VidMain.sc script in terms of its overall structure. The VidUtil.sc script also defines several procedures, writes each one in turn to a library (VidUtil.lib), and releases each procedure from memory.

Table 18.22 lists the procedures defined and written to VidUtil.lib by VidUtil.sc.

Table 18.22. Contents of the VidUtil Library (Source Script VidUtil.sc)

Procedure name	Major purpose
AppIntro( )	Displays limited information about the application while the application loads
MaxWindow( )	Customizes attributes of any window
ShowAboutBox( )	Displays system information and information specific to the video store application
RepaintProc( )	Repaints dialog canvas elements
GetAcctID( )	Prompts user for a member identification number
PrintInvoice( )	Prints a customer invoice
CheckPrinter( )	Ensures that the printer is ready before sending output
ConfirmBox( )	Presents a generic confirmation dialog box to the user
TameMemoBox( )	Customizes attributes of a Memo field window and controls interaction with the window
BadKeyTone( )	Makes a distinctive sound to warn user of an invalid action
LeaveApp( )	Cleans up after the application and leaves application

```
; *****************************************************************
; script name : VidUtil.sc
; purpose     : defines utility procedures used in the sample
;               video store application
; library     : VidUtil.lib
; procedures  : AppIntro()      : application splash screen
;               RepaintProc()   : dialog procedure - repaints dialog box
;               ShowAboutBox()  : displays system information
;               GetAcctID()     : gets account# from user thru dialog box
;               MaxWindow()     : customizes attributes of a window
;               TameMemoBox()   : customizes attributes of a memo field
;               BadKeyTone()    : notifies user of an invalid keystroke
;               LeaveApp()      : cleans up after user leaves application
;               ConfirmBox()    : creates a simple confirmation dialog bo
;               PrintInvoice()  : prints a customer invoice
;               CheckPrinter()  : checks to see if the printer is on line
; *****************************************************************
;

LibName = "VidUtil"                    ; assignment to global variable
                                       ; used in this script only


; *****************************************************************
;          Beginning of VidUtil procedure definitions
; *****************************************************************
```

The AppIntro() Procedure

The AppIntro() procedure creates a canvas window displaying limited information about the video store application. The application uses AppIntro() to display information while the application is loading.

Before the procedure creates the window, it creates a dynamic array that stores window attribute indexes. The dynamic array (named WindowAtts[]) holds only those attributes that are customized when the window is created. After the procedure defines the dynamic array, it creates a window using the optional ATTRIBUTES <<*DynArrayName*>> TO <<*WindowName*>> syntax of the WINDOW CREATE command.

AppIntro() writes introductory text to the new window canvas. The procedure uses the STYLE ATTRIBUTE to make blinking dots (...) follow the text Please wait. Blinking dots give the user the visual impression that something is happening.

```
; ................................................
; procedure   : AppIntro()
; purpose     : displays a splash screen while
;               application loads
; returns     : None
; calls procs : None
; ................................................

PROC AppIntro()
  PRIVATE WindowAtts

  DYNARRAY WindowAtts[]               ; create a dynamic array
  WindowAtts["HASFRAME"] = False      ; assign array tags and elements
  WindowAtts["ORIGINROW"] = 6
  WindowAtts["ORIGINCOL"] = 17
  WindowAtts["FLOATING"] = True
  WindowAtts["HEIGHT"] = 10
  WindowAtts["WIDTH"] = 45

  ; now create a new window with attributes from dynamic array
  WINDOW CREATE ATTRIBUTES WindowAtts TO InfoWindow
  ; InfoWindow is now the current window and the current canvas

  CURSOR OFF
  CANVAS OFF                          ; don't show updates while we
                                      ; write some formatted text to the canvas
  @1,0 ?? FORMAT("W44,AC", "Sample Video Store Application")
  @3,0 ?? FORMAT("W44,AC", "Using Paradox 4.0 Special Edition c")
  @4,0 ?? FORMAT("W44,AC", "Copyright 1992 Que Corporation")
  @7,0 ?? FORMAT("W44,D2,AC", TODAY())
  @8,12 ?? "Loading application"
                                      ; color the entire window white on blue
  PAINTCANVAS ATTRIBUTE 15+16 0,0,9,44
  STYLE ATTRIBUTE 15+16+128
  ?? "..."                            ; dots appear white on blue, blinking
  STYLE                               ; reset style
  CANVAS ON                           ; now display the canvas with text

ENDPROC                               ; end of AppIntro() procedure definition

WRITELIB Libname AppIntro             ; write procedure to library
RELEASE PROCS AppIntro                ; release procedure from memory after
                                      ; it's written to a library
```

The MaxWindow() Procedure

The MaxWindow() procedure uses a dynamic array and a WINDOW SETATTRIBUTES command to customize a window's appearance and operation. This procedure is parameterized so that it can be used with any window. Procedures (or scripts) that call MaxWindow() use the following syntax:

        MaxWindow(<<*WindowHandle*>>),

where <<*WindowHandle*>> is any valid window handle.

MaxWindow() is used by the application primarily for form images. It maximizes the window, removes the window frame, and restricts the user from closing, moving, or resizing the window.

MaxWindow() returns a logical value based on the existence of the requested window. The last statement in the procedure returns True if the window exists, and False if it does not.

```
; ...............................................................
; procedure    : MaxWindow(WinHandle)
;                WinHandle = valid window handle
; purpose      : makes an existing window full screen,
;                without a frame. restricts user from
;                closing, moving or resizing the window.
;                used primarily for form windows
; returns      : True if attributes of WinHandle are
;                changed, False if WinHandle does not exist
; calls procs  : None
; ...............................................................

PROC MaxWindow(WinHandle)
  PRIVATE ProcWin

  IF ISWINDOW(WinHandle)                ; make sure window exists before
    THEN DYNARRAY ProcWin[]             ; we change attributes
      ProcWin["MAXIMIZED"] = True       ; assign elements of new dynamic
      ProcWin["HASFRAME"] = False       ; array with tag names exactly
      ProcWin["CANMOVE"] = False        ; as the SETATTRIBUTES command
      ProcWin["CANRESIZE"] = False      ; expects to use them
      ProcWin["CANCLOSE"] = False

                                        ; then set attributes from the array
      WINDOW SETATTRIBUTES WinHandle FROM ProcWin
  ENDIF
  RETURN ISWINDOW(WinHandle)            ; True if successful, False if not

ENDPROC                                 ; end of MaxWindow()

WRITELIB libname MaxWindow              ; write to library
RELEASE PROCS MaxWindow                 ; and release from memory
```

The RepaintProc() Procedure

The RepaintProc() procedure is a dialog procedure that repaints the
dialog box canvas created in the ShowAboutBox() procedure. Because
it is called only on the IDLE trigger from within ShowAboutBox(),
the RepaintProc() doesn't need to determine what event called it.
RepaintProc() simply issues the REPAINTDIALOG command and
returns to ShowAboutBox().

RepaintProc() returns a True value after issuing REPAINTDIALOG. Dialog box procedures return True by default, so explicitly returning a
value is not required. Returning a logical value is a good habit, however, as it makes the code easier to follow. Remember from earlier
chapters that dialog boxes can return True to process the pending
event or False to deny it.

Even though this simple dialog box procedure doesn't use formal
parameters (EventType, TagValue, EventValue, and ElementValue),
they are required in all dialog procedures. The literal names are insignificant—you can name them whatever you want, but they must be
included in the procedure definition.

```
; ..............................................
; procedure   : RepaintProc()
; purpose     : repaints the dialog created by the
;                 ShowAboutBox() procedure.
; returns     : True
; calls procs : None
; ..............................................

PROC RepaintProc(EventType, TagValue, EventValue, ElementValue)

                          ; proc is called on idle trigger
    REPAINTDIALOG         ; repaint the screen constantly, to
                          ; show updates to time
    RETURN True           ; explicitly execute the idle event

ENDPROC

WRITELIB libname RepaintProc
RELEASE PROCS RepaintProc
```

The ShowAboutBox() Procedure

The following procedure, ShowAboutBox(), displays information specific to the application and available system resources. Before displaying the dialog box, the procedure uses the SYSINFO command to load a

dynamic array with information about the system. Within the SHOWDIALOG definition, the dynamic array is displayed as formatted text. The system time and date also are displayed on the canvas.

ShowAboutBox() uses the TIME() function to display the current time in the dialog. To display the current time continually, ShowAboutBox() calls the dialog procedure (RepaintProc()) when on the IDLE trigger. The dialog procedure simply repaints the dialog, refreshing the displayed time, and returns to the dialog.

ShowAboutBox() places an OK PUSHBUTTON on the dialog box as its only control element. The only way the user can leave the dialog box is to press the OK button.

```
; ..................................................
; procedure    : ShowAboutBox()
; purpose      : displays system information in
;                a dialog box
; returns      : None
; calls procs  : RepaintProc()
; ..................................................

PROC ShowAboutBox()

   SYSINFO TO InfoBag                   ; load dynamic array with system info

   SHOWDIALOG ""                        ; begin dialog box definition with no title
     PROC "RepaintProc"                 ; call RepaintProc() procedure when
     IDLE                               ; system is idle
     @4,17 HEIGHT 17 WIDTH 45           ; location and dimension of box

     STYLE ATTRIBUTE 15+16              ; subsequent text colored white on blue
                                        ; now write some information inside the box
     @1,0 ?? FORMAT("W43,AC", "Sample Video Store Application")
     STYLE
     @3,0 ?? FORMAT("W43,AC", "Using Paradox 4.0 Special Edition c")
     @4,0 ?? FORMAT("W43,AC", "Copyright 1992 Que Corporation")

     FRAME FROM 6,1 TO 6,41             ; frame a portion of the box
                                        ; put the date and time in the box
     @7,0 ?? FORMAT("W43,AC", FORMAT("D2", TODAY()) + "  " + TIME())

                                        ; use the IIF() function to determine
                                        ; whether a mouse exists, and display text
                                        ; indicating the results
     @8,0 ?? FORMAT("W43,AC",
                 "Mouse is" + IIF(InfoBag["MOUSE"],
              " ", " not ") + "installed")

                                        ; provide memory statistics
```

```
@10,4 ?? "Available expanded memory : " + STRVAL(InfoBag["EXPANDED"])
@11,4 ?? "Available extended memory : " + STRVAL(InfoBag["EXTENDED"])

PUSHBUTTON @13,16 WIDTH 10      ; place a single OK button in the dialog
   "OK"                         ; label the button OK
   OK                           ; optional action of button when pressed
   VALUE "OK"                   ; the value of this control element
   TAG "OKTag"                  ; name tag for the button
   TO PButtonVal                ; variable assigned with VALUE "OK"

 ENDDIALOG                      ; end dialog definition

ENDPROC                         ; end of procedure definition

WRITELIB Libname ShowAboutBox   ; write procedure to library
RELEASE PROCS ShowAboutBox      ; and release from memory
```

The GetAcctID() Procedure

GetAcctID() defines a dialog box to prompt the user for an account identification number. Notice from the dialog definition that three control elements are placed on the dialog box: an ACCEPT type-in box, an OK PUSHBUTTON, and a Cancel PUSHBUTTON.

The ACCEPT type-in box restricts the user's input to exactly four numbers and an entry that matches a value in the first field of the Members table. PAL enables the LOOKUP to assign validity checks to ACCEPT type-in boxes in the same way you use them in an ACCEPT statement outside the dialog box.

GetAcctID() returns the value the user entered or the logical value False to the calling procedure. Because the user can press Esc to cancel the dialog box, in which case the control variable "AcctID" is not assigned, GetAcctID() assigns a False value to the return value and returns to the calling procedure.

Customers sometimes forget their member identification number; therefore, GetAcctID() would have more flexibility if it enabled users to enter an alternate search value such as the customer's last name. You can accomplish this by redesigning the dialog box with a second ACCEPT type-in box. After the user enters a last name, place the Members table on the workspace and issue a LOCATE or LOCATE INDEXORDER command to search for the last name. After the last name is found, store the account number to a variable and continue the procedure in a way similar to the GetAcctID() described below.

```
; ..............................................
; procedure   : GetAcctID()
; purpose     : generates a dialog box to get a
;                member account number from user
; returns     : a four digit Account#, or false
;                if dialog box is cancelled
; calls procs : None
; ..............................................

PROC GetAcctID()
  PRIVATE AcctID, ButtonVal
                          ; define the dialog box with title,
                          ; location and size of box.

  SHOWDIALOG "Member Account#" @6,20 HEIGHT 7 WIDTH 40

    @1,3 ?? "Enter member account# :" ; write text inside the dialog box

    ACCEPT @1,27 WIDTH 8       ; create an accept element
      "N"                      ; accept only "N"umbers for input
      LOOKUP "Members"         ; verify entry with values from
                              ; first field in the Members table
      PICTURE "####"           ; accept exactly four numbers
      TAG "AcceptTag"          ; this is the 'name tag' of the
                              ; ACCEPT element - syntax requires this
                              ; even though we won't evaluate it
      TO AcctID               ; this is the variable which will be
                              ; assigned with the number that the
                              ; user types in

    PUSHBUTTON @3,6 WIDTH 10  ; place an OK pushbutton element
      "OK"                    ; label the button "OK"
      OK                      ; action of the button when pressed
      DEFAULT                 ; this button pressed by default
      VALUE True              ; value of the button when pressed
      TAG "OKButton"          ; name tag of pushbutton element
      TO ButtonVal            ; variable assigned with VALUE True

    PUSHBUTTON @3,23 WIDTH 10 ; place a cancel pushbutton element
      "Cancel"
      CANCEL
      VALUE False
      TAG "CancelTag"
      TO ButtonVal

  ENDDIALOG                    ; end of dialog definition
```

```
RETURN IIF(ISASSIGNED(AcctID), AcctID, False)
                              ; pass the number the user typed in
                              ; back to calling procedure


ENDPROC                       ; end of procedure definition


WRITELIB Libname GetAcctID    ; write the procedure to library
RELEASE PROCS GetAcctID       ; and release from memory
```

The PrintInvoice( ) Procedure

PrintInvoice( ) is called when the user selects **P**rint from the Rental
pull-down menu. PrintInvoice( ) runs a query on the appropriate tables,
calls the CheckPrinter( ) procedure to verify that the printer is on-line,
and prints a predesigned report.

After PrintInvoice( ) generates an Answer table with a query, it removes
the query images from the workspace and calls CheckPrinter( ).
CheckPrinter( ) is responsible for making sure that the printer is ready
to accept output. The return value of CheckPrinter( ), True or False, is
assigned to a variable. PrintInvoice( ) evaluates the result of the variable to determine whether the printer is ready for output.

If the printer is indeed ready for output, PrintInvoice( ) copies a
predesigned report specification from a dummy table to the Answer
table and sends the report to the printer.

After the invoice has been printed or the print job cancelled, the Answer table is removed from the workspace and control is returned to
RentalWaitProc( ).

```
; .................................................................
; procedure  : PrintInvoice(AcctID)   AcctID = 4 digit account#
; purpose    : runs a query to get information for an invoice,
;              copies a report spec from a dummy table, checks
;              the printer, and prints the report.
; returns    : a number: 1 if invoice was printed
;                        2 if print job was cancelled
; calls procs : CheckPrinter()
; .................................................................

PROC PrintInvoice(AcctID)
  PRIVATE PrinterOnline                 ; scope of variable limited
                                        ; to this procedure


  MESSAGE "Retrieving invoice information, please wait"
```

```
; The following query structure was saved interactively
; with Scripts|QuerySave, and then inserted into this
; procedure. Note that the use of the variable AcctID in
; the query definition, thereby parameterizing the query.

Query

    Invoice ¦    Invoice#              ¦   Account#           ¦ Tax    ¦
            ¦ Check _InvNum, ~InvoiceNum ¦ Check _AcctID, ~AcctID ¦ Check  ¦

    Members ¦ Account# ¦ Last Name ¦ First Name ¦ Street ¦ City  ¦
            ¦ _AcctID  ¦ Check     ¦ Check      ¦ Check  ¦ Check ¦

    Members ¦ State ¦ Zip   ¦ Eve Telephone ¦ Day Telephone ¦
            ¦ Check ¦ Check ¦ Check         ¦ Check         ¦

    Lineitem ¦   Invoice# ¦ Video ID ¦ Title ¦ Due Date ¦ Fee   ¦
             ¦   _InvNum  ¦ Check    ¦ Check ¦ Check    ¦ Check ¦

Endquery
DO_IT!                                  ; execute the query

MOVETO [Invoice(Q)->#] CLEARIMAGE       ; clear all query images
MOVETO [Members(Q)->#] CLEARIMAGE
MOVETO [LineItem(Q)->#] CLEARIMAGE
MOVETO "Answer"                         ; then move to the answer table

PrinterOnline = CheckPrinter()          ; CheckPrinter() makes sure the
                                        ; printer is ready, and gets
                                        ; direction from user. Calling
                                        ; the procedure in this way assigns
                                        ; the returned value to
PrinterOnline
   IF PrinterOnline

        ; if the printer is ready, copy the appropriate report from
        ; a dummy table (DummyRpt) to the Answer table, and print it,
        ; then return to the wait procedure
      THEN MESSAGE "Printing Invoice..."
           COPYREPORT "DummyRpt" "1" "Answer" "R"
           INSTANTREPORT                ; prints report "R"
           CLEARIMAGE                   ; close the Answer table window
           MESSAGE ""
           RETURN 2                     ; invoice has been printed -
                                        ; return 2 to the wait procedure
```

```
      ELSE MESSAGE "Print job cancelled"    ; otherwise, cancel the print job
           SLEEP 2000
           CLEARIMAGE                        ; close the Answer table window
           MESSAGE ""
           COEDITKEY
           RETURN 1                          ; print job was cancelled -
                                             ; return 1 to wait procedure
      ENDIF

ENDPROC                                      ; end of PrintInvoice() procedure

WRITELIB libname PrintInvoice                ; write procedure to library
RELEASE PROCS PrintInvoice                   ; release it from memory
```

The CheckPrinter() Procedure

The video store application uses the CheckPrinter() procedure to verify that the printer is on-line and ready for output. If the printer is not ready the first time the procedure checks, CheckPrinter() creates a simple pop-up menu that notifies the user and offers a chance to retry or cancel the print job completely.

If the user selects **R**etry from the pop-up menu, CheckPrinter() loops to the beginning of the WHILE loop and executes the same code again. (The user can retry the print job indefinitely.) If the user decides to cancel the print job, CheckPrinter() calls ConfirmBox() to confirm that the print job should be cancelled.

CheckPrinter() uses the PRINTERSTATUS() function in a WHILE loop to check the status of the printer. The beginning of the WHILE loop reads WHILE NOT PRINTERSTATUS(). If PRINTERSTATUS() returns True, the printer is ready to accept output, and commands inside the loop are not executed.

If the printer is not ready for output, the procedure removes the message from the screen with the statement MESSAGE "" and begins a nested WHILE loop. The body of the nested (or inner) loop displays a pop-up menu to notify the user. If the user chooses to retry the print job, CheckPrinter() issues a QUITLOOP, which breaks from the inner loop, clears the message, and begins again at the top of the outer WHILE loop.

If the user selects **C**ancel from the menu, CheckPrinter() calls ConfirmBox() to confirm that the user wants to cancel the print job. If the user confirms, CheckPrinter() returns a False value to the PrintInvoice() procedure.

CheckPrinter() restricts the user from leaving the WHILE loop until
PRINTERSTATUS is successful or the user cancels the job. After the
loop is terminated, CheckPrinter() returns a True value to the
PrintInvoice() procedure to convey the result of CheckPrinter() to the
calling procedure.

```
; ************************************************
; procedure   : CheckPrinter()
; purpose     : makes sure printer ready to receive
;                 output - gives user option to retry
;                 or cancel
; returns     : True if printer is ready
;                 False if print job is cancelled
; calls procs : ConfirmBox()
; ************************************************

PROC CheckPrinter()
  PRIVATE MenuSelection     ; limit scope of variable to this proc

  MESSAGE "Checking printer status..."

      ; *** Outer Loop ***
      ; subsequent commands are executed until printer is ready for output
  WHILE NOT PRINTERSTATUS()
    MESSAGE ""

      ; *** Inner Loop ***
      ; subsequent commands are executed until quitloop or return is issued
    WHILE True
      SHOWPOPUP "Is Printer On?" CENTERED ; show a pop-up menu
        "Retry"  : "Attempt to print invoice again" : "Retry",
        "Cancel" : "Cancel print job" : "Cancel"
      ENDMENU
      TO MenuSelection                ; assign choice to variable

      IF MenuSelection = "Retry"    ; when user selects Retry
        THEN QUITLOOP                ; leave inner loop
        ELSE                        ; call ConfirmBox() procedure
          ConfirmBox("Cancel Print Job?","","")
                                    ; parameters 2 and 3 make
                                    ; box appear at center screen
            IF Retval               ; ConfirmBox() sets retval
                                    ; True if Yes button pressed
                                    ; False if No pressed
              THEN MESSAGE ""       ; clear message
                   RETURN False     ; return False to calling procedure
                                    ; if user cancels print job
            ENDIF
```

```
        ENDIF
      ENDWHILE                        ; end of inner loop


      MESSAGE "Checking printer status..."
    ENDWHILE                          ; end of outer loop


    MESSAGE ""                    ; clear message
    RETURN True                   ; return True to calling procedure
                                  ; when printer is ready
  ENDPROC                         ; end of CheckPrinter() procedure

  WRITELIB libname CheckPrinter   ; write proc to library
  RELEASE PROCS CheckPrinter      ; release proc from memory
```

The ConfirmBox( ) Procedure

The ConfirmBox( ) procedure is a generic procedure used to confirm user actions from a dialog box. The sample application uses ConfirmBox( ) whenever the user has attempted to execute an important action such as leaving the application, deleting a customer from the database, or cancelling a print job.

ConfirmBox( ) takes three formal parameters, or arguments: QString, OriginRow, and OriginCol. The first argument is a string that ConfirmBox( ) places directly on the dialog canvas. When the application needs to confirm that the user wants to leave the application, for example, the calling procedure can substitute QString with a string such as "Are you sure you want to leave the application?"

ConfirmBox( ) uses the other two parameters, OriginRow and OriginCol, to position the dialog box on-screen. A nice feature of the ConfirmBox( ) procedure is its capability to default to the center of the screen. If the calling procedure passes empty strings ("") to OriginRow or OriginCol, the procedure automatically defines the origin row and column of the dialog box.

ConfirmBox( ) first assigns default values to OriginRow and OriginCol if necessary. ConfirmBox( ) uses an IIF( ) function to determine whether the parameters contain blank strings; if so, ConfirmBox( ) assigns the variables with predetermined values.

You can improve this default position technique by adding the flexibility to vary the width and height of the dialog box. ConfirmBox( ) only appears in one width or height. If you need to display a very long string, you can use the LEN( ) function to determine the length of the QString parameter and adjust the dialog width accordingly. If the string is longer than 78 characters, you can dynamically change the height to

accommodate a two-line (or longer) string. You also can take parameterization one step farther and build a procedure that handles simple
and complex dialog boxes; you then can rely on the parameterized
procedure to calculate placement of control elements and determine
appropriate actions.

```
; .............................................................
; procedure  : ConfirmBox(QString,   = string in form of question
;                                       max 38 characters
;                         OriginRow, = top row number of box
;                                       defaults to 6
;                         OriginCol) = left column of box
;                                       defaults to 19
; purpose    : creates a simple confirmation dialog
;              used for confirming actions with
;              Yes/No buttons
; returns    : True if Yes button is pressed
;              False if No button is pressed
; calls procs : None
; .............................................................

PROC ConfirmBox(QString, OriginRow, OriginCol)
  PRIVATE PButtonVal

    ; the following IIF() statements are used to default the
    ; box placement in the center of the screen. The calling
    ; procedure may pass an empty string ("") for each of the
    ; OriginCol and OriginRow parameters to set default position

  OriginCol = IIF(OriginCol = "", 19, OriginCol)
  OriginRow = IIF(OriginRow = "", 6, OriginRow)

  SHOWDIALOG "Confirm"          ; begin dialog box definition
    @OriginRow,OriginCol HEIGHT 7 WIDTH 40

    @1,0 ?? FORMAT("W38,AC",QString)
                                ; format the formal parameter so
                                ; the string displays in the center

    PUSHBUTTON @3,6 WIDTH 10   ; place a Yes pushbutton element
      "Yes"                    ; label the button "OK"
      OK                       ; action of the button when pressed
      VALUE True               ; the value of the button when pressed
      TAG "OKButton"           ; name tag of pushbutton element
      TO PButtonVal            ; variable assigned with VALUE value
```

```
  PUSHBUTTON @3,21 WIDTH 10 ; place a No pushbutton element
    "No"
    CANCEL
    DEFAULT
    VALUE False                  ; notice that the value of both buttons
                                 ; is not a string - buttons are assigned
                                 ; logical values
    TAG "CancelTag"
    TO PButtonVal

 ENDDIALOG                       ; end of dialog definition

 RETURN Retval                   ; note that retval will always be
                                 ; assigned (No button = False
                                 ; Yes button = True

ENDPROC                          ; end of ConfirmBox() proc definition

WRITELIB libname ConfirmBox      ; write proc to library
RELEASE PROCS ConfirmBox         ; and release from memory
```

The TameMemoBox( ) Procedure

TameMemoBox( ) handles user interaction with Memo fields in field view. The calling procedure is responsible for entering field view on the Memo field.

TameMemoBox( ) sets the attributes of the Memo field window from a dynamic array. The dynamic array is defined within the procedure; it downsizes and centers the window on-screen, removes the window title, and restricts the user from closing it.

After the procedure has customized the window attributes, it goes into a WAIT FIELD session. The user may move or resize the window and add or delete text with the usual Paradox operations. The procedure prompts the user to press Esc or F2 when finished editing the Memo field. Changes to the Memo field are canceled if the user presses Esc; if the user presses F2, they are saved.

The placement of the PROMPT command is important. Because TameMemoBox( ) is called from Wait Procedures, the PROMPT must be changed before TameMemoBox( ) goes into the WAIT FIELD session. This makes the prompt in the lower left corner of the screen change from whatever it was before, to the string specified in TameMemoBox( ). TameMemoBox( ) doesn't have to reset the prompt, because the Wait procedure that calls TameMemoBox( ) automatically changes the prompt back to the original state.

This procedure is parameterized so that it can be used with any valid window handle.

```
; ..................................................
; procedure  : TameMemoBox()
; purpose    : resizes and moves an open memo field
;              to center of screen.
;              waits on field until [F2] or [Esc]
; returns    : True if contents of box are saved ([F2])
;              False if not ([Esc])
; calls procs : None
; ..................................................

PROC TameMemoBox(WinHandle)
  PRIVATE MemoAtts                        ; restrict MemoAtts effectiveness
                                          ; to this procedure

  IF ISWINDOW(WinHandle)                  ; if WinHandle is a valid window
    THEN DYNARRAY MemoAtts[]              ; create a dynamic array
        MemoAtts["TITLE"] = ""           ; and assign elements exactly
        MemoAtts["ORIGINROW"] = 8        ; as the SETATTRIBUTES command
        MemoAtts["ORIGINCOL"] = 21       ; expects to see them --
        MemoAtts["HEIGHT"] = 8           ; these attributes move and resize
        MemoAtts["]WIDTH"] = 35          ; the window and restrict the user
        MemoAtts["CANCLOSE"] = False     ; from closing the window

                                          ; now set the window attributes
                                          ; from the dynamic array just created
        WINDOW SETATTRIBUTES WinHandle FROM MemoAtts
  ENDIF

  PROMPT " ¦ [F2] Save changes ¦ [Esc] Cancel changes ¦"
  WHILE True
    WAIT FIELD                          ; let user interact only with the memo
      MESSAGE "Begin typing to make changes to memo field..."
    UNTIL "F2", "Esc", "DOS", "DOSBIG"
    SWITCH
      CASE Retval = "F2"  : DO_IT! QUITLOOP
      CASE Retval = "Esc" : CANCELEDIT QUITLOOP
      OTHERWISE : LOOP
    ENDSWITCH
  ENDWHILE

ENDPROC                                 ; end of TameMemoBox() procedure

WRITELIB libname TameMemoBox            ; write proc to library
RELEASE PROCS TameMemoBox               ; and free memory
```

The BadKeyTone( ) Procedure

The BadKeyTone( ) procedure is a simple procedure that sounds two tones: a high note followed by a low note that audibly warns the user when an invalid action is taken. The procedure is written so that the same two tones always sound. Proceduralizing repetitive actions such as this simplifies executing them consistently.

```
; ..................................................
; procedure    : BadKeyTone()
; purpose      : generates hi-lo tones used for
;                alerting the user of a bad keystroke
; returns      : None
; calls procs  : None
; ..................................................

PROC BadKeyTone()

   SOUND 500 100        ; high tone
   SOUND 300 20         ; low tone

ENDPROC

   WRITELIB libname BadKeyTone
   RELEASE PROCS BadKeyTone
```

The LeaveApp( ) Procedure

The LeaveApp( ) procedure performs basic housekeeping chores before leaving the application in order to clean up after it.

LeaveApp( ) first plays Taps to alert the user that the application is terminating. The SYSMODE( ) function determines what mode the application is in. If SYSMODE( ) returns anything other than "Main", such as "CoEdit", LeaveApp( ) issues DO_IT! to return to main mode.

LeaveApp( ) removes all windows from the desktop, releases all variables with the RESET command, and quits to Paradox. LeaveApp does not need to release procedures explicitly from memory because Paradox releases all procedures when script play ends.

Notice that the QUIT command is followed by the string "Back in Paradox now...". Remember to inform your users what is taking place, even after you leave the application. You also can issue the EXIT command to leave Paradox altogether and return to DOS.

```
; ..............................................
; procedure   : LeaveApp()
; purpose     : does general housekeeping and
;               returns to Paradox native mode
; returns     : None
; calls procs : None
; ..............................................

PROC LeaveApp()

  MESSAGE "Leaving the application..."

  SOUND 110 500                    ; play Taps
  SLEEP 50
  SOUND 110 300
  SOUND 146 1500

  IF SYSMODE() <> "Main"
    THEN DO_IT!                    ; go back to main mode
  ENDIF
  ALTSPACE {Desktop} {Empty}       ; clear workspace
  RESET                            ; clear global variables from memory
  QUIT "Back in Paradox now..."    ; return to Paradox with a message

ENDPROC                            ; end LeaveApp proc definition

WRITELIB libname LeaveApp          ; write proc to library
RELEASE PROCS LeaveApp             ; and release from memory
```

VidUtil.sc Script End

After all the procedures have been defined, written to a library, and
released from memory, the global variable LibName is released from
memory. LibName is not used by the application; its only purpose is to
simplify writing procedures to a library in batch mode. After it has
served its purpose, it should be released to save memory.

```
;*************************************************************
;            End of VidUtil procedure definitions
;*************************************************************
;

RELEASE VARS LibName            ; release global variable used
                                ; exclusively for this script
```

Chapter Summary

This chapter explained how to design and develop the components of a PAL application. You learned how the video store sample application uses messages, menus, and dialog boxes to pull together a complete user interface. Also, you learned how to allow the user access to table data through a WAIT statement. Finally, you saw how scripts define procedures, and how procedures can be stored to libraries.

As you go on to design your own applications, keep in mind that the development process is highly individual. The sample application shown here was one of many possible ways to implement a video store application.

PAL Command and Function Reference

This chapter gives you reference information for the Paradox Application Language Version 4.0. The first section gets your existing Version 3.5 scripts running in Paradox Version 4.0 as quickly as possible. The remaining sections give you a reference guide to the capabilities and features of the PAL programming language. Use the listings that group the PAL commands and functions by category to get an idea of "what's out there" and to see what tools are available for accomplishing different types of tasks. Use the alphabetic listing of commands and functions to get more detailed information and to determine the proper syntax for using a command or function.

Version Compatibility

Paradox and PAL Version 4.0 provide downward compatibility with Version 3.5. This means that, if you have tables and scripts created with Paradox Version 3.5, then Version 4.0 is capable of using them. To take full advantage of the new features in Version 4.0 (like memo fields, dialog boxes, and multiple windows), however, you will need to make changes in your tables and scripts.

To enable your existing tables from prior versions of Paradox to completely support the new features, you must perform a **M**odify **R**estructure on each table. Paradox asks you for confirmation, and then saves the table with the standard (Version 4.0) format. Refer to Chapter 2, "Creating Database Tables," for more information on the **F**ileFormat menu selection.

Incorporating windows, pull-down menus, dialog boxes, and mouse operations in your existing scripts is somewhat more complex. From a PAL programmer's point of view, the differences between PAL Version 4.0 and Version 3.5 are substantial. Many new commands and functions have been added to the language to support the new "desktop" interface paradigm and its use of the mouse and a windowed environment (refer to Chapter 15, "An Overview of the Paradox Application Language"). Changing large scripts to take advantage of the new features available will require extensive rewriting.

You can use your Version 3.5 scripts, however, with no or only minor changes. Paradox Version 4.0 provides two different methods of providing compatibility with Version 3.5. You can select the System menu (by pressing Alt-space bar), and then select **C**ompatibility mode, or you can use the SETUIMODE command in your script. Either way, after the Paradox interface is changed to the compatibility interface, your Version 3.5 scripts will behave as if they are being executed by Version 3.5.

> **WARNING:** Do not change to Compatibility mode if table images are on the workspace in Edit or CoEdit mode or if other unsaved data is on the workspace. All edited data and Editor, Form, or Report Designer sessions will be canceled and changes discarded when the User Interface mode is changed.

If you change to Compatibility mode manually using the Paradox menus, you are asked to confirm the change. After you have changed to the Version 3.5 menu interface, you cannot change the interface back to Standard mode manually.

If you are changing the user interface in order to run a particular PAL script application, you probably should have the script change the interface mode using the SETUIMODE command. When the script is done, it then can restore the user interface to Standard mode by using the SETUIMODE command again. Then, you (or the user of your application) will not get stuck in Compatible mode.

To have your script change the user interface mode, use the method described here. At the beginning of each of your Version 3.5 scripts (or the main "driver" script—refer to Chapter 15, "An Overview of the Paradox Application Language," and Chapter 16, "Using the Paradox Application Language") add the following command:

SETUIMODE COMPATIBLE

The rest of your script will execute in Version 3.5 mode. To keep things tidy, when your Version 3.5 script has completed its work, the script should set the user interface back to Standard mode before returning to Paradox Main mode. To do this, include the following command at each point where your script has an endpoint:

SETUIMODE STANDARD

An end-point in a script is either the end of the script itself, a RETURN command that passes control back to Paradox Main mode, or a QUIT command. You do not need to change the user interface if the script terminates with an EXIT command because EXIT returns to the DOS command line.

Global Variables

Three global variables are available in PAL: AutoLib, ErrorProc, and RetVal. These variables are used in various ways and can be very important in your applications.

AutoLib

Paradox loads procedures into memory in two ways. The first technique loads the procedure explicitly by using the READLIB command. Paradox also can load a procedure implicitly by using the AutoLib variable.

AutoLib stores the name of one or more procedure libraries. If a procedure is not already in memory when your script calls it, Paradox looks for the procedure in the libraries listed in AutoLib. If AutoLib is blank, or Paradox cannot find the requested procedure in the libraries listed in AutoLib, a script error occurs.

The following example shows the AutoLib variable being set so that two procedure libraries are searched.

```
AutoLib = "GenLib, AccntLib"
```

The first library is named GenLib, and the second library is named AccntLib. Both libraries will be searched automatically for requested procedures after the assignment to AutoLib is made.

ErrorProc

When a script error occurs, PAL usually suspends script execution and enters the Debugger. Advanced programmers use the ErrorProc variable to establish a special procedure to handle errors in the script without halting or "crashing." For more information on writing error handling procedures, refer to the PAL User's Guide.

RetVal

The RetVal variable is used by Paradox for a variety of purposes. Many Paradox commands and functions use RetVal to provide additional information about their operation. Paradox even uses RetVal to store a copy of the value returned with the RETURN command from a script or procedure.

RetVal frequently is used to report the success or failure of a PAL command, or to record the keystrokes used to end WAIT sessions and many of the menu commands.

Because RetVal is used so often, and for so many different purposes, you cannot count on its value to remain the same for very long. If you intend to test RetVal to determine the success or failure of some operation, you should copy it to another variable before doing anything else.

Refer to the individual command and function descriptions to determine if the command or function affects RetVal, and what the values returned in RetVal mean.

An Overview of PAL Commands and Functions by Category

This section provides a listing and brief description of each of the PAL commands and functions, based on their category. The commands and functions are listed alphabetically within each category. Functions are distinguished from commands by placing a pair of parentheses at the end of the function name; for example, TODAY( ) indicates that the keyword TODAY is a function.

Date and Time

Date and time functions give you information about the time and date (as obtained from the computer's internal clock), and to initialize, format, or manipulate various time and date values (see table 19.1).

Table 19.1. Date and Time Functions

Function/Command	Purpose
BLANKDATE( )	Produces a blank date value
DATEVAL( )	Converts a string to a date value
DAY( )	Extracts the numeric value of the day of the month

continues

Table 19.1. Continued

Function/Command	Purpose
DOW( )	Extracts the day of the week as a string
FORMAT( )	Formats a date for output
MONTH( )	Extracts the numeric value of the month (1 to 12)
MOY( )	Extracts the month of the year as a string
TICKS( )	Reports the number of milliseconds since midnight
TIME( )	Gives a string representing the current time
TODAY( )	Gives today's date as a date value
USDATE( )	Reformats a date into U.S. format
YEAR( )	Extracts the numeric value of the year from a date

Dialog Box

Table 19.2 lists the group of commands that control the appearance, behavior, and contents of dialog boxes.

Table 19.2. Dialog Commands

Function/Command	Purpose
ACCEPTDIALOG	Like an OK button press, accepts the current dialog box
CANCELDIALOG	Like a CANCEL button press, cancels the current dialog box
CONTROLVALUE	Obtains value of any control element in a dialog box
NEWDIALOGSPEC	Describes new properties for an existing dialog box
REFRESHCONTROL	Refreshes a single control in a dialog box

Function/Command	Purpose
REFRESHDIALOG	Refreshes an entire dialog box
REPAINTDIALOG	Recalculates and redisplays a dialog box
RESYNCCONTROL	Causes a single control to be resynchronized
RESYNCDIALOG	Causes an entire dialog box to be resynchronized
SELECTCONTROL	Moves the highlight to a particular control in a dialog box
SHOWDIALOG	Creates and defines a dialog box

Editor

The editor commands shown in table 19.3 provide script control over an editor session. This is useful for editing memo fields, automating the creation of forms or reports, and even writing scripts that create or modify other scripts.

Table 19.3. Editor Commands

Function/Command	Purpose
EDITOR EXTRACT	Copies selected editor text to a variable
EDITOR FIND	Similar to using Edit Find, searches for a string
EDITOR FINDNEXT	Performs the last EDITOR FIND again
EDITOR GOTO	Moves the editor cursor to given character offset
EDITOR INFO	Initializes a dynamic array with information about an edit session
EDITOR INSERT	Copies the contents of a variable into the editor
EDITOR NEW	Starts an editor session with a new file
EDITOR OPEN	Starts an editor session with an existing file

continues

Table 19.3. Continued

Function/Command	Purpose
EDITOR READ	Copies a disk file into an active editor session
EDITOR REPLACE	Similar to **Edit Replace**, finds and replaces a string
EDITOR SELECT	Marks (selects) a block of text
EDITOR WRITE	Copies the marked (selected) text to a disk file
REPLACE	Emulates pressing the Ctrl-A key combination
REPLACENEXT	Emulates pressing the Alt-A key combination
SHIFTPRESS	Equivalent to pressing the Shift key plus a specified direction key

Information

Information functions, shown in table 19.4, give information about tables, arrays, variables, errors, and password rights.

Table 19.4. Information Functions

Function/Command	Purpose
ARRAYSIZE( )	Provides the size of a fixed array
ATFIRST( )	Checks for cursor positioned in first record
ATLAST( )	Checks for cursor positioned in last record
BANDINFO( )	Obtains the current band in the Report Generator
BOT( )	Checks for a move made past the beginning of a table

Function/Command	Purpose
CHECKMARKSTATUS( )	Indicates whether a query field has a check mark in it
COL( )	Displays current column position relative to the window
COLNO( )	Displays current column position on the workspace
DIREXISTS( )	Indicates the existence of a specified disk directory
EOT( )	Checks for move made past the end of table
ERRORCODE( )	Provides the code number of the last error; 0 if none
ERRORINFO( )	Initializes a dynamic array with data about the last error
ERRORMESSAGE( )	Provides the text of the last error message; "" if none
ERRORUSER( )	Provides the name of the network user locking an object
FAMILYRIGHTS( )	Checks for access rights to a table's family
FIELD( )	Obtains the name of the current field
FIELDINFO( )	Gets current field indicator in Form or Report designer
FIELDNO( )	Displays field position in table
FIELDRIGHTS( )	Checks for access rights to a table's field
FIELDSTR( )	Displays the current field name
FIELDTYPE( )	Displays the data type of the current field
FILESIZE( )	Provides the size of a disk file
FORM( )	Determines which form is in use for current table
FORMTYPE( )	Obtains the type of the form
HELPMODE( )	Checks to see whether Paradox help is displayed
IMAGENO( )	Obtains the current image's position on the workspace

continues

Table 19.4. Continued

Function/Command	Purpose
IMAGETYPE( )	Obtains the type of the current image
ISASSIGNED( )	Checks to see whether a variable or field has been initialized
ISBLANK( )	Checks to see whether a variable or field is blank
ISEMPTY( )	Checks to see whether a table is empty
ISENCRYPTED( )	Checks to see whether a table is encrypted (password protected)
ISFIELDVIEW( )	Checks to see whether current field is in field view
ISFILE( )	Checks for the existence of a specified disk file
ISFORMVIEW( )	Checks to see whether current image is in form view
ISINSERTMODE( )	Checks to see whether the insert mode is on
ISLINKLOCKED( )	Checks to see whether the current table is linklocked
ISMULTIFORM( )	Checks to see whether the current form has embedded tables
ISMULTIREPORT( )	Checks to see whether the current report has lookup tables linked to it
ISSHARED( )	Checks to see whether a table is in a network shared directory
ISTABLE( )	Checks to see whether a specified table exists
ISVALID( )	Tests the validity of a specified field's contents
ISWINDOW( )	Checks to see whether a window handle is valid
LINKTYPE( )	Obtains the type of link between tables on a form
LOCKSTATUS( )	Displays the number of times a specified lock type has been placed

Function/Command	Purpose
MENUCHOICE( )	Obtains the current selected Paradox menu choice (not PAL menu or application menu)
MENUPROMPT( )	Gets the current text of current type—in menu prompt
NFIELDS( )	Gets the number of fields in a table
NIMAGERECORDS( )	Gets the number of records in current image—linked or unlinked
NIMAGES( )	Gets the number of images on workspace
NKEYFIELDS( )	Gets the number of key fields in a table
NPAGES( )	Gets the number of pages in the current report or form
NRECORDS( )	Gets the number of records in a table
NROWS( )	Gets the number of rows in the current report or image
PAGEWIDTH( )	Gets the width in pages of the current report specification
RECNO( )	Gets the current record number
RECORDSTATUS( )	Reports the status of the current record
ROW( )	Gets the row position relative to the window
ROWNO( )	Gets the row position relative to the screen
TABLE( )	Gets the current table name
TABLERIGHTS( )	Checks for access rights for a specified table
TYPE( )	Provides the type of an expression, array, variable, or specified field
WINDOW( )	Gets the current text of the message bar

Input/Output

These commands and functions, shown in table 19.5, are used to display information on the screen, send data to the printer, or get information from the user.

Table 19.5. Input/Output

Function/Command	Purpose
?	Displays data values on a canvas on the line below the cursor
??	Displays data values on a canvas at the cursor
@	Positions the cursor at specified screen coordinates
ACCEPT	Gets an optionally validated value from the user
BEEP	Causes a short, low-pitched tone to be generated
CANVAS	Controls when changes to a canvas display are made
CHARWAITING( )	Checks for characters in the keyboard buffer
CLEAR	Clears the current canvas
CLEARPULLDOWN	Clears a pull-down menu from the screen
CLOSE PRINTER	Closes a printer device (usually used on networks)
CURSOR	Controls the appearance of the cursor on the PAL canvas
ECHO	Controls display of the workspace during script execution
EXECEVENT	Executes an event specified by a dynamic array
FRAME	Draws a frame on the current canvas
GETCHAR( )	Gets (or waits for) a single character from the keyboard

Function/Command	Purpose
GETEVENT	Captures mouse, keyboard, message, or idle events
GETKEYBOARDSTATE	Captures the keyboard status (CAPS LOCK on, and so forth)
GETMENUSELECTION	Activates menu created with SHOWPULLDOWN, waits for menu selection or cancel
KEYPRESS	Executes a specified keypress as if typed at keyboard
MESSAGE	Displays a message in the message bar
MOUSE CLICK	Emulates a mouse click
MOUSE DOUBLECLICK	Emulates a mouse double-click
MOUSE DRAG	Emulates a mouse drag from one x, y location to another
MOUSE HIDE	Hides the mouse cursor and disables mouse events
MOUSE SHOW	Displays the mouse cursor and enables mouse events
NEWWAITSPEC	Redefines the specification of a WAIT session
OPEN PRINTER	Opens a printer device (usually used on networks)
PAINTCANVAS	Displays colors and styles on a canvas
PRINT	Sends data to the printer or to a file
PRINTER	Turns a continuous printer echo on or off
PROMPT	Sets a custom prompt for the bottom line of the screen
SETKEYBOARDSTATE	Sets the CAPS, NUM, and SCROLL lock key status
SETMARGIN	Sets a margin for displays to both screen and printer
SHOWARRAY	Uses the contents of two arrays to display a pop-up menu
SHOWFILES	Uses disk files in a directory to display a pop-up menu

continues

Table 19.5. Continued

Function/Command	Purpose
SHOWMENU	Displays a pop-up menu at the center of the screen
SHOWPOPUP	Displays a titled pop-up menu at specified coordinates
SHOWPULLDOWN	Displays a pull-down menu with submenus
SHOWTABLES	Uses tables in a directory to create a pop-up menu
STYLE	Sets colors and styles to be used with subsequent displays
TEXT	Displays several lines of text
TYPEIN	Simulates typing a specified string at the keyboard
WAIT	Causes a script to wait for specified events

Keypress Interaction

Keypress interaction commands, shown in table 19.6, emulate the effect of pressing certain keys in various Paradox modes. When used in a script, these commands cause Paradox to act as if a user had made the indicated keystroke interactively.

Table 19.6. Keypress Interaction Commands

Command	Equivalent	Function
ALTSPACE	Alt-space bar	
BACKSPACE	Backspace key	
CHECK	F6	Check mark
CHECKDESCENDING	Ctrl-F6	Sort query in descending order

Command	Equivalent	Function
CHECKPLUS	Alt-F6	Check-plus mark
CLEARALL	Alt-F8	Clear all images
CLEARIMAGE	F8	Clear image
CLIPCOPY	Ctrl-Ins	Copy to clipboard
CLIPCUT	Shift-Del	Cut to clipboard
CLIPPASTE	Shift-Ins	Paste from clipboard
COEDITKEY	Alt-F9	CoEdit
CROSSTABKEY	Alt-X	Cross tabulate
CTRLBACKSPACE	Ctrl-Backspace	Erase current field
CTRLBREAK	Ctrl-Break	Interrupt
CTRLEND	Ctrl-End	
CTRLHOME	Ctrl-Home	
CTRLLEFT	Ctrl-←	
CTRLPGDN	Ctrl-PgDn	
CTRLPGUP	Ctrl-PgUp	
CTRLRIGHT	Ctrl-→	
DEL	Del	
DELETELINE	Ctrl-Y	
DELETEWORD	Alt-D	
DITTO	Ctrl-D	Copy from previous field of previous record
DO_IT!	F2	Perform or end operation
DOS	Ctrl-O	Shell to DOS
DOSBIG	Alt-O	Shell to DOS with maximum free RAM
DOWN	Down arrow	
DOWNIMAGE	F4	Move to next image or multitable form
EDITKEY	F9	Edit
END	End	

continues

Table 19.6. Continued

Command	Equivalent	Function
ENTER	Enter	
ESC	Esc	Go to previous menu, prompt, or workspace
EXAMPLE	F5	Query example
FIELDVIEW	Alt-F5	Begin Field view, or Ctrl-F
FORMKEY	F7	Change to or from Table or Form view
GRAPHKEY	Ctrl-F7	Graph table
GROUPBY	Shift-F6	Group records based on field in query
HELP	F1	Enter Paradox Help mode
HOME	Home	
INS	Ins	
INSTANTPLAY	Alt-F4	Plays instant script
INSTANTREPORT	Alt-F7	Instant report
KEYLOOKUP	Alt-K	Duplicate keys
LEFT	Left arrow	
LOCKKEY	Alt-L	Lock/Unlock current record
MENU	F10	Display menu
MINIEDIT	Ctrl-E	Start editor
ORDERTABLE	Alt-S	
PGDN	PgDn	
PGUP	PgUp	
REFRESH	Alt-R	Refresh screen (multiuser)
REPLACE	Ctrl-A	Replace
REPLACENEXT	Alt-A	Replace Next

Command	Equivalent	Function
RESYNCKEY	Ctrl-L	Resynchronize master and detail records in multi-table forms
REVERSETAB	Shift-Tab	
RIGHT	Right arrow	
ROTATE	Ctrl-R	Rotate field
SCROLLPRESS	Scroll-Lock and a direction key	
TAB	Tab	
TOGGLEPALETTE	Alt-C	Turn palette on/off
TOQPRO	Ctrl-F10	Go to Quattro Pro
UNDO	Ctrl-U	Undo
UP	Up arrow	
UPIMAGE	F3	Move up one workspace image
VERTRULER	Ctrl-V	Show/hide vertical ruler in Report Designer
WINCLOSE	Ctrl-F8	Close current window
WINMAX	Shift-F5	Maximize/restore current window
WINNEXT	Ctrl-F4	Move to next window
WINRESIZE	Ctrl-F5	Move/resize current window
ZOOM	Ctrl-Z	Go to first record with specified value
ZOOMNEXT	Alt-Z	Repeat Zoom

Mathematical

Paradox provides functions for the most common mathematical and trigonometric formulas, and commands for formatting their results (see table 19.7).

Table 19.7. Mathematical Functions

Function	Description
ABS( )	Provides the absolute value of a number
ACOS( )	Gives the arc cosine of a number
ASIN( )	Gives the arc sine of a number
ATAN( )	Gives the arc tangent of a number: 2-quadrant
ATAN2( )	Gives the arc tangent of a number: 4-quadrant
BLANKNUM( )	Provides a blank number, differentiated from zero
COS( )	Gives the cosine of an angle
FORMAT( )	Provides formatting control for number
EXP( )	Computes e^x
INT( )	Gives the integer part of a number
LN( )	Gives the natural logarithm of a number
LOG( )	Gives the base 10 logarithm of a number
MOD( )	Gives the modulus (remainder) result of a division
PI( )	Returns the constant p
POW( )	Raises a number to a power
RAND( )	Gives a pseudo-random number between 0 and 1
ROUND( )	Rounds a number to specified decimals or digits
SIN( )	Gives the sine of an angle
SQRT( )	Gives the square root of a number
TAN( )	Gives the tangent of an angle

Menu Equivalent

These commands, shown in table 19.8, provide script shortcuts to access Paradox menu commands, without having to write out the command sequences in detail. The following two command sequences, for example, are identical:

Menu {Tools} {Copy} {Table} {mytable} {newtable}

COPY "mytable" "newtable"

As you can see, the second form is easier to type and easier to read later. In the second form, the two table names could be replaced with string variables, providing more flexibility.

Table 19.8. Menu Equivalents

Command	Equivalent	Description
ADD	{Tools}{More}{Add}	Adds one table to another
CALCDEBUG		Turns on/off error message for calculated fields
CANCELEDIT	{Cancel}{Yes}	Cancels changes in Form, Report, or Editor session
COEDIT	{Modify}{CoEdit}	Begins coediting mode
COPY	{Tools}{Copy}{Table}	Copies a table
COPYFORM	{Tools}{Copy}{Form}	Copies a form
COPYREPORT	{Tools}{Copy}{Report}	Copies a report
CREATE	{Create}	Creates a new table
DELETE	{Tools}{Delete}{Table}	Erases a table and its family
EDIT	{Modify}{Edit}	Begins edit mode
EMPTY	{Tools}{More}{Empty}	Empties a table
EXIT	{Exit}{Yes}	Ends script and exits Paradox to DOS

continues

Table 19.8. Continued

Command	Equivalent	Description
LOCK	{Tools}{Net}{Lock}	Locks tables on a network
PICKFORM	{Image}{PickForm}	Picks the form to use for displaying a table
PLAY	{Script}{Play}	Starts a script
PROTECT	{Tools}{More}{Protect}	Encrypts (password protect) a table
QUERY/ENDQUERY	{Ask}	Defines a query
RENAME	{Tools}{Rename}{Table}	Gives a table a different name
REPORT	{Report}{Output}	Sends a specified table's report to the printer
SETDIR	{Tools}{More}{Directory}	Changes the working directory
SETPRINTER	{Report}{SetPrinter} {OverRide}{PrinterPort}	Specifies port the printer is attached to
SETPRIVDIR	{Tools}{Net}{SetPrivate}	Sets a network user's private directory
SETUSERNAME	{Tools}{Net}{UserName}	Sets the user name reported on the network
SORT	{Modify}{Sort}	Sorts a table
SUBTRACT	{Tools}{More}{Subtract}	Subtracts one table from another
UNLOCK	{Tools}{Net}{Lock}	Unlocks one or more tables
VIEW	{View}	Displays a table on the workspace

Network and Multiuser

Network and Multiuser commands, shown in table 19.9, are of use when Paradox is installed on a network.

Table 19.9. Network and Multiuser Commands and Functions

Function/Command	Description
IMAGERIGHTS	Establishes or clears access rights to an image
LOCK	Locks one or more tables
LOCKKEY	Emulates Alt-L keypress, lock/unlock current record
LOCKRECORD	Locks the current record
POSTRECORD	Posts record in CoEdit in advance of DO_IT!
PRIVDIR( )	Obtains the current private directory path
PRIVTABLES	Causes tables to be stored in user's private directory
REFRESH	Updates the display of the workspace
RETRYPERIOD( )	Obtains the current setting of the retry period
SETBATCH	Opens network lock file for high-speed updates of current table
SETPRIVDIR	Sets or changes the name of the user's private directory
SETRESTARTCOUNT	Sets the number of restarts when making query, report, or crosstab
SETRETRYPERIOD	Sets the interval between automatic retries
SETUSERNAME	Sets the user name reported to the network
UNLOCK	Unlocks one or more tables
UNLOCKRECORD	Unlocks the current record
USERNAME( )	Obtains user name as reported by network

Procedure and Procedure Library

Procedure and procedure library commands enable you to define execute procedures and create, use, and maintain procedure libraries. These functions give you a means of gathering information about the status and composition of your procedure libraries (see table 19.10).

Table 19.10. Procedure and Procedure Library Commands and Functions

Function/Command	Purpose
CONVERTLIB	Converts procedure library format from Version 3.5 to Version 4.0
CREATELIB	Creates new library; overwrites existing library
EXECPROC	Executes a procedure. The executed procedure may not have parameters.
FILEVERSION( )	Provides the Paradox version under which the library was built
INFOLIB	Displays a list of procedures in a library on-screen
PROC..ENDPROC	Defines the beginning and end of a procedure
READLIB	Loads a procedure from a library file into RAM
RELEASE	Tells Paradox to reclaim memory used by a procedure
SETSWAP	Tells Paradox the size of the memory-management swap limit
WRITELIB	Places a parsed procedure into a library file on disk

Program Flow Control

The items listed in table 19.11 are not exactly commands or functions; they are statements that control how your script executes. These items include statements for making decisions based on various criteria and statements for repeating an operation ("looping") until certain conditions are met.

Table 19.11. Program Control Statements

Statement	Purpose
EXIT	Ends script execution, and then ends Paradox
FOR..ENDFOR	Repeats for a fixed number of times
FOREACH..ENDFOREACH	Scans through all member elements of a dynamic array
IF..THEN..ELSE..ENDIF	Makes an either/or branching decision
IIF( )	Used as a function, a one-line IF..THEN..ELSE
LOOP	Forces script execution to top of current loop
QUIT	Ends script execution
QUITLOOP	Stops the current loop prematurely
RETURN	Ends current procedure or script; optionally passes a value back to the calling script or procedure
SCAN..ENDSCAN	Loops through all records in a table
SWITCH..ENDSWITCH	Makes multiple-choice branching decision
WHILE..ENDWHILE	Loops while a condition is true

Statistical and Financial

The functions listed in table 19.12 provide access to some of the more common financial and statistical formulas.

Table 19.12. Statistical and Financial Functions

Function	Purpose
CAVERAGE( )	Provides column average
CCOUNT( )	Provides count of nonblank column values
CMAX( )	Gives maximum value in a column
CMIN( )	Returns minimum value in a column
CNPV( )	Provides net Present Value of values in a column
CSTD( )	Gives standard Deviation of values in a column
CSUM( )	Gives sum of values in a column
CVAR( )	Provides variance of column values from average
FV( )	Provides future value of a series of payments
IMAGECAVERAGE( )	Returns column average of image column
IMAGECCOUNT( )	Gives count of nonblank entries in image column
IMAGECMAX( )	Provides maximum value of image column
IMAGECMIN( )	Returns minimum value of image column
IMAGECSUM( )	Provides sum of values in an image column
MAX( )	Provides greater of two numbers
MIN( )	Gives lesser of two numbers
PMT( )	Provides amortized payment of a loan
PV( )	Gives present value of a series of payments

String Manipulation

These functions, shown in table 19.13, provide tools to manipulate strings and substrings and gives a means of converting strings to and from other value types.

Table 19.13. String Functions

Function	Purpose
ASC( )	Obtains the number value of a character
CHR( )	Obtains the character value of a number
DATEVAL( )	Obtains a date from a string
FIELDSTR( )	Obtains the contents of the current field as a string
FILL( )	Fills a string with copies of a single character
FORMAT( )	Specifies display formats for a string
LEN( )	Obtains the length of a string
LOWER( )	Converts all the characters in a string to lowercase
MATCH( )	Compares a string with a pattern
NUMVAL( )	Converts a string to a number
SEARCH( )	Finds a substring in a string
SEARCHFROM( )	Finds a substring in a string at a specified starting position
SPACES( )	Obtains a string composed entirely of a specified number of spaces
STRVAL( )	Converts any value to a string
SUBSTR( )	Obtains a substring from a string
UPPER( )	Converts all the characters in a string to uppercase

System Status and Control

These commands and functions provide information about and control over the Paradox system, such as the user interface (see table 19.14).

Table 19.14. System Status Commands and Functions

Function/Command	Purpose
DEBUG	Suspends script execution and enters the PAL debugger
DIRECTORY()	Obtains current working directory path
DRIVESPACE()	Gets the amount of free space on a given disk drive
DRIVESTATUS()	Determines whether the given disk drive is valid and ready
EDITLOG	Manipulates the rollback editing log
EXECUTE	Causes PAL to execute a series of script commands
GRAPHTYPE()	Gets the current graph type
ISBLANKZERO()	Checks to see whether Blank=Zero is true
ISRUNTIME()	Checks to see whether the script is running under Paradox Runtime
MEMLEFT()	Gets the amount of free memory
MONITOR()	Gets the current monitor type
NETTYPE()	Gets the current network type
PRINTERSTATUS()	Determines whether the printer is ready
QUERYORDER()	Determines whether queries are arranged in table or image order
RESET	Clears workspace, ends script, and returns to Paradox Main mode

Function/Command	Purpose
RMEMLEFT( )	Gets the amount of free code pool memory
RUN	Executes DOS commands
SAVETABLES	Forces memory buffers for data tables written to disk
SDIR( )	Gets the DOS directory path of the currently executing script
SETAUTOSAVE	Sets the autosave interval
SETBW	Forces display mode to black and white, grayscale, or monochrome
SETKEY	Attaches a macro to a specified key
SETMAXSIZE	Establishes maximum table size
SETNEGCOLOR	Sets whether color is used when displaying negative values
SETQUERYORDER	Sets field order in which query results are arranged—table/image
SETRECORDPOSITION	Positions the current record in a specific row of the image
SETUIMODE	Changes the user interface mode— standard or compatible
SLEEP	Delays for a specified interval
SORTORDER( )	Determines which sort order has been installed
SYNCCURSOR	Synchronizes the positions of the canvas and workspace cursor
SYSCOLOR( )	Determines the color settings for a single Paradox screen element
SYSMODE( )	Determines the current Paradox mode (Main, Edit, and so forth)
SYSINFO	Initializes a dynamic array with information about the system
VERSION( )	Obtains the Paradox version in use

Variable and Array

Table 19.15 shows the commands for creating and manipulating variables and arrays.

Table 19.15. Variable/Array Commands

Command	Purpose
=	Assigns a value to a variable or array element
APPENDARRAY	Fills several table records from several fixed arrays
ARRAY	Creates and dimensions a fixed array
COPYFROMARRAY	Fills a table record from a fixed array
COPYTOARRAY	Copies a table record into an array
DYNARRAY	Creates a dynamic array
FILEREAD	Reads a disk file into a variable
FILEWRITE	Writes a string or memo variable to a disk file
FORMTABLES	Creates a list of tables embedded in a form
RELEASE	Reclaims memory allocated to variables
REPLACEFIELDS	Replaces contents of several fields with several expressions. More efficient than several separate assignment statements.
REPORTTABLES	Creates a list of tables embedded in a report
SAVEVARS	Writes script containing all of the current variables and values

Window

Table 19.16 lists the commands and functions for establishing and keeping track of windows and their associated objects.

Table 19.16. Window Commands and Functions

Command/Function	Purpose
GETCANVAS()	Obtains the handle for current canvas
GETCOLORS	Initializes dynamic array with color palette information
GETWINDOW()	Obtains the current window handle
ISWINDOW()	Determines whether a window handle is valid
LOCALIZEEVENT	Changes mouse event coordinates from screen to window
SETCANVAS	Selects the current canvas
SETCOLORS	Uses a dynamic array to set the color palette
WINDOW CLOSE	Closes a specified window
WINDOW CREATE	Creates a new window
WINDOW ECHO	Turns a window's echo on/off
WINDOW GETATTRIBUTES	Initializes a dynamic array with window attribute data
WINDOW GETCOLORS	Initializes a dynamic array with window or dialog box color information
WINDOW HANDLE	Obtains a window handle
WINDOW LIST	Creates a list of all open windows
WINDOW MAXIMIZE	Maximizes/restores a window
WINDOW MOVE	Moves a window
WINDOW RESIZE	Resizes a window

continues

Table 19.16. Continued

Command/Function	Purpose
WINDOW SCROLL	Changes a window's horizontal and vertical scroll bar positions
WINDOW SELECT	Selects the current active window
WINDOW SETATTRIBUTES	Uses a dynamic array to set window attributes
WINDOW SETCOLORS	Sets the color attributes of a single window or dialog box
WINDOWAT( )	Obtains the handle of a window enclosing a given point. If more than one window encloses the point, obtains topmost window.

Workspace and Canvas Status

These commands and functions, shown in table 19.17, pertain to control and maintenance of the workspace and canvas areas. Some workspace and canvas commands are listed elsewhere if they fit a more specific category, such as information, window, or program control.

Table 19.17. Workspace and Canvas Commands/Functions

Function/Command	Purpose
CURSORCHAR( )	Obtains the character at the current cursor location
CURSORLINE( )	Obtains the text of the line at the current cursor
FIRSTSHOW	In Compatibility mode, moves the current image to the top
INDEX	Creates a secondary index for a table
LOCATE	Locates a record based on field value(s)

Function/Command	Purpose
LOCATE INDEXORDER	Locates a record based on field value(s) using secondary index
MOVETO	Positions the cursor on a specified field, table, or image
PASSWORD	Submits one or more passwords for access to protected tables
REQUIREDCHECK	Turns the "required field" validity checking on and off
SELECT	Enters text or a menu command
SKIP	Moves one or more records forward or backwards in table
TYPEIN	Enters a string expression as if typed at the keyboard
UNPASSWORD	Revokes access to protected tables

Alphabetic Listing of Commands/Functions

This section describes all PAL commands in Paradox 4.0. The commands and functions are listed alphabetically. This section is intended as a handy quick reference; for in-depth descriptions of each command or function, consult the *PAL Reference Guide* that is supplied with Paradox. This section can assist PAL programmers in determining the correct command and function syntax. The commands and functions are presented with the command or function name and type listed in the title line. The section then describes the correct syntax, followed by a description of the purpose of the command. Often, a short example also is given.

To understand fully the syntax lines presented in this chapter, you must be familiar with a few conventions. These conventions indicate what is mandatory or optional and what components of the syntax line are variable.

Function names are followed by parentheses ( ) to distinguish them from commands.

All mandatory parts of a syntax line are shown in **boldface.** Optional elements are shown in *italic.* Alternative elements are separated by the *pipe* character (|).

In this chapter, all literal text you type in a syntax line is shown in UPPERCASE letters. All text that you replace with other text (variable text) is shown in lowercase letters.

= *Variable/Array*

Syntax

> *variable* | *array[element]* | *field specifier* = **expression1**

Description

The = command assigns the value of an expression to the specified variable, array, or field. The **expression1** parameter contains the expression that is assigned to the variable, array, or field.

You do not have to declare variables before you use them. You create a variable in a script by using the = command to give the variable a value. The variable takes on the data type of expression.

Unlike variables, arrays must be declared before they can be assigned a value (refer to the ARRAY and DYNARRAY commands). After an array is declared and dimensioned, you can use the = command to assign values to each element of the array.

To use the = command to assign a value to a field, the field must belong to a table which is in Edit or CoEdit mode and on the workspace.

Example

```
VIEW "Employee"
First = "Robert"
COEDITKEY
[Emp First Name] = First
```

This example establishes an alphanumeric variable named First by assigning this variable the value "Robert." The script then activates CoEdit mode and assigns the value of the variable First (which is "Robert") to the Emp First Name field in the current record of the current image.

?

Input/Output

Syntax

> **?** *expressionlist*

Description

The ? command moves the cursor to the beginning of the next line in the current canvas, and then displays the value or values specified in the optional *expressionlist* parameter in order from left to right. ? alone moves the cursor without affecting the display otherwise. When the ? command is finished displaying the *expressionlist*, the cursor is left at the end of the *expressionlist*.

You can include multiple expressions in the *expressionlist* parameter, separated by commas. The ? command evaluates the expressions (converting most types to strings) and lists the values side-by-side, from left to right, with no additional spaces between the values.

This command writes to the current canvas. You must select the canvas directly by using SETCANVAS or indirectly by using WINDOW CREATE. If you do not select the canvas, PAL makes the cursor movement and display on the full-screen canvas.

See also the ?? and TEXT commands.

Example

```
? "The current system time is ",TIME()
```

This example displays a message similar to the following:

```
The current system time is 15:16:37
```

??

Input/Output

Syntax

> **??** *expressionlist*

Description

The ?? command behaves exactly like the ? command, except that the optional *expressionlist* parameter is displayed at the current cursor location on the current canvas. The cursor is left at the end of the *expressionlist*. Refer to the ? command for comments regarding the current canvas. ?? by itself does not alter the display and does not move the cursor. You can include multiple expressions in the *expressionlist* parameter, separated by commas. The ?? command evaluates the expressions and lists their values side-by-side, from left to right, with no additional spaces between the values.

See also the ? and TEXT commands.

Example

```
SETCANVAS mywin
? "Today is: "
?? TODAY()

?? ", tomorrow will be: "

?? TODAY() + 1
```

This example displays a message similar to the following:

```
Today is: 1/1/1992, tomorrow will be: 1/2/1992
```

@ .... *Input/Output*

Syntax

> **@ row, column**

Description

Use the @ command to position the cursor on the current PAL canvas.

row is an integer between 0 and 24 that denotes the cursor's vertical location on the 25-line screen. The top row of the screen is row 0, and the bottom row is row 24.

column is an integer between 0 and 79 that denotes the cursor's horizontal position on the 80-column screen. The leftmost column is column 0, and the rightmost column is column 79.

The cursor is placed at the row and column coordinates of the current canvas. You must select the canvas directly by using SETCANVAS or indirectly by using WINDOW CREATE. If you do not select the canvas, PAL makes the cursor movement on the full-screen canvas.

See also the ?? and TEXT commands.

Example

```
@ 12,39
```

This example moves the cursor to the 13th row and 40th column of the screen.

ABS( )   *Mathematical*

Syntax

> **ABS(number)**

Description

ABS returns the absolute value (positive value) for any number between positive or negative 10^{-307} and positive or negative 10^{308}.

Example

```
x = ABS(-45.123)
MESSAGE x
```

This example displays the number 45.123, stripped of the minus sign.

ACCEPT   *Input/Output*

Syntax

> **ACCEPT type** *PICTURE pict MIN val1 MAX val2 DEFAULT val3 LOOKUP lookuptable REQUIRED* **TO var**

Description

ACCEPT pauses the script and enables the user to enter data. The entered data is stored as a variable identified by the **var** parameter. Data-entry editing (refer to Chapter 3, "Entering, Editing, and Viewing Data," for a discussion of data entry) and validity checking (refer to Chapter 9, "Using Power Entry and Editing Features," for a discussion of validity checks) are supported.

type is a valid Paradox field type (refer to Chapter 2, "Creating Database Tables," for a discussion of field type).

The optional keyword *PICTURE* performs validity checking in the same manner as the **ValCheck D**efine **P**icture command described in the "Controlling Data Entry through Pictures" section of Chapter 9, "Using Power Entry and Editing Features." Replace *pict* with a valid PAL picture format.

The MIN, *MAX*, and *DEFAULT* keywords are equivalent to ValCheck **D**efine LowValue, ValCheck **D**efine HighValue, and ValCheck **D**efine **D**efault, respectively. *val1* indicates the low value or minimum. *val2* indicates the high value or maximum. *val3* indicates the default value.

The *LOOKUP* keyword causes ACCEPT to perform a private lookup. The parameter *lookuptable* identifies the lookup table.

Using the *REQUIRED* keyword forces the user to enter some value for **var** before the script continues.

The various options (*PICTURE*, *MIN*, *MAX*, *DEFAULT*, *LOOKUP*, and *REQUIRED*) may be used in any combination. If the user presses the Esc key while an ACCEPT is active, the global variable RetVal is set to False.

Example

```
?? "Type your Social Security number:"
ACCEPT "A11" PICTURE "###-##-####" TO ssn
IF NOT RetVal THEN
    QUIT
ENDIF
```

This example prompts the user to type a social security number. When the user presses Enter, the script assigns the number entered to the variable *ssn*. If the user presses Esc, the script stops.

ACCEPTDIALOG *Dialog Box*

Syntax

ACCEPTDIALOG

Description

Use ACCEPTDIALOG to make your script accept the current dialog (created with SHOWDIALOG) in the same way pressing an OK button would. The ACCEPTDIALOG command takes effect when script control returns from the dialog. Use this command only in script instructions that are part of a dialog procedure or are reached from a dialog procedure.

See also the CANCELDIALOG, REFRESHDIALOG, RESYNCDIALOG, and SELECTCONTROL commands.

ACOS( )   *Mathematical*

Syntax

> **ACOS(number)**

Description

> ACOS returns the arc cosine of **number**, where **number** is be-
> tween –1 and 1. If an illegal argument is passed, Error is returned.
> Valid arc cosines range from 0 to pi.

Example

```
x = ACOS(-.022)
MESSAGE x
```

> This example displays 1.592798101848

ADD   *Menu*

Syntax

> **ADD table1 table2**

Description

> This command is equivalent to the Tools More Add menu com-
> mand. Refer to Chapter 13, "Using Paradox Tools," for a discus-
> sion of this command. **table1** is the source table, and **table2** is
> the target table.

ALTSPACE   *Keypress Interaction*

Syntax

> **ALTSPACE**

Description

> This command opens the System menu, if one is available. This is
> the same as pressing Alt-space bar.

> **WARNING:** Paradox closes an active menu or dialog box as it opens the System menu.

APPENDARRAY   *Variable/Array*

Syntax

APPENDARRAY arraylist

Description

This command adds the contents of one or several arrays to the current table on the workspace. **arraylist** is a list of fixed array variables; each array in the list is separated with a comma and must have the same structure. The APPENDARRAY command has the same effect as performing a COPYFROMARRAY command for each array in the arraylist.

The table to which APPENDARRAY adds records is the current table. The table must be in display mode and in CoEdit mode, otherwise a script error occurs. Records are added in index order if the table is keyed, otherwise they are appended at the end of the table.

The fixed arrays listed in arraylist must be structured as if they were created with the COPYTOARRAY command. APPENDARRAY ignores the first element in each of the arrays because the first element of an array created with the COPYTOARRAY command contains the table name and is ignored by the COPYFROMARRAY. Beginning with the second element in each of the arrays, the array elements are transferred to corresponding record fields in order from left to right.

Attempts to place an unassigned array element, or an array element of the wrong type into a record field, will result in a script error. If the array contains more elements than the record has fields, the extra elements are ignored.

APPENDARRAY sets the global variable RetVal to the number of arrays that were added to the table.

If a key violation occurs while APPENDARRAY is posting the new records, the command is halted. The record containing the key violation is not posted, and the remaining arrays in the list are not processed.

See also ARRAY, COPYFROMARRAY, and COPYTOARRAY.

ARRAY   *Variable/Array*

Syntax

ARRAY arrayname [number]

Description

This command creates an array. **arrayname** is the name of the
new array and must be a legal PAL variable identifier (refer to
Chapter 15, "Overview of the Paradox Application Language," for
more information on variable names and arrays). The parameter
number is an integer between 1 and 15,000 that indicates the
array's dimension.

Do not use the same name for an array and for a variable in the
same script.

Use the RELEASE VARS command to release the array from
memory.

See also DYNARRAY.

Example

```
RELEASE VARS ALL
ARRAY Fullname [3]
Fullname[1] = "Joseph"
Fullname[2] = "R."
Fullname[3] = "Green"
?? Fullname[1]," ",Fullname[2]," ",Fullname[3]
SLEEP 3000
```

This example creates a three-dimensional array named Fullname,
assigns values to each element of the array, and displays the
name Joseph R. Green.

ARRAYSIZE( )   *Information*

Syntax

ARRAYSIZE(arrayname)

Description

ARRAYSIZE returns the dimension of an array. A zero is returned
if the array was not defined or if the variable is not an array.

arrayname represents the array to be tested. The dimension is the number of values an array can store.

See also the TYPE, ISASSIGNED, and DYNARRAYSIZE functions.

Example

```
ARRAY Xray[30]
RETURN ARRAYSIZE(Xray)
```

This example displays the number 30, which is the dimension of the array named Xray.

ASC( ) *String*

Syntax

ASC(char)

Description

The ASC function returns the ASCII code for **char**, where **char** is a valid PAL keycode expression. The function returns a positive number when **char** is an ASCII code and returns a negative number when **char** is an IBM extended code.

Example

```
RETURN  ASC("F2")
```

This example returns –60.

ASIN( ) *Mathematical*

Syntax

ASIN(number)

Description

ASIN returns the arc sine of **number**, where **number** is between –1 and 1. If an illegal argument is passed, Error is returned. Valid arc sines range from –pi/2 to pi/2.

Example

```
y = -.225
MESSAGE ASIN(y)
```

This example displays .226943036178.

ATAN( )   *Mathematical*

Syntax

> **ATAN(number)**

Description

> ATAN returns the 2 quadrant arc tangent of **number** where
> **number** represents the tangent of the angle. ATAN, expressed
> in radians, returns a value between –pi/2 and pi/2.

Example

```
x = .433
RETURN ATAN(x)
```

This example displays .4086271587177.

ATAN2( )   *Mathematical*

Syntax

> **ATAN2(number1, number2)**

Description

> ATAN2 returns the 4 quadrant arc tangent of **number1** and
> **number2** where **number1** represents the cosine and **number2**
> represents the sine of an angle. ATAN2, expressed in radians,
> returns a numeric value.

Example

```
x = 1
y = .3
RETURN ATAN2(x, y)
```

This example displays .2914567944778.

ATFIRST( )   *Workspace, Canvas*

Syntax

ATFIRST()

This function accepts no arguments.

Description

ATFIRST analyzes the current record or restricted view and returns a logical value of True if the current record is the first record. True also is returned if the table is empty. False is returned when the record is not the first record in the table and when more than one record is in the table.

ATFIRST respects the limits of the restricted view in a multitable form.

Example

```
IF ATFIRST() THEN
    MESSAGE "Can't go up"
    SLEEP 2500
ELSE
    UP
ENDIF
```

This example displays the message Can't go up if the current record is already the first record in the table. Otherwise, the script activates the up-arrow key to move up one record in the table.

ATLAST( )   *Workspace, Canvas*

Syntax

ATLAST()

This function accepts no arguments.

Description

ATLAST analyzes the current table or restricted view and returns a logical value of True if the current record is the last record in the table or view. True also is returned if the table is empty. False is returned when the record is not the last record in the table and when more than one record exists in the table.

ATLAST respects the limits of the restricted view in a multitable form.

Example

```
IF ATLAST() THEN
    MESSAGE "Don't go down"
    SLEEP 2500
ELSE
    DOWN
ENDIF
```

If the current record is the last record in the table, this example displays the message Don't go down. Otherwise, the script presses the down-arrow key to move down one record in the table.

BACKSPACE   *Keypress Interaction*

Syntax

BACKSPACE

Description

The BACKSPACE command is equivalent to pressing Backspace. The effect of this command depends on the Paradox mode and the context. BACKSPACE deletes the character to the left of the cursor in Main, Edit, CoEdit, field view, Form Designer, or Report Designer modes and contexts only. If Paradox is not in one of these modes, then this command has no effect. Refer to the chapter that discusses the mode and context in which you intend to use the BACKSPACE command. Compare this command to the CTRLBACKSPACE and DEL commands.

BANDINFO( )   *Workspace, Canvas*

Syntax

BANDINFO()

This function accepts no arguments.

Description

BANDINFO returns the name of the current band (such as Report Header, Form Band, and so forth) while in Report mode. Paradox generates a script error if the function is called while not in the Report mode.

BEEP   *Input/Output*

Syntax

BEEP

Description

The BEEP command causes the computer to sound a low-pitched tone. BEEP commonly is used to draw the user's attention to the screen or to indicate an error condition of some kind.

Example

```
BEEP BEEP BEEP
MESSAGE "You must make an entry in this field."
SLEEP 3000
```

This example beeps three times and displays the message You must make an entry in this field.

BLANKDATE( )   *Date*

Syntax

BLANKDATE()

This function accepts no arguments.

Description

BLANKDATE assigns a blank date to a variable or Paradox date field. Use this function to initialize blank date values; it is the only way to obtain a blank date value.

Example

```
oldate = DATEVAL("7/01/91")
MESSAGE oldate
```

This example displays the following date:

    7/01/91

Contrast this example with the following example:

    oldate = BLANKDATE()
    MESSAGE oldate

This second example displays nothing on-screen.

BLANKNUM( )   *Mathematical*

Syntax

> **BLANKNUM()**

This function accepts no arguments.

Description

BLANKNUM assigns a blank numeric value to a numeric field or variable. A blank number is not the same as zero. For certain calculations, you may want to tell Paradox to treat blanks as zeros. Use the Paradox Custom Configuration Program to set the Blank=Zero option. To determine the current Blank=Zero setting, use the ISBLANKZERO function.

Example

    bowlscore = BLANKNUM()

This example initializes the value of the bowling score variable, bowlscore to a blank number.

BOT( ) *Information, Workspace, Canvas*

Syntax ·

> **BOT()**

This function accepts no arguments.

Description

BOT is a logical function that tests to see whether the cursor has moved beyond the beginning of the current image.

The ATFIRST function is usually preferable to the BOT.

CALCDEBUG   *Menu*

Syntax

CALCDEBUG ON | OFF string

Description

The CALCDEBUG command is equivalent to the **PAL C**alcDebug command in the Custom Configuration Program.

Starting in Version 3.5, you can use PAL functions in calculated fields in forms and reports. By default, if you are playing a script and Paradox detects an error in a calculated field, Paradox does not display an error message, but fills the calculated field with blanks. The CALCDEBUG command enables you to cause Paradox to display an error message when it detects an error in a calculated field.

The **string** parameter, referred to as the fill string, indicates the value Paradox should assign to the calculated field when an error is detected.

Example

```
CALCDEBUG ON "calc error"
```

This example toggles on the calculated-field error messages and designates the string calc error as the fill string.

CANCELDIALOG   *Dialog Box*

Syntax

CANCELDIALOG

Description

Use CANCELDIALOG to make your script cancel the current dialog (created with SHOWDIALOG) in the same way pressing a Cancel button would. The CANCELDIALOG command takes effect when script control returns from the dialog. Use this command only in script instructions which are part of a dialog procedure or are reached from a dialog procedure.

See also the ACCEPTDIALOG, REFRESHDIALOG, RESYNCDIALOG, and SELECTCONTROL commands.

CANCELEDIT   *Menu*

Syntax

>   **CANCELEDIT**

Description

> The CANCELEDIT command is an abbreviated menu command,
> equivalent to the following sequence of PAL commands:
>
> ```
> MENU {Cancel} {Yes}
> ```

CANVAS   *Input/Output*

Syntax

>   **CANVAS ON | OFF**

Description

> The CANVAS command enables you to build the current PAL can-
> vas, and then display the entire canvas at once. By default, the
> current canvas is on and all changes to the canvas display imme-
> diately. Use the CANVAS OFF command to turn off the current
> canvas while the script builds the screen. Then use CANVAS ON
> to display the entire screen at the same time.
>
> This command controls only the current canvas. You must select
> the canvas directly using SETCANVAS or indirectly by using WIN-
> DOW CREATE. If you do not select the canvas, PAL makes this
> command affect the full-screen canvas.
>
> See also the ?? , @, SETCANVAS, and TEXT commands.

CAVERAGE( )   *Statistical*

Syntax

>   **CAVERAGE(tablename, fieldname)**

Description

CAVERAGE calculates the average of the entries in the **fieldname** column. **tablename** represents the table to scan. **fieldname** represents the column to average. A script error occurs if **fieldname** is not a numeric field. CAVERAGE includes all the nonblank values in the column. CAVERAGE disregards blank values even if Blank=Zero was set in the Paradox Custom Configuration Program.

CAVERAGE in a multiuser environment places a Write Lock on **tablename**. If another user already placed a Full Lock or Prevent Write Lock on this table, by default Paradox retries to place a Write Lock on the table for the designated retry period. If the retry period is exceeded, a script error occurs.

CAVERAGE does not require the table to be on the workspace. When used with multitable forms, the function does not respect the limits of the restricted view.

CCOUNT( )   *Statistical*

Syntax

CCOUNT(tablename, fieldname)

Description

CCOUNT sums the nonblank entries in a numeric column of a table. **tablename** is the name of the table to scan. **fieldname** indicates the field (column) to count. A script error occurs if the field is not numeric. CCOUNT includes all the nonblank values in the column. CCOUNT disregards blank values even if Blank=Zero was set in the Paradox Custom Configuration Program.

CCOUNT, in a multiuser environment, places a Write Lock on the table. If an application or other user already placed a Full Lock or Prevent Write Lock on the table, by default Paradox retries to place a Write Lock on the table for the designated retry period. If the retry period is exceeded, a script error occurs.

CCOUNT does not require **tablename** to be on the workspace. When used with multitable forms, the function does not respect the limits of the restricted view.

CHARWAITING( )   *Input/Output*

Syntax

> **CHARWAITING()**

This function accepts no arguments.

Description

> Use this function to determine whether or not the keyboard buffer
> has any characters waiting to be read. CHARWAITING returns a
> logical value of True if at least one character is in the keyboard
> buffer; otherwise False is returned. CHARWAITING does not re-
> move characters from the keyboard buffer; it only checks to see if
> any characters are waiting. After using CHARWAITING to test for
> characters to be read, use GETCHAR to read the character from
> the keyboard buffer.
>
> See also GETCHAR( ).

CHECK *Workspace, Keypress Interaction*

Syntax

> **CHECK**

Description

> The CHECK command is equivalent to pressing the F6
> (Checkmark) key. Refer to Chapters 4, "Getting Started with Query
> By Example," and 7, "Using Advanced Query By Example and Mul-
> tiple Tables," for more information on using F6 (Checkmark).

CHECKDESCENDING *Workspace, Keypress Interaction*

Syntax

> **CHECKDESCENDING**

Description

The CHECKDESCENDING command is equivalent to pressing the Ctrl-F6 (Check Descending) keystroke. Refer to Chapter 4, "Getting Started with Query By Example," for more information on how to use Ctrl-F6 (Check Descending).

CHECKMARKSTATUS( )   Information, Workspace, Canvas

Syntax

CHECKMARKSTATUS()

This function accepts no arguments.

Description

The CHECKMARKSTATUS function determines whether the current field on a query form was checked, and if so, returns the kind of check assigned. Table 19.18 lists the values returned by this function.

Table 19.18. Values Returned by the CHECKMARKSTATUS Function

Status	Returned string
Not checked	"" (null string)
Check	"Check"
CheckPlus	"CheckPlus"
CheckDescending	"CheckDescending"
Groupby	"GroupBy"

CHECKPLUS

Workspace, Keypress Interaction

Syntax

CHECKPLUS

Description

The CHECKPLUS command is equivalent to pressing Alt-F6 (Check Plus). Refer to Chapter 4, "Getting Started with Query By Example," for more information about how to use Alt-F6 (Check Plus).

CHR( )

String

Syntax

CHR(num)

Description

The CHR function returns a one-character string containing the ASCII symbol corresponding to the **num**, where **num** is an integer between 1 and 255.

Example

```
RETURN = CHR(233)
```

This example returns the Greek symbol Theta (θ).

CLEAR

Input/Output

Syntax

CLEAR *EOL* | *EOS*

Description

The CLEAR command clears the current canvas. Using CLEAR by itself clears all contents from the current canvas. When used with the *EOL* keyword, the CLEAR command clears the current canvas from the cursor to the end of the line that contains the cursor. When used with the *EOS* keyword, the CLEAR command clears the current canvas from the cursor to the end of screen.

This command has no effect on images in the Paradox workspace.

This command clears only the current canvas. You must select the canvas directly using SETCANVAS or indirectly by using WINDOW CREATE. If you do not select the canvas, PAL clears the full-screen canvas.

See also the CLEARALL and CLEARIMAGE commands.

CLEARALL   *Workspace, Keypress Interaction*

Syntax

> **CLEARALL**

Description

The CLEARALL command is equivalent to pressing the Alt-F8 (ClearAll) key. Refer to Chapter 4, "Getting Started with Query By Example," for more information about using Alt-F8 (ClearAll). CLEARALL does not clear canvases from the workspace. Use the WINCLOSE keypress command or the WINDOW CLOSE command to remove canvases from the workspace.

CLEARIMAGE   *Workspace, Keypress Interaction*

Syntax

> **CLEARIMAGE**

Description

The CLEARIMAGE command is equivalent to pressing the F8 (ClearImage) key. Refer to Chapter 4, "Getting Started with Query By Example," for more information about using F8 (ClearImage).

CLEARPULLDOWN   *Input/Output*

Syntax

> **CLEARPULLDOWN**

Description

> Use CLEARPULLDOWN to remove pull-down menus displayed
> with the SHOWPULLDOWN command because they are not re-
> moved automatically from the desktop.
>
> See also the SHOWPULLDOWN command for an example of how
> to use CLEARPULLDOWN.

CLIPCOPY   *Keypress Interaction*

Syntax

> **CLIPCOPY**

Description

> Use this command to copy a marked (selected) block of text from
> the editor to the Clipboard. It has the same effect as pressing Ctrl-
> Ins. This command is only effective while in an Editor session, but
> does not produce a runtime error if not in an Editor session.
>
> See CLIPCUT and CLIPPASTE for related commands.

CLIPCUT   *Keypress Interaction*

Syntax

> **CLIPCUT**

Description

> Use this command to cut the marked (selected) block of text from
> the Editor to the Clipboard. It has the same effect as pressing
> Shift-Del. This command is effective only while in an Editor
> session, but does not produce a runtime error if not in an Editor
> session.
>
> See CLIPCOPY and CLIPPASTE for related commands.

CLIPPASTE   *Keypress Interaction*

Syntax

> **CLIPPASTE**

Description

> Use this command to place the text in the Clipboard into the Editor. The insertion occurs at the current cursor location. This command has the same effect as pressing Shift-Ins. This command is only effective while in an Editor session, but does not produce a runtime error if not in an Editor session.
>
> See CLIPCUT and CLIPCOPY for related commands.

CLOSE PRINTER   *Input/Output*

Syntax

> **CLOSE PRINTER**

Description

> The CLOSE PRINTER command closes a printer device opened by the OPEN PRINTER command. If you open a printer device, you should always close it when you are done with it. This command is usually used in network environments.
>
> See also to the OPEN PRINTER command.

Example

```
VIEW "Customer"
SETPRINTER "LPT1"
OPEN PRINTER
SCAN
   PRINT [Company Name]+"\n"
   PRINT [Cust Address]+"\n"
   PRINT [Cust City]+", "+[Cust State]+"  "+[Cust Zip]+"\n\n\n\n"
ENDSCAN
PRINT "\f"
CLOSE PRINTER
CLEARIMAGE
```

This example opens a printer device, prints an address list from the Customer table, and then closes the printer device.

CMAX( )   *Statistical*

Syntax

CMAX(tablename, fieldname)

Description

CMAX scans the numeric column specified by **fieldname** and returns the largest value of the entries. **tablename** is the name of the table to scan; it does not have to be on the workspace at the time CMAX is called. If the specified field column in the specified table contains only blank values, CMAX returns the string Error. A script error results if the **fieldname** is not a numeric field.

CMAX in a multiuser environment places a Write Lock on **tablename**. If another user already placed a Full Lock or Prevent Write Lock on the table, Paradox, by default, tries to place a Write Lock on the table for the designated retry period. If the retry period is exceeded, a script error occurs.

When used with multitable forms, the CMAX function does not respect the limits of the restricted view.

Example

```
max_electricity = CMAX( "elec_use", "kwh" )
SETCANVAS mywin
@0,0 ?? "Maximum electricity usage was: ", max_electricity,
   " kilowatt hours."
```

This script fragment finds the maximum value of a field called kwh in the table elec_use and stores it in the variable max_electricity. The current canvas is set to a previously saved window handle stored in the variable mywin, the cursor is positioned at the top left corner of the canvas, and a message similar to the following is displayed:

```
Maximum electricity usage was 750 kilowatt hours.
```

CMIN( ) *Statistical*

Syntax

CMIN(tablename, fieldname)

Description

CMIN scans a numeric column as indicated by **fieldname** and returns the smallest value of the entries. **tablename** is the table to scan. Blank entries are not regarded as minimum values (even if Blank=Zero was set in the Paradox Custom Configuration Program. A script error occurs if the field (column) is not numeric. If all of the entries in the specified field are blank, CMIN returns the string Error. This function can be used on a table that is not on the workspace.

CMIN in a multiuser environment places a Write Lock on **tablename**. If another user already placed a Full Lock or Prevent Write Lock on the table, Paradox, by default, tries to place a Write Lock on the table for the designated retry period. If the retry period is exceeded, a script error occurs. CMIN ignores blank values even if Blank=Zero was set in the Paradox Custom Configuration Program.

CMIN does not require the table to be on the workspace.

When used with multitable forms, the CMIN function does not respect the limits of the restricted view.

Example

```
minelectricity = ( CMIN "elec_use", "kwh" )
? "Minimum electricity usage was: ",
    minelectricity, " kilowatt hours."
```

This fragment finds the minimum value of a field called kwh in the table elec_use and stores it in the variable minelectricity. The current canvas is set to a previously saved window handle stored in the variable mywin and a message similar to the following is displayed:

```
Minimum electricity usage was 750 kilowatt hours.
```

CNPV( )   *Financial*

Syntax

> **CNPV(tablename, fieldname, discount)**

Description

CNPV calculates the net present value of a series of cash flows.
The cash flows are values within a column of a table. **tablename** is
the table that contains the flows. **fieldname** is a numeric column
that contains the cash flows. **discount** represents the discount
rate per period. The discount rate is represented in decimal (.09),
not in percent (9%), form. Only nonblank values are included in
the calculation. If the field is not numeric, a script error results.

The table must be set up by period, normally by month or year.
An expected cash flow must be entered for each period. Set up
with zero all periods that you expect to have zero as the cash
flow; do not leave the periods blank. CNPV ignores blank values,
and the cash flow periods are wrong.

A cash flow can be positive or negative.

If an initial cash flow is made, add this flow independently of the
CNPV calculation. Because the initial flow occurs as time 0, do not
discount the initial flow. The following formula can be used:

> initflow + CNPV(tablename, fieldname, discount)

In a multiuser environment, CNPV places a Write Lock on
tablename. If an application or other user already placed a Full
Lock or Prevent Write Lock on the table, by default Paradox retries to place a Write Lock on the table for the designated retry
period. If the retry period is exceeded, a script error occurs.

CNPV does not require the table to be on the workspace. CNPV
does not respect the limits of restricted views on multitable
forms.

Example

You just made an investment, which you expect to produce the
cash flows at the following rate:

Year	Amount
1	100
2	200
3	300
4	400
5	500

The cash is received at the end of each year for five years. The discount rate to use is 9 percent. The following example assumes that this data is stored in a table named Flowtab. The cash flow amounts are stored in the column (field) named FlowAmt.

```
MESSAGE CNPV("Flowtab", "FlowAmt", 0.09)
Sleep 2000
```

This example displays the number 1100.069939512 on-screen.

COEDIT   Menu

Syntax

> **COEDIT table1**

Description

The COEDIT command is equivalent to executing the menu command **M**odify **C**oEdit, which displays a table in CoEdit mode. The **table1** parameter indicates the table that should be displayed. Refer to Chapter 3, "Entering, Editing, and Viewing Data," for a discussion of CoEdit mode.

Example

```
COEDIT "Employee"
```

This example displays the Employee table on the workspace in CoEdit mode.

COEDITKEY   Keypress Interaction

Syntax

> **COEDITKEY**

Description

The COEDITKEY command is equivalent to pressing Alt-F9 (CoEdit). Refer to Chapter 3, "Entering, Editing, and Viewing Data," for more information about Alt-F9 (CoEdit).

Example

```
VIEW "Employee"
COEDITKEY
```

This example displays the Employee table on the workspace in Main mode, and then activates CoEdit mode. The result is the same as the following PAL command:

```
COEDIT "Employee"
```

COL( )   *Workspace, Canvas*

Syntax

COL()

This function accepts no arguments.

Description

Use this function to obtain the current column position of the cursor relative to the current PAL canvas. The left-most edge of the canvas is represented by the number 0.

COL cannot provide information about the cursor in the workspace area.

This function reports on only the current canvas. You must select the canvas directly using SETCANVAS or indirectly by using WINDOW CREATE. If you do not select the canvas, PAL reports the cursor column for the full-screen canvas.

See also the ?? and TEXT commands.

COLNO( )   *Workspace, Canvas*

Syntax

COLNO()

This function takes no arguments.

Description

Use COLNO to determine the current column position in the current display or query image of the workspace. COLNO pertains to the image and not to the window. The leftmost field of the image always corresponds to the record number and is column 1 of the image. A script error results if this function is used when there are no images present in the workspace, or if used in any context other than Main, Edit, CoEdit, or in the Form Designer or Report Designer.

COLNO returns the current line number of the cursor in Form Designer, Report Designer, and the Script Editor. A script error occurs if no images are present in the workspace.

CONTROLVALUE( )   Dialog Box

Syntax

> **CONTROLVALUE(tagname,** *labelname* **)**

Description

This function obtains the value of any control in a dialog box created with SHOWDIALOG. Use this function when the value of a control element variable differs from the value displayed by the control.

tagname is the name of the control for which the value is to be obtained. When used, the *labelname* is the label of a check box field. If the control being sampled is a check box, then the labelname must be supplied. The *labelname* option is not used for other types of controls.

See also SHOWDIALOG.

CONVERTLIB   Procedure

Syntax

> **CONVERTLIB oldlibname newlibname**

Description

This command converts a procedure library from Paradox 3.0 or 3.5 format to Version 4.0 format. **oldlibname** is the name of the old version Paradox procedure library; **newlibname** is the name of the new procedure library. Paradox cannot directly read procedure libraries from previous versions.

See also the FILEVERSION function.

Example

```
IF FILEVERSION( "mylib" ) <> "4.0" THEN
    CONVERTLIB "mylib" "mylib40"
ENDIF
```

This example uses the FILEVERSION function to determine the version of Paradox that the procedure library mylib was created with. If it was not created with Paradox Version 4.0, then CONVERTLIB is used to convert mylib to a Version 4.0 procedure library. The new procedure library is named *mylib40*.

COPY   *Menu*

Syntax

> **COPY table1 table2**

Description

The COPY command makes a copy of an existing table and its family of objects. This command is equivalent to the **Tools Copy Table** menu command. Refer to Chapter 13, "Using Paradox Tools," for a discussion of this command. **table1** is the source table, and **table2** is the new table.

> **CAUTION:** The COPY command potentially can replace an existing table and family of objects without a warning. If the destination table name (**table2** in the syntax) is the same as an existing table name, COPY replaces the old table and family with the new table and family without issuing a warning or error message. The script should, therefore, use the ISTABLE function to check for the existence of the destination table before issuing the COPY command.

COPYFORM   *Menu*

Syntax

> **COPYFORM table1 form1 table2 form2**

Description

This command is equivalent to the **Tools Copy Form** menu command. Refer to Chapter 13, "Using Paradox Tools," for a discussion of this command. **table1** is the source table, and **form1** is the source form. **table2** is the target table, and **form2** is the new form.

> **CAUTION:** Similar to the **COPY** command, the COPYFORM command potentially can replace an existing form without warning. Use the ISFILE function to check for the existence of a form—ISFILE("orders.f1"), for example—before using COPYFORM.

COPYFROMARRAY *Variable/Array*

Syntax

COPYFROMARRAY array1

Description

The COPYFROMARRAY command is the counterpart to the COPYTOARRAY command. This command copies the elements of an array to the current record of the current table. **array1** specifies the source array. The target table, which is the current image, must be in either Edit or CoEdit mode. You must structure the source array so that the first element of the array contains the table name, and the remaining elements contain the values you want to copy to the current record's fields in order. This structure is the same array structure created by the COPYTOARRAY command. If the source array is not initialized, a script error occurs. Review the multiuser considerations for COEDIT.

Example

```
VIEW "Translog"
VIEW "Orders"
@ 10,10 ?? "Type the Order # for the transaction to edit:"
ACCEPT "N" TO Order_Num
MOVETO [Order #]
LOCATE Order_Num
COPYTOARRAY Before
MOVETO [Translog ->]
```

```
END
EDITKEY
DOWN
COPYFROMARRAY Before
MOVETO [Orders ->]
WAIT RECORD UNTIL "Help", "Do_It!"
```

In this example, before the user makes changes to a record, the script uses COPYTOARRAY and COPYFROMARRAY to save a copy of the record to a transaction log table named Translog. The Translog table, which must have the same structure as Orders, in this example, enables the script to give you the opportunity to undo changes made to the Orders table—an action sometimes called "rolling back a transaction."

COPYREPORT   *Menu*

Syntax

COPYREPORT table1 report1 table2 report2

Description

This command is equivalent to the **Tools Copy R**eport menu command. Refer to Chapter 13, "Using Paradox Tools," for a discussion of this command. **table1** is the source table, and **report1** is the source report. **table2** is the target table and **report2** is the new report.

> **CAUTION:** Similar to the COPY command, the COPYREPORT command potentially can replace an existing report without warning. Use the ISFILE function to check for the existence of a report—ISFILE("orders.r1"), for example—before using COPYREPORT.

COPYTOARRAY   *Variable/Array*

Syntax

COPYTOARRAY array1

Description

The COPYTOARRAY command is the counterpart to the COPYFROMARRAY command. This command creates an array, the name of which is specified by the parameter **array1**. COPYTOARRAY then copies the field values from the current record in the current image to the new array. The first element in the array contains the table name of the current image. The remaining elements contain the values of the various fields in the current image, in table structure order.

In the script, when referring to array elements, you can use the table name and field names as subscripts. If a script uses COPYTOARRAY to create the array *emparray* from the table Employee, for example, the script can use the following notation to refer to the first element of emparray:

```
emparray ["Employee"]
```

Example

Refer to the example shown with the COPYFROMARRAY command.

COS( )   *Mathematical*

Syntax

COS(number)

Description

COS returns a value between –1 and 1, which is the cosine of **number**. **number**, expressed in radians, represents an angle.

Example

```
RETURN COS(15)
```

This example displays - .759687912858 on-screen.

CREATE   *Menu*

Syntax

CREATE table1 field_defs

CREATE table1 LIKE table2

Description

The CREATE command is equivalent to the **Create** menu command.

Using the first form of the command, **table1** contains the name of the new table. **field_defs** is a list of field names and field formats that define the structure of the new table.

In the second form of the CREATE command, the command creates **table1** using the structure of **table2.**

Refer to Chapter 2, "Creating Database Tables," for a full discussion of defining table structure.

Examples

```
CREATE "Translog"
    "Order #"        : "N*",
    "Cust ID #"      : "A4",
    "Emp ID #"       : "A11",
    "Date"           : "D",
    "Company Name"   : "A20",
    "Cust Address"   : "A20",
    "Cust City"      : "A20",
    "Cust State"     : "A2",
    "Cust Zip"       : "A5",
    "Cust Phone"     : "A14"

CREATE "Translog" LIKE "Orders"
```

Both of these examples create a table named Translog.

CREATELIB   Procedure

Syntax

CREATELIB library1 *SIZE number*

Description

The CREATELIB command creates a library for storing PAL procedures. Refer to Chapter 16, "Using the Paradox Application Language," for a discussion of PAL procedures.

The **library1** parameter indicates the name of the PAL procedure library. The library name must start with a letter and can be from one to eight characters long. The script creates a disk file by the same name and adds the file-name extension LIB.

By default, a PAL procedure library accommodates a maximum of 50 PAL procedures. To increase this capacity, use the optional keyword *SIZE* followed by *number*. The *number* parameter must be an integer between 50 and 300.

If disk space is at a premium, increase the library maximum size no more than absolutely necessary. For each additional potential procedure file, the library file increases in size by at least 44 bytes, *before* any procedures are added.

CREATELIB doesn't check for an existing library file of the same name before creating a file. The script should therefore use the ISFILE command to check for duplicate file names before executing the CREATELIB command.

After the script creates the library, the script must use the WRITELIB command to add procedures to the library. The script must first use the PROC command, however, to load each procedure into memory before it can be written to the library.

Example

```
CREATELIB "OrdEntry" SIZE 100
```

This example creates a library file named ORDENTRY.LIB, which can accommodate up to 100 PAL procedures.

CROSSTABKEY   *Keypress Interaction*

Syntax

CROSSTABKEY

Description

The CROSSTABKEY command is equivalent to pressing Alt-X (Crosstab). Refer to Chapter 12, "Using Paradox Graphics," for a complete discussion of using the Crosstab command to create graphs in Paradox.

CSTD( )   *Statistical*

Syntax

CSTD(tablename, fieldname)

Description

Calculates the variances of entries in a numeric column of a table and returns the standard deviation. **tablename** indicates the table to use. The standard deviation is calculated on the column indicated by **fieldname**. A script error occurs if the column is not numeric. If the column has no nonblank entries, the string Error is returned.

CSTD in a multiuser environment places a Write Lock on **tablename**. If an application or another user already placed a Full Lock or Prevent Write Lock on the table, by default Paradox retries to place a Write Lock on the table for the designated retry period. If the retry period is exceeded, a script error occurs. CSTD ignores blank values even if Blank=Zero was set in the Paradox Custom Configuration Program.

CSTD does not require the table to be on the workspace.

When used with multitable forms, the function does not respect the limits of the restricted view.

CSUM( )   *Statistical*

Syntax

CSUM(tablename, fieldname)

Description

CSUM returns the sum of the entries in a numeric column. **tablename** indicates the table to use. **fieldname** is the numeric column to total. The string Error is returned if the column has no nonblank values; if the column is not numeric, a script error occurs.

CSUM, in a multiuser environment, places a Write Lock on **tablename**. If an application or another user already placed a Full Lock or Prevent Write Lock on the table, Paradox retries to place a Write Lock on the table for the designated retry period. If the retry period is exceeded, a script error occurs.

CSUM does not require the table to be on the workspace.

When used with multitable forms, the function does not respect the limits of the restricted view.

CTRLBACKSPACE   *Keypress Interaction*

Syntax

CTRLBACKSPACE

Description

The CTRLBACKSPACE command is equivalent to pressing the Ctrl-Backspace keystroke. This keystroke erases the contents of the current field in the current image. This command is effective only in Edit mode, CoEdit mode, and in a query form in Main mode. In field view, this keystroke erases the current contents of the field and ends field view.

CTRLBREAK   *Keypress Interaction*

Syntax

CTRLBREAK

Description

The CTRLBREAK command is equivalent to pressing Ctrl-Break. This command generally terminates interruptible tasks. CTRLBREAK has no effect, however, on queries, sorts, and reports because the script is not in control while these tasks are in progress. If no interruptible task is ongoing and the script is in control, the CTRLBREAK command interrupts the script and starts the PAL Debugger.

CTRLBREAK cannot interrupt a password-protected script or interrupt a script running under Paradox Runtime. Use the **M**enu **M**ore **B**reakDisable command in the Custom Configuration Program to disable CTRLBREAK.

CTRLEND   *Keypress Interaction*

Syntax

CTRLEND

Description

The CTRLEND command is equivalent to pressing Ctrl-End. The effect this command has depends on the Paradox mode and the context. In Main, Edit, or CoEdit mode, the cursor moves to the last field of the current record; in the Form Designer, Report Designer, or Editor, the cursor moves to the end of the current line. In Field View, the cursor moves to the last character in the field. Refer also to the chapters that discuss the mode and context in which you intend to use the CTRLEND command.

CTRLHOME   *Keypress Interaction*

Syntax

CTRLHOME

Description

The CTRLHOME command is equivalent to pressing Ctrl-Home. The effect of this command depends on the Paradox mode and the context. In Main, Edit, or CoEdit mode, the cursor moves to the first field of the current record. In the Form Designer, the cursor moves to the beginning of the current line. In the Report Designer, the cursor moves to the first character in the current line. CTRLHOME has no effect in the Editor. In Field View, the cursor moves to the first character in the field. Refer also to the chapters that discuss the mode and context in which you intend to use the CTRLHOME command.

CTRLLEFT   *Keypress Interaction*

Syntax

CTRLLEFT

Description

The CTRLLEFT command is equivalent to pressing Ctrl-Left. The effect of this command depends on the Paradox mode and the context. In table view for Main, Edit, or CoEdit mode, the display is shifted right one screen. In the Report Designer, the display also is shifted right one screen. In Field View or the Editor, the cursor moves one word to the left. CTRLLEFT has no effect in the Form Designer or in Form View. Refer to the chapters that discuss the mode and context in which you intend to use the CTRLLEFT command.

CTRLPGDN   *Keypress Interaction*

Syntax

> **CTRLPGDN**

Description

> The CTRLPGDN command is equivalent to pressing Ctrl-PgDn. In the Editor, the cursor is moved to the end of the field or file being edited. In Form View, the cursor is moved to the same field of the next record. CTRLPGDN otherwise has no effect. Refer also to the chapters that discuss the mode and context in which you intend to use the CTRLPGDN command.

CTRLPGUP   *Keypress Interaction*

Syntax

> **CTRLPGUP**

Description

> The CTRLPGUP command is equivalent to pressing Ctrl-PgUp. In the Editor, the cursor is moved to the beginning of the field or file being edited. In Form View, the cursor is moved to the same field of the previous record. CTRLPGUP otherwise has no effect. Refer also to the chapters that discuss the mode and context in which you intend to use the CTRLPGUP command.

CTRLRIGHT   *Keypress Interaction*

Syntax

> **CTRLRIGHT**

Description

The CTRLRIGHT command is equivalent to pressing Ctrl-Right. The effect of this command depends on the Paradox mode and the context. In table view for Main, Edit, or CoEdit mode, the display is shifted left one screen. In the Report Designer, the display also is shifted left one screen. In Field View or the Editor, the cursor moves one word to the right. CTRLRIGHT has no effect in the Form Designer or in Form View. Refer to the chapters that discuss the mode and context in which you intend to use the CTRLRIGHT command.

CURSOR   Input/Output

Syntax

CURSOR *BAR* ∣ *BOX* ∣ *NORMAL* ∣ *OFF*

Description

The CURSOR command controls the appearance of the cursor on the current PAL canvas. By default, the cursor appears on the canvas as a flashing underscore character. The *BAR* keyword causes the cursor to appear as a flashing bar character. The *BOX* keyword causes the cursor to appear as a flashing filled-in box character. The *NORMAL* keyword returns the cursor to its default shape. The *OFF* keyword hides the cursor from view on the canvas. The CURSOR command affects only the cursor on the current canvas, and has no effect on the workspace cursor.

You must select the canvas directly using SETCANVAS or indirectly by using WINDOW CREATE. If you do not select the canvas, PAL makes the change in the cursor for the full-screen canvas.

See also the CANVAS and SYNCCURSOR commands.

Example

```
CURSOR OFF
```

This example turns the cursor off on the PAL canvas.

CURSORCHAR( )   *Workspace, Canvas*

Syntax

CURSORCHAR()

This function accepts no arguments.

Description

CURSORCHAR returns a one-character string, which represents the character displayed at the current cursor position on the workspace.

In Paradox Version 4.0, the CURSORCHAR function applies to the Form Designer and Report Designer only. A script error occurs if the function is used in other modes. To obtain text from the Editor, use the EDITOR SELECT and EDITOR EXTRACT commands.

See also the CURSORLINE function.

CURSORLINE( )   *Workspace, Canvas*

Syntax

CURSORLINE()

This function accepts no arguments.

Description

CURSORLINE returns the line of text from the workspace that contains the cursor.

In Paradox Version 4.0, the CURSORLINE function applies to the Form Designer and Report Designer only. A script error occurs if the function is used in other modes. To obtain text from the Editor, use the EDITOR SELECT and EDITOR EXTRACT commands.

See also the CURSORCHAR function.

CVAR( )   *Statistical*

Syntax

CVAR(tablename, fieldname)

Description

CVAR calculates the population variance (how much a set of values varies from the average) of entries in a numeric column. **tablename** indicates the table to use. **fieldname** is the numeric column for which to calculate the variance. The string Error is returned if all of the values in the specified column are blank. If the column is not numeric, a script error results. CVAR does not include blank values in its calculation, even if Blank=Zero was set using the Custom Configuration Program.

CVAR, in a multiuser environment, places a Write Lock on **tablename**. If an application or another user already placed a Full Lock or Prevent Write Lock on the table, by default Paradox retries to place a Write Lock on the table for the designated retry period. If the retry period is exceeded, a script error occurs.

CVAR does not require the table to be on the workspace.

When used with multitable forms, the function does not respect the limits of the restricted view.

DATEVAL( )   *Date, String*

Syntax

DATEVAL(string)

Description

The DATEVAL function converts a string into Paradox date format, where **string** can be transformed to a valid Paradox date. If **string** does not convert to a valid Paradox date, the string Error is returned.

Example

```
MESSAGE DATEVAL( "7/8/88" )
MESSAGE DATEVAL( "13/01/91" )
```

The first example displays the date "7/8/88" in the message area. The second example displays the string Error, because 13/01/91 is not a valid date.

DAY( )   *Date*

Syntax

> **DAY(date)**

Description

DAY returns an integer between 1 and 31 that represents the day of the month extracted from the **date** parameter, which can be any valid Paradox date expression. If the date expression is invalid, a script error occurs.

Example

> MESSAGE DAY(7/8/88)

This example displays the number 8 in the message area at the lower right corner of the screen.

DEBUG   *System Control*

Syntax

> **DEBUG**

Description

The DEBUG command interrupts execution of the script and enters the PAL Debugger. Refer to Chapter 16, "Using the Paradox Application Language," for a discussion of the Debugger. Use this command to correct problems in a script without having to trace the execution of every command in the script. Place the DEBUG command immediately before the script instructions that are suspect. Script execution occurs normally until the DEBUG command is reached. After the Debugger is activated, use the Debugger's Where? command, and then use the Trace command.

This command is not effective if your script is running under Paradox Runtime.

DEL   *Keypress Interaction*

Syntax

> **DEL**

Description

> The DEL command is equivalent to pressing Del. The effect of this command depends on the Paradox mode and the context. Refer to the chapter that discusses the mode and context in which you intend to use the DEL command.

DELETE   *Menu*

Syntax

> **DELETE table1**

Description

> The DELETE command deletes a table and the table's family of objects. **table1** is a string expression containing the name of the table to be deleted. This command is equivalent to the menu command **T**ools **D**elete **T**able, except that the DELETE command does not ask for confirmation. Refer to Chapter 13, "Using Paradox Tools," for a discussion of **T**ools **D**elete **T**able.

> If the specified table does not exist, or Paradox is not in Main mode when the script executes this command, a script error results.

Example

```
tblname = "OldEmp"
DELETE tblname
```

> This example deletes the table named OldEmp and its family of objects.

DELETELINE   *Keypress Interaction*

Syntax

DELETELINE

Description

The DELETELINE command deletes text. If the current context is the Report Designer, then the text is deleted from the current cursor position to the end of the current line. In the Editor, the entire current line (the one the cursor is on) is deleted. This command is equivalent to pressing Ctrl-Y and has no effect on the PAL Canvas. Refer to Chapter 5, "Getting Started With Reports," for a discussion of the Report Designer. Refer to Chapter 17, "Using the Script Editor and PAL Debugger," for more information about the Editor.

DELETEWORD   *Keypress Interaction*

Syntax

DELETEWORD

Description

This command deletes from the current cursor position to the end of the word, including spaces and punctuation marks. This command has an effect only in the Editor and is ignored in other contexts. It is not possible to use DELETEWORD to join lines of text, because it does not remove line breaks.

> **WARNING:** The text removed by DELETEWORD is *not* placed into the Clipboard.

See also the CLIPCUT and CLIPPASTE commands.

DIRECTORY( )   *System Status*

Syntax

> **DIRECTORY()**

This function accepts no arguments.

Description

> DIRECTORY returns a string containing the full DOS path name of the working directory currently in use. Consult your DOS manuals for help with path names.
>
> See also the SETDIR command and the DIREXISTS, PRIVDIR, and SDIR functions.

Example

```
SETDIR "c:\\telsave"
RETURN DIRECTORY()
```

This example displays the directory name C:\TELSAVE\.

DIREXISTS( )   *Information*

Syntax

> **DIREXISTS(dospath)**

Description

> DIREXISTS tests the **dospath** given and returns a numeric value showing whether the table exists. Table 19.19 lists values that can be returned by the DIREXISTS function.

Table 19.19. Values Returned by the DIREXISTS Function	
Status	**Returned value**
Directory does not exist	0
Directory exists	1
Syntax error in DOS path	−1

Example

```
DirPath = "\\MYAPP\\MYDATA"
y = DIREXISTS(DirPath)
IF y = 1
THEN
    MESSAGE "Data Found"
ELSE
    MESSAGE "Data Not Found " + " " +DirPath
        SLEEP 2500
ENDIF
```

This example displays the message Data Found if the directory \MYAPP\MYDATA exists. Otherwise, the script displays the message Data Not Found \MYAPP\MYDATA.

DITTO   *Workspace, Keypress Interaction*

Syntax

DITTO

Description

The DITTO command copies the current field value from the same field of the preceding record. This command is equivalent to the Ctrl-D (Ditto) keystroke command. Refer to Chapter 3, "Entering, Editing, and Viewing Data," for a discussion of the Ctrl-D (Ditto) command.

The DITTO command works in DataEntry mode, Edit mode, and CoEdit mode but is ignored in other modes.

DO_IT!   *Keypress Interaction*

Syntax

DO_IT!

Description

The DO_IT! command is equivalent to the F2 (Do-It!) keystroke and the DO-IT! menu command. The effect of this command depends on the Paradox mode and the context. Refer to the chapter that discusses the mode and context in which you intend to use the DO_IT! command.

DOS   *Keypress Interaction*

Syntax

DOS

Description

The DOS command suspends Paradox and enables the user to execute commands at the DOS command line. The DOS command is equivalent to the Ctrl-O (DOS) keystroke command and to the **Tools More ToDOS** menu command. Refer to Chapter 13, "Using Paradox Tools," for a discussion of these equivalent commands.

When the user types *exit*, Paradox regains control and continues execution of the script at the command that follows the DOS command.

The DOS command provides approximately 210K bytes of memory in which the user can run DOS programs or execute DOS commands. If this amount of memory is insufficient to run the desired DOS program or programs, use the DOSBIG command.

See also the RUN command.

DOSBIG   *Keypress Interaction*

Syntax

DOSBIG

Description

Like the DOS command, the DOSBIG command suspends Paradox and enables the user to execute commands at the DOS command line. The DOSBIG command provides more free memory, however, than does the DOS command. The DOS command saves the Paradox environment to disk, and then gives the user approximately 500K bytes of memory to run DOS programs or execute DOS commands.

The DOSBIG command is equivalent to the Alt-O (DOS Big) keystroke command. Refer to Chapter 13, "Using Paradox Tools," for a discussion of this command.

When the user types *exit*, Paradox regains control and continues execution of the script at the command that follows the DOSBIG command.

DOW( )   *Date*

Syntax

> **DOW(date)**

Description

> DOW returns the day of the week on which **date** falls, as one of the following three-character abbreviations: Mon, Tue, Wed, Thu, Fri, Sat, or Sun. **date** must be a valid Paradox date expression, or a script error occurs.

Example

> ```
> MESSAGE DOW(6/10/91)
> ```
>
> This example displays Mon.

DOWN   *Keypress Interaction*

Syntax

> **DOWN**

Description

> The DOWN command is equivalent to pressing the down-arrow key. The effect of this command depends on the Paradox mode and the context. Refer to the chapter that discusses the mode and context in which you intend to use the DOWN command.

DOWNIMAGE   *Workspace, Keypress Interaction*

Syntax

> **DOWNIMAGE**

Description

The DOWNIMAGE command moves the cursor on the workspace down to the next image. This command is equivalent to the F4 (Down Image) keystroke command. Refer to Chapter 3, "Entering, Editing, and Viewing Data," for a discussion of the F4 (Down Image) command.

DOWNIMAGE is effective only in Main mode, Edit mode, and CoEdit mode. This command has no effect on canvas windows.

Refer to the descriptions of the WINNEXT and WINDOW SELECT if you need to move to canvas windows.

DRIVESPACE( )   *System Status*

Syntax

DRIVESPACE(diskdrive)

Description

DRIVESPACE returns the available bytes on a disk. **diskdrive** is a single character representing a valid drive. DRIVESPACE returns 0 if the drive was not ready. If an invalid disk drive is passed, a script error occurs.

Example

```
MESSAGE DRIVESPACE("c")
```

This example displays, in bytes, the free space on drive C.

DRIVESTATUS( )   *System Status*

Syntax

DRIVESTATUS(diskdrive)

Description

DRIVESTATUS returns a logical value of True if the drive specified by **diskdrive** is ready. **diskdrive** is a single character representing a valid drive. False is returned if the drive is not ready, and a script error occurs if the **diskdrive** specification is invalid (more than one character, or a disk that does not exist).

Use this function to test that a disk drive is ready before trying to write to or read from it. If you prompt a user to enter a disk into a drive, for example, check the drive status to be sure that the disk was placed in the drive and the drive door is closed before continuing with execution of the script.

Example

```
IF DRIVESTATUS("B") THEN
    COPY "Invoices" "B:Invoices"
ELSE
    MESSAGE "Diskette Drive B:, Not Ready"
    SLEEP 2500
ENDIF
```

This example copies the table named Invoices to a disk in drive B if it is ready, or displays an error message if drive B is not ready.

DYNARRAY   *Variable/Array*

Syntax

> **DYNARRAY arrayname[ ]**

Description

This command creates a new dynamic array. **arrayname** is the name of the new array and must be a legal PAL variable identifier (refer to Chapter 15, "An Overview of the Paradox Application Language," for more information on variable names and arrays). Note that the size of the array is not specified. This is what makes dynamic arrays unique: their size (that is, the number of elements in the array) is changeable.

Use the DYNARRAYSIZE function to determine the current size of a dynamic array, and use ISASSIGNED to determine if an element of the array is initialized. To dispose of elements in a dynamic array that have become unnecessary, and to free more memory, use the RELEASE VARS command.

The FOREACH structure should be used to loop through all of the elements in a dynamic array.

You can indirectly create dynamic arrays by using any of these commands: EDITOR INFO, ERRORINFO, GETCOLORS, GETEVENT, GETKEYBOARDSTATE, SYSINFO, or WINDOW GETATTRIBUTES. Please refer to the individual command descriptions for more information.

Do not use the same name for a dynamic array and for a variable in the same script.

See also ARRAY.

Example

```
DYNARRAY DeptHeads[]
DeptHeads["OfficeName"] = "East Coast"
DeptHeads["Accounting"] = "Joe"
DeptHeads["Sales"] = "Susan"
DeptHeads["Shipping"] = "Mary"
OfficeSize = DYNARRAYSIZE( DeptHeads ) -1
@0,0 ?? "The ", DeptHeads["OfficeName"],
      " office has  ", OfficeSize, " Department Heads."
? "The Department Heads are:"
FOREACH MEMBER IN DeptHeads
    IF (MEMBER <> "OFFICENAME") THEN
        ? DeptHeads[MEMBER]
    ENDIF
ENDFOREACH
DeptHeads["Receiving"] = "Fred"
? "After adding the new department, there are
      ", DYNARRAYSIZE(DeptHeads)-1, " departments."
```

This example creates a dynamic array called DeptHeads and initializes and displays some of the array's elements. Here, the first element of the array (OfficeName) is excluded from printing during the FOREACH loop, and also is excluded from the size computations because it is not the name of a department head. The next to last line of the example creates a new element in the dynamic array. The output of this example is as follows (the exact order of the names in the list may vary):

```
The East Coast office has 3 Department Heads.
The Department Heads are:
Mary
Susan
Joe
After adding the new department, there are 4 departments.
```

DYNARRAYSIZE( )   Information

Syntax

DYNARRAYSIZE(arrayname)

Description

This function returns the size of a dynamic array as a numeric value. **arrayname** is the name of a dynamic array. The numeric value returned is the number of elements in the dynamic array. A value of 0 (zero) is returned if **arrayname** is not a dynamic array or if the dynamic array has not yet been declared or no elements of the dynamic array have been initialized. Use the ISASSIGNED function and the TYPE function to determine whether a variable is a dynamic array and whether any elements have been initialized.

See also the DYNARRAY command and the ARRAYSIZE function.

Example

See the DYNARRAY command example for an example of the DYNARRAYSIZE function.

ECHO   Input/Output

Syntax

ECHO *FAST* | *SLOW* | *OFF* | *NORMAL*

Description

The ECHO command enables you to control whether the workspace displays during execution of a script. By default, ECHO is OFF, and the workspace is frozen while each script executes. Only the PAL canvas displays during a script.

This command has the same effect as choosing **S**cripts **S**howplay. When the *FAST* keyword is added to the ECHO command, the script displays the results of each step on the workspace, but at a speed somewhat slower than full speed. The *SLOW* keyword slows execution even further. If the ECHO command includes the *NORMAL* keyword, all steps in the script are displayed at full speed.

The ECHO command affects the echo status for the entire Paradox system. You can change the echo status for individual workspace windows by using the WINDOW ECHO command. The echo status also can be set by using the WINDOW SETATTRIBUTES command.

See also WINDOW ECHO, WINDOW GETATTRIBUTES, and WINDOW SETATTRIBUTES.

EDIT   *Menu*

Syntax

> **EDIT table1**

Description

> The EDIT command enables the user to edit or add records to an existing table; the table is identified in the **table1** parameter. This command is equivalent to the **M**odify **E**dit menu command. Refer to Chapter 3, "Entering, Editing, and Viewing Data," for more details about using the **M**odify **E**dit command.

> Paradox must be in Main mode for the EDIT command to be effective.

Example

> ```
> EDIT "Employee"
> ```

> This example adds the Employee table to the workspace and places the table in Edit mode.

EDITKEY   *Keypress Interaction*

Syntax

> **EDITKEY**

Description

> The EDITKEY command places the workspace into Edit mode. This command is equivalent to the F9 (Edit) keystroke command. Refer to Chapter 3, "Entering, Editing, and Viewing Data," for more information about this keystroke command and about Edit mode.

Example

```
VIEW "Orders"
@ 10,10 ?? "Type the Order # for the transaction to edit:"
ACCEPT "N" TO Order_Num
MOVETO [Order #]
LOCATE Order_Num
EDITKEY
WAIT RECORD UNTIL "Help", "Menu", "Do_It!"
```

In this example, the script displays the Orders table on the workspace, and then asks the user to type the Order # for the transaction to edit. When the user indicates the Order #, the script locates the appropriate record in Orders and uses the EDITKEY command to place the workspace into the Edit mode. The user is then permitted to edit the specified record in Orders.

EDITLOG   *System Control*

Syntax

EDITLOG *MARK* | *REVERT* | *INDEX* | *PERMANENT*

Description

The EDITLOG command enables the script to control the transaction log that Paradox creates during DataEntry and Edit modes. In a multitable form, this command is not effective and generates a script error. Use the UNDO command to reverse changes in a multitable form data-entry or editing session. For more information about the Undo command, see Chapter 3, "Entering, Editing, and Viewing Data." The EDITLOG command is not available for Memo or Binary fields and will cause a script error if any table on the workspace contains Memo or Binary fields.

The *MARK* keyword sets a marker in the transaction log. The script can set multiple markers; all markers, however, are cleared by the DO_IT! command. The transaction log is described in Chapter 3, "Entering, Editing, and Viewing Data."

The *REVERT* keyword reverses data-entry or edit changes up to the most recent marker in the transaction log. If no marker is set (by the EDITLOG MARK command), REVERT reverses all changes up to the beginning of the data-entry or editing session.

The *INDEX* keyword causes Paradox to update primary and secondary indexes for the current table. The effect of this keyword on indexes is similar to that of pressing F2 (Do-It!) in CoEdit mode; but, EDITLOG INDEX has no effect on the transaction log. Refer to Chapter 3, "Entering, Editing, and Viewing Data," for a discussion of CoEdit mode.

The *PERMANENT* keyword causes Paradox to update the primary and secondary indexes for the current table and to reset the transaction log. Neither EDITLOG REVERT nor UNDO can reverse changes made during the session after EDITLOG PERMANENT is used (unless more changes are made).

Example

```
VIEW "Customer"
EDITKEY
WHILE (True)
   WAIT TABLE
      PROMPT "Press Ctrl-U to Undo last transaction,
         F2 when done, F1 for help."
      UNTIL "Help", "Down", "Up", "Undo", "Do_It!"
   SWITCH
      CASE RetVal = "Help":
         HELP
      CASE RetVal = "Down":
         EDITLOG INDEX
         EDITLOG MARK
         DOWN
      CASE RetVal = "Up":
         EDITLOG INDEX
         EDITLOG MARK
         UP
      CASE RetVal = "Undo":
         EDITLOG REVERT
      CASE RetVal = "Do_It!":
         DO_IT!
         QUITLOOP
   ENDSWITCH
ENDWHILE
```

This example uses the EDITLOG INDEX command to emulate in Edit mode and table view CoEdit's treatment of indexes. The script uses EDITLOG MARK and EDITLOG REVERT to maintain Edit mode's capacity for undoing changes with the Ctrl-U (Undo) keystroke.

EDITOR EXTRACT   *Editor*

Syntax

EDITOR EXTRACT TO variablename

Description

This command copies the marked (selected) block of text in the current Editor session. **variablename** is the PAL variable to which the text is copied; PAL creates the variable if necessary. The resulting variable type will be either a memo variable or a string variable, depending on the length of the selected block. EDITOR EXTRACT places any selected text into a variable and should be used instead of CURSORCHAR or CURSORLINE for large sections of text. Using this command in any context other than an editor session causes a script error. Compare this command to FILEREAD.

See also EDITOR INSERT.

EDITOR FIND   *Editor, Menu*

Syntax

EDITOR FIND string_expression

Description

This command is the same as using the **Search Find** command from the Editor Menu. **string_expression** is any valid PAL string expression. Paradox searches forward from the current cursor location. The search is case-sensitive by default; append the **..** string wild card to **string_expression** to make the search find any case text. Using this command in a context other than an editor session causes a script error.

See also EDITOR FINDNEXT, and EDITOR REPLACE for related commands.

EDITOR FINDNEXT   *Editor, Menu*

Syntax

     EDITOR FINDNEXT

Description

This command continues a search initialized with the EDITOR
FIND command. The search begins at the current cursor position
and continues searching for the string specified with the EDITOR
FIND. This command is the same as choosing **S**earch **N**ext from
the Editor Menu. Using this command in a context other than an
editor session causes a script error.

See also EDIT FIND and EDITOR REPLACE for related commands.

EDITOR GOTO   *Editor*

Syntax

     EDITOR GOTO *POSITION* **offset** | *LINE* **num**

Description

This command positions the cursor in the current Editor window.

If used with the POSITION keyword, **offset** is the character offset
at which the cursor is placed. The first character in any editor
session is character 1. Character offset is not the same as column
position. Note in the example below that character offset 24 is
actually on the third line of the file.

If used with the LINE keyword, **num** is the line number at which
the cursor is placed.

See also EDITOR INFO and EDITOR SELECT.

Example

```
CLEARALL
CLEAR
ECHO NORMAL
EDITOR OPEN "gotest.sc"
EDITOR GOTO POSITION 24
MESSAGE "Now at character offset 24 in the Editor."
SLEEP 4000
EDITOR GOTO LINE 1
MESSAGE "Now at line one of the Editor."
SLEEP 4000
```

This example clears the canvas and workspace, turns the echo on at normal speed, and then uses EDITOR OPEN to open an editor session and load the file named gotest.sc. If this example is stored in gotest.sc, the EDITOR GOTO command moves the cursor to the character "M" in the word "NORMAL" of the third line. The cursor is then moved to line 1. Because the column position of the cursor exceeds the length of the new line, it is positioned in the first column of the new line.

EDITOR INFO   *Editor*

Syntax

EDITOR INFO *COMPLETE* **TO arrayname**

Description

This command stores information about the current Editor session in a dynamic array. **arrayname** is any legal PAL variable identifier. EDITOR INFO always creates or reinitializes **arrayname** as a dynamic array. Table 19.20 lists the indexes that **arrayname** is given when it is created, and describes the information stored in each element subscripted by the given index.

The optional COMPLETE keyword forces the column position, number of characters, and the current line to recalculated. These values usually are not computed by EDITOR INFO because counting the number of characters in the file may take a significant amount of time, and may not be the information desired.

EDITOR INFO affects the value of the global variable RetVal. If EDITOR INFO is used outside the context of an Editor session RetVal is set to False, otherwise RetVal is set to True.

Table 19.20. Indexes and Elements Initialized by EDITOR INFO

Index	Element description
NUMEDITOR	Numeric: total number of Editor sessions now active
TYPE	Editor session type: Memo, File, or Script
SELSTART	Numeric: offset of the beginning of the currently selected text

Index	Element description
SELEND	Numeric: offset of the end of the currently selected text
CHARPOS	Numeric: offset of the current cursor position
CHANGED	Logical: value is false until the editor file is changed; then it's set to true
OVERWRITE	Logical: true if the editor mode is overstrike (typeover), false otherwise
AUTOINDENT	Logical: true when the editor is in auto indent mode, false otherwise
WORDWRAP	Logical: true when the editor's word-wrap feature is on, false otherwise
WRAPPOS	Numeric: indicates the column position at which word-wrapping occurs. If WORDWRAP is false, this value is 0.
CHARLEN	Number of characters in the editor file stored in memory. Initialized only if the optional keyword COMPLETE is used.
COL	Number of the column where the cursor is currently located. Initialized only if the optional keyword COMPLETE is used.
CURLINE	Number of the line where the cursor currently is. Initialized only if the optional keyword COMPLETE is used.

Example

```
EDITOR INFO TO myeditor
IF NOT RetVal THEN
    RETURN "The current context is not an editor session."
ELSE
    FOREACH member IN myeditor
        MESSAGE "[" + member + "] = " + STRVAL(myeditor[member])
        SLEEP 4000
    ENDFOREACH
ENDIF
```

This example initializes a dynamic array called myeditor, creating it if necessary. RetVal is examined to see whether the information retrieval was successful. If an editor session was not running, then a message to that effect is printed, and the script terminates execution. Otherwise, each element of the dynamic array containing the editor information is displayed in the message area.

EDITOR INSERT   *Editor*

Syntax

EDITOR INSERT expression

Description

This command places a string corresponding to **expression** into an Editor session at the current cursor location in the Editor. **expression** is any valid PAL expression; EDITOR INSERT converts it to a string value as necessary. If the current editor session contains selected (marked) text, the string derived from **expression** replaces it. This command produces a script error if used outside the context of an Editor session.

See also EDITOR EXTRACT, EDITOR INFO, EDITOR SELECT, and FILEWRITE for related commands.

Example

```
CLEARALL
CLEAR
ECHO NORMAL
EDITOR OPEN "edins.sc"
EDITOR SELECT 21 26
CLIPCUT
xstring = "SLOW"
EDITOR INSERT xstring
```

This example clears both the canvas and the workspace, turns the echo on at normal speed, and then opens an editor session with the file named *edins.sc.* If text stored in the edins.sc file is identical to the script above, then the EDITOR SELECT command selects the word "NORMAL." The CLIPCUT command is used to remove the selected text, and the EDITOR INSERT command is used to insert the word "SLOW."

EDITOR NEW   *Editor*

Syntax

> **EDITOR NEW filespec**

Description

Use this command to start an editor session and create a new file.
filespec must evaluate to a string expression containing any legal
DOS file name and path; an invalid file name produces a script
error.

> **WARNING:** If the file indicated by **filespec** already exists, it
> is destroyed and replaced by the new file without asking for
> confirmation. EDITOR NEW is valid in any of the contexts in
> which the key command Ctrl-E is available.

EDITOR OPEN   *Editor, Menu*

Syntax

> **EDITOR OPEN filespec**

Description

Use this command to start an editor session and load an existing
file into the editor. **filespec** must evaluate to a string expression
containing any legal DOS file name and path; an invalid file name
produces a script error. If the file indicated by **filespec** does not
exist, a script error occurs. EDITOR OPEN is valid in any of the
contexts in which the key command Ctrl-E is available.

Example

See EDITOR INSERT for an example of the EDITOR OPEN
command.

EDITOR READ   *Editor, Menu*

Syntax

EDITOR READ filespec

Description

This command loads a file into the current editor session at the current cursor location. **filespec** must evaluate to a string expression containing any legal DOS file name and path; an invalid file name produces a script error. If the file indicated by **filespec** does not exist, or the file already is open, a script error occurs. Using this command in any other context than an editor session produces a script error.

See also EDITOR WRITE and EDITOR INSERT.

EDITOR REPLACE   *Editor, Menu*

Syntax

EDITOR REPLACE string1 string2

Description

This command causes the editor to find **string1** and replace it with **string2**. The search begins at the current cursor location. This command is the same as choosing **S**earch **R**eplace from the Editor menu. **string1** is a string expression indicating the pattern to search for. This may be quoted strings, string variables, concatenated strings, or strings containing the Paradox wild-card patterns .. and @. Note that EDITOR REPLACE is case-sensitive. Append the .. wild-card character to **string1** to make the search match any case text. Using EDITOR REPLACE in any context other than an editing session produces a script error.

See also EDITOR FIND and EDITOR FINDNEXT.

Example

See EDITOR WRITE for an example using the EDITOR REPLACE command.

EDITOR SELECT   *Editor*

Syntax

> **EDITOR SELECT loc1 loc2**

Description

EDITOR SELECT marks (selects) text in an editor session. **loc1** is an integer value indicating the character offset of the location where the selected text begins. **loc2** is an integer value indicating the character offset of the location where the selected text ends. The first location in the file is number 1. Using this command outside the context of an editor session results in a script error.

See also the CLIPCOPY, CLIPCUT, and CLIPPASTE commands.

Example

See the EDITOR INSERT and EDITOR WRITE commands for examples of using the EDITOR SELECT command.

EDITOR WRITE   *Editor, Menu*

Syntax

> **EDITOR WRITE filespec**

Description

Use this command to write the marked (selected) block of text in the current editor session to the file specified by **filespec**. **filespec** must evaluate to a string expression containing any legal DOS file name and path; an invalid file name produces a script error.

> **WARNING:** If the file indicated by **filespec** already exists, its contents are destroyed and replaced by the selected text from the editor without asking for confirmation. Using this command outside the context of an editor session results in a script error.

See also EDITOR READ, EDITOR EXTRACT, EDITOR INSERT, FILEREAD, and FILEWRITE.

Example

```
CLEARALL
CLEAR
ECHO NORMAL                          ; show what's going on
EDITOR OPEN "edwrite.sc"             ; load this script file
                                     ; into the editor

EDITOR GOTO POSITION 1
EDITOR REPLACE "NORMAL" "SLOW"
EDITOR INFO COMPLETE TO myedit       ; create DYNARRAY
                                     ; "myedit" loaded with
                                     ; editor status
                                     ; information
EDITOR SELECT 1 myedit["CHARLEN"]    ; select all of the text
                                     ; in the editor
EDITOR WRITE "ed_slow.sc"
```

This example loads a file (containing the preceding script) into an editor session. The word "NORMAL" is replaced with the word "SLOW." All of the editor text is selected, and then written to a new file called ed_slow.sc

---

EMPTY   *Menu*

Syntax

EMPTY table1

Description

The EMPTY command deletes all records from the table specified in the **table1** parameter. This command is equivalent to the Tools More Empty menu command, except that the EMPTY command deletes all records without asking for user confirmation. Refer to Chapter 13, "Using Paradox Tools," for a discussion of the Tools More Empty menu command.

Example

```
EMPTY "Customer"
```

This example deletes all records from the Customer table without asking for confirmation from the user.

END   *Keypress Interaction*

Syntax

END

Description

The END command is equivalent to pressing End. The effect of this command depends on the Paradox mode and the context. In Main, Edit, or CoEdit mode, the cursor is moved to the last record of the current table or restricted view. In the Form and Report Designer, the cursor is moved to the last line. In the Editor, the cursor is moved to the end of the line. Refer to the chapter that discusses the mode and context in which you intend to use the END command.

ENTER   *Keypress Interaction*

Syntax

ENTER

Description

The ENTER command is equivalent to pressing Enter. The effect of this command depends on the Paradox mode and the context. Refer to the chapter that discusses the mode and context in which you intend to use the ENTER command.

EOT( )   *Information, Workspace*

Syntax

EOT()

This function accepts no arguments.

Description

EOT returns a logical answer to determine whether the cursor has moved beyond the end of the table. Three Paradox commands, MOVETO, SKIP, and LOCATE, can move the cursor beyond the bounds of the current table.

EOT returns True if the MOVETO, SKIP, or LOCATE command moved the cursor beyond the last record in the table. False is returned if the cursor is not moved beyond the last record of the current table.

EOT adheres to the limits of the restricted view.

The functionality of EOT has been replaced by the ATLAST function.

ERRORCODE( )   *Information*

Syntax

ERRORCODE( )

This function accepts no arguments.

Description

ERRORCODE returns the code of the most recent error. A zero verifies that no errors occurred. You can use ERRORCODE with a global variable ErrorProc to develop an error-handling procedure.

ERRORINFO   *Information*

Syntax

ERRORINFO TO arrayname

Description

This function creates and initializes a dynamic array containing information about the last error. **arrayname** is any valid PAL variable name. Table 19.21 describes the dynamic array elements and their subscript (index) names. Use this function and the global variable ErrorProc to build your own error-handling procedure.

Table 19.21. Dynamic Array Index and Elements Obtained from ERRORINFO

Index	Element description
SCRIPT	Name of script in which the error occurred
LINE	Line number of the script in which the error occurred
POSITION	Character offset position in the script where error occurred
CODE	Category code of the error; same as code returned by ERRORCODE
USER	Same as value returned by ERRORUSER, name of user who locked an object
MESSAGE	Same as value returned by ERRORMESSAGE, test of most recent error message
PROC	Current PROC name, blank if no PROC is executing
SQLERRORMESSAGE	If SQL is loaded, the most recent SQL error message text; blank otherwise
SQLERRORCODE	If SQL is loaded, the most recent SQL error code; 0 otherwise

ERRORMESSAGE( )   *Information*

Syntax

ERRORMESSAGE()

This function accepts no arguments.

Description

ERRORMESSAGE returns the error message that corresponds to the last ERRORCODE encountered. A blank is returned if no errors occurred.

See also the ERRORINFO function.

ERRORUSER( )   Information

Syntax

> **ERRORUSER()**

This function accepts no arguments.

Description

> ERRORUSER returns the name of the user who placed a lock on a Paradox object. ERRORUSER is appropriate after receiving an error code of 3, 4, 9, 10, 11, 50, 51, 52, or 65. The user name returned is that set with the SETUSERNAME command or the name read from the network.

ESC   Keypress Interaction

Syntax

> **ESC**

Description

> The ESC command is equivalent to pressing Esc. The ESC command returns to the preceding menu or to the workspace.

EXAMPLE   Keypress Interaction

Syntax

> **EXAMPLE**

Description

> The EXAMPLE command is equivalent to pressing F5 (Example) in a query form. Refer to Chapter 7, "Using Advanced Query By Example and Multiple Tables," for a description of how to use the F5 (Example) command in Paradox Query By Example.

```
        ENDWHILE
    ENDIF
```

This example checks to see that the table is indeed encrypted, and then asks the user to enter a password. The WHILE loop continues to execute until the user selects the correct password, or the number of tries at getting a password exceeds 3. In the second case, the script is terminated and the user is returned to the Paradox Main mode.

EXECEVENT   Input/Output

Syntax

> **EXECEVENT arrayname**

Description

This command is used to create an event under script control or to process an event trapped with GETEVENT. **arrayname** is a dynamic array name and must be correctly initialized to represent a mouse, keyboard, message, or idle event.

The dynamic array **arrayname** must have an index TYPE. The remaining indexes will vary depending on the type of event. Table 19.22 lists the indexes for keyboard events, table 19.23 lists the indexes for message events, and table 19.24 lists the indexes for mouse events. For an idle event, the dynamic array specified by **arrayname** must have only the TYPE index. **arrayname[TYPE]** must contain the string IDLE. Refer to Chapter 16, "Using the Paradox Application Language," for more information regarding events.

See also DYNARRAY, GETEVENT, and LOCALIZEEVENT.

Table 19.22. Keyboard Event Dynamic Array Indexes and Elements

Index	Element description
TYPE	Contains "KEY" to indicate keyboard event
SCANCODE	The system BIOS keyboard scan code. A numeric value
KEYCODE	The ASCII or IBM extended code. A numeric value

Note: *Use either the SCANCODE or the KEYCODE, but not both. These indexes duplicate each other. If both are initialized, the SCANCODE takes precedence.*

Table 19.23. Message Event Dynamic Array Indexes and Elements

Index	Element description
TYPE	Contains "MESSAGE" to indicate a message event
MESSAGE	Contains the text of the specific message: RESIZE, CLOSE, OK, MAXIMIZE, CANCEL, NEXT, PREV, or DEFAULT

Note: *Refer to Chapter 16, "Using the Paradox Application Language," for more information regarding message events.*

Table 19.24. Mouse Event Dynamic Array Indexes and Elements

Index	Element description
TYPE	Contains "MOUSE" to indicate a mouse event
ROW	Row number of mouse cursor relative to the screen
COL	Column number of the mouse cursor relative to the screen
BUTTONS	LEFT for the left button, RIGHT for the right button
DOUBLECLICK	True to indicate a double-click, false otherwise
ACTION	UP for button release, DOWN for button press

EXECPROC   *Procedure*

Syntax

> **EXECPROC proc1**

Description

The EXECPROC command calls a PAL procedure, but the procedure can have no arguments. Procedures normally are called by including the procedure's name as a command in the script. In some cases, however, specifying the procedure name as a variable is convenient. The EXECPROC command, and the related EXECUTE command, enable the script to call the procedure specified in the **proc1** parameter.

The distinctions between EXECPROC and EXECUTE are that EXECPROC executes more quickly than EXECUTE but can call only procedures that do not take an argument. In addition, Paradox does not swap dynamically from memory a procedure called by the EXECPROC command.

Example

The following example attempts to execute the procedure PrintJun, assuming that the user types *JUN* when prompted for a month abbreviation:

```
PROC PrintJun()
    REPORT "Orders" "6"
ENDPROC
?? "Type the three letter month abbreviation: "
ACCEPT "A3" TO monthname
printrun = "Print" + monthname
PRINTRUN
```

This script fails because Paradox cannot distinguish when to use *PRINTRUN* as a variable and when to use it as a command. The following example, however, uses EXECPROC to accomplish the desired result:

```
PROC PrintJun()
    REPORT "Orders" "6"
ENDPROC
?? "Type the three letter month abbreviation: "
ACCEPT "A3" TO monthname
printrun = "Print" + monthname
EXECPROC printrun
```

EXECUTE   *System Control*

Syntax

EXECUTE commands1

Description

The EXECUTE command executes one or more PAL commands, specified in the **commands1** parameter. The **commands1** parameter is a string value up to 255 characters long.

PAL commands normally are executed by including the command name directly in the script. In some cases, however, it is convenient to specify one or more commands in a variable. The EXECUTE command enables the script to execute commands contained in the **commands1** parameter.

The EXECUTE command creates a temporary script named Execute from the contents of the **commands1** parameter, and then runs the script as though it has been called by the PLAY command.

Example

The following script cannot work because of the ambiguous use of printrun:

```
PROC PrintJun( print_table )
   REPORT print_table "6"
ENDPROC
?? "Type the table name: "
ACCEPT "A8" TO tablename
? "Type the three letter month abbreviation: "
ACCEPT "A3" TO monthname
printrun = "Print" + monthname
PRINTRUN(tablename)
```

The preceding script fails because Paradox cannot distinguish when PRINTRUN is used as a variable and when it is used as a command. The following example, however, uses EXECUTE to accomplish the desired result:

```
PROC PrintJun( print_table )
   REPORT print_table "6"
ENDPROC
?? "Type the table name: "
ACCEPT "A8" TO tablename
? "Type the three letter month abbreviation: "
ACCEPT "A3" TO monthname
printrun = "Print" + monthname
EXECUTE printrun+"(\""+tablename+"\")"
```

EXIT   *Menu*

Syntax

EXIT

Description

The EXIT command stops execution of the script and exits Paradox. This command is equivalent to the **Exit Yes** menu command.
All changes to tables are saved and memory variables are cleared.
This command is effective only in Main mode and results in a
script error in any other mode.

EXP( )   *Mathematical*

Syntax

EXP(number)

Description

EXP returns the exponential of **number**, where **number** is a numeric expression. This is the formula e^x where *e* is the constant
2.71828182845. The inverse of this is the LN function.

Example

```
RETURN EXP(1)
```

This example displays 2.71828182845.

```
RETURN EXP(5)
```

This example displays 148.4131591025.

FAMILYRIGHTS( )   *Information*

Syntax

FAMILYRIGHTS(tablename, right)

Description

FAMILYRIGHTS returns a logical value of True if a user has rights to create or modify objects in the table's family. **tablename** is the Paradox table to check. **right** is the table family that Paradox checks. Table 19.25 lists the codes used to specify the table family rights for which you want Paradox to check.

Table 19.25. Table Family Right Codes

Code	Family right
F	Form
R	Report
S	Image Setting
V	Validity Checks

False is returned if the user does not have the family rights to alter or create objects in the family.

This function relates to Paradox security and password protection.

Example

```
RETURN FAMILYRIGHTS("Employee", "V")
```

FIELD( )   Workspace, Canvas, Information

Syntax

FIELD()

This function accepts no arguments.

Description

FIELD reports the name of the current field in the current image on the workspace. A string containing the # symbol is returned if the cursor is in the record number field. A script error occurs if the function is used with no images present.

Example

```
VIEW "Mytable"
MOVETO [Myfield]
MESSAGE FIELD()
```

This example displays the field name Myfield.

FIELDINFO( )

Workspace, Canvas, Information

Syntax

> **FIELDINFO()**

This function accepts no arguments.

Description

Use the FIELDINFO function to obtain information about the current field in a Report or Form editing session.

In the Form and Report designer, FIELDINFO returns a string containing the contents of the current field indicator at the bottom of the screen.

In the Form designer, the field indicator contains the type of field placed, such as Regular or Calculated, and the name of the placed field. If the field type is Calculated, then the formula is returned instead of the name of the field. If the cursor is not on a field, a blank string is returned.

In the Report designer, the field indicator does not contain the type of the field, but only the name of the field. If the field is a calculated field, then the formula is returned. If the cursor is not on a field, a blank string is returned.

A script error will be generated if FIELDINFO is used in any context other than the Form or Report Designer.

Example

```
MESSAGE FIELDINFO()
```

This example displays the field type and field name, such as "Regular, Emp Last Name".

FIELDNO( )   Workspace, Canvas, Information

Syntax

FIELDNO(fieldname, tablename)

Description

FIELDNO returns an integer value indicating the field position within the table. **fieldname** is the field to check. **tablename** is the table in which the field resides. The string Error is returned if the field is not found. A script error occurs if the table does not exist. FIELDNO is table specific and is not affected by changes made to the image using the ROTATE command.

FIELDRIGHTS( )   Information

Syntax

FIELDRIGHTS(tablename, fieldname, string)

Description

FIELDRIGHTS returns a logical value of True if the user has the rights you are checking for, otherwise it returns False. You can test for All rights (read and modify) or ReadOnly rights to a field. **tablename** is the table being tested. **fieldname** is the field being checked, and **string** represents the level of rights you are checking for, and must be one of the two strings "All" or "ReadOnly".

Example

```
RETURN FIELDRIGHTS("Employee", "Salary", "ReadOnly")
```

The statement in this example uses FIELDRIGHTS to test whether the current user has network privileges sufficient to read the field called Salary in the table named Employee. The logical value True is returned if the user does have access rights, or False if not.

FIELDSTR( ) *Workspace, Canvas, Strings*

Syntax

FIELDSTR()

This function accepts no arguments.

Description

FIELDSTR returns a string containing the contents of the current field. A null string, "", is returned if the field is blank. Use this function to check the contents of nonalphanumeric fields which may only be partially filled in.

FIELDTYPE( ) *Workspace, Canvas*

Syntax

FIELDTYPE()

This function accepts no arguments.

Description

FIELDTYPE determines the field type of the current field. Valid Paradox field types are listed in table 19.26.

Table 19.26. Valid FIELDTYPE Values

Value	Field Type
"A*n*"	Alphanumeric, where *n* is the length
"B"	Binary
"D"	Date
"M*n*"	Memo field, where *n* is the length of the fixed portion of the field
"N"	Numeric
"O"	Other
"S"	Short number
"$"	Currency

FIELDVIEW   Keypress Interaction

Syntax

FIELDVIEW

Description

The FIELDVIEW command switches to field view. This command is equivalent to the Alt-F5 (Field View) and Ctrl-F keystroke combinations. Refer to Chapter 1, "Navigating Paradox," for a discussion of field view. Use either the ENTER command or the DO_IT! command to return to normal table or form view.

FILEREAD   Variable/Array

Syntax

FILEREAD *BINARY* **filespec TO anyvar**

Description

This command reads a disk file into a variable. **filespec** is any legal DOS file name. **anyvar** is any valid PAL variable name; this command creates it if necessary. Depending on the size of the disk file read, a variable initialized with FILEREAD will either be a string type or a memo type variable.

By default, every carriage-return/line-feed (CR/LF) pair is replaced with a single line-feed (LF) unless the optional keyword BINARY is used to disable the conversion.

If **filespec** is not a valid DOS file name, a script error results. The maximum file size that can be read is 64 megabytes in size.

See also FILEWRITE, EDITOR EXTRACT, and EDITOR INSERT.

FILESIZE( )   Information

Syntax

FILESIZE(filename)

Description

FILESIZE returns the number of bytes in a file, including unused space in clusters allocated to the file. **filename** is an existing DOS file name. A script error occurs if the named file does not exist.

The size returned by the FILESIZE function is the number of bytes used by the clusters allocated to the file; a cluster normally is 1,024 or 2,048 bytes. Because there often is "slack" in the clusters at the end of a file (that is, a cluster used by the file but is not full), the number returned by the FILESIZE function usually is not the same as the number of bytes that DOS reports in use. Because free space on a disk also, in effect, is measured in clusters, this is a more practical method of measuring file size.

Example

```
IF DRIVESTATUS( "A" ) THEN

    IF FILESIZE("mydata") <= DRIVESPACE( "A" ) THEN
        COPY "mydata" "a:\mydata"
    ENDIF
ENDIF
```

This example checks that a disk is in drive A:, and then checks that enough room is on the disk to accommodate the table called mydata. If the disk has enough room, the table is copied to drive A:.

FILEVERSION( )   *Procedure*

Syntax

FILEVERSION(libname)

Description

Use this command to determine under which version of Paradox a procedure library was created. The function returns a string, such as 3.5 or 4.0, to indicate the Paradox version. Paradox cannot use libraries created with a previous version. Use this command in conjunction with CONVERTLIB to determine which procedure libraries need conversion, and then perform the conversion.

Example

Refer to CONVERTLIB for an example using FILEVERSION.

FILEWRITE   *Variable/Array*

Syntax

> **FILEWRITE** *BINARY APPEND* **filespec FROM varname**

Description

This command writes up to 64 megabytes to a disk file. **filespec** is any legal DOS file name. **varname** is any valid PAL variable identifier.

By default, every line-feed (LF) is replaced with a carriage-return/line-feed (CR/LF) pair unless the optional keyword BINARY is used to disable the conversion. Also by default, if the file specified by **filespec** already exists, it will be replaced completely by FILEWRITE unless the optional keyword APPEND is used. APPEND causes the new text specified by **varname** to be added to the end of an existing file.

If **filespec** is not a valid DOS file name, a script error results.

See also FILEREAD, EDITOR EXTRACT, and EDITOR INSERT.

FILL( )   *String*

Syntax

> **FILL(string, num)**

Description

The FILL function repeats the value of the first character in **string**, **num** times, where **num** is an integer value between 0 and 255.

Example

```
RETURN FILL( "@", 10 )
```

This example returns the string @@@@@@@@@@.

FIRSTSHOW   *Workspace*

Syntax

> **FIRSTSHOW**

Description

The FIRSTSHOW command scrolls the workspace until the current image starts at the top of the screen. To ensure that the current image is the only one displayed, make sure that the image is the last one in the workspace before the script issues the FIRSTSHOW command.

This command is ignored if not in Compatibility mode. Use SETUIMODE to change to Compatibility mode.

Example

```
VIEW "Employee"
VIEW "Customer"
VIEW "Orders"
MOVETO [Order#]
FIRSTSHOW
WAIT TABLE
   PROMPT "Move to the order you want to edit, then press F7."
   UNTIL "FormKey"
FORMKEY
EDITKEY
```

This example displays the tables Employee, Customer, and Orders on the workspace. The FIRSTSHOW command then scrolls the workspace so that the Orders image appears at the top of the screen. The WAIT command enables the user to scroll through the Orders table and to locate a record for editing. When the user presses F7, the script switches to form view and Edit mode.

FOR   *Program Control*

Syntax

> **FOR var1** *FROM number1 TO number2 STEP number3*
>   commands
> **ENDFOR**

Description

The FOR command and ENDFOR commands together create a program control structure, often referred to as a FOR loop, that executes a series of one or more commands a specified number of times. The commands to be executed by the FOR loop are represented in the syntax by the **commands** parameter.

var1 is a counter, a value that determines the number of times **commands** is executed. *number1, number2,* and *number3* are integer values that can be included to specify a beginning value, ending value, and increment value for **var1**.

The *FROM* keyword must precede the *number1* parameter in order to specify a beginning value for **var1**. The *TO* keyword—with the *number2* parameter—can specify an ending value. If *FROM number1* is omitted, the counter starts at the current value for **var1**. If *TO number2* is omitted, the control structure executes **commands** indefinitely.

By default, the counter is incremented (increased in value) by 1 every time the script executes **commands**. You can use the *STEP* keyword, with *number3*, to specify a different increment value.

If you include the LOOP command in the FOR loop, all commands that follow LOOP, up to ENDFOR, are not executed, but the counter is incremented and execution begins again at the top of the FOR loop. You can include the QUITLOOP command within the FOR loop to exit the control structure.

Use the FOREACH command to construct loops with dynamic arrays. Refer to Chapter 15, "An Overview of the Paradox Application Language," for more information on looping structures.

See also FOREACH, LOOP, QUITLOOP, and WHILE.

Example

```
CLEAR
VIEW "Employee"
SCAN
  FOR COUNTER FROM 1 TO 5
      ? [Emp First Name]+" "+[Emp Last Name]
      SKIP
  ENDFOR
  ?
  ? "Press Esc to Quit"
  ? "Press any other key to see five more names."
  pause = GETCHAR()
  IF pause = 27
      THEN QUITLOOP
```

```
        ENDIF
        CLEAR
        @ 0,0
    ENDSCAN
    CLEARIMAGE
```

This example uses a FOR loop to display five names from the Employee table. The user then can press any key to see five more names or can press Esc to quit.

FOREACH   *Program Control*

Syntax

> **FOREACH var1 IN arrayname**
> Commands
> **ENDFOREACH**

Description

Use this variation of the FOR loop structure to step through the elements of a dynamic array. **var1** is any valid PAL variable identifier; it is set to each index for each element in the dynamic array specified by **arrayname**. **commands** represents any single or series of legitimate PAL commands or expressions.

Do not expect the array elements to be processed in any particular order because the dynamic arrays do not use integers for their indexes, and the order of their elements is effectively random.

If you include the LOOP command in the FOREACH loop, all commands that follow LOOP, up to ENDFOREACH, are not executed, but **var1** is incremented to the next element, and execution begins at the top of the FOREACH. You can include the QUITLOOP command within the FOREACH loop to exit the control structure.

See also DYNARRAY, FOR, LOOP, QUITLOOP, and WHILE.

Example

See DYNARRAY for an example of using FOREACH.

FORM( ) Workspace, Canvas, Information

Syntax

FORM()

Description

FORM returns the name of the current form as a string. The form names returned will follow Paradox form specifying conventions and will be strings such as F or 1 through 14. If no active forms are found, the string None is returned.

A script error occurs if no tables are found on the workspace.

FORMAT( )—For Date Values Date

Syntax

FORMAT(formatcmd, date)

Description

FORMAT controls the way Paradox displays or prints a date value. **formatcmd** is a formatting command, and **date** is the date value to be formatted. Table 19.27 lists the valid formatting commands for date values.

Table 19.27. Date Formatting Commands	
Command	**Date format**
D1	MM/DD/yy
D2	Month dd,yyyy
D3	mm/dd
D4	mm/yy
D5	dd-Mon-yy
D6	Mon yy
D7	dd-Mon-yyyy

D8	mm/dd/yyyy
D9	dd.mm.yy
D10	dd/mm/yy
D11	yy-mm-dd
D12	yy.mm.dd
D13	dd.mm.yyyy

Example

```
RETURN FORMAT("D2", 6/10/1992)
```

This example returns June 10, 1992.

FORMAT( )—For Logical Values F

Syntax

FORMAT(formatcmd, logical)

Description

Format controls the way Paradox shows or prints data. **formatcmd** is a formatting command, and **logical** is a logical value to be formatted. To cause the script to display or print Yes for True and No for False, use the formatting command **LY**. Use the command **LO** to cause On to display or print for True and Off to display or print for False.

Example

```
x=512
RETURN FORMAT("LY", x > 500)
```

This example displays Yes because x is greater than 500, and the command LY causes the True value to display as Yes.

FORMAT( )—For Numerical Values Mathematical

Syntax

> FORMAT(formatcmd, number)

Description

Format controls the way Paradox displays or prints data. **formatcmd** is a formatting command and **number** is the numeric value to be formatted. Table 19.28 lists valid numeric formatting commands.

Table 19.28. Numeric Formatting Commands

Type	Command	Description
Width	Wn.m	Sets total width (n) and decimal places (m)
Edit	EC	Include commas
	EZ	Insert leading zeros (example: "001")
	EB	Insert leading blanks (example: " 1")
	ES	Use scientific notation
	E*	Insert leading * (example: "**1")
	EI	Use international numeric format
Sign	E$	Floating dollar sign
	S+	Include leading + or – sign
	S–	Include leading – sign only
	SP	Enclose negatives numbers in parentheses ( )
	SD	Include DB (debit) and CR (credit) notation
	SC	Include CR notation only

Example

```
x = 4563.1234
RETURN FORMAT("W10.2,EC",x)
```

This example displays 4,563.12. The script displays only two decimals and adds a comma.

FORMAT( )—For String Values   *String*

Syntax

> **FORMAT(formatcmd, string)**

Description

FORMAT modifies the way Paradox displays or prints information. The **formatcmd** parameter is a formatting command, and **string** is the value to be formatted. Table 19.29 lists the commands that can be used as the **formatcmd** parameter.

Table 19.29. String Formatting Commands

Type	Command	Description
Width	Wn	Sets maximum string width
	Wn.m	Sets string width and decimal places
Alignment	AL	Left justifies string
	AR	Right justifies string
	AC	Centers string within width
Case	CU	Changes string to all uppercase
	CL	Changes string to all lowercase
	CC	Changes string to initial capitals only

Example

```
RETURN FORMAT( "CC", "reading railroad" )
```

This example returns the string Reading Railroad because CC is a formatting command that displays only the initial letters as capitals.

FORMKEY   *Keypress Interaction*

Syntax

> **FORMKEY**

Description

> The FORMKEY command toggles between table view and form
> view. This command is equivalent to pressing F7 (Form Toggle).
> Refer to Chapter 1, "Navigating Paradox," Chapter 8, "Using Ad-
> vanced Form Techniques," and Chapter 9, "Using Power Entry and
> Editing Features," for more information about using F7 (Form
> Toggle).
>
> See also PICKFORM and FORMTYPE.

FORMTABLES   *Variable/Array*

Syntax

> **FORMTABLES table1 form1 array1**

Description

> The FORMTABLES command places into a specified array the
> names of all tables embedded in a given form. **table1** is the table
> that "owns" the form being tested. **form1** is the form being tested.
> FORMTABLES places the name(s) of all embedded table(s) into
> the elements of the standard array specified by **array1**. The array
> is created and dimensioned, if necessary.
>
> If FORMTABLES finds no embedded tables, Paradox assigns the
> logical value False to the system created variable named RetVal.
> Otherwise, RetVal is given the value True. You also can use the
> function ISMULTIFORM to determine whether a form has embed-
> ded tables.
>
> A script error occurs using FORMTABLES if the table does not
> exist, the form does not exist, or (in multiuser environments) if
> the table is locked or the user has insufficient access rights.
>
> See also FORM, FORMTYPE, ISMULTIFORM, and REPORTTABLES.
> Refer also to Chapter 8, "Using Advanced Form Techniques."

Example

```
FORMTABLES "Orders" "2" Embedtab
? "Form 2 of Orders has the following embedded table(s):"
?
FOR counter FROM 1 TO ARRAYSIZE(Embedtab)
   ? "   "+Embedtab[counter]
ENDFOR
SLEEP 3000
```

This example displays the name(s) of embedded tables in form 2 of the Orders table. Assuming Form 2 is the order-entry form described in Chapter 8, "Using Advanced Form Techniques," this script displays the table name Detail.

FORMTYPE( )   *Workspace, Canvas, Information*

Syntax

FORMTYPE(formstring)

Description

If the form in the current image is of the kind indicated by **formstring**, FORMTYPE returns a logical value of True. **formstring** is a string indicating which of the form types is being tested for. It must have one of the following values: MultiRecord, Linked, Detail, or DisplayOnly. FORMTYPE returns False if the current form is not the form type requested.

FRAME   *Input/Output*

Syntax

FRAME *SINGLE | DOUBLE* FROM rowstart, colstart TO rowend colend

Description

Use this command to draw a frame on the current canvas. The optional keywords SINGLE and DOUBLE specify whether the frame is drawn with a single line or double line. If neither keyword is specified, the border is drawn with a single line. **rowstart** and

colstart are integer numbers indicating the top left corner of the frame by row and column numbers relative to the current window or dialog. **rowend** and **colend** are integers indicating the bottom right corner of the frame relative to the current window or dialog. If **rowstart** and **rowend** are the same, FRAME draws a horizontal line; similarly, if **colstart** and **colend** are the same, FRAME draws a vertical line.

FRAME acts on only the current canvas. You must select the canvas directly by using SETCANVAS or indirectly by using WINDOW CREATE. If you do not select the canvas, FRAME places its output on the full-screen canvas.

See also the ?, ??, @, SETCANVAS, and TEXT commands.

FV( )   *Financial*

Syntax

FV(payment, interest, time)

Description

FV analyzes a series of equal payments and calculates the future value. **payment** is the amount of cash paid out each period. **interest** is the interest per period, and **time** is the number of periods to calculate. The **interest** parameter is expressed as a decimal (.105) and not as a percent (10.5%).

Example

```
MESSAGE FV(350,.105,10)
SLEEP 3500
```

This example displays the number 5713.602822027.

GETCANVAS( )   *Window*

Syntax

GETCANVAS()

This function takes no arguments.

Description

Use this function to get the window handle for the current canvas. GETCANVAS returns the string value corresponding to the window handle. Used in combination with SETCANVAS, the GETCANVAS function enables you to keep track of various window contexts and prevent subroutines from accidentally changing the current canvas for the calling procedure.

PAL canvas display commands always write to the current canvas. You directly select the canvas by using SETCANVAS or indirectly by using WINDOW CREATE.

See also WINDOW ECHO, WINDOW GETATTRIBUTES, WINDOW HANDLE, and WINDOW SETATTRIBUTES.

Example

```
mywin = GETCANVAS()
WINDOW CREATE TO new_win      ; make window of default size
FRAME DOUBLE FROM 4, 4 TO 8, 8  ; place a smaller frame
@ 5,5 ?? "Wow"                ; in the window and write
SLEEP 4000
WINDOW CLOSE
SETCANVAS mywin
?? "Back from our break."
SLEEP 4000
WINDOW CLOSE
```

This example uses GETCANVAS to save the current canvas's window handle in the variable mywin, and then creates a new canvas window (which becomes the current canvas). A frame is placed in the new window, and the word "Wow" is placed inside the frame. After a brief delay, the new canvas is closed. At this point, Paradox no longer knows which is the current canvas; various script errors or undesired results may occur with the next canvas painting commands. The SETCANVAS command is then used to reestablish the window handle stored in mywin as the current canvas.

GETCHAR( )

Input/Output

Syntax

GETCHAR()

This function takes no arguments.

Description

This function returns a numeric value corresponding to the next character typed at the keyboard. A positive number indicates that the number is an ASCII code, and a negative number indicates an IBM extended character code. If the keyboard buffer is empty, GETCHAR waits for a character to be typed. Use CHARWAITING to determine whether there are any characters in the keyboard buffer.

NOTE   GETCHAR discards any mouse events in the queue.

See also the GETEVENT and EXECEVENT commands and the ASC and CHR functions.

GETCOLORS   *Window*

Syntax

GETCOLORS TO arrayname

Description

This command initializes the dynamic array specified by **arrayname** with the current palette. Each index element in the array represents a specific attribute of the palette. The value of each element is the number that controls the palette attribute of the index. See Appendix D, "PAL Color Palette Codes," for a list of the dynamic array indexes, their meaning, and the palette color codes.

GETEVENT( )   *Input/Output*

Syntax

GETEVENT *eventlist* **TO arrayname**

The optional eventlist is any combination the following (in any order):

ALL

MOUSE *"ALL"* | *"UP"* | *"DOWN"* | *"MOVE"* | *"AUTO"*

KEY *"ALL"* | *keylist*

MESSAGE *"ALL"* | *"RESIZE"* | *"CLOSE"* | *"MAXIMIZE"* | *"NEXT"* | *"MENUSELECT"* | *"MENUKEY"*

IDLE

The optional keylist for the KEY event selection is a list of one or more keys separated by commas.

Description

Use this command to trap specific events with your script. Normally, events are passed directly on to Paradox. In order to capture events for your script to act on, you must use the GETEVENT command. Events not trapped with GETEVENT continue to be passed on to Paradox. **arrayname** is any valid dynamic array name. The dynamic array is reinitialized (or created) with the type and data corresponding to the event that is trapped. The dynamic array **arrayname** will have an index TYPE. The remaining indexes will vary depending on the type of event. Table 19.30 lists the indexes for keyboard events, table 19.31 lists the indexes for message events, and table 19.32 lists the indexes for mouse events. For an idle event, the dynamic array specified by **arrayname** will have only the TYPE index. **arrayname["TYPE"]** will contain the string IDLE. Refer to Chapter 16, "Using the Paradox Application Language," for more information regarding events.

GETEVENT has several options. The options can be used singly or in combination. The type of events trapped may be more closely defined by using the additional option modifiers (such as ALL, UP, and so forth) You can use none, one, or several of the option modifiers at one time. If using more than one, separate them with commas.

The ALL keyword causes all events to be trapped, including idle events. By default, GETEVENT does not usually capture idle events because they are internal to the computer system.

The MOUSE keyword causes mouse events to be trapped. The ALL modifier traps all mouse events. The other modifiers can be used to trap button presses (UP or DOWN), or mouse movement (MOVE). AUTO describes the event occurring when a mouse button is held down but the mouse is not moved.

KEY ALL causes all keyboard events to be trapped, and KEY **keylist** causes only the listed key presses to be trapped.

The MESSAGE keyword causes message events to be trapped. The modifier ALL will trap all message events. Messages events usually occur in the context of a window or menu. All the following messages that might be received with a message event relate to the current window and/or current menu activities. The RESIZE message indicates a move into Resize/move mode. CLOSE indicates closing the window, MAXIMIZE indicates that the window should be made as large as possible. NEXT indicates a move to the next window. MENUSELECT and MENUKEY indicate menu and key selections in a pull-down menu created with SHOWPULLDOWN.

IDLE causes only idle events to be trapped.

Table 19.30. Keyboard Event Indexes

Index	Element description
TYPE	Always contains KEY for keyboard events
SCANCODE	Contains the key scancode generated by the system BIOS
KEYCODE	The ASCII or IBM Extended character code

Note: *The keyboard status information indexes described in GETKEYBOARDSTATE also are included in this dynamic array.*

Table 19.31. Message Event Indexes

Index	Element description
TYPE	Always contains "MESSAGE" for message event.
MESSAGE	String for the message event, "RESIZE", "MAXIMIZE", and so forth
MENUTAG	Contains the TAG for the pull-down menu item selected

Note: *The MENUTAG index is created only if the MESSAGE element contains MENUSELECT or MENUKEY.*

Table 19.32. Mouse Event Indexes

Index	Element description
TYPE	Contains MOUSE to indicate a mouse event
ROW	Row number of mouse cursor relative to the screen
COL	Column number of the mouse cursor relative to the screen
BUTTONS	LEFT for the left button; RIGHT for the right button
DOUBLECLICK	True to indicate a double-click, false otherwise
ACTION	UP for button release; DOWN for button press

Note: *The keyboard status information indexes described in GETKEYBOARDSTATE also are included in this dynamic array.*

See also DYNARRAY, EXECEVENT, LOCALIZEEVENT, SHOWPULLDOWN, and SHOWDIALOG.

Example

```
ECHO NORMAL
WINDOW CREATE TO mywin
WHILE True <> False
   GETEVENT MOUSE "UP", "DOWN" MESSAGE "CLOSE" TO myevent
   IF myevent["TYPE"] = "MOUSE" THEN
      SWITCH
         CASE myevent["ACTION"] = "UP" :
            MESSAGE "Mouse button up at: ", myevent["ROW"], " ",
               myevent["COL"]
         CASE myevent["ACTION"] = "DOWN" :
            MESSAGE "Mouse button down at: ", myevent["ROW"], " ",
               myevent["COL"]
      ENDSWITCH
   ENDIF
IF myevent["TYPE"] = "MESSAGE" THEN
      IF myevent["MESSAGE"] = "CLOSE" THEN
         MESSAGE "Closing the window and ending script."
         SLEEP 2000
         WINDOW CLOSE
         SLEEP 2000
         RETURN
```

```
      ELSE
          MESSAGE "Untrapped message event--this should never happen!"
      ENDIF
    ENDIF
  ENDWHILE
```

This example first creates a window. An infinite loop is set up, and GETEVENT is used to trap any changes in the mouse buttons and to trap the CLOSE message event. The message bar shows output indicating at what screen coordinates a mouse button was either pressed or released. When the user presses Alt-space bar for the System menu and then selects Close, the message bar shows that the close message was received. Note that the Untrapped message event message will never be displayed, because the one and only message event being trapped is the CLOSE message.

This example is not intended to do any useful work, merely demonstrate the use of the GETEVENT command.

GETKEYBOARDSTATE( )   *Input/Output*

Syntax

> **GETKEYBOARDSTATE TO arrayname**

Description

This command initializes a dynamic array with information relating to the keyboard. Your keyboard has several keys that produce certain controlling or modifying effects on other keys. Use GETKEYBOARDSTATE to determine which of these keys have been pressed or are being held down. **arrayname** is the name of a Paradox dynamic array. It is reinitialized or created to have the indexes and elements described in table 19.33. All the elements contain Logical values.

Not all keyboards will have all of the keys listed in the table, and not all BIOS programs make the distinction between the left and right Alt, Ctrl, and Shift keys. If this is the case, GETKEYBOARDSTATE will initialize the dynamic array with only a subset of the fields listed in the table.

See also DYNARRAY and SETKEYBOARDSTATE.

Table 19.33. GETKEYBOARDSTATE Dynamic Array Elements

Index	Element description
ALT	Alt key held down = True; otherwise False
CAPS LOCK	Caps Lock on = True; otherwise False
CTRL	Any Ctrl key held down = True; otherwise False
LEFT ALT	Left Alt key held down = True; otherwise False
LEFT CTRL	Left Ctrl key held down = True; otherwise False
LEFT SHIFT	Left Shift key held down = True; otherwise False
NUM LOCK	Num Lock on = True; otherwise False
RIGHT SHIFT	Right Shift key held down = True; otherwise False
SCROLL LOCK	Scroll Lock on = True; otherwise False

Note: *If CTRL is True and LEFT CTRL is False, then the right Ctrl key is being held down. This usually is true for the keys Alt, Ctrl, and Shift.*

GETMENUSELECTION   *Input/Output*

Syntax

GETMENUSELECTION KEYTO keyvar TO choice

Description

This command activates a menu created with SHOWPULLDOWN and is valid only when used with SHOWPULLDOWN. GETMENUSELECTION is used to force the user to interact only with the menu, and not with other objects on the workspace. The menu defined with SHOWPULLDOWN becomes active immediately; the user does not press F10 first. **keyvar** is a variable used to hold a Paradox keycode. **choice** is a Paradox variable used to hold the Tag belonging to the selected menu choice.

If a user clicks the mouse outside of the menu, or the user presses the Esc key, then the SHOWPULLDOWN menu is deactivated and the string "Esc" is assigned to choice.

The optional KEYTO keyword is used when the SHOWPULLDOWN command is used with the optional UNTIL keyword. The Paradox keystroke code that resulted in the SHOWPULLDOWN menu ending is stored in the keyvar variable.

The global variable RetVal is set to True if the user made a menu selection, False otherwise.

See also SHOWPULLDOWN.

GETWINDOW( ) *Window*

Syntax

GETWINDOW()

This function takes no arguments.

Description

Use this function to obtain the handle of the current window. In Paradox, the current window may not be the same as the current canvas or current workspace. This function returns a string value corresponding to the current window handle.

See also GETCANVAS, SETCANVAS, and WINDOW HANDLE.

GRAPHKEY *Keypress Interaction*

Syntax

GRAPHKEY

Description

The GRAPHKEY command displays a graph using the current graph settings and data from the current image. This command is equivalent to pressing Ctrl-F7 (Graph). Refer to Chapter 12, "Using Paradox Graphics," for a full discussion of Paradox graphics and the Ctrl-F7 (Graph) keystroke.

GRAPHTYPE( )   *System Status*

Syntax

GRAPHTYPE( )

This function accepts no arguments.

Description

GRAPHTYPE returns the current graph type. This function returns one of the following strings, describing the current graph type: `Bar`, `Line`, `Marker`, `Marker Line`, `Pie`, `Rotated Bar`, `Stacked Bar`, `3-D Bar`, `Area`, or `X-Y`. Refer to Chapter 12, "Using Paradox Graphics," for a full discussion of Paradox graphics.

GROUPBY   *Workspace, Keypress Interaction*

Syntax

GROUPBY

Description

The GROUPBY command causes records to be grouped in a query by the current field. This command is equivalent to pressing Shift-F6 (Groupby) keystroke. Refer to Chapter 7, "Using Advanced Query By Example and Multiple Tables," for more information about grouping records in queries and use of the Shift-F6 (GroupBy) keystroke.

HELP   *Keypress Interaction*

Syntax

HELP

Description

The HELP command accesses the Paradox help system. This command is equivalent to pressing F1 (Help). Refer to Chapter 1, "Navigating Paradox," for a discussion of the Paradox help facility.

HELPMODE( )   *Information*

Syntax

> **HELPMODE()**

This function accepts no arguments.

Description

HELPMODE returns the kind of help currently in use. This function returns one of the following strings describing the current help mode: Help, LookupHelp, or None if no help is in use. Refer to Chapter 1, "Navigating Paradox," for a discussion of the Paradox help facility.

HOME   *Keypress Interaction*

Syntax

> **HOME**

Description

The HOME command is equivalent to pressing Home. The effect of this command depends on the Paradox mode and the context. Refer to the chapter that discusses the mode and context in which you intend to use the HOME command.

IF   *Program Control*

Syntax

> **IF condition1**
>
> > **THEN** *commands1*
> >
> > *ELSE commands2*
>
> **ENDIF**

Description

Together, the IF command and the supporting keywords, THEN, ELSE, and ENDIF, form a branching control structure that gives a script the capability to "decide" between two options, based on the existence or nonexistence of a given condition or group of conditions. The parameter **condition1** is any PAL expression which evaluates as a Logical value and represents the condition for which the script is testing.

PAL commands inserted in place of the **commands1** parameter are executed only if **condition1** evaluates to a logical value of True. When **condition1** is False, these **commands1** are skipped. If you include the optional *ELSE* keyword, however, PAL commands inserted in place of the *commands2* parameter are executed only if **condition1** is False.

For more complex decision-making requirements, you can nest IF control structures (often called IF statements); but either the SWITCH control structure or the WHILE control structure often is a better choice as a matter of programming structure and clarity.

Refer to Chapter 15, "An Overview of the Paradox Application Language," for more information on various program control structures.

Example

```
IF TIME() < "12:00:00" THEN
    ? "Good morning!"
ELSE
    IF TIME() < "18:00:00" THEN
        ? "Good afternoon!"
    ELSE
        ? "Good evening!"
    ENDIF
ENDIF
SLEEP 3000
```

This example displays the message Good morning! if the time is before noon, Good afternoon! from noon until 6:00 pm, and Good evening! if the system time is from 6:00 pm until midnight.

IIF( )   *Program Control*

Syntax

  IIF(condition, val1, val2)

Description

This program-control function returns one of two values depending on a condition. **condition1** is any Paradox logical expression. **val1** is any Paradox expression and represents the value IIF returns if **condition1** is True. **val2** also is a Paradox expression and represents the value returned by IIF if **condition1** is False.

Use this function in calculated fields on forms or reports.

See also IF.

Example

```
MESSAGE IIF(ISBLANK([therms]), "Missing data!", [therms])
```

This example displays the text Missing data! in the message bar if the field therms in the current record of the current image is blank. Otherwise, the value contained in the therms field is displayed in the message bar.

IMAGECAVERAGE( )   *Statistical*

Syntax

IMAGECAVERAGE()

This function accepts no arguments.

Description

IMAGECAVERAGE calculates the current column's average value. The function applies to the current image on the workspace or multitable form. A script error results if the current column is not numeric. Blank values are not included in the calculation even if Blank=Zero is set by using the Customer Configuration Program.

IMAGECAVERAGE, in a multiuser environment, places a Write Lock on the current table. If an application or another user already placed a Full Lock or Prevent Write Lock on the table, by default Paradox retries to place a Write Lock on the table for the designated retry period. If the retry period is exceeded, a script error occurs.

IMAGECAVERAGE respects the limits of the restricted view.

IMAGECCOUNT( )   *Statistical*

Syntax

> **IMAGECCOUNT()**

This function accepts no arguments.

Description

> IMAGECCOUNT counts the number of nonblank entries in the current column of the current image. A script error results if the current column is not numeric. Blank values are not included in the calculation even if Blank=Zero was set using the Customer Configuration Program.
>
> IMAGECCOUNT, in a multiuser environment, places a Write Lock on the current table. If an application or another user already placed a Full Lock or Prevent Write Lock on the table, by default Paradox retries to place a Write Lock on the table for the designated retry period. If the retry period is exceeded, a script error occurs.
>
> IMAGECCOUNT respects the limits of the restricted view.

IMAGECMAX( )   *Statistical*

Syntax

> **IMAGECMAX()**

This function accepts no arguments.

Description

> IMAGECMAX returns the largest nonblank value of the current column of the current image. The string Error is returned if the column contains no nonblank values. A script error results if the current column is not numeric. Blank values are not included in the calculation even if Blank=Zero is set by using the Customer Configuration Program.
>
> In a multiuser environment, IMAGECMAX places a Write Lock on the current table. If an application or another user already placed a Full Lock or Prevent Write Lock on the table, Paradox retries to place a Write Lock on the table for the designated retry period. If the retry period is exceeded, a script error occurs.
>
> IMAGECMAX respects the limits of the restricted view.

IMAGECMIN( )   *Statistical*

Syntax

IMAGECMIN()

This function accepts no arguments.

Description

IMAGECMIN returns the smallest nonblank value of the current column of the current image. The string Error is returned if the column contains no nonblank values. A script error results if the current column is not numeric. Blank values are not included in the calculation even if Blank=Zero is set by using the Customer Configuration Program.

In a multiuser environment, IMAGECMIN places a Write Lock on the current table. If an application or another user already placed a Full Lock or Prevent Write Lock on the table, Paradox retries to place a Write Lock on the table for the designated retry period. If the retry period is exceeded, a script error occurs.

IMAGECMIN respects the limits of the restricted view.

IMAGECSUM( )   *Statistical*

Syntax

IMAGECSUM()

This function accepts no arguments.

Description

IMAGECSUM calculates the sum of the current column of the current image. A script error results if the current column is not numeric. The string Error is returned if no nonblank entries are found.

IMAGECSUM, in a multiuser environment, places a Write Lock on the current table. If an application or another user already placed a Full Lock or Prevent Write Lock on the table, by default Paradox retries to place a Write Lock on the table for the designated retry period. If the retry period is exceeded, a script error occurs.

IMAGECSUM respects the limits of the restricted view.

IMAGENO( )   *Workspace, Canvas*

Syntax

>   **IMAGENO()**

This function accepts no arguments.

Description

>   IMAGENO returns a number that indicates the position of the current image on the workspace. Paradox counts the images from the top of the workspace to the bottom. If no images are present, a is returned. Query forms are grouped at the top of the workspace, regardless of the order in which they are placed. Therefore, query forms always have lower image numbers than other types of images.

>   Displaying a multitable form places the image of each linked table on the workspace in the order in which they appear on the form. Linked tables which were placed on the workspace before the multitable form was picked, are given the image number of the original placement on the workspace.

IMAGERIGHTS   *Multiuser*

Syntax

>   **IMAGERIGHTS** *UPDATE | READONLY*

Description

>   The IMAGERIGHTS command enables the script to place further restrictions on the user's rights to a particular table, or to remove restrictions. The UPDATE keyword restricts the current user's rights in the current image to making changes to nonkey fields. The READONLY keyword limits the user to merely viewing the values in the current image.

>   When the IMAGERIGHTS command is used alone (without a keyword), the command clears additional restrictions that may have been placed by any previous IMAGERIGHTS command(s). This command does not effect any restrictions placed through the **Tools More Protect** command or the Paradox Protection Generator.

Refer to Chapter 13, "Using Paradox Tools," for a discussion of assigning Paradox table rights, family rights, and field rights.

IMAGETYPE( )   *Workspace, Canvas, Information*

Syntax

> **IMAGETYPE()**

This function accepts no arguments.

Description

IMAGETYPE indicates the current image type. It returns one of the following strings describing the image type: None, Display (a table or form view), or Query (a query form). To use IMAGETYPE, Paradox must be in the Main, Edit, or CoEdit mode; otherwise, a script error occurs.

Example

```
IF IMAGETYPE() = "Query" THEN
    CLEARIMAGE
ENDIF
```

This example clears the query form from the workspace only if the image type is Query.

INDEX   *Menu*

Syntax

> **INDEX** *optionlist* **table1 ON field1**

optionlist may be any one of the following keywords. Note that if field1 is a list of fields instead of a single field name, then the MAINTAINED keyword is required.

> **MAINTAINED**
>
> **LABEL labelname**
>
> **CASESENSITIVE**

Description

The INDEX command creates a secondary index for a specified table and nonkey field. This command is equivalent in its creation of a secondary index to the **T**ools **Q**uery **S**peedup menu command. Unlike the menu command, however, the use of the INDEX command is not restricted to query forms. The **table1** and **field1** parameters indicate the table and field to be indexed, respectively. Creating a secondary index speeds queries and operation of the LOCATE and ZOOM commands with respect to **field1**.

Adding the optional *MAINTAINED* keyword to the INDEX command causes Paradox to incrementally update the index file as data in the table is changed. This keyword improves performance by decreasing the time needed to update the index; however, MAINTAINED can be used only when indexing a keyed table.

The LABEL keyword is used to give the index a particular name. **labelname** is a string or string expression that cannot exceed 31 characters in length. Each **labelname** must be unique for a given table.

By default, indexes created with the INDEX command are not case-sensitive. The CASESENSITIVE keyword causes the index to be case-sensitive.

Secondary indexes can be based on more than one field. To create an index using more than one field, you must use the MAINTAINED keyword. Instead of supplying a single field name with **field1**, a list of field names is used. The LABEL and CASESENSITIVE options work the same with multifield indexes.

Use the ORDERTABLE command to view a table in the order of a secondary index.

Example

```
VIEW "Employee"
INDEX MAINTAINED "Employee" ON "Emp Last Name", "Emp First Name"
MOVETO [Emp Last Name]
? "Type the employee's last name: "
ACCEPT "A20" TO last
LOCATE last
```

This example creates a multifield secondary index on the Emp Last Name and Emp First Name fields in the Employee table (assuming that these fields are not already the table's key fields). Creating the secondary indexes then increases the speed of subsequent LOCATE commands on the Emp Last Name field.

INFOLIB   *Procedure*

Syntax

> **INFOLIB library1**

Description

> The INFOLIB command creates and adds to the workspace a temporary table named List, which contains the names of procedures contained in the specified procedure library. The parameter **library1** is the name of the procedure library evaluated. The INFOLIB command works only from Main mode.

> Paradox Version 4.0 cannot read libraries created with earlier versions of Paradox. Use the FILEVERSION function to determine the version of the procedure library file and CONVERTLIB to convert it, if necessary.

INS   *Keypress Interaction*

Syntax

> **INS**

Description

> The INS command is equivalent to pressing Ins. The effect of this command depends on the Paradox mode and the context. Refer to the chapter that discusses the mode and context in which you intend to use the INS command.

INSTANTPLAY   *Keypress Interaction*

Syntax

> **INSTANTPLAY**

Description

> The INSTANTPLAY command plays the script named Instant. This command is equivalent to pressing Alt-F4 (Instant Script Play). Refer to Chapter 6, "Getting Started with Scripts and Keyboard

Macros," for a discussion of recording and playing an instant
script.

INSTANTREPORT   *Keypress Interaction*

Syntax

> **INSTANTREPORT**

Description

> The INSTANTREPORT command prints a report from the current
> image using the standard report specification. This command is
> equivalent to press Alt-F7 (Instant Report). When working in the
> Report Generator, the Instant Report command prints a report
> using the current table and the current report specification. Refer
> to Chapter 5, "Getting Started With Reports," Chapter 10, "Using
> Tabular Reports," and Chapter 11, "Using Free-Form Reports," for
> more information about using Alt-F7 (Instant Report).

INT( )   *Mathematical*

Syntax

> **INT(number)**

Description

> INT returns the integer portion of **number**, where **number** is a
> numeric value.

Example

> ```
> RETURN INT(7.156)
> ```

> This example displays the number 7.

ISASSIGNED( )   *Information*

Syntax

> **ISASSIGNED(varname)**

Description

ISASSIGNED returns a logical value of True if **varname** was assigned a value. **varname** represents a variable or an array (fixed or dynamic) or an array element. Blank values are considered assignments. The function returns False if **varname** was not assigned a value. Use this function to avoid script errors that can occur if your script refers to an unassigned variable.

ISBLANK( )   *Information*

Syntax

ISBLANK(palval)

Description

ISBLANK returns a logical value of True if the value of **palval** is a blank value such as a blank string, blank number, or blank date. **palval** must be a valid Paradox expression.

ISBLANK is an important function and frequently is used to determine whether a Paradox field was assigned a value.

See also BLANKNUM and BLANKDATE.

Example

```
IF ISBLANK([Last Name]) THEN
   MESSAGE "Error -> you must enter a last name"
   SLEEP 2500
ENDIF
```

This example displays an error message if the Last Name field is blank.

ISBLANKZERO( )   *System Status*

Syntax

ISBLANKZERO()

This function accepts no arguments.

Description

ISBLANKZERO returns a logical value of True if blanks are treated as zeros in calculations, and returns False if blanks are not treated as zeros. Blank=Zero is a Custom Configuration Program setting.

PAL returns script errors when a calculation is attempted on a blank numerical field. Blank=Zero instructs Paradox to replace the blank value with a zero for the purpose of the calculation.

ISEMPTY( )   *Information*

Syntax

ISEMPTY(tablename)

Description

ISEMPTY returns a logical value of True if **tablename** contains no records. **tablename** represents the table name that you want tested. A script error occurs if **tablename** does not exist.

ISEMPTY does not respect the limits of a restricted view.

ISENCRYPTED( )   *Information*

Syntax

ISENCRYPTED(tablename)

Description

ISENCRYPTED returns a logical value of True if **tablename** is password protected. **tablename** represents the table that you want tested.

ISFIELDVIEW( )   *Workspace, Canvas*

Syntax

ISFIELDVIEW()

This function accepts no arguments.

Description

ISFIELDVIEW returns a logical value of True if the current field is in field view (Alt-F5). False is returned if the field is not in field view. Refer to Chapter 3, "Entering, Editing, and Viewing Data," for more information about Field View.

ISFILE( )   *Information*

Syntax

ISFILE(filename)

Description

ISFILE returns a logical value of True if **filename** exists. **filename** must be a valid DOS file name, including the file extension. False is returned if the file does not exist.

T I P	To test for a Paradox table, use the ISTABLE function, not the ISFILE function. You may see a delay between the time a table is created in Paradox and the time the table is copied to disk. Use the SAVETABLES command to force the disk entries to be updated.

Example

```
IF ISFILE("C:\\AUTOEXEC.BAT") THEN
    MESSAGE "I hope so."
    SLEEP 2500
ELSE
    MESSAGE "Where is it?"
    SLEEP 2500
ENDIF
```

This example displays different messages depending on whether a file named AUTOEXEC.BAT is stored in the root directory of drive C.

ISFORMVIEW( )   *Workspace, Canvas*

Syntax

ISFORMVIEW()

This function accepts no arguments.

Description

ISFORMVIEW returns a logical value of True if the current table image is in form view. False is returned if the image is a table view or a query image. To use ISFORMVIEW, Paradox must be in the Main, Edit, or CoEdit mode; otherwise, a script error occurs. If no images are on the workspace, a script error is issued.

See also ISFIELDVIEW for a related function.

Example

```
IF ISFORMVIEW() = "False" THEN
    FORMKEY
ENDIF
```

This example executes the FORMKEY command, to toggle on form view, only if the workspace is not already in Form view.

ISINSERTMODE( )   *Workspace, Canvas*

Syntax

ISINSERTMODE()

This function accepts no arguments.

Description

ISINSERTMODE returns a logical value of True if Paradox insert mode is currently active. False is returned if overwrite mode is active. An indicator in the upper right corner of the screen displays Ins when the insert mode is active. This function is effective only in the Form or Report Designer, and in the Editor. In other modes, this function generates a script error.

ISLINKLOCKED( )   *Workspace, Canvas*

Syntax

> **ISLINKLOCKED()**

This function accepts no arguments.

Description

ISLINKLOCKED returns a logical value of True if the current table is link locked. False is returned if the table is not link locked. A table becomes link locked if the table is part of a multitable form and a user begins editing or co-editing. After a table is link locked by Paradox, the table remains locked throughout the duration of the multitable session. Link locking is a method Paradox uses to maintain referential integrity by preventing a user from editing individual tables currently linked to an open multitable form. This lock prevents a user from modifying data that can destroy the linking relationships between the related tables.

ISMASTER( )   *Information*

Syntax

> **ISMASTER(table1, pass1)**

Description

This function is used to test a password for a table without registering the password with the table. **table1** is a string expression representing a table name. **pass1** is a string expression evaluating to the password being tested. ISMASTER returns True if the table being tested is encrypted, and the password matches the one being checked; a value of False is returned otherwise.

Example

```
IF ISENCRYPTED( mytable ) THEN
    pwrd = ""
    tries = 0
    WHILE NOT ISMASTER( mytable, pwrd )
        @1, 1, "Enter your password: "
        ACCEPT "A15" REQUIRED TO pwrd
        tries = tries + 1
        IF tries > 3 THEN
```

```
        QUIT
      ENDIF
    ENDWHILE
  ENDIF
```

This example checks to see that the table is indeed encrypted, and then asks the user to enter a password. The WHILE loop continues to execute until the user selects the correct password, or the number of tries at getting a password exceeds 3. In the second case, the script is terminated and the user is returned to the Paradox Main mode.

ISMULTIFORM( ) *Workspace, Canvas*

Syntax

ISMULTIFORM(tablename, formname)

Description

ISMULTIFORM analyzes the form and returns a logical value of True if the form is a multitable form (contains embedded forms). False is returned if the form has no embedded forms. **tablename** represents the Paradox table to be passed to the function and **formname** represents the form within the table's family of objects. Valid form names are "F" and "1" through "14." Paradox accepts, and converts to string values, integer values of 1 through 14 for form names.

A script error occurs if the form or table do not exist, if the table is locked, or if the user doesn't have adequate table rights.

See also the command FORMTABLES.

ISMULTIREPORT( ) *Workspace, Canvas*

Syntax

ISMULTIREPORT(tablename, reportname)

Description

ISMULTIREPORT returns a logical value of True if a report has linked lookup tables. If the report is a single table report, meaning that the report does not have any linked lookup tables, False is returned. **tablename** is the Paradox table, and **reportname** is the report name. Valid Paradox report names are "R" and "1" through "14." Paradox accepts, and converts to string values, integer values of 1 through 14 for table names.

A script error occurs if the report or table does not exist, if the table is locked, or if the user doesn't have adequate table rights.

See also the REPORTTABLES command.

ISRUNTIME( )   *System Status*

Syntax

ISRUNTIME( )

This function accepts no arguments.

Description

ISRUNTIME returns a logical value of True if Paradox Runtime is executing the script. False is returned if Paradox is executing the script.

ISSHARED( )   *Information*

Syntax

ISSHARED(tablename)

Description

ISSHARED returns a logical value of True if **tablename** is in a shared directory. A script error occurs if the table does not exist or is in another user's private directory.

If **tablename** is shared, you may need to check for locks placed by other users and place locks on the table dependent on your application.

ISTABLE( ) *Information*

Syntax

ISTABLE(tablename)

Description

ISTABLE returns a logical value of True if **tablename** exists, where **tablename** represents a Paradox table. False is returned if the table does not exist.

Always use the ISTABLE function, not the ISFILE function, to test for a Paradox table. The ISTABLE function checks both the workspace and the disk to determine the existence of the table.

ISVALID( ) *Information*

Syntax

ISVALID()

This function accepts no arguments.

Description

ISVALID returns a logical value of True if the contents of the current field are valid, based on the field type and validity checks defined for the field. By default, Paradox performs validity checks when exiting the field. ISVALID can be used to test the field while the cursor remains in the field. ISVALID returns False if the fields do not comply with the field type and validity checks.

See FIELDSTR, FIELDTYPE, and RECORDSTATUS for related functions.

ISWINDOW( ) *Information, Window*

Syntax

ISWINDOW(winhandle)

Description

This function is used to determine whether a window handle corresponds to any active windows. **winhandle** is any Paradox window handle. ISWINDOW returns True if the window specified by **winhandle** is active (open); it returns False otherwise.

Each time a window is opened on the workspace or canvas, Paradox assigns it a unique integer. This number is referred to as the "window handle." Each number is used only once during a Paradox session; if the window is closed, its handle is not reused.

A window handle is assigned directly by using WINDOW HANDLE or GETWINDOW and is assigned indirectly by using WINDOW CREATE.

Use this function to ensure that a window handle is valid before using commands such as SETCANVAS or WINDOW SELECT.

KEYLOOKUP   *Keypress Interaction*

Syntax

KEYLOOKUP

Description

The KEYLOOKUP command is equivalent to the Alt-K (Key Viol) keystroke. Refer to the "Handling Key Violations in CoEdit Mode" section of Chapter 3, "Entering, Editing, and Viewing Data," for a discussion of how to use Alt-K (Key Viol). The KEYLOOKUP command is effective in only CoEdit mode.

KEYPRESS   *Input/Output*

Syntax

KEYPRESS keycode1

Description

The KEYPRESS command enables the script to simulate pressing any key on the keyboard, as well as any valid keystroke combination. The **keycode1** parameter indicates the keystroke to be emulated. **keycode1** is either a PAL keycode string, an ASCII decimal code, or an extended code. Appendix C, "PAL Keycodes and Extended Codes," lists all the available PAL keycodes, ASCII codes, and extended codes.

LEFT   *Keypress Interaction*

Syntax

> **LEFT**

Description

> The LEFT command is equivalent to pressing the left-arrow key. The effect of this command depends on the Paradox mode and the context. Refer to the chapter that discusses the mode and context in which you intend to use the LEFT command.

LEN( )   *String*

Syntax

> **LEN(string)**

Description

> LEN returns the numeric value length of string. The **string** parameter must be a valid PAL string expression.

Example

> ```
> MESSAGE LEN( "Elizabeth" )
> ```

> This example displays 9.

LINKTYPE( )   *Workspace, Canvas*

Syntax

> **LINKTYPE( )**

> This function takes no arguments.

Description

> LINKTYPE returns a string representing the type of link between the master table and the current subordinate table. Table 19.34 lists the link type values returned by the LINKTYPE function.

Table 19.34. Link Types

Link type	Description
None	No links between the tables, master table is current, or the form is not a multitable form
Group	Many master table records to one detail table record, or many master table records to many detail table records
1-1 Group	One master table record to one detail table record
1-M Group	One master table record to many detail table records

LN( )   *Mathematical*

Syntax

> **LN(number)**

Description

LN returns the natural logarithm of **number**, where **number** is any positive value. The string Error is returned if **number** is zero or negative. LN returns the logarithm to base *e* of **number**, where *e* is the constant value 2.7182845905.

See also EXP.

Example

```
RETURN LN(5)
```

This example displays the number 1.609437912434.

```
RETURN LN(0)
```

This example displays Error.

LOCALIZEEVENT   *Window*

Syntax

> **LOCALIZEEVENT arrayname**

Description

> This command changes the screen-relative coordinates of a mouse event to window-relative coordinates, and adds the window handle of the window that the mouse event occurred in to the elements in **arrayname**. **arrayname** is a dynamic array initialized as a mouse event.

> When GETEVENT is used to capture a mouse event, the row and column coordinates that are retrieved to show the even location are relative to the whole screen. It usually is more useful to know where the mouse event occurred relative to the window.

> LOCALIZEEVENT adds an index called WINDOW to the dynamic array and stores the handle of the window in which the mouse event occurred in the new element.

Example

```
WHILE True <> False
    GETEVENT MOUSE "UP", "DOWN" MESSAGE "CLOSE" TO myevent
    IF myevent["TYPE"] = "MOUSE" THEN
        LOCALIZEEVENT myevent
        SWITCH
            CASE myevent["ACTION"] = "UP" :
                MESSAGE "Mouse button up at: ",
                    myevent["ROW"], " ", myevent["COL"]
            CASE myevent["ACTION"] = "DOWN" :
                MESSAGE "Mouse button down at: ",
                    myevent["ROW"]," ", myevent["COL"]
                IF myevent["WINDOW"] = mywin THEN
                    @ myevent["ROW"]-1, myevent["COL"]-1
                        ?? "*"
                    ENDIF
        ENDSWITCH
    ENDIF
    IF myevent["TYPE"] = "MESSAGE" THEN
        IF myevent["MESSAGE"] = "CLOSE" THEN
            MESSAGE "Closing window and ending script."
```

```
            SLEEP 2000
            WINDOW CLOSE
            SLEEP 2000
            RETURN
         ENDIF
      ENDIF
   ENDWHILE
```

This example uses LOCALIZEEVENT to shift the mouse coordinates from screen-relative to window-relative measurements. After GETEVENT, LOCALIZEEVENT is used. If the mouse button down was in our window, then an * is placed there.

LOCATE   *Workspace*

Syntax

> **LOCATE** *NEXT PATTERN* **val1**
>
> **LOCATE** *NEXT* **vallist1**

Description

The LOCATE command searches the current image for a record that contains a given value in the current field. The search value is represented by the **val1** parameter in the first of the preceding syntax lines.

Sometimes you want the script to match values in multiple fields. In such a case, you can specify a list of values, represented by **vallist1** in the second syntax line. The values in the list are separated by commas. The LOCATE command then attempts to match the values in **vallist1** to the first n fields in the current image, where n is the number of values in **vallist1**.

If LOCATE finds a match, the script makes the matching record the current record and sets the system variable RetVal to the logical value True. When no match is found, the cursor does not move, but RetVal is set to False.

When the current image is a multitable form, LOCATE respects the limits of the restricted view. In a linked detail table, LOCATE searches only records linked to the current master record.

By default, LOCATE starts searching at the first record in the current image. The *NEXT* keyword causes LOCATE to begin the search with the current record.

The *PATTERN* keyword enables you to include Paradox wild-card characters (@ and ..) in **val1.** You cannot use *PATTERN* when LOCATE is searching for matches in multiple fields (**vallist1**). Refer to Chapter 4, "Getting Started with Query By Example," for a discussion of matching patterns with wild cards.

When searching a nonkey field, you can improve the performance of the LOCATE operation by using INDEX to create a secondary index on the search field.

Example

```
VIEW "Employee"
INDEX MAINTAINED "Employee" ON "Emp Last Name"
MOVETO [Emp Last Name]
? "Type the employee's last name: "
ACCEPT "A20" TO last
LOCATE last
WHILE (RetVal = True)
    PROMPT "Press F2 to find next employee, Esc to stop."
    WAIT RECORD UNTIL "F2", "Esc"
    IF RetVal = "F2" THEN
        DOWN
        LOCATE NEXT last
        IF RetVal = False THEN
            UP
        ENDIF
    ELSE
        QUITLOOP
    ENDIF
ENDWHILE
```

This example first permits the user to type the name of an employee whose record the user wants to display. The script then moves to the Emp Last Name field and uses LOCATE to find the first matching record. The user is prompted to

```
Press F2 to find next employee, Esc to stop.
```

If the user presses F2, the script uses LOCATE NEXT to find the next matching record, if any. If the user presses Esc, the script ends. The script also ends when LOCATE fails to find a matching record (when RetVal is False).

LOCATE INDEXORDER   *Workspace*

Syntax

This command has six syntax variations:

LOCATE INDEXORDER *NEXT* | *PREV PATTERN* **val1**

LOCATE INDEXORDER *NEXT* | *PREV* **valuelist**

LOCATE INDEXORDER BESTMATCH val1

LOCATE INDEXORDER BESTMATCH valuelist

LOCATE INDEXORDER *FIRST* | *LAST*

LOCATE INDEXORDER BY label valuelist

Description

Use this command to locate records in fields that are keyed (primary indexes) or have a secondary index. **val1** is the value being searched for. **valuelist** is a list of two or more values, each separated with a comma. Use this command only in fields that are indexed and only on tables currently displayed in table or form view, or a script error occurs. All variations of LOCATE INDEXORDER respect the limits of a restricted view. LOCATE INDEXORDER scans through the table in the order of the secondary index (primary indexes if using the second or fourth form) and stops at the first record matching **val1** or **valuelist**. A successful search will set RetVal to True; an unsuccessful search will set RetVal to False.

To use the first form of LOCATE INDEXORDER, the cursor must be placed in the field in which **val1** is to be located. The optional keywords NEXT and PREV indicate whether the locate operation should go forward or backward in the table. The PATTERN keyword tells PAL that **val1** contains the wild-card search characters .. and @.

In the second form of LOCATE INDEXORDER, the command searches for a match based on several fields. The number of fields used in the search depends on the number of separate values in the **valuelist**. The values are matched up with the table's fields starting at the leftmost field and moving to the right. All of the fields used in this form must be key (primary index) fields.

LOCATE INDEXORDER BESTMATCH, the basis for the third and fourth forms of this command, substitutes the first record with a field (or fields) greater than the **val1** (or **valuelist**) fields(s) originally specified if it cannot find an exact match for **val1** (or **valuelist**).

Use the fifth variation of LOCATE INDEXORDER by first placing the cursor in an indexed field. Then execute LOCATE INDEXORDER with either the FIRST or LAST keyword. FIRST will make the record that is first in the index order the current record. LAST will make the record that is last in the index order the last record.

The sixth variation of LOCATE INDEXORDER uses an optional label. The label is the secondary index label. When the label is used, LOCATE INDEXORDER finds a record whose first fields match the number and value of the fields specified in the valuelist. If the secondary index is based on several fields, then the cursor must be in the leftmost field of the index; if the secondary index is based on a single field, the cursor must be on that field. If the field is indexed with more than one secondary index, and no label is specified, then Paradox will use the index which produces a match in the least amount of time.

See also ORDERTABLE, LOCATE, and ZOOM.

LOCK   *Menu*

Syntax

LOCK locklist1

Description

The LOCK command places one or more locks on one or more specified shared tables. The **locklist1** parameter consists of one or more comma-separated tables and lock pairs. Lock types include the following: FL (full lock), WL (write lock), PFL (prevent full lock), and PWL (prevent write lock). Refer to "Creating Tables on a Network," in Chapter 2, "Creating Database Tables," for a description of each lock type.

As explained in Chapter 2, Paradox places appropriate locks on tables and records as needed. A good PAL programming practice, however, is to lock tables using the LOCK command before the script begins an operation that explicitly requires a particular type of lock for completion. Otherwise, the script may complete only part of the operation and then become "stalled" while waiting for a table to become available for locking. This practice avoids the potential of two Paradox users each waiting for a resource currently in use by the other—so called *deadlock* or *deadly embrace*.

When the script succeeds in placing all specified locks, Paradox assigns the system variable RetVal the logical value True. If LOCK cannot complete all specified locks, the command doesn't lock any table but assigns False to RetVal. Use the ERRORCODE command to diagnose why a lock attempt is unsuccessful.

Example

```
LOCK "Orders" WL, "Detail" WL
IF RetVal = False THEN
    ?? "Lock failed."
    SLEEP 3000
ELSE
    EDIT "Orders"
    FormKey
    PROMPT "Press F2 when done. Press Esc to cancel."
    WAIT TABLE UNTIL "F2", "Esc"
    IF RetVal = "F2" THEN
        DO_IT!
    ELSE
        MENU {Cancel} "Y"
    ENDIF
    CLEARIMAGE
ENDIF
UNLOCK "Orders" WL, "Detail" WL
```

This example displays Orders in form view only if Orders and Detail can be write locked. Otherwise, the script displays the message

```
Lock failed.
```

LOCKKEY Multiuser, Keypress Interactive

Syntax

LOCKKEY

Description

The LOCKKEY command is a toggle that either locks or unlocks the current record. This command is equivalent to pressing Alt-L (Lock Toggle). Refer to Chapter 3, "Entering, Editing, and Viewing Data," for a discussion of using Alt-L (Lock Toggle) to explicitly lock records. Chapter 3 also explains how to use Alt-L (Lock Toggle) and Alt-K (Key Viol) to resolve key violations. LOCKKEY is effective only on CoEdit mode.

Contrast the lock-toggling effect of LOCKKEY to the effects of LOCKRECORD and UNLOCKRECORD. LOCKRECORD only locks records and UNLOCKRECORD only unlocks records.

LOCKRECORD   *Multiuser*

Syntax

> **LOCKRECORD**

Description

In CoEdit mode, the LOCKRECORD command locks the current record. Paradox also sets the value of RetVal to True when LOCKRECORD successfully locks the current record. If the lock is not successful (RetVal is False), the ERRORCODE function is available to help diagnose the reason.

When LOCKRECORD is executed on a new record, the record is added to the table; the record is locked; and the table is sorted by any key values. The new record becomes the current record.

Refer to Chapter 3, "Entering, Editing, and Viewing Data," for a discussion of table and record locking. LOCKRECORD is effective only on CoEdit mode.

LOCKSTATUS( )   *Workspace, Canvas*

Syntax

> **LOCKSTATUS(tablename, locktype)**

Description

LOCKSTATUS returns an integer that represents the number of times you placed a certain lock type on a table. **tablename** is the Paradox table to check. **locktype** is a valid Paradox lock type-PFL (Prevent Full Lock), PWL (Prevent Write Lock), FL (Full Lock), or WL (Write Lock). In addition, you also can check for ANY. (Refer to the "Creating Tables on a Network" section of Chapter 2, "Creating Database Tables," for a description of each lock type.)

If you placed no locks of the specified type on the table, LOCKSTATUS returns 0. LOCKSTATUS does not count locks placed by Paradox but includes only locks directly placed by you. When checking for ANY, Paradox returns the total locks placed by you on the table.

LOG( )   *Mathematical*

Syntax

> **LOG(number)**

Description

> LOG returns the base 10 logarithm of **number**, where **number** is any positive value. Script error is returned if number is zero or negative. LN returns the logarithm to base e of **number**.

Example

> ```
> RETURN LOG(5)
> ```

This example displays `.6989700043360`.

> ```
> RETURN LOG(0)
> ```

This example displays `Error`.

LOOP   *Program Control*

Syntax

> **LOOP**

Description

> The LOOP command skips to the beginning of the nearest control FOR, FOREACH, SCAN, or WHILE control structure (loop). In general, the logic of most loop structures and the script instructions that they enclose can be constructed so that the LOOP instruction is never needed.

Example

> ```
> VIEW "Employee"
> CLEAR
> @ 0,0
> ```

```
? "The following employees are not in the Sales Department:"
?
SCAN
    IF [Department] = "Sales" THEN
        LOOP
    ENDIF
    ?[Emp First Name]+" "+[Emp Middle Initial]+" "+[Emp Last Name]
ENDSCAN
?
? "Press any key to return to Paradox"
x = GETCHAR()
CLEARIMAGE
```

This example uses the LOOP command to return to the top of the SCAN loop whenever an employee is from the Sales department.

LOWER( )   *String*

Syntax

LOWER(expr)

Description

This function returns a string composed entirely of lowercase characters. **expr** is an expression of any type. LOWER will convert it to a string automatically.

See also UPPER.

Example

```
MESSAGE LOWER( "the QUICK red fox" )
```

This example displays the quick red fox. The following example displays 100 thousand.

```
MESSAGE LOWER( "100 THOUSAND" )
```

MATCH( )   *String*

Syntax

MATCH(string, patternstring, *varnamelist*)

Description

The **string** parameter is the string Paradox is searching. **patternstring** is the value for which you want Paradox to search. *varnamelist* is a list of variable names.

MATCH returns a logical value of True if the value in **patternstring** is found within **string**. False is returned if **patternstring** is not found within **string**.

If you include a *varnamelist*, then the variables in the list are assigned values (from left to right) as the pieces matching **patternstring** are found in **string**.

Example

```
RETURN MATCH( "Kyle", "Ky" )
```

This example would display "True".

MAX( )   *Statistical*

Syntax

MAX(x, y)

Description

MAX determines the larger of two numbers, returning it as the function result. **x** and **y** are numeric values to compare. The arguments must be numeric.

Example

```
MESSAGE MAX(10,-100)
```

This example displays 10.

MEMLEFT( )   *System Status*

Syntax

MEMLEFT( )

This function accepts no arguments.

Description

MEMLEFT returns the amount of RAM, in bytes, which is available to your application.

Example

```
IF MEMLEFT() < 6500 THEN
    MESSAGE "Available memory is getting low"
    SLEEP 2500
ENDIF
```

This example displays a message if the free RAM is less than 6,500 bytes.

MENU   *Keypress Interaction*

Syntax

MENU

Description

The MENU command displays the current Paradox menu. This command is equivalent to pressing F10 (Menu).

MENUCHOICE( )   *Workspace, Canvas*

Syntax

MENUCHOICE( )

This function takes no arguments.

Description

Use MENUCHOICE to return the currently highlighted menu choice as a string. If no menu is displayed, MENUCHOICE returns the string Error. This command does not apply to menus created with SHOWMENU or similar commands, nor does it apply to the PAL Menu. Use MENUCHOICE only when a Paradox menu is active.

MENUDISABLE   Input/Output

Syntax

MENUDISABLE string

Description

Use MENUDISABLE to disable (gray) a menu item on a menu created with SHOWPULLDOWN or SHOWPOPUP command. **string** is a string expression evaluating to a *Tag* associated with the menu item. A script error occurs if the Tag isn't found, or if no menu is displayed.

See also MENUENABLE, SHOWPOPUP, and SHOWPULLDOWN.

Example

Refer to the sample application in Chapter 18 for an example of MENUDISABLE.

MENUENABLE   Input/Output

Syntax

MENUENABLE string

Description

Use MENUENABLE to enable a menu item on a menu created with SHOWPULLDOWN or SHOWPOPUP command. **string** is a string expression evaluating to a *Tag* associated with the menu item. A script error occurs if the Tag isn't found, or if no menu is displayed.

See also MENUDISABLE, SHOWPOPUP, and SHOWPULLDOWN.

Example

Refer to the sample application in Chapter 18 for an example of MENUENABLE.

MENUPROMPT( )   Workspace, Canvas

Syntax

MENUPROMPT( )

This function takes no arguments.

Description

Use this function to get the text contents of a type-in field in a Paradox dialog box. MENUPROMPT returns a string corresponding to the text in the type-in box. Use MENUPROMPT only with Paradox dialog boxes that have type-in fields; the function returns the string Error otherwise. MENUPROMPT will not work with list boxes or menus, nor can it be used with dialog boxes created with SHOWDIALOG.

See also the MENUCHOICE function.

MESSAGE

Input/Output

Syntax

MESSAGE list1

Description

The MESSAGE command displays information in the lower right corner of the PAL canvas. The **list1** parameter is a list of one or more PAL expressions. The MESSAGE command concatenates (combines as a string) the values in the list and displays the result near the lower right corner of the canvas. The message is in reverse video or in a contrasting color, depending on your monitor type.

When operating in compatibility mode, Paradox clears the message whenever a new message is displayed, the canvas is refreshed, or the workspace is displayed. You may often need to use the SLEEP command, therefore, to prevent the message from being cleared from the screen before the user can read the message's content.

In standard mode, however, the message is removed only when another message is displayed, or Paradox stops running. If a blank message is displayed, the message bar is removed completely.

Example

```
@ 1, 1 ACCEPT "N" TO number
WHILE ISBLANK( number )
   BEEP BEEP BEEP
   MESSAGE "You must make an entry in this field."
   SLEEP 3000
   @ 1, 1 ACCEPT "N" TO number
ENDWHILE
```

This example uses Compatibility mode message techniques to allow the user to see the message. The following example accomplishes the same task with Standard mode techniques:

```
@ 1, 1 ACCEPT "N" TO number
WHILE ISBLANK( number )
   BEEP BEEP BEEP
   MESSAGE "You must make an entry in this field."
   @ 1, 1 ACCEPT "N" TO number
ENDWHILE
MESSAGE ""              ; clears the message bar away
```

MIN( )   *Statistical*

Syntax

MIN(x, y)

Description

MIN determines the smaller of two numbers. **x** and **y** are numeric values to compare. The arguments must be numeric.

Example

```
RETURN MIN(10,-100)
```

This example displays the number -100.

MINIEDIT   *Keypress Interaction*

Syntax

MINIEDIT

Description

This command has the same effect as pressing Ctrl-E. Refer to Chapter 17, "Using the Script Editor and PAL Debugger," for more information.

MOD( )   *Mathematical*

Syntax

> **MOD(dividend, divisor)**

Description

> MOD returns the modulus, which is the remainder after dividing **dividend** by **divisor**. **dividend** and **divisor** must be numeric.
>
> The formula for the Modulus (or remainder) is
>
> $$MOD(x, y) = x - (y * INT(x/y))$$

Example

> ```
> RETURN MOD(77,16)
> ```
>
> This example displays 13, which is the result of the following expression:
>
> ```
> (77 - (16 * INT(77/16))
> ```

MONITOR( )   *System Status*

Syntax

> **MONITOR( )**
>
> This function takes no arguments.

Description

> MONITOR returns the kind of monitor as set in the Custom Configuration Program. If no PARADOX.CFG file is found, Paradox checks the hardware for monitor type. MONITOR returns one of the following strings: B&W, Mono, or Color.

Example

> ```
> IF MONITOR() = "Color" THEN
>    PICKFORM "1"         : Form 1 uses color
> ELSE
>    PICKFORM "2"         ; Form 2 uses monochrome
> ENDIF
> ```

This example chooses data-entry forms based on the value returned by the MONITOR( ) function.

MONTH( )   Date

Syntax

> **MONTH(date)**

Description

MONTH returns an integer between 1 and 12, representing the month in which **date** occurs. A script error is returned if the value of **date** is not a valid date.

Example

> MESSAGE MONTH(25-DEC-91)

This example displays the number 12.

MOUSE CLICK   Input/Output

Syntax

> **MOUSE CLICK** *LEFT* | *RIGHT* | *BOTH* **num1, num2**

Description

Use this command to simulate a mouse click. **num1** is the row coordinate for the mouse, and **num2** is the column coordinate. If you do not use any of the optional keywords, PAL assumes that a left-button click is to be simulated. The keywords RIGHT and BOTH instruct PAL to simulate a right-button click or both buttons pressed, respectively.

MOUSE CLICK is not affected by MOUSE HIDE. If no mouse is present, a script error occurs. You should use the SYSINFO command to determine whether a mouse is present before using any of the mouse commands.

See also MOUSE DOUBLECLICK, MOUSE DRAG, MOUSE HIDE, and MOUSE SHOW.

MOUSE DOUBLECLICK   Input/Output

Syntax

> **MOUSE DOUBLECLICK** *LEFT* | *RIGHT* | *BOTH* **num1, num2**

Description

Use this command to simulate a mouse double-click. **num1** is the row coordinate for the mouse, and **num2** is the column coordinate. If you do not use any of the optional keywords, PAL assumes that a left-button double-click is to be simulated. The keywords RIGHT and BOTH instruct PAL to simulate a right-button double-click or both buttons double-clicked, respectively.

MOUSE DOUBLECLICK is not affected by MOUSE HIDE. If no mouse is present, a script error occurs. You should use the SYSINFO command to determine whether a mouse is present before using any of the mouse commands.

See also MOUSE CLICK, MOUSE DRAG, MOUSE HIDE, and MOUSE SHOW.

MOUSE DRAG   Input/Output

Syntax

> **MOUSE DRAG** *LEFT* | *RIGHT* | *BOTH* **FROM rowstart, colstart TO rowend, colend**

Description

Use this command to simulate a mouse drag. **rowstart** and **colstart** are number values indicating the row and column coordinates of the mouse cursor's location at the start of the dragging operation. **rowend** and **colend** are number values indicating the row and column coordinates of the mouse cursor's location at the end of the dragging operation. If you do not use any of the optional keywords, PAL assumes that the drag is being made with the left button of the mouse. The keywords RIGHT and BOTH instruct PAL to simulate a right-button drag or a drag operation using both buttons held down.

Your script can use MOUSE DRAG to move objects in windows or on the screen. If the starting location of the drag (indicated by **rowstart** and **colstart**) corresponds with the location of dragging handle (like the top bar of a window), then the object is moved by the simulated drag.

MOUSE DRAG is not affected by MOUSE HIDE. If no mouse is present, a script error occurs. You should use the SYSINFO command to determine whether a mouse is present before using any of the mouse commands.

See also MOUSE CLICK, MOUSE DOUBLECLICK, MOUSE HIDE, and MOUSE SHOW.

MOUSE HIDE   *Input/Output*

Syntax

> **MOUSE HIDE**

Description

This command disables the processing of mouse events and hides the mouse cursor. The event queue is cleared of mouse events, and further mouse events are ignored. Mouse event processing will remain disabled until the script ends, or until a MOUSE SHOW command is executed.

If no mouse is present, a script error occurs. You should use the SYSINFO command to determine whether a mouse is present before using any of the mouse commands.

See also MOUSE CLICK, MOUSE DOUBLECLICK, MOUSE DRAG, and MOUSE SHOW.

MOUSE SHOW   *Input/Output*

Syntax

> **MOUSE SHOW**

Description

This command enables the processing of mouse events and displays the mouse cursor. If mouse event processing was previously stopped because of a MOUSE HIDE command, it is resumed.

If no mouse is present, or the mouse is already enabled, MOUSE SHOW is ignored. You should use the SYSINFO command to determine whether a mouse is present before using any of the mouse commands.

See also MOUSE CLICK, MOUSE DOUBLECLICK, MOUSE DRAG, and MOUSE SHOW.

MOVETO   *Workspace*

Syntax

> **MOVETO fieldspecifier1**
>
> **MOVETO FIELD fieldname1**
>
> **MOVETO RECORD recno**
>
> **MOVETO imageno**
>
> **MOVETO table1**

Description

The MOVETO command moves the workspace cursor to a particular field, record, or image, depending on which form of the command you use.

The **MOVETO fieldspecifier1** form of the command moves the cursor to a particular field in the current record of a specified image. **fieldspecifier1** must be a valid field specifier. Refer to Chapter 15, "An Overview of the Paradox Application Language," for a discussion of field specifiers.

Use the **MOVETO FIELD fieldname1** form of the command when you want to move the cursor to a field in the current image that is specified in the script as a variable. This command is equivalent to the Image Zoom Field menu command. Refer to Chapter 3, "Entering, Editing, and Viewing Data," for a discussion of the Zoom menu options.

The **MOVETO RECORD recno** form of the MOVETO command moves the cursor to the record specified by **recno**, where **recno** is a valid record number. This command is equivalent to the Image Zoom Record menu command.

The **MOVETO imageno** form of the MOVETO command moves to a particular image on the workspace or multitable form. **imageno** is the relative position of the image, expressed as a number where the first (top) image in the workspace is image number 1; the next image is image number 2; and so on. The script can use the IMAGENO function to determine the image number of a particular image on the workspace. This version of the MOVETO command changes the current workspace image, but does not affect the current canvas.

The **MOVETO table1** form of MOVETO moves the workspace cursor to the first display image or query form on the workspace or multitable form for **table1**. **table1** must contain the name of a table that has an image on the workspace or in the current multitable form. This version of the MOVETO command changes the current workspace image, but does not affect the current canvas.

When the current image is a multitable form, MOVETO can move the cursor only to images in the same form. In DataEntry mode, the MOVETO command can move the cursor between images only if the current image is a multitable form and only if the images are contained in that multitable form.

Example

```
 VIEW "Translog"
VIEW "Orders"
@ 10,10 ?? "Type the Order # for the transaction to edit:"
ACCEPT "N" TO Order_Num
MOVETO [Order #]
LOCATE Order_Num
COPYTOARRAY Before
MOVETO [Translog ->]
END
EDITKEY
DOWN
COPYFROMARRAY Before
MOVETO "Orders"
WAIT RECORD UNTIL "Help", "Do_It!"
```

This example shows three MOVETO commands:

MOVETO [Order #] uses the MOVETO fieldspecifier1 form to move the cursor to the Order # field.

MOVETO [Translog ->], like the preceding example, uses a field specifier. Here, however, the field specifier indicates an image, Translog, rather than a field.

The third example, MOVETO Orders, moves to the first image on the workspace for the Orders table.

MOY( ) *Date*

Syntax

> **MOY(date)**

Description

MOY returns a string representing the month contained in a given date. **date** is any valid PAL date expression. MOY returns one these abbreviations: Jan, Feb, Mar, Apr, May, Jun, Jul, Aug, Sep, Oct, Nov, Dec.

Example

```
MESSAGE MOY(8/10/90)
```

This example displays Aug.

NETTYPE( ) *System Status*

Syntax

> **NETTYPE( )**

This function accepts no arguments.

Description

NETTYPE returns the type of network on which the script is running. When the script is running on a stand-alone system, this function returns the string SingleUser. Possible strings returned by the NETTYPE function include the following: Novell, 3Com, IBM, AT&T Starlan, Banyan, Lanman, Dec, Other, and SingleUser.

NEWDIALOGSPEC *Dialog Box*

Syntax

> **NEWDIALOGSPEC list1**

Description

Use this command to respecify the event list for the currently active dialog box. **list1** is an event list as described under the entry for the SHOWDIALOG command. You should use NEWDIALOGSPEC only in a dialog procedure or in script instructions reached from a dialog box. This command is useful if changing the behavior of a dialog box becomes necssary. Refer to Chapter 15, "An Overview of the Paradox Application Language," for more information on dialog boxes.

See also SHOWDIALOG.

NEWWAITSPEC   *Input/Output*

Syntax

NEWWAITSPEC list1

Description

Use this command to respecify the event list for the currently active wait session. **list1** is an event list as described under the entry for the WAIT command. You should use NEWWAITSPEC only in a wait session or in script instructions reached from a wait session. This command is useful if changing the behavior of a wait session becomes necessary. Refer to Chapter 15, "An Overview of the Paradox Application Language," for more information on wait sessions.

See also WAIT.

NFIELDS( )   *Workspace, Canvas*

Syntax

NFIELDS(tablename)

Description

NFIELDS counts the number of fields in a table. **tablename** is the table to examine.

A script error occurs if the table does not exist.

Example

```
RETURN NFIELDS("Customer")
```

This example displays the number 7, assuming that the Customer table has seven fields in its structure.

NIMAGERECORDS( ) *Workspace, Canvas*

Syntax

> **NIMAGERECORDS( )**

This function takes no arguments.

Description

NIMAGERECORDS counts the number of records in the current image, which may be different from the number of records you see on-screen (see the function NROWS). In a multitable form, NIMAGERECORDS respects the restricted view. When the cursor is resting in an embedded detail table, NIMAGERECORDS returns the number of detail records that are associated with the current master record. If no images are on the workspace, a script error occurs.

NIMAGES( ) *Workspace, Canvas*

Syntax

> **NIMAGES( )**

This function takes no arguments.

Description

NIMAGES scans the workspace and returns the number of images on the workspace. The function returns 0 if no images are found on the workspace. When a multitable form is placed on the workspace, NIMAGES is increased by the amount of tables embedded on the form. Tables embedded on the multitable form—and placed on the workspace before the form is placed—do not increase NIMAGES. Canvas images are not included in the count returned by NIMAGES.

NKEYFIELDS( )   *Workspace, Canvas*

Syntax

NKEYFIELDS(tablename)

Description

NKEYFIELDS examines a table and reports the number of key fields in the table. **tablename** represents the table to examine. NKEYFIELDS returns 0 if the table has no key fields. A script error occurs if the table does not exist.

Example

```
RETURN NKEYFIELDS("Customer")
```

This example returns the number 1, assuming that the Customer table has one key field.

NPAGES( )   *Workspace, Canvas*

Syntax

NPAGES( )

This function takes no argument.

Description

NPAGES scans the current form or report specification and returns the number of pages in the specification. In a report specification, NPAGES determines the number of page widths. In a single table form, the actual number of pages is returned. Linked detail tables always return 1, the Paradox maximum for embedded forms.

NRECORDS( )   *Workspace, Canvas*

Syntax

NRECORDS(tablename)

Description

NRECORDS returns the number of records in a table. **tablename** represents a Paradox table. A script error occurs if the table does not exist.

In a multitable form, the limits of a restricted view are not respected by NRECORDS.

NROWS( )   *Workspace, Canvas*

Syntax

NROWS( )

This function accepts no arguments.

Description

NROWS totals the rows in a report specification or the current display or query image. When a table display image or query form is current, NROWS returns a number between 1 and 22, indicating the number of rows or the image or query currently displayed on-screen. When used in a report specification NROWS determines the number of rows in the specification.

NUMVAL( )   *String*

Syntax

NUMVAL(string)

Description

Use NUMVAL to convert a string expression to a number. The string Error is returned if **string** does not evaluate as a numeric representation.

See also DATEVAL and STRVAL.

Example

```
MESSAGE NUMVAL( "HAL9000" )
MESSAGE NUMVAL( "-12.5")
```

The first line in the example will display the message Error, because HAL9000 does not represent a number. The second line will display –12.5, the successfully converted string.

OPEN PRINTER   *Input/Output*

Syntax

> **OPEN PRINTER**

Description

> The OPEN PRINTER command opens a printer device. See also the CLOSE PRINTER command. This command usually is only necessary in network environments.

Example

```
VIEW "Customer"
SETPRINTER "LPT1"
OPEN PRINTER
SCAN
    PRINT [Company Name]+"\n"
    PRINT [Cust Address]+"\n"
    PRINT [Cust City]+", "+[Cust State]+"  "+[Cust Zip]+"\n\n\n\n"
ENDSCAN
PRINT "\f"
CLOSE PRINTER
CLEARIMAGE
```

> This example opens a printer device, prints an address list from the Customer table, and then closes the printer device.

ORDERTABLE   *Keypress Interaction*

Syntax

> **ORDERTABLE**

Description

> This command simulates pressing Alt-S. Refer to Chapter 4, "Getting Started with Query By Example," for more information regarding the Alt-S command.

PAGENO( )   Workspace, Canvas

Syntax

> **PAGENO( )**

This function accepts no arguments.

Description

> PAGENO reports the current page number for a report or form specification. When working with a report specification, PAGENO returns the number of the current page width. When working with a form specification or with a table in form view, PAGENO returns the number of the current page of the form specification.

PAGEWIDTH( )   Workspace, Canvas

Syntax

> **PAGEWIDTH( )**

This function accepts no arguments.

Description

> PAGEWIDTH returns the current page width setting of a report specification.
>
> A script error occurs if PAGEWIDTH is used in all modes but Report Mode.

Example

> ```
> RETURN PAGEWIDTH( )
> ```
>
> Assuming that the page width is set to 132 columns, this example returns the number 132.

PAINTCANVAS   Input/Output

Syntax

> **PAINTCANVAS** *BORDER FILL string1 monolist1* | *ATTRIBUTE number1* | *BACKGROUND* **row1, col1, row2, col2** | *ALL*

Description

The PAINTCANVAS command adds color, screen display attributes, or filler text to a specified area of the current canvas. The **row1** and **col1** parameters specify the screen coordinates of the upper left corner of the portion of the canvas to be affected. **row2** and **col2** are the screen coordinates for the lower right corner of the area to be affected.

The *BORDER* keyword applies color and/or display attributes to a one-character-wide border defined by the screen coordinates contained in the **row1**, **col1**, **row2**, and **col2** parameters.

The keyword *FILL* causes Paradox to fill the designated area of the current canvas with the character contained in the *string1* parameter.

The optional *monolist1* parameter is a comma-separated list of one or more of the following options:

BLINK	Screen area blinks continuously
INTENSE	Foreground characters display in high-intensity video
REVERSE	Characters display in reverse video

The *ATTRIBUTE* keyword sets colors or monochrome-character-display attributes on the current canvas. The *number1* parameter must evaluate to an integer between 0 and 255. Compute the value for *number1* from the attribute codes listed in the tables in Appendix D, "PAL Color Palette Codes." For a color screen, the *number1* parameter is the sum of the foreground color and the background color numbers. To create blinking text, add 128 to the color or monochrome attribute numbers.

The BACKGROUND keyword causes only the fill string to be changed. The style and color attributes remain unchanged.

The ALL keyword causes PAINTCANVAS to affect the entire current canvas.

The PAINTCANVAS command applies color and screen attributes to characters that already are placed on the canvas. Use the STYLE command to control the color and display attributes of characters before the script writes the characters to the canvas.

See also SETCANVAS, GETCANVAS, and STYLE.

Example

```
PAINTCANVAS ATTRIBUTE 62 5,10,20,70
SLEEP 5000
```

This example causes the area of the canvas from row 5, column 10 to row 20, column 70 to display with yellow foreground characters and cyan background color.

PASSWORD   Workspace

Syntax

> PASSWORD passwordlist1

Description

The PASSWORD command supplies to Paradox one or more passwords as a group, for access to protected tables. The **passwordlist1** parameter contains one or more passwords separated by commas. By including all the passwords needed to access protected tables in an application, the user is not later interrupted by a request to enter a password.

Refer to Chapter 13, "Using Paradox Tools," for a discussion on creating and using passwords to protect tables and scripts.

Example

```
PASSWORD "safe", "safer", "safest"
```

This example passes all three passwords—safe, safer, and safest—to Paradox at once. Paradox uses these passwords throughout the script, whenever a protected table script is encountered.

PGDN   Keypress Interaction

Syntax

> PGDN

Description

The PGDN command is equivalent to pressing PgDn. The effect of this command depends on the Paradox mode and the context. Refer to the chapter that discusses the mode and context in which you intend to use the PGDN command.

PGUP   *Keypress Interaction*

Syntax

PGUP

Description

The PGUP command is equivalent to pressing PgUp. The effect of this command depends on the Paradox mode and the context. Refer to the chapter that discusses the mode and context in which you intend to use the PGUP command.

PI( )   *Mathematical*

Syntax

PI()

This function accepts no arguments.

Description

PI returns the constant *pi*, which is approximated by 3.141592653589.

PICKFORM   *Menu*

Syntax

PICKFORM formname

Description

The PICKFORM command chooses a form for use in form view. This command is equivalent to the Image PickForm menu command. The **formname** parameter contains the name of the form you want the script to select. Refer to Chapter 8, "Using Advanced Form Techniques," for a complete discussion of designing and using Paradox forms. Chapter 3, "Entering, Editing, and Viewing Data," also describes how to use the Image menu.

Example

```
EDIT "Orders"
PICKFORM "2"
```

This example displays the Orders table in the workspace in Edit mode and then uses the PICKFORM command to select form 2.

PLAY   *Menu*

Syntax

> **PLAY script1**

Description

The PLAY command executes another script. This command is equivalent to the **S**cript **P**lay menu command. Playing one script from within another script often is referred to as *calling a subroutine*. Refer to Chapter 15, "An Overview of the Paradox Application Language," for a discussion of playing scripts as subroutines.

Example

```
SHOWMENU
    "Benefits": "Add, change, display, print benefit info",
    "Employee": "Add, change, display, print employee info",
    "Salary": "Add, change, display, print salary info",
    "Leave": "Leave the application"
TO response
SWITCH
    CASE response = "Benefits":
        PLAY "Exben"
    CASE response = "Employee":
        PLAY "Exemp"
    CASE response = "Salary":
        PLAY "Exsal"
    CASE response = "Leave":
        QUIT
ENDSWITCH
```

This example calls any of three other scripts, depending on the user's menu selection.

PMT( )   *Financial*

Syntax

PMT(principal, interest, period)

Description

PMT calculates the periodic payment needed to pay off a loan. **principal** is the outstanding loan balance. **interest** is the interest rate of the loan, expressed in decimal format. **period** is the number of payment periods.

The interest rate used must match the period calculated. If the payment periods are monthly, the rate of interest also must be monthly.

The PMT function is used with amortization loans. With an amortization loan, the payment includes interest on the outstanding principal. The remainder of the payment is applied to the principal. Home mortgages are amortization loans.

Example

```
RETURN PMT(120000,.00875,360)
```

This example displays the number 1097.687153391.

POSTRECORD   *Multiuser*

Syntax

POSTRECORD *violcode LEAVELOCKED*

Description

Use this command to post a record during an edit or CoEdit. POSTRECORD provides a way to have your script post the record early, before the entry is complete (or DO_IT! is executed). If the optional keyword LEAVELOCKED is specified, the record is left locked after the post; if the post is unsuccessful, LEAVELOCKED is ignored. If you do not use the LEAVELOCKED option, the record remains unlocked and may not remain current after the post.

The optional *violcode* is used to control the action of the command if a key violation occurs and may be any one of the following keywords: NOPOST, FORCEPOST, KEYVIOL. NOPOST is the default. If the *violcode* option is NOPOST, then Paradox will not post the record when a key violation occurs. The FORCEPOST code will always post the record, and the KEYVIOL code will leave the record in a key violation state if a key violation occurs. FORCEPOST cannot be used on the master record in a linked form. In this last condition, you can use the KEYLOOKUP command to investigate the key violation.

If the POSTRECORD command is unsuccessful for any reason, the global variable RetVal is set to False, otherwise RetVal is true.

See also KEYLOOKUP, and refer to Chapter 3, "Entering, Editing, and Viewing Data," for more information on key violations.

POW( )   *Mathematical*

Syntax

> **POW(x, y)**

Description

POW returns the value of **x** raised to the power of **y**, where **x** and **y** are numeric values.

Example

```
RETURN POW( 3, 2 )
```

This example displays the number 9.

PRINT   *Input/Output*

Syntax

> **PRINT** *FILE filename1* **list1**

Description

The PRINT command sends output to a printer or to a file. The **list1** parameter contains a comma-separated list of values. By default, the PRINT command sends the values contained in **list1** to the selected printer (see the SETPRINTER command). The FILE keyword causes PRINT to send output to the file specified in the *filename1* parameter. If you use the FILE keyword, you must also supply the *filename1* parameter.

The PRINT command sends characters to the printer or to a file as ASCII characters. The PRINT command does not filter out control characters, except that PRINT sends the NULL character (ASCII 0) in place of ASCII 255.

Refer to the section, "Constants," in Chapter 15, "An Overview of the Paradox Application Language," for a discussion of special *backslash sequences* that send certain control codes that control a printer.

Example

```
VIEW "Customer"
SETPRINTER "LPT1"
OPEN PRINTER
SCAN
    PRINT [Company Name]+"\n"
    PRINT [Cust Address]+"\n"
    PRINT [Cust City]+", "+[Cust State]+"  "+[Cust Zip]+"\n\n\n\n"
ENDSCAN
PRINT "\f"
CLOSE PRINTER
CLEARIMAGE
```

This example opens a printer device, prints an address list from the Customer table, and then closes the printer device.

PRINTER   *Input/Output*

Syntax

PRINTER ON | OFF

Description

By default, the ?, ??, and TEXT commands send output to the screen only. The PRINTER ON command also causes these three commands to send screen output to the printer. After the printer is turned on with PRINTER ON, you can use the PRINTER OFF command to turn off the printer.

PRINTERSTATUS( )　　　*System Status*

Syntax

> **PRINTERSTATUS( )**

This function takes no arguments.

Description

> PRINTERSTATUS returns a logical value of True when a printer is
> connected to the system and the printer is ready to print output.
> This function tests the printer connected to LPT1 (the default), to
> the port designated in the Custom Configuration Program, to the
> port designated by a SETPRINTER command, or to the port desig-
> nated by the Report SetPrinter OverRide command.

Example

```
IF PRINTERSTATUS() THEN
    REPORT "Employee" "1"
ELSE
    MESSAGE "Printer is not ready, please check it"
ENDIF
```

This example sends output to the printer only if the printer is
ready to print. Otherwise, the script displays an error message.

PRIVDIR( )　　　*System Status*

Syntax

> **PRIVDIR( )**

This function accepts no arguments.

Description

> PRIVDIR returns the name of the user's private directory. This
> function is important when running Paradox on a network be-
> cause every network user must have their own private directory
> where temporary tables are placed. The private directory can be
> placed on the local drive or on a network drive.

PRIVTABLES   *Multiuser*

Syntax

PRIVTABLES list1

Description

The PRIVTABLES command assigns one or more specified tables to the user's private directory. Each user on a multiuser system must have a *private directory* assigned to them. This private directory can be assigned using either the Custom Configuration Program or using the **T**ools **N**et **S**etPrivate menu command.

Paradox stores temporary files (such as Answer tables) in the private directory. Use PRIVTABLES to cause other files to be stored in the private directory as well. Typically, you should use the PRIVTABLES command to assign to the private directory tables that do not need to be shared, but are temporary in nature.

The RESET command, among other things, clears all table assignments to the private directory.

Example

```
PRIVTABLES "Translog", "Emptemp"
```

This example assigns the tables Translog and Emptemp to the user's temporary directory. When the application that contains this PRIVTABLES command creates one of the specified tables, Paradox places the table, and its family of objects, into the user's private directory, rather than in the working directory that contains shared files.

PROC   *Procedure*

Syntax

PROC *CLOSED* **proc1** (*varlist1*) *USEVARS varlist2 PRIVATE varlist3* **commands ENDPROC**

Description

The PROC command creates a PAL procedure. Refer to Chapter 15, "An Overview of the Paradox Application Language," for a discussion of PAL procedures and procedure libraries.

The *CLOSED* keyword makes the procedure a closed procedure. Closed procedures are completely self-contained procedures that can take special advantage of PAL's automatic memory-management features. To use closed procedures, you must observe several special restrictions. Closed procedures, for example, can be called only from a procedure library. Refer to the *PAL Programmer's Guide*, supplied with Paradox, for more information on when and how to use this powerful option.

By default, all variables in a closed procedure are local to the procedure. As a rule, closed procedures ignore the previously assigned values of all variables. If you want a closed procedure to use certain global variable values, add the *USEVARS* keyword followed by the list of global variables in the *varlist2* parameter.

varlist1 is an optional parameter that contains a list of arguments which is passed to the procedure when the procedure is called. You must enclose *varlist1* in parentheses. Include the parentheses even if you don't specify *varlist1*. It is good programming practice to have a procedure refer to global variables through the parameter list. That way, procedures do not have to be rewritten if a global variable has its name changed and also helps avoid accidentally changing the wrong global variable. Refer to Chapter 15, "An Overview of the Paradox Application Language," for more information on procedure parameters.

When a non-closed procedure creates a variable, the variable is, by default, global. Global variables are not cleared when a procedure ends. Use the *PRIVATE* keyword to create variables that are private (local) to the procedure. When the procedure execution ends (either by reaching the ENDPROC or a RETURN command) all of the variables listed after the PRIVATE keyword are removed from memory. This is desirable, because it keeps more of the computer's memory available for data or variables in other procedures. It is good programming practice to ensure that as many as possible of the variables that a procedure uses are local. When you use the *PRIVATE* keyword, include the list of private variables as the *varlist3* parameter.

commands may be any number of PAL commands or expressions. The commands are executed until the flow of execution (as determined by various program control commands) reaches the ENDPROC or a RETURN command. Script execution resumes with the first command after the procedure was called. The procedure, and the entire script, also stops executing if an EXIT or QUIT command is encountered.

In addition to causing the procedure to stop executing and return control to the calling script or procedure, the RETURN command can be used to make the procedure return a value as if it were a function. The procedure can then be used in an expression, just like a PAL function. In this way, you can create your own specialized functions (often referred to as a user-defined function, abbreviated as UDF).

The ENDPROC keyword is required to indicate that the end of the procedure has been reached.

See also CREATELIB, EXECPROC, READLIB, RELEASE PROCS, RETURN, and WRITELIB.

Example

```
PROC Month_Rpt( print_table, month_name )
   months = "JanFebMarAprMayJunJulAugSepOctNovDec"
   monthno =(SEARCH(month_name, months)+2)/3
   REPORT print_table monthno
ENDPROC
?? "Type the table name: "
ACCEPT "A8" TO tablename
? "Type the three letter month abbreviation: "
ACCEPT "A3" TO monthname
Month_Rpt(tablename, monthname)
```

This example creates a procedure named Month_Rpt. The procedure takes two arguments: a table name (table_name) and a month name (month_name). The procedure first converts the month name (the three letter abbreviation of a month name) to a month number. Finally, the procedure executes the REPORT command to print a report by using the month number to select the appropriate report specification.

PROMPT   *Input/Output*

Syntax

> **PROMPT** *prompt*

> **PROMPT** *prompt1, prompt2*

Description

The first form of the PROMPT command displays a custom prompt in the global prompt line at the bottom of the workspace display. This form is for use with Standard (Version 4.0) mode. *prompt* is any PAL string expression.

The second form of the PROMPT command is for use in Compatibility (Version 3.0, 3.5) mode. *prompt1* and *prompt2* are PAL string expressions. The two strings are displayed in the top two lines of the Paradox workspace, the menu area. *prompt1* is displayed in the top line of the workspace and is displayed below *prompt1*, in the second line of the menu area.

For Standard or Compatibility mode, the PROMPT command issued alone, with no parameters, cancels all currently defined custom prompts and Paradox resumes control of the affected display areas.

The prompts generated by the PROMPT command are visible only if ECHO is set to NORMAL, FAST or SLOW.

See also the WAIT command.

PROTECT *Menu*

Syntax

> **PROTECT table1 password1**

Description

The PROTECT command is equivalent to the **T**ools **M**ore **P**rotect **P**assword **T**able menu command. Refer to Chapter 13, "Using Paradox Tools," for a discussion of this menu command. **table1** is the table to be protected. **password1** is the owner password for the table.

Example

> PROTECT "Customer" "Safest"

This example encrypts the Customer table and assigns Safest as the owner password.

PV( ) *Financial*

Syntax

> **PV(payment, interest, periods)**

Description

PV calculates the present value of a series of equal payments. **payment** is the periodic payment amount. **interest** is the interest rate expressed as a decimal. **periods** is the number of equal payments to be made.

The interest rate used must correspond to the period used. If the period calculated is monthly, the interest rate also must be monthly.

Example

```
RETURN PV(1000,.150,360)
```

This example displays the number 66353.24174122 on-screen.

QUERY   *Menu*

Syntax

QUERY queryimage ENDQUERY

Description

The QUERY command places a query on the workspace. The easiest and most foolproof way to build a QUERY command is through the **S**cripts **Q**uerySave menu command. Refer to the Chapter 4 section, "Saving a Query," for a description of how to use this menu option.

A query saved as a script can be modified with the Script Editor. You should not, however, try to edit a query saved with the **Q**uerySave option. The syntax of scripts created by the **Q**uerySave option is much different from that of other PAL commands. And Paradox doesn't help you with the construction of the query, as the program does when you build a query interactively in Main mode. Instead of using the Script Editor to correct a script saved with the **Q**uerySave option, you first should play the existing script and then modify the query, using the techniques described in Chapters 4 and 7. After the query produces the results you want, you should save it again by using **Q**uerySave with the same script name, thus replacing the old version. You then can use the **R**ead option in the Script Editor to add the corrected query to your program.

After you read the query into a script, you can add PAL variables in a query by preceding the variable name with a tilde (~). Such variables are then referred to as *tilde variables*. Variables also can be added while you are creating interactively. Because the underscore character is used in a query form to indicate an example, do not use variable names that contain the underscore character.

The QUERY command places the query image on the workspace, but does not execute the query itself. To execute the query, add the **DO_IT!** command immediately following the *ENDQUERY* keyword.

By default, Paradox sorts fields in a query according to the order set in the Custom Configuration Program. This order can be changed by using the SETQUERYORDER command. The current order that results is displayed in can be obtained by using the QUERYORDER function.

See also QUERYORDER, SETQUERYORDER, and SETRESTARTCOUNT.

Example

```
@ 0,0
CLEAR
?? "Type a customer ID number: "
ACCEPT "A4" TO custno
QUERY
Orders | Order # | Cust ID #      | Company Name | Date  |
       | Check   | Check ~custno  | Check        | Check |
       |         |                |              |       |
       |         |                |              |       |
ENDQUERY
DO_IT!
FIRSTSHOW
```

This example accepts a customer ID number to the tilde-variable custno. The QUERY command then displays a query image on the workspace with ~custno in the Cust ID # field. The **DO_IT!** command executes the query, and the FIRSTSHOW command ensures that the Answer table is displayed at the top of the screen.

QUERYORDER( )   System Status

Syntax

QUERYORDER( )

This function takes no arguments.

Description

QUERYORDER is used to find out the current sort order for fields in the answer table. The function returns the string TableOrder or ImageOrder, indicating the default order of fields in the Answer table. The default query order is set in the Custom Configuration Program, but can be changed by using the SETQUERYORDER command. In TableOrder the columns of the Answer table appear in the same order as the fields appear in the table structure. When query order is set to ImageOrder, the Answer table columns are arranged in the same order as columns in the query form, which may not be the same order as the table structure field order.

QUIT   *Program Control*

Syntax

> **QUIT** *message1*

Description

The QUIT command stops execution of the currently playing script and all higher level scripts that may have called the current script or procedure. Control is returned to Paradox, even if the script was initiated from the DOS command line.

The optional *message1* parameter displays a message in the message bar at the lower right corner of the screen.

If QUIT is not followed by the optional *message1* parameter, it must be the last command on the line to avoid a script error. QUIT may be followed by a comment.

Example

> QUIT "All Done!"

This example returns control to Paradox and displays the message All Done! in the lower right corner of the screen.

QUITLOOP   *Program Control*

Syntax

> **QUITLOOP**

Description

The QUITLOOP command jumps out of the current FOR, FOREACH, SCAN, or WHILE loop and executes the command following the ENDFOR, ENDFOREACH, ENDSCAN, or ENDWHILE command, without executing any more commands in the loop. A script error occurs if QUITLOOP is used outside of one of the loop structures listed above.

RAND( ) *Mathematical*

Syntax

RAND()

This function accepts no arguments.

Description

RAND returns a random number between 0 and 1.

Example

```
RETURN RAND( )
```

This example may display .9410375557813 one time, display .2225995804566 the next, and so on.

READLIB *Procedure*

Syntax

READLIB library1 *IMMEDIATE* **proclist1**

Description

The READLIB command loads into memory PAL procedures that are stored on disk in a PAL procedure library. The **library1** parameter contains the name of the procedure library. **proclist1** contains a comma-separated list of procedures from the library to be called at some time during the script.

By default, Paradox loads as many procedures from the library that can fit into available memory. Paradox swaps procedures in and out of memory as needed to maintain adequate memory to run the script.

The optional *IMMEDIATE* keyword causes the script to load all specified procedures into memory at once. A script error results when there remains insufficient memory to load all the requested procedures.

When loading closed procedures, using an autoloading library rather than the READLIB command usually is most efficient. To make one or more procedure libraries autoloading, insert the following command in the script at a point that precedes any calls to procedures contained in the library(s):

```
AutoLib = librarylist
```

Substitute the procedure library name(s) for **librarylist** (separate multiple names with commas, not spaces). Any subsequent procedure call causes Paradox to search the named library(s) for the called procedure and, when found, to load the procedure into memory.

The following AutoLib = librarylist command makes the libraries named OrdEntry and Inventory autoloading libraries:

AutoLib = "OrdEntry, Inventory"

Paradox cannot directly load procedures from libraries created with earlier versions. Use the FILEVERSION function to determine library versions, and use the CONVERTLIB command to convert the library to Version 4.0 format.

See also CREATELIB, INFOLIB, RELEASE PROCS, PROC, and WRITELIB.

Example

```
READLIB "OrdEntry" Month_Rpt, Roll_Back
```

This preceding example loads the procedures Month_Rpt and Roll_Back into memory from the READLIB library.

RECNO( )   *Workspace, Canvas*

Syntax

RECNO( )

This function accepts no arguments.

Description

RECNO reports the record number of the current record. A script error occurs if no images exist on the workspace or the image is not a display image.

In a multitable form, RECNO respects the limits of a restricted view. With linked detail tables, the function returns a record count including only the records in the view.

RECORDSTATUS( )　　　　*System Status*

Syntax

>   **RECORDSTATUS(status)**

Description

In CoEdit mode, RECORDSTATUS returns a logical value of True if the record's status matches the value of **status**. **status** must have one of the following values: New, Locked, Modified, or KeyViol.

Table 19.35 lists the values returned by the RECORDSTATUS function under various circumstances. Using RECORDSTATUS in any mode other than CoEdit results in a script error.

Table 19.35. Values Returned by RECORDSTATUS

Record Status	New	Locked	Modified	KeyViol
New, blank record	True	False	False	False
New record after input	True	False	True	False
New record key violation	True	True	True	True
Unchanged existing record	False	False	False	False
Unchanged locked existing record	False	True	False	False
Modified existing record	False	True	True	False
Modified existing record key violation	False	True	True	True

REFRESH *Multiuser, Keypress Interaction*

Syntax

REFRESH

Description

The REFRESH command updates the display images on the workspace to reflect all previous changes made by other users on a multiuser system. This command is equivalent to pressing Alt-R (Refresh Image). Refer to Chapter 6, "Getting Started with Scripts and Keyboard Macros," for a discussion of the Paradox auto refresh feature and the use of Alt-R (Refresh Image).

The Paradox canvases are not refreshed with this command; REFRESH applies only to the workspace. Your script must directly refresh images on the canvas.

REFRESHCONTROL   *Dialog Box*

Syntax

REFRESHCONTROL tagname

Description

This command refreshes the individual dialog box control element specified by **tagname**. Refer to Table 19.36 for a list of the valid values for **tagname** (listed in the Control column of the table), and the refresh action that takes place. REFRESHDIALOG must be called from a dialog procedure or from script instructions reached from a dialog procedure.

This command is useful, for example, if the directory for a file picklist is changed as part of the dialog action. Using a REFRESHCONTROL "PICKTABLE" command would cause the picklist to be regenerated with the new file path specification.

Using REFRESHCONTROL causes a RESYNCCONTROL to be executed, as well.

See also REFRESHDIALOG and SHOWDIALOG.

Table 19.36. REFRESHCONTROL Elements and Actions

Control tag	Action
ACCEPT	DataType element and values assigned with PICTURE updated
CHECKBOX	Check box elements specified by the TO variables are highlighted
LABEL	None
PICKARRAY	Regenerates pick list based on fixed array contents, highlights the list element most closely matching the TO variable
PICKDYNARRAY	Regenerates pick list based on dynamic array contents, highlights the list element most closely matching the TO variable
PICKDYNARRAYINDEX	Regenerates pick list based on dynamic array index names, highlights the list element most closely matching the TO variable
PICKFILE	Regenerates pick list based on the Path statement, highlights the list element most closely matching the TO variable
PICKTABLE	Regenerates pick list based on the Path statement, highlights the list element most closely matching the TO variable
PUSHBUTTON	None
RADIOBUTTON	Radio button element specified by the TO variable is highlighted
SLIDER	Updates MIN, MAX, ARROWSTEP, PAGESTEP values, places scroll box at location specified by the TO variable

REFRESHDIALOG   Dialog Box

Syntax

> **REFRESHDIALOG**

Description

> This command refreshes all of the control elements in a dialog
> box. REFRESHDIALOG has the same effect as issuing a
> REFRESHCONTROL command for every control element in the
> dialog box, followed by a REPAINTDIALOG. Refer to the descrip-
> tion of REFRESHCONTROL for a list of the control elements
> affected, and the action resulting from the refresh operation.
> REFRESHDIALOG must be called from a dialog procedure or
> from script instructions reached from a dialog procedure. A
> RESYNCDIALOG command automatically is issued each time
> REFRESHDIALOG is used.
>
> See also ACCEPTDIALOG, CANCELDIALOG, and SHOWDIALOG.

RELEASE   Procedure, Variable/Array

Syntax

> **RELEASE PROCS** *ALL* | *proclist1*
>
> **RELEASE VARS** *ALL* | *varlist1*

Description

> The RELEASE command clears procedures, global variables, and
> arrays from memory. For most situations—particularly with Para-
> dox Version 2.0 or greater—you do not need to explicitly release
> procedures from memory because of the automatic memory man-
> agement feature. You usually use this command when an applica-
> tion must run in Paradox Version 1.1, or at the start of a script to
> clear out any procedures that may remain in memory from previ-
> ous scripts.
>
> Using the *ALL* keyword with RELEASE PROCS clears from memory
> and undefines all procedures defined previously during the cur-
> rent session. Alternatively, you can cause the script to release
> specific procedures by listing them in the *proclist1* parameter.

RELEASE VARS ALL clears all variables and arrays from memory. To release specific variables or arrays, list them in the *varlist1* parameter instead of using the optional ALL keyword.

In Paradox 4.0, when the RELEASE VARS ALL command is used in a closed procedure, it frees any global variables that were listed with USEVARS. In previous versions of Paradox, if RELEASE was used in a closed procedure, the command cleared only variables, arrays, and procedures defined or called by the procedure itself.

Example

```
PROC CLOSED TestRelease()
USEVARS glbl1, glbl2
   x = 1
   y = 2
   z = "snore"
   glbl1 = "Test"
   glbl2 = 3
   RELEASE VARS ALL
ENDPROC
```

This example creates a closed procedure, called TestRelease, which uses two external variables, called glbl1 and glbl2. When the RELEASE command is executed, the local variables x, y, and z will be destroyed, and their memory returned to the central pool. The external variables glbl1 and glbl2 also will be destroyed and have their memory returned to the central pool.

RENAME   *Menu*

Syntax

> **RENAME table1 table2**

Description

The RENAME command changes the name of the table specified in the **table1** parameter to the name contained in the **table2** parameter. If **table1** does not exist, a script error is generated. This command is equivalent to the **T**ools **R**ename **T**able menu command. Refer to Chapter 13, "Using Paradox Tools," for a discussion of this menu command.

REPAINTDIALOG   *Dialog Box*

Syntax

REPAINTDIALOG

Description

This command redisplays the current dialog box, updating the results of changes (like canvas painting commands) that have occurred in the current SHOWDIALOG. This command should be called from a dialog procedure or from script instructions reached from a dialog procedure.

See also SHOWDIALOG, REFRESHDIALOG, and RESYNCDIALOG.

REPLACE   *Keypress Equivalent*

Syntax

REPLACE

Description

This command emulates pressing the Ctrl-A key combination. Selected text in the editor is replaced with a string that was specified previously by using the Editor Replace command or menu choice. If the current image is not an open editor session, the command is ignored. The REPLACE command is also ignored—no text is selected or no replacement string is specified.

REPLACEFIELDS   *Variable/Array*

Syntax

REPLACEFIELDS fld1 expr1, ..., fldN exprN

Description

Use this command to make several assignments to fields in a record at one time. This is faster than making several separate assignments. **fld1** is a valid field name in the current record. **expr1** is a valid PAL expression of the same type as the field named by **fld1**. The value of **expr1** is assigned to the field named by **fld1**. The remaining parameters for this command are similar pairs of field names and expressions: **fldN** and **exprN**.

The record must be in a table which is in both display and CoEdit mode; any other use of REPLACEFIELDS will result in a script error. Only one record at a time may be manipulated with REPLACEFIELDS.

If a key violation occurs when the modified record is posted at the completion of the REPLACEFIELDS command, the command terminates and the record is not posted.

REPLACEFIELDS sets the global variable RetVal True if it is successful, False if not.

REPLACENEXT　　　*Keypress Emulation*

Syntax

REPLACENEXT

Description

This command emulates pressing the Alt-A key combination. The previously established search and replace action is repeated.

The REPLACENEXT command is ignored if used when no editor session is active, or if no search or replacement strings are specified.

Use menu selection commands or the EDITOR REPLACE command to establish the search string and the replacement string.

REPORT　　　*Menu*

Syntax

REPORT table1 report1

Description

The REPORT command sends output to the printer using a report specification created in the Paradox Report Designer. This command is equivalent to the **R**eport **O**utput **P**rinter menu command. The **table1** parameter contains the name of the table whose data is to be printed. **report1** must evaluate to the name of the report specification (R or 1 through 14) you want the script to use in creating the printout. Refer to Chapter 5, "Getting Started with Reports," Chapter 10, "Using Tabular Reports," and Chapter 11, "Using Free-Form Reports," for discussions on creating and using report specifications created in the Report Designer.

The REPORT command is effective only from Main mode.

Example

```
PROC Month_Rpt( print_table, month_name )
    months = "JanFebMarAprMayJunJulAugSepOctNovDec"
    monthno =(SEARCH(month_name, months)+2)/3
    REPORT print_table monthno
ENDPROC
?? "Type the table name: "
ACCEPT "A8" TO tablename
? "Type the three letter month abbreviation: "
ACCEPT "A3" TO monthname
Month_Rpt(tablename, monthname)
```

This example creates a procedure named Month_Rept. The procedure takes two arguments: a table name (table_name) and a month name (month_name). The procedure first converts the month name (the three letter abbreviation of a month name) to a month number. Finally, the procedure executes the REPORT command to print a report using the month number to select the appropriate report specification.

REPORTTABLES   *Variable/Array*

Syntax

REPORTTABLES table1 report1 array1

Description

The REPORTTABLES command generates an array that contains the name or names of any lookup table(s) linked into a multitable report.

table1 contains the name of the master table for the report. **report1** contains the name of the report specification, and must be one of R or 1 through 14. The REPORTTABLES command creates and dimensions an array using the name specified in **array1**. The command places the names of all linked lookup tables into the elements of the specified array.

If the specified report is linked to no lookup tables, Paradox sets the system variable RetVal to the logical value False. When the report has one or more linked lookup tables, RetVal is assigned a value of True.

REQUIREDCHECK   *Workspace*

Syntax

> **REQUIREDCHECK** *ON* | *OFF*

Description

> The REQUIREDCHECK command turns off, or back on, the *required* validity check for the current workspace image. This command does not establish the *required* validity check, but can disable and enable the check. To establish the *required* validity check—to make a field a required field—use the ValCheck **D**efine **R**equired menu command (for more information about this menu command, see the related discussion in Chapter 9, "Using Power Entry and Editing Features").

RESET   *System Control*

Syntax

> **RESET**

Description

> The RESET command clears all images from the workspace and ensures that Paradox is in Main mode. This command often is used at the beginning of a script to make sure that the script starts in a known state. RESET also causes Paradox to write to disk all changed memory blocks, ensuring that changes to tables are not lost due to a power interruption (see also the SAVETABLES command).

> On a multiuser system, the RESET command also removes all locks that an application explicitly has set and clears private table names.

RESYNCCONTROL   *Dialog Box*

Syntax

> **RESYNCCONTROL tagname**

Description

> This command causes a dialog box control to be redisplayed, showing the actual value of its variable contents. **tagname** specifies the dialog control to be resynchronized. Refer to REFRESHCONTROL for a list of the valid values for the **tagname** and the actions accompanying it. RESYNCCONTROL must be called from a dialog procedure or from script instructions reached from a dialog procedure.

> As the user interacts with other controls in a dialog, or due to explicit changes made by your script, a dialog box control may have its description or settings changed. If, for example, a user uses one control in a dialog to change a directory path and another control in the same dialog contains a pick list of tables, then the pick list should be resynchronized.

> See also REFRESHCONTROL, REFRESHDIALOG, and SHOWDIALOG.

RESYNCDIALOG   *Dialog Box*

Syntax

> **RESYNCDIALOG**

Description

> This command is the same as issuing a RESYNCCONTROL command for every control element in the current dialog box, followed by a REPAINTDIALOG. Refer to REFRESHCONTROL for a list of control tags and the actions taken during the resynchronization. RESYNCDIALOG must be called from a dialog procedure or from script instructions reached from a dialog procedure.

> See also RESYNCCONTROL, REFRESHCONTROL, REFRESHDIALOG, and SHOWDIALOG.

RESYNCKEY — *Keypress Interaction*

Syntax

> **RESYNCKEY**

Description

> The RESYNCKEY command resynchronizes the master and detail records in a multitable form. This command is equivalent to the Ctrl-L (Resynchronize) keystroke.

> When the master-to-detail table relationship is many-to-one or many-to-many, the current master record does not own the detail record(s). Any change to the value in the link field(s) in the master record creates no corresponding change in the detail record(s). The master record and detail record(s) are out-of-sync. The screen no longer displays the correct detail record(s) for the displayed link field value. By moving the cursor to another master record, Paradox resynchronizes master and detail record(s). The RESYNCKEY command accomplishes the same goal without moving to another record.

RETRYPERIOD( ) — *System Status*

Syntax

> **RETRYPERIOD( )**

> This function accepts no arguments.

Description

> RETRYPERIOD returns the current retry period as set in the Custom Configuration Program or with the SETRETRYPERIOD command. The function returns an integer value that represents seconds. Valid retry periods are 0 to 30,000 seconds.

> The retry period is the number of seconds that Paradox continuously attempt to access a locked network resource. A retry period of 0 means that no further attempts are made for the object after the first attempt fails.

RETURN   *Program Control*

Syntax

> **RETURN** *expression1*

Description

> The RETURN command returns control from a script or procedure to the script, to the procedure that called it, or to Paradox if the current script is the top level script. The RETURN is not required in every script or procedure. Scripts and procedures always return to the calling script or procedure when they finish executing. The RETURN command provides a method to return to the calling routine before reaching the end of the called routine.
>
> The optional *expression1* parameter can be added to return a value to the calling script or procedure or to display the value as a message in the bottom right corner of the workspace.
>
> If the RETURN command is used to return from the top-level script, and the optional *expression1* parameter is used, the string equivalent of the parameter will be displayed in the message area at the bottom right corner of the screen. This is the same message area used by the MESSAGE command.

Example

```
PROC Nmonth( month_name )
    IF LEN(month_name) <> 3 THEN
       BEEP
       ? "Month name is too long or too short!"
       RETURN 0
    ENDIF
    months = "JanFebMarAprMayJunJulAugSepOctNovDec"
    monthno =(SEARCH(month_name,  months)+2)/3
    RETURN monthno
ENDPROC
? Nmonth( "Oct" )
```

> This example creates a procedure, Nmonth, that returns the month number (1 to 12) when passed the three-letter month abbreviation. The procedure first checks to determine whether the parameter passed is three characters long. If not, the procedure displays an error message and returns the value 0 to the calling script. If the parameter passed is three characters long, the procedure calculates the month number and passes the answer back to the calling script.

When the script calls the procedure with the value Oct, the procedure returns the number 10.

REVERSETAB   *Keypress Interaction*

Syntax

> **REVERSETAB**

Description

> The REVERSETAB command is equivalent to pressing Shift-Tab. The effect of this command depends on the Paradox mode and the context. Refer to the chapter that discusses the mode and context in which you plan to use the REVERSETAB command.

RIGHT   *Keypress Interaction*

Syntax

> **RIGHT**

Description

> The RIGHT command is equivalent to pressing the right-arrow key. The effect of this command depends on the Paradox mode and the context. Refer to the chapter that discusses the mode and context in which you plan to use the RIGHT command.

RMEMLEFT( )   *System Status*

Syntax

> **RMEMLEFT( )**
>
> This function accepts no arguments.

Description

> RMEMLEFT returns the amount of RAM, in bytes, which is available in the code pool. You can use this function to test if an application is violating the code pool.

The code pool is a reserved memory area in which Paradox programs are stored. The code pool consists of an upper and lower area. Applications that consume all memory in the central pool may extend into the code pool area. A low memory error occurs if your PAL script invades the code pool.

An application may use a portion of the upper code pool, although performance is degraded. If an application extends from the upper code area to the lower code area, Paradox displays a low memory error message. An application that uses a portion of the lower code pool may produce unpredictable results and eventually fail. If only the upper part of the code pool is being used, RMEMLEFT will clear the low memory error code, otherwise RMEMLEFT will set the low memory error code.

ROTATE   Workspace, Keypress Interaction

Syntax

> **ROTATE**

Description

The ROTATE command is equivalent to pressing Ctrl-R (Rotate), which rotates the fields to the right of the cursor in the current image. Refer to Chapter 3, "Entering, Editing, and Viewing Data," for a discussion of the Ctrl-R (Rotate) keystroke command.

ROUND( )   Mathematical

Syntax

> **ROUND(number1, precision1)**

Description

ROUND returns the value of **number1** rounded to the precision as indicated by **precision1**. **precision1** is an integer value between −15 and 15 inclusive. If **precision1** is positive, the rounding is performed to the right of the decimal point. If **precision1** is negative, the rounding is performed on the whole digits, or to the left of the decimal.

Example

```
RETURN ROUND(3.7653,0)
```

The preceding example displays the number 4.

```
RETURN ROUND(3.7653,3)
```

The preceding example displays the number 3.765.

```
RETURN ROUND(3765.3,-2)
```

The preceding example displays the number 3800.

ROW( )   *Workspace, Canvas*

Syntax

ROW

This function accepts no arguments.

Description

Use this function to obtain the current row position of the cursor relative to the current PAL canvas. The top edge of the canvas is represented by the number 0.

ROW cannot provide information about the cursor in the workspace area.

This function reports on only the current canvas. You must directly select the canvas using SETCANVAS or indirectly by using WINDOW CREATE. If you do not selected the canvas, PAL will report the cursor column for the full-screen canvas.

See also the ?? and TEXT commands.

ROWNO( )   *Workspace, Canvas*

Syntax

ROWNO( )

This function takes no arguments.

Description

Use ROWNO to determine the current row position in the current display or query image of the workspace. ROWNO pertains to the image and not to the window. A script error results if this function is used when no images are present in the workspace, or if used in any context other than Main, Edit, CoEdit, or in the Form Designer or Report Designer.

ROWNO returns the current line number of the cursor in Form Designer and Report Designer, and the Script Editor. A script error occurs if no images are present in the workspace.

RUN   *System Control*

Syntax

    RUN *BIG SLEEP number1 NOREFRESH NORESTORE NOSHELL doscommand1*

Description

The RUN command suspends Paradox and executes a DOS program or command. After executing the DOS command, the script returns to Paradox and executes the next PAL command.

By default, the RUN command provides approximately 200K of memory to the DOS command or program. Using the BIG keyword gives an additional 300K of available memory by swapping the entire Paradox environment out to disk (or swap device).

You can add the SLEEP keyword to insert a time delay between the completion of the DOS command and resumption of the PAL commands. The *number1* parameter is a numeric value that denotes the size of the delay in milliseconds (thousandths of a second).

When the DOS command or program being executed by the RUN command has no meaningful screen output, you can use the NOREFRESH command to keep the PAL canvas on-screen during execution of the RUN command.

Conversely, to keep the DOS screen output on-screen while the script executes the PAL commands, use the NORESTORE keyword.

By default, the RUN command loads a second copy of the DOS command interpreter, COMMAND.COM, before executing the specified DOS command or program. Beginning with Paradox 3.5, you can use the NOSHELL keyword to prevent Paradox from loading COMMAND.COM. This option provides more memory for the DOS program but is not capable of executing internal DOS commands (such as COPY or DIR) or batch files.

Refer to Chapter 13, "Using Paradox Tools," for more information about accessing the operating system.

SAVETABLES

Syntax

> **SAVETABLES**

Description

> The SAVETABLES command ensures that all changes to tables are written to disk.

SAVEVARS   *Variable/Array*

Syntax

> **SAVEVARS** *ALL | varlist*

Description

> The SAVEVARS command creates a script named *Savevars*, which saves the contents of specified variables and arrays. The Savevars script can be played later to restore the values of the named variables and arrays. The ALL keyword causes the command to save the value of all current variables and arrays. To specify particular variables and/or arrays, use the *varlist1* parameter.

SCAN   *Program Control*

Syntax

> **SCAN** *FOR condition1 commands1* **ENDSCAN**

Description

The SCAN command processes the records of the current image one-by-one, from top to bottom. Each PAL command in the optional *commands1* parameter executes for each record in the current image. By adding the FOR keyword, you can cause SCAN to process only records that meet the condition specified in the optional *condition1* parameter.

See also the discussions of the LOOP, QUITLOOP, and SKIP commands.

Example

```
CLEAR
VIEW "Employee"
SCAN
    ??
    FOR COUNTER FROM 1 TO 5
        ? [Emp First Name]+" "+[Emp Last Name]
        SKIP
    ENDFOR
    ?
    ? "Press Esc to Quit"
    ? "Press any other key to see five more names."
    pause = GETCHAR()
    IF pause = 27 THEN
        QUITLOOP
    ENDIF
    CLEAR
    @ 0,0
ENDSCAN
CLEARIMAGE
```

This example uses a SCAN to process all the records in the Employee table. The script displays five names from the table and then prompts the user to press Esc to quit or press any other key to see five more names. If the user presses Esc, the script uses the QUITLOOP command to break out of the SCAN loop.

SCROLLPRESS   *Keypress Interaction*

Syntax

SCROLLPRESS palkey

Description

This command simulates pressing the Scroll Lock key in combination with the specified direction key. For more information on this command, refer to Chapter 1, "Navigating Paradox," for more information. **palkey** must be one of the following PAL key code strings: Up, Down, Left, Right, CtrlRight, CtrLeft, CtrlPgDn, CtrlPgUp, PgUp, PgDn, Home, End.

SETBATCH   *Multiuser*

Syntax

SETBATCH ON | OFF

Description

Use this command to speed up operations on a network. SETBATCH holds the network lock file open, reducing the time required for file I/O and concurrency control by preventing other users from accessing the table. The ON keyword turns the SETBATCH lock on, and the OFF keyword removes the SETBATCH lock.

SETBATCH locks the file; if another user attempts to write to the table, or access the network lock file, that user's system will freeze until your application releases the lock file and table by using the SETBATCH OFF command. If your application ties up the lock file for too long, other users may receive time-out errors. For this reason, use the SETBATCH OFF command as soon as possible after issuing the SETBATCH ON.

SETBATCH affects the current table only. If the current table changes for any reason, the SETBATCH will be turned off automatically.

SDIR( )   *System Status*

Syntax

SDIR()

This function takes no arguments.

Description

SDIR returns the full DOS path name of the current script.

Example

Assume that the current directory is C:\USERS\DAVID\DBFILES. The following command displays the full directory name:

```
RETURN SDIR()
```

SEARCH( )   *String*

Syntax

SEARCH(substring, string)

Description

SEARCH returns the numeric starting position of **substring** within **string**. **substring** is the value for which to search and may not exceed 255 characters in length. **string** is the string you want Paradox to search and may be of any length.

If **substring** is not found, the SEARCH function returns 0. The SEARCH function is not sensitive to case.

Example

```
y = SEARCH( "grity", "Integrity" )
```

In this example, y = 5.

SEARCHFROM( )   *String*

Syntax

SEARCHFROM(substring, string, pos)

Description

SEARCHFROM returns the numeric starting position of **substring** within **string**, with the search beginning at **pos**. **substring** is the value for which to search and may not exceed 255 characters in length. **string** is the string you want Paradox to search and may be of any length. **pos** is a numeric value indicating the position in **string** at which the search should begin.

If **substring** is not found, the SEARCHFROM function returns 0. The SEARCHFROM function is not sensitive to case.

Example

```
source = "How now, brown cow?"
sample = "O"
y = SEARCH( sample, source )
WHILE y <> 0
   ? y
   y = SEARCHFROM( sample, source, y +1 )
ENDWHILE
```

This example prints the numbers 2, 6, 12, 17, each on a separate line.

SELECT   *Workspace*

Syntax

SELECT expression1

Description

The SELECT command simulates choosing an option from a Paradox menu. The **expression1** parameter contains the name of the menu option. The effect of a SELECT command is the same as including the specified menu option name in braces (refer to the "Keypress Interactions" section of Chapter 15, "An Overview of the Paradox Application Language"). Often, an abbreviated menu command also may be available. For example, the following script statements have identical effect:

```
SELECT "View" SELECT "Employee"
```

```
{VIEW}{Employee}
```

```
VIEW "Employee"
```

You occasionally must use the SELECT command rather than the equivalent keypress interaction command or abbreviated menu command; each menu choice can be a variable or calculated expression that gives added programming flexibility.

Using SELECT with the ZOOM command is especially helpful.

See also TYPEIN.

SELECTCONTROL   Dialog Box

Syntax

SELECTCONTROL tagname

Description

This command is used to select a control in the current dialog box. **tagname** evaluates to a legitimate control tag. SELECTCONTROL does not invoke the dialog procedure, nor does it produce ARRIVE, DEPART, or UPDATE event triggers. SELECTCONTROL must be called from a dialog procedure or from script instructions reached from a dialog procedure.

See also REFRESHCONTROL and SHOWDIALOG.

SETAUTOSAVE   System Control

Syntax

SETAUTOSAVE secs

Description

This command sets the number of seconds that Paradox waits before checking the internal memory buffers for changes. **secs** is an integer between 0 and 255 and represents the total number of seconds to wait.

When changes are made to Paradox tables, the copy of the table (or part of the table) stored in memory is changed, but the disk is not immediately updated. At regular intervals, Paradox checks to see if memory buffers have changed, and then updates the disk. The default autosave value when Paradox starts up is 0.

To determine the current autosave value, use the SYSINFO function and check the value of the resulting dynamic array element referenced by the AUTOSAVE index.

SETBW   System Control, Workspace

Syntax

SETBW

Description

This command forces Paradox to use the Black and White monitor palette. If the monitor type is CGA, EGA, or VGA, a grayscale shading is used. Otherwise, the monochrome palette is put to use. SETBW will clear settings made with the SETCOLORS command.

See also SYSINFO and SYSCOLOR.

SETCANVAS   *Window*

Syntax

SETCANVAS *DEFAULT* | *winhandle*

Description

Use SETCANVAS to establish the current canvas. **winhandle** is a variable containing a valid window handle number. Use the DEFAULT keyword instead to select the full-screen canvas.

Note that SETCANVAS selects the current canvas, but does not select the current window.

See also GETCANVAS, ?, ??, and @.

Example

See also GETCANVAS for an example using the SETCANVAS command.

SETCOLORS   *Window*

Syntax

SETCOLORS FROM arrayname

Description

The SETCOLORS command can be used to set the global color palette. **arrayname** is a dynamic array initialized to contain palette information. Refer to GETCOLORS and Appendix D, "PAL Color Palette Codes," for information on the dynamic array structure and the specific color attribute codes.

See also GETCOLORS and SYSCOLOR.

SETDIR   *Menu*

Syntax

> **SETDIR path1**

Description

The SETDIR command establishes a new Paradox working drive or directory. The **path1** parameter contains the DOS path for the new working drive or directory. This command is equivalent to the **Tools More Directory** menu command. Refer to the section "Changing the Working Directory" in Chapter 13, "Using Paradox Tools," for more information.

Like the equivalent menu command, the SETDIR command clears all temporary tables (such as the Answer or Changed tables) from memory. But unlike the **Tools More Directory** menu command, SETDIR does not ask for user confirmation before clearing memory.

Example

```
SETDIR "C:\\PDOX40\\P40DATA2"
```

This example changes the working directory to C:\PDOX40\P40DATA2. Notice that two backslash characters (\\) must be used to denote a single backslash in the path.

SETKEY   *System Control*

Syntax

> **SETKEY keycode1** *commands1*

Description

The SETKEY command creates a *keyboard macro*, which is a set of PAL commands assigned to a particular key or key combination. The **keycode1** parameter contains the PAL keycode, ASCII code, or extended code for the key or key combination you want to re-define. PAL keycodes, ASCII codes, and extended codes are listed in Appendix C, "PAL Keycodes and Extended Codes." Refer to the discussion in Chapter 6, "Getting Started with Scripts and Keyboard Macros," for more information about creating and using keyboard macros.

To cancel assignment of a keyboard macro, include the SETKEY command and appropriate PAL keycode, but without the *commands1* parameter.

Example

```
SETKEY 3 PLAY "Centry"
```

This example assigns the command PLAY "Centry" to the key combination Ctrl-C because the number 3 is the ASCII code for the key combination Ctrl-C.

SETKEYBOARDSTATE *Input/Output*

Syntax

> **SETKEYBOARDSTATE FROM arrayname**

Description

This command allows you change the condition of the on/off keys on the keyboard. **arrayname** is a dynamic array initialized with the indexes listed in table 19.37. The second column of the table describes the types of the dynamic array elements and the effect they will have. Each of the elements is a Logical type.

See also to GETKEYBOARDSTATE.

Table 19.37. SETKEYBOARDSTATE Dynamic Array Structure	
Index	**Element action**
CAPS LOCK	True sets CAPS LOCK on, False sets it to off.
NUM LOCK	True sets NUM LOCK on, False sets it to off.
SCROLL LOCK	True sets SCROLL LOCK on, False sets it to off.

SETMARGIN   Input/Output

Syntax

> **SETMARGIN** *OFF* | *margin1*

Description

> The SETMARGIN command sets the left margin for text displayed on the canvas using the ? command or the TEXT command. By default, the left margin is set to the left edge of the screen. The *margin1* parameter contains the margin setting. Include the *OFF* keyword to reset the left margin to the left edge of the screen. SETMARGIN also affects the margin for printer output with the PRINTER ON command.

> See also ?, ??, TEXT, WINDOW GETATTRIBUTES, and WINDOW SETATTRIBUTES.

SETMAXSIZE   System Control

Syntax

> **SETMAXSIZE size1**

Description

> The SETMAXSIZE command sets the maximum table size. The table size, in M (1,048,576 bytes), is specified in the **size1** parameter and can have a value of 64, 128, 192, or 256.

> By default, Paradox determines maximum table size by assigning the block size used to store data. Each table can contain a maximum of 64K blocks (K = 1,024) and Paradox stores data in 2K, 3K, or 4K blocks. The maximum table size, therefore, is 128M, 192M, or 256M, depending on which block size was chosen by Paradox. Changing the maximum size to 192 causes Paradox to save data in no smaller than 3K blocks; changing the maximum table size to 256 causes block size to become 4K.

> The SETMAXSIZE command affects tables created or restructured after the command is executed.

Example

```
SETMAXSIZE 192
```

This example sets the maximum table size to at least 192M. This command also causes Paradox to save data in at least 3K blocks.

SETNEGCOLOR   *Workspace*

Syntax

> **SETNEGCOLOR** *NUMERIC | CURRENCY | BOTH ON | OFF*

Description

The SETNEGCOLOR command turns on or off the use of color to highlight negative numeric and currency values on the Paradox workspace.

By default, Paradox displays negative numeric and currency values as white numbers on a red background (on a color monitor). You can change the color scheme through the Custom Configuration Program (see Appendix B, "Configuring Paradox"). You can use the SETNEGCOLOR command to turn off (or back on) this use of color for numeric values, currency values, or both.

Use *NUMERIC* to apply the SETNEGCOLOR command only to numeric data on the workspace. Use the *CURRENCY* keyword to cause the SETNEGCOLOR command to apply to only currency values. The *BOTH* keyword causes the command to apply to numeric values and to currency.

The *OFF* keyword turns off the use of color for negative values. The *ON* keyword turns use of color back on.

See also SYSCOLOR.

Example

```
SETNEGCOLOR BOTH OFF
```

This example turns off the use of color for negative currency values and also for negative numeric values.

SETPRINTER   *Input/Output*

Syntax

> **SETPRINTER port1**

Description

The SETPRINTER command determines the printer port to which print data is sent. The default port is LPT1. The **port1** parameter can have a value of LPT1, LPT2, LPT3, COM1, COM2, or AUX.

This command is equivalent to the **R**eport **S**etPrinter **O**verRide **P**rinterPort command, discussed in Chapter 10, "Using Tabular Reports."

Example

```
SETPRINTER "LPT2"
```

This example sets the printer port to LPT2.

SETPRIVDIR   *Menu, Multiuser*

Syntax

SETPRIVDIR path1

Description

The SETPRIVDIR command establishes a new Private directory for the current user on a multiuser system, for the current session. The **path1** parameter contains the DOS path for the new private directory.

This command is equivalent to the **T**ools **N**et **S**etPrivate menu command. Refer to the section "Assigning a Private Directory" in Chapter 13, "Using Paradox Tools," for more information.

Example

```
SETPRIVDIR "C:\\PDOX35\\P35DATA2"
```

This example changes the private directory to C:\PDOX35\P35DATA2. Notice that two backslash characters (\\) must be used to denote a single backslash in the path.

SETQUERYORDER   *Workspace*

Syntax

SETQUERYORDER *TABLEORDER* | *IMAGEORDER*

Description

The SETQUERYORDER command determines whether Paradox arranges the columns (fields) of Answer tables in table-structure order or in query-image order.

By default, Paradox arranges the columns in Answer tables in the order that the respective fields are listed in the table structure. You can use the Custom Configuration Program to change this setting so that Paradox displays the columns of query Answer tables in the same order as the columns in the query form. The SETQUERYORDER command overrides the current setting.

Use the *TABLEORDER* keyword to cause Answer table columns to be arranged in table-structure order. Use the *IMAGEORDER* keyword to cause table columns for Answer tables to be arranged in query-form order.

Refer to Chapters 4, "Getting Started with Query By Example," and Chapter 7, "Using Advanced Query By Example and Multiple Tables," for details on query by example and the significance of column order.

SETRECORDPOSITION   *Workspace*

Syntax

SETRECORDPOSITION recno1 row1

Description

The SETRECORDPOSITION command scrolls a multirecord form to a specified screen position. **recno1** is the record number of the record to be displayed. **row1** is the row in the multirecord form at which you want the specified record to be displayed.

Example

```
VIEW "Employee"
PICKFORM 4
MOVETO [Emp Last Name]
LOCATE "Jones"
SETRECORDPOSITION RECNO() 1
```

This example places the Employee table on the workspace in a multirecord form. The script moves to the Emp Last Name field and locates the first record for an employee with last name Jones. The SETRECORDPOSITION command then scrolls the records in the form to position the located record in the first row.

SETRESTARTCOUNT　　*Multiuser*

Syntax

SETRESTARTCOUNT *OFF* | *count1*

Description

The SETRESTARTCOUNT command determines the maximum number of times Paradox attempts to execute a query on a multiuser system before canceling the operation. The *count1* parameter contains the maximum number of attempts before Paradox cancels the query operation.

By default, when you are executing a query using shared tables, Paradox takes a snapshot of all tables required to process the query immediately before it executes the query. If another user modifies one of the tables as the snapshot is taken, Paradox abandons the snapshot and tries again. Paradox continually tries to take a snapshot of all tables required to process the query until successful.

Use the SETRESTARTCOUNT command to limit the number of times Paradox takes a snapshot. The default condition is OFF, meaning that Paradox will continue to try infinitely.

If the query does not succeed, Paradox sets the error code to 27.

See also the ERRORCODE command.

Example

```
SETRESTARTCOUNT 15
```

This example limits the number of attempts at successfully performing a snapshot to 15.

SETRETRYPERIOD　　*Multiuser*

Syntax

SETRETRYPERIOD period1

Description

The SETRETRYPERIOD command determines the amount of time, in seconds, that Paradox attempts to access a shared resource before canceling the operation.

When running a Paradox script on a multiuser system, your script may attempt to access a shared table or other shared resource while another user on the network has control of the resource. By default, Paradox displays an error message and aborts the attempted operation. The SETRETRYPERIOD causes Paradox to try continuously to access the blocked resource for the period of time specified in the **period1** parameter. **period1** must evaluate to a number between 0 and 30,000. This parameter represents seconds. When the retry period is set to 0, Paradox makes only the initial attempt to gain control of the resource and then cancels the operation.

See also the discussion of the RETRYPERIOD.

Example

```
SETRETRYPERIOD 90
```

This example sets the retry period to 90 seconds.

SETSWAP *Procedure*

Syntax

> **SETSWAP memory1**

Description

The SETSWAP command sets the minimum amount of memory that Paradox keeps free in the central memory pool, the so-called *swap point*. The **memory1** parameter is a number representing the number of bytes Paradox should keep free of PAL-related allocations. The free memory then can be used for Paradox tables, forms, reports, and so on. If loading another PAL procedure crosses the swap point, Paradox attempts to swap an unused procedure out of memory. Sometimes Paradox cannot swap out a sufficient number of procedures to maintain the required minimum amount of free central memory pool and cancels the running application. In such a case, you need to either redesign your application or set a lower swap point.

See also MEMLEFT and RMEMLEFT.

Example

```
SETSWAP 65536
```

This command sets the swap point to 64K (64 × 1,024).

SETUIMODE   *System Control*

Syntax

SETUIMODE *COMPATIBLE* | *STANDARD*

Description

This command enables your script to change the user interface mode. STANDARD mode is the Version 4.0 interface; COMPATIBLE mode corresponds to the user interface in Paradox 3.5. Do not change the user interface while tables on the workspace are in Edit or CoEdit mode. Changes to these tables is lost with the change in interface mode.

Most scripts written for Version 3.5 of Paradox will run successfully in Version 4.0. If the scripts contain canvas painting commands, or many menu/keypress commands, they should be run in compatibility mode. Add the command SETUIMODE COMPATIBLE to the very beginning of your Version 3.5 script and the command SETUIMODE STANDARD at the very end.

SETUSERNAME   *Menu, Multiuser*

Syntax

SETUSERNAME user1

Description

The SETUSERNAME command sets the user name for the current user on a multiuser system. This command is equivalent to the **Tools Net UserName** menu command. Refer to the section "Assigning a User Name" in Chapter 13, "Using Paradox Tools," for more information about this subject.

SHIFTPRESS   *Editor, Keypress Interaction*

Syntax

SHIFTPRESS palkey

Description

This command simulates pressing the Shift key in combination with the specified direction key. For more information on this command, refer to Chapter 1, "Navigating Paradox," for more information. **palkey** must be one of the following PAL key code strings: Up, Down, Left, Right, CtrlRight, CtrLeft, CtrlPgDn, CtrlPgUp, PgUp, PgDn, Home, End.

SHOWARRAY   *Input/Output*

Syntax

> **SHOWARRAY menu1 prompts1** *UNTIL keyslist1 KEYTO var1*
> *DEFAULT defchoice1* **TO var2**

Description

The SHOWARRAY command enables a script or procedure to construct a pick list style menu displayed inside a dialog box with "OK" and "Cancel" command buttons. The dialog box is placed in the center of the screen. The **menu1** parameter is an array that contains the names of the menu choices to appear in the pick list. The **prompts1** parameter is an array that contains descriptions to appear in the bottom line of the screen area, one for each menu option. The user selects a menu option by placing the highlight over the desired choice and pressing Enter or choosing "OK". The selection is assigned to the variable specified as the **var2** parameter.

The UNTIL keyword tells the script to recognize particular key presses in addition to the menu selections. Specify a list of PAL key codes (see Appendix C, "PAL Keycodes and Extended Codes") in the *keylist1* parameter. If you use the UNTIL keyword, you also can add the KEYTO keyword to cause the script to store any keypress in the variable specified as the *var1* parameter.

The DEFAULT keyword determines the menu option to be highlighted when the menu is initially displayed. The *defchoice1* parameter contains the menu name of the default menu option. If you don't include the DEFAULT keyword, the first menu option is highlighted as the default choice.

If the user selects a menu option pressing Enter or choosing "OK", Paradox stores the logical value True to the system variable RetVal and stores the name of the menu selection to the **var2** parameter. If the user presses Esc, or chooses "Cancel" instead of making a menu choice, Paradox removes the dialog box from the screen, sets **var2** equal to Esc and sets RetVal to False.

Example

```
ARRAY Menu1[4]
ARRAY Prompts1[4]
Menu1[1] = "Employee"
Menu1[2] = "Customer"
Menu1[3] = "Orders"
Menu1[4] = "Quit"
Prompts1[1] = "View the Employee table"
Prompts1[2] = "View the Customer table"
Prompts1[3] = "View the Orders table"
Prompts1[4] = "Return to Paradox"
WHILE (True)
    SHOWARRAY Menu1 Prompts1 TO choice1
    SWITCH
        CASE choice1 = "Employee":
            View "Employee"
        CASE choice1 = "Customer":
            View "Customer"
        CASE choice1 = "Orders":
            View "Orders"
        CASE choice1 = "Quit":
            QUITLOOP
        CASE choice1 = "Esc":
            QUITLOOP
    ENDSWITCH
    PROMPT "Press Esc to return to menu."
    WAIT TABLE UNTIL "Esc"
    CLEARIMAGE
ENDWHILE
```

This example uses the SHOWARRAY command to create a pick list menu inside a dialog box which displays the following four options:

```
Employee
Customer
Orders
Quit
```

If the user chooses one of the first three options, the script displays the appropriate table. If the user selects **Quit**, or presses Esc, or chooses "Cancel", the script terminates.

SHOWDIALOG   Dialog Box

Syntax

> **SHOWDIALOG title**
>   **PROC procname eventlist**
>   **@rownum,colnum HEIGHT hnum WIDTH wnum**
>   **CanvasItems**
>   **ControlItems**
> **ENDDIALOG**

Description

Use this command to create a dialog box in your application. You can create a dialog box with any combination of command button, radio button, or check box controls, as well as a variety of pick list types.

The dialog box definition begins with the keyword SHOWDIALOG. **title** may be any string expression and is displayed at the top of the dialog box's window frame as the dialog box's title. **rownum** and **colnum** are numeric expressions; combined with the @ symbol they specify the screen coordinates for the top left corner of the dialog box. The HEIGHT keyword is followed by a numeric expression (**hnum**) specifying the height of the dialog box in rows. The WIDTH keyword is followed by a numeric expression (**wnum**) specifying the width of the dialog box in columns.

If the optional keyword PROC is used, then the procname must be supplied. **procname** is the name of the procedure that is played after one of the trigger events in the **eventlist** occurs. **eventlist** is list of trigger events; if no **eventlist** is specified, all events except IDLE are assumed. The syntax for an **eventlist** uses any one or several of the following keywords and options, in any order:

```
ALL

MOUSE "ALL" | "UP" | "DOWN" | "MOVE" | "AUTO"

KEY "ALL" | keylist

MESSAGE "ALL" | "RESIZE" | "CLOSE" | "MAXIMIZE" | "NEXT" |
"MENUSELECT" | "MENUKEY"

TRIGGER "ALL" | "OPEN" | "ARRIVE" | "UPDATE" | "DEPART" |
"CLOSE" | "SELECT" | "ACCEPT" | "CANCEL"

IDLE
```

The dialog procedure must have four parameters. In order from left to right, the parameters represent the trigger type, a tag value, an event value, and a dialog element value.

For mouse, key, message, or idle events, the trigger type passed to the dialog procedure will be "EVENT". The tag value passed to the dialog procedure is the tag expression associated with the active control in the dialog. The event value passed to the dialog procedure is a dynamic array structured to contain event information like the dynamic array used by the GETEVENT command. The element value for this type of trigger type is a null string.

For the remaining triggers, the trigger type passed to the dialog procedure will correspond to the actual trigger: UPDATE, DEPART, SELECT, ACCEPT, CANCEL, ARRIVE, OPEN, or CLOSE. The tag value passed to the dialog procedure is the value of the tag expression associated with the active control element in the dialog. The event value and element value passed to the dialog procedure varies, depending on the type of the trigger event. If the trigger is UPDATE, the event value is the current value of the active control element variable associated with the control. If the control is a check box, the element value for the UPDATE trigger is the label string for the control; otherwise the element value is a null string. If the trigger is the DEPART trigger, the event value passed to the dialog procedure is the tag expression associated with the control, which will be moved to NEXT. The element value for the DEPART trigger is a null string. For the SELECT trigger, the event value is the current value of the variable associated with the active control. The element value for the SELECT trigger is a null string. For all remaining triggers, the event value is blank, and the element value is a null string.

Note that the event or trigger that initiates the dialog procedure will still be in the event queue when the dialog procedure returns. This event will be passed on to Paradox and processed normally. To prevent the event from being processed (denied), have the dialog procedure return a value of False. Refer to the RETURN command.

After specifying the optional dialog procedure, the position, height, and width of the dialog box, you can specify a series of CanvasItems. CanvasItems may be one, some, or none of the following keywords and their options: STYLE, STYLE ATTRIBUTE, @, ?, ??, FRAME, CLEAR EOL, CLEAR EOS, and PAINTCANVAS. Refer to each of these commands individually for information on what they do and what their required and optional parameters are. These canvas painting commands are used in the dialog box in the same way that they would be used for any other Paradox canvas.

ControlItems in the SHOWDIALOG syntax is a list of any one or several of the following control definitions. The controls may be defined in any combination. In the syntax shown below, **rownum** and **colnum** are numeric expressions that specify the row and column coordinates for the top left corner of the control item in the dialog box. The coordinates are window-relative. The HEIGHT keyword is followed by a numeric expression (**hnum**) to specify the height of the control in rows, and the WIDTH keyword is followed by another numeric expression (**wnum**) to specify the width of the control in columns. For pick lists, the optional COLUMNS keyword is followed by a numeric expression (**cnum**) to indicate the width of the picklist in columns.

```
PICKARRAY @rownum, colnum HEIGHT hnum WIDTH wnum COLUMNS cnum
    arrayname
    TAG TagExpression
    TO ControlVariable
```

The PICKARRAY element creates a pick list from the elements of a fixed array named by **arrayname**. When the dialog is accepted, the selected item in the pick list is returned in the variable specified by **ControlVariable**. The **TagExpression** is the tag that is passed to the dialog procedure.

```
PICKDYNARRAY @rownum, colnum HEIGHT hnum WIDTH wnum COLUMNS cnum
    arrayname
    TAG TagExpression
    TO ControlVariable
```

The PICKDYNARRAY element creates a pick list from the elements of the dynamic array named by **arrayname**. When the dialog is accepted, the selected item in the pick list is returned in the variable specified by **ControlVariable**. The **TagExpression** is the tag that is passed to the dialog procedure.

```
PICKDYNARRAYINDEX @rownum, colnum HEIGHT hnum WIDTH wnum COLUMNS cnum
    arrayname
    TAG TagExpression
    TO ControlVariable
```

The PICKDYNARRAYINDEX element creates a pick list from the index tags of the dynamic array named by **arrayname**. When the dialog is accepted, the selected item in the pick list is returned in the variable specified by **ControlVariable**. The **TagExpression** is the tag that is passed to the dialog procedure.

```
PICKFILE @rownum, colnum HEIGHT hnum WIDTH wnum COLUMNS cnum
   pathname
   NOEXT
   TAG TagExpression
   TO ControlVariable
```

The PICKFILE element creates a pick list from files in the directory specified by **pathname**. **pathname** is a string expression that evaluates to a legal DOS path specification. You may use the DOS wild cards "?" and "*" in the file specification as part of the path. (Refer to your DOS manual for more information about path names and file specifications.) When the dialog is accepted, the selected file in the pick list is returned in the variable specified by **ControlVariable**. The **TagExpression** is the tag that is passed to the dialog procedure. The optional NOEXT keyword causes the files in the pick list to be displayed without their extensions.

```
PICKTABLE @rownum, colnum HEIGHT hnum WIDTH wnum COLUMNS cnum
   pathname
   TAG TagExpression
   TO ControlVariable
```

The PICKTABLE element creates a pick list from tables in the directory specified by **pathname**. **pathname** is a string expression that evaluates to a legal DOS path specification. You may use the DOS wild cards "?" and "*" in the file specification part of the path. (Refer to your DOS manual for more information about path names and file specifications.) When the dialog is accepted, the selected table in the pick list is returned in the variable specified by **ControlVariable**. The **TagExpression** is the tag that is passed to the dialog procedure.

```
PUSHBUTTON @rownum, colnum WIDTH wnum
   labelname
   OK | CANCEL
   DEFAULT
   VALUE expression
   TAG TagExpression
   TO ControlVariable
```

The PUSHBUTTON element creates a push button in the dialog box. The **labelname** is a string expression that is used as the label for the push button. The optional OK and CANCEL keywords determine the action that the push button performs. OK accepts the dialog box, and CANCEL cancels the dialog box. The optional DEFAULT keyword indicates whether or not this push button is the default button activated when the user presses the Enter key.

Each dialog box may have only one DEFAULT push button. The VALUE keyword is followed by any valid PAL expression (expression). When the dialog is accepted, the result of the evaluating expression is returned in the variable specified by **ControlVariable** if the button was pressed. The **TagExpression** is the tag that is passed to the dialog procedure.

```
RADIOBUTTONS @rownum, colnum HEIGHT hnum WIDTH wnum
    labelname1, labelname2, ..., labelnameN
    TAG TagExpression
    TO ControlVariable
```

The RADIOBUTTONS element creates a bank of radio buttons in the dialog box. The **labelname1, labelname2, ..., labelnameN** is a comma-separated list of string expressions. Each string expression is used as the label for a distinct radio button in the bank of radio buttons. When the dialog is accepted, the ordinal value of the selected radio button is returned in the variable specified by **ControlVariable** (if the third radio button is selected, for example, the number 3 is returned). The **TagExpression** is the tag that is passed to the dialog procedure.

```
CHECKBOXES @rownum, colnum HEIGHT hnum WIDTH wnum
    TAG TagExpression
    label1 TO var1
    label2 TO var2
    ...
    labelN TO varN
```

The CHECKBOXES element creates a bank of check boxes in the dialog box. **label1** is a string expression used as the label for the first check box element. **var1** is the variable that will contain the result of the check box status for the check box designated **label1**. This scheme is repeated for **label2** and **var2**, and so on, for as many labels and variables as are needed. When the dialog is accepted, the variables associated with each check box element is set to True if the check box was marked, or False if the check box was not marked. The **TagExpression** is the tag that is passed to the dialog procedure.

```
ACCEPT @rownum, colnum WIDTH wnum
    typestring
    PICTURE picturestring
    MIN minvalue MAX maxvalue
    LOOKUP tname
    REQUIRED
    HIDDEN
    TAG TagExpression
    TO ControlVariable
```

The ACCEPT element creates a type-in control in the dialog box. **typestring** is a string expression that evaluates to a valid Paradox data type. Refer to the ACCEPT command for information on using the optional keywords PICTURE, MIN, MAX, LOOKUP, and REQUIRED. The HIDDEN keyword is unique to the use of ACCEPT in a dialog box. The HIDDEN keyword prevents the text that is typed in from being displayed, which is useful if the dialog box is used to obtain passwords. When the dialog is accepted, the text that was entered is returned in the variable specified by **ControlVariable**. The **TagExpression** is the tag that is passed to the dialog procedure.

```
SLIDER @rownum, colnum
    VERTICAL | HORIZONTAL
    LENGTH lnum
    MIN minvalue
    MAX maxvalue
    ARROWSTEP stepvalue
    PAGESTEP pagevalue
    TAG TagExpression
    TO ControlVariable
```

The SLIDER element creates scroll bar sliders for the dialog box. The VERTICAL or HORIZONTAL keywords indicate the orientation of the slider control. The LENGTH keyword is followed by a numeric expression (**lnum**) indicating how long the slider control is. If the slider is vertical, the length is measured in rows; if the slider is horizontal, the length is measured in columns. The MIN and MAX keywords, respectively, determine the minimum and maximum values that the slider control can have. The ARROWSTEP keyword uses the numeric expression following it to indicate the amount that the slider value changes when the scroll arrows are clicked. The PAGESTEP keyword uses the numeric expression following it to indicate the amount the slider value changes when the scroll bar is clicked. When the dialog box is accepted, the current value of the slider is returned in the variable specified by **ControlVariable**. The **TagExpression** is the tag that is passed to the dialog procedure.

```
LABEL @rownum, colnum
    labelname
    FOR TagExpression
```

The LABEL element creates a hot-key label for any dialog box control element. If the label is clicked, or the hot-key is pressed, the associated control element becomes the active control in the dialog box. The **labelname** is a string expression used as the text for the label. The **TagExpression** is a string expression that evaluates to the tag expression of the dialog box control for which the hot-key label is being created.

Example

Refer to the section "Working with Dialog Boxes" in Chapter 16 for an example of the SHOWDIALOG command.

SHOWFILES   Input/Output

Syntax

> **SHOWFILES** *NOEXT* **path1 prompt1** *UNTIL keylist1 KEYTO*
> *var1* **TO var2**

Description

The SHOWFILES command enables a script or procedure to construct a dialog box with a pick list of file names from a specified directory, with "OK" and "Cancel" buttons.

The **path1** parameter contains the name of the directory that contains the file names to be listed in the second line of the menu area. You can include DOS wild-card characters (? or *) in this parameter to limit the file names listed. Otherwise, Paradox assumes you want all file names listed. You can use the optional NOEXT keyword to suppress the display of file name extensions in the menu.

The **prompt1** parameter contains a string that appears as a prompt in the bottom line of the screen area.

When the user selects a file from the menu, the selection is assigned to the variable specified as the **var2** parameter.

If no files can be found in the specified directory that meet the specification in **path1**, Paradox assigns the value None to the variable named **var2**.

Use the UNTIL keyword when you want the script to recognize particular key presses, in addition to the menu selections. Specify a list of PAL key codes (see Appendix C, "PAL Keycodes and Extended Codes") in the *keylist1* parameter. If you use the *UNTIL* keyword, you also can add the KEYTO keyword to cause the script to store any keypress in the variable specified as the *var1* parameter.

If the user selects a menu option, or chooses "OK", Paradox stores the logical value True to the system variable RetVal and stores the name of the highlighted menu selection to the **var2** parameter. If the user presses Esc, or chooses "Cancel", instead of making a menu choice, Paradox removes the menu from the screen, sets **var2** equal to Esc and sets RetVal to False.

Example

```
WHILE (True)
   SHOWFILES NOEXT "c:\\p40data\\*.sc" "Script:" TO script1
   SWITCH
      CASE script1 = "None":
         BEEP
         RETURN "No scripts found"
         QUITLOOP
      CASE script1 = "Esc":
         QUITLOOP
   ENDSWITCH
   PLAY script1
   CLEARIMAGE
ENDWHILE
```

This example displays a list of scripts from the C:\P40DATA directory. After the user selects a file name, the selected script is displayed.

SHOWMENU   Input/Output

Syntax

> **SHOWMENU menulist1** *UNTIL keylist1 KEYTO var1 DEFAULT defchoice1* **TO var2**

Description

The SHOWMENU command enables a script or procedure to construct a pop-up style menu in the center of the screen.

The **menulist1** parameter contains a list of menu-prompt pairs. Each menu option name is listed first, followed by a colon and then the associated menu prompt. When the menu name is highlighted, the associated prompt displays in the bottom line of the screen area. When the user selects a menu option, the selection is assigned to the variable specified as the **var2** parameter.

Use the UNTIL keyword to tell the script to recognize particular key presses, in addition to the menu selections. Specify a list of PAL key codes (see Appendix C) in the *keylist1* parameter. If you use the UNTIL keyword, you also can add the KEYTO keyword to cause the script to store any keypress in the variable specified as the *var1* parameter.

The DEFAULT keyword determines the menu option to be highlighted when the menu is initially displayed. The *defchoice1* parameter contains the menu name of the default menu option. If you don't include the DEFAULT keyword, the first menu option is highlighted as the default choice.

If the user selects a menu option, Paradox stores the logical value True to the system variable RetVal and stores the name of the menu selection to the **var2** parameter. If the user presses Esc instead of a menu choice, Paradox removes the menu from the screen, sets **var2** equal to Esc, and sets RetVal to False.

Example

```
SHOWMENU
    "Benefits": "Add, change, display, print benefit info",
    "Employee": "Add, change, display, print employee info",
    "Salary": "Add, change, display, print salary info",
    "Leave": "Leave the application"
TO response
SWITCH
    CASE response = "Benefits":
        PLAY "Exben"
    CASE response = "Employee":
        PLAY "Exemp"
    CASE response = "Salary":
        PLAY "Exsal"
    CASE response = "Leave":
        QUIT
ENDSWITCH
```

This example displays a pop-up menu at the center of the screen with the choices **B**enefits, **E**mployee, **S**alary, and **L**eave. If the user selects **B**enefits, Paradox plays the Exben script. If the user selects **E**mployee, Paradox plays the Exemp script, and so on. The last menu option, **L**eave, causes the script to QUIT, which stops execution of the script and returns the user to Paradox.

SHOWPOPUP   Input/Output

Syntax

> **SHOWPOPUP title** *CENTERED* | *@rownum,colnum*
> **menuitem1,**
> **menuitem2,**
> **...,**
> **menuitemN**
> **ENDMENU** *UNTIL keylist KEYTO var1* **TO selvar**

A **menuitem** is a statement using one of the following three syntax options:

1. **choice : description :** *DISABLE* **tagname**

2. **choice : description :** *DISABLE* **tagname**

> **SUBMENU**
> **menuitem1,**
> **menuitem2,**
> **...,**
> **menuitemN**
> **ENDSUBMENU**

3. **SEPARATOR**

Description

Use this command to create a pop-up menu. **title** is any valid string expression. **title** is displayed on the top of the window frame containing the pop-up menu.

The optional keyword CENTERED places the menu at the center of the screen. To place the menu at a specific location, use the @ symbol instead. When the @ symbol is used, **rownum** and **colnum** are numeric expressions specifying the row and column coordinates of the menu. The top left corner of the pop-up menu is placed at the specified coordinates.

Following the placement options, a comma-separated list of menu choices is listed. Each **menuitem** must use one of the three syntax forms shown above. The **menuitem** syntax is described after the ENDMENU keyword.

The ENDMENU keyword indicates the end of the pop-up menu definition. The optional keyword UNTIL enables the user to exit from the menu by using a keystroke that does not result in a menu selection. The keylist is a list of Paradox keystroke values, such as "F2", "F9", "Esc", and so on. To record the keystroke that ended the pop-up menu interaction when the UNTIL keyword was used, add the optional KEYTO keyword. The KEYTO option stores the keystroke value in the PAL variable specified by var1.

selvar is any valid PAL variable and is used to return the menu choice made by the user. The value placed in **selvar** is the same as the tagname specified for each menu choice. Refer to the descriptions of the menuitem syntax below.

The first form for a menuitem consists of a string expression (**choice**) that gives the name of the menu selection, followed by a colon, followed by another string expression (**description**). The description string is displayed in the bottom line of the screen. The description string is followed by another colon. Now the optional keyword DISABLE can be used. When the menu is initially displayed, the DISABLE keyword disables the menu selection being defined. Finally, a tagname is supplied. **tagname** is any valid string expression. The tagname string expression corresponding to the user's selection is returned in the variable indicated by **selvar**.

The second form for a menuitem defines a menu selection that leads to a submenu. The first part of the submenu definition is the same as the first form for a menuitem. **choice**, **description**, and DISABLE are all used the same. In the case of a submenu definition, the tagname is optional. The major difference from the first syntax form begins with the use of the keyword SUBMENU. After SUBMENU, another comma-separated list of menuitem definitions appears. These menuitem definitions follow the same three syntax rules and define the menu choices on the submenu. Submenus may be nested up to 50 levels. The submenu definition is ended with the ENDSUBMENU keyword.

The third form of the menuitem syntax consists of the single keyword SEPARATOR. This option places a single horizontal bar on the pop-up menu. Use this bar to group related items on the menu. The SEPARATOR does not produce a selectable menu item.

See also MENUENABLE, MENUDISABLE.

Example

Refer to the section of Chapter 16 titled "Creating Menus" for an example of the SHOWPOPUP command.

SHOWPULLDOWN   *Input/Output*

Syntax

> **SHOWPULLDOWN**
> > **menuitem1,**
> > **menuitem2,**
> > **...,**
> > **menuitemN**
> **ENDMENU** *UNTIL keylist*

A menuitem is a statement using one of the following three syntax options:

1. **choice : description :** *DISABLE* **tagname**

2. **choice : description :** *DISABLE tagname*

   > **SUBMENU**
   > > **menuitem1,**
   > > **menuitem2,**
   > > **...,**
   > > **menuitemN**
   > **ENDSUBMENU**

3. **SEPARATOR**

Description

Use this command to create a menu bar with pull-down menus. The menu bar created with the SHOWPULLDOWN menu covers the Paradox Main Menu. Like the Paradox Main Menu, menus created with the SHOWPULLDOWN command are always present, even if they are not active. When the user presses the F10 key or clicks on the menu bar with the mouse, the menu is activated. The menu also is activated if the GETMENUSELECTION command is issued by your script. When the user makes a selection, a MENUSELECT message event is generated. Refer to GETEVENT for more information on this event type.

Following the SHOWPULLDOWN keyword, a comma-separated list of menu choices is listed. Each menuitem must use one of the three syntax forms shown above. The menuitem syntax is described after the ENDMENU keyword.

The ENDMENU keyword indicates the end of the pull-down menu definition. The optional keyword UNTIL enables the user to exit from the menu by using a keystroke that does not result in a menu selection. The keylist is a list of Paradox keystroke values, such as "F2", "F9", "Esc", and so on.

The first form for a menuitem consists of a string expression (**choice**) which gives the name of the menu selection, followed by a colon, followed by another string expression (**description**). The description string is displayed in the bottom line of the screen. The description string is followed by another colon. Now the optional keyword DISABLE can be used. When the menu is initially displayed, the DISABLE keyword disables the menu selection being defined. Finally, a tagname is supplied. **tagname** is any valid string expression. The tagname string expression corresponding to the user's selection is returned as part of the message event generated when the selection is made.

The second form for a menuitem defines a menu selection that leads to a submenu. The first part of the submenu definition is the same as the first form for a menuitem. **choice**, **description**, and DISABLE, are all used the same. In the case of a submenu definition, the tagname is optional. The major difference from the first syntax form begins with the use of the keyword SUBMENU. After SUBMENU, another comma-separated list of menuitem definitions appears. These menuitem definitions follow the same three syntax rules and define the menu choices on the submenu. Submenus may be nested up to 50 levels. The submenu definition is ended with the ENDSUBMENU keyword.

The third form of the menuitem syntax consists of the single keyword SEPARATOR. This option places a single horizontal bar on the pull-down menu. Use this bar to group related items on the menu. The SEPARATOR does not produce a selectable menu item.

See also GETMENUSELECTION, GETEVENT, MENUENABLE, and MENUDISABLE.

Example

Refer to the section of Chapter 16 titled "Creating Menus" for an example of the SHOWPULLDOWN command.

SHOWTABLES   *Input/Output*

Syntax

> **SHOWTABLES path1 prompt1** *UNTIL keylist1 KEYTO var1*
> **TO var2**

Description

The SHOWTABLES command enables a script or procedure to construct a dialog box containing a pick list of table names from a specified directory, and "OK" and "Cancel" buttons.

The **path1** parameter contains the name of the directory that contains the table names to be listed in the second line of the menu area. You can include DOS wild-card characters (? or *) in this parameter to limit the names listed; otherwise, Paradox assumes that you want all table names listed.

The **prompt1** parameter contains a string that appears as a prompt in the bottom line of the screen area.

When the user selects a table from the menu, the selection is assigned to the **var2** parameter.

If no table names can be found in the specified directory that meet the specification in **path1**, Paradox assigns the value None to **var2**.

Use the UNTIL keyword when you want the script to recognize particular key presses, in addition to the menu selections. Specify a list of PAL key codes (see Appendix C, "PAL Keycodes and Extended Codes") in the *keylist1* parameter. If you use the UNTIL keyword, you can add the KEYTO keyword to cause the script to store any keypress in the *var1* parameter.

If the user selects a menu option, or chooses "OK", Paradox stores the logical value True to the system variable RetVal and stores the name of the highlighted menu selection to **var2**. If the user presses Esc or chooses "Cancel" instead of making a menu choice, Paradox removes the menu from the screen, sets **var2** equal to Esc, and sets RetVal to False.

Example

```
WHILE (True)
   SHOWTABLES "c:\\p40data\\" "Table:" to table1
   SWITCH
      CASE table1 = "None":
         BEEP
         RETURN "No tables found"
         QUITLOOP
      CASE table1 = "Esc":
         QUITLOOP
   ENDSWITCH
   VIEW table1
```

```
        PROMPT "Press F2 to return to menu, Esc to Quit"
        WAIT TABLE UNTIL "F2"
        CLEARIMAGE
    ENDWHILE
```

This example displays a list of tables from the C:\P40DATA directory. After the user selects a file name, the script displays the table on the workspace in Main mode.

SIN( )   *Mathematical*

Syntax

> **SIN(number)**

Description

> SIN returns the sine of an angle. The sine is between –1 and 1. **number** represents an angle in radians. ASIN is the inverse function.

Example

> ```
> RETURN SIN(.5)
> ```

This example displays the number `.4794255386042`.

SKIP   *Workspace*

Syntax

> **SKIP** *increment1*

Description

> The SKIP command moves the cursor up or down a specified number of records on a display image in the workspace. The optional *increment1* parameter contains the number of records to move. If *increment1* is positive, the cursor moves down the number of records indicated. If the number is negative, the cursor moves upward. By default, the SKIP command moves the cursor forward (down) one record.

In a detail (linked) table on a multitable form, SKIP can move only within the linked records shown on the form (the *restricted view*).

If you don't use the *increment1* parameter in a particular SKIP command, you cannot follow this command with any other PAL command on the same line.

Example

```
CLEAR
VIEW "Employee"
SCAN
    FOR COUNTER FROM 1 TO 5
        ? [Emp First Name]+" "+[Emp Last Name]
        SKIP
    ENDFOR
    ?
    ? "Press Esc to Quit"
    ? "Press any other key to see five more names."
    pause = GETCHAR()
    IF pause = 27 THEN
        QUITLOOP
    ENDIF
    CLEAR
    @ 0,0
ENDSCAN
CLEARIMAGE
```

This example uses the SKIP command in a FOR loop to display five names from the Employee table.

SLEEP   *System Control*

Syntax

SLEEP period1

Description

The SLEEP command inserts a time delay in the script. The **period1** parameter is an integer value that denotes the size of the delay in milliseconds (thousandths of a second). The delay can be from 0 to 30,000 milliseconds (which is 30 seconds). The SLEEP command frequently is used to give the user sufficient time to read a message on-screen before the script continues with the next step.

SORT   *Menu*

Syntax

> **SORT table1** *ON fieldlist1 D TO table2*

Description

The SORT command sorts a specified table. This command is equivalent to the **M**odify **S**ort menu command. Refer to the "Sorting Tables" section in Chapter 9, "Using Power Entry and Editing Features," for more information about this menu command.

The **table1** parameter contains the name of the table to be sorted. By default, Paradox sorts the table in ascending order on each field in the table, moving from left to right in the table structure. By including the ON keyword, you can specify a different sort order. Include in the *fieldlist1* parameter a list of fields from **table1**. List the fields in the order of sorting priority. Paradox sorts first on the first field listed in *fieldlist1* and then settles ties based on the values in the second field listed in *fieldlist1*. All remaining ties are settled by the third field, and so on.

The optional D keyword, placed after a field name in the *fieldlist1* parameter, causes sorting to be in descending order, rather than the default ascending order.

By default, when **table1** is not keyed, the sorted output of the SORT command replaces the original **table1**. If **table1** is a keyed table, however, you must include the TO keyword and also a destination table name—the *table2* parameter.

SORT does not warn the user before an existing table is replaced. You usually should add commands to your scripts, such as the ISTABLE function, to determine whether a table already exists by a particular name before doing a sort to this table.

Example

```
SORT "Employee" ON "Emp Last Name", "Emp First Name" TO
"Empsort"
```

This example sorts the Employee table on the Emp Last Name and Emp First Name fields. The command places the resulting table into the new table named Empsort.

SORTORDER( )   System Status

Syntax

SORTORDER( )

This function accepts no arguments.

Description

SORTORDER returns the current setting for sort order. SORTORDER manages the order in which Paradox data is sorted by altering the collating sequence. In the United States, ASCII is the default sort order. Possible sort orders include the following: Ascii, Intl, Nordan (Versions 3.5 and earlier), Nordan4 (Version 4.0), and Swedfin.

The sort order setting is stored in the PARADOX.SOR file. To change the sort order, copy a new sort-order file from the Installation/Sample Tables distribution disk (such as INTL.SOR or NORDAN.SOR). Delete PARADOX.SOR and rename the new sort-order file to PARADOX.SOR. You then must restructure *all* of your tables. Be sure to restructure detail tables in one-to-many relationships before restructuring the master table, or the links between tables will be lost.

SOUND   Input/Output

Syntax

SOUND frequency duration

Description

This command causes the IBM sound chip to generate a tone at the given frequency for a given number of milliseconds. **frequency** is the frequency of the sound in Hertz, and **duration** is the time the sound is played measured in milliseconds.

See also BEEP.

SPACES( )   *String*

Syntax

> **SPACES(x)**

Description

> SPACES inserts **x** number of spaces in a string.

Example

> MESSAGE "Summer" + SPACES(10) + "time"

> This example displays the following line on-screen:

> Summer   time

SQRT( )   *Mathematical*

Syntax

> **SQRT(number)**

Description

> SQRT returns the square root of **number**. **number** must represent
> a positive value. A script error occurs if **number** is less than zero.

Example

> RETURN SQRT(81)

> This example displays 9.

STRVAL( )   *Date and String*

Syntax

> **STRVAL(expression)**

Description

> This function converts numeric values, date values, and logical
> values to string values. **expression** is any valid PAL expression.

STRVAL evaluates the expression and returns the resulting value as a string. STRVAL uses the current interactive date format for date values.

See also DATEVAL and NUMVAL.

STYLE   Input/Output

Syntax

> **STYLE** *monolist1*
>
> **STYLE ATTRIBUTE** *number1*

Description

The STYLE command adds color and other screen display attributes to text displayed with the ?, ??, and TEXT commands. STYLE applies to text placed on the canvas after the command is executed.

The optional *monolist1* parameter is a comma-separated list of one or more of the following options:

BLINK	Screen area blinks continuously
INTENSE	Foreground characters display in high-intensity video
REVERSE	Characters display in inverse video

The ATTRIBUTE keyword sets colors or monochrome-character-display attributes on the canvas. The *number1* parameter must evaluate to an integer between 0 and 255. Compute the value for *number1* from the attribute codes listed in the tables in Appendix D, "PAL Color Palette Codes." For a color screen, the *number1* parameter is the sum of the foreground color and the background color numbers. To create blinking text, add 128 to the color or monochrome attribute numbers.

To revert all text attributes and colors back to the normal settings, issue the STYLE command with no keyword or parameter.

See also PAINTCANVAS, WINDOW GETATTRIBUTES, and WINDOW SETATTRIBUTES.

SUBSTR( )   *String*

Syntax

> **SUBSTRING(string, start, length)**

Description

> SUBSTRING extracts a subset of **string**. **string** indicates the string to be searched. **start** indicates the position of the extract, and **length** denotes the length of the string to be returned.
>
> See also MATCH and SEARCH.

Example

```
MESSAGE SUBSTRING("Goodnite", 1, 4) + " " + SUBSTRING("Commander", 1, 7)
```

> This function displays the following line:

```
Good Command
```

SUBTRACT   *Menu*

Syntax

> **SUBTRACT table1 table2**

Description

> The SUBTRACT command subtracts the records of one table from those of another table. This command is equivalent to the **T**ools **M**ore **S**ubtract menu command. Refer to the "Subtracting Tables" section in Chapter 13, "Using Paradox Tools," for a discussion of this menu command.
>
> The **table1** parameter is the name of the table that contains the records to be deleted. **table2** is the target parameter. The SUBTRACT command does not ask for confirmation before deleting the matching records.

SWITCH   *Program Control*

Syntax

> **SWITCH**
> > **caselist1**
> > **OTHERWISE: commands1**
> **ENDSWITCH**

Each entry in caselist1 has the following form:

> **CASE condition1 : commands2**

Description

The SWITCH command operates like multiple independent IF statements but is a more compact structure when many decisions must be made. You use the SWITCH command with multiple CASE statements, where each CASE statement tests for the occurrence of a different condition. You can use the optional OTHERWISE statement to specify what command(s) should be executed if none of the CASE conditions are met. SWITCH often is combined with SHOWMENU, SHOWPOPUP, or SHOWPULLDOWN to enable the user to control the sequence of script execution interactively. Any number of PAL statements are represented by commands1 and commands2.

Example

```
SHOWMENU
    "Benefits": "Add, change, display, print benefit info",
    "Employee": "Add, change, display, print employee info",
    "Salary": "Add, change, display, print salary info",
    "Leave": "Leave the application"
TO response
SWITCH
    CASE response = "Benefits":
        PLAY "Exben"
    CASE response = "Employee":
        PLAY "Exemp"
    CASE response = "Salary":
        PLAY "Exsal"
    CASE response = "Leave":
        QUIT
ENDSWITCH
```

This example displays at the center of the screen a pop-up menu using the SHOWMENU command. The script then uses the SWITCH command to test the user's response to the menu. If the user selects Employee, Paradox plays the Exemp script, and so on. The last menu option, **Leave**, causes the script to QUIT, which stops execution of the script and returns the user to Paradox.

SYNCCURSOR   Workspace

Syntax

> **SYNCCURSOR**

Description

The SYNCCURSOR command synchronizes the cursor on the current canvas with the cursor position on an associated object. If the current canvas is the full screen, the cursor is positioned at the same place as the workspace cursor. If the current canvas is an image window, the cursor is placed to correspond with the image cursor. If the current window is a canvas window, the cursor is positioned at row 0 and column 0 of the window.

SYSCOLOR( )   System Status

Syntax

> **SYSCOLOR(element)**

Description

SYSCOLOR returns a screen element's color attribute. **element** is an integer between 0 and 31 or between 1,000 and 1,071 that represents a Paradox screen element. Refer to Appendix D, "PAL Color Palette Codes," for information regarding the various color codes.

Example

```
RETURN SYSCOLOR(8)
```

This example returns the color attribute for the workspace area.

SYSINFO   System Control

Syntax

SYSINFO TO dynarray

Description

Use this command to obtain information about the system on which Paradox is running. **dynarray** is any valid name for a dynamic array. If dynarray does not exist, it will be created. If dynarray already exists, it will be redefined. Table 19.38 lists the indexes of the dynamic array created by SYSINFO.

Table 19.38. SYSINFO Dynamic Array Structure

Index	Element meaning
BUILD	A string indicating the current build of Paradox
EXPANDED	Amount of currently available expanded memory
EXTENDED	Amount of currently available extended memory
LANGUAGE	Three-digit string indicating the language that DOS is using
MOUSE	True if a mouse is present, False otherwise
PROTECTED	True if running in protected mode, False otherwise
SCREENHEIGHT	Number of physical vertical rows on display screen
SCREENWIDTH	Number of physical horizontal columns on-screen
UIMODE	A string value: "COMPATIBLE" if user interface is in compatibility mode, "STANDARD" otherwise

SYSMODE( ) *System Status, Workspace, Canvas*

Syntax

SYSMODE( )

This function takes no arguments.

Description

SYSMODE reports the current Paradox mode by returning a string containing the description of the mode. Paradox modes include the following: Main, CoEdit, Create, Form, DataEntry, Edit, File Editor, Graph, Index, Password, Preview, Report, Restructure, Script, and Sort.

See also CANCELEDIT, RESET, IMAGENO, IMAGETYPE, ISFORMVIEW, ISINSERTMODE, and NIMAGES.

Example

```
IF SYSMODE() <> "CoEdit" THEN
    COEDITKEY
ENDIF
```

This example executes the COEDITKEY command that switches to CoEdit mode, but only if Paradox is not already in CoEdit mode.

TAB *Keypress Interaction*

Syntax

TAB

Description

Using the TAB command is the same as pressing Tab. The effect of this command depends on the Paradox mode and the context in which it is used. Refer to the chapter that discusses the mode and context in which you intend to use the TAB command.

TABLE( )   *Workspace, Canvas*

Syntax

> **TABLE( )**

This function takes no arguments.

Description

TABLE returns the name of the current table. The image can be a table in form view or table view, or a query image. A script error occurs if no tables exist on the workspace.

Example

```
View "Customer"
RETURN Table()
```

This example displays the string Customer in the message area at the lower right side of the screen.

TABLERIGHTS( )   *Information*

Syntax

> **TABLERIGHTS(tablename, rights)**

Description

TABLERIGHTS returns a logical value of True if the user has table rights to a shared table, as expressed in **rights**. **tablename** is the table to be checked. **rights** contains the level of rights for which to test. Valid entries for the **rights** parameter are as follows: ReadOnly, Update, Entry, InsDel, and All.

TABLERIGHTS returns False if the user does not have the rights requested.

TAN( )   *Mathematical*

Syntax

> **TAN(number)**

Description

TAN returns the tangent of an angle. The angle is expressed in radians and is represented by **number**, a value in radians.

Example

```
RETURN TAN(333)
```

This example displays the number $-.008821509334$.

TEXT   *Input/Output*

Syntax

TEXT text1 ENDTEXT

Description

The TEXT command displays on the current canvas text that is specified in the **text1** parameter. Paradox begins displaying the specified text at the current cursor position on the current canvas.

The TEXT command and the keyword ENDTEXT each must be on a line by themselves (comment lines preceded by a semicolon are permitted). All characters, including blanks, between the TEXT and ENDTEXT commands are displayed on the canvas literally. Quotation marks should not be included unless you also want them to display.

You can use the STYLE command to control color and display attributes.

You should keep the number of lines displayed by TEXT less than the height of the canvas because when the display reaches the bottom, text is wrapped to the top of the display and the new lines will display over lines previously placed.

This command writes to the current canvas. You must directly select the canvas using SETCANVAS or indirectly by using WINDOW CREATE. If you do not select the canvas, PAL makes the cursor movement and is displayed on the full-screen canvas.

See also the ? and ?? commands.

Example

```
TEXT
```

The TEXT command is the most convenient command for displaying multiple lines of text on the canvas.

```
ENDTEXT
SLEEP 3000
```

This example displays on the current canvas, beginning at the cursor, a blank line, two lines of text, and another blank line.

TICKS( )   *Time*

Syntax

TICKS( )

This function takes no arguments.

Description

TICKS returns the time since midnight, measured in milliseconds. The time is obtained from the system clock.

See also the TIME and TODAY functions.

TIME( )   *Date*

Syntax

TIME( )

This function accepts no arguments.

Description

TIME returns the time of day in 24-hour format. The time is taken from the system clock.

See also the TIME and TODAY functions.

Example

```
IF TIME() > "14:59:00" THEN
    MESSAGE "Deposit is credited tomorrow"
ENDIF
```

This example displays the message `Deposit is credited tomorrow` if the system time is after 2:59 PM.

TODAY( )   *Date*

Syntax

> **TODAY( )**

This function takes no arguments.

Description

> TODAY returns the current date as taken from your computer's system date.

Example

```
IF TODAY() = 5/28/92 THEN
    MESSAGE "Happy Birthday Pat"
ENDIF
```

This example displays the message Happy Birthday Pat if the system date is May 28, 1992.

TOGGLEPALETTE   *Keypress Interaction*

Syntax

> **TOGGLEPALETTE**

Description

> The TOGGLEPALETTE command is equivalent to pressing Alt-C. The effect of this command depends on the Paradox mode and the context in which it will be used. Refer to the chapter that discusses the mode and context in which you intend to use the TOGGLEPALETTE command.

TOQPRO   *Keypress Interaction*

Syntax

> **TOQPRO**

Description

> The TOQPRO command is equivalent to pressing Ctrl-F10. This command is not available unless Quattro Pro also is running.

Refer to the chapter that discusses the mode and context in which you intend to use the TOQPRO command.

TYPE( )   *Information*

Syntax

> **TYPE(expression)**

Description

TYPE returns the type of the expression. **expression** is any valid Paradox expression. Table 19.39 lists values that can be returned by the TYPE function.

Table 19.39. Expression Types Returned by TYPE

Returned value	Type
A*n*	String, where *n* represents the length of the string
AY	Fixed array
D	Date
DY	Dynamic Array
L	Logical
M	Memo (alphanumeric data greater than 255 characters in length)
N	Numeric
S	Short integer
$	Dollars

TYPEIN   Input/Output, Workspace

Syntax

> **TYPEIN expression1**

Description

> The TYPEIN command simulates typing keystrokes into Paradox.
> The **expression1** parameter contains the values to be typed. By
> default, Paradox converts values to strings, unless the value de-
> rives from a mixed expression. The TYPEIN command is useful for
> dynamically modifying report forms, answering prompts, and so
> forth.

> The effect of TYPEIN can be the same as placing characters in the
> script within quotation marks. The two following statements have
> the same effect:

> "This is a test."

> TYPEIN "This is a test"

> With the TYPEIN command, however, you can use a variable to
> specify the text to be typed:

> string = "This is another test"

> TYPEIN string

UNDO   Keypress Interaction

Syntax

> **UNDO**

Description

> The UNDO command reverses the last transaction in the Paradox
> transaction log. This command is equivalent to the Ctrl-U (Undo)
> keystroke command DataEntry, Edit, and CoEdit modes. Refer to
> Chapter 3, "Entering, Editing, and Viewing Data," for a complete
> discussion of the Undo feature.

UNLOCK   *Menu, Multiuser*

Syntax

> **UNLOCK** *locklist1* | *ALL*

Description

The UNLOCK command removes one or more locks on one or more specified shared tables. The *locklist1* parameter consists of one or more comma-separated tables and lock pairs. Lock types include the following: FL (full lock), WL (write lock), PFL (prevent full lock), and PWL (prevent write lock). Refer to the section "Creating Tables on a Network" in Chapter 2, "Creating Database Tables," for a description of each lock type.

As explained in Chapter 2, Paradox places and removes locks on tables and records as needed. A good PAL programming practice, however, is to explicitly lock and unlock tables often, using the LOCK and UNLOCK commands when the script performs an operation that requires a particular type of lock for completion. This practice avoids the potential of two Paradox users each waiting for a resource currently in use by the other, which is referred to as a *deadlock* or *deadly embrace*.

Use the ALL keyword to unlock all tables explicitly locked by the current user.

Example

```
LOCK "Orders" WL, "Detail" WL
IF RetVal = False THEN
   ?? Lock failed. SLEEP 3000
ELSE
   EDIT "Orders"
   FormKey
   PROMPT "Press F2 when done, Esc to cancel."
   WAIT TABLE UNTIL "F2", "Esc"
   IF RetVal = "F2" THEN
      DO_IT!
   ELSE
      MENU {Cancel} "Y"
   ENDIF
   CLEARIMAGE
ENDIF
UNLOCK "Orders" WL, "Detail" WL
```

This example locks Orders and Detail at the beginning of the script segment and unlocks the same tables at the end.

UNLOCKRECORD   *Multiuser*

Syntax

UNLOCKRECORD

Description

The UNLOCKRECORD command unlocks the current record, if the record is locked. This command is equivalent to the Alt-L (Lock Toggle) keystroke command. Refer to "Handling Key Violations in CoEdit Mode" in Chapter 3, "Entering, Editing, and Viewing Data," for more information. This command is effective only in CoEdit mode.

UNPASSWORD   *Menu, Workspace*

Syntax

UNPASSWORD passwordlist1

Description

The UNPASSWORD command deactivates one or more Paradox passwords to protected tables. The **passwordlist1** parameter contains one or more passwords separated by commas. After this command is executed, a user has to enter a valid password before he or she can access protected tables on the network.

Refer to Chapter 13, "Using Paradox Tools," for a discussion on creating and using passwords to protect tables and scripts.

Example

```
UNPASSWORD "safe", "safer", "safest"
```

This example revokes three previously given passwords: safe, safer, and safest.

UP   *Keypress Interaction*

Syntax

> **UP**

Description

> The UP command is equivalent to pressing the up-arrow key. The effect of this command depends on the Paradox mode and the context. Refer to the chapter that discusses the mode and context in which you intend to use the UP command.

UPIMAGE   *Keypress Interaction* *Workspace*

Syntax

> **UPIMAGE**

Description

> The UPIMAGE command moves the cursor to the previous image on the workspace. This command is equivalent to pressing the F3 (Up Image) keystroke command. Refer to Chapter 3, "Entering, Editing, and Viewing Data," for a discussion of the F3 (Up Image) command.

> UPIMAGE is effective only in Main mode, Edit mode, and CoEdit mode.

> See also DOWNIMAGE.

UPPER( )   *String*

Syntax

> **UPPER(expr)**

Description

> This function returns a string composed entirely of uppercase characters. **expr** is an expression of any type. UPPER will convert a string automatically.

> See also LOWER.

Example

```
MESSAGE UPPER("Some are Caps Some are Not")
```

> This function displays the following line:

```
SOME ARE CAPS SOME ARE NOT
```

USDATE( )   Date

Syntax

> **USDATE(date1)**

Description

> This function returns a date in United States date format. **date1** is any expression that evaluates to a date.

Example

```
MESSAGE USDATE( DATEVAL( "2/29/92" ) )
```

> This example displays the date value 2-Feb-1992.

USERNAME( )   System Status

Syntax

> **USERNAME( )**

> This function accepts no arguments.

Description

> USERNAME reports the name of the current user. The user name can be set in three ways: through the network operating system;

through the Custom Configuration Program (which overrides any LAN user name); or through the SETUSERNAME PAL command or equivalent **Tools Net UserName** interactive menu command (which overrides any user name set in the Custom Configuration Program).

The USERNAME function is useful when assigning user information to complete a transaction register.

Example

```
[Changed By] = USERNAME()
[Changed time] = TIME()
[Changed Date] = TODAY()
```

This example uses the user name, system date, and system time to maintain a transaction register.

VERSION( )   *System Status*

Syntax

VERSION( )

This function takes no argument.

Description

VERSION reports the current Paradox version number. Paradox versions to date include 1, 1.1, 2, 3, 3.5, and 4.0.

See also CONVERTLIB and FILEVERSION.

VERTRULER   *Keypress Interaction*

Syntax

VERTRULER

Description

The VERTRULER command toggles the vertical ruler in the Paradox Report Designer. This command is equivalent to the Ctrl-V (Vertical Ruler Toggle). Refer to the section "Displaying a Vertical Ruler" in Chapter 5, "Getting Started with Reports," for more information about this feature.

VIEW   Menu

Syntax

> **VIEW table1**

Description

> The VIEW command places a display image on the workspace. This command is equivalent to the **View** menu command. The **table1** parameter contains the name of the table to display. The VIEW command can be executed only from Main mode.

Example

> ```
> VIEW "Employee"
> ```

> This command displays the Employee table on the workspace in Main mode.

WAIT   Input/Output

Syntax

> The WAIT command syntax has two versions:

> > **WAIT FIELD | RECORD | TABLE | WORKSPACE**
> > **PROMPT string1, string2**
> > **MESSAGE string3**
> > **UNTIL keylist**

> and

> > **WAIT FIELD | RECORD | TABLE | WORKSPACE**
> > **PROC procname eventlist**
> > **ENDWAIT**

Description

> Use the WAIT command to cause your application to wait while the user interacts with a field, record, table, or the workspace. The WAIT is terminated by specified keystrokes (used with the UNTIL keyword in the first form) or depending on the return value of the WAIT procedure (in the second form).

> The first form of the WAIT command is provided primarily for compatibility with applications developed under previous versions of Paradox. When the WAIT command is encountered, the

workspace is made visible, and the user's interaction is limited to the current field, record, table, or workspace, depending on which keyword is used. All function keys and other control keys are blocked, except those listed in the keylist (and the FieldView commands). The keylist is a comma-separated list of Paradox keystroke values (like "F2," "Esc," "Enter," and so on). If a SHOWPULLDOWN menu is defined, then the F10 key will remain enabled so that the user can access the pull-down menu. If the F1 key is not explicitly named in the keylist and fields have help-and-fill lookup tables associated, then the F1 key is enabled for the help-and-fill lookup.

The second form of the WAIT command limits the user's interaction to the current field, record, table, or workspace, depending on the keyword used. **procname** is the name of the procedure that is invoked when specified events or triggers occur. The events and triggers that will call the WAIT procedure are listed in the eventlist. Refer to the GETEVENT and SHOWDIALOG command for information about events and triggers.

The WAIT procedure is required to have three parameters. In order from left to right, the parameters are the trigger type, the event record, and the cycle number. The first two parameters, the trigger type and the event record, are assigned their values based on the specific event that resulted in the WAIT procedure call. The last parameter, the cycle number, is assigned by Paradox. If the WAIT procedure is called for a trigger, the specific name of the trigger is assigned to the trigger type parameter. If the WAIT procedure is called for an event (mouse, key, message, or idle), then the trigger type parameter is given the value "EVENT".

The event record that is passed as the second parameter of the WAIT procedure is initialized with indexes and element values appropriate for the type of event or trigger being processed. Refer to GETEVENT for more information about how this dynamic array is structured.

The cycle number that is passed as the third parameter of the WAIT procedure is a unique number. This number will remain the same for as long as the individual triggers being processed were created by the same event. For example, a single keypress or mouse click may move the cursor out of a field. The following triggers may all be generated as the result of this single event: EVENT, DEPARTFIELD, DEPARTROW, ARRIVEROW, ARRIVEFIELD. All of these triggers would have the same cycle number because they all resulted from the same event.

The WAIT procedure must return a value. The value returned must be the number 0, 1, or 2. A return value of 0 indicates that the current event should be processed by Paradox and that processing should proceed to the next event in the queue. A return value of 1 indicates that the current event should be blocked or denied and that the current trigger cycle should be broken out of with the WAIT session remaining active. A return value of 3 indicates that the current event should be denied and that both the current trigger cycle and the WAIT should be terminated.

The WAIT procedure also changes the value in the global variable RetVal. RetVal returns a series of numeric codes, which indicate what actions occurred inside the WAIT procedure. A RetVal value of 2000 indicates that the return value of the WAIT procedure is 0. A RetVal value of 2001 indicates that the return value of the WAIT procedure is 1. A RetVal value of 2002 indicates that the return value of the WAIT procedure is 2. A RetVal value of 2003 indicates that the WAIT procedure results in a DEPARTFIELD or DEPARTTABLE trigger when the active WAIT is specified for FIELD or TABLE. A RetVal value of 2004 indicates that the WAIT procedure results in a DEPARTTABLE trigger when the WAIT table is a help lookup table. A RetVal value of 2005 indicates that the WAIT procedure results in closing the last table on the workspace when the active WAIT is specified for the WORKSPACE. Refer to the *PAL Programmer's Guide* (supplied with Paradox) for more information on using the WAIT command with lookup tables.

Example

Refer to the section, "Building WAIT Sessions," in Chapter 16, for an example of the WAIT command.

WHILE   *Program Control*

Syntax

WHILE condition1 *commands* **ENDWHILE**

Description

Together, the WHILE and ENDWHILE commands create a program control structure that repeats a specified sequence of commands when a certain condition is logically True. A WHILE control structure often is called a WHILE loop.

The **condition1** parameter specifies the condition that must be met for the script to repeatedly execute the commands specified in the *commands* parameter. If **condition1** evaluates to a value of True, the commands listed between WHILE and ENDWHILE are executed.

You can use the LOOP command in a WHILE loop to return to the top of the WHILE loop without executing all the commands in the loop. The QUITLOOP command terminates a WHILE loop.

Example

```
VIEW "Employee"
INDEX MAINTAINED "Employee" ON "Emp Last Name"
MOVETO [Emp Last Name]
? "Type the employee's last name: "
ACCEPT "A20" TO last
LOCATE last
WHILE (RetVal = True)
    PROMPT "Press F2 to find next employee, Esc to stop."
    WAIT RECORD UNTIL "F2", "Esc"
    IF RetVal = "F2" THEN
        DOWN LOCATE NEXT last
        IF RetVal = False THEN
            UP
        ENDIF
    ELSE
        QUITLOOP
    ENDIF
ENDWHILE
```

This example uses the WAIT command to permit the user to view a specific record that the script finds on the workspace. The data is safe because the workspace is in Main mode. The only active keystrokes are F2 and Esc so that the user cannot accidentally enter Edit or CoEdit.

WINCLOSE   *Keypress Interaction*

Syntax

> **WINCLOSE**

Description

Closes the current window, if the window is closeable. This command is the equivalent of Ctrl-F8. WINCLOSE will ask for

confirmation if the window is an editor window, or a Report or
Form Designer window. You can determine if a window can be
closed by using WINDOW GETATTRIBUTES and then examining
the CANCLOSE element of the resulting dynamic array. Refer also
to Chapter 3, "Entering, Editing, and Viewing Data," for more information on Ctrl-F8.

See also WINDOW CLOSE, CLEARIMAGE, and CLEARALL.

WINDOW( )   *Workspace, Canvas*

Syntax

WINDOW( )

This function accepts no arguments.

Description

WINDOW returns the contents of the currently displayed Paradox
message window as a string. If the workspace is not showing a
message window at the time, the string returned is blank.

The WINDOW function works with system-generated messages
only. Messages created by the application using the MESSAGE
command cannot be returned with WINDOW. The function can be
used only in scripts. Interactive use of WINDOW does not work
because the Alt-F10 command sequence required to get to the PAL
Menu clears the message.

WINDOW CLOSE   *Window*

Syntax

WINDOW CLOSE

Description

WINDOW CLOSE closes the currently active window. Unlike
WINCLOSE, the window is closed regardless of its CANCLOSE
attribute. If there is an image in the window, it is closed also.
WINDOW CLOSE does not ask for confirmation and will cancel
sessions in the Editor, Report Designer, or Form Designer without
warning.

WINDOW CREATE   Window

Syntax

> **WINDOW CREATE** *FLOATING @rownum,colnum*
> *HEIGHT hnum*
> *WIDTH wnum*
> *ATTRIBUTES dynarray* **TO winhandle**

Description

Use this command to create a new canvas window. The handle of the new window is stored in winhandle. Optionally, the window may be placed at specified screen coordinates and have a specified size.

The new window becomes the current canvas and all subsequent output will go to the new window canvas, unless explicitly changes with a WINDOW SETCANVAS command.

The FLOATING keyword causes the window to be created as a "floating" window; it is placed as the topmost window on the screen and will always be visible.

The @ symbol, followed by the numeric expressions *rownum* and *colnum,* optionally specifies row and column coordinates for the origin of the window. The top left corner of the window will be placed at the coordinates specified.

Use the optional HEIGHT keyword, followed by the numeric expression *hnum* to specify the height, in rows, of the new window.

Use the optional WIDTH keyword, followed by the numeric expression *wnum* to specify the width, in columns, of the new window.

To set customized attributes for the window, use the optional ATTRIBUTES keyword followed by a dynamic array initialized with the same indexes and element values as a dynamic array used by the WINDOW GETATTRIBUTES or WINDOW SETATTRIBUTES commands.

See also WINDOW GETATTRIBUTES, WINDOW SETATTRIBUTES.

Example

Refer to the GETCANVAS function for an example of the WINDOW CREATE command.

WINDOW ECHO   *Window*

Syntax

> **WINDOW ECHO winhandle logic1**

Description

> This command turns the canvas echo on or off for a specified
> canvas. **winhandle** is any valid window handle. **logic1** is a Logical
> value controlling whether the echo is turned on or off. If **logic1**
> evaluates as True, then the echo is turned on, otherwise the echo
> is turned off.

WINDOW GETATTRIBUTES   *Window*

Syntax

> **WINDOW GETATTRIBUTES winhandle TO arrayname**

Description

> Use this command to obtain the current attributes of a specified
> window. **winhandle** is any valid window handle. **arrayname** is any
> valid dynamic array name. **arrayname** is reinitialized or created
> with the indexes and elements described in table 19.40.

> You can use WINDOW GETATTRIBUTES and WINDOW
> SETATTRIBUTES to change the attributes of a window.

> See also WINDOW SETATTRIBUTES.

Table 19.40. Window Attribute Dynamic Array Indexes and Elements

Index	Element description
CANCLOSE	Logical: whether or not user can close the window
CANMAXIMIZE	Logical: whether or not the user can maximize/restore window

continues

Table 19.40. Continued

Index	Element description
CANMOVE	Logical: whether or not the user can move the window
CANRESIZE	Logical: whether or not the user can resize the window
CANVAS	Logical: whether or not canvas writes are displayed immediately
CANVASHEIGHT	Number: the canvas buffer height
CANVASWIDTH	Number: the canvas buffer width
ECHO	Logical: whether or not the echo is on
FLOATING	Logical: whether or not the window is above the echo layer
HASFRAME	Logical: whether or not the window has a frame
HASSHADOW	Logical: whether or not the window has a shadow
HEIGHT	Number: number of rows including the frame
MARGIN	Number/String: Size of left margin, OFF if there is none
MAXIMIZED	Logical: whether or not the window is maximized
ORIGINCOL	Number: the column in which the top left window corner starts
ORIGINROW	Number: the row in which the top left window corner starts
SCROLLCOL	Number: the column offset location of the window

Index	Element description
SCROLLROW	Number: the row offset location of the window
STYLE	Number: color and attribute codes for the canvas
TITLE	String: the window's title
WIDTH	Number: number of columns including the frame

WINDOW GETCOLORS   *Window*

Syntax

WINDOW GETCOLORS winhandle TO dynarray

Description

Use this command to obtain information about the color attributes of a window's components. **winhandle** is any expression evaluating to a valid window handle. **dynarray** is any valid PAL variable name. The WINDOW GETCOLORS command will create **dynarray** if it does not exist, or will reinitialize it if it already exists.

WINDOW GETCOLORS places the attributes from the current palette for the window or dialog box specified by **winhandle** into the dynamic array specified by **dynarray**. Table 19.41 lists the dynamic array indexes and the window components they describe. Table 19.42 lists the dynamic array indexes and the dialog box components they describe. In either case, the elements of the dynamic array will contain a number indicating the color of the component. Refer to Appendix D for a list of PAL color codes.

Window color attributes may be set for all windows by using the SETCOLORS command, or individually by using the WINDOW SETCOLORS command.

Table 19.41. Window Component Codes for a Window

Index	Element description
0	Frame for Inactive window
1	Frame for Active window
2	Frame icons (close/size) and selected frame (used when dragging window)
3	Scroll bar
4	Scroll bar controls
5-7	Undefined—reserved for future use

Table 19.42. Window Component Codes for a Dialog Box

Index	Element description
0	Frame for Inactive window
1	Frame for Active window
2	Selected frame (used when dragging window)
3	Scroll bar page area
4	Scroll bar controls
5	Default background for text
6	Label color for inactive control
7	Label color for active control
8	Hot-key color for control label
9	Normal push-button label text color
10	Default push-button label text color
11	Selected push-button text color
12	Undefined—reserved for future use
13	Hot-key color for push-button label

Index	Element description
14	Button shadow
15	Normal radio button or check box item
16	Highlighted radio button or check box item
17	Hot key for radio button or check box
18	Normal text for type-in boxes
19	Selected text for type-in box
20	Arrows for type-in box
21-24	Undefined—reserved for future use
25	Normal pick list item
26	Selected pick list item in an active pick list
27	Selected pick list item in an inactive pick list
28	Column dividers in pick list
29-31	Undefined—reserved for future use

WINDOW HANDLE

Window

Syntax

> **WINDOW HANDLE** *IMAGE num1* | *FORM DESIGN* | *REPORT DESIGN* | *CURRENT* | *DIALOG* **TO winhandle**

Description

Use WINDOW HANDLE to obtain the handle of a specified window, including images, forms, reports, and dialog boxes. However specified, the window handle is returned in **winhandle**.

The *IMAGE num1* option obtains a window handle based on the window's image number. *num1* is a numeric expression. Use IMAGENO to get an image's number.

FORM obtains the window handle of the current form. Use the additional option keyword DESIGN for the current Form Designer window handle.

REPORT obtains the window handle of the current report. Use the additional option keyword DESIGN for the current Report Designer window handle.

Use the CURRENT option to get the handle of the current window. This is equivalent to using the GETWINDOW function.

Use the DIALOG option to get the handle of the current dialog box (created with SHOWDIALOG).

See also GETCANVAS and other WINDOW commands.

WINDOW LIST   *Window*

Syntax

WINDOW LIST TO arrayname

Description

This command generates a list of all window handles for all windows on the desktop. **arrayname** is a fixed array. It is reinitialized or created to have as many elements as there are windows on the desktop. If no windows are on the desktop, **arrayname** is unassigned.

See also WINDOW HANDLE.

WINDOW MAXIMIZE   *Window*

Syntax

WINDOW MAXIMIZE winhandle

Description

This command maximizes (make as large as possible) a specified window. **winhandle** is an expression resulting in a valid window handle. Note that this command will maximize the window regardless of the setting of CANMAXIMIZE in the window's attributes. If **winhandle** is invalid, a script error occurs. WINDOW MAXIMIZE sets the global variable RetVal to False if it is unsuccessful, otherwise RetVal is set to True.

See also WINDOW GETATTRIBUTES, WINDOW HANDLE, GETWINDOW, and GETCANVAS.

WINDOW MOVE   *Window*

Syntax

WINDOW MOVE winhandle TO rownum, colnum

Description

This command moves a window. **winhandle** is an expression resulting in a valid window handle. **rownum** is the new row location for the top left corner of the window, and **colnum** is the new column location for the top left corner of the window. Note that this command will move the window regardless of the CANMOVE setting in the window's attributes. If **winhandle** is invalid, a script error occurs. WINDOW MOVE sets the global variable RetVal to False if it is unsuccessful, otherwise RetVal is set True.

See also WINDOW GETATTRIBUTES, WINDOW HANDLE, GETWINDOW, and GETCANVAS.

WINDOW RESIZE   *Window*

Syntax

WINDOW RESIZE winhandle TO heightnew, widthnew

Description

This command resizes a window. **winhandle** is an expression resulting in a valid window handle. **heightnew** is an expression resulting in a numeric value and specifies the new window height in rows. **widthnew** is an expression resulting in a numeric value and specifies the new window height in columns. Note that this command will resize the window regardless of the CANRESIZE setting in the window's attributes. If **winhandle** is invalid, a script error occurs. WINDOW RESIZE sets the global variable RetVal to False if it is unsuccessful, otherwise RetVal is set to True.

WINDOW SCROLL   *Window*

Syntax

> **WINDOW SCROLL winhandle TO rownum colnum**

Description

Use this command to change (scroll) the view inside a window vertically and/or horizontally without interactively using the scroll bars. **winhandle** is an expression which evaluates to a valid window handle. **rownum** and **colnum** are numeric expressions indicating the row and column offsets of the new scroll position.

The offset is specified differently, depending on the type of image displayed in the window being scrolled. If the window being scrolled is an Editor window, then **rownum** represents the character offset, and **colnum** represents the number of columns for the offset. If the window being scrolled contains a table image, then **rownum** represents the record offset, and **colnum** represents the number of fields for the offset. If the window being scrolled is a canvas, report previewer, or form designer window, then **rownum** represents the number of rows, and **colnum** represents the number of columns for the offset.

Use the WINDOW GETATTRIBUTES command to determine the current column and row offset for a window.

See also WINDOW GETATTRIBUTES, and WINDOW SETATTRIBUTES.

WINDOW SELECT   *Window*

Syntax

> **WINDOW SELECT winhandle**

Description

Use this command to make a specified window current and active. **winhandle** is an expression resulting in a valid window handle. The action of WINDOW SELECT is like that of a mouse click on a window to select it. If **winhandle** is invalid, a script error occurs.

See also GETWINDOW, WINDOW HANDLE, WINDOW LIST, WINDOW GETATTRIBUTES, and WINDOW SETATTRIBUTES.

WINDOW SETATTRIBUTES   *Window*

Syntax

WINDOW SETATTRIBUTES winhandle FROM arrayname

Description

Use this command to change the current attributes of a specified window. **winhandle** is any valid window handle. **arrayname** is an expression resulting in a dynamic array name. The dynamic array specified by **arrayname** must be initialized with the indexes and elements described with the WINDOW GETATTRIBUTES command (see table 19.39).

You can use WINDOW GETATTRIBUTES and WINDOW SETATTRIBUTES to change the attributes of a window. To change the scroll position of the view in a window, use the WINDOW SCROLL command.

See also WINDOW GETATTRIBUTES and WINDOW SCROLL.

WINDOW SETCOLORS   *Window*

Syntax

WINDOW SETCOLORS winhandle DEFAULT | FROM dynarray

Description

Use this command to set the color attributes of the window components for a specified window or dialog box. **winhandle** is an expression that evaluates to a valid window handle. If the DEFAULT keyword is used, then the default color attributes are given to the window. If the FROM keyword is used, then **dynarray** represents a valid PAL dynamic array name. The dynamic array must be structured the same as a dynamic array created with the WINDOW GETCOLORS command. Refer to the description of the WINDOW GETCOLORS command for information on the array indexes and their meanings. Each value in the dynamic array elements contains a PAL color code, defining the color to be displayed. Refer to Appendix D for a list of the supported color codes and their meanings.

WINDOWS SETCOLORS is used to set the colors for a specific window. To set the colors for all windows, use the SETCOLORS command.

See also WINDOW GETCOLORS, GETCOLORS, SETCOLORS, and other window commands.

WINDOWAT( )   *Window*

Syntax

> **WINDOWAT(rnum, cnum)**

Description

This function returns a valid window handle for the window on the desktop that encloses a specified set of row and column coordinates. **rnum** is a numeric expression indicating the row coordinate, and **cnum** is a numeric expression indicating the column coordinate. If no windows are enclosing the specified co-ordinates, then WINDOWAT returns 0. If more than one window is enclosing the specified coordinates, the handle of the window closest to the surface (that is highest in the *z-order*) is returned.

See also LOCALIZEEVENT and WINDOW HANDLE.

WINMAX   *Keypress Interaction*

Syntax

> **WINMAX**

Description

The WINMAX command has the same effect as pressing Shift-F5. If the window can be made larger, it is maximized (made as large as possible). If the window is already maximized, it is returned to its previous size. Refer to Chapter 3, "Entering, Editing, and Viewing Data," for more information.

WINNEXT   *Keypress Interaction*

Syntax

> **WINNEXT**

Description

> The WINNEXT command has the same effect as pressing Ctrl-F4. Refer to Chapter 3, "Entering, Editing, and Viewing Data," for more information.

WINRESIZE   *Keypress Interaction*

Syntax

> **WINRESIZE**

Description

> The WINRESIZE command has the same effect as pressing Ctrl-F5. Refer to Chapter 3, "Entering, Editing, and Viewing Data," for more information.

WRITELIB   *Procedure*

Syntax

> **WRITELIB library1 proclist1**

Description

> The WRITELIB command stores procedures in an existing procedure library created by the CREATELIB command. The **library1** parameter contains the name of the procedure library file. **proclist1** contains the name(s) of the procedures to be added to the library.

> See also CREATELIB, READLIB, and CONVERTLIB.

YEAR( )   *Date*

Syntax

YEAR(date)

Description

YEAR returns the year as a number, extracted from value of **date**.

Example

MESSAGE YEAR (4 - APR - 94)

This example displays the number 1994.

ZOOM   *Keypress Interaction*

Syntax

ZOOM

Description

The ZOOM command is equivalent to pressing Ctrl-Z (Zoom) or using the **Image Zoom Value** menu command. This command searches for a record that has a specified value in the current field. Refer to the section "Finding a Record with Zoom and Zoom Next," in Chapter 3, "Entering, Editing, and Viewing Data." It often is very useful to use the ZOOM command in combination with the SELECT command.

See also to the LOCATE and SELECT commands.

ZOOMNEXT   *Keypress Interaction*

Syntax

ZOOMNEXT

Description

The ZOOMNEXT command is equivalent to pressing Alt-Z (Zoom Next). This command finds the next record that contains a previously specified value in the current field. Refer to discussion of the ZOOM command in this command reference, and to the discussion of Alt-Z (Zoom Next) in Chapter 3, "Entering, Editing, and Viewing Data," for more information.

See also the LOCATE command.

Paradox 4.0 Installation and Start-Up

This appendix explains how to install Paradox 4.0 and how to begin using the program. Installation of Paradox on a local area network server is not discussed in this appendix. Network administrators should refer to the *Network Installation Guide* included in the Paradox documentation.

Understanding System Requirements

Before installing Paradox 4.0, make sure that your system meets the minimum requirements to run Paradox 4.0 as a single-user program. You must have a PC that uses an Intel 80286, 80386, 80386SX, or 80486 central processing unit (CPU) and that can run in protected mode. The PC must have a hard disk with approximately 3.5M of free storage space to install Paradox 4.0. Your system also must have a minimum of 2M random access memory (RAM), and MS-DOS or IBM DOS 3.0 or higher.

To take advantage of all the capabilities of Paradox, you also need a graphics-capable monitor and graphics printer or plotter.

Installing the Main Program

Paradox 4.0 is distributed on both 5 1/4-inch 1.2M and 3 1/2-inch 1.44M disks. The installation process is similar for either disk size.

To begin installing Paradox, you must be at the DOS prompt. The current drive should be the hard disk on which you want to install Paradox 4.0. To install Paradox on your hard drive (usually drive C), you should be at the DOS prompt, C>. (C> is the default prompt, but many systems are set up to display C:\>.)

Place the distributed Paradox disk, Install disk 1 into drive A (the first floppy drive). Type *a:install* and press Enter. Paradox displays the initial installation screen. Read this screen and press Enter to continue.

The second screen asks for the source drive, the drive from which you want the installation program to copy the Paradox 4.0 files. This screen suggests A as the source drive. Press Enter to confirm drive A or type a different drive letter and press Enter.

Select the type of installation from the following options:

- *Stand-alone Installation.* Select this option when you want to install Paradox 4.0 on your computer's hard disk.

- *Network Installation.* Select this choice to start the network installation procedure on a local area network. (**Note:** Network installation is not covered fully in this appendix. Refer to the *Network Installation Guide* distributed with Paradox 4.0 for more information on installing Paradox on a local area network.)

- *Optional Software Installation.* Choose this option when you want to install the sample tables, the sample application, the Paradox Application Workshop (PAW), or the sample PAW application.

If you choose to install Paradox to a stand-alone PC, the next screen asks you to type a User name, your company's name, and the Paradox 4.0 serial number. With the highlighted selection bar resting in the User Name line, press Enter to open a small data-entry window. Type your name, including up to 30 characters and blanks, and press Enter.

If you are installing Paradox on your company's computer, move the highlighted bar to the Company Name line and press Enter to display a small window. Type your company's name and press Enter.

Move the highlighted bar to the Serial Number line and press Enter to display a data-entry window. Type the serial number, found on Installation Disk 1, and press Enter.

Use the Country Group and Sort Order lines to select another country group (United States, English International, Europe, Sweden and Finland, Norway and Denmark). This setting affects date formats and whole number separators. You also use the Country Group and Sort Order lines to change the order in which Paradox sorts Paradox tables (ASCII or dictionary order).

Press F2 (Do-It!) to continue.

The installation program examines the CONFIG.SYS file on your hard disk and informs you if you need to modify the file. When a change is necessary, Install gives you the option to have Install make the change to CONFIG.SYS or to make the change yourself. If Paradox makes some change to the file, the program saves a copy of the original version first as CONFIG.PDX.

NOTE DOS reads CONFIG.SYS each time you restart the computer. For Paradox 4.0 to work properly, the following lines need to appear in this file:

```
FILES = 40
BUFFERS = 40
```

Paradox ensures that these lines exist as part of the installation process, but you may accidentally change or delete this file later. If you have trouble getting Paradox to start, look at this file by using the DOS type command:

TYPE CONFIG.SYS

If necessary, add the FILES and BUFFERS lines listed previously, using any text editor that produces pure ASCII text files.

The next screen enables you to specify the installation directory and to indicate whether you want to install the sample tables, the sample application, the Paradox Application Workshop (PAW), and the sample PAW application.

The first line indicates that the default directory for the installation of Paradox 4.0 files is C:\PDOX40. If you want to install Paradox in a different directory, press Enter, backspace over this directory name, type the new path specification, and press Enter. Press F2 (Do-It!) to continue the Installation process.

Paradox displays the message `Reading files...` and then `Writing files...` and instructs you to insert Installation Disk 2 into the source drive.

Insert the distributed Installation Disk 2 and press Enter. Install continues to copy files to your system's hard disk.

Installing Optional Software

The Paradox 4.0 disks include many optional programs and files. If you don't install these programs and files, you still can use the Paradox program. You may decide later to install the optional software, however.

To install the optional software, start Install, as described in the preceding section of this appendix, and select the Optional Software Installation option from the third Install screen.

The next screen enables you to specify the installation directory and to indicate whether you want to install the sample tables, the sample application, the Paradox Application Workshop (PAW), and the sample PAW application.

The first line indicates that the default directory for the installation of Paradox 4.0 files is `C:\PDOX40`. If you prefer to install Paradox in a different directory, press Enter, backspace over this directory name, type the new path specification, and press Enter. Press F2 (Do-It!) to continue the Installation process.

Paradox displays the message `Reading files...` and then `Writing files...` and instructs you to insert the appropriate Installation Disk into the source drive. When you are prompted, insert the remaining Installation disks.

Getting Started

Now that your program is installed, you're ready to start Paradox. This section explains how to access Paradox and how to start the Paradox Personal Programmer.

Starting Paradox 4.0

The simplest way to start Paradox is to change to the directory in which Paradox is installed, type *paradox*, and press Enter. This method works every time but isn't usually the best method.

When you create database files with Paradox, the program usually places these files in the directory from which you start the program. If you start Paradox from the directory containing the Paradox program, you mix data files with program files. This poor file management leads to problems when you create more and more database tables.

A better way to use Paradox is to create a separate directory on your hard disk for each database application and to start Paradox from that directory. This method, however, requires a little preparation. The following discussion explains how to enter the necessary DOS commands and shows you how to use a *batch* file to consolidate the commands.

To create a directory on your hard disk for a Paradox database, start at the DOS prompt with the root directory of your hard disk current. If your hard disk is designated drive C, for example, the prompt is C> or C:\>. Create a directory with the MD command (for Make Directory). To create a directory with the name PDOXDATA, type *md \pdoxdata* at the DOS prompt and press Enter. Change to the new directory by typing *cd \pdoxdata* and pressing Enter. Starting Paradox from this directory stores new database files in this directory.

So that DOS can find the Paradox program files, draw a map by defining the *path* to the Paradox directory. For example, assume that your DOS files are in the DOS directory and that the Paradox 4.0 program files are stored in \PDOX40. Type *path c:\pdox40;c:\;c:\dos* and press Enter. Insert the appropriate directory name into the PATH statement for your system.

To start Paradox 4.0, type *paradox* and press Enter. As Paradox loads, you see a title screen showing the *signature* information you supplied during the installation process (user name, company, and serial number). This screen is followed by the Paradox Main menu. Paradox is ready to use.

Using a Batch File To Start Paradox 4.0

Consolidate the commands that start Paradox into one command by creating a batch file. Access DOS at the root directory of your hard disk and type the following commands, pressing Enter at the end of each line:

```
copy con p40.bat
echo off
cls
path c:\pdox40;c:\;c:\dos
cd \pdoxdata
paradox
cd \
```

After the last line, press F6. DOS displays ^Z. Press Enter. You should see the message 1 File(s) copied. This process creates a batch file named P40.BAT.

To start Paradox, type *p40* at the DOS prompt and press Enter.

Create several batch files to start Paradox, each of which makes a different directory the working directory, to ensure that unrelated data is not mixed in the same directory. If you build a database to process orders for your company's merchandise, for example, you may place the database in a directory named C:\ORDERS. You can create a batch file named ORDERS.BAT that starts Paradox from this directory, ensuring that all data for this database is placed in the C:\ORDERS directory. To create this batch file, type the following at the DOS prompt, pressing Enter at the end of each line:

```
copy con orders.bat
echo off
cls
path c:\pdox40;c:\;c:\dos
cd \orders
paradox
cd \
```

Press F6 and Enter. Place this file in the root directory so that you can use it from any directory. When you type *orders* and press Enter, Paradox starts, and the working directory is C:\ORDERS.

Starting the Paradox Application Workshop

You start the Paradox Application Workshop (PAW) from within Paradox 4.0. You need to create a separate directory for each application you want to generate with the Application Workshop. You also need to add the directory containing the Application Workshop to the path. After you complete these two steps, you can create an application in that directory. Use the *CD* command to change to the proper directory for the application, type *paradox*, and press Enter. After Paradox starts, click the System menu button or press Alt-space bar to display the System menu. Select Utilities, **P**AW from the System menu. Paradox starts the Application Workshop. Refer to Chapter 14 for a detailed discussion of this powerful program generator.

Configuring Paradox

This appendix describes how to use the Custom Configuration Program (CCP), a utility for customizing many Paradox features. The program modifies the file PARADOX.CFG located in the directory containing Paradox (usually C:\PDOX40 for Paradox 4.0).

Starting, Leaving, and Canceling the CCP

You can start the Custom Configuration Program (CCP) in several different ways. The easiest way to start the CCP is from the System menu. Click on the System menu button (the ≡ symbol in the upper left corner of the screen) or press Alt-space bar to display the System menu. Select Utilities, Custom to cause Paradox to start the Custom Control Program.

The Custom Configuration Program is actually a Paradox Application Language script named Custom. Consequently, you also can start the CCP in the same manner that you start any PAL script. To run Custom from the DOS command line, change to the directory that contains the Paradox program files, type *paradox custom*, and press Enter.

Alternatively, to run the Custom script after you already have started Paradox, access the Main menu and select **S**cripts, **P**lay. At the `Script:` prompt, type the name of the directory containing the Paradox program, *c:\pdox40*, and press Enter. Paradox displays a list of scripts. Select Custom and press Enter. Paradox starts the CCP and briefly displays an initial logo screen.

The first time you start the CCP, the program displays the Monitor Type dialog box that asks you to indicate whether you have a color or black and white monitor. Select **C**olor if you are viewing Paradox on a color monitor. Choose **B**&W if you are using a black and white monitor.

Paradox displays the Main CCP menu with the following selections:

> **M**achine Information
> **V**ideo
> **R**eports
> **G**raphs . . .
> **S**tandard Settings . . .
> **F**ormat Data . . .
> **N**etwork . . .
> **P**AL . . .
> **A**SCII . . .
> **D**O-IT!
> **C**ancel

Make all selections from this menu to configure Paradox with the CCP. When you finish customizing Paradox, select **D**O-IT! to save the new configuration. You also can press F2 (Do-It!) from any CCP screen to save all changes made up to that point.

Paradox gives you a choice of saving the new configuration to one of the following:

■ *HardDisk.* Choose this option when using Paradox on a stand-alone computer. Paradox saves the new configuration file to the directory containing the Paradox system files.

■ *Network.* Select this option if you are using Paradox on a network. Paradox prompts you to enter a directory. Type the name of your *private directory* and press Enter. See "Assigning a Private Directory" in Chapter 13 for information on how to determine which directory is your private directory.

After you indicate where the new configuration file should be stored, Paradox returns you to the Main menu and uses the new settings you established with the CCP.

To cancel the Custom Control Program session without saving changes, select **C**ancel from the Main CCP menu.

The remaining sections of this appendix discuss changes you can make to the Paradox default settings with the Custom Configuration Program.

Obtaining Machine Information

Select the **M**achine Information option on the CCP Main menu to generate a report (to screen, printer, or file) about your computer's configuration. CCP displays two choices:

> **B**asic . . .
> **D**etailed . . .

Select **B**asic to generate a report that includes the following information about your system:

> DOS version
> BIOS version
> BIOS ID string
> CPU type
> Coprocessor
> Total main memory
> Extended memory
> Expanded memory
> Display Adapter
> Monitor
> Mouse driver version
> Configuration signature

Choose **D**etailed to generate a report that includes all the information about the basic report and information about available disk drives, the contents of CONFIG.SYS, and the contents of AUTOEXEC.BAT.

Setting Video Defaults

Select **V**ideo on the Main CCP menu to alter the default video settings. Paradox displays the following menu:

- *Video Settings.* Select this option to indicate monitor type, to inhibit screen flicker (*snow*), to hide the color palette in the Form Designer, and to specify that negative numbers should be shown in a different color than positive numbers.

- *Color Palettes.* Choose this option to customize Paradox screen colors. Refer to the next section, "Customizing Screen Color," for a full discussion of this option.

When you select the **V**ideo Settings option on the Main CCP menu, the CCP displays the Video Settings dialog box. This dialog box lists four settings:

- *Monitor type.* Paradox knows the type of video adapter installed in your computer, but the program cannot determine the type of monitor you are using. If you usually can read highlighted text on-screen when you use Paradox, don't change this option. If highlighted text on-screen usually is difficult to read, select **C**olor, **M**onochrome, or **B**&W. If you're using a black-and-white monitor with a CGA adapter, for example, you need to choose **B**&W.

- *Snow Prevention.* Click the box ([ ]) to the right of this setting to eliminate snow-like interference on color/graphics cards.

- *Form Palette.* Use this setting to specify whether the color palette should be displayed during form design.

- *Negative Colors.* Use this setting to indicate when you want Paradox to use color with negative numbers. Select the Numbers option to color negative numbers differently. Choose Currency to color negative currency values differently.

T I P

Another way to identify your monitor type is by using *command line configuration.* To use the black-and-white setting without running the CCP and changing default video settings, for example, type the following command to start Paradox 4.0: *paradox -b&w.*

The following options also can be used in the same way:

-color. Add this command to the start-up command to indicate that a color monitor is attached to a compatible adapter.

-snow. Use this command to eliminate snow-like interference on color/graphics cards.

-mono. Use this command-line option to indicate that you are using a monochrome monitor and adapter.

Customizing Screen Color

To customize screen colors in Paradox 4.0, choose **C**olor Palettes from the Video menu. Paradox displays the Color Settings dialog box containing the following command buttons:

Assign
Use Default
New
Edit
Copy
Rename
Delete
DO-IT!

These options enable you to create up to 10 color palettes and then assign the palette that you want Paradox to use. The Color Settings dialog box also displays a list box that lists the currently defined palettes. Use the command buttons as follows:

- Use Assign to indicate that you want to assign the selected palette as the color scheme used for the Standard video setting, the Compatible video setting, or the B&W setting.

- Select Use Default to cause Paradox to reassign the original Paradox colors as the current palette assignments.

- Choose New to create a new palette.

- Select Edit to modify a color palette.

- Use the Copy command button to create another copy of the currently selected palette.

- Select Delete to erase the selected palette.

- Select DO-IT! to save your changes and to return to the Main CCP menu.

Customizing the Report Generator

Choose **R**eport from the Main CCP menu to alter the default Report Generator settings and the predefined setup strings used to control your printer. Paradox displays the following menu:

Report Settings
Printer Setup

To establish new default settings for the Report Designer, select the **R**eport Settings options. CCP displays the Report Settings dialog box, which lists the following settings:

- *Width.* Select this setting to set the default page width for report specifications. The original setting is 80.

- *Left margin.* Select this setting to set the default left margin. The original setting is 0.

- *Length.* Select this setting to set the default number of lines per page for report specifications. The original setting is 66.

- *Pause between pages.* Select this setting to make Paradox pause the printer between pages so that you can insert a new sheet of paper. By default, Paradox does not pause the printer because the program assumes that you're using continuous paper.

- *Eject page with.* Select this setting to determine whether form feeds should be used at the end of pages instead of line feeds. The original setting is Formfeed.

- *Group Repeats.* Choose this setting to indicate whether to retain or suppress group repeats in a report that has a group band.

To add a printer setup or to edit an existing printer setup, choose **P**rinter Setup from the Reports menu. The CCP displays the Printer table, which lists all currently defined printer setups. Each setup includes a printer name, printer port assignment, setup string, and reset string. (The available setup strings are included in table 10.1.)

Paradox indicates the default printer by an asterisk (*) placed at the rightmost end of the printer name. When you run the CCP for the first time, the asterisk appears at the rightmost end of the StandardPrinter setup.

To assign a different printer setup as the default, use field view (Alt-F5, Ctrl-F, or double click) to delete the asterisk next to the original default printer's name, and add an asterisk to the right of the new default printer's name in the Printer table's Name field.

You also can use the Printer table to change the printer port assigned to the printer, and to edit the printer's setup string and reset string.

When you're finished making changes to the Printer table, press F2 (Do-It!). The CCP returns to the Main CCP menu.

Customizing Graph Settings

Choose **G**raphs from the Main CCP menu to change the default graph settings. The original settings are listed in table 12.1. Paradox displays the following menu:

- *GraphSettings.* Select this option to modify the main graph settings listed in table 12.1. See Chapter 12 for information about these settings. Make changes to default graph settings only if you manually change a setting frequently from within Graph mode.

■ *Printers.* Choose this option to establish your default graphics printer. You can define up to four printers or plotters. Choose the manufacturer, model, mode (resolution—for example, 150×150 dpi is medium resolution) and device (printer port-parallel port, serial port, or EPT) and decide whether to pause between pages.

■ *Screen.* Select this option to set the screen display for graphics. This option is independent of the Monitor type setting in the Video Settings dialog box (described in the section "Setting Video Defaults," earlier in this chapter.) Unless Paradox fails to recognize your screen type, leave the setting on Auto.

After making your selections, select the OK command button to return to the CCP Main menu.

Controlling the Interface Settings

The CCP groups several default settings under the menu choice, Standard Settings. To change these settings, select Standard Settings from the Main CCP menu. The Standard Settings dialog box appears and lists the following settings:

■ *Working Directory.* By default, when you start Paradox, the start-up directory becomes the working directory. To establish a particular directory as the default working directory, type a directory path in the working directory text box. If you want Paradox always to store tables in the C:\PDOXDATA directory, for example, you can type *c:\pdoxdata* in the Working directory text box. If you have several unrelated databases, however, you should establish a separate working directory for each database because you don't want to put unrelated tables in the same directory. Leave blank the Working directory text box in the Interface settings dialog box. Refer to Appendix A for an explanation of how to use batch files to control working directories.

■ *Interface Mode.* Paradox 4.0 presents a different user interface (the way the screen looks and interacts with the user) than all previous versions of the program. Scripts and PAL applications written for use with Paradox Version 3.5 and earlier may not work properly in Paradox 4.0, without modification, because of differences in the user interface. To ease the transition between Paradox 3.5 and 4.0, Paradox 4.0 enables you to switch back to the Paradox 3.5 interface—referred to as *compatibility* mode (refer to "Switching to the 3.5 Interface" in Chapter 1). You can make the 3.5 interface the default by selecting the Compatible option on the Interface line of the Interface Settings dialog box.

- *Mouse Use.* Select an option in this line to cause Paradox to recognize or ignore a mouse input device and to specify whether the mouse is a right- or left-handed mouse. Select the No option to cause Paradox to ignore any mouse input. Choose the Yes option (the default) to cause Paradox to recognize right-handed mouse input. Select the Left-handed option to cause Paradox to recognize left-handed mouse input.

- *Disable break.* Select this option to disable the normal capability to interrupt an operation in Paradox with the Ctrl-Break keystroke combination. When you choose the European country group during installation, Paradox disables the effect of Ctrl-Break in Paradox because several European keyboard drivers can produce the Ctrl-Break signal even when Ctrl-Break is not pressed.

- *Query order.* Use the Image Order and Table Order options in the Query order line to cause Paradox to construct answer tables with fields in image order or in table order, respectively. See Chapters 4 and 7 for details on Query By Example (QBE) and the significance of field order. The original setting is Table Order.

- *Blank = Zero.* Choose this option to indicate that Paradox should treat blanks in numeric fields as zeros in arithmetic operations. The original setting ignores blanks.

- *Autosave.* Use this option to enable the Autosave feature. When this feature is on, Paradox uses idle time between keystrokes to save data to disk, reducing the potential for data loss through a power failure. The original default setting is Yes (enabled).

- *File format.* Use the File format line in the Standard Settings dialog box to indicate whether Paradox 4.0 should create and maintain tables in full-featured Paradox 4.0 format (including such new options as memo fields), or in the file format used by earlier versions of Paradox. Choose the Standard option (the default) to cause Paradox to create and maintain files in Paradox 4.0 format. Choose the Compatible option to cause Paradox to create and maintain tables using the Paradox 3.5 file format.

After making your selections, select the OK command button to return to the CCP Main menu.

Customizing Data Format Settings

Select Format Data from the Main CCP menu to alter the default number format and date format used to display data on-screen and in reports. The Data Format dialog box appears and lists the following settings:

- *Number format.* Use an option on this line to set the format used to display separators in currency values and decimal numbers. Choose the United States option (the default) to cause Paradox to separate whole numbers with commas and to use periods (.) to divide whole numbers from decimal digits. Select the International option to separate whole numbers with periods and use commas to separate whole numbers from decimal digits.

- *Date format.* Select an option on this line to set the default date format. Choose one of the following options: mm/dd/yy, dd-Mon-yy, or dd.mm.yy. The original setting is mm/dd/yy.

- *Accept ISO dates?* Select this option to cause Paradox to accept dates in the ISO format.

After making your selections, select the OK command button to return to the CCP Main menu.

Customizing Network Settings

Choose **N**etwork from the Main CCP menu to alter the network-related default settings. Paradox displays the Network Settings dialog box that lists the following settings:

- *User Name.* If the network operating system you're using doesn't support user names, use this line to specify a default user name. Paradox identifies your workstation by this name when other users need shared resources you have locked. You don't have to manually set the user name for each Paradox session. During a Paradox session, this option also overrides the user name established by your network administrator.

- *Private directory.* Use this line to establish your Paradox private directory. This directory is used for files that cannot be shared, such as temporary tables.

- *Refresh interval.* Use this line to modify the interval at which Paradox refreshes your screen with changes made to a shared table. The original default time is three seconds. Specify a new time in seconds. 0 disables the feature.

- *When data changes.* When you are running a Paradox report or query involving shared tables over a local area network, it's possible that another user will make a change to a value in one of the tables on which the report or query is based. By default, Paradox restarts the query or report whenever a user changes data in a shared table on which the query or report is based. If such an event occurs infrequently, leave this setting alone. If queries and/or reports are interrupted frequently because users are updating a table, select the Continue Queries And Reports option. This option enables queries and reports to continue, uninterrupted, even when another user begins to make changes in a table upon which the query or report is based.

After making your selections, select the OK command button to return to the CCP Main menu.

Customizing PAL Settings

Choose **P**AL from the Main CCP menu to modify the default PAL settings. Paradox displays the PAL dialog box that lists the following settings:

- *Show calc field errors?* Select this option to cause Paradox to display an error message if a calculated field error message occurs. By default, Paradox does not display an error message when it detects an error in a calculated field.

- *Error string.* Use this text box to specify the value Paradox should substitute into a calculated field when Paradox detects an error in the calculations.

- *Script editor.* Use this option to link to Paradox a different ASCII text editor.

- *Blob editor.* Use this option to link to Paradox an editor that you want to use to edit BLOB fields.

After making your selections, select the OK command button to return to the CCP Main menu.

Customizing ASCII Export/ Import Settings

Select **A**SCII from the Main CCP menu to modify the settings for exporting and importing ASCII database files. Paradox displays the ASCII Export/Import settings dialog box that lists the following settings:

■ *String delimiter.* Use the text box in this line to modify the default characters used to enclose or *delimit* fields in ASCII files. The original setting is a double quotation mark. Paradox also recognizes by default single quotation marks as delimiters.

■ *Delimit.* Use this setting to specify which type of field should be delimited: Strings only or All fields.

■ *Field Separator.* Use the text box in this line to change the character used to separate fields when importing and exporting ASCII files. The original setting is a comma.

■ *Export Blank Fields.* Use this choice to determine whether Paradox places zeros in blank numeric fields during ASCII export. The original default setting is As Nothing. To cause Paradox to place zeros in blank fields, select As Zeros.

■ *Decimal Point.* Select an option in this line to indicate whether to export or import ASCII files in International format. The original setting is Period, which causes Paradox to recognize a period as a decimal point. Select the Comma option to cause Paradox to recognize a comma as the decimal point

After making your selections, select the OK command button to return to the CCP Main menu.

PAL Keycodes and Extended Codes

This appendix presents PAL keycodes and extended codes along with the ASCII character, Paradox keystroke, and PAL commmand equivalents. PAL keycodes are used with the PAL commands KEYPRESS and SETKEY and with PAL commands that include the UNTIL keyword (refer to Chapters 15 and 16).

PAL Keycode	ASCII Character	Paradox Keystroke	PAL Command
0		Ctrl-2	
1	☻	Ctrl-A	REPLACE
2	•	Ctrl-B	
3	♥	Ctrl-C	
4	♦	Ctrl-D	DITTO
5	♣	Ctrl-E	
6	♠	Ctrl-F	FIELDVIEW

PAL Keycode	ASCII Character	Paradox Keystroke	PAL Command
7	·	Ctrl-G	GO
8	■	Ctrl-H, Backspace	BACKSPACE
9	°	Ctrl-I, Tab	TAB, \t
10	◙	Ctrl-J	\n
11	♂	Ctrl-K	
12	♀	Ctrl-L	RESUME, \f
13	♪	Ctrl-M	ENTER
14	♫	Ctrl-N	
15	☼	Ctrl-O	
16	►	Ctrl-P	
17	◄	Ctrl-Q	
18	↕	Ctrl-R	ROTATE
19	‼	Ctrl-S	
20	¶	Ctrl-T	
21	§	Ctrl-U	UNDO
22	▬	Ctrl-V	VERTRULER
23	↨	Ctrl-W	
24	↑	Ctrl-X	
25	↓	Ctrl-Y	DELETELINE
26	→	Ctrl-Z	ZOOM
27	←	Ctrl-[, Esc, Ctrl-Esc	ESC
28	∟	Ctrl-\	
29	↔	Ctrl-]	
30	▲	Ctrl-6	
31	▼	Ctrl-_	
32		Space	SPACEBAR
33	!	!	
34	"	"	
35	#	#	
36	$	$	
37	%	%	
38	&	&	
39	'	'	
40	(	(	
41	)	)	

PAL Keycode	ASCII Character	Paradox Keystroke	PAL Command
42	*	*	
43	+	+	
44	,	,	
45	-	-	
46	.	.	
47	/	/	
48	0	0	
49	1	1	
50	2	2	
51	3	3	
52	4	4	
53	5	5	
54	6	6	
55	7	7	
56	8	8	
57	9	9	
58	:	:	
59	;	;	
60	<	<	
61	=	=	
62	>	>	
63	?	?	
64	@	@	
65	A	A	
66	B	B	
67	C	C	
68	D	D	
69	E	E	
70	F	F	
71	G	G	
72	H	H	
73	I	I	
74	J	J	
75	K	K	

PAL Keycode	ASCII Character	Paradox Keystroke	PAL Command
76	L	L	
77	M	M	
78	N	N	
79	O	O	
80	P	P	
81	Q	Q	
82	R	R	
83	S	S	
84	T	T	
85	U	U	
86	V	V	
87	W	W	
88	X	X	
89	Y	Y	
90	Z	Z	
91	[	[	
92	\	\	
93	]	]	
94	^	^	
95	_	_	
96	'	'	
97	a	a	
98	b	b	
99	c	c	
100	d	d	
101	e	e	
102	f	f	
103	g	g	
104	h	h	
105	i	i	
106	j	j	
107	k	k	
108	l	l	
109	m	m	
110	n	n	
111	o	o	
112	p	p	

PAL Keycode	ASCII Character	Paradox Keystroke	PAL Command
113	q	q	
114	r	r	
115	s	s	
116	t	t	
117	u	u	
118	v	v	
119	w	w	
120	x	x	
121	y	y	
122	z	z	
123	{	{	
124	|	|	
125	}	}	
126	~	~	
127	Δ	Ctrl-Backspace CTRLBACKSPACE	
128	Ç	Alt-128	
129	ü	Alt-129	
130	é	Alt-130	
131	â	Alt-131	
132	ä	Alt-132	
133	à	Alt-133	
134	å	Alt-134	
135	ç	Alt-135	
136	ê	Alt-136	
137	ë	Alt-137	
138	è	Alt-138	
139	ï	Alt-139	
140	î	Alt-140	
141	ì	Alt-141	
142	Ä	Alt-142	
143	Å	Alt-143	
144	É	Alt-144	
145	æ	Alt-145	
146	Æ	Alt-146	
147	ô	Alt-147	
148	ö	Alt-148	
149	ò	Alt-149	

PAL Keycode	ASCII Character	Paradox Keystroke	PAL Command
150	û	Alt-150	
151	ù	Alt-151	
152	ÿ	Alt-152	
153	Ö	Alt-153	
154	Ü	Alt-154	
155	¢	Alt-155	
156	£	Alt-156	
157	¥	Alt-157	
158	û	Alt-158	
159	ƒ	Alt-159	
160	á	Alt-160	
161	í	Alt-161	
162	ó	Alt-162	
163	ú	Alt-163	
164	ñ	Alt-164	
165	Ñ	Alt-165	
166	ª	Alt-166	
167	º	Alt-167	
168	¿	Alt-168	
169	⌐	Alt-169	
170	¬	Alt-170	
171	1/2	Alt-171	
172	1/4	Alt-172	
173	¡	Alt-173	
174	«	Alt-174	
175	»	Alt-175	
176	░	Alt-176	
177	▓	Alt-177	
178	█	Alt-178	
179	│	Alt-179	
180	┤	Alt-180	
181	╡	Alt-181	
182	╢	Alt-182	
183	╖	Alt-183	
184	╕	Alt-184	
185	╣	Alt-185	
186	║	Alt-186	

PAL Keycode	ASCII Character	Paradox Keystroke	PAL Command
187	╗	Alt-187	
188	╝	Alt-188	
189	╜	Alt-189	
190	╛	Alt-190	
191	┐	Alt-191	
192	└	Alt-192	
193	┴	Alt-193	
194	┬	Alt-194	
195	├	Alt-195	
196	─	Alt-196	
197	┼	Alt-197	
198	╞	Alt-198	
199	╟	Alt-199	
200	╚	Alt-200	
201	╔	Alt-201	
202	╩	Alt-202	
203	╦	Alt-203	
204	╠	Alt-204	
205	═	Alt-205	
206	╬	Alt-206	
207	╧	Alt-207	
208	╨	Alt-208	
209	╤	Alt-209	
210	╥	Alt-210	
211	╙	Alt-211	
212	╘	Alt-212	
213	╒	Alt-213	
214	╓	Alt-214	
215	╫	Alt-215	
216	╪	Alt-216	
217	┘	Alt-217	
218	┌	Alt-218	
219	█	Alt-219	
220	▄	Alt-220	
221	▌	Alt-221	
222	▐	Alt-222	
223	▀	Alt-223	

PAL Keycode	ASCII Character	Paradox Keystroke	PAL Command
224	∝	Alt-224	
225	β	Alt-225	
226	Γ	Alt-226	
227	π	Alt-227	
228	Σ	Alt-228	
229	σ	Alt-229	
230	μ	Alt-230	
231	τ	Alt-231	
232	ō	Alt-232	
233	Θ	Alt-233	
234	Ω	Alt-234	
235	δ	Alt-235	
236	∞	Alt-236	
237	φ	Alt-237	
238	∈	Alt-238	
239	∩	Alt-239	
240	≡	Alt-240	
241	±	Alt-241	
242	≥	Alt-242	
243	≤	Alt-243	
244	⌠	Alt-244	
245	⌡	Alt-245	
246	÷	Alt-246	
247	≈	Alt-247	
248	°	Alt-248	
249	·	Alt-249	
250	.	Alt-250	
251	√	Alt-251	
252	n	Alt-252	
253	2	Alt-253	
254	■	Alt-254	
255		Alt-255	

Extended Keyboard Codes

Certain keystrokes cannot be represented by the standard ASCII codes. To represent these keystrokes, Paradox uses negative numbers.

A two-character sequence is used. The first character is always an ASCII NUL (0). The second character and its translation are listed in the following table. Some codes expand to multi-keystroke characters.

PAL Keycode	Paradox Keystroke	PAL Command
–2	Alt-Space bar	ALTSPACE
–3	Null (null character)	
–4	Ctrl-Ins	CLIPCOPY
–5	Shift-Ins	CLIPPASTE
–7	Shift-Del	CLIPCUT
–15	Shift-Tab	REVERSETAB
–16	Alt-Q	
–17	Alt-W	
–18	Alt-E	MINIEDIT
–19	Alt-R	REFRESH
–20	Alt-T	
–21	Alt-Y	
–22	Alt-U	
–23	Alt-I	
–24	Alt-O	DOSBIG
–25	Alt-P	
–30	Alt-A	REPLACENEXT
–31	Alt-S	ORDERTABLE
–32	Alt-D	DELETEWORD
–33	Alt-F	
–34	Alt-G	
–35	Alt-H	
–36	Alt-J	
–37	Alt-K	KEYLOOKUP
–38	Alt-L	LOCKKEY
–44	Alt-Z	ZOOMNEXT
–45	Alt-X	CROSSTAB
–46	Alt-C	TOGGLEPALETTE
–47	Alt-V	
–48	Alt-B	
–49	Alt-N	
–50	Alt-M	
–59	F1	HELP
–60	F2	DO_IT!
–61	F3	UPIMAGE

PAL Keycode	Paradox Keystroke	PAL Command
–62	F4	DOWNIMAGE
–63	F5	EXAMPLE
–64	F6	CHECK
–65	F7	FORMKEY
–66	F8	CLEARIMAGE
–67	F9	EDITKEY
–68	F10	MENU
–71	Home	HOME
–72	¡	UP
–73	PgUp	PGUP
–75	··	LEFT
–77	«	RIGHT
–79	End	END
–80	»	DOWN
–81	PgDn	PGDN
–82	Ins (Insert)	INS
–83	Del (Delete)	DEL
–84	Shift-F1	F11
–85	Shift-F2	F12
–86	Shift-F3	F13
–87	Shift-F4	F14.
–88	Shift-F5	WINMAX, F15
–89	Shift-F6	GROUPBY, F16
–90	Shift-F7	F17
–91	Shift-F8	F18
–92	Shift-F9	F19
–93	Shift-F10	F20
–94	Ctrl-F1	F21
–95	Ctrl-F2	F22
–96	Ctrl-F3	F23
–97	Ctrl-F4	WINNEXT, F24
–98	Ctrl-F5	WINRESIZE, F25
–99	Ctrl-F6	CHECKDESCENDING, F26
–100	Ctrl-F7	GRAPHKEY, F27
–101	Ctrl-F8	WINCLOSE, F28
–102	Ctrl-F9	F29
–103	Ctrl-F10	TOQPRO, F30

PAL Keycode	Paradox Keystroke	PAL Command
−104	Alt-F1	F31
−105	Alt-F2	F32
−106	Alt-F3	INSTANTRECORD, F33
−107	Alt-F4	INSTANTPLAY, F34
−108	Alt-F5	FIELDVIEW, F35
−109	Alt-F6	CHECKPLUS, F36
−110	Alt-F7	INSTANTREPORT, F37
−111	AltF8	CLEARALL, F38
−112	Alt-F9	COEDITKEY,F39
−113	Alt-F10	PALMENU, F40
−114	Ctrl-PrtSc	
−115	Ctrl-¨	CTRLLEFT
−116	Ctrl-«	CTRLRIGHT
−117	Ctrl-End	CTRLEND
−118	Ctrl-PgDn	CTRLPGDN
−119	Ctrl-Home	CTRLHOME
−120	Alt-1 (keyboard)	
−121	Alt-2 (keyboard)	
−122	Alt-3 (keyboard)	
−123	Alt-4 (keyboard)	
−124	Alt-5 (keyboard)	
−125	Alt-6 (keyboard)	
−126	Alt-7 (keyboard)	
−127	Alt-8 (keyboard)	
−128	Alt-9 (keyboard)	
−129	Alt-0 keyboard)	
−130	Alt- (keyboard)	
−131	Alt-= (keyboard)	
−132	Ctrl-PgUp	CTRLPGUP

PAL Color Palette Codes

This appendix lists the color attribute codes used with the PAL commands that can set or change screen colors or attributes. Some of these commands include STYLE, PAINTCANVAS, WINDOW GETATTRIBUTES, WINDOW SETATTRIBUTES, and so on.

For the monochrome and color attributes, the display attribute is stored in a single byte of data. The way the contents of this byte are interpreted depends on whether you are using a monochrome or color display. Use the MONITOR function to determine what monitor type is in use.

Monochrome Attributes

Use the codes in table D.1 to select the desired attribute. To make any of the monochrome text styles in the table blink, add 128 to the code from the table. To make up the correct code number for blinking inverse video, for example, you use an attribute code of 240 (128 + 112).

Table D.1. Monochrome Display Attributes

Code	Attribute
0	No display (same as black on black)
1	Underline text
2	Normal text
9	Underlined, high-intensity text
10	High-intensity text
112	Inverse text (dark letters on a light background)

Color Attributes

Use the codes in tables D.2 and D.3 to select the desired attribute. When working with color attributes, the lowest four bits of the attribute byte determine the color or attribute of the foreground. The highest four bits of the attribute byte determine the color or attribute of the background. To combine a foreground and background color, add the two numbers together. To make up the correct code for light red text on a light gray background, for example, you use an attribute code of 124 (12+112).

Table D.2. Color Foreground Attributes

Code	Attribute
0	Black
1	Blue
2	Green
3	Cyan
4	Red
5	Magenta
6	Brown
7	Light Gray
8	Dark Gray

Code	Attribute
9	Light Blue
10	Light Green
11	Light Cyan
12	Light Red
13	Light Magenta
14	Yellow
15	White

Table D.3. Color Background Attributes

Code	Attribute
0	Black
16	Blue
32	Green
48	Cyan
64	Red
80	Magenta
96	Brown
112	Light Gray

Symbols

A

D

data
  combining, 537
  entering, 19-22
    in BLOB (Binary large
      OBject) field, 104
    in DataEntry mode, 99-100
    in memo field, 103-104
  entering and editing
    in CoEdit mode, 119-120
    in Edit mode, 109-110
  finding with Zoom, 105
  format settings, configuring
    with Custom Configuration
    Program (CCP), 1002-1003
  saving or abandoning, 101
data series, *see* series
data types, PAL (Paradox
  Programming Language),
  525-527
databases, 19
  building, 242-245
  creating, 17-19
  designing, 68-71
  entering data, 19-22
  normalizing, 262-263
  obtaining information about,
    426-427
  printing, 25-26
  relational, 64-65
  sorting, 24-26
  tables, defining structure,
    72-82
  terminology, 64-67
DataEntry KeepEntry command,
  338
DataEntry menu options,
  105-106
DataEntry mode, 31-32, 98
  adding multiple Entry tables,
    435-436
  dittoing field contents, 103
  entering data, 99-100
  handling keys and key
    violations, 106-107

saving or abandoning entered
  data, 101
undoing transactions, 101-103
on networks, 107-108, 337-338
with multitable forms,
  335-338
validity checks, 324
with source and map tables,
  342-344
DataEntry ValCheck Clear
  command, 335
DataEntry ValCheck Define
  Default command, 325
DataEntry ValCheck Define
  HighValue command, 325
DataEntry ValCheck Define
  LowValue command, 324
DataEntry ValCheck Define
  Picture command, 331
DataEntry ValCheck Define
  Required command, 334-335
DataEntry ValCheck Define
  TableLookup
  AllCorrespondingFields
    command, 328-330
  JustCurrentField HelpAndFill
    command, 327
  JustCurrentField
    PrivateLookup command,
    326
date and time PAL functions,
  705-706
date arithmetic, 175-176
date constants, 530-531
date fields, 76
  formatting screen displays,
    134-135
  placing in report
    specifications, 210-211
  range operators, 174
  reformatting, 212
DATEVAL( ) PAL function,
  773-774
DAY( ) PAL function, 774
DB file-name extension, 67
Debug option, 224

L

2535